Understanding
CURRENT PROCEDURAL TERMINOLOGY AND HCPCS
Coding Systems

2020

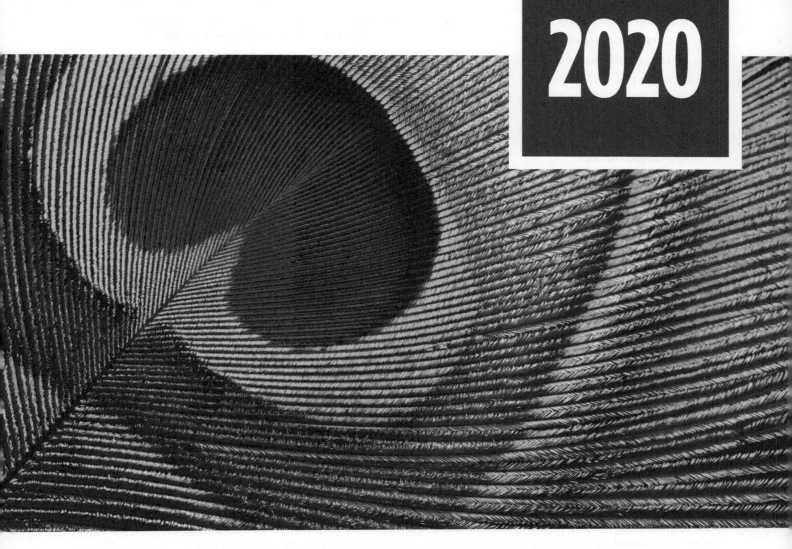

Mary Jo Bowie
MS, BS, AAS, RHIA, RHIT

 CENGAGE

Australia • Brazil • Mexico • Singapore • United Kingdom • United States

Understanding Current Procedural Terminology and HCPCS Coding Systems, 2020 edition
Mary Jo Bowie

SVP, Higher Education & Skills Product: Erin Joyner

Product Director: Matthew Seeley

Sr. Product Manager: Stephen G. Smith

Director, Learning Design: Rebecca von Gillern

Senior Manager, Learning Designer: Leigh Hefferon

Learning Designer: Kaitlin Schlicht

Product Assistant: Dallas Wilkes

Marketing Manager: Jonathan Sheehan

Director, Content Creation: Juliet Steiner

Manager, Content Creation: Stacey Lamodi

Content Manager: Mark Peplowski

Digital Delivery Lead: Lisa Christopher

Sr. Designer: Angela Sheehan

Compositor Name: MPS Limited

For product information and technology assistance, contact us at **Cengage Customer & Sales Support, 1-800-354-9706.**

For permission to use material from this text or product, submit all requests online at **www.cengage.com/permissions.** Further permissions questions can be emailed to **permissionrequest@cengage.com.**

Library of Congress Control Number: 2019911678

ISBN: 978-0-357-37848-9

Cengage
200 Pier 4 Boulevard
Boston, MA 02210
USA

Cengage is a leading provider of customized learning solutions with employees residing in nearly 40 different countries and sales in more than 125 countries around the world. Find your local representative at: **www.cengage.com.**

Cengage products are represented in Canada by Nelson Education, Ltd.

To learn more about Cengage platforms and services, register or access your online learning solution, or purchase materials for your course, visit **www.cengage.com.**

Notice to the Reader

Publisher does not warrant or guarantee any of the products described herein or perform any independent analysis in connection with any of the product information contained herein. Publisher does not assume, and expressly disclaims, any obligation to obtain and include information other than that provided to it by the manufacturer. The reader is expressly warned to consider and adopt all safety precautions that might be indicated by the activities described herein and to avoid all potential hazards. By following the instructions contained herein, the reader willingly assumes all risks in connection with such instructions. The publisher makes no representations or warranties of any kind, including but not limited to, the warranties of fitness for particular purpose or merchantability, nor are any such representations implied with respect to the material set forth herein, and the publisher takes no responsibility with respect to such material. The publisher shall not be liable for any special, consequential, or exemplary damages resulting, in whole or part, from the readers' use of, or reliance upon, this material.

Printed at CLDPC, USA, 1-20

TABLE OF CONTENTS

Understanding Current Procedural Terminology and HCPCS Coding Systems represents a comprehensive approach to learning and mastering procedural coding. This book provides detailed instruction for CPT coding as well as additional resource information that is essential for coders. This book can be used in an academic setting and also as a reference in a working environment. Space has been provided in the text for the learner to work on exercises to promote a hands-on approach to coding.

This book approaches procedural coding in a fresh and innovative manner. Many clinical examples are used throughout the text to provide the student with real-life coding examples and practice. The book also provides a review of human anatomy that is relevant to selecting procedural codes. Learning is reinforced by the use of illustrations of anatomy and operative procedures.

Organization of the Text

Understanding Current Procedural Terminology and HCPCS Coding Systems has 23 chapters, which present an introduction to CPT coding and detail on all of the main sections of CPT. Each chapter contains Internet links, a summary, and a chapter review to facilitate learning. Case studies are used throughout the text to enrich the learning process.

Special Features of the Text

Several features are incorporated into the chapters to facilitate learning:

- **Chapter outlines** located at the beginning of each chapter help organize the material.
- **Learning objectives** establish goals for each chapter and can be used as a checklist for reviewing concepts.
- **Key terms** are identified at the beginning of the chapter, are boldfaced throughout the chapter, and appear in the glossary to assist readers in learning the technical vocabulary associated with coding.
- **Exercises** challenge the learner's knowledge and reinforce understanding of presented materials.
- **Examples** illustrate key concepts to promote understanding.
- **Illustrations** of human anatomy and procedures appear throughout the book. These help the student visualize operative procedures and are a valuable resource for coders.
- **Internet links** encourage users to expand their knowledge and stay current with the most up-to-the-minute information.
- **Coding assignments** require learners to assign codes using coding manuals.
- **Case studies** encourage readers to apply concepts taught within the text to actual clinical scenarios.

New to the 2020 Edition

The 1995 and1997 Documentation Guidelines for Evaluation and Management Services are available at the CMS website at: https://www.cms.gov/Outreach-and-Education/Medicare-Learning-Network-MLN /MLNEdWebGuide/Downloads/95Docguidelines.pdf and https://www.cms.gov/Outreach-and-Education /Medicare-Learning-Network-MLN/MLNEdWebGuide/Downloads/97Docguidelines.pdf, respectively.

- The most current code sets available at the time of publication
- Additional coding exercises and coding assignments

- Additional comprehensive operative reports added in Appendix VI to simulate cases that would be coded by an outpatient coder

Learning Package for the Student

MINDTAP

MINDTAP is the first of its kind in an entirely new category: the Personal Learning Experience (PLE). This personalized program of digital products and services uses interactivity and customization to engage students, while offering a range of choice in content, platforms, devices, and learning tools. MINDTAP is device agnostic, meaning that it will work with any platform or learning management system, and will be accessible anytime, anywhere: on desktops, laptops, tablets, mobile phones, and other Internet-enabled devices. *Understanding Current Procedural Terminology and HCPCS Coding Systems,* 2020 edition, on MINDTAP includes:

- An interactive eBook with highlighting, note-taking functions, and more
- Flashcards for practicing chapter terms
- Computer-graded activities and exercises
- Case studies
- Medical Coding Trainer

Teaching Package for the Instructor

Instructor Resources

The *Instructor Resources Website to Accompany Understanding Current Procedural Terminology and HCPCS Coding Systems,* 2020 edition, contains a variety of tools to help instructors successfully prepare lectures and teach within this subject area. This comprehensive package provides something for all instructors, from those teaching coding for the first time to seasoned instructors who want something new. The following components in the website are free to adopters of the text:

- A downloadable, customizable *Instructor's Manual* containing a semester plan, course outlines, lesson plans, answers to text questions, and more.
- A *Test Bank* with several hundred questions and answers for use in instructor-created quizzes and tests.
- Chapter slides created in PowerPoint® to use for in-class lecture material and as handouts for students.

MINDTAP

On the MINDTAP platform in the new *Understanding Current Procedural Terminology and HCPCS Coding Systems,* 2020 edition, instructors customize the learning path by selecting Cengage Learning resources and adding their own content via apps that integrate into the MINDTAP framework seamlessly with many learning management systems. The guided learning path demonstrates the relevance of basic principles in coding through engagement activities, interactive exercises, and animations, elevating the study by challenging students to apply concepts to practice. To learn more, visit www.cengage.com/mindtap.

Optum360® EncoderPro.com

Enhance your course with Cengage learning materials and online coding tools from Optum360®. *EncoderPro. com Expert* is an online coding and reference tool designed to enhance your coding capabilities.

- Using online coding tools can help by: saving you time and money;

- increasing accuracy, reducing denials, and ensuring you receive complete reimbursement; and
- reducing required storage space and paper.

Features of EncoderPro.com Expert include:

- ICD-10-CM code content search
- ICD-10 mapping tools
- Coders' Desk Reference
- Complete code history
- Local Coverage Determinations (LCDs) and Medicare Pub. 100 access
- Medicare CCI edits
- Modifier crosswalk
- Enhanced compliance editor
- Enhanced LCD/NCD policy searching
- Cross-coder relationships from seven coding and billing specialty reference books

To make the switch and start saving on coding materials with Cengage and Optum360®, contact your Cengage Learning Consultant today at cengage.com/repfinder.

About the Author

MARY JO BOWIE, MS, BS, AAS, RHIA, RHIT

Consultant and Owner, Health Information Professional Services, Binghamton, New York. Active member, American Health Information Management Association (AHIMA). Mary Jo has over 35 years experience in the health information and coding profession. Professionally she has served the New York State Health Information Management Association as Education Director and was a member of the Board of Directors, 1989–1991; Ambulatory Care Coding Guidelines (ACGC) Committee, 1995–2001; and was Chairperson of the ACGC Committee, 1993–1995. She was the New York State Nominee for the American Health Information Management Association National Award for Literary Contribution to Profession, 1993 and 1994. Mary Jo has completed numerous national professional seminars on ICD-9-CM, ICD-10-CM, and CPT coding. She was the lead trainer for Cengage Learning's ICD-10-CM Peer-to-Peer Training. She is an AHIMA approved Trainer for ICD-10-CM/PCS.

Dedication

To my husband Bill, who is always by my side no matter what we face together, you are my motivation for all I do. To my daughter Sarah, and daughter Bethannie, son-in-law Jesse, and grandchildren Isabella, Jesse, Adelyn and other grandchildren yet to arrive. My love is always with you. To my parents, who are always there to support everything I do.

In memory of Ted Bowie, who taught us all to fight until we hear the referee blow the whistle.

A special thanks to Kaitlin Schlicht, Stephen Smith, and Mark Peplowski, who keep me on track and make authoring a joy. To my extended Cengage family, thanks for all the work you do in marketing and promoting my books. A very special thanks to Lou Ann Decker for her time and work that she put into reviewing these pages and attaching the hot pink notes!

—*Mary Jo Bowie*

HOW TO USE THE TEXTBOOK

Chapter Outline

At the beginning of each chapter, you will find an outline of all major headings. Review these headings of topic areas before you study the chapter. They are a road map.

Learning Objectives

Learning Objectives provide a framework for study of the chapter content.

Key Terms

Key Terms represent new vocabulary that is highlighted within the chapter at first usage. Use the end-of-book Glossary to study definitions of all key terms.

CHAPTER 1

Chapter Outline

Introduction
History of Current Procedural Terminology
The Structure and Design of CPT
CPT as Part of HCPCS
Summary

Internet Links
Chapter Review
Coding Assignments
Short Answer

Learning Objectives

At the conclusion of this chapter, you should be able to:

1. Explain the purpose of Current Procedural Terminology (CPT).
2. Identify key parties and dates in the development and revision of CPT.
3. Summarize the format and contents of the sections of the CPT code manual.
4. Interpret the symbols and punctuation used in CPT.
5. Locate a CPT code in the CPT code manual.
6. Differentiate between Level I and Level II codes in HCPCS.

Key Terms

add-on code symbol (+)
bullet symbol (●)
Category I proprietary laboratory analyses (PLA) tests symbol ↑↓
Category II
Category III

Current Procedural Terminology (CPT)
flash symbol (✔)
forbidden symbol (⊘)
guidelines
Healthcare Common Procedure Coding System (HCPCS)

hollow circle symbol (o)
horizontal triangles symbol (►◄)
Level I codes
Level II codes
National Codes
number symbol (#)

prohibitory symbol (⊘)
proprietary laboratory analyses (PLA) tests symbol (⊬)
star symbol (★)
triangle symbol (▲)

Introduction

The coding system known as **CPT**, or **Current Procedural Terminology**, was developed by the American Medical Association (AMA). The AMA annually updates the code sets within CPT, and the new codes become effective on January 1 of each year. These five-digit codes are part of the language used by physicians and insurance companies to convey the services provided to a patient during an encounter. Just as the ICD-10-CM diagnostic codes explain what brought the patient to the provider for the encounter, CPT tells the insurance carrier what service or services were provided to the patient during that encounter.

The biggest hurdle that a coder might have with CPT coding is translating the physician's terminology or documentation into a billable service. Physicians communicate in medical terminology, whereas insurance carriers communicate in reimbursement language (CPT). For this reason, a working knowledge of CPT coding is necessary for the correct coding of procedures and services. Insurance carriers require that CPT codes be submitted on claims to determine the appropriate payment for the services rendered.

This chapter will provide an overview of the CPT manual as well as the terms and symbols used to guide coders to the proper selection of CPT codes.

History of Current Procedural Terminology

The CPT coding system was first published in 1966 by the AMA. The system provided uniform reporting of physician services performed in the outpatient setting. The first CPT manual was pocket sized and contained only 163 pages. It contained four-digit codes, along with brief descriptions.

Chapter Review

Chapter Review sections appear in every chapter, and test your understanding of the material through questions in varying formats.

Exercises

Sprinkled throughout the chapters, Exercises encourage readers to stop periodically and apply critical thinking skills to solve coding challenges.

Exercise 2.1—Check Your Understanding

List the modifiers given in the series in the proper order. If the order does not make a difference, indicate this with ND.

1. 62, 22 _____
2. GW, US _____
3. 56, QT _____
4. AA, 47 _____
5. 59, 51 _____

Coding Assignments

For each code listed, note the main section of the CPT manual in which you would find the code. The first one is done for you.

1. 00142   Anesthesia
2. 23076   _____
3. 88348
8. 75810   _____
9. 37766   _____
10. 93283

Coding Assignments

Coding Assignments invite you to use CPT and HCPCS coding manuals to identify proper procedural codes.

Internet Links

For more information about CMS and the HCPCS coding system, visit *http://www.cms.gov*.

Chapter Review

True/False

Instructions: Indicate whether the following statements are true (T) or false (F).

1. _____ CPT codes tell the insurance carrier what brought the patient to the physician's office.
2. _____ Text, symbols, and the history of CPT are found in the introduction of the book.
3. _____ The CPT code book is updated annually on July 1.
4. _____ The Surgery section of codes begins with code 10001 and goes through code 69999.
5. _____ ▲ is the symbol for a revised code.

Fill in the Blank

Instructions: Fill in the blanks in the statements that follow.

6. The CPT coding system was first published in 1966 by _____.
7. A complete and detailed description of all modifiers used in CPT is found in _____.
8. The CPT manual contains _____ main sections.
9. The _____ separates the common portion of the code description from additional portions of the code.
10. The _____ is organized by main terms.

Coding Assignments

For each code listed, note the main section of the CPT manual in which you would find the code. The first one is done for you.

Internet Links

Internet Links encourage you to expand your knowledge base with the most up-to-date information available on the Web.

Case Studies

Case Studies challenge you to carefully select codes appropriate to the scenarios described.

Introduction to Current Procedural Terminology

Chapter Outline

Learning Objectives

At the conclusion of this chapter, you should be able to:

1. Explain the purpose of Current Procedural Terminology (CPT).
2. Identify key parties and dates in the development and revision of CPT.
3. Summarize the format and contents of the sections of the CPT code manual.
4. Interpret the symbols and punctuation used in CPT.
5. Locate a CPT code in the CPT code manual.
6. Differentiate between Level I and Level II codes in HCPCS.

Key Terms

add-on code symbol (+)

bullet symbol (●)

category I proprietary laboratory analyses (PLA) tests symbol ↑↓

Category II

Category III

Current Procedural Terminology (CPT)

flash symbol (✓)

forbidden symbol (⊘)

guidelines

Healthcare Common Procedure Coding System (HCPCS)

hollow circle symbol (o)

horizontal triangles symbol (►◄)

Level I codes

Level II codes

National Codes

number symbol (#)

prohibitory symbol (⊘)

proprietary laboratory analyses (PLA) tests symbol (✗)

star symbol (★)

triangle symbol (▲)

Introduction

The coding system known as **CPT,** or **Current Procedural Terminology,** was developed by the American Medical Association (AMA). The AMA annually updates the code sets within CPT, and the new codes become effective on January 1 of each year. These five-digit codes are part of the language used by physicians and insurance companies to convey the services provided to a patient during an encounter. Just as the ICD-10-CM diagnostic codes explain what brought the patient to the provider for the encounter, CPT tells the insurance carrier what service or services were provided to the patient during that encounter.

The biggest hurdle that a coder might have with CPT coding is translating the physician's terminology or documentation into a billable service. Physicians communicate in medical terminology, whereas insurance carriers communicate in reimbursement language (CPT). For this reason, a working knowledge of CPT coding is necessary for the correct coding of procedures and services. Insurance carriers require that CPT codes be submitted on claims to determine the appropriate payment for the services rendered.

This chapter will provide an overview of the CPT manual as well as the terms and symbols used to guide coders to the proper selection of CPT codes.

History of Current Procedural Terminology

The CPT coding system was first published in 1966 by the AMA. The system provided uniform reporting of physician services performed in the outpatient setting. The first CPT manual was pocket sized and contained only 163 pages. It contained four-digit codes, along with brief descriptions.

The CPT manual has grown in size and descriptions since 1966. The CPT manual now contains six main sections, which are divided into subsections, and then further divided into subcategories and headings. It now contains thousands of codes, which continue to be revised and updated annually.

The Structure and Design of CPT

The CPT update notifications are released in early fall to allow time for providers to become educated and update their systems to be in compliance with the January 1 code changes. Coding changes that are announced include additions, deletions, and code revisions from the previous year. Coders need to review the annual updates in CPT so that they have an understanding of the most current codes; therefore, submitted claims will not be rejected because of invalid or outdated codes.

The CPT manual consists of an introduction, the main body of the book, the appendices, and the index. To locate a procedure completed during an encounter, the coder may need to look for the service in several different ways. Becoming familiar with the layout and format of the book will help the coder to better locate a code.

In order to become familiar with the contents of the CPT manual, you should use your CPT manual and locate the following (the table of contents for CPT is found at the front of the manual):

- Introduction
- Evaluation and Management Services Guidelines
- Evaluation and Management
- Anesthesia Guidelines
- Anesthesia
- Surgery Guidelines
- Surgery
- Radiology Guidelines
- Radiology
- Pathology and Laboratory Guidelines
- Pathology and Laboratory
- Medicine Guidelines
- Medicine

- Category II Codes
- Category III Codes
- Appendices
- Index

The Introduction

The introduction to the CPT manual contains valuable information that will help you navigate through the manual. Text, symbols, history, and how to use the book are all explained within the introduction section of the manual.

Also found in the introduction is a breakdown of the section numbers and their sequence, instructions for using the CPT manual and for formatting, and an explanation of guidelines, add-on codes, and modifiers. To become familiar with the information found within the introduction, read the introduction contained within the CPT manual.

Symbols

Various symbols are used to alert the coder to unique features of the CPT manual. Symbols that are included in the CPT manual are discussed below. The symbols are located in front of the code numbers within the various sections to denote that the symbol applies to a specific code.

Triangle Symbol ▲

The **triangle symbol** is used to denote that a code has been revised from the previous edition of CPT with a substantial change in the CPT description of the procedure or service. Appendix B contains a summary of codes that have been revised, as well as additional and deleted codes. When a code is revised, the triangle symbol will appear before the code number in the main body of the CPT manual. In Appendix B, the triangle symbol will appear before the code number, and the deleted language in the code description will be noted with a strikethrough. The newly added information will be underlined.

In the 2020 edition of CPT, for example, code number 54640 was revised.

> **EXAMPLE:** In 2019, the code descriptor stated:
>
>   54640   Orchiopexy, inguinal approach, with or without hernia repair
>
> In 2020, the code descriptor was revised as follows:
>
>   54640   Orchiopexy, inguinal or scrotal approach

Reference code 54640 in the CPT manual and in Appendix B to note how this symbol is used.

Bullet Symbol ●

The **bullet symbol** is used to denote a new code that has been added since the previous edition of CPT. In the body of the CPT manual, the bullet symbol will appear before the code number. A summary of these newly added codes appears in Appendix B of the CPT manual. In Appendix B, the bullet symbol appears next to the new code number with the phrase "Code added." The full description of the new code does not appear in Appendix B.

In the 2020 edition of CPT, the following appeared as a new code:

> **EXAMPLE:** 49014 Re-exploration of pelvic wound with removal of preperitoneal pelvic packing, including repacking, when performed.

Review this code addition in both Appendix B and in the CPT manual Surgery code section and note how the bullet symbol is used.

Horizontal Triangles Symbol ►◄

The **horizontal triangles symbol** is used to indicate new or revised text in the CPT manual. When the horizontal triangle symbol appears, the coder must note the information that has been added or revised from the previous edition of the CPT manual.

> **EXAMPLE:** In the 2020 edition of CPT, revised text appears before code 19300. Reference this section in the CPT manual to review the revised information, and note the location of the horizontal triangles that appear around the paragraph that starts with "Mastectomy procedures (with the exception of gynecomastia [19300]) ....".

Add-on Code Symbol +

The **add-on code symbol** is used within CPT to list procedures that are completed in addition to the primary procedure or service performed. Appendix D in the CPT manual lists these codes, and they are denoted in the body of the CPT manual when the add-on code symbol appears before the code number. Add-on codes must be reported in addition to the primary procedure or service code and can never be reported alone. In addition, they are to be reported by the same provider of the service. Additional information on add-on codes is located in the Introduction of the CPT manual under the heading of "Add-on Codes."

> **EXAMPLE:** 11000 Debridement of extensive eczematous or infected skin; up to 10% of body surface +11001 each additional 10% of the body surface, or part thereof (List separately in addition to code for primary procedure)

The placement of the symbol alerts the coder that code 11001 is an add-on code and can be used only in conjunction with code 11000.

Number Symbol

The **number symbol** indicates codes that are out of numerical sequence. As CPT codes have been added over the years, codes have been listed out of numerical order to allow the placement of procedures with related concepts within code families, regardless of the availability of sequential numerical code numbers. The number symbol is used in the body of the CPT manual to indicate a code that is out of numerical order. The symbol will precede other symbols that have been assigned to a code.

> **EXAMPLE:**
>
> Excision
>
>   (For bone biopsy, see 20220–20251)
> 21550 Biopsy, soft tissue of neck or thorax
>   (For needle biopsy of soft tissue, use 20206)
> 21552 Code is out of numerical sequence. See 21550–21558
> 21554 Code is out of numerical sequence. See 21550–21558
> 21555 Excision, tumor, soft tissue of neck or anterior thorax, subcutaneous; less than 3 cm
> # 21552 3 cm or greater

Code 21552 is the code that is out of numerical sequence. Appendix N lists a summary of resequenced CPT codes, thus indicating the codes that do not appear in the body of the CPT manual in numerical order.

Forbidden or Prohibitory Symbol ⃠

The **forbidden or prohibitory symbol** indicates that a code is exempt from modifier –51 and also has not been denoted as a CPT add-on code. Modifier –51 indicates that multiple procedures have been performed. The use of modifiers will be discussed later in the textbook. Appendix E of the CPT manual lists the summary of CPT codes that are exempt from modifier –51. Review Appendix E for the complete list of codes that are exempt from the use of modifier –51.

> ⃠ 20974   Electrical stimulation to aid bone healing; noninvasive
> (nonoperative)

When code 17004 is reported with other codes, a modifier is not added to the code.

Hollow Circle Symbol ○

The **hollow circle symbol** indicates a reinstated or recycled code in CPT. This symbol is used in the CPT manual only if a code has been reinstated. In those years in which no codes are reinstated or recycled, the hollow circle symbol will not appear in the code book.

In 2010, code 1127F was deleted, and then it was reinstated in 2012. Thus, the following example appeared in the 2012 edition of CPT:

> **EXAMPLE:**
> ○1127F   New episode for condition   (NMA–No Measure Associated)

This symbol only appears the year it has been reinstated, therefore, the 2020 edition of CPT does not have the hollow circle symbol next to this code.

Flash Symbol ⚡

The **flash symbol** indicates codes for vaccines that are pending FDA approval. To see examples of vaccines awaiting FDA approval, reference Appendix K in the CPT manual.

Proprietary Laboratory Analyses (PLA) Tests Symbol ⚕

The **proprietary laboratory analyses (PLA) tests symbol**, ⚕, is used to denote duplicate proprietary laboratory analyses (PLA) tests. The PLA codes define proprietary clinical laboratory analyses. Appendix O, of the CPT manual, includes all codes that are included in the Proprietary Laboratory Analyses subsection of the Pathology and Laboratory Section of the CPT manual. PLA test codes will be further defined in the Pathology and Laboratory chapter of this textbook. **The Category I proprietary laboratory analyses (PLA) tests symbol ↑↓** is used to identify Category I PLA codes. For a full explanation of PLA codes and the use of sysmbols that relate to PLA reference the information found in the CPT manual prior to code 0001U found at the end of the Pathology and Laboratory section of the coding manual.

Star Symbol ★

The **star symbol** was added in the 2017 edition of CPT to denote codes that may be used to report synchronous (real-time) telemedicine services when modifier –95 is appended to the code. Telemedicine services are services that are rendered using electronic communication and encompasses interactive telecommunications, which, at a minimum, includes video and audio communication between the patient and the provider. The star symbol is listed in the CPT manual preceding the code number. Appendix P of the CPT manual lists the CPT codes that can be used as telemedicine codes.

> **EXAMPLE:** Dr. Jones treats patients with a diagnosis of Parkinson's Disease who reside in a nursing home facility via telemedicine services to evaluate the progression of the disease. Dr. Jones selects the evaluation and management code 99309 to report the subsequent nursing facility care services. Code 99309-95 is used to report this service since this is performed via telemedicine.

Reference code 99309 in the evaluation and management section of the CPT manual and note that the star symbol appears before the code to indicate that this service can be provided via telemedicine. Further explanation of the use of modifier –95 will be explained in Chapter 2 of this textbook.

Sections, Subsections, Categories, Subcategories, and Headings of the CPT Manual

There are six main sections in CPT. These main sections are as follows. (Note that the sections do not appear in numerical order within the CPT manual.)

Section Title	Code Range
Evaluation and Management	99201–99499
Anesthesia	00100–01999, 99100–99140
Surgery	10004–69990
Radiology	70010–79999
Pathology and Laboratory	80047–89398, 0001U–0138U
Medicine	90281–99199, 99500–99607

Each main section is divided further into subsections arranged by anatomic site, procedure, descriptors, or condition subheadings.

EXAMPLE: Referencing the Surgery section of the CPT manual you will see the following arrangement for codes that relate to incision and drainage procedures of the integumentary system. I have selected the specific code 10080 for this illustration:

```
(Section) Surgery
   (Subsection) Integumentary System
      (Subcategory) Skin, Subcutaneous, and Accessory Structures
         (Heading) Incision and Drainage
            (Procedure) 10080 Incision and drainage of pilonidal cyst; simple
```

The coder should keep in mind that the CPT manual is also arranged from head to toe and from the trunk outward. The Surgery section illustrates this clearly with the procedures for the Musculoskeletal System.

EXAMPLE:
```
(Section) Surgery
   (Subsection) Musculoskeletal System
      (Subcategory) Head
         (Heading) Incision
            (Procedure) 21010 Arthrotomy, temporomandibular joint
```

The next subcategory is the Neck (Soft Tissues) and Thorax, with the heading of "Incision," starting with procedure code 21501. Then the code subcategories move on to the Back and Flank, Spine (Vertebral Column), Abdomen, Shoulder, Humerus (Upper Arm) and Elbow, Forearm and Wrist, and Hand and Fingers. The subcategories continue in the same manner, beginning with the Pelvis and Hip Joint and moving the rest of the way down the body.

The codes are in numeric order within each section of the code manual, except for those cases when codes have been added out of sequence. These out-of-sequence codes are identified by the number symbol (#), as discussed earlier in this chapter. Locating specific codes will be discussed later in this chapter.

When a code is located in the main section of the CPT manual, please be aware of semicolon (;) use within the code descriptions. The semicolon is a very important symbol in CPT; it is the key to making proper code selections. The semicolon separates the common portion of the procedure description from the unique portion of the procedure description.

EXAMPLE: The provider documentation states, "I&D of a pilonidal cyst was performed today. Extensive amounts of pus were exudated. Patient tolerated procedure well. This is considered a complicated I&D because of the presence of infection."

The procedure codes for this case are found in the Surgery section and read as follows:

```
10080    Incision and drainage of pilonidal cyst; simple
10081        complicated
```

The code 10081 would be selected to report this procedure.

The way to read the code description for code 10081 properly is, "Incision and drainage of pilonidal cyst; complicated." The indentation indicates that after the semicolon, the term "complicated" is used for code 10081.

Exercise 1.1 – Check Your Understanding

For the codes given, indicate the section and subsection where the code is found. The first one is done for you.

Code	Section/Subsection	Code	Section/Subsection
1. 70300	Radiology/Diagnostic Radiology (Diagnostic Imaging)	10. 65112	_____
		11. 90371	_____
		12. 99203	_____
2. 60220	_____	13. 10160	_____
3. 26034	_____	14. 33120	_____
4. 88036	_____	15. 50100	_____
5. 43651	_____	16. 21811	_____
6. 38115	_____	17. 66184	_____
7. 99304	_____	18. 52441	_____
8. 97010	_____	19. 61000	_____
9. 77021	_____	20. 59074	_____

Guidelines

At the start of each of the CPT main sections, section-specific guidelines are presented. **Guidelines** define items that are necessary for appropriately interpreting and reporting the procedures and services contained within that section of the CPT manual. The guidelines specific to each section of CPT codes are strictly followed. Guidelines are provided at the start of each main section, but guidelines, or notes, may also appear at the beginning of a subsection.

EXAMPLE: In the Surgery section, prior to the description for code 11200, the following note appears after the heading "Removal of Skin Tags":

Removal by scissoring or any sharp method, ligature strangulation, electrosurgical destruction, or combination of treatment modalities, including chemical destruction or electrocauterization of wound, with or without local anesthesia.

This note further explains that if the skin tag was removed by any method listed, it would be proper to assign the appropriate CPT code from this subsection.

Coders should read and review each of the guideline sections at the start of each year for any noted changes that may have been made from the prior year's guidelines. As discussed earlier in this chapter, when text changes are made the revised text will appear within the horizontal triangles symbol.

Index

The Index is located in the back of the CPT manual. Instructions for the use of the CPT Index appear in the back of the CPT manual prior to the Index. The Index is organized by main terms. The main terms, which are in bold print, are organized by one of the following:

1. Procedure or Service
2. Organ or other Anatomic Site
3. Condition
4. Synonyms, Eponyms, and Abbreviations

When locating a term in the index, always follow this order. First, attempt to locate the main term by the name of the procedure or service, then attempt to identify it by organ or anatomic site, then by condition, and last by synonyms, eponyms, or abbreviations.

Main terms in the Index can be followed by a series of subterms that modify the main term. Subterms further define or clarify the main term. The coder must review the subterms because they have an effect on the selection of the appropriate code for the procedure. Some entries in the Index will have more than one code that applies to a given index entry; a range of codes will be listed. You will notice a comma separating the two codes. If more than two codes in a series apply, they will be separated by a hyphen. The coder must reference all the codes listed in the Index in the main section of the CPT manual. The coder should select the code after referencing the main sections. Always verify codes in the main text of CPT.

Appendices

The appendices are located in the back of the CPT manual, before the Index. Locate the appendices in the CPT manual and review the content found in each appendix of the manual. The appendices in CPT can be summarized as follows.

Appendix	Description
Appendix A—Modifiers	Detailed description of each of the modifiers used with CPT codes.
Appendix B—Summary of Additions, Deletions, and Revisions	Additions, deletions, and revised CPT codes for the current edition of CPT. This is a good reference at the beginning of the year when a new edition of CPT is published as it can be referenced for updating billing sheets and code summary sheets used by clinical staff. The appendix shows the actual changes that have been made to the code descriptions, new codes that have been added and deleted codes. In Appendix B of the CPT manual, read through the paragraph following the heading for additional information about how the symbols are used in this appendix.
Appendix C—Clinical Examples	Clinical examples for codes found in the Evaluation and Management section of CPT. This appendix provides valuable information about the selection of Evaluation and Management, E/M, codes and provides clinical examples of cases for various E/M codes.
Appendix D—Summary of CPT Add-on Codes	List of add-on codes found throughout CPT. Add-on codes can be recognized within the sections of the CPT manual because proceeding the code number the + symbol is listed in the CPT manual.

(continues)

(*continued*)

Appendix	Description
Appendix E—Summary of CPT Codes Exempt from Modifier 51	The codes listed here are exempt from use of a −51 modifier.
Appendix F—Summary of CPT Codes Exempt from Modifier 63	The codes listed here are exempt from use of a −63 modifier.
Appendix G—Summary of CPT Codes That Include Moderate (Conscious) Sedation	On January 1, 2017, the summary of CPT codes that include moderate (conscious) sedation, Appendix G, was removed from the CPT appendices. Appendix G now states that for information and guidance on reporting moderate sedation services the coder should reference the guidelines for codes 99151, 99152, 99153, 99155, 99156, and 99157.
Appendix H—Alphabetical Clinical Topics Listing (AKA, Alphabetical Listing)	This appendix, which included the Alphabetical Clinical Topics Listing, has been removed from the CPT manual. The appendix now lists the AMA website for obtaining this information.
Appendix I—Genetic Testing Code Modifiers	Genetic testing code modifiers have been removed from the CPT manual. The appendix now lists a website to reference for up-to-date information.
Appendix J—Electrodiagnostic Medicine Listing of Sensory, Motor, and Mixed Nerves	This appendix contains a listing of sensory, motor, and mixed nerves and the appropriate nerve conduction study code that is used. This should be referenced when selecting codes 95907–95913.
Appendix K—Product Pending FDA Approval	This appendix contains a listing of vaccines pending FDA approval.
Appendix L—Vascular Families	Appendix L contains a listing of vascular families, the branch order, and those families commonly reported during arteriographic procedures.
Appendix M—Renumbered CPT Codes–Citations Crosswalk	This appendix contains a listing of renumbered and crosswalked codes and their descriptions.
Appendix N—Summary of Resequenced CPT Codes	Appendix N contains a listing of the CPT codes that are not in numerical order in the CPT manual. This appendix can be referenced to identify the codes out of numerical order.
Appendix O—Multianalyte Assays with Algorithmic Analyses	This appendix lists codes that are unique to a single clinical laboratory or manufacturer.
Appendix P—CPT Codes That May Be Used for Synchronous Telemedicine Services	This appendix is a summary of the CPT codes that may be used to report real-time telemedicine services.

Become familiar with the contents of the appendices because they provide an excellent source for reference information.

CPT as Part of HCPCS

Until 1983, CPT codes were recognized only by private insurance companies. After that time, the Healthcare Financing Administration developed the **Healthcare Common Procedure Coding System (HCPCS)**, using CPT codes as part of the HCPCS system for reporting Medicare services. The Healthcare Financing Administration is now known as the Centers for Medicare and Medicaid Services (CMS). The CPT codes that were already in use became the Level I or Category I codes of the new HCPCS coding system for the Medicare program. Some third-party payers also recognize the additional codes in HCPCS.

HCPCS

The Healthcare Common Procedure Coding System, commonly referred to as HCPCS (pronounced "hicpics"), is divided into Level I and Level II.

HCPCS Level I

The CPT codes are **Level I codes**. These codes are divided into Category I, Category II, and Category III. **Category I** codes are the codes from the main sections of CPT:

- Evaluation and Management
- Anesthesia
- Surgery
- Radiology
- Pathology and Laboratory
- Medicine

These codes are used to report services rendered by providers. They are mandatory.

Category II codes are not mandatory and are considered tracking codes. In the CPT manual, following the Medicine section, Category II codes can be located. Category II codes should never be used as a primary procedure code.

> **EXAMPLE:** The following code represents a Category II code:
>
> 1005F   Asthma symptoms evaluated (includes documentation of numeric frequency of symptoms or patient completion of an asthma assessment tool/survey/questionnaire) (NMA-No Measure Associated)

Category III codes, located in the CPT codebook after the Category II codes, are temporary codes for emerging technologies, services, procedures, and service paradigms, and are used for the collection of statistical data. With the creation of new procedures and technologies, these temporary codes can be assigned as additional codes to track their use. To become familiar with the reporting guidelines for Category III codes, reference the Category III code listing in the CPT manual. (The Category Code listing is found in the section prior to the start of the Appendices in the CPT manual.) As stated in this section of the CPT manual, if a Category III code is available, the Category III code must be reported instead of a Category I unlisted code. This will be discussed further later in the textbook.

> **EXAMPLE:** The following represents a Category III code:
>
> 0085T   Breath test for heart transplant rejection

HCPCS Level II

HCPCS **Level II codes** are commonly referred to as **National Codes**. These codes are published annually by the Medicare program and are used to bill for services and procedures that are not included in the Level I codes. These codes can be obtained on the Centers for Medicare and Medicaid Services (CMS) website and from the published annual edition of the codes. HCPCS Level II codes consist of one alpha character (A through V) followed by four digits. HCPCS Level II codes are discussed in Chapter 23 of this textbook.

Summary

- Current Procedural Terminology (CPT) comprises codes and guidelines used by the medical profession to report procedures and services provided to a patient during an encounter.
- The introduction of CPT contains explanations of the symbols used, how to maneuver through the book, and instructions for using the book.
- The main sections of CPT contain the codes used to report procedures to the insurance company/payer.

- The index helps the coder find the service that needs to be reported.
- The appendices further assist the coder with quick references to modifiers and coding changes.

Internet Links

For more information about CMS and the HCPCS coding system, visit *http://www.cms.gov*.

Chapter Review

True/False

Instructions: Indicate whether the following statements are true (T) or false (F).

1. _____ CPT codes tell the insurance carrier what brought the patient to the physician's office.

2. _____ Text, symbols, and the history of CPT are found in the introduction of the book.

3. _____ The CPT code book is updated annually on July 1.

4. _____ The Surgery section of codes begins with code 10001 and goes through code 69999.

5. _____ ▲ is the symbol for a revised code.

Fill in the Blank

Instructions: Fill in the blanks in the statements that follow.

6. The CPT coding system was first published in 1966 by _____.

7. A complete and detailed description of all modifiers used in CPT is found in _____.

8. The CPT manual contains _____ main sections.

9. The _____ separates the common portion of the code description from additional portions of the code.

10. The _____ is organized by main terms.

Coding Assignments

For each code listed, note the main section of the CPT manual in which you would find the code. The first one is done for you.

1.	00142	Anesthesia	8.	75810	_____
2.	23076	_____	9.	37766	_____
3.	88348	_____	10.	93283	_____
4.	62281	_____	11.	64400	_____
5.	65091	_____	12.	77003	_____
6.	90935	_____	13.	30520	_____
7.	99456		14.	89264	_____

15. 92326	_____	**18.** 77307	_____
16. 90651	_____	**19.** 33955	_____
17. 80345	_____	**20.** 99188	_____

Short Answer

Using the introduction to the CPT manual as a reference, define the following.

1. Unlisted procedure or service

   _____

   _____

   _____

2. Add-on codes

   _____

   _____

   _____

3. Modifiers

   _____

   _____

   _____

4. Special Report

   _____

   _____

   _____

5. Alphabetical Reference Index

   _____

   _____

   _____

6. Section Numbers and Their Sequences

   _____

   _____

   _____

7. Using Appendix D of the CPT manual, review the following codes to determine if the code listed is an add-on code.

   Next to the code, write "Yes" if the code is an add-on code or "No" if the code is not an add-on code.

Code	Is this an add-on code?	Code	Is this an add-on code?
11047	_____	63082	_____
60540	_____	81416	_____
36100	_____		

8. Using Appendix E of the CPT manual, review the following codes to determine if the code listed is exempt from modifier –51 use.

   Next to the code, write "Yes" if the code is exempt or "No" if the code is not exempt.

Code	Is this code exempt from the use of modifier –51?	Code	Is this code exempt from the use of modifier –51?
99201	_____	93618	_____
20975	_____	36620	_____
97535	_____		

Modifiers

Chapter Outline

Introduction

Definition and Purposes of Modifiers

Use of Modifiers for Various Procedures
   and Service Locations

Modifiers Used for Hospital
   Outpatient Services

CPT Level I Modifiers

HCPCS Level II Modifiers

Summary

Internet Links

Chapter Review

Case Studies

Learning Objectives

At the conclusion of this chapter, you should be able to:

1. Identify where a list of CPT modifiers can be found in the CPT manual.
2. Sequence pricing and statistical modifiers in the proper order.
3. Differentiate between pricing and statistical modifiers.
4. Define the various CPT modifiers used.
5. Identify modifiers approved for hospital outpatient services.
6. Define the various HCPCS Level II modifiers used.
7. Assign CPT and HCPCS Level II modifiers to procedural statements.
8. Identify where modifiers are listed on the CMS-1500 form.

Key Terms

alternative laboratory
   platform testing—
   modifier 92

anesthesia by surgeon—
   modifier 47

assistant surgeon—
   modifier 80

assistant surgeon (when
   qualified resident
   surgeon is not
   available)—modifier 82

bilateral procedure—
   modifier 50

CPT modifier

decision for surgery—
   modifier 57

discontinued outpatient
   hospital/ambulatory
   surgery center (ASC)
   procedure after
   administration of
   anesthesia—modifier 74

discontinued outpatient
   hospital/ambulatory
   surgery center (ASC)
   procedure prior to
   the administration of
   anesthesia—modifier 73

discontinued
   procedure—modifier 53

distinct procedural service—modifier 59

habilitative services—modifier 96

increased procedural services—modifier 22

informational modifiers

Level I (CPT) modifiers

Level II (HCPCS/National) modifiers

mandated services—modifier 32

minimum assistant surgeon—modifier 81

multiple modifiers—modifier 99

multiple outpatient hospital E/M encounters on the same date—modifier 27

multiple procedures—modifier 51

postoperative management only—modifier 55

preoperative management only—modifier 56

preventive service—modifier 33

pricing modifiers

procedure performed on infants less than 4 kg—modifier 63

professional component—modifier 26

reduced services—modifier 52

reference (outside) laboratory—modifier 90

rehabilitative services—modifier 97

repeat clinical diagnostic laboratory test—modifier 91

repeat procedure or service by another physician or other qualified health care professional—modifier 77

repeat procedure or service by same

physician or other qualified health care professional—modifier 76

significant, separately identifiable E/M service by the same physician or other qualified health care professional on the same day of the procedure or other service—modifier 25

staged procedure

staged or related procedure or service by the same physician or other qualified health care professional during the postoperative period—modifier 58

statistical modifiers

surgical care only—modifier 54

surgical team—modifier 66

synchronous telemedicine service rendered via a real-time interactive

audio and video telecommunications system—modifier 95

two surgeons—modifier 62

unplanned return to the operating/procedure room by the same physician or other qualified health care professional for a related procedure during the postoperative period—modifier 78

unrelated E/M service by the same physician or other qualified health care professional during postoperative period—modifier 24

unrelated procedure or service by the same physician or other qualified health care professional during the postoperative period—modifier 79

unusual anesthesia—modifier 23

Introduction

At times, a CPT code needs to be reported with the addition of a modifier. Modifiers give additional information, when necessary, about the CPT code to a third-party payer to ensure that claims are paid correctly.

Definition and Purposes of Modifiers

A **CPT modifier** is a two-digit code that is appended to the CPT code to indicate that a service or procedure has been altered for some reason, but it does not change the main definition of the code. The modifier further describes the service performed. Two types of modifiers are used with CPT codes: **Level I (CPT) modifiers** are two-digit numeric codes, whereas **Level II (HCPCS/National) modifiers** are two-digit alphanumeric modifiers. A complete listing of Level I modifiers is contained in Appendix A of the CPT manual. To become familiar with the modifier codes and descriptions, review Appendix A of the CPT manual.

Modifiers are used for various reasons, including the following:

- A service or procedure has both a technical and professional component.
- A service or procedure was performed by more than one physician.
- A service or procedure was performed in more than one location.

- A service or procedure has taken more time to complete than routinely would occur.
- A service or procedure was reduced or increased.
- Only part of a procedure was completed.
- A bilateral procedure was performed.
- A service or procedure was completed multiple times.
- An unusual event occurred during the procedure.
- An accompanying or adjunctive procedure was performed.

Use of Modifiers for Various Procedures and Service Locations

As mentioned earlier in this chapter, Appendix A of the CPT manual lists the Level I modifiers. It should be noted that instruction is also given as to which modifiers are used for physician services and which modifiers are appropriate for ambulatory surgery center hospital outpatient use.

Modifiers Used with Physician Services

When billing physician services, place modifiers in item 24d of the CMS-1500 form, following the CPT code. Appendix I of this textbook provides an example of the CMS-1500 form. Reference Appendix I, Figure A1-1, of this textbook to see where to place the modifier on the CMS-1500 form.

When reporting modifiers for Medicare claims, the CPT code is followed by the modifier. It should be noted that some third-party payers use different instructions for reporting modifiers. It is important to review the modifier instructions for the payer you are billing. This will be explained further when we discuss the various modifiers.

The CMS-1500 claim form contains modifier fields. For Medicare claims, when you enter only one modifier, enter it in the first modifier field. When more than one modifier is submitted, the modifiers must be ranked according to whether the modifier will affect the fee for the service. Modifiers that affect pricing are listed in Table 2-1 and should be reported in the first modifier field because they directly affect the fee for a service. The modifiers listed in Table 2-1 are often referred to as **pricing modifiers**, and they either increase or decrease the fee for the service.

The remaining modifiers, often referred to as **statistical modifiers** or **informational modifiers**, are used for informational purposes and have an impact on the processing or payment of the code billed but do not affect the fee. Table 2-2 lists the statistical/informational modifiers.

It is important for the coder to also enter the pricing modifier in the first modifier field.

> **EXAMPLE:** Ranking of Two Modifiers—One pricing modifier and one statistical modifier.
>
> Assume that Dr. Smith performed an open incision and drainage of an appendiceal abscess and reported code 44900. Two days later, Dr. Smith repeated the same procedure on the same patient. During this episode of care, he only performed the surgical care; therefore, modifier 54, surgical care only, would be appended to the code 44900. Because this is a repeat procedure by the same physician, modifier 76 also would have to be reported. Therefore, modifier 54 should be reported in the first modifier field, because it affects pricing, and modifier 76 would be entered in the second modifier field, because it does not affect pricing.

TABLE 2-1 Pricing Modifiers That Affect Fees

AA	AD	AH	AJ	AS	GM	QB	QK	QU	QX	QY	QZ
SG	TC	UN	UP	UQ	UR	US	22	26	50	51	52
53	54	55	56	62	66	73	74	78	80	82	99

TABLE 2-2 Statistical and Informational Modifiers

AE	AF	AG	AK	AR	AT	AM	CC	CG	E1	E2	E3
E4	EJ	EM	EP	ET	F1	F2	F3	F4	F5	F6	F7
F8	F9	FA	FP	G1	G2	G3	G4	G5	G6	G7	G8
G9	GA	GB	GC	GE	GG	GH	GJ	GN	GO	GP	GQ
GT	GV	GW	GY	GZ	KO	KP	KQ	KX	LC	LD	LR
LS	LT	Q3	Q4	Q5	Q6	Q7	Q8	Q9	QA	QC	QD
QL	QM	QN	QP	QQ	QS	QT	QV	QW	RC	RD	RP
RT	SF	SW	SY	T1	T2	T3	T4	T5	T6	T7	T8
T9	TA	VP	23	24	25	32	47	57	58	59	76
77	79	90	91	95							

When reporting more than one statistical or informational modifier with no other pricing modifiers, you can report the statistical or information modifiers in any order, with the exception of the QT, QW, and SF modifiers. These three modifiers are valid for use only in the first modifier field. Assume that modifiers T7 and 58 are being reported together. The modifiers can be sequenced in any order because they are both statistical modifiers.

Exercise 2.1—Check Your Understanding

List the modifiers given in the series in the proper order. If the order does not make a difference, indicate this with ND.

1. 62, 22 _____
2. GW, US _____
3. 56, QT _____
4. AA, 47 _____
5. 59, 51 _____

Use of Multiple Modifiers—Modifier 99

Modifier 99—multiple modifiers indicates that multiple modifiers are needed for an individual CPT code. This modifier is not recognized by all insurance plans, so coders must review the coding guidelines for plans that are being billed. Medicare recognizes modifier 99, and coders should refer to Medicare administrative contractor information for instructions on reporting this modifier. Many Medicare administrative contractors require modifier 99 to be entered in the first modifier field when more than two modifiers apply. Additional information is required in the narrative field (item 19 on the claim form), listing all modifiers in the correct ranking order.

Exercise 2.2—Check Your Understanding

Pricing and Statistical/Informational Modifiers

For the following modifiers, state whether the modifier is a pricing modifier or a statistical/informational modifier.

Modifier	Type	Modifier	Type
1. 52	_____	6. 23	_____
2. E3	_____	7. 59	_____
3. 82	_____	8. 50	_____
4. 78	_____	9. 77	_____
5. GN	_____	10. QD	_____

Modifiers Used for Hospital Outpatient Services

Hospital outpatient services are reported on the UB-04 form, also known as the CMS-1450 form. When modifiers are reported for these services, they should be placed in field 44 of that form. Reference Appendix I, Figure A1-2, of this textbook to determine where modifiers should be placed on a UB-04/CMS-1450 form.

Modifiers Approved for Ambulatory Surgery Center Hospital Outpatient Use

Not all modifiers are approved for use on ambulatory surgery claims. The list of approved modifiers is reviewed annually. Table 2-3 lists the currently approved modifiers. Appendix A of the CPT manual also lists the modifiers that are approved for the ambulatory surgery setting. Familiarize yourself with the modifiers used in this setting by reading the listing and the modifiers' descriptions in Appendix A of the CPT manual.

TABLE 2-3 Modifiers Approved for Ambulatory Surgery Center Hospital Outpatient Use

Level I Modifiers												
25	27	50	52	58	59	73	74	76	77	78	79	91
Level II Modifiers												
LT	RT	E1	E2	E3	E4	FA	F1	F2	F3	F4	F5	F6
F7	F8	F9	TA	T1	T2	T3	T4	T5	T6	T7	T8	T9
LC	LD	LM	RC	RI	GG	GH	QM	QN	XE	XS	XP	XU

Exercise 2.3—Check Your Understanding

Modifiers Used for Ambulatory Surgery Center Hospital Outpatient Claims

Mary Smith is an outpatient surgery coder at Sunny Valley Hospital, and she is developing a list of modifiers that can be used in this setting. Next to the modifier listed, write "Yes" if the modifier should be used in this setting or "No" if the modifier should not be used in this setting.

Modifier	Use in Outpatient Surgery Setting?	Modifier	Use in Outpatient Surgery Setting?
1. 22	_____	9. E4	_____
2. 50	_____	10. RT	_____
3. 53	_____	11. F3	_____
4. 59	_____	12. TC	_____
5. 62	_____	13. RC	_____
6. 66	_____	14. GG	_____
7. 73	_____	15. T1	_____
8. 76	_____		

CPT Level I Modifiers

The best way to understand how to use modifiers is to review the definition for each modifier found in Appendix A of the CPT manual. Here, we discuss the use of each modifier and give examples of cases that require modifier use. The titles of the modifiers are listed as they appear in the CPT manual.

Increased Procedural Services—Modifier 22

Assign **modifier 22** when the service provided is greater than that usually required for the listed procedure. This modifier should not be appended to an Evaluation and Management code.

> **EXAMPLE:** A radical abdominal hysterectomy with bilateral total pelvic lymphadenectomy and para-aortic lymph node biopsy was performed on Peg Smith. The procedure took 50 minutes longer than normal because, during the surgery, the patient experienced prolonged bleeding.

The code to report would be 58210-22 because of the unusual amount of time that it took to complete the procedure.

The use of modifier 22 is tracked by insurance companies. This should be used only for cases that are truly unusual and for which documentation of the case can justify the unusual aspect of the service. The surgeon needs to identify the additional work, such as technical difficulties during the procedure, or an increased intensity and/or time, just to name a few items. When this modifier is reported, an operative note will be requested and a special report may be requested, which would require the following information:

- A complete description of the procedure performed.
- The reason the service fell outside the parameters of the CPT code description.
- The time, effort, and equipment used during the procedure.
- The complexity of the case, describing the patient's condition and symptoms that occurred during the procedure.
- The preoperative and postoperative diagnoses.
- Pertinent physical findings that influenced the case and procedure.
- Any diagnostic and therapeutic services that were rendered in association with the procedure.
- Concurrent diagnosis, symptoms, and problems that were present.
- The anticipated follow-up care.

Unusual Anesthesia—Modifier 23

Occasionally, a procedure that routinely is not completed with any type of anesthesia or local anesthesia requires the use of general anesthesia. When this occurs, **modifier 23** is appended to the CPT code.

> **EXAMPLE:** Randy Hill is a patient with a psychiatric condition who needs to undergo surgery for a simple drainage of a finger abscess. Because the patient has much anxiety about the procedure, the physician uses general anesthesia on him.

The code to report is 26010-23.

Unrelated Evaluation and Management Service by the Same Physician or Other Qualified Health Care Professional During Postoperative Period—Modifier 24

For each procedure, a postoperative period is established that denotes the usual postoperative period for the condition related to the surgery. When a patient is seen for an **unrelated Evaluation and Management service during a postoperative period**, **modifier 24** is appended to the Evaluation and Management code, abbreviated

E/M code. This would indicate that an E/M service was performed during a postoperative period for a reason or reasons unrelated to the original procedure. The diagnosis code reported for the unrelated Evaluation and Management service must reflect the reason for the unrelated service.

> **EXAMPLE:** Sally Monk had an open cholecystectomy. Five days after the surgery, she experienced chest pain and was seen by the same physician who performed the surgery. He evaluated the chest pain.

The physician reported code 99213-24 to indicate that she was seen for a condition unrelated to the surgery. The diagnosis code for this visit would be chest pain, which is a condition that is not related to the cholecystectomy.

Significant, Separately Identifiable Evaluation and Management Service by the Same Physician or Other Qualified Health Care Professional on the Same Day of the Procedure or Other Service—Modifier 25

Modifier 25 is added to any appropriate level of an Evaluation and Management service when the physician needs to indicate that on the day a procedure or service was performed, the patient's condition required a significant, separately identifiable Evaluation and Management service that was above and beyond the other service provided or beyond the usual preoperative and postoperative care associated with the procedure that was performed.

> **EXAMPLE:** Devon presented to the doctor's office with knee pain that was a result of a sports injury. The physician examined Devon and determined that he had tendonitis. In the course of his examination, several warts were noted on the plantar side of Devon's left foot. The doctor felt that treatment should be started due to the size of two of the three warts. Devon did state that he has pain when wearing his shoe gear.

The physician reported code 99213-25 with a diagnosis of knee pain and tendonitis; in addition, he reported 17110 for cryotherapy treatment of the warts. The diagnosis code assigned to 17110 would be plantar warts. As per the definition of modifier 25, there are times when the Evaluation and Management service may be prompted by the same symptom or condition for which the procedure and/or service was provided; therefore, in these cases, different diagnoses are not required for the reporting of the E/M service on the same date.

Professional Component—Modifier 26

A number of CPT procedures have both a professional and a technical component. Examples of codes that have both a professional and a technical component include codes in the Pathology and Radiology chapters and cardiology codes found in the Medicine chapter of CPT. When a physician is reporting only the professional component, the service is identified by adding **modifier 26** to the usual procedure number.

> **EXAMPLE:** Dr. Ty, a radiologist, interprets a four-view x-ray examination of the cervical spine.

This is reported using code 72050-26.

Modifier 26 should not be appended to codes that represent a professional component but do *not* have a technical component as part of the code definition. An example of a code that represents only the professional component is code 93042—Rhythm ECG, one to three leads; interpretation and report only.

Multiple Outpatient Hospital E/M Encounters on the Same Date—Modifier 27

Modifier 27 is appended to an E/M service code when separate and distinct E/M encounters are performed in multiple outpatient hospital settings on the same date. This modifier is not to be used for physician reporting of multiple E/M services performed by the same physician on the same day. This is to be used for the reporting of services in the Hospital Outpatient Prospective Payment System.

> **EXAMPLE:** Jack Jones is seen by Dr. Smith in the podiatry clinic at Sunny Valley Hospital, and Dr. Smith selects code 99213 to report the services provided. Later that day, Jack Jones goes to the oncology clinic at Sunny Valley Hospital, and Dr. Johnson selects code 99214.

Dr. Smith would report code 99213, and Dr. Johnson would report code 99214-27.

Mandated Services—Modifier 32

At times, services are performed because the service is required or mandated by an insurance company or by a governmental, legislative, or regulatory agency. When this occurs, **modifier 32** is appended to the CPT code to indicate that the service was a mandated service.

> **EXAMPLE:** Joe Wenn was in an automobile accident. His auto insurance company is mandating that he be examined by Dr. Spy to determine the extent of his injuries. Joe has already been seen by his own primary care physician. Because Dr. Spy's examination of Joe is mandated by the auto insurance company, modifier 32 should be appended to the E/M code that Dr. Spy submits.

Dr. Spy submits code 99214-32.

Preventive Service—Modifier 33

Modifier 33 is used for the purpose of identifying the delivery of an evidence-based service in accordance with a U.S. Preventive Services Task Force A or B rating. The modifier is appended to codes representing preventive services. For separately reported services specifically identified as preventive, the modifier should not be used.

Anesthesia by Surgeon—Modifier 47

Modifier 47 is used by physicians or surgeons only when regional or general anesthesia is provided by the same physician or surgeon who is completing a procedure or service. This modifier is not to be used when local anesthesia is used. This modifier is appended to a procedure code or service code and is never appended to the anesthesia code.

> **EXAMPLE:** Dr. Smith performs a dilation of the esophagus by unguided bougie under general anesthesia on patient Bobby Jones.

Dr. Smith reports 43450-47.

Bilateral Procedure—Modifier 50

Modifier 50 is used by both facilities and professionals when bilateral procedures are performed in the same operative session. It is used only with codes that describe a unilateral procedure. Modifier 50 is not used on codes that describe bilateral procedures, such as code 31231—Nasal endoscopy, diagnostic, unilateral, or bilateral. It should be noted that some payers prefer RT (right) or LT (left) modifiers instead of modifier 50 and require the code to be reported twice.

> **EXAMPLE:** Dr. Sinus completed a bilateral intranasal maxillary sinusotomy on Linda New.

The code to report this procedure for Medicare patients would be 31020-50. Some insurance companies instruct providers to report the codes as follows: 31020 and 31020-50 or 31020-RT and 31020-LT.

Multiple Procedures—Modifier 51

At times, during the same operative/procedural session, multiple procedures are performed by the same provider. When multiple procedures, other than E/M services, Physical Medicine and Rehabilitation services, or provision of supplies (e.g., vaccines), are performed at the same session by the same provider, the primary procedure or service code would be reported as listed in the CPT manual. The additional procedure(s) or service(s) would be reported by adding **modifier 51** to the additional procedure or service code(s).

> **EXAMPLE:** John Jones has a puncture aspiration of an abscess on his left shoulder. During the same session, the cutting of three benign hyperkeratotic lesions also occurred.

Code 10160 would be reported for the puncture aspiration, whereas code 11056-51 would be reported for the cutting of the lesions.

This modifier is used only by providers and is not used by facilities. It should also be noted that this modifier should not be appended to designated add-on codes or Evaluation and Management codes. Appendix E within the CPT manual contains a list of codes that are exempt from modifier 51.

Reduced Services—Modifier 52

When a service or procedure is partially reduced or eliminated at the physician's discretion, **modifier 52** should be appended to the service or procedure code. This modifier should be used to report reduced services without changing the identification of the basic service. In other words, modifier 52 is used when part of the procedure was performed, but part of the procedure or service was not completed, at the provider's discretion. The use of modifier 52 may prompt a payer to request supporting documentation. The provider documentation should clearly state the reason for the reduced service.

> **EXAMPLE:** Kevin is 10 years old and is presenting for a physical for soccer camp. His physician reviews the camp forms and performs the required physical, but no comprehensive history is obtained. The examination is detailed but not comprehensive.

Kevin's physical is coded with a 99393—Periodic comprehensive preventive medicine; late childhood (age 5–11). A 52 modifier is appended because the history and examination do not meet the requirements for the comprehensive physical code that is used.

CMS states that for outpatient hospital reporting, modifiers 73 and 74 are used in place of modifier 52 for previously scheduled procedures/services that are partially reduced or canceled as a result of extenuating circumstances or those that threaten the well-being of the patient prior to or after administration of anesthesia. Reference the definition of modifier 52 in Appendix A of the CPT manual for additional clarification.

Discontinued Procedure—Modifier 53

At times, the physician may terminate a surgical or diagnostic procedure because of extenuating circumstances that threaten the well-being of the patient. **Modifier 53** would be used for cases in which the surgical or diagnostic procedure was started but discontinued. However, this modifier is not used to report the elective cancellation of a procedure prior to the patient's anesthesia induction and/or surgical preparation in the operating suite.

> **EXAMPLE:** Dr. Rissen brought Danielle into the OR for an endoscopic resection of a renal tumor. Danielle was put out under general anesthesia, and the procedure was started. As Dr. Rissen moved the scope into place through the established nephrostomy and touched the tumor to prep for removal, Danielle's blood pressure dropped from 150/80 to 100/50. Dr. Rissen stopped the procedure immediately, and Danielle was sent to recovery. The surgery was rescheduled when Danielle's blood pressure was stabilized.

Dr. Rissen reported code 50562 with a 53 modifier. The code reflects the renal endoscopy through established nephrostomy with resection of tumor, and the 53 modifier indicates that the procedure was discontinued by the surgeon due to the condition of the patient. The use of the 53 modifier indicates that additional services may be provided in the future.

As noted earlier for modifier 52, modifiers 73 and 74 are required for outpatient hospital ambulatory surgery center reporting in place of modifier 53. Reference the definition of modifier 53 for further clarification on the reporting for outpatient hospital/ambulatory surgery center reporting.

Surgical Care Only—Modifier 54

For most surgeries, the preoperative care, the surgery, and the postoperative care are completed by the same provider. However, in some cases, elements of surgical care are divided among providers. When this occurs, modifiers are used to indicate which provider performed various elements of the surgical care. **Modifier 54** is used when one physician performed the surgical procedure and another provider or providers completed the preoperative and/or postoperative management.

EXAMPLE: Dr. Hill performed a repair of a ruptured spleen with a partial splenectomy on Mary Smith. A different provider performed the pre- and postoperative care.

Because Dr. Hill did not provide the preoperative and postoperative care, the code to report for Dr. Hill would be 38115-54.

Modifier 54 is not used for any procedures that have zero global surgical days. Documentation must show transfer of care between physicians to justify the separation of the reporting of the surgical code. The pre- and postoperative services provided by the physician other than the surgeon would be coded with an appropriate E/M code.

Postoperative Management Only—Modifier 55

Modifier 55 indicates that one provider performed the postoperative management and another provider performed the surgical procedure.

EXAMPLE: Dr. Hill performed a repair of a ruptured spleen with a partial splenectomy on Mary Smith. However, following the surgery, Dr. Cook provided the postoperative care.

Dr. Cook would report code 38115-55.

Preoperative Management Only—Modifier 56

At times, a different provider will perform the preoperative care and evaluation, and another provider will perform the surgical procedure. When this occurs, **modifier 56** is used to report the preoperative care.

EXAMPLE: Prior to surgery, Dr. House evaluated and cared for Mary Smith. Then Dr. Hill performed a repair of a ruptured spleen with a partial splenectomy on Mary Smith.

Because Dr. House performed the preoperative care, the code to report this service would be 38115-56.

Decision for Surgery—Modifier 57

Modifier 57 is appended to an Evaluation and Management service code when, during the service, the initial decision was made to perform surgery.

EXAMPLE: Dr. Jones examined Jenise, a 27-year-old female patient, and determined that she needed to have a tonsillectomy and adenoidectomy. This was scheduled to occur in two weeks. Dr. Jones completed a comprehensive history and a comprehensive examination and documented medical decision making of high complexity.

Dr. Jones would report 99215-57.

The use of modifier 57 on a minor procedure performed on the same day as the decision for the procedure should be checked with the particular insurance carrier. Some insurance companies allow this; Medicare does not. Medicare prefers the use of a 25 modifier on the Evaluation and Management code for minor procedures with global days of 0 or 10. The coder should check with the payer to find out how they would like the decision for surgery reported.

Staged or Related Procedure or Service by the Same Physician or Other Qualified Health Care Professional During the Postoperative Period—Modifier 58

Modifier 58 is used during the postoperative period of a procedure when

- During the original procedure, a second procedure is planned as part of the care. (This is known as a **staged procedure**.)
- During the postoperative period, more extensive care is needed than what was rendered in the original procedure.
- During the postoperative period, therapy is required following the surgical procedure.

> **EXAMPLE:** A patient presents for insertion of Heyman capsules for clinical brachytherapy. The documentation states that this is the first of two procedures.

The code for the first treatment would be 58346, and the second time the patient presents would be recorded as 58346-58.

Although this modifier indicates that more extensive care was needed, it is not to be used to report the treatment of a problem that requires a return to the operating room. In these situations, modifier 78 is appropriate.

Distinct Procedural Service—Modifier 59

Under certain circumstances, the physician may need to indicate that a procedure or service was independent from other non-E/M services performed on the same day. **Modifier 59** identifies procedures that are not typically reported together but are appropriate under the circumstances. Different anatomical sites or procedures that are not ordinarily encountered or performed on the same day by the same physician may require use of this modifier. It should be noted that when another, already established modifier is appropriate, it should be used rather than modifier 59.

> **EXAMPLE:** Six-year-old Elizabeth fell down in her driveway. She had a 3-cm laceration on her right arm and gravel embedded in the forearm of her left arm. There was an intermediate repair of the laceration on her right arm. There was a 10-squre cm debridement of subcutaneous tissue, epidermis, and dermis of her left arm.

The intermediate repair of the laceration includes the debridement of the gravel and would be reported using code 12032. The debridement of the gravel that was embedded in the left arm would be coded 11042 with a 59 modifier. It should be noted that modifier 59 is not appended to an E/M service.

Effective January 1, 2015, four new HCPCS modifiers (XE, XP, XS, XU) were implemented to define specific subsets of modifier 59. The modifiers are collectively referred to as the −X {EPSU} modifiers. Please note that modifier 59 will continue to be used after January 1, 2015 with the new −X {EPSU} modifiers. Modifier 59 is one of the most widely used modifiers, and CMS felt that it was necessary to have more specific information from providers and facilities regarding the submission of the modifier, thus they established the −X {EPSU} modifiers to provide that information.

The −X {EPSU} modifiers are defined as follows:

- XE Separate Encounter—A service that is distinct because it occurred during a separate encounter.
- XS Separate Structure—A service that is distinct because it was performed on a separate organ/structure.

- XP Separate Practitioner—A service that is distinct because it was performed by a different practitioner.
- XU Unusual Non-Overlapping Service—The use of a service that is distinct because it does not overlap usual components of the main service.

CMS will continue to recognize the –59 modifier, but note that Current Procedural Terminology instructions indicate that modifier 59 should not be used when a more descriptive modifier is available. Therefore if an –X {EPSU} modifier is used for a code, it is incorrect to include modifier 59 as an additional modifier for the code.

Two Surgeons—Modifier 62

Modifier 62 is used when two primary surgeons work together to perform a distinct part(s) of a single reportable procedure. In this situation, each surgeon should report his or her own distinct operative work by adding modifier 62 to the single definitive procedure code. In addition, each surgeon should report any associated add-on codes for the procedure, as long as the two surgeons continued to work as primary surgeons, and append the add-on procedure codes with modifier 62.

> **EXAMPLE:** Mr. Pearl needed surgery to insert a pacemaker. Dr. Johnson made the incision and created the generator pocket. At this point in the procedure, Dr. Hyder inserted the atrial electrode and programmed the pacemaker. The electrode was tested, and then Dr. Johnson closed the incision.

Both surgeons in our example would document their piece of the surgery and report the surgery using 33206-62. It should also be noted that if additional procedure(s) (including add-on procedure[s]) were performed during the same surgical session and one of the surgeons acts as an assistant, those services are reported with modifier 80 or 82 added. The separate code(s) would be reported without modifier 62 added.

Procedure Performed on Infants Less Than 4 kg—Modifier 63

Modifier 63 reports procedures performed on neonates and infants up to a body weight of 4 kg. This modifier is not to be appended to codes from the Evaluation and Management section, Anesthesia section, Radiology section, Pathology/Laboratory section, or Medicine section. As per the definition in Appendix A of the CPT manual, this modifier is to be used on codes 20100–69990, unless otherwise designated in the manual.

> **EXAMPLE:** Tiny Tim, a 3.6-kg male infant, underwent a repair of a congenital arteriovenous fistula of the thorax and abdomen.

This procedure would be reported with code 35182-63 because of the weight of the child.

Surgical Team—Modifier 66

Some highly complex procedures require the services of several physicians, often of different specialties, plus other highly skilled, specially trained personnel and various types of complex equipment during the operative procedure. When this occurs, it is known as the *surgical team* concept. To indicate this on the claim, each provider should append **modifier 66** to the basic procedure number used for reporting services.

> **EXAMPLE:** Mr. Daniels underwent the repair of some complex cardiac anomalies by the modified Fontan procedure. It was also necessary to perform a cavopulmonary anastomosis to a second superior vena cava. It was necessary for several cardiothoracic surgeons to work together as a team to accomplish this procedure successfully.

Codes 33617 and 33768 would be used to report this procedure. A 66 modifier is appended to the services to indicate the surgery was performed by a team of surgeons, not just one or two. Each surgeon would need to document the procedure, indicating the need for a team of surgeons, unless one op note can clearly delineate each surgeon's role in the procedure.

Discontinued Outpatient Hospital/Ambulatory Surgery Center (ASC) Procedure Prior to the Administration of Anesthesia—Modifier 73

Modifier 73 is used for outpatient or ambulatory surgery centers and is used when, due to extenuating circumstances or situations that threaten the well-being of the patient, the physician cancels a surgical or diagnostic procedure after the patient's surgical preparation. The preparation includes sedation, when provided, and being taken to the room where the procedure is to be performed; however, the surgery is cancelled prior to the administration of anesthesia. Under these circumstances, the procedure code for the intended procedure is used and appended with modifier 73.

EXAMPLE: Mrs. Evans was wheeled into the OR for her breast biopsy. As she was being prepped, minutes prior to the administration of the anesthesia, there was a mechanical problem with the electrical power to the operating room. The generator was not responding, and the other operating rooms were being utilized. The surgeon had to cancel the surgery until a later date.

It should be noted that modifier 73 is not used for the elective cancellation of a service prior to the administration of anesthesia and/or surgical preparation of the patient.

Discontinued Outpatient Hospital/Ambulatory Surgery Center (ASC) Procedure After Administration of Anesthesia—Modifier 74

Like modifier 73, modifier 74 is used for outpatient or ambulatory surgery centers. Modifier 74 is used when, due to extenuating circumstances or those that threaten the well-being of the patient, the physician terminates a surgical or diagnostic procedure *after* the administration of anesthesia or after the procedure was started. Modifier 74 is appended to the usual procedure code for the intended procedure.

Repeat Procedure or Service by Same Physician or Other Qualified Health Care Professional—Modifier 76

At times, it is necessary for a physician or other qualified health care professional to repeat a procedure or service subsequent to the original procedure or service. When this occurs, modifier 76 is used. The original procedure or service code is the same for both sessions.

EXAMPLE: Mrs. Roberts underwent a needle thoracentesis aspiration of the pleural space by Dr. Clark. Later that day, another thoracentesis was necessary, and Dr. Clark performed it.

Dr. Clark reported the second procedure with code 32554-76. Note that this modifier is not to be appended to an E/M code.

Repeat Procedure or Service by Another Physician or Other Qualified Health Care Professional—Modifier 77

Modifier 77 is used when a physician or other qualified health care professional needs to indicate that a basic procedure or service performed by another physician had to be repeated. The physician who repeated the procedure would append modifier 77 to the repeated procedure or service code, which would be the same procedure or service code as the original procedure or service code. By slightly modifying our previous example, we can see how to use modifier 77:

EXAMPLE: Mrs. Roberts underwent a needle thoracentesis aspiration of the pleural space by Dr. Clark. The next day, another needle thoracentesis aspiration of the pleural space was necessary; however, Dr. Clark was not available. Dr. Lewis performed the procedure.

Dr. Lewis reported it with code 32554-77. This modifier is not be be appended to an E/M code.

Unplanned Return to the Operating/Procedure Room by the Same Physician or Other Qualified Health Care Professional Following Initial Procedure for a Related Procedure During the Postoperative Period—Modifier 78

At times, a patient is taken back to the operating room for a *related* procedure during the postoperative period of the initial procedure. The claim would indicate that another procedure was performed during the postoperative period of the initial procedure by appending **modifier 78** to the procedure code of the subsequent procedure. It is possible that an unforeseen complication may arise from the original surgery and that the patient may need to be returned to the operating room.

> **EXAMPLE:** Mr. Mitchell had hip replacement surgery performed by Dr. Weiss. Two days postop, the incision developed a hematoma. This required a return trip to the OR, where Dr. Weiss performed a superficial wound dehiscence with a simple closure.

To report this service properly, you would use code 12020-78. Should documentation be requested by a payer, it needs to support the use of this modifier.

Unrelated Procedure or Service by the Same Physician or Other Qualified Health Care Professional During the Postoperative Period—Modifier 79

During a postoperative period, it may be necessary for the performance of another procedure that was unrelated to the original procedure. When this situation occurs, **modifier 79** is used.

> **EXAMPLE:** Mr. Duncan underwent an excision of two lesions on the small intestine by Dr. Cass. Mr. Duncan was experiencing pain in the area of the diaphragm 30 days postop. Several tests were done, and a diaphragmatic hernia was diagnosed. Mr. Duncan underwent surgical repair of a paraesophageal hiatal hernia via thoracotomy.

Dr. Cass reported code 43334-79.

Assistant Surgeon—Modifier 80

During surgery, it is not uncommon for a surgeon to assist another surgeon. To report the services of the assistant surgeon, add modifier 80 to the usual procedure code. The assistant surgeon reports the same code(s) as the primary surgeon, but a **modifier 80** is added to his or her services.

> **EXAMPLE:** Dr. Barton performed an anastomosis on the extrahepatic biliary ducts and gastrointestinal tract. Dr. Carrey assisted Dr. Barton with this procedure.

In our example, Dr. Barton would bill code 47780, whereas Dr. Carrey would report 47780-80 for his services.

It should be noted that Medicare Part B does not cover the services of an assistant surgeon for certain procedures. The physician fee schedule on the CMS Web site lists the modifier 80 exemptions. Payment cannot be collected from the patient for these services if the provider is enrolled as a participating Medicare provider.

Minimum Assistant Surgeon—Modifier 81

Modifier 81 would be used if the circumstances required a second surgeon for a short time, but not throughout the whole procedure. Another instance that would warrant an 81 modifier would be when a second or third assistant surgeon was needed during a procedure.

EXAMPLE: Dr. Grace was performing an open revision of arteriovenous fistula with an autogenous dialysis graft with thrombectomy. At one point, he required the assistance of Dr. Brown to help with some bleeding. Dr. Grace got the patient stable and finished the procedure. Dr. Brown was present only during the critical portion of the surgery and left the surgical suite after the patient stabilized.

Dr. Grace would report his services with CPT code 36833, whereas Dr. Brown would report his services with code 36833-81.

Assistant Surgeon (When Qualified Resident Surgeon Is Not Available in a Teaching Facility)—Modifier 82

Modifier 82 is used when there is the unavailability of a qualified resident surgeon. In the teaching hospital setting, some residency programs allow their residents to participate as assistants-at-surgery. Modifier 82 is appended if a qualified resident surgeon is not available. CMS guidelines require a certification on file for each claim submitted with this modifier as part of section 1842 of the Social Security Act.

EXAMPLE: Dr. Evans was the surgeon on call at 3:00 a.m. when four people were brought into Mercy Hospital, a teaching facility. The four patients had been seriously injured in a motor vehicle accident. All four patients needed immediate surgical attention, which left the surgical teams shorthanded. Dr. Evans asked a colleague in his practice, Dr. Donaldson, to assist because all the surgical residents were caring for other patients.

Dr. Donaldson's services are reported with an 82 modifier to indicate that no surgical residents were available to assist Dr. Evans.

Reference (Outside) Laboratory—Modifier 90

Modifier 90 is used on laboratory procedure codes to indicate that the laboratory procedures are performed by a party other than the treating or reporting physician.

EXAMPLE: Dr. McGuire ordered a urine culture to be done on a patient who he suspected had a bladder infection but who was sensitive to certain antibiotics. The culture was to be done by an outside laboratory because Dr. McGuire's lab does not perform cultures.

The urine culture would be reported with a 90 modifier to indicate that the test was sent out to be run.

Repeat Clinical Diagnostic Laboratory Test—Modifier 91

Modifier 91 is used to indicate that the same laboratory test was repeated on the same day to obtain subsequent (multiple) test results. Problems with equipment or collected specimen, confirmation of initial test results, and the availability of an all inclusive code are *not* considered valid reasons to append this modifier.

EXAMPLE: Jenny presented to her physician with a blood sugar reading of 325. Jenny had a quantitative blood glucose test in the doctor's office, which confirmed her high blood sugar reading. She was given Glucophage, p.o., right then in the office. The physician asked her to wait for an hour, and the test was rerun, with results showing Jenny's blood sugar back in a more acceptable range.

The first test would be reported with code 82947, and the second with code 82947-91.

It should also be noted that this modifier is not used when the code description includes a series of test results that are run on the same day.

Alternative Laboratory Platform Testing—Modifier 92

Modifier 92 is used when laboratory testing is performed by the use of a kit or transportable instrument for HIV testing: codes 86701–86703 and 87389. The kit's components can include a single-use, disposable analytical chamber, which can be carried or transported to the vicinity of the patient.

The code used to report the HIV-1 test is code 86701-92.

Synchronous Telemedicine Service Rendered Via a Real-Time Interactive Audio and Video Telecommunications System—Modifier 95

Modifier 95 is used to report synchronous telemedicine services that occur using a real-time interactive audio and video telecommunications system. This modifier can only be appended to services that are listed in Appendix P of the CPT manual. The CMS HCPCS modifier GT (defined as via interactive audio and video telecommunication systems) also currently exists to report telemedicine services to Medicare, but the GT modifier is not accepted by all payers. Modifier 95 was added to provide for the reporting of telemedicine services for payers that do not accept the GT modifier.

When using the 95 modifier the following criteria must be met:

1. The CPT code that is to be reported is listed in appendix P of the CPT manual and the telemedicine star icon appears next to the CPT code description in the CPT manual. (Reference the code description for code 99214 in the CPT manual and in Appendix P of the CPT manual to see how this displays in the CPT manual.)
2. All components of the CPT code description are completed via telemedicine and are documented by the provider of service.
3. A real-time audio and video telecommunication system is used and the provider and patient are in different locations when the service is performed.

Remember, prior to using the 95 modifier you must determine that the code may be used for synchronous telemedicine services.

Habilitative Services—Modifier 96

There are services and procedures that are completed for either habilitative or rehabilitative purposes. For example physical or occupational therapies are such services. **Modifier 96**, is be used by a physician or other qualified health care professional, to denote when a service or procedure is provided for habilitative purposes.

Within the CPT manual habilitative services are defined as services that teach an individual learned skills and functions for daily living that the individual has not yet developed. The habilitative services will then additionally help the individual to maintain and improve the learned skills or also help the individual maintain, learn, or improve skills and functioning for daily living.

Rehabilitative Services—Modifier 97

Modifier 97 is used to denote services or procedures that are rehabilitative in nature and can be used by a physician or other qualified health care professional. Rehabilitative services are services that occur after an individual was sick, hurt, or disabled. The purpose of the rehabilitative service is to help the individual maintain, get back, or improve skills and functions for daily living that were impaired or lost due to the sickness, injury, or a disability that the individual sustained.

Multiple Modifiers—Modifier 99

Under certain circumstances, more than two modifiers may be necessary to delineate a service completely. When more than two are necessary, modifier 99 is used.

> **EXAMPLE:** Marty presented to Dr. Taggert for treatment of his mycotic nails. He had the great toe on both feet treated, as well as the fourth and fifth toes on the right, and the third and fourth toes on the left.

Dr. Taggert would report his treatment of mycotic nails, code 11721, with the modifiers for the toes that were treated: TA, T2, T3, T5, T8, T9. Since all these modifiers will not fit in the modifier field, the use of modifier 99 would be appropriate. To report this on a claim, most insurance companies require the 99 modifier in the first field, followed by the next three modifiers and the remaining modifiers in the narrative.

HCPCS Level II Modifiers

HCPCS Level II modifiers accompany the HCPCS Level II codes. The Healthcare Common Procedure Coding System (HCPCS) is an alphanumeric system that describes services provided by physicians and other providers. The HCPCS system also provides codes for ambulance and durable medical equipment (DME). DME services include such things as crutches, walkers, and canes. These codes may or may not be reimbursed. The coder, as well as the providers, needs to know that just because a CPT code for a service exists does not mean that the service is reimbursable. This is something that the insurance carriers should be contacted about. More details about the HCPCS code set are explained later in this textbook.

HCPCS modifiers are assigned for the same reason that the other modifiers are assigned: the service being provided needs to be explained further. The author referenced the HCPCS Level II modifier information at *http://www.cms.gov/Medicare/Coding/MedHCPCSGenInfo/index.html.* Listed below are some of the modifiers that are used. The list is not exhaustive. Coders should use the Web sites of the various insurance carriers, as well as the CMS site for clarification on usage of these modifiers. A comprehensive list is found in Appendix 2 of the HCPCS Level II book. The purpose of the following partial listing of Level II HCPCS modifiers is to provide an overview of the use and types of Level II modifiers that are used when reporting HCPCS Level II codes.

Level II—HCPCS Alphanumeric Modifiers

The following is a partial list of the Level II HCPCS modifiers:

A1—Dressing for 1 wound.

A2—Dressing for 2 wounds.

A3—Dressing for 3 wounds.

A4—Dressing for 4 wounds.

A5—Dressing for 5 wounds.

A6—Dressing for 6 wounds.

A7—Dressing for 7 wounds.

A8—Dressing for 8 wounds.

A9—Dressing for 9 or more wounds.

AA—Anesthesia services performed by anesthesiologist.

AD—Medical supervision by a physician, more than four concurrent anesthesia procedures.

AE—Registered Dietician.

AF—Specialty Physician.

AG—Primary Physician.

AH—Clinical Psychologist (CP) services. [Used when a medical group employs a CP and bills for the CP's service.]

AI—Principal physician of record.

AJ—Clinical Social Worker (CSW). [Used when a medical group employs a CSW and bills for the CSW's service.]

AK—Nonparticipating Physician.

AM—Physician, team member service.

AP—Determination of refractive state not performed in the course of diagnostic ophthalmological examination.

AQ—Physician providing a service in an unlisted health professional shortage area (HPSA).

AR—Physician Provider Services in a Physician Scarcity Area (PSA). [Effective for dates of service on or after January 1, 2005.]

AS—Physician Assistant, Nurse Practitioner, or Clinical Nurse Specialist services for assistant at surgery.

AT—Acute treatment. (This modifier should be used when reporting a spinal manipulation service [codes 98940, 98941, and 98942].) Effective dates of service October 1, 2004, and after.

CB—Service ordered by a renal dialysis facility (RDF) physician as part of the ESRD beneficiary's dialysis benefit. It is not part of the composite rate, and it is separately reimbursable.

CC—Procedure code changed. [This modifier is used when the submitted procedure code is changed either for administrative reasons or because an incorrect code was filed.]

CR—Catastrophe/disaster related.

EJ—Subsequent claims for a defined course of therapy (example: EPO, sodium hyaluronate).

EM—Emergency reserve supply (for ESRD benefit only).

EP—Service provided as part of Medicaid early periodic screening diagnosis and treatment (EPSDT) program.

The following modifiers are used to identify various body parts that might need to be identified when multiple procedures are reported.

E1—Upper Left, Eyelid.

E2—Lower Left, Eyelid.

E3—Upper Right, Eyelid.

E4—Lower Right, Eyelid.

FA—Left Hand, Thumb.

F1—Left Hand, Second Digit.

F2—Left Hand, Third Digit.

F3—Left Hand, Fourth Digit.

F4—Left Hand, Fifth Digit.

F5—Right Hand, Thumb.

F6—Right Hand, Second Digit.

F7—Right Hand, Third Digit.

(continues)

(continued)

F8—Right Hand, Fourth Digit.

F9—Right Hand, Fifth Digit.

LM—Left Main Coronary Artery.

LT—Left Side. [Used to identify procedures performed on the left side of the body.]

RC—Right Coronary Artery.

RI—Ramus Intermedius Coronary Artery.

RT—Right Side. [Used to identify procedures performed on the right side of the body.]

TA—Left Foot, Great Toe.

T1—Left Foot, Second Digit.

T2—Left Foot, Third Digit.

T3—Left Foot, Fourth Digit.

T4—Left Foot, Fifth Digit.

T5—Right Foot, Great Toe.

T6—Right Foot, Second Digit.

T7—Right Foot, Third Digit.

T8—Right Foot, Fourth Digit.

T9—Right Foot, Fifth Digit.

Additional Modifiers F to G9

The following is a partial listing of the F to G9 modifiers. Modifiers G1 to G6 are used to report information about dialysis services. End Stage Renal Disease (ESRD) facilities report CPT code 90999 (unlisted dialysis procedure), and one of the G modifiers (G1, G2, G3, G4, and G5) on all claims for hemodialysis to reflect the most recent urea reduction ratio (URR). Medicare reviews the reported G1 to G5 modifier to determine the adequacy of dialysis to measure the quality of dialysis services. Code 90999-G6 reports to Medicare that less than six dialysis sessions have been provided in a month.

FP—Service provided as part of Medicaid Family Planning Program.

FX—X-ray taken using film.

G1—Most recent urea reduction ratio (URR) reading of less than 60.

G2—Most recent urea reduction ratio (URR) reading of 60 to 64.9.

G3—Most recent urea reduction ratio (URR) of 65 to 69.9.

G4—Most recent urea reduction ratio (URR) of 70 to 74.9.

G5—Most recent urea reduction ratio (URR) reading of 75 or greater.

G6—ESRD patient for whom less than six dialysis sessions have been provided in a month.

G7—Pregnancy resulted from rape or incest, or pregnancy is certified by physician as life threatening.

G8—Monitored Anesthesia Care (MAC) for deep complex, complicated, or markedly invasive surgical procedure.

G9—Monitored Anesthesia Care (MAC) for patient who has history of severe cardio-pulmonary condition.

G Modifiers

Knowledge of the following G modifiers is important if you are reporting services for Medicare patients; use of these modifiers will help prevent Medicare payment denials and allows for the proper payment of Medicare claims.

GA—Waiver of Liability Statement on file. [Effective for dates of service on or after October 1, 1995, a physician or supplier should use this modifier to note that the patient has been advised of the possibility of noncoverage.]

GC—This service has been performed in part by a resident under the direction of a teaching physician.

GE—This service has been performed by a resident without the presence of a teaching physician under the primary care exception.

GG—Performance and payment of a screening mammogram and diagnostic mammogram on the same patient, same day.

GH—Diagnostic mammogram converted from screening mammogram on same day.

GJ—"Opt Out" physician or practitioner emergency or urgent service.

GM—Multiple patients on one ambulance trip.

GN—Services delivered under an outpatient speech language pathology plan of care.

GO—Services delivered under an occupational therapist plan of care.

GP—Services delivered under a physical therapist plan of care.

GQ—Via asynchronous telecommunications system.

GT—Via interactive audio and video telecommunication systems.

GV—Attending physician not employed or paid under arrangement by the patient's hospice provider.

GW—Service not related to the hospice patient's terminal condition.

GY—Item or service statutorily excluded or does not meet the definition of any Medicare benefit.

GZ—Item or service expected to be denied as not reasonable and necessary.

Modifiers J through V

The following is a partial list of modifiers J to V. A complete listing of modifiers J to V is found in the HCPCS Level II manual. This partial listing helps to outline the types of modifiers that are found in this range of modifiers.

J1—Competitive Acquisition Program (CAP), no-pay submission for a prescription number.

J2—Competitive Acquisition Program (CAP), restocking of emergency drugs after emergency administration and a prescription number.

J3—Competitive Acquisition Program (CAP), drug not available through CAP as written, reimbursed under average sales price (ASP) methodology.

KL—DMEPOS item delivered via mail.

KO—Single drug unit dose formulation.

KP—First drug of a multiple drug unit dose formulation.

KQ—Second or subsequent drug of a multiple drug unit dose formulation.

KX—Therapy cap exception has been approved, or it meets all the guidelines for an automatic exception.

(continues)

(continued)

LC—Left circumflex coronary artery.

LD—Left anterior descending coronary artery.

LR—Laboratory round-trip.

LS—FDA-monitored intraocular lens implant.

Q3—Live kidney donor and related services.

Q4—Service for ordering/referring physician qualifies as a service exemption.

Q5—Service furnished by a substitute physician under a reciprocal billing arrangement.

Q6—Service furnished by a locum tenens physician.

Q7—One Class A finding.

Q8—Two Class B findings.

Q9—One Class B and Two Class C findings.

QA—FDA investigational device exemption.

QB—Physician providing service in a rural Health Professional Shortage Area (HPSA).

QC—Single channel monitoring.

QD—Recording and storage in solid-state memory by digital recorder.

QK—Medical direction of two, three, or four concurrent anesthesia procedures involving qualified individuals.

QL—Patient pronounced dead after ambulance called.

QM—Ambulance service provided under arrangement by a provider of services.

QN—Ambulance service furnished directly by a provider of services.

QP—Documentation is on file showing that the laboratory test(s) was ordered individually or ordered as a CPT-recognized panel other than automated profile codes 80002–80019, G0058, G0059, and G0060.

QS—Monitored anesthesia care service.

QT—Recording and storage on a tape by an analog tape recorder.

QW—Clinical Laboratory Improvement Amendment (CLIA) waived test. (Modifier used to identify waived tests.)

QX—CRNA service with medical direction by a physician.

QY—Anesthesiologist medically directs one CRNA.

QZ—CRNA service without medical direction by a physician.

RD—Drug provided to beneficiary but not administered "incident to."

SF—Second opinion ordered by a Professional Review Organization (PRO) per Section 9401, P.L. 99-272 (100% reimbursement—no Medicare deductible or coinsurance).

SG—Ambulatory Surgical Center (ASC) facility service.

SL—State supplied vaccine.

SW—Services provided by a Certified Diabetic Educator.

SY—Persons who are in close contact with member of high-risk population (use only with codes for immunizations).

TC—Technical Component. Under certain circumstances, a charge may be made for the technical component alone. Under those circumstances, adding modifier TC to the usual procedure number identifies the technical component charge. **Note:** The TC modifier should not be appended to procedure codes that represent the technical component (e.g., 93005).

TG—Complex/higher level of care.

UN—Two patients served.

UP—Three patients served.

UQ—Four patients served.

UR—Five patients served.

US—Six or more patients served.

VP—Aphakic patient.

Ambulance Origin and Destination Modifiers

The following modifiers are used to designate the place of origin and destination of a transport. The first position identifies the place of origin, and the second position identifies the destination.

EXAMPLE: A patient is picked up at the scene of an accident and transported to a hospital. Place "S" (scene of accident or acute event) in the first modifier position to indicate the place of origin. Place "H" (hospital) in the second modifier position to indicate the destination of the patient.

D—Diagnostic or therapeutic site other than "P" or "H" when these are used as origin codes.

E—Residential, domiciliary, custodial facility (other than an 1819 facility).

G—Hospital Based Dialysis Facility (hospital or hospital related).

H—Hospital.

I—Site of transfer (e.g., airport or helicopter pad) between modes of ambulance transport.

J—Non-Hospital-Based Dialysis Facility.

N—Skilled Nursing Facility (SNF; 1819 facility).

P—Physician's office.

R—Residence.

S—Scene of Accident or Acute Event.

X—(Destination code only) Intermediate stop at physician's office on the way to the hospital.

Summary

- Modifiers offer additional information to insurance payers and Medicare to release payment for services.
- Modifiers work as adjectives in describing services provided to patients.
- Some modifiers affect payment.
- Some modifiers are for information only.
- Modifiers indicate that additional information may be found in the supporting documentation.
- The two types of modifiers are CPT Level I modifiers and HCPCS Level II modifiers.

Internet Links

For federal regulatory information about physician billing and payment, go to *http://www.cms.gov* and search physician billing.

Chapter Review

Fill in the Blank

Instructions: Fill in the blanks in the statements that follow.

1. A CPT modifier is a(n) _____ digit modifier appended to a CPT code to indicate that a service or procedure has been altered.

2. A complete listing of Level I modifiers commonly found in the CPT coding book can be found in _____.

3. When billing physician services, place modifiers in item _____ of the CMS-1500 form.

4. Statistical modifiers, also known as _____ modifiers, are used for informational purposes and affect the processing or payment of the code billed but do not affect the fee.

5. Modifier 99 indicates that _____ modifiers are needed for an individual CPT code.

6. Modifier 56 is used only when _____ management is provided.

7. A mandated service is reported using modifier _____.

8. When a surgeon completes only the surgical care, modifier _____ should be appended to the CPT procedure code.

9. To report the services of the assistant surgeon, add modifier _____ to the procedure code.

10. Modifier 90 is used on _____ laboratory or reference laboratory procedure codes to indicate that the procedure was performed by a party other than the treating or reporting physician.

Identify the Modifier

Instructions: For the following situations, list the correct modifier to use, or supply a short answer.

1. Two surgeons _____

2. Unusual anesthesia _____

3. Increased procedural services _____

4. Reduced services _____

5. Postoperative management only _____

6. Explain when modifier 26 is used. _____

7. Explain when modifier 47 is used. _____

8. When a bilateral procedure is performed in the same operative session and the CPT code describes a unilateral procedure, which modifier should be appended to the CPT code? _____

9. Which modifier is used to indicate that a different provider performed the preoperative procedure management of a patient? _____

10. Repeat procedure or service by the same physician or other qualified health care professional
    _____

11. Discontinued procedure _____

12. Decision for surgery _____

13. Surgical team _____

14. Assistant surgeon _____

15. Professional component _____

16. What modifier would be added to code 90999 to indicate that a patient's most recent URR reading
    was 61.4? _____

17. Right hand, fourth digit _____

18. Multiple patients were transported on one ambulance trip. Which modifier should be appended to the
    service code? _____

19. Minimum assistant surgeon _____

20. Repeat clinical diagnostic laboratory test _____

Case Studies

Review each case and indicate the correct code(s).

Case 1

Marty went to the doctor's office with a sore throat and an upset stomach. The doctor
performed an exam and evaluation of Marty. In the course of the evaluation, Marty
mentioned he was having some back pain. The doctor also evaluated this issue and
performed an osteopathic manipulation on one body region. The doctor reported a 99213
with a(n) _____ modifier and a 98925 for the OMT.

Case 2

Dr. Albert is performing a complicated pyeloplasty on Kelly. Kelly was tolerating the
procedure fairly well until her blood pressure began to drop dangerously low. After having
trouble stabilizing her, Dr. Albert discontinued the procedure because he felt it would be
too dangerous to continue. The doctor reported the part of the service he performed with a
50400 and a(n) _____ modifier.

Case 3

Jamie South was out of town playing football two weeks ago, and he sustained a broken ankle. He was taken to the local hospital, and Dr. Books performed a closed treatment of trimalleolar ankle fracture with manipulation. Today he is being seen by Dr. Thompson for the postoperative care for the fracture treatment. Dr. Thompson should report code 27818 with modifier _____.

Case 4

Mary Beth is a 19-day-old neonate who weighs 3.2 kg and who is undergoing an arthrotomy with biopsy of the interphalangeal joint. The surgeon reports code 28054 with modifier _____.

Case 5

Dr. Cook is performing a pulmonary valve replacement. Dr. Samson is the assistant surgeon for the case. Dr. Cook reports code 33475, whereas Dr. Samson should report _____.

Case 6

Sam is a 10-year-old child who has had chronic ear infections for the last year. Today Dr. Abbes has decided that Sam needs to have tubes inserted into his ears. This is scheduled to occur in three weeks. Today's visit was coded with 99214 appended with modifier _____.

Case 7

James Tree is a patient at an intermediate care facility. Today he is being seen by Dr. Rip because of a state mandate for the resident to be seen every six months. Code 99315 was reported with modifier _____ to report the mandated service.

Case 8

Dr. Whoo interprets an MRI of the temporomandibular joint. This is reported with code 70336, appended with modifier _____.

Case 9

Drs. Jones and Smith work as a surgical team to perform a double lung transplant with cardiopulmonary bypass. Dr Jones would report code 32854, and Dr. Smith would report code 32854-66. Is this correct? _____

Case 10

Dr. Jackson performed a therapeutic pneumothorax on Sally Small and reported code 32960. Later that same day, the procedure was repeated by Dr. Jackson. How should the second procedure be reported? _____

Evaluation and Management

Chapter Outline

Learning Objectives

At the conclusion of this chapter, you will be able to:

1. Define key terms related to evaluation and management coding.
2. Locate codes in the subsection and subcategory of the CPT Evaluation and Management section.
3. Identify the documentation needed to justify the selection of a code from the Evaluation and Management section of the CPT manual.
4. Differentiate between a new and an established patient.
5. Select place of service codes for CPT services and codes.
6. Explain the consequences of submitting an incorrect place of service code.
7. Classify parts of the patient's SOAP note and medical history.
8. State documentation requirements for the selection of a consultation code.
9. Choose the correct E/M code for services provided.
10. Explain the rules related to coding for hospital observation services, critical care services, nursing facility services, and preventive medicine services.
11. Identify and code procedures for evaluation and management from case studies.

Key Terms

brief HPI

care plan oversight

case management

chief complaint (CC)

complete PFSH

comprehensive examination

comprehensive history

consultations

contributory factors

coordination of care

counseling

critical care

detailed examination

detailed history

elements of examination

emergency department (ED)

established patient

Evaluation and Management (E/M)

expanded problem-focused examination

expanded problem-focused history

extended HPI

face-to-face time

family history

high–complexity medical decision making

history

history of the present illness (HPI)

Initial Observation Care

low birth weight (LBW)

low-complexity medical decision making

moderate-complexity medical decision making

nature of the presenting problem

new patient

observation

observation status

past, family, and social history (PFSH)

past history

pertinent PFSH

place of service (POS)

preventive medicine services

problem-focused examination

problem-focused history

psychiatric residential treatment center

referral

review of systems (ROS)

SOAP note

social history

Standby Services

straightforward medical decision making

unit/floor time

very low birth weight (VLBW)

Introduction

The first section of CPT is titled **Evaluation and Management (E/M)** and is commonly referred to as the E and M section. *Evaluation and Management* means exactly what it says. The patient is first evaluated by a physician, nurse practitioner, physician assistant, or in some cases a nurse. After the evaluation is completed, a management plan is implemented and recorded in the patient's medical record. The evaluation of the patient, along with the management plan, are considered billable services, and the CPT codes are used to delineate the type of service given to the patient, thus determining the revenue amount generated by the service provided.

Documentation Guidelines for Evaluation and Management Services

In 1995 and 1997, the American Medical Association (AMA) and the Centers for Medicare and Medicaid Services (CMS; formerly known as the Health Care Financing Administration) developed documentation guidelines for Evaluation and Management services. This was done to provide the health-care industry with a reference tool that could be used to give providers guidance in documenting and selecting Evaluation and Management codes, as well as a way to measure code selection.

The author has chosen the 1997 *Documentation Guidelines for Evaluation and Management Services* as the basis for writing this chapter. The Internet links for both the 1995 and 1997 guidelines can be found on the CMS

website at: https://www.cms.gov/Outreach-and-Education/Medicare-Learning-Network-MLN
/MLNEdWebGuide/Downloads/95Docguidelines.pdf and https://www.cms.gov/Outreach-and-Education
/Medicare-Learning-Network-MLN/MLNEdWebGuide/Downloads/97Docguidelines.pdf, respectively.

All coders are encouraged to be familiar with and reference these guidelines frequently.

Overview of the Evaluation and Management Section

The Evaluation and Management section contains categories for office visits, hospital visits, emergency room visits, preventive medicine visits, consultations, and skilled nursing facility and other types of visits, as summarized in Table 3-1. To become familiar with the various categories within the Evaluation and Management section, simply use Table 3-1 to walk through the section by identifying the categories listed in the table.

TABLE 3-1 Categories and Code Ranges in the Evaluation and Management Section

Category	Code Range
Office and Other Outpatient Services	99201–99215
Hospital Observation Services	99217–99220, 99224–99226
Hospital Inpatient Services	99221–99223, 99231–99239
Consultations	99241–99255
Emergency Department Services	99281–99288
Critical Care Services	99291–99292
Nursing Facility Services	99304–99318
Domiciliary, Rest Home (e.g., Boarding Home), or Custodial Care Services	99324–99337
Domiciliary, Rest Home (e.g., Assisted Living Facility), or Home Care Plan Oversight Services	99339–99340
Home Services	99341–99350
Prolonged Services	99354–99360, 99415–99416
Physician Standby Services	99360
Case Management Services	99366–99368
Care Plan Oversight Services	99374–99380
Preventive Medicine Services	99381–99429
Non-Face-to-Face Physician Services	99441–99458
Special Evaluation and Management Services	99450–99456
Newborn Care Services	99460–99463
Delivery/Birthing Room Attendance and Resuscitation Services	99464–99465
Inpatient Neonatal Intensive Care Services and Pediatric and Neonatal Critical Care Services	99466–99486
Cognitive Assessment and Care Plan Services	99483
Care Management Services	99487, 99489, 99490, 99491
Psychiatric Collaborative Care Management Services	99492–99494
Transitional Care Management Services	99495–99496
Advance Care Planning	99497, 99498
General Behavioral Health Integration Care Management	99484
Other Evaluation and Management Services	99499

Exercise 3.1—Check Your Understanding

Subsection and Subcategories of the CPT Evaluation and Management Section

Using a CPT manual, identify the subsection and subcategory of the CPT Evaluation and Management section for the following codes. The first two are completed for you.

CPT Code(s)	Subsection and Subcategory of E/M Section	CPT Code(s)	Subsection and Subcategory of E/M Section
1. 99211–99215	Office and other outpatient services; established patient	4. 99238–99239	
		5. 99251–99255	
		6. 99217	
2. 99281–99285	Emergency department services; new or established patient	7. 99231–99233	
		8. 99241–99245	
		9. 99497–99498	
3. 99341–99345		10. 99360	

Evaluation and Management Coding

The Evaluation and Management section of CPT has some unique guidelines that coders must understand in order to code effectively within this section. The guidelines for the Evaluation and Management section are located in the CPT manual at the beginning of the section. The guidelines define commonly used terms and instructions for selecting a level of E/M service. Three major questions must be asked when you are identifying an Evaluation and Management code:

1. Is the patient a new or an established patient?
2. Where was the service provided?
3. What was the degree of the service rendered?

New Patients versus Established Patients

The majority of the categories in this chapter (i.e., office visits, hospital visits, and skilled nursing facility) are divided according to whether the patient is a new or established patient. For example, the Office or Other Outpatient Services codes, 99201–99215, are divided as follows:

New Patient codes—99201–99205

Established Patient codes—99211–99215

It should be noted, however, that not all categories within the Evaluation and Management section differentiate between new and established patients. For example, the Emergency Department Service codes do not differentiate between new and established patients. In referencing the Emergency Department Service codes, 99281–99285, it should be noted that CPT states that this range of codes is for new *or* established patients.

New Patient

The criteria for what constitutes a new patient need to be understood when it is time to assign a code from the Evaluation and Management section of the CPT manual. The CPT manual defines a **new patient** as a patient who has not received any professional services from the physician/qualified health care professional, or from another physician/qualified health care professional of the exact same specialty and subspeciality who belongs to the same group practice, within the past three years. Important components of the definition to be considered when you select a code include the terms

- same specialty or subspeciality,
- same group practice,
- three years.

Same-Specialty Consideration

EXAMPLE: Bob Light is a patient at Troy Medical Associates, which is a multispecialty group practice. This practice includes family practice physicians and various specialists. Bob is a regular patient of Dr. Sign, who is a family practice physician. Bob is experiencing back pain, and he has made an appointment with Dr. Hey, an orthopedic surgeon who is also a physician for Troy Medical Associates.

In this case, when Bob is seen by Dr. Hey, Dr. Hey's office can bill Bob as a new patient because the physicians are of a different specialty, even though they are within the same multispecialty group. Remember, each first encounter in a different specialty can be considered new when the patient has not been seen by that specialty within the same group practice.

Another consideration you must take into account is whether the patient has been seen by different groups or by different physicians who are not in the same group practice but are of the same specialty.

Same versus Different Group Practice Considerations

EXAMPLE: Mrs. Smith called Valley Medical Associates to make an appointment with internist Dr. Case. When asked if she was a patient of Dr. Case, Mrs. Smith replied that she had never seen Dr. Case. However, she had been a patient of Dr. Kelly, who was also an internist, but he was located at Hilltop Associates, another group of internists in town. Dr. Kelly had recently retired, and Mrs. Smith needed to refill her blood pressure medicine and establish herself with a new doctor.

In our example, Mrs. Smith is seen by Dr. Case, who will bill her as a new patient. Dr. Case and Dr. Kelly are both internists; however, because they do not belong to the same group practice, Dr. Case can code Mrs. Smith's visit as a new-patient visit.

Also, when determining if a patient is a new or an established patient, coders must consider the last time that a patient was seen. Remember, the definition states, "within the last three years."

Three-Year Consideration

EXAMPLE: Sue Lutes lived in New York and was an established patient with Dr. Jones. In May 2009, she was seen by Dr. Jones before she moved to Florida. She lived in Florida until June 2010 and then moved back to New York. In July 2013, she was experiencing symptoms of an upper-respiratory infection and was seen by Dr. Jones.

In this example, when Sue was seen by Dr. Jones in July 2013, she can be billed as a new patient because she was not seen by Dr. Jones for more than three years. However, if she had been seen within the three-year period by Dr. Jones, she would not have been billed as a new patient.

This understanding is critical because assignment of the wrong code can result in a denial from the insurance company, stating that new-patient guidelines have not been met. Should this type of denial occur, it would be corrected by identifying the level of service for an established patient that is supported in the documentation, and by reprocessing it using the correct code.

Established Patient

An **established patient** is a patient who has received professional services from the physician/qualified health care professional, or another physician/qualified health care professional of the same exact specialty and subspeciality, who belongs to the same group practice, within the past three years.

> **EXAMPLE:** Mike Roberts is a patient of the ABC Family Practice. Mike was ill and called the office to get an appointment with Dr. James, his primary care provider. Mike had seen Dr. James one month earlier for an annual physical. For today's visit, Dr. James was away, but Dr. Matthews (a partner in the group) had an opening in his schedule, which Mike agreed to take. This was the first time that Mike had ever seen Dr. Matthews.

In our example, Dr. James and Dr. Matthews are both family practice providers who belong to the same group practice, ABC Family Practice. Because the established patient criteria was met, Mike would be billed as an established patient, even though he was a new patient to Dr. Matthews. Remember, in cases where another physician was covering or was on call for a physician, the patient's encounter is billed as though the patient had been seen by the physician who was not available.

Location of the Service Provided

As we noted earlier in this chapter, the Evaluation and Management section of CPT is divided into categories according to the location of the service. Therefore, in order to select a code, the coder must know where the service was provided: was the service provided in a physician's office, the hospital, or a skilled nursing facility? When attempting to locate the correct CPT code for an Evaluation and Management service from the index, the coder can reference the location of the service to locate the correct Evaluation and Management code. For example, if the patient was seen in the hospital, the term to reference in the index would be "hospital," which would lead the coder to "Hospital Discharge Services" and "Hospital Services." To become familiar with the locations, review Table 3-1 of this chapter.

When services are billed on professional claims, the claim form requires a place-of-service code. See Appendix I for an example of a CMS-1500 professional claim form. Coders need to understand the concept of **place of service (POS)**, so we will note it here because there is a correlation between Evaluation and Management codes and place of service codes. The place of service code is a different code from the Evaluation and Management code.

A place of service code is required in box 24B of the CMS-1500 form. Place of service codes are maintained by the Centers for Medicare and Medicaid Services (CMS) and are used by payers (Medicare, Medicaid, and other private insurance companies) to specify where a service was rendered. POS is described using a numeric code that is usually listed in the beginning of the CPT manual. Table 3-2 lists POS codes.

The POS lets the payer know where care was rendered, such as the office (POS 11) or an urgent care facility (POS 20). Use of an incorrect place of service with an E/M code can result in a rejection by the insurance carrier.

> **EXAMPLE:** Dr. Calvin, an emergency-department physician, saw Matt for abdominal pain and cramping. After evaluating Matt, it was determined that he needed to be admitted under the care of a surgeon for an appendectomy.

In our example, Dr. Calvin would be submitting a code from the Emergency Department Service codes 99281–99285, because he was the emergency-department doctor. The place-of-service code that would be submitted on the claim with Dr. Calvin's charges would be 23-Emergency Room—Hospital. The POS code and Evaluation and Management code are "connected" in that they have a correlation.

Evaluation and Management coding requires attention to documentation in the patient's medical record, the severity of the problem encountered, and the medical necessity of the service being billed. Each of these issues will be discussed in this chapter, along with explanations on choosing the correct CPT code for the E/M service rendered.

TABLE 3-2 Place of Service Codes

Place of Service Code(s)	Place of Service Name
01	Pharmacy
02	Telehealth
03	School
04	Homeless Shelter
05	Indian Health Service Freestanding Facility
06	Indian Health Service Provider-Based Facility
07	Tribal 638 Freestanding Facility
08	Tribal 638 Provider-Based Facility
09	Prison-Correctional Facility
10	Unassigned
11	Office
12	Home
13	Assisted Living Facility
14	Group Home
15	Mobile Unit
16	Temporary Lodging
17	Walk-in Retail Health Clinic
18	Place of Employment—Worksite
19	Off Campus—Outpatient Hospital
20	Urgent Care Facility
21	Inpatient Hospital
22	On Campus—Outpatient Hospital
23	Emergency Room—Hospital
24	Ambulatory Surgical Center
25	Birthing Center
26	Military Treatment Facility
27–30	Unassigned
31	Skilled Nursing Facility
32	Nursing Facility
33	Custodial Care Facility
34	Hospice
35–40	Unassigned
41	Ambulance—Land
42	Ambulance—Air or Water
43–48	Unassigned
49	Independent Clinic
50	Federally Qualified Health Center
51	Inpatient Psychiatric Facility
52	Psychiatric Facility—Partial Hospitalization
53	Community Mental Health Center

(continues)

TABLE 3-2 *(continued)*

Place of Service Code(s)	Place of Service Name
54	Intermediate Care Facility/Individuals with Intellectual Disabilities
55	Residential Substance Abuse Treatment Facility
56	Psychiatric Residential Treatment Center
57	Non-residential Substance-Abuse Treatment Facility
58–59	Unassigned
60	Mass Immunization Center
61	Comprehensive Inpatient Rehabilitation Facility
62	Comprehensive Outpatient Rehabilitation Facility
63–64	Unassigned
65	End-Stage Renal Disease Treatment Facility
66–70	Unassigned
71	Public Health Clinic
72	Rural Health Clinic
73–80	Unassigned
81	Independent Laboratory
82–98	Unassigned
99	Other Place of Service

Exercise 3.2—Check Your Understanding

POS and Evaluation and Management Codes

Using Table 3-2, select the correct POS code for the following CPT services and codes. The first two are completed for you.

CPT Code	POS Code	CPT Code	POS Code
1. 99215, office visit	11	6. 99307, subsequent skilled nursing facility care	
2. 99221, initial hospital care	21	7. 99238, hospital discharge	
3. 99341, home visit		8. 99205, new office visit	
4. 99315, skilled nursing facility visit		9. 99384, physical exam, office	
5. 99252, initial inpatient consultation		10. 99283, emergency room	

Office or Other Outpatient Services (99201–99215)

Office or Other Outpatient Services is the first category of codes in the Evaluation and Management chapter of the CPT manual. The code range for office visits begins with 99201 and concludes with 99215. The category is further broken down into the subcategories of New Patient (99201–99205) and Established Patient (99211–99215). The note at the beginning of the category instructs the coder that codes in this subcategory are used for services provided in an outpatient setting, such as a doctor's office or an ambulatory setting.

Levels of Evaluation and Management Services

The third question that a coder must ask is, "What was the degree of the service that was rendered?"

To choose an E/M level of service, you should understand the degree of the service rendered and what makes up each of the levels used for reporting. The subsections and subcategories within the E/M chapter of CPT are made up of different levels of service codes, which have different criteria depending on the level of service rendered. New patient codes have different documentation requirements than established patient codes. The American Medical Association and CMS have established *Documentation Guidelines for Evaluation and Management Services*. These guidelines were established in 1995 and revised in 1997. This book uses the 1997 guidelines as a point of reference. The Internet links for both the 1995 and 1997 guidelines can be found on the CMS website at: https://www.cms.gov/Outreach-and-Education/Medicare-Learning-Network-MLN /MLNEdWebGuide/Downloads/95Docguidelines.pdf and https://www.cms.gov/Outreach-and-Education /Medicare-Learning-Network-MLN/MLNEdWebGuide/Downloads/97Docguidelines.pdf, respectively.

Seven components go into making up the levels of service for E/M codes:

- History
- Examination
- Medical decision making
- Counseling
- Coordination of care
- Nature of presenting problem
- Time

History, examination, and medical decision making are considered the key components. Counseling, coordination of care, and nature of the presenting problem are considered contributory components. Time is unique in that it can or cannot contribute to code selection, depending on other factors of the case. To understand fully how these seven components should influence your choice of a level of E/M service code, we will look at each one individually.

The first three components are key because they are universally recognized as the basis for choosing a level of service for a patient encounter.

History

Four types of history appear in the Evaluation and Management codes:

- Problem focused
- Expanded problem focused
- Detailed
- Comprehensive

Coders must determine the type of history documented in the patient's record in order to select the appropriate level of history. This will be discussed later in this chapter because coders must first have an understanding of the elements that determine the various history types.

Each type of **history** is based on the following elements:

- Chief complaint (CC)
- History of presenting illness (HPI)
- Review of systems (ROS)
- Past, family, and social history (PFSH)

Chief Complaint (CC)   For each patient history, a **chief complaint (CC)**, defined as the reason for the patient encounter, should be recorded in the patient's record. In other words, why did the patient need to seek care? A chief complaint is usually stated in the patient's own words and should be recorded for each encounter.

History of the Present Illness (HPI)   Also recorded as part of the history is the **history of the present illness (HPI)**, a chronological description of the patient's present illness. The HPI is based on elements that describe the location of the problem, how long the problem has been going on, the severity, the quality, timing, context, and modifying factors, as well as the associated signs and symptoms relating to the problem. Refer to Table 3-3 for a listing of the elements of the HPI. The HPI can be brief or extended. A **brief HPI** consists of one to three elements of the HPI, whereas an **extended HPI** consists of at least four elements of the HPI or the status of at least three chronic or inactive conditions.

TABLE 3-3 History Components and Elements Within the Component

Component	Element
History of present illness	Location
	Quality
	Severity
	Duration
	Timing
	Context
	Modifying factors
	Associated signs and symptoms
Review of systems	Constitutional symptoms
	Eyes
	Ears, nose, mouth, throat
	Cardiovascular
	Respiratory
	Gastrointestinal
	Genitourinary
	Musculoskeletal
	Integumentary (skin and/or breast)
	Neurological
	Psychiatric
	Endocrine
	Hematologic/lymphatic
	Allergic/immunologic
Past, family, and social history	Past medical history: past illnesses, injuries, surgeries, and treatments that would be pertinent to today's visit or are medically significant
	Family history: history of immediate family members whose condition would impact the medical decision making process
	Social history: review of past current activities that impact the health status of the patient, such as smoking, drinking, drug use (the frequency and amount used), occupational history, sexual history, and education

Review of Systems (ROS)   The **review of systems (ROS)** is an inventory of body systems that is obtained from the patient to identify signs and/or symptoms that the patient may be experiencing or may have experienced. A total of 14 systems, listed in Table 3-3, are recognized in the guidelines. There are three types of ROS:

- Problem-Pertinent ROS—The patient's response to one system
- Extended ROS—The patient's response to two to nine systems
- Complete ROS—The patient's responses to at least ten systems

Remember, the ROS is obtained by querying the patient. It is most commonly completed by a series of questions from the provider to the patient.

Past, Family, and/or Social History (PFSH)   The last portion of the HPI consists of **past, family, and social history (PFSH)**. The **past history** includes information regarding major illnesses, surgeries, injuries, and hospitalizations, as well as current medications and allergies. Past history refers to any past medical information that may affect the medical decision making process.

Family history includes information regarding immediate family members who suffer from a chronic or acute illness that would impact care of the patient during either the current encounter or future encounters. Typically, a complete family history is obtained during the annual physical examination or an initial visit to initiate care and is updated as needed.

Social history is the portion of the HPI that discusses the patient's marital status; use of tobacco, alcohol, and drugs; the patient's occupation; sexual history; and other social factors that would affect care of the patient or that the provider feels may be relevant to comprehensive patient care.

A past, family, and/or social history can be pertinent or complete. A **pertinent PFSH** is a review of the history area that is related to the problem identified in the HPI. To justify a pertinent PFSH, there must be one specific item from any of the three history areas documented. A **complete PFSH** is the review of two or all three of the past, family, and/or social history areas. The definition of a complete PFHS is dependent on the category of E/M service. (Reference the Internet links for both the 1995 and 1997 guidelines can be found on the CMS website at: https://www.cms.gov/Outreach-and-Education/Medicare-Learning-Network-MLN/MLNEdWebGuide /Downloads/95Docguidelines.pdf and https://www.cms.gov/Outreach-and-Education/Medicare-Learning -Network-MLN/MLNEdWebGuide/Downloads/97Docguidelines.pdf, respectively, under the heading "Past, Family, and/or Social History" for the specific definitions that pertain to the various E/M categories.)

At this time, it may seem impossible for a coder to keep all these definitions straight. However, with practice and review, the guidelines and definitions can be understood and learned. A coder needs to learn not only the definitions that relate to history, but also the definitions that relate to the other key components. Exam and medical decision making must also be mastered.

SOAP Notes   Many providers record encounters by using a *SOAP note*. The HPI is sometimes referred to as the "S," or subjective, portion of a SOAP note. A **SOAP note** contains a subjective portion (the history), an objective portion (the exam), an assessment portion (the diagnosis), and a plan (the plan for the patient's care). The following diagram may help you visualize how this information is connected.

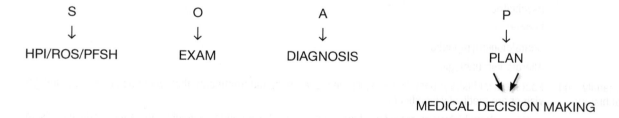

The author has found that when training students and providers, this example has helped to visualize the components of an Evaluation and Management code. Keep this in mind as we discuss the exam and medical decision-making components as well.

Selecting a Type of History   As discussed in this chapter, each type of history is based on the chief complaint; history of presenting illness; review of systems; and past, family, and social history. All these components of the history must be reviewed because they are all integral pieces of the final decision as to which level of history is chosen. As mentioned earlier, the different levels of history are referred to in CPT as the problem focused history, expanded problem-focused history, detailed history, and comprehensive history.

All histories must include a chief complaint. The **problem-focused history** is a brief HPI, which is related to the problem that brought the patient to the office. In the documentation for the encounter, one to three elements of the history of the presenting illness are needed. No review of systems or past, family, and/or social history is required. An **expanded problem-focused history** includes documentation of one to three elements of the HPI, as well as a review of the system directly related to the chief complaint. No past, family, and/or social history is required. A **detailed history** includes documentation of four or more elements of the HPI, a review of two to nine systems, and an element from the past, family, and/or social history, which may be related to the patient's problem. The **comprehensive history** contains documentation of four or more elements of the HPI, a complete review of systems, and a complete past, family, and social history.

For a better understanding of how to read a provider's note, let's review some examples that show various types of histories.

Example of Problem Focused History:

Sara presents with a sore throat and fever (chief complaint). She has had a sore throat and fever for two days (brief HPI).

Example of Expanded Problem-Focused History:

Sara presents with a sore throat and fever (chief complaint). She has had a sore throat and has been running a fever of 101 to 102 for the past two days (brief HPI). She states that she has had difficulty swallowing (a review of system related to problem—ENT).

Example of Detailed History:

Sara presents with a sore throat and fever (chief complaint). She has had a sore throat and has been running a fever of 101 to 102 for the past two days. She states that she has had difficulty swallowing, but her ears do not hurt, and she has had no shortness of breath (extended HPI with pertinent review of systems that includes not only ENT, but also lungs). Sara's brother is ill with strep throat, but no one else in the house is sick (family history).

Example of Comprehensive History:

Sara presents with a sore throat and fever (chief complaint). She has had a sore throat and has been running a fever of 101 to 102 for the past two days. She states that she has had difficulty swallowing, but her ears do not hurt, and she has had no shortness of breath, diarrhea, nausea, vomiting, or abdominal pain or cramping, and her bowel and bladder habits have not changed (extended HPI with pertinent review of systems in addition to other body systems—ENT, lungs, gastrointestinal, abdomen, urinary). Sara's brother is ill with strep throat, but no one else in the house or at school is sick. She is not exposed to secondhand smoke at home. Until today, she has been very healthy with no serious illness to speak of (past, family, and social history).

An important coding guideline to remember is that the review of systems and the past, family, and social history should be reviewed and updated as needed, but they do not need to be rerecorded at each visit. However, if they directly impact the current visit, documentation needs to reflect this. Any changes should be noted, along with the date and location of the note being referenced.

EXAMPLE: Bobby presented today for symptoms of a sinus infection. Review of systems as well as review of past, family, and social history were taken during the patient's annual physical dated April 12, 20XX, and are located in this record. Information was reviewed and discussed with the patient. The following changes were noted: ROS is positive for facial pain and postnasal drip. The PFSH is unchanged from the April 12, 20XX, note.

The coder should reference Table 3-4 to become more familiar with the types of history components. This table and a further explanation can be found in the 1995 and 1997 guidelines located on the CMS website at: https://www.cms.gov/Outreach-and-Education/Medicare-Learning-Network-MLN/MLNEdWebGuide /Downloads/95Docguidelines.pdf and https://www.cms.gov/Outreach-and-Education/Medicare-Learning -Network-MLN/MLNEdWebGuide/Downloads/97Docguidelines.pdf, respectively.

● ● ● Guideline

To qualify for a given type of history, all three elements in the table must be met. (A chief complaint is indicated at all levels.)

TABLE 3-4 History

History of Present Illness (HPI)	Review of Systems (ROS)	Past, Family, and/or Social History (PFSH)	Type of History
Brief	N/A	N/A	Problem Focused
Brief	Problem Pertinent	N/A	Expanded Problem-Focused
Extended	Extended	Pertinent	Detailed
Extended	Complete	Complete	Comprehensive

Exercise 3.3—Check Your Understanding

Documentation of Patient History

The following documentation represents a history for a patient encounter. Identify the parts of the history using the terms listed. The first one is done for you.

1. Social history
2. Chief complaint
3. Past history
4. Severity

5. Family history
6. Quality
7. Review of systems
8. Associated signs and symptoms

Beth presents today with a cough and nasal congestion (1) ___2___. She says she has an extremely painful (2) _____, nonproductive cough (3) _____. She has had a fever, which the patient states ran between 101 and 102 over the last few days (4) _____. Her sister is just getting over strep throat, but no other family members are ill (5) _____.

Beth says she has never been hospitalized and has no drug allergies (6) _____.

She has no ear pain, no nausea, no vomiting, and no change in bowel habits (7) _____.

Beth is not a smoker, does not consume alcohol, and is not a recreational drug user (8) _____.

Examination

The next key component in choosing an Evaluation and Management level of service is the examination. The examination is also recognized as the "O," or objective, portion of the provider's note. This is the portion of the visit in which the provider conducts an examination of the patient. The examination portion of the Evaluation and Management services is based on four types of examination.

The first type of examination is a **problem-focused examination**. A problem-focused examination addresses only the problem that brought the patient into the office. An **expanded problem-focused examination** addresses the affected area, along with other body systems or areas that might also be affected by the problem that brought the patient into the office. The next level of examination is known as a **detailed examination**, which involves not only the affected area, but also related systems or organs. The final and most extensive examination is known as a **comprehensive examination**, which is the highest level of examination and consists of a multisystem, or complete, examination of a single-organ system.

The *Documentation Guidelines for Evaluation and Management Services* specify that there are various types of exams: general multisystem examinations and single-organ examinations. The following is a list of the single-organ examinations:

Cardiovascular

Ear, nose, and throat

Eye

Genitourinary

Hematologic/lymphatic/immunologic

Musculoskeletal

Neurological

Psychiatric

Respiratory

Skin

Any type of exam can be performed by any physician or qualified health care professional, regardless of specialty. However, certain specialties are not paid for multisystem exams as they fall out of their particular scope of practice (e.g., podiatry—unless there is cardiovascular or neurologic involvement, the exam would focus on the area of the body from the knee down).

The type of the examination is selected by the examining provider and is based on the nature of the presenting problem, the patient's history, and the physician's clinical judgment. The level or type of the examination depends on the **elements of examination**, which, in lay terms, is the system or body area that was examined by the provider. To understand the elements of examination fully, a coder must understand the specific elements required for each exam type. This is explained in the Documentation Guidelines found on the CMS website at: https://www.cms.gov/Outreach-and-Education/Medicare-Learning-Network-MLN/MLNEdWebGuide/Downloads/95Docguidelines.pdf and https://www.cms.gov/Outreach-and-Education/Medicare-Learning-Network-MLN/MLNEdWebGuide/Downloads/97Docguidelines.pdf, respectively. To demonstrate how to read the tables found in the guidelines, we will discuss the guidelines for a general multisystem examination and then give examples of various levels of exams. For a multisystem exam, and all single-organ examinations, there are four types of examinations. Table 3-5 lists the type of exam and the number of elements that must be performed and documented by the provider to justify the examination level of a multisystem exam.

TABLE 3-5 Level of Examination

Level of Examination	Perform and Document
Problem focused	One to five elements identified by a bullet
Expanded problem focused	At least six elements identified by a bullet
Detailed	At least two elements identified by a bullet from each of the six areas/systems or at least 12 elements identified by a bullet in two or more areas/systems
Comprehensive	At least two elements identified by a bullet from each of the nine areas/systems. Refer to *1997 Documentation Guidelines for Evaluation and Management Services* for specific information by type of examination.

Content and documentation requirements exist for the multisystem exam and for each type of single-organ system. Table 3-6 outlines the elements of examination, or bullets, that have to be met to justify a given exam level for a multisystem exam.

TABLE 3-6 Content and Documentation Requirements for General Multisystem Examination

System/Body Area	Elements of Examination
Constitutional	Measurement of *any three* of the following seven vital signs: 1. sitting or standing blood pressure 2. supine blood pressure 3. pulse rate and regularity 4. respiration 5. temperature 6. height 7. weight

(*continues*)

TABLE 3-6 (*continued*)

System/Body Area	Elements of Examination
	(Vital signs may be measured and recorded by ancillary staff.)
	General appearance of patient (e.g., development, nutrition, body habitus, deformities, attention to grooming)
Eyes	Inspection of conjunctivae and lids
	Examination of pupils and irises (e.g., reaction to light and accommodation, size, and symmetry)
	Ophthalmoscopic examination of optic discs (e.g., size, C/D ratio, appearance) and posterior segments (e.g., vessel changes, exudates, hemorrhages)
Ears, Nose, Mouth, and Throat	External inspection of ears and nose (e.g., overall appearance, scars, lesions, masses)
	Otoscopic examination of external auditory canals and tympanic membranes
	Assessment of hearing (e.g., whispered voice, finger rub, tuning fork)
	Inspection of nasal mucosa, septum, and turbinates
	Inspection of lips, teeth, and gums
	Examination of oropharynx: oral mucosa, salivary glands, hard and soft palates, tongue, tonsils, and posterior pharynx
Neck	Examination of neck (e.g., masses, overall appearance, symmetry, tracheal position, crepitus)
	Examination of thyroid (e.g., enlargement, tenderness, mass)
Respiratory	Assessment of respiratory effort (e.g., intercostal retractions, use of accessory muscles, diaphragmatic movement)
	Percussion of chest (e.g., dullness, flatness, hyperresonance)
	Palpation of chest (e.g., tactile fremitus)
	Auscultation of lungs (e.g., breath sounds, adventitious sounds, rubs)
Cardiovascular	Palpation of heart (e.g., location, size, thrills)
	Auscultation of heart with notation of abnormal sounds and murmurs
	Examination of
	carotid arteries (e.g., pulse amplitude, bruits)
	abdominal aorta (e.g., size, bruits)
	femoral arteries (e.g., pulse amplitude, bruits)
	pedal pulses (e.g., pulse amplitude)
	extremities for edema and/or varicosities
Chest (Breasts)	Inspection of breasts (e.g., symmetry, nipple discharge)
	Palpation of breasts and axillae (e.g., masses or lumps, tenderness)
Gastrointestinal (Abdomen)	Examination of abdomen with notation of presence of masses or tenderness
	Examination of liver and spleen
	Examination for presence or absence of hernia
	Examination of anus, perineum, and rectum, including sphincter tone, presence of hemorrhoids, rectal masses
	Obtain stool sample for occult blood test when indicated
Genitourinary	MALE:
	Examination of the scrotal contents (e.g., hydrocele, spermatocele, tenderness of cord, testicular mass)
	Examination of the penis
	Digital rectal examination of prostate gland (e.g., size, symmetry, nodularity, tenderness)

(*continues*)

TABLE 3-6 *(continued)*

System/Body Area	Elements of Examination
	Examination of urethra (e.g., masses, tenderness, scarring)
	Examination of bladder (e.g., fullness, masses, tenderness)
	Cervix (e.g., general appearance, lesions, discharge)
	Uterus (e.g., size, contour, position, mobility, tenderness, consistency, descent or support)
	Adnexa/parametria (e.g., masses, tenderness, organomegaly, nodularity)
Lymphatic	Palpation of lymph nodes in *two or more* areas: Neck Axillae Groin Other
Musculoskeletal	Examination of gait and station Inspection and/or palpation of digits and nails (e.g., clubbing, cyanosis, inflammatory conditions, petechiae, ischemia, infections, nodes) Examination of joints, bones, and muscles of *one or more* of the following six areas: 1. head and neck 2. spine, rib and pelvis 3. right upper extremity 4. left upper extremity 5. right lower extremity 6. left lower extremity The examination of a given area includes Inspection and/or palpation with notation of presence of any misalignment, asymmetry, crepitation, defects, tenderness, masses, effusions Assessment of range of motion with notation of any pain, crepitation, or contracture Assessment of stability with notation of any dislocation (luxation), subluxation, or laxity Assessment of muscle strength and tone (e.g., flaccid, cog wheel, spastic) with notation of any atrophy or abnormal movements
Skin	Inspection of skin and subcutaneous tissue (e.g., rashes, lesions, ulcers) Palpation of skin and subcutaneous tissue (e.g., induration, subcutaneous nodules, tightening)
Neurologic	Test cranial nerves with notation of any deficits Examination of deep tendon reflexes with notation of pathological reflexes (e.g., Babinski) Examination of sensation (e.g., by touch, pin, vibration, proprioception)
Psychiatric	Description of patient's judgment and insight Brief assessment of mental status, including orientation to time, place, and person recent and remote memory mood and affect (e.g., depression, anxiety, agitation)

After you compare the medical record documentation and the documentation content requirements, you would base the level of examination for a general multisystem examination on the number of elements of examination that were recorded by the provider.

● ● ● Guideline

Content and Documentation Requirements (Reference Documentation Guidelines)

Problem Focused	**One to five elements identified by a bullet.**
Expanded Problem Focused	**At least six elements identified by a bullet.**
Detailed	**At least two elements identified by a bullet from each of six areas/systems or at least twelve elements identified by a bullet in two or more areas/systems.**
Comprehensive	**Perform all elements identified by a bullet in at least nine organ systems or body areas and document at least two elements by a bullet from each of the nine areas/systems.**

Determining the level of service for an examination becomes easier over time. The documentation *must* reflect what your provider actually did so that you can bill the most accurate level of service determination possible for the visit.

The following examples illustrate the four levels of examination that are found in provider documentation. These examples also illustrate the increasing detail that is needed to move from a problem-focused examination to a comprehensive examination.

Example of Problem-Focused Examination

Provider documentation is as follows:

Vital signs: BP, 120/70; Weight, 120 lb; Temp, 99

HEENT: TMs clear, PND, throat is very red and tonsils swollen

Bullets documented within this example would be

- Constitutional, as represented by the three vital signs recorded counts as one bullet point.
- HEENT would count as two bullet points.

Thus, justifying a problem-focused examination requires one to five bullet points.

Example of Expanded Problem-Focused Examination

Provider documentation is as follows:

Vital signs: BP, 120/70; Weight, 120 lb; Temp, 99

GENERAL APPEARANCE: NAD

HEENT: TMs clear, PND, throat is very red and tonsils swollen; Facial pain in the sinus area

LUNGS: Clear to percussion

Bullets documented within this example would be

- Constitutional, as represented by the three vital signs recorded and general appearance counts as two bullets.
- HEENT would count as three bullet points.
- Lungs would count as one bullet point for the percussion.

Thus, justifying an expanded problem-focused examination requires at least six elements.

Example of Detailed Examination

Provider documentation is as follows:

Vital signs: BP, 120/70; Weight, 120 lb; Temp, 99

GENERAL APPEARANCE: NAD

HEENT: TMs clear, PND, throat is very red and tonsils swollen. Facial pain in the sinus area

LUNGS: Clear to auscultation and percussion

HEART: RRR

EXTREMITIES: No swelling; pedal pulses normal bilaterally

ABDOMEN: Soft, nontender

NECK: No mass or tenderness; thyroid appears normal

Bullets documented within this example would be

- Constitutional, as represented by the three vital signs recorded and general appearance counts as two bullets.
- HEENT would count as three bullet points.
- Lungs would count as two bullet points because auscultation counts as one bullet point and percussion counts as a separate bullet point.
- Heart would count as two bullet points because RRR would count as one bullet point and pedal pulses would count as a separate bullet point. This is listed under extremities because this is how most providers document.
- Extremities count as one bullet point because the examination included the notation about swelling.
- Abdomen counts as one bullet point for the examination noted.
- Neck: Because the provider mentions the thyroid separately, count this as an additional bullet point, giving two bullets for the neck.

Thus, justifying a detailed examination requires at least two elements identified by a bullet from each of six areas/systems *or* at least 12 elements identified by a bullet in two or more areas/systems. In this example, at least 12 elements in two or more areas are documented.

Example of Comprehensive Examination

Provider documentation is as follows:

Vital signs: BP, 120/70; Weight, 120 lb; Temp, 99

GENERAL APPEARANCE: Well-developed, well-nourished 78-year-old male who appears to show some signs of anxiety and depression. Patient is oriented to time, place, and person

HEENT: TMs clear, PND, throat is very red and tonsils swollen. Facial pain in the sinus area

LUNGS: Clear to auscultation and percussion

HEART: RRR

EXTREMITIES: No swelling; pedal pulses normal bilaterally

NEUROLOGIC: DTR normal bilaterally; patient exhibits decreased sensation to touch in the left foot

ABDOMEN: Soft, nontender, no splenomegaly or enlargement of liver

NECK: No mass or tenderness; thyroid appears normal

SKIN: No rashes noted. Palpation of skin shows subcutaneous nodule in the axillary area

Bullets documented within this example would be

- Constitutional, as represented by the three vital signs recorded and general appearance counts as two bullets.
- Psychiatric elements of the exam are documented under General Appearance. The provider documented the patient's anxiety and depression. The provider also documented that the patient was "oriented to time, place, and person," which allows for an additional bullet point, giving a total of two for the psychiatric elements.
- HEENT would count as three bullet points.

- Lungs would count as two bullet points because auscultation counts as one bullet point and percussion counts as a separate bullet point.
- Heart would count as two bullet points because RRR would count as one bullet point and pedal pulses would count as a separate bullet point.
- Extremities count as one bullet.
- Neurologic examination included deep tendon reflex and sensation to touch, which counts as two bullet points.
- Abdomen examination counts as two bullet items because the examination of the liver and spleen, along with examination of the abdomen, are documented.
- Neck: Because the provider mentions the thyroid separately, count this as an additional bullet point, giving two bullet points for the neck.
- Skin examination counts as two bullet points for inspection and palpation.

Thus, justifying a comprehensive examination requires all elements identified by a bullet in at least nine organ systems or body areas, and documents at least two elements identified by a bullet from each of the nine areas/systems. In this example, at least two elements from nine systems are documented.

The preceding examples reflect how a provider can move from a problem-focused examination to a comprehensive examination. The author has found from shadowing many doctors over the years that documentation doesn't always reflect the work actually being done in the exam rooms. Remember, if you didn't document it, you didn't do it!

Medical Decision Making

The final key component of selecting an Evaluation and Management code is the element of medical decision making. Medical decision making is the process that a provider completes to determine a diagnosis and decide on a plan of care for the patient.

The provider must consider several factors during the medical decision-making process: the number of diagnoses or management options, and the amount and/or complexity of the data reviewed, as well as the risk of complications and/or morbidity or mortality. These all play a role in selecting the type of medical decision making reflected in the CPT code. The documentation of the assessment (the "A" in the SOAP note) and the supporting thought process, which lead to the plan (the "P" in the SOAP note), must be recorded. When you are trying to appeal payment of a service, it is very important to include notes that can logically present the thought process or reasoning behind the service provided.

The Documentation Guidelines for Evaluation and Management Services outline four levels of medical decision making that are referred to in CPT: **straightforward**, **low-complexity**, **moderate-complexity**, and **high-complexity**, as well as provide a more detailed description of each of these types of medical decision making.

• • • Guideline

To select the proper type of decision making, two of the three elements in the table must be either met or exceeded to qualify for a given type of decision making.

As the complexity of these factors increases, the level of medical decision making increases. The *Documentation Guidelines for Evaluation and Management Services* offer the following table, Table 3-7, to guide the coder in selecting the correct type of medical decision making.

TABLE 3-7 Type of Medical Decision Making

Number of Diagnoses or Management Options	Amount and/or Complexity of Data to Be Reviewed	Risk of Complications and/ or Morbidity or Mortality	Type of Decision Making
Minimal	Minimal or None	Minimal	Straightforward
Limited	Limited	Low	Low Complexity
Multiple	Moderate	Moderate	Moderate Complexity
Extensive	Extensive	High	High Complexity

The type of medical decision making is based on three factors:

- The number of diagnoses or management options
- The amount and/or complexity of data to be reviewed
- The risk of complications and/or morbidity or mortality

Number of Diagnosis or Management Options For each encounter, the provider will assess the patient to determine a clinical impression or diagnosis, and this information will be used to determine the number of diagnoses that the provider will address or treat. After assessing the patient, the provider will initiate treatment for the diagnosis, order testing to determine a diagnosis, or refer the patient to another provider for a consultation. This reflects the management options that the provider is using to treat the patient. Both diagnosis and management options should be documented in the patient's record to determine clearly the number of diagnosis and management options that are relevant to the encounter. The *Documentation Guidelines for Evaluation and Management Codes* do not give specific values for the terms used in the table: *minimal*, *limited*, *multiple*, and *extensive*. However, some logical assumptions can be made about these terms. *Minimal* and *limited* require that at least one diagnosis or management option be documented. *Multiple* and *extensive* require that at least two or more diagnoses or management options be recorded.

When reviewing the patient's medical record to select the number of diagnosis and management options, keep the following points in mind:

- A diagnosed problem generally requires less medical decision making than an undiagnosed problem.
- Conditions that are improving or resolving generally reflect less decision making than problems or conditions that are increasing in severity, worsening, or failing to respond to treatment.
- If a referral or consultation is sought, decision making is generally more complex.
- For an encounter with an established diagnosis, the patient's record should reflect the status of the problem: improved, controlled, resolving, not controlled, worsening, and so on.
- For an encounter without an established diagnosis, the patient's medical record should reflect that the diagnosis is not clearly established at this time. Terms such as *probable, possible*, and *rule out* are typically recorded by the provider.
- Review the record to determine the types and amount of further diagnostic testing ordered. The greater the number of tests ordered generally indicates a higher complexity of medical decision making.
- Review the record to identify the instructions given to the patient, nursing instructions, and treatment ordered. Treatments ordered can include medications as well as therapies. Typically, the more treatment that is provided, the higher level of medical decision making.

Amount and/or Complexity of the Data to Be Reviewed The second factor that has to be determined to select an appropriate type of medical decision making is the amount and/or complexity of data to be reviewed. The more information the provider reviews, the higher level of medical decision making that is justified. Providers must document that they have reviewed diagnostic findings, reports, and old records to justify the amount and complexity of the data reviewed.

Five terms are used to describe the amount and/or complexity of data to be reviewed: *none, minimal, limited, moderate,* and *extensive.* These terms are not defined further in the *Documentation Guidelines for Evaluation and Management Services.* The author recommends that facilities and offices discuss with all coders the interpretation of these terms and consistently interpret their meanings. Important points to remember when you review the record to determine the amount and complexity of the data reviewed are as follows:

- The more tests and procedures reviewed by the provider, the higher the level of this element.
- The review of a report can be documented by the provider either in a note or by the provider initialing and dating the report of the test results.
- If a provider personally reviews an image, tracing, or specimen that she or he ordered, the complexity of the data reviewed increases.
- When documenting the complexity of the data reviewed, providers should clearly document the information obtained in order to justify the types of data reviewed.

Risk of Significant Complications, Morbidity, and/or Mortality   The third factor that determines the type of medical decision making is the risk of significant complications, morbidity, and/or mortality. The risks are described as minimal, low, moderate, or high and are based on the risks associated with presenting problem(s), the diagnostic procedure(s), and possible management options. The *Documentation Guidelines for Evaluation and Management Services* define these three areas in the "Table of Risk". Reference the Internet links for both the 1995 an 1997 guidelines which can be found on the CMS website at: https://www.cms.gov/Outreach -and-Education/Medicare-Learning-Network-MLN/MLNEdWebGuide/Downloads/95Docguidelines.pdf and https://www.cms.gov/Outreach-and-Education/Medicare-Learning-Network-MLN/MLNEdWebGuide /Downloads/97Docguidelines.pdf, respectively, to review this table. Because the determination of risk is not quantifiable, the table should be used to guide the coder in selecting the type of risk.

● ● ● **Guideline**

The highest level of risk in any one area (presenting problem[s], diagnostic procedure[s], or management options) determines the overall risk for the encounter.

The following should be considered when selecting the type of risk:

- Comorbidities and underlying diseases increase the complexity of the risk.
- Surgical and invasive procedures performed during an encounter increase the risk. The procedures need to be documented in the record.
- Undiagnosed problems, multiple diagnoses, and acute and chronic conditions that pose a threat to life or bodily function increase risk.
- The more complex the diagnostic tests ordered are, the greater the level of risk.
- The more complex the management options ordered are (e.g., prescription medications, procedures, need to resuscitate, etc.), the greater the level of risk.

Because of the complexity of the elements of medical decision making, the coder must have a working knowledge of the guidelines as they pertain to the types of medical decision making. For this reason, see the Internet links for both the 1995 and 1997 guidelines which can be found on the CMS website at: https:// www.cms.gov/Outreach-and-Education/Medicare-Learning-Network-MLN/MLNEdWebGuide /Downloads/95Docguidelines.pdf and https://www.cms.gov/Outreach-and-Education/Medicare -Learning-Network-MLN/MLNEdWebGuide/Downloads/97Docguidelines.pdf, respectively, for a complete and detailed explanation of how the coder should review and choose a level of medical decision making based on the documentation provided.

The CPT manual guides the coder on the combination of key components (history, examination, and medical decision making) needed to determine a level of service for each Evaluation and Management code in CPT. In the E/M code 99202, the coder will see the following entry:

EXAMPLE:

99202   Office or other outpatient visit for the Evaluation and Management of a new patient, which requires these three key components:

- an expanded problem-focused history;
- an expanded problem-focused examination;
- straightforward medical decision making.

Counseling and/or coordination of care with other physicians, other qualified health care professionals, or agencies are provided consistent with the nature of the problem(s) and the patient's and/or family's needs.

Usually the presenting problem(s) are of low to moderate severity.

Typically, 20 minutes are spent face-to-face with the patient and/or family.

The coder's task is to review the documentation in the patient's record and to select the Evaluation and Management code that accurately reflects the services provided during the encounter.

Exercise 3.4—Check Your Understanding

Evaluation and Management Coding

Using a CPT manual, choose the correct code for the level of E/M service rendered (99211–99215), based on the following examination and medical decision making given. The first one is done for you.

1. Detailed examination/moderate medical decision making   99214

2. Problem-focused examination/straightforward medical decision making   _____

3. Expanded problem-focused examination/low-complexity medical decision making   _____

4. Detailed examination/low-complexity medical decision making   _____

5. Comprehensive examination/high-complexity medical decision making   _____

Remaining Elements

The remaining elements that factor into choosing a level of service are counseling, coordination of care, and nature of the presenting problem. These components, known as **contributory factors**, can contribute to the work that goes into an encounter and should be considered when determining a level of service to code. They are closely related and in many instances overlap. A description of the coordination of care and nature of the presenting problem appears in most Evaluation and Management codes, but in reality, these factors do not greatly influence code selection. **Coordination of care** is not formally defined in CPT; however, it represents services that are completed to organize or direct the patient's care. **Nature of the presenting problem** is defined in CPT as one of five types:

- Minimal
- Self-limited or minor
- Low severity
- Moderate severity
- High severity

The complete definition for each of these types of nature of the presenting problem is found in the *Evaluation and Management Services Guidelines* in the CPT manual.

The seventh factor that is indicated in some E/M codes is *time*. It should be noted that the time included in the codes represents an average for a specific code. CPT offers two definitions for time:

- **Face-to-face time**

    This definition is used for office and other outpatient visits and consultations. According to the definition found in the CPT manual, *time* is defined as the time a physician spends face-to-face with the patient and/or family. Although the definition in CPT specifies that the time includes time with the family, most payers, including Medicare, do not recognize the time spent with the family. They include only the time spent with the patient.

- **Unit/floor time**

    This definition is used for hospital observation services, inpatient hospital care, initial and follow-up hospital consultations, and nursing facilities. According to CPT, this time includes the time that the physician is present on the patient's unit and at the bedside rendering services. Also included is the time in which the physician documents patient information and reviews the patient's chart, examines the patient, records medical information, and communicates with other professionals and the patient's family. This is another area where the various payers interpret the definition differently.

It is important for providers to document the time they spend with patients, especially when they are counseling a patient about an aspect of their treatment or care. As described in the *Documentation Guidelines for Evaluation and Management Services,* time is considered the key or controlling factor that determines the particular level of E/M service when more than 50 percent of the physician time is spent counseling and/or coordinating care for the patient. **Counseling** is defined as a discussion with a patient and/or family concerning one or more of the following:

- Diagnostic results, impressions, and/or recommended diagnostic studies
- Prognosis
- Risk and benefits of management (treatment) options
- Instructions for management (treatment) and/or follow-up
- Importance of compliance with chosen management (treatment) options
- Risk-factor reduction
- Patient and family education

Reference the Evaluation and Management Services Guidelines in the CPT manual for more information on the definition of counseling.

Counseling a patient and/or family member usually involves a discussion of treatment options, prognosis of a condition, instructions on medications, diet and exercise, results of ancillary studies, or risks and benefits of any number of treatment options. Time spent counseling should be documented along with the total time of the visit, as well as what the patient was counseled on. It is very important to justify a higher level of Evaluation and Management code when you use time as the key factor in code selection.

● ● ● **Guideline**

In a case where counseling and/or coordination of care dominates (more than 50%) the physician patient and/or family encounter (face-to-face in the office or other outpatient setting, floor/unit time in the hospital or nursing facility), time is considered the key, or controlling, factor in qualifying for a particular level of E/M service.

Example of the Recording of Time in a Provider Note

Today, Dr. Gomez saw Jill, an established patient, to complete an assessment and plan. Because Jill is an established patient, Dr. Gomez documented only an expanded problem-focused history and an expanded problem-focused examination, thus justifying code 99213. However, the following information was entered as part of Dr. Gomez's office note:

A: Anorexia nervosa

P: I spent 30 minutes with Jill counseling her on anorexia and other eating disorders. The total time of the visit was 40 minutes. I spent time on an explanation of the risks to her health if she doesn't get the disorder under control. I referred her to the Eating Disorder Clinic and have given her orders for a Comp Panel, and we will also check her lytes.

Because the time Dr. Gomez spent counseling Jill is documented, as well as the overall time of the visit, code 99215 is justified because time becomes the key factor in code selection when counseling and/or coordination of care dominates (more than 50 percent) the physician-patient encounter.

The coder needs to keep in mind that no matter how much documentation a provider generates for a visit, the questions that need to be answered when you assign codes are "What brought the patient in for this encounter?", "What service did we provide once the patient came in?", and "Is the service we are billing supported by medical necessity and documentation?" Once the coder has answered these questions, a code assignment can be made with confidence. Tying all the information together becomes easier with experience and familiarity with the CPT manual. Coders may differ on how elements are looked at, but overall, the code selected needs to be supported in the documentation. *Remember:* In the eyes of a Medicare auditor or an insurance auditor, "If care is not documented, it was not done!"

Hospital Coding

CPT has a specific code range for hospital coding. This category of CPT is divided into initial hospital care codes for admissions and subsequent hospital care codes for additional visits after the admission. These categories include both new and established patients.

To have a complete understanding of the hospital inpatient service codes, coders must read the detailed notes that appear in the CPT manual under the headings "Hospital Inpatient Services," "Initial Hospital Care," and "Subsequent Hospital Care."

Initial Hospital Care (99221–99223)

Initial hospital care codes, 99221–99223, depend on the level of service that is rendered. These codes are used by the admitting physician to report the first hospital inpatient encounter. This range of codes is *not* used by other physicians; it is for only the admitting physician and is reported only once per hospital admission.

When referencing codes 99221–99223, the language used to describe the service should be noted. The term *per day* is used to describe the code. This means that only one of these codes should be reported per day. The descriptions found in codes 99221–99223 also state that all three key E/M components must be met to justify the code. Therefore, the level of history, examination, and medical decision making must all meet or exceed the level of service described in the code. If time is used as an element in assigning a code, the total face-to-face time and the floor/unit time related to the patient's care also count, so long as they are supported in the documentation. Once the admitting physician has assigned an admission code, this code set can no longer be used with relation to this patient's admission. Subsequent hospital visit codes will be discussed later in this chapter.

Another unique feature of this range is described in the fourth paragraph under the heading Initial Hospital Care in the CPT manual. The note states that when a patient is admitted to the hospital after having been seen by the admitting physician at another site of service, all the services that were performed by the physician are considered part of the initial hospital care when they are performed on the same date as the admission.

> **EXAMPLE:** Mr. Weber presented to Dr. Potter's office with abdominal pain. The doctor obtained a history from the patient and performed an examination. As part of the medical decision-making process, Dr. Potter admitted Mr. Weber to the hospital from her office for testing to determine the cause of the pain.

Mr. Weber saw Dr. Potter on the same day as the admission. Dr. Potter will be the physician following Mr. Weber in the hospital. The initial hospital care code will include the services provided in the office earlier in the day. No E/M office visit code would be charged for this visit.

Table 3-8 lists and describes each of the initial hospital care codes and the three key components that need to be performed and documented in the patient medical record to support the initial hospital services.

TABLE 3-8 Initial Hospital Care (99221–99223)

Initial Hospital Care Code	Description (All three elements need to be met or exceeded for the level of service billed.)
99221	Code 99221 is considered a low level code for initial hospital care. This code is used for a new or established patient. Prior to assigning this code the coder needs to read and reference the CPT manual for a complete listing of all the instructional notes that apply to this code as well as codes 99222 and 99223. Code 99221 includes a: • detailed or comprehensive history • detailed or comprehensive examination • straightforward or low complexity medical decision making. The documentation found in the patient's record must contain a history, examination and medical decision making at the level specified in the CPT manual to report the code.
99222	Code 99222 reports a mid-level code for an initial hospital care visit. This code is utilized for new and established patients. To report this code the documentation must record the following three elements: • comprehensive history • comprehensive examination • moderate medical decision making. Reference the CPT manual for a complete description of the code and additional information about the reporting of this code.
99223	Code 99223 is considered a high level code for initial hospital care as the documentation must record the following: • comprehensive history • comprehensive examination • high complexity medical decision making. Code 99223 is the most comprehensive of codes 99221, 99222 and 99223. The history and examination are comprehensive and the level of medical decision making is of high complexity, therefore is it essential that the documentation in the patient's record is recorded to support these components.

Subsequent Hospital Visits (99231–99233)

After the initial code for admission is used, subsequent hospital visits are billed with codes from the 99231–99233 code range. These codes reflect the physician's work for subsequent days of service performed in the hospital. These codes are summarized in Table 3-9.

TABLE 3-9 Subsequent Hospital Visits (99231–99233)

Subsequent Hospital Visit Code	Description (Two of the three key components need to be met to code the level of service.)
99231	The lowest level code for subsequent hospital care is code 99231. Subsequent hospital care codes 99231, 99232 and 99233 require that two of the three key components of the code be documented. Code 99231 has the following key components:

(continues)

TABLE 3-9 (*continued*)

Subsequent Hospital Visit Code	Description (Two of the three key components need to be met to code the level of service.)
	• problem-focused history • problem-focused examination • straightforward or low-level medical decision making. To review the complete description of code 99231 reference the CPT manual and note the instructional notations that appear prior to the code. The information that appears prior to code 99231 also governs codes 99232 and 99233.
99232	Code 99232 is considered a mid-level code that reports subsequent hospital care. This code has the following three key components: • expanded problem-focused interval history • expanded problem-focused examination • moderate medical decision making. Reference the CPT manual to review the additional components for code 99232. To report code 99232 two of the three key components must be documented.
99233	The highest level code for a subsequent hospital care visit is code 99233. To report code 99233 documentation must record two of the following components: • detailed interval history • detailed examination • high-level medical decision making Please review the CPT manual for the additional components for code 99233. Remember this is the highest level code for subsequent hospital care.

Hospital Discharge Codes (99238, 99239)

To indicate that a patient has been discharged from the hospital, the coder would use code 99238 or 99239. These codes are time based and include all services provided to a patient on the date of discharge. Code 99238, "Hospital discharge day management; 30 minutes or less," is the standard discharge and is used to indicate that the work involved in discharging a patient took approximately 30 minutes or less. If the provider needs to take more time in the discharge process, code 99239, "Hospital discharge day management; more than 30 minutes," would be used. It is essential that the time spent in the discharge process is documented when code 99239 is used.

Exercise 3.5—Check Your Understanding

Hospital Service Codes

Select the correct hospital inpatient code based on the information given using a CPT manual.

1. Dr. Calvin admitted Ms. Jones, and, after taking a comprehensive history, he completed a comprehensive examination and medical decision making of moderate complexity. The code chosen for this visit is _____.

2. Dr. Smith saw his patient on the medical unit of the hospital. This was a follow-up visit from the day before. The history and examination were expanded problem-focused, and medical decision making was of a moderate level. The code chosen for this visit is _____.

3. Dr. Cary sent Ms. Kelley to the hospital from his office. He saw her later that day, when he added to the information he had gathered at his office. The history and examination were comprehensive. The medical decision making was of high complexity. The level of service chosen for this hospital visit is _____.

(continues)

Exercise 3.5—*continued*

4. Sandy was being discharged from the hospital. The doctor gave her a brief examination, discharge instructions, and prescriptions for medications. He talked to her family about follow-up care. This all took approximately 25 minutes. The correct code for this hospital visit is _____.

5. Mr. Alexander was admitted to the hospital two days ago by Dr. Simmons. Dr. Simmons had been seeing Mr. Alexander each day. Today, Dr. Simmons documented an expanded problem-focused interval history and an examination of the same level. Because a new problem developed, medical decision making was of a moderate level. The level of service chosen for this hospital visit is _____.

Hospital Observation Services (99217–99226)

When a patient is admitted for **observation** or **observation status**, the patient has not been admitted to the hospital as an inpatient but needs to be admitted under observation status for assessment. *Observation* indicates that the patient is in the hospital for a short time (usually less than 24 hours but sometimes as long as 48 hours) to determine the course of care. The patient ultimately may be released to go home or may be admitted to the hospital as an inpatient in an effort to offer more extensive care. The observation codes are reported by the supervising physician. This is explained in the CPT manual prior to code 99218 in the instructional notation that appears after the heading Initial Observation Care.

CPT code range 99218–99220 is used for new or established patients who are admitted under outpatient hospital observation status. CPT code 99217, "Observation care discharge," is used when a patient is discharged from outpatient hospital observation on a date that may be different from the date of admission to observation.

> **EXAMPLE:** Cindy was admitted for a 23-hour observation in the chest pain unit on May 10. On May 11, Cindy was discharged because no evidence of a cardiac problem was evident.

In our example, Cindy was admitted on May 10 and discharged on May 11. On May 10, the code selected would reflect the level of service the doctor performed, and a code from the 99218–99220 code range would be assigned. On May 11, the code selected would be 99217 to represent the discharge. The 99217 code includes discharge instructions for the patient and continuing care.

If admission and discharge to observation occur on the same date, a code from the 99234–99236 code range would be chosen.

Observation Care

Codes 99218, 99219, and 99220, **Initial Observation Care**, are assigned for patients who are seen for Evaluation and Management services during their time in observation. The correct code is chosen based on the level of history, examination, and medical decision making that are rendered. These codes are allowed only once per day. Typically, these observation codes can be billed for any time the patient is seen in observation, from 23-hour admits up to 48-hour admits, depending on the hospital guidelines regarding how long a patient can stay in observation.

Codes 99224 to 99226 are used to report subsequent observation care. The reporting of these codes includes the following services:

- Review of patient's medical record and diagnostic studies.

- Reviewing the patient's physical condition and response to care since the patient was last seen.

Codes 99234–99236, Observation or Inpatient Care Services (including admission and discharge), are used when a patient is admitted and discharged on the same date of service. The important point to remember is that codes 99234–99236 are used *only* in cases where all the services are performed on the same date. In the CPT manual, following the heading "Observation or Inpatient Care Services (Including Admission and Discharge Services)," prior to code 99234, instructional notations instruct coders as follows:

- When a patient is admitted to the hospital from observation status on the same date, the provider should report only the initial hospital care code.

- When observation status is part of the course of an encounter in another site of service, all evaluation and management services provided by the supervising physician or other qualified health care provider are considered part of the initial observation care when all of the services are performed on the same date.

- When a patient is admitted to observation or inpatient care and discharged on a different date, the following code ranges should be reported:

  99218–99220, 99224–99226, 99217, or 99221–99223, 99238 and 99239, as appropriate.

Exercise 3.6—Check Your Understanding

Observation Coding

Indicate whether the following statements are true (T) or false (F).

1. _____ Beth was admitted on August 10 at 4:30 a.m. for observation for stomach cramps. She was discharged that same day at 7:30 p.m., when she began feeling better. Based on the doctor's documentation meeting the levels of service, this visit should be coded with codes in the range 99234–99236.

2. _____ Marie presented in the ED with dehydration due to nausea and vomiting. Dr. Barnes (the hospitalist) was present when Marie came in. He took a comprehensive history and performed a comprehensive examination. He decided to admit Marie under his service as a 23-hour admit in observation. He ordered labs and an IV to rehydrate her.

   Dr. Barnes should have billed a 99282-25 for his evaluation in the emergency department and then billed a 99219 for Marie's continued care in observation.

3. _____ Discharge from observation status includes instructions for care, examination, and preparation of discharge records.

4. _____ When a doctor codes an encounter by using code 99236, there needs to be at least a comprehensive history and examination, and medical decision making of high complexity.

5. _____ Initial observation codes 99218 through 99220 are used once per day while the patient is in the hospital under observation to report the initial observation care.

6. _____ The observation care level of service code 99218 includes services related to expanded history, expanded examination, and problem-focused medical decision making.

7. _____ There are average times associated with the observation care discharge code 99217.

8. _____ Code 99235 would be reported if there is a detailed history, detailed examination, and medical decision making of high complexity.

9. _____ A patient can be admitted to the hospital as an inpatient and then discharged to observation.

10. _____ The observation care level of service reported by the supervising physician should include the services related to initiating observation status provided in other sites of service.

Consultations

Consultations are services rendered by providers when their opinion or expertise is requested by another provider or appropriate source. If you follow the rule of "3 Rs," you should be able to distinguish a consult from other Evaluation and Management services. The 3 Rs are as follows: your provider receives a *request* to *render* an opinion or give advice and, in doing so, they are *responding* to the request.

The response to the request closes the circle, and the decision can then be made as to whether this is actually a consult. The patient's medical record must reflect all three of these components before a consult code is assigned. The request can be a verbal request, but documentation by both the provider making the request and the provider rendering the opinion must reflect the fact that a request was made. See Figure 3-1 for an example of a consult circle.

For every consultation billed, the record should contain documentation stating the following:

- The request for the consultation
- A written consultation report that identifies:
  - The specific problem for which the consultation was requested
  - The extent of the history, exam, and medical decision making that occurred during the encounter
  - The consultant's findings and recommendations
- A written report of the findings that is sent to the referring provider

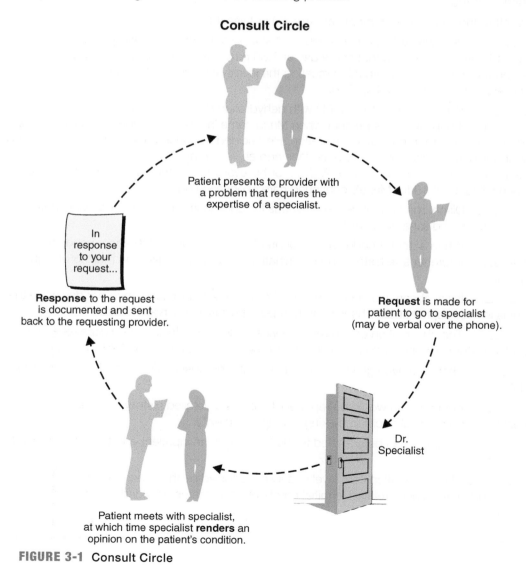

Consult Circle

Patient presents to provider with a problem that requires the expertise of a specialist.

In response to your request...

Response to the request is documented and sent back to the requesting provider.

Request is made for patient to go to specialist (may be verbal over the phone).

Dr. Specialist

Patient meets with specialist, at which time specialist **renders** an opinion on the patient's condition.

FIGURE 3-1 Consult Circle

When reporting consultation services for Medicare patients, consultation codes are not to be billed according to the CMS policy. If a consultation for a Medicare patient occurs, the services should be reported as follows:

- *Consultations completed in the office or hospital outpatient setting*—These services are reported with codes from the Office or Other Outpatient Services category.
- *Consultations completed in the Inpatient setting*—These services are reported with codes from the Hospital Inpatient Service category.
- *Consultations completed in a Nursing Facility*—These services are reported with the Nursing Facility Services category.

It should be noted that when initial hospital care or initial nursing facility services are provided to Medicare patients, the attending physician needs to report modifier A1, denoting the Principal Physician of Record. This distinguishes the services provided by the attending physician from the consultation services provided.

The consultation codes are divided according to the site of service. Code range 99241–99245 is for consultations that are performed in the office or other outpatient setting. Codes 99251–99255 are for consultations that are performed when the patient is a hospital inpatient, a resident of a nursing facility, or a patient in a partial hospital setting. These code ranges are for new and established patients and can be reported only once per setting. Documentation requirements for assigning inpatient or outpatient consults require that all three key components—history, examination, and medical decision making—be met or exceeded for the level of service billed. If, after the completion of the consultation, the consultant assumes care for the management of the patient, the appropriate Evaluation and Management service code should be assigned according to the site of service in which the service was performed.

EXAMPLE: Dr. Jones is a cardiologist who is called into Sunny Valley Hospital for a consultation to see Ms. Brown, who is experiencing chest pain.

Depending on the level of service rendered, Dr. Jones would bill the consultation using code range 99251–99255. Dr. Jones determines that Ms. Brown has a cardiac condition that he is going to follow.

● ● ● Guideline

Code range 99251–99255, Inpatient Consultations, is used to report consultations for hospital inpatients, residents of nursing facilities, or patients in a partial hospital setting. Only one consultation should be reported by a consultant per admission.

Providers should not bill consult codes when the request for a second opinion comes from the patient or a family member. In these cases, the service is billed using the appropriate code from the office visit codes or other site-of-service codes.

A second opinion may be requested by an insurance company or a peer-review organization. If this is the case, modifier 32, mandated services, needs to be appended. Modifier 32 indicates that the service was mandated to be performed. If a decision for major surgery (usually surgery with 90-day global) is made at the time of the visit, modifier 57, decision for surgery, is appended to the Evaluation and Management service code.

Conditions that are diagnosed and require treatment from another provider do not constitute a consult.

EXAMPLE: Kevin was sent to Dr. Derm by his primary care physician in the hope that Dr. Derm would be able to treat the three plantar warts on Kevin's left foot. Dr. Derm looked at Kevin's foot and performed cryosurgery on each wart.

The example given is categorized as a referral. A **referral** is when a patient is sent, or referred, to a specialist for treatment of a condition that has been diagnosed and the specialist doesn't need to render an opinion on a patient's condition. These cases are billed using the appropriate Evaluation and Management code that depends on the site of service.

Emergency Department Services (99281–99288)

CPT defines an **emergency department (ED)** as "an organized hospital-based facility for the provision of unscheduled episodic services to patients who present for immediate medical attention." Codes 99281–99285 are used by providers who perform services in the ED of a hospital-based facility, which is open 24 hours a day, seven days a week. Codes in the range of 99281–99285 are used by ED doctors, nurse practitioners, and physician assistants. These codes are not used by other physicians who may be called into the ED to consult or admit the patient.

> **EXAMPLE:** Dr. Jones is the treating provider for the ED at ABC Hospital. Dr. Jones saw Sara Daniels regarding heartburn and pressure in her chest. Tests were run, and Dr. Jones contacted Ms. Daniels's primary care provider, Dr. Calvin. Dr. Calvin was already in the hospital rounding. He came to the ED, reviewed the test results, performed his own examination, and decided to admit Sara to the chest pain clinic for further evaluation.

Dr. Jones would bill an Emergency Department code from the 99281–99285 range for the visit because he was the treating ED provider and needs to submit a charge for the services he performed when Sara Daniels presented at the hospital. Dr. Calvin would code his part of the visit using the 99221–99223 range because he admitted Sara to the chest pain clinic for further evaluation. The fact that Dr. Calvin saw Sara in the ED does not affect the code choice.

The codes in this series require certain levels in all three key components (history, examination, and medical decision making) and are used for both new and established patients. This code set contains information that is not typically found in other Evaluation and Management code explanations with in the component of nature of the presenting problem. The component of time is not established for ED service codes and, therefore, would not be considered a factor when a code is selected.

Code 99281 requires a problem-focused history and examination, and the medical decision making is straightforward. Codes 99282 and 99283 require an expanded problem-focused history and a problem-focused examination. The medical decision-making piece is where the difference is evident when you choose between these two codes. Code 99282 requires medical decision making of low complexity, whereas code 99283 requires medical decision making of moderate complexity.

Codes 99284 and 99285 have different history and examination documentation requirements. The medical decision making for these codes is also different. For code 99284, medical decision making is of moderate complexity, requiring an urgent evaluation but when there is not "an immediate significant threat to life or physiologic function." For code 99285, medical decision making is of "high severity and poses an immediate significant threat to life or physiologic function." When patients present to the ED, they may not be capable of giving a comprehensive history due to their state of consciousness or other modifying conditions that may prevent a patient's response to questions.

The differences noted in medical decision making are of importance in the instance of the ED because the patients are usually new to these providers and require a more extensive history and examination. Coders will encounter some difficulty when trying to educate an ED physician about levels of service due to the nature of the environment in which these doctors are practicing. Severe problems and life-threatening conditions are a daily occurrence in this setting, so the doctors' view of severity of a presenting problem may be somewhat skewed. A coder will sometimes need to reeducate a doctor on what constitutes the levels of medical decision making.

Code 99288—"Physician direction of emergency medical systems (EMS) emergency care, advanced life support" is available to physicians who are communicating by two-way radio when a physician is located in the hospital and the patient is outside the hospital with emergency rescue personnel. The physician is giving direction on care of the patient that might include telemetry, cardiopulmonary resuscitation, intubation, and administration of fluids or drugs. This code is not used very often for some payers, because it is considered bundled into the ED code billed after the patient arrives at the hospital ED.

Critical Care Services (99291, 99292)

Critical care refers to a patient who requires constant attention by the provider due to situations related to their medical condition, and whose illness or injuries would put the patient at high risk should they not get this constant attention. Typically, there is organ system failure or the threat of organ system failure involved. The patient does not have to be admitted to the intensive care unit (ICU) or a critical care unit of a hospital to be considered as receiving critical care services. If the criteria outlined in CPT at the start of the Critical Care Service category are met, the codes can be billed. A new coder should review this information in detail.

Critical care codes (99291 and 99292) are time-based codes. It is essential that the total time billed for critical care codes reflect the time spent exclusively on care of this patient, whether the time is face to face or is spent on the floor providing services for this one patient.

The time billed can reflect the time coordinating care, discussing (with family members or other doctors) necessary information needed for treatment, or any other work directly related to the individual patient's care, which could include the following:

- Reviewing test results and radiological images
- Documenting the critical care service provided in the patient's medical record
- Time spent obtaining a medical history from the patient or other persons involved in the event that the patient's medical condition affected his or her ability to give a history

Remember: The time reported must be directly related to the management of one and only one patient! If the doctor is caring for other patients during downtime while he or she is administering the critical care services to the original patient, this intermittent time *cannot* be counted.

Certain services are considered an integral part of critical care services. The CPT manual lists these services in the note preceding the codes for critical care services. If the service is not included in the list provided, it is allowed as a separately billable service.

> **EXAMPLE:** Dana was admitted to ICU with severe chest pain, shortness of breath, and vomiting. The doctor ordered a pulse oximetry, EKG monitoring, blood gases, and a chest x-ray. Shortly after arrival, Dana required an emergency tracheostomy. The doctor spent 2½ hours at Dana's bedside trying to stabilize her, which he had detailed documentation to support.

In our example, Dana's doctor wanted to bill 2½ hours of critical care services. The coder would be able to bill out the following:

99291 × for the first hour and 14 minutes and a 99292 × 3

If additional services are provided that are not in the list provided in CPT, they are allowed as a separately billable service and can be submitted as a separate charge. So, going back to our example, in addition to our critical care codes, the emergency tracheostomy (code 31603) would also be coded because this procedure is not included in the critical care services. The critical care code would require a 25 modifier be appended to it to indicate that this was a separately identifiable service.

Critical care services have their own set of guidelines, which are detailed at the start of the Critical Care Services category. The coder should read and thoroughly understand these guidelines before assigning a code from this section.

Coding for critical care services requires that the documentation contain at least a sentence summarizing how much time was spent directly caring for the patient, even if the time spent was not continuous or face to face. If the time spent was less than 30 minutes another E/M code would be assigned, depending on whether the patient was an inpatient or an outpatient. An unlimited amount of time can be billed under critical care codes, but the documentation *must* support *any* time billed with critical care codes.

Pediatric Critical Care Patient Transport (99466, 99467, 99485, and 99486)

At times, critically ill pediatric patients (*pediatric* being defined here as 24 months of age or less) are transported to facilities, accompanied by a provider. When this occurs, code range 99466–99467, Pediatric Critical Care Patient Transport, should be reported. The guidelines for these two codes are specific. The physician is required to accompany the patient during interfacility transport. Face-to-face care is required, and the time associated with the face-to-face care needs to be documented.

The coder will note the plus sign (+) attached to code 99467. This indicates that code 99467 is an add-on code and cannot be billed alone. Code 99466 is used for the first 30 to 74 minutes, adding code 99467 for each additional 30 minutes.

> **EXAMPLE:** Dr. Howard wanted her 18-month-old female patient transported to a facility that specialized in pediatric heart patients. Because of the age of the patient and the severity of the heart condition, Dr. Howard decided to accompany the baby in the ambulance to be sure she remained stable during the 1-hour, 45-minute drive.

In this example, Dr. Howard is able to bill for this service. She would need to bill 99466 for the first 30 to 74 minutes and then code 99467×1 for the remainder of the time.

Codes 99485 and 99486 are used to report non-face-to-face supervision by a control physician during an interfacility transport for a critically ill or injured pediatric patient, 24 months or younger. Code 99485 reports the first 30 minutes while code 99486 reports each additional 30 minutes. Thus code 99486 must be reported following code 99485 when reported on a claim. Before reporting codes 99466, 99467, 99485, and 99486, coders should review the guidelines in the CPT manual that precede code 99466. At this time, reference the guidelines that are present in the CPT manual that pertain to codes 99466, 99467, 99485, and 99486.

Exercise 3.7—Check Your Understanding

Critical Care Services

Using a current CPT coding book, indicate whether each statement is true (T) or false (F).

1. _____ Codes 99291 and 99292 are used to report the total time spent by a physician providing critical care services to a critically ill or critically injured patient.

2. _____ Critical care services provided to infants 29 days through 24 months of age in an inpatient setting are reported with codes 99291 and 99292.

3. _____ The time that can be reported as critical care is the time spent engaged in work directly related to the individual patient's care.

4. _____ The physician needs to be immediately available to the patient to bill critical care services.

5. _____ Code 99291 can be used only once per date, even if time spent by the physician is not continuous on that date.

6. _____ Activities performed in the critical care unit that directly impact care of the patient can be counted as time in coding critical care services.

7. _____ Gastric intubation and ventilatory management are separately billable when performed with other critical care services.

8. _____ Physician attendance during transport of a 3-year-old is reported with codes 99466 and 99467.

9. _____ If a patient is unable to give a history, obtaining that history through discussion with family members may be reported as critical care.

10. _____ A provider may bill critical care services if he is on the floor and available for questions but is seeing other patients during the same period.

Inpatient Neonatal and Pediatric Critical Care Services (99468–99480)

Codes 99468–99480 are for neonatal and pediatric critical care services provided in an inpatient setting. These codes require the neonate or pediatric patient to be in the hospital and include the same services noted in the guidelines at the beginning of the Critical Care code range. The guidelines at the beginning of this section of CPT, prior to code 99468, list all services bundled in the neonatal and pediatric critical care codes. Before assigning a code, in addition to the critical care codes, the coder should pay close attention to the list of bundled services.

Code range 99468–99476 is differentiated according to initial or subsequent services and the age of the patient. Neonatal critical care services, for patients 28 days or younger, are coded using 99468 for initial inpatient neonatal critical care and 99469 for subsequent visits. Code 99468 for initial inpatient neonatal critical care can be billed in addition to the following: 99464, "Attendance at delivery;" and 99465, "Newborn resuscitation," if any of these codes apply to the physician's role during delivery. Review the guidelines that appear before code 99468 and after the heading Inpatient Neonatal and Pediatric Critical Care for additional information pertaining to these codes.

Pediatric critical care services for children 29 days through 24 months of age are reported with code 99471 for initial care and code 99472 for subsequent care. For children 2 through 5 years of age, code 99475 reports the initial inpatient pediatric critical care, and code 99476 reports the subsequent inpatient pediatric critical care.

As part of critical care, the Initial and Continuing Intensive Care Services codes, 99477–99480, are found at the end of the pediatric and neonatal critical care section of CPT. These codes are used to indicate that an infant needs services that do not fall under critical care guidelines but are intensive enough to require more care than a typical hospital code. There is typically continuous monitoring and a team of healthcare professionals involved in the care of an infant, with the physician coordinating the care.

Codes 99478, 99479, and 99480 are based on present body weight. Keep in mind when you are looking at body weight, that 1,000 grams is equal to 35.27 ounces. Table 3-10 summarizes the assignment of these codes.

TABLE 3-10 Continuing Intensive Care Services

Instructions for Assigning Codes
Prior to assigning codes 99478, 99479 and 99480 the coder must reference the CPT manual and review the information that appears prior to code 99477. Code 99478 is the lowest level of the subsequent intensive care service codes. Codes 99478, 99479 and 99480 are only reported once per day, for the evaluation and management of the recovering very low birth weight infant. A very low body weight is a weight less than 1,500 grams. The record needs to reflect the present body weight of the infant to justify the use of this code.
Code 99479 reports subsequent intensive care services for the evaluation and management of the recovering low birth weight infant. The present body weight for this code is from 1,500 to 2,500 grams. Reference the CPT manual for additional information that applies to this code.
Code 99480 is the final subsequent intensive care service code, for the evaluation and management of the recovering infant. This code is used when the present body weight of the infant is 2501 to 5000 grams. Documentation in the record needs to record the body weight of the infant to justify the use of this code.

A coder may encounter abbreviations such as for **low birth weight (LBW)** and **very low birth weight (VLBW)**. Should you encounter such abbreviations when coding, be aware that to be considered VLBW, the weight of the infant would be less than 1,500 grams. LBW would be an infant with present body weight of 1,500–2,500 grams. Normal weight for a newborn would be a present body weight of 2,501–5,000 grams.

Exercise 3.8—Check Your Understanding

Critical Care Services

The following questions relate only to critical care services. Please fill in the blanks in the following statements with the term(s) that correctly complete the sentences. Reference the CPT manual for the complete language used for the coding of critical care services.

1. In addition to the history, examination, and medical decision making, the physician is also required to document _____ spent in direct care of the patient to support the billing of codes 99291 and 99292.

2. When coding Pediatric Critical Care Transport, the coder needs to use code 99466 for the first 30 to 74 minutes and code _____ for each additional 30 minutes thereafter.

3. Initial inpatient neonatal critical care services are coded using code _____.

4. _____ is the abbreviation that a coder may see when coding an infant chart when the infant's present birth weight is less than 1,500 grams.

5. Mr. Mills was admitted to ICU, where Dr. Brown spent 1 hour and 20 minutes performing critical care services. Dr. Brown submitted the following code(s) for his services: _____.

6. Sandrine required constant observation by a health-care team in the neonate ICU. She is 5 days old and has been in the ICU for the past 3 days. Day 4 services in ICU are billed with code _____.

7. Critically ill or injured children over the age of _____ years of age or older would be reported with hourly critical care service codes 99291 and 99292.

8. If the same physician provides critical care services for a pediatric patient 23 months of age in an outpatient setting and an inpatient setting on the same day, critical care services would be reported using code(s) _____.

9. _____ is the direct delivery by a physician(s) of medical care for a critically ill or critically injured patient.

10. Time spent that can be reported as critical care is the time spent _____ related to the patient's care, whether it is face-to-face or floor/unit time.

Nursing Facility Services (99304–99318)

Code range 99304–99318 is used to report evaluation and management services provided to patients in Skilled Nursing Facilities (SNF), Long Term Care Facilities (LTCF), or Intermediate Care Facilities (ICF) codes. This range of codes is referred to as Nursing Facility Services codes. If your provider refers to the place of service as any of the preceding, this is the code range you would use. Convalescent care and rehabilitative care are also provided in these facilities, and these services also fall under this code range.

In addition to these sites, patients in a psychiatric residential treatment center would have services coded from this section of CPT as well. A **psychiatric residential treatment center** provides 24-hour care that includes a therapeutically planned and professionally staffed group-living and learning environment.

Physician assessment and care plans are required, and in most cases, affect the payment received by the facility. Resident Assessment Instrument (RAI), Minimum Data Set (MDS), and Resident Assessment Protocols (RAPs) are the most common assessments that are referred to in the nursing facility setting. These assessments are required at admission/readmission to a facility. Should a patient's condition substantially change, a reassessment must be completed on the patient.

There is no distinction made between new and established patients, but a distinction is made between initial and subsequent care. Initial Care codes (99304–99306) require that the three key components meet or exceed the level of service being billed. These codes usually require updates, revisions, or initiation of a new care plan. The instructions for the use of nursing facility initial care codes are noted in Table 3-11.

TABLE 3-11 Nursing Facility Initial Care (99304–99306)

Instructions for Use of Codes (*All three* key components must be met.)
Code 99304 reports an initial nursing facility care service for the evaluation and management of a patient. This code contains the following three key components that must be met to report this code: • detailed/comprehensive history • detailed/comprehensive examination • medical decision making that is straightforward or of low complexity. • The record must document all three of the components. Prior to code 99304 there is an extensive notation that applies to all codes for initial nursing facility care codes. Review the CPT manual for this additional information.
Code 99305 reports the mid level code for an initial nursing facility care service for the evaluation and management of a patient. The key components for code 99305 are: • comprehensive history • comprehensive examination • medical decision making that is of moderate complexity These three key components must be recorded in the documentation for the visit for this code to be justified.
Code 99306 is considered the highest level of the initial nursing facility care service codes for the evaluation and management of a patient. As with codes 99304 and 99305, code 99306 is a "per day" code. Review the CPT manual for the full description of these codes. • comprehensive history • comprehensive examination • medical decision making of high complexity

Subsequent Care codes (99307–99310) require that two of the three key components meet or exceed the level of service billed. Bundled into the subsequent care codes are review of the patient's medical record and review of any ancillary studies. The assessment forms are not affected. The codes, with descriptions, are found in Table 3-12.

Nursing facility discharge services are coded using codes 99315 and 99316. These codes are time based, and if code 99316 is used, documentation must be provided to substantiate why the discharge took more than 30 minutes. The codes include final examination, final instructions and prescriptions given, and any discussion of nursing facility stay, even if the time is not continuous. Table 3-13 summarizes these codes.

Code 99318, "Evaluation and management of a patient involving an annual nursing facility assessment," is used for a patient who requires an annual nursing facility assessment. This code requires a detailed interval history, a comprehensive examination, and medical decision making of low to moderate complexity. This code cannot be reported on the same date of service as the other nursing facility services codes (99304–99316).

TABLE 3-12 Nursing Facility Subsequent Care (99307–99310)

Instructions for the Use of Codes (At least *two* of the three key components must be met.)
The lowest level of the subsequent nursing facility care codes for evaluation and management of a patient is code 99307. To report this code two of the three key components must be documented: • problem-focused interval history • problem-focused examination

(*continues*)

TABLE 3-12 *(continued)*

Instructions for the Use of Codes (At least *two* of the three key components must be met.)
• straightforward medical decision making.
The additional components of the code are recorded in the code description in the CPT manual. Reference the CPT manual for the complete code description. It should be noted that codes 99307, 99308, 99309 and 99310 are "per day" codes.
Code 99308 reports subsequent nursing facility care for evaluation and management of a patient. This is considered a higher level code than code 99307 since the history, examination and medical decision level is as follows for this code: • expanded problem-focused interval history • expanded problem-focused examination • medical decision making of low complexity.
Subsequent nursing facility care for evaluation and management of a patient is reported with code 99309 when two of the following key components are documented by the provider: • detailed interval history • detailed examination • medical decision making of moderate complexity. The description of the additional components of this code can be reviewed by reading the code description in the CPT manual.
Code 99310 is the highest level code for the reporting of subsequent nursing facility care for evaluation and management of a patient. To report this code two of the following key components must be recorded by the provider: • comprehensive interval history • comprehensive examination • medical decision making of high complexity. This is considered the highest level code for subsequent care and therefore the medical documentation should be reviewed to ensure that the reporting of this code is justified prior to submitting a claim.

TABLE 3-13 Nursing Facility Discharge Services (99315, 99316)

Instructions for the Use of Codes
Time is a deciding factor when assigning codes for nursing facility discharge services. 99315 is used to report nursing facility discharge day management. This code is used when the management for discharge is 30 minutes or less. The best practice is to have providers record the time they spend in completing the discharge management.
Code 99316 reports a nursing facility discharge day management with a time of more than 30 minutes. It is essential that the provider records that more than 30 minutes is spent to justify the use of this code.

Exercise 3.9—Check Your Understanding

Nursing Facility Services

Using the CPT manual, indicate whether the following statements are true (T) or false (F).

1. _____ A subsequent nursing facility visit that has a comprehensive exam and a problem-focused interval history with moderate medical decision making would be coded with CPT code 99309.

(continues)

Exercise 3.9—*continued*

2. _____ The primary screening and assessment tool used by skilled nursing facilities is an RAI.

3. _____ A subsequent nursing facility visit that has a problem-focused interval history, a detailed examination, and straightforward medical decision making is coded with CPT code 99307.

4. _____ Hospital discharge services performed on the same date as a nursing facility admission may be reported separately.

5. _____ Codes 99304–99306 are billable using time as a determining element.

6. _____ If a patient is admitted to a nursing facility, any services related to the admission, even if the other services related to the admission were performed in another setting, are included in the code for this admission if performed on the same date as the admission.

7. _____ Nursing Facility Service codes are broken down between new and established patients.

8. _____ Mr. Wallace was readmitted to the nursing home from the hospital. His doctor completed a required annual nursing facility assessment upon return to the nursing home. Mr. Wallace's doctor submitted code 99318 because of changes to the annual facility assessment. The code assignment is correct.

9. _____ Dottie was being discharged to home from her convalescent stay at Sunny Valley nursing facility. Her doctor spent 1 hour discussing discharge orders, preparing the prescriptions, and giving Dottie a comprehensive physical prior to discharge. Her doctor submitted code 99309 for these services. The code assignment is correct.

10. _____ If a patient is in a psychiatric residential treatment center and is also receiving psychotherapy, the psychotherapy is a separately billable service.

Domiciliary, Rest Home, and Custodial Care Services

Domiciliaries, rest homes, and custodial care services are also referred to as boarding homes. The home or facility may assist patients with activities of daily living (ADLs) if needed, but no medical supervision is rendered in this type of setting. Patients typically are living in these settings for long periods. This subcategory of CPT is divided into services provided to new and established patients. Table 3-14 lists the codes and requirements associated with each new patient code.

TABLE 3-14 Domiciliary, Rest Home, and Custodial Care Services—New Patients (99324–99328)

Code(s)	Instructions for Use of Codes (*All three* key components must be met.)
99324	Code 99324 is the first level code for a domiciliary or rest home visit for the evaluation and management of a new patient. Documentation for this code must include the following three key components: • problem-focused history • problem-focused examination • straightforward medical decision making. Reference the CPT manual and compare the level of history, examination and medical decision making for codes 99325 to 99328.
99325	Code 99325 is the second listed code in the range of 99324 to 99328. Reference the CPT manual and note the three key components that are required to report this code.

(*continues*)

TABLE 3-14 (*continued*)

Code(s)	Instructions for Use of Codes (*All three* key components must be met.)
99326	Code 99326 is the third code in this code range and note that the history and examination to be reported for this code is detailed and the medical decision making is moderate.
99327 and 99328	Codes 99327 and 99328 are the final codes for this range and they report a comprehensive history and comprehensive examination. The codes differ in that code 99327 reports moderate medical decision making while code 99328 reports high medical decision making. All three key components must be documented to report these codes. • comprehensive history • comprehensive examination • medical decision making of moderate complexity

Approximate time spent with the patient is given for these codes, so documentation of the time spent can be used as an element in code selection. Time is not considered a key factor. Travel time is not considered a billable service.

Codes for established patients fall under the same guidelines, except that instead of three key components being required or a level of service to be met, only two are required. Table 3-15 notes the codes and descriptions.

TABLE 3-15 Domiciliary, Rest Home, and Custodial Care Services—Established Patients (99334–99337)

Code	Description (At least *two* of the three key components must be met.)
99334	Code 99334 is the lowest level of codes in the code range 99334 to 99337. When reporting this code only two of the three key components need to be documented.
99335	Reference the CPT manual and note that code 99335 is the second code listed in this code range. This code reports a higher level of history and examination than code 99334. The medical decision making for this code is of low complexity.
99336	The third code in this range reports the following: • detailed interval history • detailed examination • moderate medical decision making. Reference the CPT manual for a full description of the code.
99337	Code 99337 is the most comprehensive code for this code range. Documentation of two of the following components must be recorded in the patient's record to report this code: • comprehensive interval history • comprehensive examination • moderate to high medical decision making. Reference the CPT manual for the complete description of this code.

Care Plan Oversight codes, 99339 and 99340, also are present in this range of codes. Table 3-16 lists the codes and definitions for care plan oversight services in the domiciliary, rest home, assisted living, or home care setting.

TABLE 3-16 Care Plan Oversight Services in Domiciliary, Rest Home, and Custodial Care Settings (99339, 99340)

Code(s)	Description
99339 and 99340	Reference the CPT manual and note that codes 99339 and 99340 report individual physician supervision of a patient (patient not present) in home, domiciliary, or rest home. Review the CPT manual for the specific modalities that are included in these codes. Code 99339 reports 15 to 29 minutes while code 99340 reports 30 minutes or more of time spent within a calendar month.

It is essential for a coder to read all notes related to the visit as well as get clarification of any services rendered, if needed, before assigning a code to the physician's services. A good understanding of the actual setting is also essential in correct code selection.

Home Services (99341–99350)

This category is broken down into new versus established patient visits. The unique thing about home services is that the provider must document why the patient was seen at home (in a private residence) and not in the office. This series of codes should not be billed for care plan oversight. Time is allowed as an element when you are choosing a code for services rendered, but travel time is not billable, so only face-to-face time should be documented and included in code selection. Table 3-17 lists the codes and criteria associated with the new-patient home service codes.

TABLE 3-17 Home Services—New Patients (99341–99345)

Code(s)	Description (*All three* key components must be met.)
99341, 99342, 99343, 99344, and 99345	Codes 99341 to 99345 report home visits for the evaluation and management of a new patient. Code 99341 reports the lowest level of E/M service and includes: • problem-focused history • problem-focused examination • straightforward medical decision making. Reference the CPT manual and note that the level of E/M for the patient increases throughout the code range. When reporting these codes it is necessary to document all three key components as listed in the code descriptions.

The Established Patient Home Visit codes are described in Table 3-18.

TABLE 3-18 Home Services—Established Patients (99347–99350)

Code(s)	Description
99347, 99348, 99349, and 99350	Home visits for the evaluation and management of an established patient are reported with code 99347 to 99350. As like the codes for E/M services for new home visit patients the codes for established patients increase in the level of history, examination and medical decision making. Note that code 99350 reports moderate- to high-complexity medical decision making. Reference the CPT manual for the full descriptions of the code range.

The coder should make the provider aware of a few things when looking at these codes. The description of the presenting problem in CPT includes a note with regard to 99350, indicating that "the patient may be unstable or may have developed a significant new problem requiring immediate physician attention." Another element that should be noted here is that the provider should decide if a Consult code might be a better choice if another provider asks for the patient to be seen and an opinion is rendered on a condition.

Prolonged Services (99354–99360)

The first subcategory of the Prolonged Service codes comprises code range 99354–99357, Prolonged Physician Service with Direct (Face-to-Face) Patient Contact, which is used when face-to-face time with a patient exceeds the normal service time reported in an inpatient or outpatient E/M code. This code range is further subdivided into inpatient and outpatient settings. Total face-to-face time does not have to be continuous, but the codes are to be used only once per date of service. Time must be clearly documented. These codes are considered add-on codes and can be used only if the time of the basic E/M code billed is exceeded by at least 30 minutes. Table 3-19 summarizes these codes.

TABLE 3-19 Prolonged Services with Direct (Face-to-Face) Patient Contact (99354–99357)

Code(s)	Description
99354 and 99355	Prolonged evaluation and management or psychotherapy service(s) in the office or other outpatient setting requiring direct patient contact beyond the usual service is reported with code 99354 and 99355. The codes are time based codes. Reference the CPT manual and review the full description for these codes and note that these codes are add-on codes.
99356 and 99357	Prolonged physician service in the inpatient or observation setting, requiring unit/floor time beyond the usual service are reported with codes 99356 and 99357. These two codes are time based codes.

EXAMPLE: Chris, with a chief complaint of shortness of breath, was seen by Dr. Newman, a hospitalist. Dr. Newman clearly documented a level 99232 hospital visit, which has 25 minutes of face-to-face time attached to the code. In addition to the E/M service, Dr. Newman ordered a nebulizer treatment and some stat blood work. He spent 1 hour and 25 additional minutes in face-to-face time with Chris while she had two nebulizer treatments, to be sure her breathing stabilized. Dr. Newman also reviewed lab results and adjusted Chris's plan of care so that the problem would not recur.

In our example, Dr. Newman would be submitting a 99232 (first 25 minutes). To bill prolonged service codes, the time spent must exceed the basic time, in this case 25 minutes, by at least 30 minutes. Dr. Newman exceeded this time by 60 minutes. The codes that apply here would be 99232 and 99356.

The next subcategory in this category of codes is Prolonged Physician Service Without Direct (Face-to-Face) Patient Contact. The guidelines for billing these codes mirror the guidelines for billing prolonged services with direct patient contact, with the exception that there are only two codes in this subcategory, which includes inpatient and outpatient services. The service time does not have to be continuous, but it must exceed the basic service rendered by 30 minutes or more. These codes are used in addition to other services rendered on the same day, but they can be used only once per date of service. These codes are typically used when there is extensive extra work regarding review of records and/or communicating with family members, specialists, or other health care professionals. If other codes are available that will accurately reflect the services rendered, they should be used instead because these codes are not often reimbursed by insurance carriers. Table 3-20 summarizes these codes.

TABLE 3-20 Prolonged Service Without Direct (Face-to-Face) Patient Contact (99358, 99359)

Code(s)	Description
99358 and 99359	Codes 99358 and 99359 report prolonged evaluation and management service before and/or after direct patient care. These codes can be listed in addition to code[s] for other physician service[s] and/or inpatient or outpatient evaluation and management service. It should also be noted that these codes are time based codes. Prior to code 99358 the CPT manual contains extensive information about the use of these codes. Read the information prior to code 99358 found in the CPT manual.

The third subcategory in the Prolonged Services category of codes is entitled Prolonged Clinical Staff Services With Physician or Other Qualified Health Care Professional Supervision. This subcategory includes codes 99415 and 99416. These services are provided in the office or outpatient setting and are to be reported when a physician or qualified health care professional provided direct supervision of clinical staff that provided prolonged face-to-face services that is beyond the typical face-to-face time of the E/M service. Codes 99415 and 99416 are reported in addition to the designated E/M service code. Code 99415 reports the first hour of prolonged clinical staff service during an E/M service and code 99416 reports each additional 30 minutes. Prior to assigning these codes coders, need to read the guidelines that are found prior to code 99415 which provide detailed instructions on the use of these codes. As stated in this section of the CPT manual, code 99415, is to be reported only once per date. Reference the table that follows code 99416 in the CPT manual for further explanation of the assignment of these codes.

Standby Services (99360) is the last code in the Prolonged Services section. This code is used when a physician requests that another physician stand by in the event his services are needed. Standby service does not require direct patient contact. A physician cannot use this code when precepting another physician or if the standby physician performs a service that has a global period attached to it, because the standby service is considered bundled into the surgical package. Typically, this code may be used with regard to a problematic delivery. You must clearly show that the physician spent more than 30 minutes on standby. Do not report code 99360 along with 99464, "Attendance at delivery."

Case Management Services (99366–99368)

Case management is a service provided by an attending physician in which the physician not only supervises but also coordinates direct care received by a patient. This category of CPT contains codes for Medical Team Conferences. Table 3-21 summarizes the code for Medical Team Conferences with direct (face-to-face) contact with the patient and/or the patient's family. Extensive notations appear in the CPT manual, which you should review before assigning codes 99366 to 99368. Locate and review the notations found in the CPT manual prior to code 99366.

TABLE 3-21 Medical Team Conference, Direct Contact with Patient and/or Family (99366)

Code	Description
99366	Code 99366 is a time based code that reports a medical team conference. Review code 99366 and note the description of the code.
	(Please note that an instructional notation within the CPT manual states that for team conference services less than 30 minutes, the service should not be reported separately.)

The codes are used to report medical team conferences in which at least three qualified health-care professionals from different specialties or disciplines meet face to face to develop, revise, coordinate, or implement health-care services needed by the patient. Table 3-22 summarizes the codes that report conferences without direct contact with the patient and/or family.

TABLE 3-22 Medical Team Conferences Without Direct Contact with Patient and/or Family (99367–99368)

Code(s)	Description
99367 and 99368	Codes 99367 and 99368 report medical team conferences when the patient and/or family member is not present during the conference. These conferences must be at least 30 minutes or longer to be reported. Reference the CPT manual to review the full description of the codes and note the code differences.

When reporting these codes, note that no more than one individual from the same specialty may report these codes at the same encounter. These codes also should not be reported when the medical team conference is part of a facility or organizational service that is contractually provided by the facility or organizational provider.

Care Plan Oversight Services (99374–99380)

Care plan oversight is a service that is billed once a month and includes all care rendered to a patient over a 30-day period. These codes are billed by only one physician in a group practice over the 30-day period to reflect services coordinated or rendered by a physician. Patients in nursing facilities or under the care of a home health agency should not be billed with these codes. These codes are summarized in Table 3-23.

TABLE 3-23 Care Plan Oversight Services (99374–99380)

Code(s)	Description
99374 and 99375	Supervision of a patient under care of home health agency (patient not present) in home, domiciliary, or equivalent environment is reported with codes 99374 and 99375. Reference the CPT manual and note the full description of the codes. The codes are time based and are reported based on services completed within a calendar month. Code 99374 reports 15 to 29 minutes and code 99375 reports 30 minutes or more.
99377 and 99378	Supervision of a hospice patient (patient not present) is reported with code 99377 and 99378. Review the CPT manual for the full description of these codes and note the time associated with each code.
99379 and 99380	Supervision of a nursing facility (patient not present) is reported with code 99379 and 99380. Reference the CPT manual and read the full descriptions of these codes and note the time used for each code.

Preventive Medicine Services (99381–99429)

Preventive medicine services are provided to a patient who is presenting to a medical office for a "well visit" or a "physical examination." They include a routine checkup, annual gynecologic examinations, and other examinations whose focus is promoting health, such as smoking and tobacco use cessation counseling visits and alcohol and/or substance abuse structures screening and intervention services. Because preventive services are age driven, no HPI is associated with the visit.

Preventive medicine does not typically entail problems, but it can be reported with a problem-oriented Evaluation and Management code should the occasion arise. If you find it necessary to code two levels of service, keep the following in mind:

- Modifier 25 is necessary to indicate that a separate Evaluation and Management service was rendered during the same visit.

- A separate note is needed, identifying the problem encountered along with any additional history, examination, and/or medical decision making that was deemed necessary to show how this problem was greater than the preventive service rendered.

- When the coder intends to "split bill," or break out a separate E/M service, the insurance carrier should be contacted to see if the separate service will be recognized and if any adjustment to the fee submitted needs to be made.

As you will note when reviewing the codes listed, preventive medicine codes are assigned by whether the patient is new or established, and then by the age of the patient.

Preventive Medicine Services—New Patient (99381–99387)

Initial preventive medicine services are categorized according to age, as summarized in Table 3-24.

TABLE 3-24 Preventive Medicine Services—New Patient (99381–99387)

Code(s)	Description
99381	Codes 99381 to 99387 report initial comprehensive preventive medicine evaluation and management of an individual new patient. The codes are differentiated by the age of the patient. Reference the CPT manual and note the components of the codes. Code 99381 is used for infants that are under 1 year old.
99382, 99383, and 99384	These codes report services provided to child under 17. Reference the CPT manual to identify the age range associated with each of these codes.
99385, 99386, and 99387	These codes report service provided to individuals 18 years old and over. Reference the CPT manual for the specific age ranges.

Preventive Medicine Services—Established Patient (99391–99397)

Preventive medicine services for established patients are categorized by age, as listed in Table 3-25.

TABLE 3-25 Preventive Medicine Services—Established Patient (99391–99397)

Code(s)	Description
99391	Code 99391 reports comprehensive preventive medicine reevaluation and management of an established patient that is under 1 year of age. Reference the CPT manual and review the specific components for this code.
99392, 99393, and 99394	These codes report preventative medicine services for established patients that are 17 years or younger. Reference the CPT manual for the specific age ranges.
99395, 99396, and 99397	These codes report preventative services for an established patient that is 18 years and over. Reference the CPT manual to identify the specific age ranges.

Counseling and/or Risk-Factor Reduction Intervention and Behavioral-Change Interventions (99401–99409)

Preventive Medicine, Individual Counseling, and Behavior Change Interventions, Individual Code range 99401–99409, Counseling Risk-Factor Reduction and Behavior Change Intervention, Individual, is used to report counseling and/or risk-factor reduction interventions for new and established patients. The codes are organized as shown in Table 3-26.

TABLE 3-26 Preventive Medicine, Individual Counseling, and Behavior Change Interventions, Individual (99401–99409)

Code(s)	Description
99401 to 99404	Preventive medicine counseling and/or risk-factor reduction interventions(s) provided to an individual are reported with codes 99401 to 99404. The codes are separate procedure codes and are differentiated by time. Reference the CPT manual for the specific times reported by each code.
99406–99407	Smoking and tobacco use cessation counseling visit (The codes are differentiated by the length of time spent counseling.)
99408–99409	Alcohol and/or substance (other than tobacco) abuse structured screening and brief intervention services (These codes are differentiated by the length of time.)

Preventive Medicine, Group Counseling   Table 3-27 describes the codes for preventive medicine group counseling.

TABLE 3-27 Preventive Medicine, Group Counseling (99411, 99412)

Code(s)	Description
99411 and 99412	Preventive medicine counseling and/or risk factor reduction intervention(s) provided to individuals in a group setting are reported with codes 99411 and 99412. These are separate procedure codes that are differentiated by time. Reference the CPT manual and note the full description of the codes and the time associated with each code.

Other Preventive Medicine Services   Table 3-28 describes the code for other preventive medicine services.

TABLE 3-28 Other Preventive Medicine Services (99429)

Code	Description
99429	The final code that relates to the reporting of preventative medicine services is code 99429. This code reports unlisted preventative services.

Non-Face-to-Face Physician Services (99091, 99421–99423, 99441–99458, 99473 and 99474)

Non-face-to-face physician services codes are used to report telephone services, online medical evaluations, and interprofessional telephone/internet consultations. During these services, the physician does not see the patient. Extensive notations appear in CPT about the use and definitions for these codes. Note that numerous codes in this subsection are time based codes.

Special Evaluation and Management Services (99450–99456)

The next group of CPT codes in the Evaluation and Management chapter of the CPT manual is used only for evaluation services performed to gather information for insurance certificates. A separate note should be documented to support use of these codes because work done for the 99450–99456 range cannot be included in the other E/M services. Special report code 99080, found in the Medicine section of CPT, would not be billed in addition to these codes.

These codes would be used for disability insurance, life insurance, or work-related medical certifications. Insurance companies or the workers' compensation board may request these evaluations. Payment by any other carriers should be explored before a patient is seen. These codes may not be paid by the patient's carrier.

Basic Life and/or Disability Evaluation Services (99450)

Code 99450 is used to report a basic life and/or disability examination that includes measurement of height, weight, and blood pressure; completion of a medical history following a life insurance pro forma; collection of blood sample and/or urinalysis complying with "chain of custody" protocols; and completion of necessary documentation/certificates.

Work-Related or Medical Disability Evaluation Services (99455, 99456)

Code 99455 reports work-related or medical disability examinations by the treating physician that include completion of a medical history commensurate with the patient's condition; performance of an examination commensurate with the patient's condition; formulation of a diagnosis, assessment of capabilities and stability, and calculation of impairment; development of a future medical treatment plan; and completion of necessary documentation/certificates and reports.

Code 99456 reports a work-related or medical disability examination by someone other than the treating physician that includes completion of a medical history commensurate with the patient's condition; performance of an examination commensurate with the patient's condition; formulation of a diagnosis, assessment of capabilities and stability, and calculation of impairment; development of a future medical treatment plan; and completion of necessary documentation/certificates and reports.

These two codes are used only in the event that an insurer is asking for a work-related examination or an examination with regard to a medical disability problem.

Newborn Care (99460–99463)

Newborn care codes from this section are used when care is provided for normal or high-risk newborns in the settings listed. Careful attention to the setting is key in assigning the correct newborn care code. Discharge services provided on the same date as assessment services should be coded using 99463. Table 3-29 lists these codes.

TABLE 3-29 Newborn Care and Delivery/Birthing Room Attendance and Resuscitation Services (99460–99465)

Code(s)	Description
99460 and 99461	Codes 99460 and 99461 report initial care for evaluation and management of normal newborn infant. Review the full descriptions of these codes in the CPT manual and note that the codes are "per day" codes and are differentiated by the site where the service is performed.
99462	Code 99462 is used to report subsequent care of a normal newborn that is provided in a hospital. Note that this code is reported per day.
99463	Code 99463 is reported for evaluation and management of normal newborn infant that was admitted and discharged on the same date. Review the CPT manual and note that the care is provided as initial care in a hospital or birthing center.
99464 and 99465	Codes 99464 and 99465 are delivery/birthing room attendance and resuscitation service codes. Review the codes descriptions of these codes in the CPT manual and note the instructional notations that appear after each of the codes at delivery (when requested by delivering provider) and initial stabilization of newborn

Delivery/Birthing Room Attendance and Resuscitation Services (99464, 99465)

Code 99464 reports an additional provider's attendance at delivery, when it is requested by the delivering provider, and the initial stabilization of the newborn. Code 99464 can be reported with codes:

- 99460—initial hospital or birthing center care, per day, for the evaluation and management of normal newborn infant
- 99468—initial inpatient neonatal critical care, per day, for the evaluation and management of a critically ill neonate 28 days of age or younger
- 99477—initial hospital care, per day, for the evaluation and management of the neonate, 28 days of age or younger, who requires intensive observation, frequent interventions and other intensive care services

Code 99465, per the CPT description, reports delivery or birthing room resuscitation, provision of positive pressure ventilation, and/or chest compressions in the presence of acute inadequate ventilation and/or cardiac output. This code can be reported with codes 99460, 99468, and 99477. The instructional notation that follows code 99465 in the CPT manual also states that additional procedures, such as intubation, are to be reported separately. Make note of this instructional notation found in the CPT manual following code 99465.

It should also be noted that codes 99464 and 99465 are not to be reported in conjunction with each other.

Care Management Services (99487, 99489, 99490, 99491)

Codes 99487, 99489, 99490, and 99491 are used to report services provided to patients who reside at home, in a domiciliary home, a rest home, or an assisted living facility who receive care management services from a physician or other qualified health care professional. These codes are time based and are used to report the management of services for specific patients that have been identified to need these services based on their continuous or episodic health conditions that are expected to be present for the next 12 months or until the death of the patient. These codes are reported only once per calendar month by a single provider who assumes the responsibility of the care management services. To become familiar with the many care management activities and office capabilities that must be present for the use of these codes, read the instructional notations that are found prior to code 99490. The notations appear after the heading of "Care Management Services." Code 99490 reports chronic care management services that include at least 20 minutes of clinical staff time. Code 99491 reports at least 30 minutes of time. Code 99487 reports the first hour of complex chronic care management services. Reference this code in the CPT manual and review the required elements for this code. One of the most important elements for this code and code 99489 is that there is moderate-or high-complexity medical decision making. This must be documented in the patient's medical record. Code 99489 is an add-on code and reports each additional 30 minutes of time and is reported in conjunction with codes 99487.

Transitional Care Management Services (99495, 99496)

Transitional care management services are reported with codes 99495 and 99496. These codes are used when a new or an established patient is transitioning from an inpatient setting to a community setting and needs these services because of medical and/or psychosocial conditions that require moderate- or high-complexity medical decision making. In the CPT manual, extensive guidelines are written for these codes. Read the guidelines that precede code 99495. Code 99495 reports transitional care management services that include communication with the patient and/or caregiver within two business days of discharge, medical decision making of least moderate complexity during the service period, and a face-to-face visit within 14 calendar days of discharge. Code 99496 reports transitional care management services that include communication with the patient and/or caregiver within two business days of discharge, medical decision making of high complexity during the service period, and a face-to-face visit within seven calendar days of discharge. Reference the CPT manual for an extensive listing of codes that cannot be reported with codes 99495 or 99496.

Advance Care Planning (99497, 99498)

Codes 99497 and 99498 are time-based codes and are used to report advance care planning. Advance care planning includes face-to-face services in which advance directives for health care are discussed. These services can or cannot include the completion of legal forms such as a Health Care Proxy, Durable Power of Attorney for Health Care, Living Will, and so on. Code 99497 reports the first 30 minutes of face-to-face time, and code 99498 is an add-on code that reports each additional 30 minutes. Codes 99497 and 99498 are not to be reported on the same date of service with codes:

- 99291, 99292—Critical care, evaluation and management of the critically ill or critically injured patient
- 99468, 99469, 99471, 99472, 99475, and 99476—Inpatient Neonatal and Pediatric Critical Care
- 99477, 99478, 99479, 99480, and 99483—Initial and Continuing Intensive Care Services for a child who requires intensive care services

See the instructional notation in the CPT manual that follows code 99498 that denotes these codes that cannot be used on the same date of service as codes 99497 and 99498.

Other Evaluation and Management Services (99499)

This code is used *only* in the event that there are *no* other E/M codes that accurately reflect the service provided. This code is used very infrequently and will generate an inquiry from the insurance carrier as to the service actually provided; in other words, supporting documentation will be required.

Summary

- When a patient comes into a physician's office, skilled nursing facility, or hospital, code assignment should begin with the Evaluation and Management chapter of the CPT manual. The patient is evaluated, and then the management or plan of care is recorded in the medical record.
- When you choose a level of service, the history, examination, and medical decision making are the three key elements in the criteria for proper code assignment.
- Seven elements play a role in code assignment. Time, the nature of the presenting problem, coordination of care, and counseling are taken into account in addition to the three key elements.
- To assign codes properly, you should know whether a patient is new or established, whether the patient is an inpatient or an outpatient, and what the place of service was.
- Emergency Service codes report both new and established patients.
- POS, or place of service, codes represent where the service or care was rendered.

- A new patient is a patient who has *not* received services from a provider of the same specialty, who belongs to the same group practice within the past three years.
- An established patient is a patient who *has* received services from the physician or another physician of the same specialty, who belongs to the same group practice within the past three years.
- A chief complaint (CC) is the reason the patient is seen.
- Past, family, and social history (PFSH) are recorded as part of the review of systems.
- The four types of histories are problem-focused, expanded problem-focused, detailed, and comprehensive.
- The four types of examinations are problem-focused, expanded problem-focused, detailed, and comprehensive.
- The four levels of medical decision making are straightforward, low complexity, moderate complexity, and high complexity.
- Hospital inpatient coding is divided into initial hospital care codes, subsequent hospital care codes, and discharge services.
- Observation codes are for patients who have not been admitted as inpatients but who need to be observed for assessment of their medical condition.
- Consultations are services rendered by a provider whose opinion or advice is requested by another provider.

Internet Links

Visit **www.cms.gov** and search the Medicare Learning Network (MLN) homepage for E/M documentation guidelines and other references that relate to billing and coding. The link for the MLN Homepage is found on the CMS homepage under the section entitled "Top 5 Resources."

Chapter Review

True/False

Instructions: Indicate whether the following statements are true (T) or false (F).

1. _____ After a patient is evaluated, a management plan is implemented and recorded in the medical record.

2. _____ A new patient is one who has not received face-to-face care from their provider within two years.

3. _____ There are seven key components to choosing a level of E/M service.

4. _____ The lowest level of code for an office visit when you are charging for a problem-focused new-patient visit is code 99211.

5. _____ The ROS is the part of the note in which the provider documents any body system(s) that might be affected by the chief complaint.

6. _____ When time is used as a key component in billing an E/M service, the provider must document face-to-face time with the patient and how much time was spent counseling the patient with the family.

7. _____ An incorrect place of service can result in a rejection by insurance carriers.

8. _____ A 99233 is coded for a high-level initial hospital care visit.

9. _____ To code a preventive physical exam, the coder must first determine the level of history the provider has recorded.

10. _____ The POS for an office visit is 23.

Fill in the Blank

Instructions: Using a current CPT manual, finish the statements using the correct term(s).

11. The location where care was rendered is called the _____.

12. Services provided to a patient who is presenting for a well visit are called _____ services.

13. Critical care codes are _____ -based codes.

14. When a patient is admitted and discharged on the same date of service, _____ codes are used.

15. _____ a patient and/or family member usually involves treatment options and instruction on medications.

16. A patient who has not received face-to-face services from a provider of the same specialty within the same group practice would be considered a(n) _____ patient.

17. A patient who has received face-to-face services from a provider of the same specialty within the same group practice would be considered a(n) _____ patient.

18. A service rendered by a provider when his or her opinion or expertise is requested by another provider or appropriate source is called a(n) _____.

19. An organized hospital-based facility that renders unscheduled episodic services to patients who require immediate attention is known as a(n) _____.

20. For services to a neonate in the intensive care unit to be coded with a 99479, the birth weight of the infant must fall between _____ and _____.

21. Transitional care management service code, _____, reports communication with a patient within two business days, high-complexity medical decision making, and a face-to-face visit within seven calendar days of discharge.

22. Seventy minutes of complex chronic care management services with one face-to-face visit would be reported with code(s) _____.

23. Add-on code 99467 would be reported for each additional 30 minutes of face-to-face services during an interfacility transport of a critically ill or injured pediatric patient, 24 months of age or younger with code _____.

24. Initial birthing center care for the evaluation and management of a normal newborn infant is reported with code _____.

25. An eight minute smoking and tobacco use cessation counseling visit is reported with code _____.

26. A preventative medicine individual counseling session of 35 minutes is reported with code _____.

27. One hour and five minutes of advance care planning would be reported with code(s) _____.

28. Joan Seap lives at home, has COPD and ASHD, and is functionally declining. Dr. Smith has revised her comprehensive care plan. Thirty minutes was spent this month completing these services. The code to report is _____.

29. Jason was seen in Dr. Jone's office as a new patient. An expanded problem focused history, a detailed exam, and straightforward medical decision was completed and documented in the patient's record. Code _____ should be reported for this visit.

30. Suzie, an established patient of Dr. Smith's, was seen in the office. Dr. Smith completed and documented a problem focused history, an expanded problem focused examination, and medical decision making of low complexity. Code _____ should be reported for this service.

Case Studies

Review each case and indicate the correct code(s).

Case 1

Mrs. Edison was having trouble eating some of the foods the nutritionists had set up on her diabetic diet menu. Mrs. Edison talked with her doctor who, in turn, called the nutritionist overseeing Mrs. Edison's diet. The doctor and the nutritionist were on the phone, had a lengthy phone conversation, and decided to integrate a new menu that both of them felt would be more beneficial to Mrs. Edison and for the management of her diabetes. The doctor then called the patient to discuss the diet changes and decided to bill for the telephone call with the patient. The call length was 24 minutes.

CPT code(s): _____ _ _____ _ _____ _

Case 2

Daisy, a 10-year-old girl, was very sick when she presented for an office visit at her pediatrician's office. She was running a high fever, was very lethargic, had swollen glands, and showed signs of dehydration because of the vomiting she had been doing the previous night. The doctor decided, after a comprehensive history and physical, that Daisy needed to be admitted to the hospital for lab workup, rehydration, antibiotics, and monitoring. Daisy's pediatrician stopped in to the hospital that evening to evaluate her condition and check on lab results. Medical decision making was high complexity.

CPT code(s): _____ _ _____ _ _____ _

Case 3

Colin was having great difficulty living alone since his recent fall down the back steps of his house. His family decided that Colin should move to a skilled nursing facility (SNF), which he finally agreed to do. The physician at the SNF did a comprehensive history and physical. The medical decision making was of moderate complexity, and there was a very detailed plan of care implemented that would work on building Colin's strength and reteaching him how to get around in a safer manner.

CPT code(s): _____ _ _____ _ _____ _

Case 4

Nick was riding his dirt bike and collided with a tree. The EMTs stabilized Nick at the scene and transported him to the nearest hospital. His doctor, Dr. Shanequa, had been contacted by the family and would meet them at the hospital emergency room. In the emergency room, Dr. Shanequa took a detailed history, did a comprehensive physical, and ordered lab work and x-rays of the head, neck, and back, along with the right leg, because Nick was complaining of severe pain in the lower portion of the leg. Dr. Shanequa determined that although Nick was pretty banged up and should not ride the dirt bike for a while, he was fine. The x-rays showed a bad sprain in the ankle area, but nothing was broken.

CPT code(s): _____ _ _____ _ _____ _ (*Hint:* **Keep in mind that Dr. Shanequa is Nick's primary care physician, not the ED doctor.**)

Case 5

Megan was admitted to the hospital on May 31 at 5:00 a.m. for chest pain with nausea and heartburn. A comprehensive history was taken, and a comprehensive exam was done. Another 12 hours later, after labs, x-rays, and monitoring had been completed, and with no repeat in symptoms, it was determined that Megan had suffered a bout of GERD, and she was released to go home.

CPT code(s): _____ _ _____ _ _____ _

Case 6

Skilled Nursing Facility Discharge Summary

This 83-year-old has been a resident for the past 1½ years. She was admitted because she had polio with left hemiparesis with speech impediment. She was hospitalized four months ago with an exacerabation of COPD, dehydration, and low blood pressure. After physical, speech, and occupational therapy, the patient has now become more independent and is able to walk behind her wheelchair. She is able to perform all of her ADLs. Routine lab work was completed last week and was found to be within normal ranges. The patient is being discharged to her daughter's home.

(continues)

(continued)

Final Examination of Patient

The patient is alert. Vital signs: BP 120/66, P-64, R-12 weight –165 lb.

HEENT: Head—normocephalic EENT: clear.

NECK: No lymphadenopathy or thyromegaly.

LUNGS: Clear, good air entry.

HEART: Regular rhythm, no murmurs. Distal pulses palpable.

ABDOMEN: Soft, nondistended.

NEUROLOGICAL: Cranial nerves 2–12 grossly intact except for speech impediment. Has left hemiparesis.

Discharge records were completed, and instructions and prescriptions were given to the patient's daughter.

CPT code(s): _____ _ _____ _ _____ _

Case 7

Office Visit

This patient has been a patient of mine for six years, and I saw him three months ago for his annual physical. Today he presents with a cough, which he has had for the last two days, with a fever of 101 and is short of breath.

Personal medical history is significant for appendicitis in 2003.

This well-nourished, well-developed 25-year-old patient presents with a cough and fever. BP 120/70. Height: 5 feet 9 inches. Weight: 175 lb.

Ears: Auditory canals and tympanic membranes within normal limits.

Oropharynx: No significant findings.

Lungs: Bilaterally congested.

Heart: Regular sinus rhythm.

Abdomen: Soft.

Liver and spleen: Not palpable.

Assessment: Acute bronchitis.

Plan: Patient was prescribed an antibiotic. See medication order for details.

CPT code(s): _____ _ _____ _ _____ _

Case 8

This 93-year-old was seen today in her home to reevaluate a rash that she has had for the last three weeks.

Patient appears alert and responsive. BP: 130/80.

Heart: Normal rate and rhythm.

Abdomen: Soft with no masses present.

Skin: The rash that was previously present on the patient's left arm and shoulders is resolved.

Patient was instructed to call if the rash reappears.

CPT code(s): _____ _ _____ _ _____ _

Case 9

Office Note

This 16-year-old presents today for his annual physical. This patient has been under my care since he was 6 years old.

This patient has no known medical problems.

Please see previous family history taken in May of last year. There are no additional items to add to that history.

Social History

The patient is a junior in high school and denies use of drugs or alcohol. He is a swimmer and trains year round and is hoping to secure a college swimming scholarship. Denies any other social risk factors at this time. Patient was given patient educational materials on social risks that are relevant to his age.

Physical Exam

Vital Signs: As recorded by nurse.

HEENT: Within normal limits.

Neck: Examination and thyroid are normal.

Abdomen: There are no masses or tenderness noted. Scar from previous appendectomy at age 12.

Heart: Normal sounds, no murmurs.

Musculoskeltal: There are no significant findings. Patient has better than average muscle strength and tone.

No laboratory tests or procedures were ordered. Patient is current on all immunizations. Patient instructed to return in one year for physical, or sooner if an acute condition occurs.

CPT code(s): _____ _ _____ _ _____ _

Case 10

Smoking Cessation Program Note

This 30-year-old male patient presents today for his fifth counseling visit as part of the Smoking Cessation Program. Reviewed self-relaxation techniques and monitoring of physical symptoms of stress that precede cravings for nicotine. Client reports reduction of three to five cigarettes per day since last visit. Patient was instructed to continue to record nicotine use and stress levels. Patient to schedule appointment in two weeks.

Time of today's session: 10:00 a.m. to 10:35 a.m.

CPT code(s): _____ – _____ – _____ –

Chapter Outline

Learning Objectives

At the conclusion of this chapter, you should be able to:

1. Locate CPT codes for anesthesia services.
2. Identify the various types of anesthesia.
3. Define the abbreviations associated with anesthesia.
4. List the professionals who are certified to administer anesthesia.
5. Identify situations in which modifiers specific to anesthesia are necessary.
6. Calculate the anesthesia reimbursement amount for patient procedures.
7. Identify and code procedures for anesthesia from case studies.
8. Assign the appropriate CPT codes with modifiers for anesthesia services.

Key Terms

anesthesia	block	conscious sedation	intraspinal anesthesia
anesthesiologist	block anesthesia	epidural anesthesia	local anesthesia
balanced anesthesia	bundled	epidural blocks	moderate sedation
base unit	certified registered	general anesthesia	modifying units
base unit value	nurse anesthetist	inhalation	peridural anesthesia
basic value	(CRNA)	injection	physical status
Bier blocks	conduction anesthesia	instillation	modifiers

postanesthesia recovery period

qualifying circumstances

regional anesthesia

relative value

Relative Value Guide (RVG)

spinal anesthesia

subarachnoid anesthesia

time unit

Introduction

This chapter introduces you to the Anesthesia section of the CPT manual, codes 00100–01999, and additional qualifying circumstance anesthesia codes 99100–99140, which are found in the Medicine section of CPT. In this chapter, we also discuss some of the nuances specific to coding anesthesia services. Anesthesia services are usually billed by a physician or certified specialist whose sole purpose is administering and monitoring anesthesia and its effect on the patient. The anesthesia provider or specialist is not typically performing the procedure in addition to the anesthesia. However, at times, a provider performing the procedure also administers the anesthetic agent.

Guidelines Related to the National Correct Coding Initiative (NCCI)

You will need to reference the following website to obtain the most current coding guideline information related to this chapter. Follow the steps given here to access the information online:

1. Log on to *http://www.cms.gov/Medicare/Coding/NationalCorrectCodInitEd/index.html*.
2. Scroll to the section titled "Downloads."
3. Click the link for the most current "NCCI Policy Manual for Medicare Services."
4. A box may appear that requires you to click "Open."
5. Click "Chapter 2" for guidelines specific to anesthesia coding.

Abbreviations Relating to Anesthesia

Abbreviation	Definition
ABP	arterial blood pressure
anes	anesthesia
BaE	barium enema
CBF	cerebral blood flow
CPR	cardiopulmonary resuscitation
EUA	examine under anesthesia
IVD	intervertebral disc
IVPB	intravenous piggy back
LBBB	left bundle branch block
mg/dl	milligrams per deciliter
MVV	maximum voluntary ventilation
TPR	temperature, pulse, respiration

What Is Anesthesia, and How Is It Administered?

Anesthesia, which means "loss of sensation," is administered to patients to relieve pain brought on by any number of causes, including surgery. Anesthesia can be administered by a qualified professional through injection, inhalation, and agent instillation. A physician qualified to administer anesthesia and who is board certified is referred to as an **anesthesiologist**. A **certified registered nurse anesthetist (CRNA)** is a registered nurse with 36 months additional training in anesthesiology who is certified to administer anesthesia.

Various scenarios can exist for the delivery of anesthesia services, including the following:

- An anesthesiologist performing the anesthesia services alone
- A certified registered nurse anesthetist performing the anesthesia services alone
- An anesthesiologist directing one certified registered nurse anesthetist
- An anesthesiologist directing multiple CRNAs performing concurrent procedures

It is important for the coder to determine who administered the anesthesia because reimbursement will vary depending on the provider. Modifiers are used to indicate whether an anesthesiologist or a CRNA delivered the anesthetic. (The use of modifiers will be discussed later in this chapter.)

Types of Anesthesia

Multiple techniques are used to anesthetize a patient. **General anesthesia** alters the patient's perception and affects the whole body, causing a loss of consciousness. This type of anesthesia typically is administered by injection, inhalation, instillation, or a combination of these techniques.

Injection of an anesthetic agent involves the anesthetic being administered directly into the bloodstream. A venous access device is used, which allows the medication to circulate through the bloodstream. **Inhalation** of anesthetic agents requires the use of the circulatory and respiratory systems to move the agent efficiently through the body. Typically, a vaporizer is used to administer this type of anesthesia. **Instillation** of an anesthetic agent is used if there are problems administering the agent by injection or inhalation. During instillation, the anesthetic agent is introduced into a cavity of the body that has a mucous membrane, such as the rectum. The mucous membrane allows the anesthetic agent to be absorbed into the circulatory system and then transported to the central nervous system, thus anesthetizing the patient. The technique is not commonly used, but it is necessary in cases where the patient is not cooperative or when other approaches have failed.

At times, general anesthesia is delivered by a combination of inhalation, injection, and instillation. This is known as **balanced anesthesia**.

Regional anesthesia, as the name suggests, anesthetizes a particular area or region of the body. This is accomplished through nerve or field blocking. The anesthetic is injected along a major nerve tract, thus interrupting the nerve conductivity in that region of the body. This type of anesthesia is also referred to as a **block**, **block anesthesia**, or **conduction anesthesia**. Common types of regional anesthesia include:

- **Bier blocks**—injection of an anesthetic agent into the arm below the elbow or in the leg below the knee.
- **Epidural blocks**—injection of an anesthetic agent into the epidural space above the dura mater, which contains the spinal nerves and cerebrospinal fluid. This is most commonly performed in the lumbar area. This also is commonly called **epidural anesthesia**, **intraspinal anesthesia**, **peridural anesthesia**, **spinal anesthesia**, and **subarachnoid anesthesia**.

Local anesthesia numbs a small area, such as a finger or toe, and occurs when an anesthetic agent is applied topically to the skin or injected subcutaneously. Local anesthesia is used for dental procedures and brief surgical procedures.

Coding and Billing Anesthesia Services

In the hospital setting, anesthesia codes are not reported because these codes represent the professional services provided by the anesthesiologist or CRNA. Anesthesia codes are used to report the professional services of the providers who anesthetized the patient. If the hospital is billing for the professional services of the anesthesiology staff, the anesthesia codes are used.

The coding and billing of anesthesia services vary significantly depending on the payer and the state in which the service is performed. Medicare requires the use of CPT anesthesia codes, whereas some third-party payers require the use of surgery codes to bill for anesthesia services. It is of the utmost importance that coders verify the coding requirements for the area in which they are reporting the services. The codes submitted for the same anesthesia service can also differ depending on the payer.

> **EXAMPLE:** An anesthesiologist provided anesthesia services for a Medicare patient for a cranioplasty for a 2-cm skull defect. The code reported should be 00215.
>
> The same service was performed for a patient with a private payer that requires the reporting of the surgery code by the anesthesiologist. In this case, the code reported should be 62140.

Before coding from the Anesthesia section of CPT, the coder must become familiar with the guidelines that appear at the start of the section. These guidelines outline the specific features of the coding system that are unique to the Anesthesia section.

Arrangement of the Anesthesia Section

Referencing the Anesthesia section of CPT, you will note that the subsections are organized first by anatomic site, and then by procedure. However, the following four subsections of Anesthesia, do not follow this arrangement:

Subsection	Code Range
Anesthesia for Radiologic Procedures	01916–01936
Anesthesia for Burn Excisions or Debridement	01951–01953
Anesthesia for Obstetrics	01958–01969
Anesthesia for Other Procedures	01990–01999

Locating Anesthesia Procedure Codes

Locating the CPT codes for anesthesia procedures is not as complicated as locating other procedure codes. The main term to reference in the index is "Anesthesia." The index is divided after that term by the type of procedure performed or the body site of the procedure. For example, the start of the index for Anesthesia looks like this:

Anesthesia

See Analgesia

Abbe-Estlander Procedure	00102
Abdomen	
Abdominal Wall	00700, 00730, 00800–00802, 00820, 00836

Therefore, if the patient underwent anesthesia for a Abbe-Estlander procedure, the coder should reference the main term *Anesthesia* in the index and then the subterm *Abbe-Estlander Procedure*.

If you look through the Anesthesia section of CPT, you will notice that anesthesia codes are general or specific. An example of a general code is Code 00500—"Anesthesia for all procedures on esophagus." However, Code 00906, "Anesthesia for vulvectomy," represents a specific code.

Exercise 4.1—Check Your Understanding

Locating Anesthesia Codes

Using a CPT manual, locate the codes or code ranges listed in the index for the procedures that follow. This exercise will help familiarize you with the index. (To select the specific code for the procedures listed, you would need to have an operative report to identify the specific procedure completed.) The first two are completed for you.

1. Anesthesia for partial hepatectomy   00792
2. Anesthesia for procedure of the ankle   00400, 01462–01522
3. Anesthesia for cast application on leg   _____
4. Anesthesia for childbirth, vaginal delivery   _____
5. Anesthesia for inferior vena cava ligation   _____
6. Anesthesia for stomach restriction for obesity   _____
7. Anesthesia for renal procedure   _____
8. Anesthesia for cervical cerclage   _____
9. Anesthesia for procedure on the pharynx   _____
10. Anesthesia for procedure on the urinary tract   _____
11. Anesthesia for orchiectomy   _____
12. Anesthesia for reconstruction of bronchi   _____
13. Anesthesia for great vessels of chest   _____
14. Anesthesia for liver hemorrhage   _____
15. Anesthesia for hip procedure   _____
16. Anesthesia for gastrocemius recession   _____
17. Anesthesia for biopsy of ear   _____
18. Anesthesia for humeral osteotomy   _____
19. Anesthesia for thoracotomy   _____
20. Anesthesia for procedure on the larynx   _____

Anesthesia Modifiers

After selecting the correct CPT anesthesia code, select modifiers to describe the case further. Numerous types of modifiers are used with anesthesia codes.

CPT Modifiers

The following CPT modifiers are used for anesthesia services:

22	Unusual Procedural Services	51	Multiple Procedures
23	Unusual Anesthesia	53	Discontinued Procedure
32	Mandated Services	59	Distinct Procedural Service

One common error that new coders make is assigning modifier 47, anesthesia by surgeon. This modifier is to be used only by a surgeon who administered regional or general anesthesia. Modifier 47 is added to the procedure code for the service performed. This modifier is not used for the anesthesia procedure codes 00100–01999.

 NOTE:

The complete definition of each of the preceding modifiers is located in Appendix A, Modifiers, of the CPT manual.

HCPCS Level II Modifiers

As mentioned earlier in this chapter, anesthesia services are performed by anesthesiologists and CRNAs. Medicare and some other payers require the use of the two-digit alpha HCPCS modifiers. Use the following HCPCS Level II modifiers with anesthesia codes to identify the exact nature of the service provided:

AA—Anesthesia services performed personally by anesthesiologist. This modifier is used only by the anesthesiologist.

AD—Medical supervision by a physician: more than four concurrent anesthesia procedures. This modifier is used only by the anesthesiologist.

G8—Monitored anesthesia care (MAC) for deep complex, complicated, or markedly invasive surgical procedures.

G9—Monitored anesthesia care for a patient who has a history of a severe cardiopulmonary condition.

QK—Medical direction of two, three, or four concurrent anesthesia procedures involving qualified individuals. This modifier is used only by the anesthesiologist.

QS—Monitored anesthesia care services.

QX—CRNA service with medical direction by a physician.

QY—Medical direction of one certified registered nurse anesthetist (CRNA) by an anesthesiologist.

QZ—CRNA service without medical direction by a physician.

Physical Status Modifiers

For each anesthesia code reported, a physical status modifier code also should be reported. (Physical status modifiers will be discussed in more detail later in this chapter.) It should be noted that Medicare does not accept physical status modifiers.

Calculating Anesthesia Charges

To calculate the reimbursement amount for professional anesthesia services, the following formula is commonly used by third-party payers:

Basic Value + Time Units + Modifying Units = Total Units

Total Units × Conversion Factor = Total Reimbursement Amount

To understand this formula, you must understand the elements in the formula and the development of these elements.

Basic Value

As mentioned previously, the American Medical Association (AMA) developed the CPT codes, including those for anesthesia. The American Society of Anesthesiologists (ASA) publishes supplemental codes and guidelines similar to those in CPT, as well as the **Relative Value Guide (RVG)**. The RVG contains the basic value of each of the anesthesia services and additional codes that act as supplements to the regular CPT codes, along with narratives similar to those in the CPT manual. Because anesthesiologists perform other services, the RVG contains CPT codes from the Evaluation and Management, Medicine, and Surgery sections of the CPT manual.

Each anesthesia code has a basic value attached to it. The **basic value**, **base unit**, or **base unit value** has two elements. The basic value is also referred to as the **relative value**. The first element of the basic value reflects the usual services attached to anesthesia services, which refer to services included in, or bundled into, the anesthesia procedure code. These would include the following:

- Preoperative visits—including the history and exam performed by the anesthesiology staff

- Intraoperative care—including the administration of fluids and blood products; monitoring of noninvasive vitals, such as electrocardiography (ECG), temperature, blood pressure, pulse oximetry, capnography, and mass spectrometry; and the administration of anesthesia

- Postoperative visits—also known as the **postanesthesia recovery period**, includes all care until the patient is released to the surgeon or to another physician.

These services are considered to be services provided at the time of the procedure and are not paid separately. If the care provided is beyond the scope of the services listed previously, those unusual services can be reported in addition to the basic anesthesia services. Unusual services that can be billed include intra-arterial, central venous, and Swan-Ganz monitoring, as well as pain management services for relief of severe postoperative pain. It should be noted that in some states, anesthesia practitioners are allowed to bill postoperative management services after the anesthesia service time ends. This would include services unrelated to the anesthesia procedure, such as postoperative pain management and ventilator management.

The second element is the value of the work associated with the anesthesia service provided. Therefore, these two elements determine the basic value for the anesthesia code.

Time Units

The second factor in the formula to calculate the charge for anesthesia services is time. Anesthesia time is defined as the actual time spent providing the anesthesia service. This is recorded in minutes and is converted to a time unit. The **time unit** is independently determined by payers and represents a defined time increment. Commonly, the increment is 15 minutes, but some carriers use a 30-minute increment. When a 15-minute increment is used, one time unit would be reported for each 15 minutes. To determine the time to report, the time starts when the provider is in personal attendance to prepare the patient for the induction of anesthesia, and the time ends when the provider is no longer in attendance and the patient may safely be sent to the post surgery recovery area.

Modifying Units

The last factor in the formula is the modifying units. **Modifying units** are determined by a patient's physical condition and qualifying circumstances that affect the administration of anesthesia.

All surgeries are not equal. Like people, circumstances for procedures differ. Sometimes conditions are unusual or out of the ordinary and significantly influence the administration of anesthesia. These situations are known as **qualifying circumstances** and are reported using codes 99100–99140. When these happen, an additional qualifying circumstance code is reported with the anesthesia service code. It should be noted that Medicare does not recognize the qualifying circumstances codes. The qualifying circumstance codes are never to be reported alone. Note that in the CPT manual, in front of each of the codes 99100, 99116, 99135, and 99140, is the add-on notation (+). This notation alerts the coder that these codes are used in addition to the code for the anesthesia service. The ASA assigned these codes as additional units because of the extenuating circumstances that surround their use. The qualifying circumstances codes are summarized in Table 4-1.

TABLE 4-1 Qualifying Circumstances (99100–99140)

Code	Description	Units Assigned by ASA
99100	Anesthesia for patient of extreme age, <1 year old and >70 years old	1
99116	Anesthesia complicated by utilization of total body hypothermia	5
99135	Anesthesia complicated by utilization of controlled hypotension	5
99140	Anesthesia complicated by emergency conditions (specify)	2

The qualifying circumstances codes are located in the Medicine section of CPT but are explained under Qualifying Circumstances in the guidelines of the Anesthesia section. These guidelines should be read and understood fully before you assign any of these codes.

As mentioned previously, the physical status of the patient can also affect the modifying-units value. **Physical status modifiers** are used to describe the patient's health status. The explanation of physical status modifiers is found in the CPT manual in the Anesthesia Guidelines. It should be noted that Medicare does not recognize physical status modifiers. These modifiers are summarized in Table 4-2.

When a patient is given a physical status modifier of P3, P4, or P5, the modifying units are increased.

To determine the total units for the anesthesia service, add the basic value, time units, and modifying units. The total reimbursement amount can be calculated by multiplying the total units by the conversion factor used in the geographical region in which the service was performed.

EXAMPLE: A patient undergoes a cardiac procedure with a basic value of 20. The procedure requires 60 minutes of anesthesia time. The time units are calculated in 15-minute increments. Therefore, there are four time units for this procedure. The patient has a severe systemic disease and is 82 years old.

Therefore, modifier P3 and code 99100 are assigned.

Calculation for Total Units	
Basic Value	20
Time Units	4
Physical Status	1
Qualifying Circumstances	1
Total Units	26

TABLE 4-2 Physical Status Modifiers

Modifier	Description	Units Assigned by ASA
P1	Normal healthy patient	0
P2	Patient with mild systemic disease	0
P3	Patient with severe systemic disease	1
P4	Patient with severe systemic disease that is a constant threat to life	2
P5	A moribund patient who is not expected to survive without the operation	3
P6	A declared brain-dead patient whose organs are being removed for donor purposes	0

Assume that the conversion factor for this geographical area is $50 per unit of anesthesia. Using the following formula, calculate the total reimbursement amount:

Total Units × Conversion Factor = Total Reimbursement Amount
26 × $50 = $1300

The total reimbursement amount for this service would be $1300.

CMS posts the anesthesiology base unit values and the conversion factors at *http://www.cms.hhs.gov /center/anesth.asp*. These units are used by Medicare to determine reimbursement amounts. The 2019 base unit values and conversion factors are also in Appendices V and VI of your textbook.

Exercise 4.2—Calculating Anesthesia Fees

For each of the following cases, calculate the anesthesia reimbursement amount based on the information given. Assume that the anesthesia time unit is 15 minutes. Use the base unit values and conversion factors found in Appendices IV and V of your textbook. The unit values for the qualifying circumstances and physical status modifiers are located in Tables 4-1 and 4-2, respectively. Assume that the payer recognizes the physical status and qualifying circumstance units.

1. John Smith is an 86-year-old male patient who was placed under general anesthesia for 30 minutes. The code used to report the anesthesia service rendered was code 00300. John had a history of an MI and, therefore, is classified with a physical status modifier of P3. This service was performed in Birmingham, Alabama.

   _____

2. Mary Jones is a 36-year-old patient who had anesthesia for sternal debridement, reported with anesthesia code 00550. Anesthesia time was 15 minutes. She has no complicating medical diagnoses. The service was performed at a hospital in the state of Alaska.

   _____

3. Helen is a 76-year-old female placed under general anesthesia for a vulvectomy. Dr. Smith, the anesthesiologist, submitted code 00906 to his staff. The patient has anemia, and the doctor assigned modifier P2. Total anesthesia time was 30 minutes. This service was performed in Danbury, Connecticut.

   _____

4. Jackie is a 9-month-old child who had an arthroscopic procedure completed on her left hip joint while under general anesthesia for 45 minutes. The anesthesia code selected by the anesthesiologist was 01202. She has renal dysfunction; therefore, the physical status modifier for the case is P4. The procedure was performed in Madera, California.

   _____

5. Mandee is an 87-year-old patient with severe cardiovascular disease who lives in Shreveport, Louisiana. She had a needle biopsy of the thyroid, anesthesia, code 00322, and was anesthetized for 15 minutes.

   _____

Special Billing Consideration—Anesthetic Administered by Physician

When a physician performs a surgery or procedure, anesthesia administered by the same physician performing the service is considered a bundled service. The term *bundled* means that the preoperative services, the postoperative services, and the procedure itself are included in the price that the physician receives for the procedure and should not be broken out and billed separately. This would include administering anesthesia.

EXAMPLE: A 10-year-old boy presented today with a 3-cm laceration on the anterior portion of the left hand, which he received while playing baseball. The wound was cleaned with Betadine, and it was determined that several stitches were needed. Xylocaine was injected, and four sutures were placed. Patient tolerated procedure well and will return in 10 days for suture removal.

In this example, the services included would be the brief evaluation, the administering of the Xylocaine anesthetic, the procedure itself, and the postoperative suture removal in 10 days. These services are considered bundled into the single procedure code and are not broken out separately for claims submission.

Moderate or Conscious Sedation

Bundled services have been discussed; however, certain services may be billed separately if the situation warrants. Services that fall outside normal anesthesia services, for example, would be billed separately. Examples of such services would include insertion of central venous or intra-arterial catheters, prolonged preoperative or postoperative care, and moderate sedation.

Moderate sedation, or conscious sedation is a form of anesthetizing a patient, with or without analgesia, that causes a controlled state of depressed consciousness so that the patient is able to respond to stimulation. Coders are given instructions in the Anesthesia Guidelines of the CPT manual for the reporting of moderate (conscious) sedation. Codes 99151 to 99153 are reported for moderate sedation provided by a physician who is also performing the service for which the conscious sedation is being provided. Codes 99155 to 99157 are used to report moderate sedation when a second physician, other than the health care professional performing the diagnostic or therapeutic service, provides the the moderate sedation in a facility setting.

Billing Concerns

Anesthesiologists bill their services separately from the surgeon. Their charges must, however, mirror the charges submitted by the surgeon. The same diagnosis and the same procedure codes should be reported if the payer requires the anesthesiologist to submit the surgery code in place of the anesthesia code. If an anesthesia code is submitted by anesthesia staff, it should reflect the same procedure submitted by the surgeon.

Summary

- Anesthesia services are performed by anesthesiologists and CRNAs.
- General anesthesia can be administered by injection, inhalation, and instillation.
- Regional anesthesia includes Bier blocks and epidural blocks and can be referred to as *conduction anesthesia*.
- Physical status modifiers are used to identify the physical condition of the patient.
- HCPCS modifiers are used for Medicare patients and some third-party payers.
- The RVG was developed by the American Society of Anesthesiologists.

Internet Links

To learn more about anesthesiology and the completion of anesthesia services, visit the following sites:

http://www.asahq.org

http://www.cms.gov/center/anesth.asp

Chapter Review

True/False

Instructions: Indicate whether the following statements are true (T) or false (F).

1. _____ Documentation of time is necessary in billing anesthesia services.

2. _____ Anesthesia complicated by emergency conditions is reported with the add-on code 99140.

3. _____ Anesthesia-specific modifiers are required only if the anesthesiologist deems it necessary.

4. _____ RVG stands for *Relative Value Guide* and is published by the AMA.

5. _____ The P4 modifier is required for services rendered to a patient who has a mild systemic disease.

Fill in the Blank

Instructions: Fill in the blanks in the statements that follow.

6. When an agent is administered into the peridural space of the spinal cord, _____ anesthesia is accomplished.

7. Preoperative and postoperative services are considered _____ into the procedure.

8. Each anesthesia code has a(n) _____ attached to it.

9. A physician who is board certified to administer anesthesia is called a(n) _____.

10. Anesthesia complicated by utilization of total body hypothermia would be assigned the add-on code _____.

Matching

Instructions: Match the physical status modifier with the example that best reflects it.

Modifier	Description
_____ 1. P1	A. Patient undergoes a lung transplant due to end-stage lung disease.
_____ 2. P2	B. Patient with poorly controlled hypertension undergoes a colonoscopy.
_____ 3. P3	C. Patient with controlled diabetes mellitus undergoes an appendectomy.
_____ 4. P4	D. Patient is a healthy 80–year-old patient undergoing a bronchoscopy.
_____ 5. P5	E. Patient pronounced dead following a brain aneurysm; harvesting of organs occurred.
_____ 6. P6	F. Patient with advanced cardiovascular disease undergoes open reduction of fracture.

Coding Assignments

Instructions: Assign the correct anesthesia CPT code for each of the following procedures.

1. Anesthesia for procedure on the eye; corneal transplant _____

2. Anesthesia for procedure on the lumbar sympathectomy _____

3. Anesthesia for procedure on upper posterior abdominal wall _____

4. Anesthesia for interpelviabdominal amputation _____

5. Anesthesia for radical perineal procedure _____

6. Anesthesia for diagnostic arthroscopic procedures of shoulder joint _____

7. Anesthesia for femoral artery ligation _____

8. Anesthesia for total knee arthroplasty _____

9. Anesthesia for physiological support for harvesting of organ(s) from brain-dead patient _____

10. Anesthesia complicated by utilization of controlled hypotension _____

11. Anesthesia for embolectomy of femoral artery _____

12. Anesthesia for induced abortion _____

13. Anesthesia for cast application to wrist _____

14. Anesthesia for ophthalmoscopy _____

15. Anesthesia for electroconvulsive therapy _____

16. Anesthesia for heart transplant _____

17. Anesthesia for percutaneous liver biopsy _____

18. Anesthesia for amniocentesis _____

19. Anesthesia for perineal prostatectomy _____

20. Anesthesia for arthroscopy on wrist _____

21. Anesthesia for tenoplasty elbow to shoulder _____

22. Anesthesia for pancreatectomy _____

23. Anesthesia for hernia repair in upper abdomen _____

24. Anesthesia for partial rib resection _____

25. Anesthesia for subdural taps _____

26. Anesthesia for thoracoplasty _____

27. Anesthesia for CSF shunting procedure _____

28. Anesthesia for biopsy of the clavicle _____

29. Anesthesia for pneumocentesis _____

30. Anesthesia for bone marrow biopsy, iliac anterior crest _____

31. Anesthesia for iridectomy _____

32. Anesthesia for permanent transvenous pacemaker insertion _____

33. Anesthesia for procedure on seminal vesicles _____

34. Anesthesia for cervical cerclage _____

35. Anesthesia for total ankle replacement _____

Case Studies

Instructions: Select the correct CPT anesthesia code for each of the following cases.

Case 1

Patient Name: Matino, Greta

MRN: 2223232

Date: 02/02/20XX

Procedure: Excision of orbital mass, left superior orbit

Anesthesiologist performed the following:

Anesthesia: Proparacaine was instilled in the left eye. The eye was then prepped and draped in the usual sterile manner. The superior aspect of the left orbit was injected with 2% Lidocaine with 1:200,000 epinephrine.

Procedure was performed by the eye surgeon.

CPT code assignment for the anesthesiologist would be: _____

Case 2

Patient Name: Wyon, Gabbie

MRN: 049586

Date: 3/4/20XX

Procedure: Radical hysterectomy

Anesthesiologist performed the following:

General anesthesia was administered prior to the completion of a radical hysterectomy.

CPT code assignment for the anesthesiologist would be: _____

Case 3

Patient Name: Jones, Joanne

MRN: 029384

Date: April 16, 20XX

Procedure: Tubal ligation

Anesthesiologist performed the following:

The patient was placed under general anesthesia prior to the completion of a laparoscopic tubal ligation.

CPT code assignment for the anesthesiologist would be: _____

Case 4

Patient Name: Stan Tanks

MRN: 774950

Date: January 15, 20XX

Procedure: Closed reduction of humerus

Dr. Jones, anesthesiologist, used general anesthesia to sedate this patient prior to a closed reduction of the humerus.

CPT code assignment for the anesthesiologist would be: _____

Case 5

Patient Name: Mary Thomas

MRN: 102938

Date: December 14, 20XX

Procedure: Cesarean delivery of twin girls

This 29-year-old patient was placed under general anesthesia for the delivery of two infant females.

CPT code assignment for the anesthesiologist would be: _____

Case 6

Patient Name: Mark Jumps

MRN: 394567

Date: June 18, 20XX

Procedure: Arthroscopic total knee arthroplasty

This 19-year-old soccer player sustained an injury to his left knee, and an arthroscopic total knee arthroplasty was performed with Dr. Jones administering the anesthesia.

CPT code assignment for the anesthesiologist would be: _____

Case 7

Patient: Natalie Smith

MRN: 893568

Date: July 7, 20XX

Procedure: Liver biopsy

This 29-year-old female with a history of liver disease was placed under anesthesia for a percutaneous liver biopsy to rule out a malignant condition.

CPT code assignment for the anesthesiologist would be: _____

Case 8

Patient: Jackie Edwards

MRN: 209385

Date: September 19, 20XX

Procedure: Craniotomy

This 38-year-old female has a hematoma, and a craniotomy was performed for the evacuation of the hematoma. She was placed under general anesthesia.

CPT code assignment for the anesthesiologist would be: _____

Case 9

Patient: Roberto Rodriguez

MRN: 683940

Date: October 19, 20XX

Procedure: Repair of cleft palate

This 2-year-old male was placed under general anesthesia for a repair of a congenital cleft palate.

CPT code assignment for the anesthesiologist would be: _____

Case 10

Patient: Jose Booth

MRN: 549762

Date: April 19, 20XX

Procedure: Needle biopsy of thyroid

This 9-month-old was placed under general anesthesia so that a needle biopsy of the thyroid could be performed.

CPT code assignment for the anesthesiologist would be: _____

Surgery and the Integumentary System

Chapter Outline

Learning Objectives

At the conclusion of this chapter, you should be able to:

1. Define key terms related to coding procedures performed within the integumentary system.
2. Explain the organization of the Surgery section of the CPT manual.
3. Explain what is included in a surgical package.
4. Identify bundled services.
5. Explain the purpose of the National Correct Coding Initiative (NCCI).
6. Define abbreviations related to the integumentary system.
7. Define the basic anatomy and functions of the integumentary system.
8. Define common procedures performed within the integumentary system.
9. Identify and code the different types of grafts.
10. Assign the appropriate CPT code(s) and modifier(s) for surgical procedures performed within the integumentary system.
11. Identify and code procedures for surgery and the integumentary system from case studies.

Key Terms

acellular dermal replacement	aspiration	benign lesion	class findings
adjacent tissue transfer	autogenous graft	biopsy	clean-contaminated wound
	autograft	burn	

clean wound

complex repair

contaminated wound

debridement

decubitus ulcer

defect site

dermal autograft

dermatome

dermis

destruction

diagnostic procedures

dirty and infected wound

donor site

epidermal autograft

epidermis

escharotomy

fine needle aspiration

first-degree burn

free graft

full thickness graft

global days

global package

graft

hematoma

heterodermic graft

homograft

homologous graft

hyperkeratotic

imaging guidance

incision and drainage (I&D)

integumentary system

intermediate repair

malignant lesion

mammary ductogram

mastectomy

mastotomy

metastasis

Mohs micrographic surgery

National Correct Coding Initiative (NCCI)

ostectomy

pedicle flap

pilonidal cyst

pinch graft

recipient site

repair

scalpel

second-degree burns

shaving

simple repair

skin tags

split-skin graft

split-thickness autograft

split-thickness graft

subcutaneous

surgical package

therapeutic procedures

third-degree burns

tissue-cultured epidermal autograft

ulcers

unbundling

wedge excision

xenografts

Introduction

The Surgery section is the largest and most complicated section in the CPT manual. The Surgery section is organized by body system and types of procedures. Specialists may find that they code mainly from one subsection of the Surgery section, whereas general surgeons code from various subsections within the section.

Careful attention to the details of the procedure and a working knowledge of the CPT manual are essential for proper code assignment. For surgical procedures, the operative note provides the most accurate source of information for the service rendered and should be documented accordingly.

This chapter will discuss the organization of the Surgery section of the CPT manual.

The Surgery section of the CPT manual begins with general information and surgical guidelines. Prior to selecting codes, coders need to review the definitions and concepts included in the Surgery Guidelines found in the CPT manual prior to the surgery codes. The Surgery guidelines address the following:

- Services
- CPT surgical package definition
- Follow-up care for diagnostic procedures
- Follow-up care for therapeutic surgical procedures
- Supplied materials
- Reporting more than one procedure/service
- Separate procedure
- Unlisted service or procedure
- Special report
- Imaging guidance
- Surgical destruction

Locate the Surgery Guidelines in the CPT manual and read the information contained in this part of the manual. Following the guidelines, the various subsections of the Surgery section appear. The Surgery section of the CPT manual is arranged by body system as follows:

- General—Codes 10004–10021
- Integumentary System—Codes 10030–19499
- Musculoskeletal System—Codes 20100–29999
- Respiratory System—Codes 30000–32999
- Cardiovascular System—Codes 33010–37799
- Hemic and Lymphatic System—Codes 38100–38999
- Mediastinum and Diaphragm—Codes 39000–39599
- Digestive System—Codes 40490–49999
- Urinary System—Codes 50010–53899
- Male Genital System—Codes 54000–55899
- Reproductive System Procedures—Code 55920
- Intersex Surgery—Codes 55970–55980
- Female Genital System—Codes 56405–58999
- Maternity Care and Delivery—Codes 59000–59899
- Endocrine System—Codes 60000–60699
- Nervous System—Codes 61000–64999
- Eye and Ocular Adnexa—Codes 65091–68899
- Auditory System—Codes 69000–69979
- Operating Microscope—Code 69990

Locate these subsections in the CPT manual. After each body system, the subsections are further divided by anatomical site, beginning with the top of the body (i.e., head or scalp) and working down to the feet and toes, and then from the trunk of the body outward. Understanding the organization of the Surgery section is valuable when a coder is attempting to determine if he or she is reviewing the correct section of the CPT manual for code selection.

Understanding whether the procedure performed is a diagnostic or therapeutic procedure can also be helpful when determining a code assignment. **Diagnostic procedures** are completed to determine a diagnosis and establish a care plan. **Therapeutic procedures** are part of the care plan and are used as treatment for a diagnosis. This chapter will discuss the Integumentary System subsection of the Surgery section in further detail.

Surgery Guidelines

Prior to the code listings in the CPT manual, the Surgery-section-specific guidelines are presented.

Services

The first guideline alerts the coder that codes for services that are provided in the office, home, or hospital, as a consultation or other medical service, are found in the Evaluation and Management section (codes 99201–99499) or in the Medicine section (codes 99000–99091) for Special Services and Reports.

Surgical Package

Prior to code assignment, it is important to understand what is included in a **surgical package**, also known as a **global package**. When a code is selected, it represents specific services that are included in a CPT surgical code. This term is defined differently by various payers, but the CPT manual defines the surgical package as follows:

- Local infiltration, metacarpal/metatarsal/digital block, or topical anesthesia
- Subsequent to the decision for surgery, one related Evaluation and Management (E/M) encounter on the date immediately prior to or on the date of procedure (including history and physical)
- Immediate postoperative care, including dictating operative notes and talking with the family and other physicians and qualified health care professionals
- Writing orders
- Evaluating the patient in the postoperative recovery area
- Typical postoperative follow-up care

This definition can be found in the Surgery Guidelines section of the CPT manual.

Many payers establish specific time periods for the postoperative period. This is referred to as the **global days** or global period. For example, Medicare defines surgeries as major or minor surgeries. Major surgeries have 90 postoperative days, whereas minor surgeries have 0 or 10 postoperative days.

> **EXAMPLE**: Brittney presented to her doctor's office with toe pain and swelling. After looking at her toe and discussing treatment options, Brittney and her doctor, Dr. Kilts, decided that she should have the nail plate removed to relieve the problem of an ingrown toenail, which was slightly deformed and causing problems. Dr. Kilts had a cancellation in his schedule for the next day, so Brittney's procedure was scheduled. She presented, had the procedure done, and was told to return in two days for a dressing change. Two days later, the dressing was changed, and the surgical site was healing nicely.

In the example, the decision for surgery was made one day prior to the procedure. The intent of the visit in the example was to determine a plan of care that would take care of the pain Brittney presented with. Since the intent of the visit was not to have the procedure performed, the evaluation of her problem is a separately billable service and should be coded with the appropriate E/M code. The procedure code reported in our example would be code 11750. This code has a 10-day global period attached to it by most payers. The dressing change is also included in the surgical package, so it would not be reported separately because it was a service performed as an integral part of the surgery. Keep in mind that most types of anesthesia, as well as airway access, are essential and would not be reported separately.

Payers should be consulted regarding their individual policies regarding surgical packages. Medicare's surgical package protocol is explained on the Centers for Medicare and Medicaid Services (CMS) website. For Medicare, approved payment amounts for procedures include payment for the following services related to the surgery. The payments are made according to this policy when the services are completed by the physician who performs the surgery.

Services that are included in Medicare's global surgical package include:

- Preoperative visits—All preoperative visits are included in the package after the decision is made to operate, beginning with the day before the day of surgery for major procedures and the day of surgery for minor procedures.
- Intraoperative services—Intraoperative services that are normally a usual and necessary part of a surgical procedure, including the prep for surgery, wound irrigation and closure, placement and removal of surgical drains, and dressing applications, are included here.
- Complications following surgery—These are all additional medical or surgical services required of the surgeon during the postoperative period of the surgery due to complications that do not require additional trips to the operating room.
- Postoperative visits—These are follow-up visits during the postoperative period of the surgery that are related to recovery from the surgery. Keep in mind that the postoperative period will be 0, 10, or 90 days based on the complexity of the surgery.
- Postsurgical pain management—Pain management that is managed by the surgeon is included in the package.

- Supplies—These are supplies other than those identified as exclusions in the CMS manual.
- Miscellaneous services—The following services, such as dressing changes; local incisional care; removal of an operative pack; removal of cutaneous sutures, staples, lines, wires, tubes, drains, casts, and splints; insertion, irrigation, and removal of urinary catheters; routine peripheral intravenous lines, nasogastric, and rectal tubes; and changes and removal of tracheostomy tubes.

Follow-Up Care for Diagnostic and Therapeutic Surgical Procedures

Within the Surgery Guidelines of CPT, the guidelines state that follow-up care includes only the care related to the recovery from the procedure. Care for conditions, complications, exacerbations, recurrence, or the presence of other diseases or injuries is to be reported separately. Failure to report care for an unrelated condition, complication, exacerbation, recurrence, disease, or injury related to the recovery from the procedure performed is a loss of revenue for the provider.

Supplied Materials

If additional supplies and materials are used over what is typically used for the procedure, the provider can bill drugs, trays, supplies, and other materials. However, caution should be used when billing these codes because the documentation has to provide evidence of the necessity for these additional materials.

Reporting More Than One Procedure/Service

The next section in the Surgery Guidelines states that if more than one procedure/service is completed on the same date, session, or during the postoperative period, codes should be appended with CPT modifiers. This was discussed in Chapter 2 of this book.

Separate Procedure

Following some code descriptions are the words "separate procedure." These codes report procedures that are typically part of a larger service or procedure and, therefore, are not reported if the larger procedure is performed. However, if the code description designated as a separate procedure is completed alone, then the code is reported.

Unlisted Service or Procedure and Special Reports

Within the Surgery Guidelines is a listing of all the unlisted surgery service or procedure codes found in the CPT manual. These codes should be used only when a more specific code is not available for use. When these codes are used, it is common for payers to request a special report that outlines the description of the following:

- The nature, extent, and need for the procedure
- The time, effort, and equipment necessary to provide the service/procedure

  Use of the unlisted codes should be rare.

Imaging Guidance

This guideline give directions that state "when imaging guidance or imaging supervision and interpretation is included in a surgical procedure, guidelines for image documentation and report, included in the guidelines for Radiology (Including Nuclear Medicine and Diagnostic Ultrasound), will apply." Reference this guideline, located in Surgery Guideline section of the CPT manual, for additional information.

Surgical Destruction

The last guideline found in the Surgery Guidelines states that surgical destruction is considered a part of a surgical procedure. Exceptions to this are listed as separate code numbers.

Exercise 5.1—Check Your Understanding

Surgical Coding

Indicate whether the following statements are true (T) or false (F).

1. _____ Vascular surgeons must assign codes from the Cardiovascular section of the Surgery chapter.

2. _____ CPT coders need to pay attention to detail and also have a working knowledge of the codes that their doctor usually assigns.

3. _____ Diagnostic procedures are part of the care plan and are used for treatment of a diagnosis that has already been rendered.

4. _____ Within the subsections of the Surgery section, the CPT codes are first arranged by body system, and then by anatomical site.

5. _____ Surgery and normal follow-up care are included in the surgical package.

The National Correct Coding Initiative (NCCI)

The **National Correct Coding Initiative (NCCI)** was implemented to standardize proper coding and payment for Medicare Part B claims. The purpose of the NCCI has evolved to include outpatient hospital services and fiscal intermediaries. Payment denials are generated when a pair of codes is submitted together on one claim and the processing system rejects the claim based on coding conventions. Medicare does not allow beneficiaries to be billed if a denial occurs based on NCCI edits, which could put your practice at financial risk. The coder should study these denials in detail and avoid repeating the same mistakes. Education to avoid further denials is usually enough to stop the denials from occurring with any frequency.

The NCCI is set up in table format. Column 1/Column 2 of the Correct Coding Edits is the first table. This used to be known as the Comprehensive/Component edits. The second table is known as the Mutually Exclusive edits. The code(s) listed in column 2 of the Mutually Exclusive edits table are not payable services when billed with the code(s) in column 1.

EXAMPLE:

Column 1	Column 2
10021	36000, 36410, 64415, 64417, etc.

In the example, if we billed code 10021 and code 36410 together, our claim would be rejected, or edited out due to NCCI coding guidelines. CPT code 10021 encompasses the services rendered in 36410, and, therefore, 36410 cannot be billed separately when reported with code 10021.

Mutually exclusive codes are codes that cannot physically be performed together during one encounter on the same anatomical site, or are code pairs that, by definition, would not be performed at the same encounter. Mutually exclusive code pairs, in certain instances, can be billed together if a modifier indicator is noted. Remember the following:

1. The standard of care is to accomplish the overall procedure.

2. To complete a procedure successfully, another procedure may also need to be performed, but these procedures may not be separately billable depending on NCCI.

Guidelines Related to the National Correct Coding Initiative (NCCI)

The Centers for Medicare and Medicaid Services (CMS) maintains guidelines that relate and affect code selection. At the beginning of each surgical chapter in this textbook, the website and the link for the National Correct Coding Initiative information that relates to the chapter will be listed. The student will need to reference the following website to obtain the most current coding guideline information related to the Integumentary chapter. The student should follow these steps to access the information online:

1. Log on to *http://www.cms.gov/Medicare/Coding/NationalCorrectCodInitED/index.html.*
2. Scroll to the section titled "Downloads."
3. Click the link for the most current "NCCI Policy Manual for Medicare Services."
4. A box will appear that requires you to click "Open."
5. Click on "Chapter 3" for guidelines specific to the Integumentary System coding.

Unbundling

Correctly coding a service means that the coder needs to be reporting the service rendered with the most comprehensive code available. Knowledge of the component parts of the procedure are important elements in coding a service correctly.

At times procedure codes are reported incorrectly by reporting additional codes. This is known as unbundling codes. **Unbundling** occurs when procedures and/or services are performed and they are separately coded and submitted to the insurance company for payment when there exists a single code to report them.

> **EXAMPLE:** Scarlet was scheduled in Dr. Johnson's office for the paring of two corns. Dr. Johnson performed the removal of the corns. (CPT code 11056 would be the correct code to report.) He filled out the encounter form as follows:
>
> 99211—For the examination
> 11055—Paring or cutting of benign hyperkeratotic lesion (eg, corn or callus); single lesion
> 11055—Paring or cutting of benign hyperkeratotic lesion (eg, corn or callus); single lesion

Dr. Johnson unbundled the services he rendered. The 99211 is inappropriate because the patient was scheduled for the removal of the corns due to a previous examination by Dr. Johnson. The determination had been made prior to this visit to do the procedure, so this evaluation is not separately billable. The coding of 11055 twice is also inappropriate because the description for code 11055 states only a single lesion and the description for code 11056 includes two to four lesions. Therefore code 11056—"Paring or cutting of benign hyperkeratotic lesion (eg, corn or callus); 2 to 4 lesions"—is the appropriate code to report. Reporting code 11055 twice is considered unbundling because two codes were reported in place of one code that would accurately report the procedure performed.

The NCCI will help a coder immensely when it comes to more complex procedures that are often performed together. It is important to use all resources available when you are trying to determine whether to code a procedure with one comprehensive code or to break it out into separate codes to capture all the work done.

Medicare and other insurance carriers review claims submitted to detect billing errors. Repeated denials for unbundling of codes can be a red flag to Medicare and other insurance carriers. This red flag may trigger an audit of coding habits to determine whether the unbundling is intentional or not. If it is determined that there is intentional unbundling of services to receive additional payment, legal action may be taken by the payer.

Abbreviations Related to the Integumentary System

Please reference the following for common abbreviations associated with the Surgery and Integumentary section of CPT.

Abbreviation	Definition
Bx or bx	biopsy
C&S	culture and sensitivity
derm	dermatology
FS	frozen section
HSV	herpes simplex virus
ID	intradermal
I&D	incision and drainage
KOH	potassium hydroxide
sc or sub-q	subcutaneous
UV	ultraviolet

Anatomy of the Integumentary System

The **integumentary system**, also known as the *skin*, acts as a shield for the body and is considered the largest body system. The functions of the integumentary system include the protection of deeper tissue by retaining fluid in the body and regulation of body temperature by controlling the amount of heat loss. A natural shield, the integumentary system also works as a factor in the immune system by blocking bacteria and other foreign bodies from entering the body. Receptors for touch are located on the skin. Because the skin is porous, it protects the body from ultraviolet radiation from the sun while also letting in ultraviolet light so that vitamin D can be produced by the body. The skin also temporarily stores fat, glucose, water, and salts that are absorbed by the blood and used by various organs of the body.

Coding some of the procedures listed in the Integumentary chapter of the CPT manual requires knowledge of how deep into the layers of skin the provider was when performing a surgery or procedure. The provider may use terms such as *epidermis*, *dermis*, and *subcutaneous*. The coder needs to know what these terms mean and where they are in relation to the depth of a procedure in order to assign a code properly.

The **epidermis** is the outermost layer of the skin. There are no blood vessels or connective tissue within the epidermis, so this layer of skin depends on lower layers for nourishment.

The **dermis** is the thick layer of tissue located directly below the epidermis. This is the layer of skin that enables a person to recognize touch, pain, pressure, and temperature changes. This layer of skin contains blood and lymph vessels, so it is more sensitive and self-sufficient than the epidermis.

The **subcutaneous** layer of skin connects the skin to the muscle surface. When a provider writes that he or she went "subcu" (you may see it written "sub-q"), this is the layer referred to. Figure 5-1 illustrates the three layers of the skin and the structures contained within these layers.

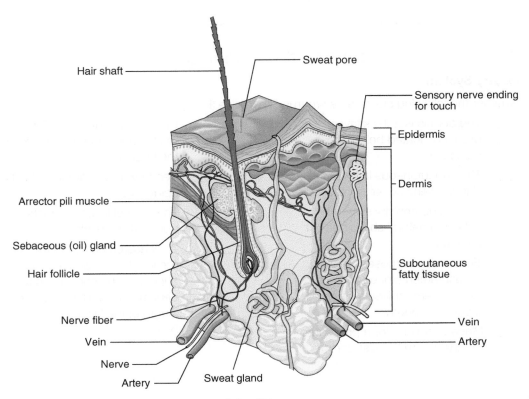

FIGURE 5-1 Layers and Structures of the Skin

The procedures in the Integumentary subsection of the Surgery section begin with incision and drainage and then move on to excision-debridement, paring or cutting, biopsy, removal of skin tags, shaving of epidermal or dermal lesions, and excision of benign and malignant lesions. To begin coding these procedures, the coder must have a basic understanding of the procedure being performed, the approach used, and the site of the procedure. You cannot even begin to code a procedure without knowing at least these three things.

As with every other aspect of coding a service, documentation is key. The more complicated the procedure, the more elements that become important when you select a code and the more detailed the documentation. You will see as you move through this chapter that size, or measurements, of lesions in centimeters is critical, as is the number of lesions. If measurements are given in inches or meters, the conversion to centimeters is necessary. Table 5-1 lists some of the more commonly referenced conversions for you.

A note of caution: *Never* assign a code based only on what doctors *tell* you they did. A procedure note should always be referenced when you assign a procedure code to a service. Everything goes back to "If you didn't document it, you didn't do it."

In the first subsection of the Integumentary section of Surgery, the procedures may be performed in a physician's office, an outpatient ambulatory setting, or a hospital. This is not an all-inclusive place-of-service list, but place of service makes a difference, in some instances, to insurance carriers. Be aware that just because a procedure is considered surgery does not mean that it is required to be done as an inpatient in the hospital.

TABLE 5-1 Conversion Table

1 inch = 2.54 centimeters (cm)
1 cm = 10.0 millimeters (mm)
20 grains = 1 pennyweight
20 pennyweight = 1 ounce (oz)

Exercise 5.2—Check Your Understanding

Integumentary System

Indicate whether the following statements are true (T) or false (F).

1. _____ The dermis is a thick layer of tissue located below the epidermis.

2. _____ The subcutaneous layer of the skin contains sweat pores.

3. _____ The integumentary system acts as a natural shield against bacteria.

4. _____ For coding purposes, measurements need to be in centimeters for lesion size and laceration length.

5. _____ Place of service for a procedure reported from the first part of the Integumentary section of the Surgery chapter has to be the hospital.

6. _____ Sensory nerves are found in the epidermis.

7. _____ The dermal layer connects the skin to the muscle.

8. _____ A measurement given for the length of a laceration is 2 inches. The conversion to centimeters would make the length of the laceration 5.08 cm.

Procedures Performed on the Integumentary System

As we proceed into the different systems included in the Surgery section, we will note different guidelines specific to that section as a further resource for coders.

General (10004–10021)

The Surgery section begins with codes for Fine Needle Aspiration (FNA) Biopsy. **Aspiration** is a procedure in which fluid is surgically removed from the body. **Fine needle aspiration** is a type of aspiration in which a very fine needle is inserted into the site, and fluid is drawn. Lumps or masses that are located by touch do not typically require imaging. If a lump cannot be located by touch, imaging may need to be used. **Imaging guidance** is a radiologic procedure that assists a physician in locating the area to be addressed, usually by ultrasound or computed tomography (CT) imaging. A marker may be placed at the site so that if further surgery is necessary, the site will be easily located.

In the CPT manual, reference codes 10004 to 10021. Please note that these codes are out of numerical sequence. The coder needs to be guided by the symbols that are used in front of codes to denote that a code is out of numerical sequence. It also should be noted that the descriptions of the codes denote if imaging guidance is used or if the procedure occurs without imaging guidance. For example, code 10021 is for fine needle aspiration biopsy, without imaging guidance for the first lesion, while code 10005 reports a fine needle biopsy including ultrasound guidance for the first lesion. This range of codes denotes the following types of imaging guidance: ultrasound, fluoroscopic, CT, or MR guidance. Please review the codes in the CPT manual for the specific descriptions for each code and note the type of imaging guidance listed in the code description.

In the CPT manual, reference the instructional notation that appears after the heading of Fine Needle Aspiration (FNA) Biopsy. This is located after the guidelines for the Surgery section of the CPT manual. The instructional notation that appears after the heading for Fine Needle Aspiration (FNA) Biopsy provides guidance to coders in relation to the reporting of additional codes that relate to procedures that typically are performed at the same time as an FNA biopsy or when multiple FNA biopsies are completed at the same operative session. Read through the instructional notation noting the various guidance it provides. An example of such guidance is: "When more than one FNA biopsy is performed on separate lesions at the same session, same day, same imaging modality, use the appropriate imaging add-on code for the second and sequent lesions." If you are coding using a CPT manual, I would suggest that you highlight the sentences in this instructional notation that give you guidance as to the reporting for this range of codes.

Introduction and Removal (10030, 10035, 10036) and Incision and Drainage (10040–10180)

Code 10030 reports image-guided fluid collection drainage by a catheter for an abscess, hematoma, seroma, lymphocele or cyst, or the like found in soft tissue via a percutaneous approach. Code 10035 reports a placement of soft tissue localization device(s), percutaneous, including imaging guidance for the first lesion. Code 10036 is an add on code and reports the placement of the localization devices for each additional lesion. The notations that follow code 10036 need to be referenced as they provide additional instructions for the reporting of these codes. **Incision and drainage (I&D)** involves surgically cutting over the area to be drained, and then withdrawing the fluid or draining it. An I&D may be performed for any number of reasons, such as drainage of a cyst or abscess.

The codes are differentiated by the type of abscess or cyst to be incised, and whether the I&D was simple or complicated. The coder would choose a simple procedure code unless the provider indicated that surgical closure was delayed or that a Z-plasty (repair) was required. In these cases, the coder may need to select a code indicating that a more complicated procedure was performed. It should be noted that this section of codes reports incision and drainage, not excisions. Following code 10081, a note informs the coder that, if an excision of a pilondial cyst occurs, code range 11770–11772 should be referenced for proper code selection.

Codes 10120–10121 would be used for foreign body removal no deeper than the subcutaneous level. Code 10121, for complicated removal, is used only if underlying tissue is involved and documented accordingly.

Debridement (11000–11047)

Debridement is a type of cleansing. It involves removal of dirt or foreign objects along with tissue that is necrotic or damaged in a way that hinders the healing process. In the CPT manual, code range 11042–11047 is used to report debridement services for injuries, infections, wounds, and chronic ulcers. For proper code selection, the depth of the tissue removed and the surface area of the wound must be known.

The percentage of body surface debrided must be documented to use the 11000–11047 codes. Additional documentation requirements for debridement code usage would be the anatomical location and the depth of the tissue removed. Any comorbidities that would affect the patient's ability to heal should also be noted.

Diabetes or peripheral vascular disease, for example, are conditions that would directly affect healing and should be noted in the documentation and listed on claims submitted to an insurance company for payment of procedures.

Codes 11000 and 11001 are used to reflect extensive removal of infected or eczematous skin. Conditions such as aggressive streptococcal skin infections or extensive skin trauma would support use of these codes. Documentation of necrotic or damaged tissue supports the medical necessity of extensive debridement and is essential in supporting use of these codes.

The coder should note the plus sign (+), also known as the add-on symbol, in front of code 11001. This plus sign indicates that code 11001 is an add-on code and cannot be used alone. It is always coded in conjunction with code 11000.

Codes 11004–11006 are used to report the debridement of skin, subcutaneous tissue, muscle, and fascia for a necrotizing soft tissue infection. The codes are differentiated according to body site. Code 11008 is an add-on code used to report the removal of prosthetic material or mesh of the abdominal wall due to infection.

Codes 11010–11012 are used for debridement in conjunction with open fractures and dislocation(s). The use of these codes depends on the depth of the open wound.

Codes 11042–11047 are used for debridement of localized areas, such as skin ulcers and circumscribed dermal infections. This code series involves simple debridement of the dermis down to the muscle and bone level. This code series begins with code 11042 for debridement of subcutaneous tissue for the first 20 sq cm or less.

Add-on code 11045 reports each additional 20 sq cm or part thereof. It should be noted that code 11045 does not appear in numerical order in the CPT manual. Codes 11043 and 11046 report the debridement of muscle and/or fascia, with code 11046 being an add-on code used to report additional tissue debrided. The debridement of bone is reported with code 11044 and add-on code 11047. To become familiar with these codes, reference the CPT manual and note how many of the codes in the code range 11042–11047 are out of numerical sequence in the code book.

When reading documentation, the coder would look for the instrument(s) used to perform the debridement. A scalpel or dermatome is typically the instrument used. A **scalpel** is actually the handle part of a surgical knife. Variously sized knife blades are attached to the scalpel, which is then used for surgical cutting. A **dermatome** is also a cutting instrument, but the dermatome cuts slices of skin—the thickness is determined by the surgeon—and can be handheld or powered, depending on its usage. Dermatomes are used for debridement but are more often used for skin grafting.

Paring or Cutting (11055–11057)

Codes in the 11055–11057 range are assigned based on the number of lesions that are being cut or pared. This code set is used when a provider is taking care of corns, calluses, or other **hyperkeratotic** lesions. *Hyperkeratotic* refers to an overgrowth of skin.

> **EXAMPLE:** Mrs. Mops presented with two corns on the right foot and one on the left. Dr. Smith decided to pare them down so she would have some comfort in her shoe gear. All three corns were pared.

In the example, Dr. Smith would code the procedure with code 11056—"Paring or cutting of benign hyperkeratotic lesion (e.g., corn or callus); two to four lesions." Because the code reads "two to four lesions," only one code would be reported, even though three corns were pared.

Routine Foot Care

Codes 11055, 11056, and 11057 are sometimes referred to as part of the "routine foot care" codes. Since Medicare does not cover routine foot care, coders must understand the Medicare definition of "routine foot care" and the specific conditions for which foot care is covered by Medicare. Routine foot care can be submitted by any provider, but it is most often submitted by podiatrists.

Routine foot care, as defined by Medicare, is defined as the following:

- Cutting or removal of corns and calluses
- Clipping, trimming, or debridement of nails, including debridement of mycotic nails
- Shaving, paring, cutting, or removal of keratoma, tyloma, and heloma
- Nondefinitive simple, palliative treatments like shaving or paring of plantar warts that do not require thermal or chemical cautery and curettage

- Other hygienic and preventive maintenance care in the realm of self-care, such as cleaning and soaking the feet and the use of skin creams to maintain skin tone of both ambulatory and bedridden patients
- Any services performed in the absence of localized illness, injury, or symptoms involving the foot

Also included in the category of routine foot care are codes 11719, "Trimming of nondystrophic nails, any number;" and 11720–11721, "Debridement of nail(s) by any method." These codes require knowledge of how many toes have been treated, use of specific modifiers indicating the toes treated, and awareness of whether any comorbidities might affect the patient.

Medicare will pay for routine foot care:

- When the patient has a systemic disease, such as diabetes mellitus, peripheral vascular disease, and metabolic or neurologic diseases of sufficient severity that puts the patient at risk if the foot care is not completed by a professional.
- When the services are performed as a necessary and integral part of other covered services, such as services that are completed for the treatment of ulcers, wounds, or infections.
- When the care is for the treatment of warts on the foot, which is covered to that same extent as the treatment of warts located elsewhere on the body.
- When there is documentation of the class findings or presence of a qualifying systemic illness for the treatment of mycotic nails. **Class findings** (Class A, Class B, or Class C) reflect clinical findings of patients with severe peripheral involvement. Modifiers are assigned to the CPT code to indicate the category of class findings related to a particular patient. These modifiers are referred to as Q modifiers. Table 5-2 lists the class findings, along with the Q modifiers.

The preceding list is not exclusive for the specific conditions for which foot care is covered by Medicare. The complete listings of coverage guidelines can be found by searching online for Medicare Local Coverage Determinations (LCD). For example, to reference the LCD for routine foot care and debridement of nails found on the National Government Services (NGS) website, go to *www.NGSMedicare.com* and then search on the words "LCD for Routine Foot Care and Debridement of Nails (L33636)." This will display the full policy.

TABLE 5-2 Class Findings and Q Modifiers

Class	Description Including Modifier
Class A	Non-traumatic amputation of foot or integral skeletal portion thereof A Q7 modifier reflects one Class A finding.

Class B	Absent posterior tibial pulse
	Absent dorsalis pedis pulse
	Advanced trophic changes as evidenced by three or more of the following:
	  1. Increase or decrease in hair growth
	  2. Change in nail texture—thickening
	  3. Change in color—discoloring
	  4. Change in skin texture—thin or shiny
	  5. Change in skin color—redness
	A Q8 modifier is used if there are two Class B findings.

Class C	Claudication Temperature changes, such as cold feet Edema Abnormal spontaneous sensations in the feet, known as paresthesias Burning A Q9 modifier would be used if there is one Class B finding accompanied by two Class C findings.

Exercise 5.3—Check Your Understanding

Codes 10021–11047

Fill in the blank with the correct term(s) or code to complete the sentence. Reference the CPT manual.

1. The handle part of the surgical knife is called the _____.

2. A complicated incision and drainage of a pilonidal cyst is reported with code _____.

3. _____ is the removal or cleansing of foreign objects or dirt to help in the healing process.

4. A puncture aspiration of a hematoma is reported with code _____.

5. A(n) _____ lesion is made up of an overgrowth of skin.

6. _____ is a procedure using a very fine needle to draw fluid out of the body.

7. The surgical cutting of an area and then the withdrawing of fluids from this area is a procedure known as a(n) _____.

8. A simple incision and removal of a foreign body from subcutaneous tissue is reported with code _____.

9. Debridement of infected skin, 8% of body surface, is reported with code _____.

10. The debridement of 12 sq cm of muscle and fascia is reported with code _____.

Biopsy (11102–11107)

A **biopsy** is a procedure in which a sampling of tissue is removed for pathological examination to differentiate between malignant and benign tissue. A definitive diagnosis is determined by a biopsy.

In the integumentary system, the codes 11102 to 11107 are used for biopsies of skin. Codes for other anatomical sites can be located in the CPT Index under the term Biopsy.

As described in the notation that precedes code 11102, the coder should be aware that these codes are assigned when the procedure was independently performed to obtain tissue solely for diagnostic histopathologic examination or the procedure was unrelated or distinct from other procedures/services provided at that time. Read this extensive instructional notation in the CPT manual that explains how to report biopsies performed on different lesions or different sites. For example, the "instructional notation" states: "Biopsies performed on different lesions or different sites on the same date of service may be reported separately, as they are not considered components of other procedures."

For codes 11102 to 11107, one of three distinct biopsy techniques are described. The codes are differentiated as a tangential biopsy, a punch biopsy, or an incisional biopsy. For the complete definition of each type of biopsy, reference the instructional notation that appears in the CPT book prior to code 11102.

Skin Tags (11200–11201)

Skin tags are skin growths that are found on many areas of the body, but usually the neck, axillae, and inguinal areas. A skin tag is a small lesion that can be brownish or flesh colored and is raised away from the body. Skin tags tend to grow with age but are almost always benign. Removal of skin tags is usually done with scissors, a scalpel, or ligature strangulation. Sometimes chemical or electrical cautery is also used.

Code 11200 is used to report the first 15 skin tags. The 11201 code is used for each additional 10 lesions or part thereof after the first 15.

EXAMPLE: Mr. Johnson was bothered by some small growths around his neck. His shirt collar was rubbing against some of them and irritating them. The doctor examined Mr. Johnson and said the growths were skin tags and could be removed at this visit. Mr. Johnson agreed. The doctor removed 25 skin tags.

The doctor coded the visit using 11200 (this code would be for the first 15 lesions removed) and then 11201 (this code with a quantity of 1 for the remaining 10 lesions) to report the remaining lesions.

Shaving of Epidermal or Dermal Lesions (11300–11313)

Shaving a lesion involves removal of a lesion from the epidermal or dermal layer by a transverse incision or slicing to remove epidermal and dermal lesions. A full-thickness dermal excision does not occur during this type of removal. This technique is most often used when a lesion is raised from the skin; the scalpel blade is moved horizontally to remove the lesion.

The code range for this procedure is 11300–11313. To code from this range, the coder needs to know the anatomical site and the size of the lesion. When this procedure is performed, typically local anesthesia is used. To close the wound, chemical cauterization or electrocauterization is performed, and the wound is not closed via sutures. If the specimen is sent to pathology, diagnosis coding should wait until the final diagnosis determination is rendered before a code is assigned.

Excision—Benign Lesions (11400–11471)

The code range 11400–11471 is used for removal of benign lesions. A benign lesion is one in which the cell growth is abnormal but not life-threatening. These types of lesions also are known as *nonmalignant tumors*.

The physician or provider may refer to the lesion as a *cyst*, a *neoplasm*, a *tumor,* or a *growth*. The coder might also see the terms *cicatricial, fibrous, inflammatory, congenital*, or *cystic*. These terms all refer to a benign lesion. The procedure note should be referenced with regard to type of lesion, anatomical site, method of lesion removal, number of lesions, and lesion size in centimeters. The lesion size, in addition to the size of the excised margins, should drive the code selection. The notation that appears before code 11400 states that the excision is defined as full-thickness removal of a lesion and the margins of tissue that surround the lesion that were also removed. To determine the size of tissue and lesion excised, the coder needs to know the clinical diameter of the lesion plus the margin required for excision.

When referencing the procedure note, attention should be drawn to whether the closure was intermediate or complex. These types of closures should be coded in addition to the excision, as explained in the paragraphs preceding code 11400 in the CPT manual. In some instances, layered closures pay more than the procedure itself. The procedure note should also indicate whether there was a skin graft or other type of closure, such as a flap. If the procedure note indicates that this is the case, the CPT code for the additional procedures would also be coded.

Excision—Malignant Lesion (11600–11646)

A malignant lesion is one in which the abnormal cell growth is found to be cancerous.

The terms that a coder might see in relation to a malignant lesion are *basal cell carcinoma, papillocystic carcinoma, squamous cell carcinoma*, and *melanoma of the skin*. It should be noted that an assumption is sometimes made that melanoma is present only in skin cancers. This is not true. Malignant melanoma can also be present in mucous membranes and the eye. This is rare, but it does occur.

Malignant tumors can grow deep and can also spread or metastasize. When a malignant growth or tumor spreads from one part of the body into another part of the body, it is called metastasis. This section of CPT should not be referenced if the tumor that is to be excised is part of deeper structures other than the skin. Other surgery sections within the Surgery chapter would be referenced for these types of deep excisions.

Code range 11600–11646 differentiates the codes relating to the site of the excision and the excised diameter of the lesion. Prior to code 11600, extensive notations instruct the coder to report separately each malignant lesion that is excised. The notation also states that the excision of the malignant lesion also includes a simple nonlayered closure. Intermediate or complex closures should be reported separately. Also note that, when there is a re-excision at a subsequent operative session to widen the margins, modifier 58 should be appended to the code if the procedure was performed during the postoperative period of the first excision.

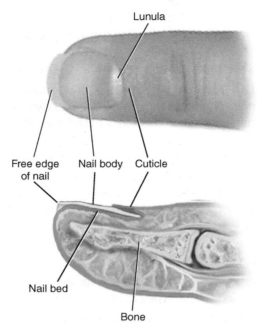

FIGURE 5-2 **Structures of the Fingernails and Toenails**

Nails (11719–11765)

We briefly discussed routine nail care earlier in this chapter. For example, the trimming of nondystrophic nails falls into this category. Also in this section of CPT are codes for avulsion of nail plates, evacuation of a subungual hematoma, biopsy of the nail unit, and repair and reconstruction of the nail bed. The code set for these procedures is 11719–11765. Figure 5-2 illustrates the structure of nails.

The debridement section of the Surgery chapter goes into detail regarding the first several codes of the nails subsection of CPT, so they will not be repeated here. The codes for the Nails subsection can be assigned when the procedure performed is in relation to toenails or fingernails. Unless the code specifically makes a distinction, these codes can be used for procedures on either set of nails.

We will begin with codes 11730—avulsion of the nail plate, partial or complete, simple, single, and 11732—each additional nail plate (list these separately in addition to the code for primary procedure). In this procedure, the physician takes the nail away from the nail bed using blunt dissection. The procedure may involve the whole nail or a part of the nail. If more than one nail is done, the 11732 code is used for each additional nail.

EXAMPLE: Joe presented to his podiatrist with painful great toes. The right toe was inflamed and was painful with shoe gear on. The left toe was not as inflamed, but there was a slight area of infection, and Joe stated that it was just as painful with shoe gear. After examination and discussion, it was decided that the doctor would perform an avulsion on each nail. On the right great toe, a complete avulsion was performed, as the nail bed was totally inflamed once the nail plate was lifted. The left great toe required only a partial avulsion, as the nail irritation occurred only on one side of the nail.

The podiatrist in our example would code 11730 for the first nail on the right toe and 11732 for the second nail, which required a partial avulsion.

Code 11740 reports an evacuation of a subungual hematoma. A **hematoma** is a collection of blood in a particular space or organ. A subungual hematoma is the collection of blood under the fingernail or toenail. Code 11740 reflects the draining of this blood collection. An electrocautery needle is used to pierce the nail so that the blood can drain.

Code 11750 is used when the nail and nail matrix are excised. This code represents a more permanent form of removal. Should the medical record documentation indicate that the nail plate was dissected away from the nail bed and that the entire tuft of the distal phalanx was removed, the coder should be using code 11750. The verbiage in a procedure note will help the coder in determining whether an avulsion or an excision took place. If there are any questions, the doctor needs to be asked to clarify what was actually done. In some cases, the doctor may refer to a wedge excision when trying to relieve problems with an ingrown toenail. A **wedge excision** is a procedure where the physician excises skin in the area of the ingrown portion of the nail in the hopes of freeing the nail enough to relieve pain. This is reported with code 11765—"Wedge excision of skin of nail fold."

Code 11755 reports a biopsy of a nail unit. Note that this code is a separate procedure code. When a biopsy is performed on a nail unit, any part of the nail can be sent to pathology, including the nail itself, along with samplings from the nail bed or soft tissue under the nail.

Repair and reconstruction of a nail bed are completed when the nail bed is damaged and is reported with codes 11760 and 11762.

During the repair of the nail bed, reported with code 11760, the defective nail is removed from the nail bed and the nail bed is sutured. A separate code for the suturing is not reported. Code 11762 reports a reconstruction of the nail bed by use of a skin graft, which is sutured in place. Repair may involve sutures. Reconstruction may involve grafting.

Pilonidal Cyst (11770–11772)

Codes 11770–11772 report excisions of pilonidal cysts. A **pilonidal cyst** is a closed sac, located in the sacrococcygeal area, that contains epithelial tissue with hair nested within the sac. The hair is referred to as ingrown hair. Code 11770 reports a simple excision that involves the excision of the cyst and a sutured closure in a single layer. Codes 11771 and 11772 report more complex excisions. The coder needs to determine that the cyst has subcutaneous extensions to report codes 11771 and 11772. Code 11771 is reported for the excisions of cysts to the underlying fascia that are closed in several layers. Code 11772 reports the most complex excisions in which there are multiple subcutaneous extensions. Closure of these excisions varies depending on the size of the defect area to be closed. Because the CPT manual does not contain explicit definitions for the terms *simple*, *extensive*, and *complicated* listed in codes 11770 to 11772, it is best practice to develop specific coding guidelines for coders to follow. When assigning these codes, the coder should query the provider if the documentation contained in the record does not clearly state the extent of the excision.

Introduction (11900–11983)

Codes 11900–11983 report various types of injections, procedures involving tissue expanders, and procedures involving drug delivery implants. Codes 11900 and 11901 report intralesional injections according to the number of lesions injected. During these procedures, the lesions are injected with a pharmacologic agent, such as a steroid or anesthetic solution, for therapeutic purposes. The instructional notation that follows code 11901 in the CPT manual states that these codes are not to be used for preoperative local anesthetic injections.

Codes 11920–11922 report procedures in which insoluble opaque pigments are injected into the skin to correct skin color defects. This is known as tattooing. The codes are differentiated according to the size of the area tattooed. Code 11920 reports an area of 6.0 sq cm or less, whereas code 11921 reports 6.1 to 20.0 sq cm. Code 11922 is used in conjunction with 11921 when greater than 20.0 sq cm is tattooed. Code 11922 is an add-on code used to report each additional 20.0 sq cm, or part thereof, tattooed above 20.0 sq cm. For example, if 25 sq cm is tattooed, code 11921 would be reported for the first 20 sq cm, and code 11922 would be reported for the additional 5 sq cm above the initial 20 sq cm reported with code 11921.

Codes 11950–11954 are used to report procedures that are completed to correct soft tissue defects or deformities by the injection of filling material into subcutaneous tissue. The injection is used to correct acne scars, facial wrinkles, or traumatic or postoperative defects. The injection fills in the dermal layer of tissue and thus decreases the depressions or defects of the skin. The codes are differentiated according to the amount of the injected substance. Code 11950 reports the injection of 1 cc or less, code 11951 reports 1.1 to 5.0 cc, code 11952 reports 5.1 to 10.0 cc, and code 11954 reports over 10.0 cc.

Codes 11960–11971 report procedures that involve the insertion, replacement, and removal of tissue expanders. Code 11960 reports the insertion of tissue expanders for sites other than the breast. Breast reconstruction with tissue expanders are reported with code 19357. At times, the tissue expanders are removed and then replaced with a permanent prosthesis; this is reported using only one code, 11970. When a previously implanted tissue expander is removed and there is no insertion of a prosthesis, code 11971 is reported.

Procedures that involve the removal of implantable contraceptive capsules are reported with code 11976. This procedure involves the placement of subdermal capsules, typically in the upper arm, of a female patient. When an insertion of an implantable contraceptive capsule occurs, code 11981 is used. Removal of a capsule without the reinsertion of a capsule is reported with code 11976, whereas removal of a capsule with a reinsertion of a contraceptive capsules is reported with codes 11976 and 11981.

The remaining codes report the following:

- Code 11980 reports the implantation of a subcutaneous hormone pellet implanted below the skin.
- Code 11981 reports the insertion of a nonbiodegradable drug delivery implant. A cylinder, containing a drug, is placed under the skin and sutured in place. The drug is then continuously released to the patient as prescribed.
- Code 11982 reports the removal of a nonbiodegradable drug delivery implant system. This code is reported when the system is not replaced.
- Code 11983 reports the removal of a nonbiodegradable drug delivery implant with reinsertion of another. Only one code is reported for both the removal and reinsertion.

Repair (12001–13160)

The **repair** of a wound is a surgical closure of an area that may have been injured as a result of trauma or surgery. Prior to selecting codes from the 12001–13160 repair codes, coders need to become familiar with the instructional notations that appear prior to code 12001. The instructional notation states that these codes can be used for any repair involving sutures, staples, or tissue adhesives, such as Dermabond. These codes can be used when the repair is a combination of these techniques, one of the techniques, or any of these techniques in combination with adhesive strips. For example, the lower layer of the skin may be sutured while the outermost layer is stapled.

Note that, if only adhesive strips are used for closure, this range of codes is not reported. For example, the use of Steri-Strips to butterfly-close a wound does not constitute a repair code. In the event Steri-Strips are used, an Evaluation and Management code should be selected to report the services rendered.

Also defined in the CPT manual are three types of repair codes. The first is a **simple repair**. A simple repair is one in which there is a simple, single-layer closure of a laceration that does not go any deeper than the subcutaneous tissue. There is no involvement of muscle fascia or of deeper structures.

Simple repair codes are not billed separately when any other procedure is performed on the same wound because it is included in the other service. For example, lesion excisions include a simple closure, so the simple closure should not be billed separately.

An **intermediate repair** of a laceration or wound is defined as a repair of the epidermis, dermis, and subcutaneous tissue with a layered closure of one or more of the deeper layers of subcutaneous tissue and superficial (nonmuscle) fascia, in addition to the skin (epidermal and dermal) closure. The wound layers do not go deeper than nonmuscle fascia. If a layered closure is not performed, and there is a single-layer closure of a heavily contaminated wound, and the wound site requires extensive cleaning or removal of foreign materials, then codes 12031–12057 can be assigned. There must be documentation supporting the fact that there was extensive cleansing and/or heavy contamination of the site.

The last type of repair is a **complex repair**. A complex repair requires more than a layered closure (that is, scar revision, debridement, extensive undermining, stents, or retention sutures). Prior to the repair, it may be necessary to prepare the area by the creation of a limited defect or the debridement of complicated lacerations or avulsions. It should be noted that the following are not included as components of a complex repair and, therefore, are reported separately:

- Excision of benign lesion (codes 11400–11446)
- Excision of malignant lesion (codes 11600–11646)
- Excisional preparation of a wound bed (codes 15002–15005)
- Debridement of an open fracture or open dislocation (codes 11010–11012)

In the CPT manual following the definitions of the type of repairs, additional instructions are given for the reporting of repairs. The first instruction states that the size of a wound needs to be recorded in the medical record and reported in centimeters.

The second instruction gives coding instructions for when multiple wounds are repaired. As discussed, the code ranges are divided according to the type of repair: simple, intermediate, and complex. The codes are then further divided by anatomical site and the size of the repair. When multiple wounds are repaired, the coder needs to determine the wounds that fall into the same classification of repair: simple, intermediate, or complex. The coder then needs to review the wound in each classification of repair and determine which anatomic sites are involved. If the wounds are from the same classification and the same anatomical site, then the lengths of the repair for the specific classification are added together and reported with one code from the classification of repair.

> **EXAMPLE:** Lindsay fell off her bike and was taken to the emergency department (ED) for evaluation. She was found to have a laceration on her left arm and left knee. After cleaning the area, the doctor determined that the two areas needed to be sutured. A simple 2.8-cm repair of the laceration on her left arm and a simple 4-cm repair of the laceration on her leg was completed.

To determine the correct code assignment, the coder should first note that the repairs are both simple repairs. Second, the coder needs to determine whether the anatomical sites, arm and leg, are both grouped into the same code descriptor within the CPT manual. Using the CPT index, the coder should reference the term "Integumentary system," then "repair," and then "simple" to code these repairs. The index lists codes 12001–12021. Referencing this range of codes, the coder notes that code 12001 reads, "Simple repair of superficial wounds of scalp, neck, axillae, external genitalia, trunk and/or extremities (including hands and feet); 2.5 cm or less." The coder can now conclude that the arm and leg are grouped into the same anatomic site: extremities. Now the coder should add together the lengths of the lacerations repaired. The laceration on the arm is 2.8 cm, and the laceration on the knee is 4 cm. Because the procedure code is in the same category for both lacerations, the coder would add the two lengths together for a total of 6.8 cm. Code 12001 reads, "2.5 cm or less," and the laceration in the example is longer than 2.5 cm. Reviewing the codes in the CPT manual, the coder would notice that code 12002 reads the same as code 12001, except when you get to the semicolon (;). At that point, the coder would read it as 2.6 cm to 7.5 cm, which is where the sum of the two areas would fall. Therefore, the CPT code assignment for our example would be 12002.

The third coding instruction found for repair codes addresses decontamination and/or debridement. Although not discussed in the CPT manual, understanding types of wounds helps a coder assign the proper CPT code and also the correct ICD-10-CM, or diagnosis, code. Roman numerals are used to note each type of wound classification. The surgical wound classification is not assigned until after the procedure is completed. The various classes of wounds are:

- Class I—A **clean wound** has a very low infection rate (1–5%) and involves no inflammation or break in sterile technique.
- Class II—A **clean-contaminated wound** has a low infection rate (8–11%) and involves a minor break in sterile technique, but no inflammation is present. The wound may involve the genitourinary, respiratory, or digestive tracts.
- Class III—A **contaminated wound** involves a major break in sterile technique, and acute nonpurulent inflammation is present. The wound is less than four hours old, and the tracts mentioned in the Class II classifications may be involved, along with the biliary tract. There is usually spillage involved. This would be referenced as a Class III.

- Class IV—This class of wounds involves nonsterile conditions in which infection and inflammation are present. The wound is more than four hours old. The viscus would be perforated, and there may be a foreign body, fecal contamination, or necrotic tissue present. This is referred to as a **dirty and infected wound**.

Knowing the classifications will help the coder determine whether debridement of a wound should be reported. Debridement of a wound is considered bundled into the repair code. However, as outlined in the instructions in the CPT manual, a separate code for debridement should be reported in the following circumstances:

- Gross contamination of a site requires prolonged cleaning.
- Appreciable amounts of devitalized or contaminated tissue are removed.
- Debridement is carried out separately without immediate primary closure.

To report the debridement, documentation needs to reflect the extra time involved, along with details regarding any removal of necrotic or devitalized tissue. Therefore, the class of the wound will also support the reporting of the debridement.

The fourth instruction discussed in the CPT manual states that, for repairs of nerves, blood vessels, and tendons, the procedures should be reported from the appropriate body system within the CPT manual: nervous system, cardiovascular system, or musculoskeletal system. The instructional notation also states the following:

- Simple ligation of a vessel is part of any wound closure.
- Exploration of the wound also is included in the repair code, as is exploration of nerves, blood vessels, and tendons that may be exposed because of injury.

Exercise 5.4—Check Your Understanding

Surgical Procedures

Fill in each blank with the correct term(s) or code to complete the statement. Reference the CPT manual.

1. A 1-cc subcutaneous injection of collagen is reported with code _____.

2. To examine and differentiate between malignant and benign tissue, a(n) _____ of the lesion would be taken and sent to pathology.

3. Code _____ would be used to report partial avulsion of the nail plate for a single nail.

4. A surgical closure of an area that may have been damaged as a result of trauma or injury, or even as a result of surgery, is called a(n) _____.

5. A(n) _____ has a very low infection rate and involves no inflammation or break in sterile technique.

6. Debridement of two nails is reported with code _____.

7. An excision of a malignant lesion of the arm with an excised diameter of 2.2 cm is reported with code _____.

8. Evacuation of a subungal hematoma is reported with code _____.

9. Repair of a nail bed is reported with code _____.

10. Excision of a pilonidal cyst, complicated is reported with code _____.

Adjacent Tissue Transfer or Rearrangement (14000–14350)

As we discussed earlier, the skin is the safeguard for the internal organs of the body against infection and other outside elements that can cause damage. When the skin is damaged in such a way that suturing or stapling cannot be performed to close a wound, a physician may perform an adjacent tissue transfer. **Adjacent tissue transfer** is exactly what its name implies: healthy tissue is manipulated or rearranged—transferred—from a site close to or next to an area that is open because of disease or injury.

Techniques indicating adjacent tissue transfer or rearrangement that may be mentioned in an operative note include rotation, Z-plasty, W-plasty, VY-plasty, advancement, Rhombic flaps, and double pedicle flaps. A **pedicle flap** is a flap of skin that hangs on a stem of skin that contains a blood vessel. This skin flap is rotated around and sutured to an adjacent site to supply blood to the new site until the injury or diseased site is healed.

When reporting codes from the 14000–14350 series, the coder would not report debridement codes or repair codes separately, because these services are included in the 14000–14350 series. Also included in this code set are the excisions of lesions. If the adjacent tissue transfer or rearrangement was performed at a different operative setting from an incision, a 58 modifier would need to be appended to indicate a staged or related procedure. If a skin graft is performed, and the type of graft performed is not noted in the 14000–14350 code set, the graft may be billed in addition to one of the 14000 codes. The coder would need to research the codes being used carefully to be sure that the proper code selection was made.

To assign a code from this series properly, the coder needs to know the site and the size of the defect in square centimeters.

Surgical Preparation (15002–15005)

The coder will need to have an understanding of certain terms before being able to code procedures from the Surgical Preparation subsection of the Integumentary System section. Understanding terminology associated with graft procedures is essential to code from this subsection of the Surgery chapter. When surgeons refer to the **defect site** or **recipient site**, they are referring to the area that will receive a graft. This site is in need of repair because of lesion removal, a burn or other injury, or the graft itself. The **donor site** is the area that provides the tissue used to make the repair.

When coding grafts, a coder must select the code very carefully by reviewing all documentation available. Some codes include the repair of the donor site, but most codes do not, so an additional code is allowed when repair of the donor site is necessary. The coder should also keep in mind that a lesion excision is not reported separately if adjacent tissue transfer or rearrangement is performed at the site. The excision is considered an integral part of graft procedures. Other terminology that the coder may encounter and have a need to understand are *flaps*, *free skin graft*, *pedicle graft*, and *adjacent tissue transfer* or *rearrangement*. We will be explaining these terms as we progress through this chapter.

Skin Replacement Surgery and Skin Substitutes

A **graft** is a section of tissue that is moved from one site to another in an effort to heal or repair a defect. There are different types of grafts that are performed, depending on several factors. A **homograft**, or **homologous graft**, involves tissue from an individual of the same species. An **autogenous graft** is a type of graft where tissue is taken from one part of a person's body and put on another part of the same person's body. A **heterodermic graft** is a type of graft where tissue from a different species is used for the repair. Other terms that a coder might encounter would be *free graft* and *split-skin graft*. A **free graft** is one in which the tissue is totally freed from its original site. A **split-skin graft**, or **split-thickness graft**, is one in which the tissue is about half or more of the thickness of the skin (i.e., the epidermis with a bit of the dermis layer).

To begin to code from this subsection, the coder needs to know the type of graft, the graft's location, and the size, in square centimeters, of the defect that is going to be repaired.

The 15002–15005 codes are the surgical preparation codes and are used for the preparation of a recipient site. The surgical preparation of a recipient site involves cleaning and excising tissue to a level where there is a healthy vascular bed on which to set the donor graft and promote healing. An excisional preparation of the skin is necessary to receive the graft: the surgeon excises tissue, scars, or lesions to the point where a healthy vascular tissue bed is exposed to receive the graft. In order for a graft to be successful, the site should be free of debris and infection, have a good blood supply source, and bleeding needs to be controlled.

TABLE 5-3 Surgical Preparation (15002–15005)

Instructions for Use of Codes
Review the CPT manual and note that code 15002 reports the preparation or creation of recipient site by excision. This code is used for defects that occur on the trunk, arms or legs. To properly code the coder must identify the size or % of the defect. When assigning this code the coder needs to identify that the size of the excision is documented or that the percentage of the body area of the wound is recorded. This code can be used alone or with code 15003.
Review the CPT manual for the full description of code 15003. This code is an add-on code and is only reported when the documentation records the size of the area is greater than 100 sq cm. Code 15003 must be used as a second or greater listed code in conjunction with code 15002. Note that code 15003 can be used multiple times based on the size of the area treated.
Like code 15002 code 15004 reports the preparation or creation of recipient site by excision. This code reports the same procedure as code 15002 except that the site of the procedure for code 15004 is the face, scalp, eyelids, mouth, neck, ears, orbits, genitalia, hands, feet, and/or multiple digits. Review the CPT manual for the full code description.
Code 15005 is reported as an add-on code to 15004, therefore code 15005 is never reported alone. The number of times that code 15005 is reported is based on the size of the area treated. Review the CPT manual for the full description of the code.

The cleansing and excising of tissue can involve lesion removal or release of scar tissue that may be causing excessive tightening. When scar tissue is released, an open wound may result, which would require some type of closing.

Table 5–3, summarizes the code descriptions for codes 15002, 15003, 15004, and 15005.

> **EXAMPLE:** A 62-year-old woman was admitted from the Emergency Department with second- and third-degree burns received while cooking dinner for her grandchildren. Both hands and part of the forearm were burned. A total of 10% of her body surface suffered from second- and third-degree burns. Under general anesthesia, the eschar was excised to viable subcutaneous tissue. Between the hands and forearm, a total of 125 sq cm was excised. The area was prepped for immediate skin grafting.

Code 15002 would be used to report the first 100 sq cm, and add on code 15003 reports the remaining 25 sq cm.

Grafts (15040–15278)

To select a code properly from the Grafts subsection of CPT, the coder would need to know the following:

- Location of the defect
- Size in centimeters of the defect
- The type of graft (flap, free, pedicle, etc.)

The best manner in which to determine the location, size, and type of graft is for the coder to review the patient's history, the procedure note, and any additional documentation that is present in the patient's record. Keep in mind that the size of the defect must be known for the assignment of certain codes. For adults and children 10 years of age and older the measurement of 100 sq cm is used in the code descriptions. For infants and children younger than 10 years of age the percentages of body surface area is used to describe the defect area. These measurements apply to the defect area only. For example, the description for code 15100 reads: "Split-thickness autograft, trunk, arms, legs; first 100 sq cm or less, or 1% of body area of infants and children (except 15050)."

An **autograft** is a type of graft that involves only one individual; the donor and recipient sites are from the same individual. Autograft codes are described in Table 5-4.

TABLE 5-4 Autograft (15040–15157)

Definitions of Grafts and Use of Codes
Reference the CPT manual and note that code 15040 is used when skin is harvested for a tissue-cultured skin autograft. This code is only used when the area is 100 sq cm or less. This is essential that the documentation found in the patient's records support the size of the area stated in the code. Do not report this code if the area is over 100 sq cm.
A pinch graft is a smaller form of autograft. Code 15050 reports a single graft or multiple pinch grafts, except those completed on the face, that are completed for a defect of up to a defect size of a 2 cm diameter. This code is only used when the graft is completed to cover a small open area. Reference the code in the CPT manual for examples.
Code 15100 reports a split-thickness autograft. To use this code the autograft must be completed on the trunk, arms, and/or legs. The size of the area treated is specified as the first 100 sq cm or less, or 1% of body area of infants and children. Review the CPT manual for additional instructions for this code.
Split-thickness autograft contains only part of the dermal layer, but the epidermis and dermis would be included.
Note that code 15101 is an add-on code that reports each additional 100 sq cm, or each additional 1% of body area of infants and children, or part thereof. This code can not be reported alone and must be reported with code 15100. The number of times that code 15101 is based on the size of the area treated.
Epidermal autograft is a graft of the epidermal layer only. Code 15110 is used to report epidermal autografts that are completed on the trunk, arms and/or legs. It is important for coders to note that this code reports only the first 100 sq cm or less or 1% of the body area of infants and children. If the size of the area treated is larger the use of add-on code 15111 should occur.
Code 15111 is an add-on code for code 15110 and is reported for each additional 100 sq cm, or each additional 1% of body area of infants and children, or part thereof when the area treated is larger than the area stated in code 15110. Code 15111 is used as an add-on code to code 15110 and code 15111 must be reported after code 15110.
As with code 15110, code 15115 reports epidermal autografts. The differences is that code 15115 reports grafts of the face, scalp, eyelids, mouth, neck, ears, orbits, genitalia, hands, feet, and/or multiple digits. The size of the area treated is specified as the first 100 sq cm or less, or 1% of body area of infants and children.
Code 15116 is the add-on code to be used with code 15115 and is used to report each additional 100 sq cm, or each additional 1% of body area of infants and children, or part thereof. To report this code the coders must verify the size of the area treated and use code 15116 for procedures in which the size of the area treated exceeds the size stated for code 15115.
A split-thickness autograft of the face, scalp, eyelids, mouth, neck, ears, orbits, genitalia, hands, feet, and/or multiple digits is reported with code 15120. This code is used for the first 100 sq cm or less, or 1% of body area of infants and children. When the size of the area treated exceeds the size listed in code 15120 the add-on code of 15121 should be listed as an additional code.
Code 15121 is an add-on code for code 15120 and is used to report each additional 100 sq cm, or each additional 1% of body area of infants and children, or part thereof when the size of the area treated exceeds what is stated in code 15120. Code 15121 must be used in conjuction with code 15120. Note: This add-on code should be checked against codes 67961–67975 if the site of the graft is the eyelids.
Code 15130 reports a dermal autograft of the trunk, arms, and/or legs. Code 15130 reports the first 100 sq cm or less, or 1% of body area of infants and children. The documentation of the size of the area treated must align to the size description stated in the CPT manual for this code. Coders should note that a dermal autograft involves only the dermal tissue in the harvest process.
Code 15131 is an add-on code for code 15130 and it is used to report each additional 100 sq cm, or each additional 1% of body area of infants and children, or part thereof. Code 15131 is not be reported alone, it must be reported with code 15130. Prior to reporting these codes the coder needs to ensure that the record documentation supports the reporting of both of these codes.
Code 15135 reports a dermal autograft of the face, scalp, eyelids, mouth, neck, ears, orbits, genitalia, hands, feet, and/or multiple digits. This code is only used for the first 100 sq cm or less, or 1% of body area of infants and children. When the size of the area treated is larger than the area stated in code 15135, code 15135 is to be reported with code(s) 15136.
Review the CPT manual and note that code 15136 is an add-on code that is used with code 15135 for each additional 100 sq cm, or each additional 1% of the body area of infants and children, or part thereof. Code 15136 is reported only with 15135 and code 15136 can not be reported alone.

(continues)

TABLE 5-4 (*continued*)

Definitions of Grafts and Use of Codes
Reference the CPT manual and note that code 15150 reports a tissue-cultured skin autograft, involving the skin of the trunk, arms or legs. Please note that code 15150 is used only for the first 25 sq cm or less. When a larger area is treated the add-on codes of 15151 and 15152 are used with code 15150. Reference the CPT manual for the full code description. A **tissue-cultured epidermal autograft** is a type of graft where tissue is harvested in a split-tissue autograft and the cultured tissue is grafted back to the donor.
Code 15151 is an add-on code that is used with code 15150 when the area of the autograft treated exceeds 25 sq cm. Code 15151 is used to report an additional 1 sq cm to 75 sq cm. Documentation in the record must justify the use of this add-on code. Note: This code can be reported only once per session.
Code 15152 is an add-on code that is reported with codes 15150 and 15151, when the size of the area treated exceeds the size of the descriptions found in codes 15150 and 15151. Code 15152 reports each additional 100 sq cm, or each additional 1% of body area of infants and children, or part thereof. Code 15152 is only used when codes 15150 and 15151 are reported. Review these three codes in the CPT manual.
Code 15155 is similar to code 15150 as both codes report tissue-cultured skin autograft. The difference is that code 15155 specifies that this code is for grafts of the face, scalp, eyelids, mouth, neck, ears, orbits, genitalia, hands, feet, and/or multiple digits. Code 15155 is for the first 25 sq cm or less. If a larger area is grafted the use of add-on codes 15156 and 15157 may be needed.
Code 15156 is an add-on code that is used with code 15155 when more than 25 sq cm are grafted. Code 15156 reports an additional 1 cm to 75 sq cm. Code 15156 must be used with code 15155 to be valid. Documentation must justify the area grafted when using both codes. 1 sq cm to 75 sq cm. (List separately in addition to the code for the primary procedure.) Note: This code should be used only once per session.
Code 15157 is an add-on code that is used when the area grafted exceeds the area described in codes 15155 and 15156. Code 15157 documents each additional 100 sq cm, or each additional 1% of body area of infants and children, or part thereof. Code 15157 is used as the third listed code after codes 15155 and 15156 when the documentation supports the total size of the graft completed.

Exercise 5.5—Check Your Understanding

Autograft Coding—Table 5-4

Fill in the blank with the correct term(s) or code to complete the sentence.

1. Epidermal autograft, back—75 sq cm

   _____

2. Split-thickness autograft, calf—200 sq cm

   _____

3. Tissue-cultured epidermal autograft, cheek— 25 sq cm _____

4. Pinch graft, tip of index finger—1 cm

   _____

5. Dermal autograft, neck—85 sq cm

   _____

6. A small-type graft, or _____, is used to cover small ulcers or the tip of digits.

7. The _____ autograft involves only the dermal layer in the harvest process.

8. This type of autograft is a type of graft in which tissue is harvested in a split-tissue autograft and the cultured tissue is grafted back to the donor. This is called a(n) _____ autograft.

9. What code(s) are assigned when a 32-sq-cm epidermal autograft of the back is performed? _____

10. What code(s) are assigned when a 145-sq-cm split-thickness graft is performed on the left leg and the trunk? _____

Acellular dermal replacement is a skin substitute for areas that require a temporary closure. Porous lattice fibers and a synthetic substance are combined to make the replacement. A surgeon will excise a full or partial thickness until viable tissue is reached. Then the surgeon will cover the open wound with an acellular dermal replacement graft until skin autografts can be placed. Table 5-5 defines the codes used for acellular dermal replacement.

TABLE 5-5 Full Thickness Grafts and Skin Substitute Grafts (15200–15278)

Instructions for Use of Codes
Code 15200 reports a full thickness graft, free, including direct closure of donor site, trunk. This is important for the coder to note that this code only reports a graft of 20 sq cm or less. If a graft of a larger size is completed than add-on code 15201 should be used in conjunction with this code.
A **full thickness graft** contains a portion of both the epidermis and dermis of the donor site with a section that is equal, continuous, and totally free for transfer.
Code 15201 is an add-on code that is used with code 15200 to report each additional 20 sq cm, or part thereof beyond what is reported using code 15200. If the graft is over 20 sq cm than code 15200 is listed first followed by code 15201. The coder needs to review the documentation to determine how many times code 15201 would be reported. Remember code 15201 reports each additional 20 sq cm.
Code 15220 reports a full thickness graft, free, including direct closure of donor site involving the scalp, arms, and/or legs. Prior to assigning this code the coder should verify the location of the graft and ensure that it involves the scalp, arms and or legs. The coder should also note that this code reports 20 sq cm or less. If a larger graft is completed than add-on code 15221 will need to be assigned as additional code(s).
Code 15221 is an add-on code that is used with code 15220 for each additional 20 sq cm, or part thereof when grafts over 20 sq cm are completed. Code 15221 is never reported alone and must be reported as a secondary code to code 15220 when the documentation supports the size of the graft described in the codes.
Code 15240 reports a full thickness graft, free, including direct closure of donor site. The sites for this code are the forehead, cheeks, chin, mouth, neck, axillae, genitalia, hands, and/or feet. As with code 15220 this code reports grafts of 20 sq cm or less. The coder needs to ensure that when selecting this code the site and size in the documentation are reflected in the code description. Reference the CPT manual for the description. Note: CPT code 15050 should be referenced if a graft is performed on a fingertip. CPT codes 26560–26562 should be referenced if repair is performed on a web finger.
Code 15241 is an add-on code that is used with code 15240 to report each additional 20 sq cm, or part thereof when the graft completed is larger than 20 sq cm. Code 15240 is to be listed first followed by code 15241 to accurately reflect the size of the graft as stated in the documentation for the procedure. Note that code 15241 can be reported more than once depending on the size of the graft.
Code 15260 is similar to codes 15200, 15220 and 15240 in that they all report a full thickness graft, free, including direct closure of donor site. The codes are differentiated by site and code 15260 reports the sites of the nose, ears, eyelids, and/or lips. Code 15260 reports a graft of 20 sq cm or less. When larger grafts are performed code 15261 is used with code 15260.
Code 15261 is an add-on code that is reported with code 15260 for each additional 20 sq cm, or part thereof. The procedural note needs to clearly reflect the size of the graft for this code to be assigned with code 15260.
Codes 15271–15278 reports the application of skin substitute grafts. Codes are differentiated by site of graft and wound surface area. Codes 15273, 15274, 15277, and 15278 designate specific criteria for body area of infants and children. Coders need to reference the CPT manual for the full description of these codes and the instructional notation that follows the heading entitled Skin Substitute Grafts.

Exercise 5.6—Check Your Understanding

Full Thickness Grafts

Code the following:

1. Full-thickness free graft, trunk—60 sq cm

_____

2. Full-thickness free graft with direct closure of donor site, trunk—10 sq cm _____

3. Full-thickness free graft, lip—10 sq cm

_____

4. Full-thickness free graft of scalp, including direct closure of donor site, scalp—17 sq cm

_____

(continues)

Exercise 5.6—*continued*

5. Full-thickness free graft, chin—15 sq cm
_____

6. Free, full thickness graft, right side of nose and upper lip—10 sq cm _____
7. Free, full thickness graft, forehead, cheek, neck, and hands (all on the left side)—28 sq cm _____
8. Free, full thickness graft, back—40 sq cm
_____

For each of the following statements, say whether the statement is true or false.

9. The supply of skin substitute grafts should be reported separately in conjunction with 15271 to 15278. _____

10. For a biologic implant for soft tissue reinforcement, use code 15777 in conjunction with the code for the primary procedure. _____

Exercise 5.7—Check Your Understanding

Code Range 15271–15278

Complete the following statements.

1. Code 15272 is used in conjunction with code _____.

2. Code 15274 is used in conjunction with code _____.

3. Do not report codes 15275 and 15276 in conjunction with code 15277 and code _____.

4. Use code 15276 in conjunction with code _____.

5. Do not report codes 15271 and 15272 in conjunction with code 15273 and code _____.

Sometimes grafts are made up of material that is nonhuman, such as pig tissue. These grafts are known as **xenografts** and are temporary coverings used until appropriate, more compatible material is available. The location and size of the defect determine code selection and are reported with codes 15271–15278.

Flaps (Skin and/or Deep Tissues) (15570–15738) and Other Flaps and Grafts (15740–15777)

Coding from this code range can be challenging, so attention to the detail in the code descriptions is necessary. In the CPT manual, several notations appear before code 15570. Locate these notations that appear before the code 15570 and follow the heading entitled Flaps (Skin and/or Deep Tissue). The first sentence informs the coder that the regions that are listed for this code range refer to the recipient site when a flap is being attached in a transfer or to a final site. The second sentence informs the coder that the regions listed refer to a donor site when a tube is formed for later transfer or when a delay of flap occurs prior to the transfer. Reference the CPT manual for additional notations that are found in this section of the manual.

Codes 15570–15576 report the formation of either a direct or tubed pedicle flap that is used to reconstruct the defect area. Codes 15600–15630 are reported when the direct or tubed pedicle flap is sectioned several weeks following the reconstruction of the defect. Codes 15733–15738 are described by donor site and are reported when the defect is repaired using a muscle, muscle and skin, or a fasciocutaneous flap.

The remaining graft codes, 15740–15777, in the Flaps subsection of the Integumentary section, are for other types of flaps and grafts, which include island pedicle, composite, and punch grafts (for hair transplants).

The coder should be very careful when coding flaps, grafts, and tissue transfers. As was discussed earlier, all documentation on the current procedure should be reviewed, along with any staged procedures that were performed. Review of these notes will allow for proper code assignment.

Table 5-6 summarizes flap-type repairs.

TABLE 5-6 Flap-Type Repairs (15570–15738)

Code(s)	Description
15570 to 15576	Codes 15570 to 15576 report the formation of direct or tubed pedicle. All of these code descriptions are with or without transfer. The differentiating factor for these codes is the site of the procedure. Reference the CPT manual prior to code 15570 for additional information that applies to this code range.
15600 to 15630	Codes 15600 to 15630 report delay of flap or sectioning of flap (division and inset). The codes are differentiated by site. Reference the CPT manual for the specific sites listed for each code.
15650	Code 15650 reports the intermediate transfer of any pedicle flap. This code description is not specific to any one location.
15730	In order to report this code the coder needs to ensure that the documentation states that the flap is a midface flap and there is preservation of the vascular pedicle(s).
15731	In order to report this code the documentation needs to identify a forehead flap with preservation of vascular pedicle.
15733 to 15738	Codes 15733 to 15738 report a muscle, myocutaneous, or fasciocutaneous flap. The codes are differentiated by site. Reference the CPT manual for the specific sites.

Other Procedures (15780–15879)

There is an array of codes in this subsection that should be reviewed. This subsection includes dermabrasion, chemical peel, rhytidectomy, blepharoplasty, and suture removal. Codes in this subsection are used by plastic surgeons and dermatologists, but they can be used by other providers as well.

Codes 15850–15852 involve suture removal and dressing change. The codes are quite clear, in that the patient must be under anesthesia other than local anesthesia. These codes should *not* be used for suture removal unless the patient needs to be sedated to remove the sutures. If a primary procedure is being performed, or the patient is returned to the operating room for complications of a surgery that require the incision to be reopened, these codes are not to be used.

Pressure Ulcers (Decubitus Ulcers) (15920–15999)

Ulcers are erosions of the skin in which the tissue becomes inflamed and is then lost. In patients who have continuous pressure in an area such as the elbows, buttocks, coccyx, hands, or wrists, the limited circulation eventually causes a breakdown, and an ulcer is formed. A **decubitus ulcer** is the result of continuous pressure in an area that eventually limits or stops the oxygen flow to the area, causing a sore. This can sometimes be referred to as a *pressure ulcer* or *bedsore*.

Codes 15920–15999 report procedures in which the physician excises the ulcer and cleanses the area until viable tissue is found. The area is then prepared for a flap or skin graft. If the underlying bone is removed before the area is repaired, the coder would select the excision code that lists the term **ostectomy**, which denotes that bone was removed. When reviewing claims, insurance companies look for the stage of the ulcer. This is reflected in documentation and the proper assignment of the ICD-10-CM diagnosis code. The coder should verify that medical documentation supports the procedural and diagnostic codes selected.

Burns, Local Treatment (16000–16036)

A **burn** is an injury to body tissue that is a result of heat, flame, sun, chemicals, radiation, and/or electricity. The procedure codes in code range 16000–16036 encompass only local treatment of the burned surface. If the burn patient needs further related medical treatment, evaluation and management codes are used to report the management of the victim.

The degree of the burn also needs to be understood by the coder. A **first-degree burn** is the least severe burn and presents no danger to the patient. Code 16000—"Initial treatment, first-degree burn, when no more than local treatment is required," would be assigned to simple treatment of a burn. Simple treatment includes application of cream and/or a dressing. Documentation should indicate the location and size of the area treated.

Second-degree burns are partial-thickness burns that form blisters. A second-degree burn, if not properly treated, could result in an infection at the burn site. **Third-degree burns** also are called *full-thickness burns.* The burn goes to the subcutaneous skin layers or further. Documentation should always indicate the location, size, and depth of the burn.

Code range 16020–16030 is assigned based on body surface area treated and reports the initial or subsequent dressings and/or debridement of partial-thickness burns. The coder would need to know the percentage of body surface area affected to assign the correct code. Codes in this range address cleansing the area, as well as some debridement and dressing application. These codes can be billed each time the service is performed.

Codes 16035, "Escharotomy; initial incision," and 16036, "Each additional incision" (list separately, in addition to the code for the primary procedure) are also reported from this range of codes. Note that code 16036 is an add-on code. In the CPT manual following code 16036 a notation appears that alerts the coder that for debridement or curettement of a burn wound the coder should reference codes 16020–16030.

Escharotomy is the removal of necrosed tissue of severely burned skin. This procedure involves the physician releasing the underlying tissue. Repairs are made using flaps, grafts, or tissue advancement, which are separately billable.

EXAMPLE: Dennis received second-degree burns to his left arm and hand, including three fingers. The burns were received while attending to a campfire on a recent camping trip. He is here for a dressing change on this area.

The bandages were removed after the arm and hand were submerged in the whirlpool. The area is healing nicely. The burn area was carefully cleansed and ointment was applied to it, and impregnated gauze was laid over the same area. The 4 × 4s were placed over the gauze, and then Kerlix was fluffed and applied to the arm and hand prior to the Ace wraps. Patient will return in two days for a dressing change.

The doctor should report services rendered in the example above using code 16025.

Destruction (17000–17286)

Destruction describes a procedure that totally destroys or removes a lesion. In this subsection of CPT, *destruction* refers to cryosurgery, laser, electrosurgery, surgical currettement, or chemosurgery. These procedures can take place alone or in conjunction with each other.

The coder will need to determine whether the type of lesion is benign, premalignant, or malignant. This determination will help the coder in deciding which code to select.

Locate codes 17000 to 17003 in the CPT manual. Note that code 17000 can be used with code 17003 since code 17003 is an add-on code for 17000. Following code 17003 a notation appears that states: "Use 17003 in conjunction with 17000." Now locate code 17004 in the CPT manual and review the notation following the code that states: "Do not report 17004 in conjunction with 17000–17003." When you are coding for lesions up to and including 14 lesions, codes 17000 and 17003 are used. When there is destruction of 15 or more lesions, code 17004 is used.

EXAMPLE: Megan presented to Dr. Barnes with 13 plantar warts to be treated. There were six warts on the right foot and seven warts on the left. Dr. Barnes used a combination of cryosurgery and surgical currettement to treat these warts.

Dr. Barnes reported her services using 17000 × 1 (quantity is always 1 for this code) and 17003 × 12 for each additional lesion. Now, if we modify this same example, treating 15 warts instead of 13, Dr. Barnes will report her charges as follows: 17004 × 1 (the quantity is always 1 for this code). Table 5-7 summarizes codes 17000, 17003, and 17004.

TABLE 5-7 Destruction of Lesions (17000–17004)

Code	Description
17000	Code 17000 reports the destruction of premalignant lesions other than skin tags or cutaneous vascular proliferative lesions. The various types of destruction used are listed in the CPT code description. Reference the CPT manual for the listing. This code is used to report the destruction of the first lesion.
17003	Code 17003 is an add-on code and is used to report the second through fourteenth lesions, each. Code 17003 is not to be reported without using code 17000 as the first listed code.
17004	Code 17004 reports the destruction of 15 or more premalignant lesions. For this code to be used the documentation must report the number of lesions.

The next range of codes, 17106–17108, involves destruction of cutaneous vascular proliferative lesions. These codes are reported when the destruction occurs with a laser and does not involve invasive procedures, such as cutting. The coder needs to know the size of the area in square centimeters.

Codes 17110 and 17111 are used to report the destruction of benign lesions other than skin tags or cutaneous vascular proliferative lesions. The procedural note needs to state specifically that the lesions destroyed were these types of lesions. These codes are never reported together. The code 17110 is for the first 14 lesions. After that, code 17111 would be reported for 15 or more lesions. Following code 17111, an instructional notation appears in the CPT manual that states: "For destruction of extensive cutaneous neurofibroma over 50–100 lesions, see 0419T, 0420T."

For code 17250—Chemical cauterization of granulation tissue (ie, proud flesh)—the provider applies a chemical substance (e.g., silver nitrate) to destroy the granulation tissue. Referencing the instructional notations that follow code 17250, the coder is instructed that this code is not to be reported with removal or excision codes for the same lesion, when chemical cauterization is used to achieve wound hemostasis, or reported in conjunction with codes 97597, 97598, and 97602 for the same lesion.

Destruction, Malignant Lesions, Any Method (17260–17286)

Destruction of a malignant lesion is coded from this section. A malignant lesion contains cells that are showing abnormal growth. These lesions also are referred to as *cancerous* lesions. To assign the proper code from this subsection, the coder needs to know the location of the lesions and the size of the lesions with the margins of the tissue before excision or destruction. The size of the lesion needs to be expressed in centimeters to select a code.

EXAMPLE: Casey was diagnosed with a melanoma on his hand, which measured 1.2 cm. Due to the lesion's location, it was decided to remove it using laser surgery. The lesion and a small area around it were treated. In total, the area measured 1.4 cm.

Code 17272 was used to report this procedure.

Exercise 5.8—Check Your Understanding

Coding Destruction of Lesions

Using a CPT manual, indicate the correct code(s) for the destruction of malignant lesions. If the diagnostic statement specifies the side, use the modifier RT or LT.

1. Chemosurgery on left hand—0.4 cm _____

2. Laser surgery, nose—2.0 cm _____

3. Cryosurgery, trunk—4.8 cm _____

4. Cryosurgery, feet—1.0 cm on left _____ 1.1 cm on right _____

5. Laser surgery, upper lip—0.5 cm _____

6. Surgical curettement, back—3.4 cm _____

7. Laser surgery, left ear—0.1 cm _____

8. Cryosurgery, right leg—2.7 cm _____

9. Chemosurgery, scalp—1.8 cm _____

10. Laser surgery, eyebrow—1.0 cm _____

Mohs Micrographic Surgery (17311–17315)

Mohs micrographic surgery is a type of chemosurgery. A chemical agent, which acts as a chemical fixative, is placed onto the lesion before it is excised. This chemical fixative allows the surgeon to access the extent of the tumor and the margins surrounding it. Once the tumor is excised, the surgeon also acts as a pathologist as the tissue samples are divided and examination is performed. These codes are not applicable if the surgeon does not act in both capacities.

Separate procedure codes can be assigned if a repair is performed. If Mohs surgery is performed the same day as a biopsy, and no prior pathology confirmation of a malignant diagnosis was made, the Mohs surgery would be reported with the diagnostic skin biopsy code(s) and the frozen section pathology code (88331) with a modifier 59. A coder can determine the correct code by knowing the stage performed, as noted in the documentation, and the number of specimens obtained.

Other Procedures (17340–17999)

These procedures tend to fall under the term *cosmetic*. This means that most insurance carriers do not recognize these CPT codes for payment because they are performed at the patient's request and not for medical necessity.

Breast (19000–19499)

The coding in this subsection involves only unilateral procedures. Depending on the insurance carrier, a modifier 50, RT (right) and/or LT (left), might be needed if the procedure is performed bilaterally.

If a biopsy is done on the same lesion that is excised, the biopsy is *not* coded separately. The biopsy is considered inclusive to the lesion removal.

Incision (19000–19030)

Code 19000—"Puncture aspiration of cyst of breast"—involves a physician inserting a needle into the breast cyst and drawing cyst fluid into a syringe. Each cyst is reported separately after the first cyst by using code 19001. The 19001 is an add-on code and must be used in conjunction with code 19000.

> **EXAMPLE:** Mrs. Page presented for a puncture aspiration of the breast. Dr. Calvin explained to her that there were three cysts that they would be aspirating fluid from. The first cyst was at the "2 o'clock" position, the second cyst was at "3 o'clock," and the third was at "6 o'clock." Mrs. Page tolerated the procedure well.

Dr. Calvin reported his services in this example using codes 19000 × 1, 19001 × 2.

A **mastotomy** is also known as a surgical incision of the breast. Code 19020 involves an incision over the tissue where a suspicious abscess, or tissue that might be suspicious, might be located. The abscess would be drained and sent for culture.

Code 19030— "Injection procedure only for mammary ductogram or galactogram"—involves injection of contrast material for radiographic study. A **mammary ductogram** is the study done on the mammary duct to the mammary gland that secretes milk from the breast. When reporting this code, remember to include the radiological piece of the procedure.

Excision (19081–19126)

Breast biopsies, cryosurgical ablation of fibroadenoma, and nipple exploration are reported with code range 19081 to 19126. A biopsy may be taken through an open or percutaneous procedure and may be completed with or without imaging guidance. If excision of the lesion is performed on the same lesion and at the same time as the biopsy, the code for the biopsy would not be reported in addition to the code for the excision. Review the extensive notation that appears in the CPT manual prior to code 19081 for additional information that applies to this range of codes.

Introduction (19281–19298)

These codes are for placement of devices into the breast for markers or other reasons. The markers indicate where lesions are for upcoming surgery. These markers make it easy for the surgeon to locate nonpalpable masses so the breast surgery can be done quickly and efficiently.

Mastectomy Procedures (19300–19307)

A **mastectomy** is the excision of the breast or breast tissue. This range of codes is used to report open procedures such as a partial or complete mastectomy. Coding from this range depends on documentation. If at all possible, the coder should read the operative report before assigning a code.

Mastectomy for gynecomastia (19300) is a code that is considered gender specific. This procedure is performed on the breast tissue of a male. This procedure does not include removal of muscle or lymph nodes.

The coder needs to review documentation to see how extensive the surgery was in order to determine whether the procedure was simple, subcutaneous, or radical. Talking with your surgeon is extremely helpful in understanding what was done during the procedure. A simple mastectomy (19303) does not involve the removal of muscle or lymph nodes. The lymph nodes may be biopsied, which would be included in the surgery. As the surgeon goes deeper, the code changes. Subcutaneous mastectomies involve the removal of breast tissue, but the outer skin and nipple are left intact. An implant may or may not be performed during the same operative session.

Repair and/or Reconstruction (19316–19499)

Justifying medical necessity is important when you are reporting these codes because some of them are looked at as cosmetic by insurance carriers. The reconstruction procedures include the insertion of prostheses or implants. The codes are reported for unilateral procedures, but they must be reported with a 50 modifier if done bilaterally.

Summary

- The integumentary system relates to the skin.
- There are three layers of the skin: the epidermis, dermis, and subcutaneous.
- The coder should determine whether the procedure performed is diagnostic or therapeutic.
- The surgical package includes E/M services performed the day of or one day prior to surgery, the surgery itself, and any postoperative management that falls within the norm of follow-up care.
- Understanding how to read the National Correct Coding Initiative is essential for any coder reporting surgical services.
- Incision and drainage (I&D) refer to surgically cutting over an area and then draining it.
- Debridement is a type of cleansing.
- Procedures performed on skin tags, benign and malignant lesions, and hyperkeratotic lesions are found in this subsection of the chapter.
- Wounds are classified into four classes: clean wound (Class I), clean-contaminated wound (Class II), contaminated wound (Class III), and dirty and infected (Class IV).
- Adjacent tissue transfer, rearrangements, and grafts are all coded to their respective subsections of the Surgery section.

Internet Links

To learn more about issues that relate to the integumentary system visit: ***https://www.aad.org/ and search on the word "procedure." Here you will find information about procedures, billing issues and other information that relates to the field of dermatology.***

Chapter Review

Fill in the Blank

Instructions: Fill in the blanks in the statements that follow.

1. Procedures completed to determine a diagnosis and establish a care plan are referred to as _____ procedures.

2. Procedures completed as part of the care plan and used as treatment for a diagnosis are called _____ procedures.

3. The surgical package is also referred to as the global package or _____.

4. The _____ was implemented to standardize proper coding and payment for Medicare Part B claims.

5. Unbundling occurs when procedures are performed and services are _____ coded, and submitted to an insurance company for payment.

6. A wound that has a very low infection rate (1–5%) and involves no inflammation or break in sterile technique is called a(n) _____.

7. A skin substitute for areas that require a temporary closure is called an acellular dermal _____.

8. Epidermal autograft is a graft of the _____ layer only.

9. Mohs micrographic surgery is a type of _____.

10. Incision and drainage refer to surgically cutting over an area and then _____ the area.

Coding Assignments

Instructions: Using a CPT manual, select the appropriate code for each of the following procedures:

1. I&D of pilonidal cyst _____

2. Debridement of seven nails _____

3. Repair of 5.3-cm superficial wound of neck _____

4. Dermabrasion for tattoo removal _____

5. Sacral pressure ulcer excision with primary closure _____

6. Cryotherapy for acne _____

7. Subcutaneous mastectomy _____

8. Excision of lactiferous duct fistula _____

9. Removal of intact mammary implant _____

10. Revision of reconstructed breast _____

11. Complex repair of nose—2.1 cm _____

12. Harvest of skin for tissue cultured skin autograft—85 sq cm _____

13. Destruction of malignant lesion of neck 2.5 cm by electrosurgery _____

14. Periprosthetic capsulectomy, breast _____

15. Correction of inverted nipples _____

16. Shaving of dermal lesion on face, 1.3-cm lesion diameter _____

17. Paring of three benign hyperkeratotic lesions _____

18. Excision of benign lesion of foot, excised diameter—3.3 cm _____

19. Intermediate repair of laceration on face—4.5 cm _____

20. Excision of ischial pressure ulcer with primary suture _____

21. Incision and drainage of seroma _____

22. Removal of 13 skin tags from upper trunk _____

23. Excision of benign lesion and margins of skin of ear, 0.8 cm _____

24. Treatment of superficial wound dehiscence with packing _____

25. Dermal facial chemical peel _____

26. Excision of excessive skin and subcutaneous tissue from the arm _____

27. Trochanteric pressure ulcer excision with skin flap closure _____

28. Removal of 12 skin tags _____

29. Excision of malignant lesion of face with an excised diameter of 2.3 cm _____

30. Intermediate repair of wound of neck measuring 13.1 cm _____

Case Studies

Review each case and indicate the correct code(s).

Case 1

Preoperative and postoperative diagnosis: 4-cm laceration of the left thigh.

Procedure: Repair of laceration

This 4-year-old male was prepped and draped in the usual fashion. The left thigh was cleansed, and 1% lidocaine was used to anesthetize the area. The laceration was measured and found to be 4 cm in length. The wound was examined, and no foreign bodies were found in the area. Eight sutures, placed in the subcutaneous fat layer of the skin, were used to close the wound. Additional sutures were placed to close the skin. The patient tolerated the procedure with no complications and was sent to the recovery area.

CPT code(s): _____

Case 2

Preoperative diagnosis: Warts

Postoperative diagnosis: One wart on third toe of right foot and two warts on fourth toe of left foot.

Due to the size of the warts, the patient was taken to the operating room for wart removal. The left foot was infiltrated with 1% lidocaine. The CO_2 laser was prepared, and the wart on the right third toe was vaporized. The two larger warts on the fourth toe of the left foot were then vaporized. All areas were vaporized to a depth of 1.5 cm. A 3-mm margin was vaporized around all the lesions. Noting no complications, the patient was transferred to the recovery room in stable condition.

CPT code(s): _____

Case 3

Preoperative and postoperative diagnosis: Scar on left eyebrow/forehead

Operation: Left eyebrow/forehead scar revision

Anesthesia: General

This 14-year-old female sustained an oblique laceration to the medial aspect of the left eyebrow. The laceration extended superiorly above the eyebrow hairs to the lower aspect of the forehead. Initially, this was repaired in the emergency department over a year ago. The scar has not healed well.

The patient was placed in the supine position and prepped and draped in the normal fashion. IV Kefzol was given. The portion of the scar was marked out with a marking pen marking the 1-cm inferomedial area. After this, 1 cc of 1% Lidocaine with 1:2000,000 of epinephrine was injected. Using a #15 blade, the widened portion of the scar was incised and then excised deeply in the subcutaneous area. The superior aspect of the incision undermining was completed, and the wound was brought together without tension. The deep layers were closed with buried 4-0 PDS sutures and a running subcuticular 5-0 Moncryl was used to close the skin. There was minimal blood loss. The patient was sent to the recovery room in satisfactory condition.

CPT code(s): _____

Case 4

Preoperative and postoperative diagnosis: Painful enlarging right vulvar cyst

Operation performed: Excision of right vulvar cyst

Reason for surgery: This 34-year-old female patient has a vulvar cyst that is causing pain and discomfort.

The patient was taken to the OR and placed in the supine position. IV analgesia was started, and then she has placed in the dorsal lithotomy position. The surgical site was prepared with Lidocaine 1%, and then epinephrine and bicarb was administered. A 20-mm cyst was seen on the medial right upper labia minora. A #15 blade was used to make a 1.2-cm incision, freeing the cyst. The cyst was removed. The area was closed with 5-0 Vicryl running interrupted sutures. The patient tolerated the procedure. She was placed back in the supine position and transferred to the recovery room in satisfactory condition.

CPT code(s): _____

Case 5

Preoperative and postoperative diagnosis: Laxity of skin and muscle of the abdomen

Procedure: Abdominoplasty

The 46-year-old female patient desired to have an abdominoplasty because of the lax skin, subcutaneous tissue, and muscle of her abdomen. The risks of the procedure were explained to the patient, and she signed the consent to have the procedure.

When the patient presented to the operatory area, the midline of the abdomen was marked for the planned incisions. The abdomen was prepped, and 45 cc of a local infiltration of 1% Lidocaine with 1:1000000 dilution of epinephrine was administered along the planned incisional lines.

A skin incision was made along the marking, which was carried through the skin and subcutaneous tissue with Bovie electrocautery. Dissection of the tissue was completed down to the fascial musculature of the abdomen. A periumbical incison was made, and the umbilical stalk was freely dissected. Additional dissection occurred, and a moderate amount of redundant skin was assessed. Using a #15 blade and Bovie electrocautery, a superior incision was made. The tissue along the upper incision was thinned, and, with hemostatis achieved, the site was irrigated with aline. Above and below the umbilicus, a plication of the rectus muscle was performed. With the patient in the semiflexed position, several tacking 2-0 Vicryl sutures were placed. An incision was then made at the iliac crest bilaterally using a #15 blade. Using Bovie electrocautery, the periumbilical area was defatted. 3-0 Vicryl sutures were used to close. On both sides, drains were placed and sutured in place. Closure

(continues)

(continued)

was completed with additional 3-0 Vicryl sutures and subcuticuar 4-0 Vicryl sutures. 3-0 and 4-0 Vicryl sutures, followed by 5-0 nylon sutures, were used to close the periumbical area. The wound was dressed. There was approximately 55 cc of blood loss. After extubating the patient, she was transferred to the recovery area in stable condition.

CPT code(s): _____

Case 6

Preoperative and postoperative diagnosis: Bilateral breast hypoplasia and symmetry

Operation performed: Bilateral augmentation mammoplasty

The patient was prepped and draped in the usual sterile fashion, and then general anesthesia was achieved. Local infiltration with 1% Lidocaine with 1:100,00 dilution of epinephrine was performed. On the right breast, using a #15 blade, an inframmammary incision was made and carried through the skin and subcutaneous issue. A Bovie electrocautery dissection was completed down to the pectoralis muscle, and a submuscular pocket was created. Saline was used to irrigate the site. Hemostasis was achieved.

The same procedure then was completed on the left breast, with dissection performed in a symmetric fashion to recreate a submuscular pocket. Two implants were inspected, and they were placed in the submuscular pockets. Additional dissection was performed on the left side to achieve symmetry. 3-0 Vicryl sutures were used to close the muscle layer. The subcutaneous deep dermal layer was then closed with 3-0 Vicryl sutures and the subcuticlar with 4-0 Vicryl sutures. The wounds were dressed, and a Velcro breast band was placed on the superior aspect of the breast. After extubing the patient, she was sent to recovery in stable condition.

CPT code(s): _____

Case 7

Preoperative diagnosis: Cyst

Postoperative diagnosis: Pending review of pathology findings

Procedure: Fine needle aspiration cyst

This 59-year-old male patient was prepped and draped in the usual fashion for a fine needle aspiration. The cyst on his right shoulder was identified, and the area was cleansed. A 25-gauge needle was guided, by palpation, into the cyst, and the fluid was removed from the cyst. The fluid was sent to pathology. The needle was withdrawn, and a bandage was placed over the wound site. There were no complications.

CPT code(s): _____

Case 8

Podiatry Note

This 67-year-old diabetic patient is seen today for debridement of all nails on his right and left feet. He states that he is having a problem walking, and his feet are painful. The nails on both feet were debrided. There were no signs of infection or open wounds. He was instructed to continue to follow up with me on a regular basis to monitor any possible podiatric conditions due to his diabetes.

CPT code(s): _____

Case 9

ER Note

This 15-year-old male patient was playing and ran into a tree, and his hand was injured. His left thumb is swollen, and there is blood present beneath the nail. After the hand was cleansed, Lidocaine was used to anesthetize the area, and then an electrocautery needle was used to pierce the nail plate. The hematoma was drained successfully. For the site to drain, a loose dressing was put in place. Instructions were given on dressing changes. He was instructed to see his primary care provider if he experiences increased pain and to schedule a follow-up appointment within seven days.

CPT code(s): _____

Case 10

Office Procedure Note

This 39-year-old patient returns to the office today because of a defect on the nail of his left big toe. He was seen three times in the last four months for this problem. This defect is very suspicious, and I felt it best to biopsy a portion of the nail plate and bed. The sample was sent to pathology. I told the patient that he will be called with the results, and then I will decide how to proceed.

CPT code(s): _____

Musculoskeletal System

Chapter Outline

Introduction

Guidelines Related to the National Correct Coding Initiative (NCCI)

Abbreviations Related to the Musculoskeletal System

Anatomy of the Musculoskeletal System

General Procedures (20100–20999)

Procedures for Musculoskeletal System by Body Site

Arthrodesis

Application of Casts and Strapping (29000–29799)

Endoscopy/Arthroscopy (29800–29999)

Summary

Internet Links

Chapter Review

Coding Assignments

Case Studies

Learning Objectives

At the conclusion of this chapter, you should be able to:

1. Define key terms related to coding procedures performed on the musculoskeletal system.
2. Define abbreviations related to the musculoskeletal system.
3. Describe the basic anatomy and functions of the musculoskeletal system.
4. Define common procedures performed on the musculoskeletal system.
5. Apply the specific guidelines for the musculoskeletal system to this chapter.
6. Select CPT codes for procedures completed on the musculoskeletal system.
7. Identify and code procedures for the musculoskeletal system from case studies.

Key Terms

arthrodesis	arthroscopy	cartilage	closed treatment
arthroplasty	arthrotomy	casts	curettage
arthroscope	augmentation	closed reduction	debridement

diagnostic arthroscopy

diagnostic endoscopy

dislocation

dynamic splint

endoscope

excision

exostosis

external fixation

fascia

fasciectomy

fixation

genioplasty

hip arthroplasty

imaging guidance

incisions

internal fixation

knee arthroplasty

Le Fort fracture

ligaments

local autograft

manipulation

morselized allograft

morselized autograft

muscle

open reduction

open reduction internal fixation (ORIF)

open treatment

ostectomy

osteoclasis

osteoectomy

osteoplasty

osteotomy

percutaneous skeletal fixation

reconstruction

reduction

sinogram

skeletal traction

skin traction

static splint

strapping

structural allograft

structural autograft

surgical arthroscopy

surgical endoscopy

synovectomy

tendon

wound exploration

Introduction

Procedures performed on the musculoskeletal system involve the bones, muscles, tendons, cartilage, and soft tissue. The range of codes that is used for the musculoskeletal system section of CPT includes codes 20100–29999. Coders need to become familiar with the definitions that are found throughout this section of the CPT manual. At the start of the section, under the General heading, codes 20100–20999 describe a number of general procedures. The remaining sections are then further organized from head to toe. Within each subsection, the codes are organized by the type of procedure. For example, code range 21010–21499 is used to code procedures performed on the head, and code range 21501–21899 is used to code procedures performed on the neck (soft tissue) and thorax. At the start of the chapter, an extensive note discusses coding guidance and definitions that are used for codes within the musculoskeletal system. Prior to code selection, read the note and become familiar with the coding guidance and definitions.

Guidelines Related to the National Correct Coding Initiative (NCCI)

The student will need to reference the following website to obtain the most current NCCI guideline information related to the musculoskeletal system.

1. Log on to *http://www.cms.gov/Medicare/Coding/NationalCorrectCodInitED/index.html*.
2. Scroll to the section titled "Downloads."
3. Click the link for the most current "NCCI Policy Manual for Medicare Services."
4. A box will appear that requires you to click "Open."
5. Click on "Chapter 4" for guidelines specific to the Musculoskeletal System coding.

Abbreviations Related to the Musculoskeletal System

The following is a list of abbreviations that are common to the musculoskeletal system.

Abbreviations	Definitions
AE	Most often-seen in documentation when referencing above-elbow amputation
AK	Most often-seen in documentation when referencing above-knee amputation
AP	anterioposterior
BE	below elbow—same context as AE
BK	below knee—same context as AK
C1, C2, etc.	cervical vertebra
C1–C7	cervical vertebrae, 1 through 7
CR	closed reduction
CTS	carpal tunnel syndrome
DIP	distal interphalangeal joint
DJD	degenerative joint disease
DTR	deep tendon reflex
EMG	electromyography
FM	fibromyalgia
Fx	fracture
IS	intracostal space
L1, L2, etc.	lumbar vertebra
L1–L5	lumbar vertebrae, 1 through 5
MCP	metacarpophalangeal joint
OA	osteoarthritis
ORIF	open reduction internal fixation
PKR	partial knee replacement
PIP	proximal intraphalangeal joint
ROM	range of motion
S1, S2, etc.	sacral vertebra
T1, T2, etc.	thoracic vertebra
T1–T12	thoracic vertebrae, 1 through 12
TENS	transcutaneous electric nerve stimulation
THA	total hip arthroplasty
THR	total hip replacement
TKA	total knee arthroplasty
TKR	total knee replacement

Anatomy of the Musculoskeletal System

To code correctly for the musculoskeletal system, coders must have an understanding of the anatomy of the musculoskeletal system and medical terms that are used in describing procedures. Table 6-1 summarizes common terms that are used in relation to the musculoskeletal system. Figure 6-1 illustrates a lateral view of the adult human skeleton. Figure 6-2 shows the anterior view of the human skeleton, and Figure 6-3 shows the posterior view of the human skeleton.

TABLE 6-1 Musculoskeletal System Terms

Term	Definition
Arthrodesis	Surgical repair or reconstruction fixation of a joint.
Arthroplasty	Plastic surgery of a joint.
Arthroscopy	Examination of the interior of a joint by use of an arthroscope.
Arthrotomy	A surgical incision of a joint.
Cartilage	Thin sheets of fibrous connective tissue.
Closed treatment	Treatment of fracture sites. When closed treatment occurs, the fracture site is not surgically exposed or opened. There are three types of closed treatment: (1) treatment without manipulation, (2) treatment with manipulation, (3) treatment with or without traction.
Debridement	The removal of foreign material or devitalized or contaminated tissue from an area.
Dislocation	The displacement of a bone from normal anatomical position.
Exostosis	A benign bony growth that projects from the surface of a bone.
Fascia	A sheet of fibrous tissue.
Fixation	The process of suturing or fastening a structure in place.
Ligaments	Bands of connective tissue that bind the joints together and connect the articular bones and cartilages to cause movement.
Manipulation	The reduction of a dislocation or fracture.
Muscle	Tissue that is composed of fibers and cells that cause movement and are able to contract. There are three types of muscle: striated, cardiac, and smooth.
Open treatment	Treatment of a fracture when the site is surgically exposed and visualized. The site may have been opened for placement of internal fixation, but this does not always occur.
Ostectomy	Removal of bone.
Osteoclasis	The process of creating a surgical fracture of a bone to correct a deformity.
Osteoplasty	Plastic surgery completed on bone tissue.
Osteotomy	Sawing or cutting of a bone.
Percutaneous skeletal fixation	Fracture treatment in which the fracture site is neither open nor closed. Fixation is placed across the fracture site, typically under the guidance of x-ray imaging.
Skeletal traction	The application of force to a limb by a clamp, pin, screw, or wire that is attached to bone.
Skin traction	The application of force to a limb using felt that is applied to the skin.
Tendon	A dense fibrous band of connective tissue that attaches muscles to bones.

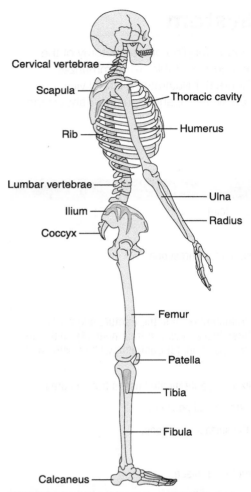

FIGURE 6-1 Lateral View of the Adult Human Skeleton

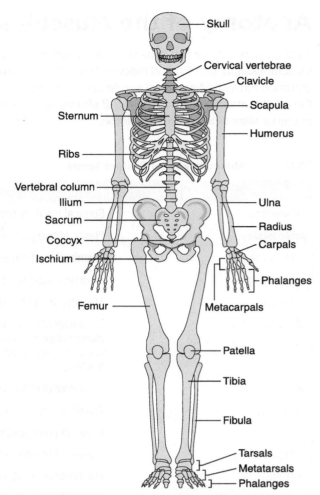

FIGURE 6-2 Anterior View of the Adult Human Skeleton

General Procedures (20100–20999)

Codes 20100–20999 represent general procedures that are performed on the musculoskeletal system. These codes are used for various anatomical structures and are not limited to any one body area, such as the head or shoulder.

Wound Exploration—Trauma (20100–20103)

Codes 20100–20103—wound exploration—trauma—are used to code wounds that occur because of a traumatic injury. **Wound exploration** is completed to determine the extent of an injury and includes surgical exploration of the wound area with enlargement of the wound. Also included is the debridement of the area, removal of any foreign material, coagulation or ligation of minor subcutaneous and/or muscular blood vessels, or the subcutaneous tissues, muscle fascia, and/or muscle. It should also be noted that this range of codes contains only separate procedure codes. Therefore, if additional procedures are reported, these codes are not reported. Coders should be familiar with the additional information that is noted in the CPT manual under the heading Wound Exploration. The codes are differentiated by site: neck, chest, abdomen/flank/back, or extremity.

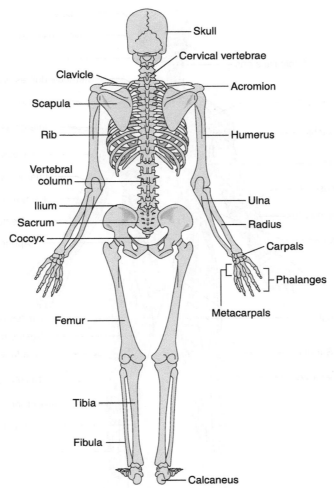

FIGURE 6-3 **Posterior View of the Adult Human Skeleton**

Excisions (20150–20251)

Excisions of the epiphyseal bar and biopsies of muscles and bones are coded using the range 20150–20251. When selecting codes for the biopsies of muscle or bone, the coder needs to determine the following:

- What was the site of the biopsy?
- Was the biopsy superficial or deep?
- Was a percutaneous needle used?
- Was the procedure completed as an open procedure?

Documentation must be reviewed to answer these questions in order to select the proper code. For example, code 20206 is used to report a percutaneous needle biopsy of a muscle, while code 20251 is used to report an open biopsy of a lumbar or cervical vertebral body.

Figure 6-4 illustrates the anterior view of the major muscles of the body, and Figure 6-5 illustrates the posterior view of the major muscles of the body.

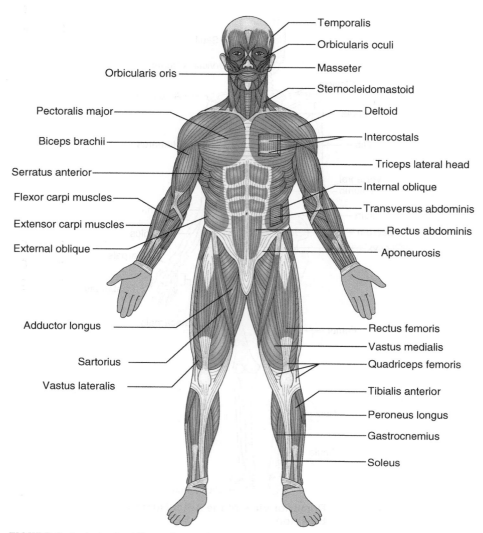

FIGURE 6-4 Anterior View of the Major Muscles of the Body

Introduction or Removal (20500–20697)

Code range 20500–20697 is used to report aspiration and injection procedures, as well as the application of halo devices, pins, wires, and other external fixation systems. Table 6-2 describes the codes from this subsection. It should be noted that many of these procedures are completed with **imaging guidance**. Imaging guidance is the use of radiological techniques or procedures to visualize the placement of a needle, a catheter, or another device. When imaging guidance is used, additional codes are reported. Notations are found after the code, directing coders to use the additional imaging guidance codes.

TABLE 6-2 Introduction or Removal (20500–20697)

Code(s)	Description
20500–20501	This code range is used to report injections into the sinus tract.
	These codes differentiate between therapeutic and diagnostic procedures. Code 20500 is used to report a therapeutic injection and is a separate procedure code. Code 20501 is a diagnostic procedure, performed on the sinus tract, also referred to as a **sinogram**. An additional code, 76080, is used to report the radiological supervision and interpretation when it occurs.

(continues)

TABLE 6-2 *(continued)*

Code(s)	Description
20520–20525	Removal of a foreign body is reported with this range of codes. Foreign bodies can become embedded in the muscle or tendon sheath. When this occurs, the foreign body is removed. These codes are used to report the removal of the foreign body and are differentiated by the term *simple, deep,* or *complicated.* Provider documentation must support the use of code 20525 by indicating the depth of the foreign body at the time of the procedure.
20526	Local anesthetics or steroids therapeutically injected into the carpal tunnel area to relieve pain are reported with this code. The code reports an injection into one extremity; however, treatment can be completed on one extremity or bilaterally. When completed bilaterally, modifier 50 is required by some payers; other payers prefer that the code be reported twice.
20550–20561	Codes 20550-20553 are used to report injections into the tendon sheath, ligament, or aponeurosis and muscles. When reporting codes 20552–20553, the coder must be able to identify the number of muscles involved, because the codes differentiate among the number of muscles involved in the procedure. Codes 20560 and 20561 report needle insertions without injections and are differentiated by the numbers of muscles.
20555	Placement of needles or catheters into muscle and/or soft tissue for subsequent interstitial radioelement application (at time of or subsequent to the procedure) is reported with this code. Prior to using this code, the CPT manual should be referenced because it provides notes that clarify proper use of this code specific to the services rendered.
20600–20611	This range of codes reports arthrocentesis, aspiration, and/or injections into joints and bursa. Code selection depends on the site of the procedure: • Small joint or bursa—such as fingers or toes, reported with code 20600 without ultrasound guidance. Code 20604 reports the procedure with ultrasound guidance, with permanent recording and reporting. • Intermediate joint or bursa—such as temporomandibular, acromioclavicular, ankle, elbow, wrist, or olecranon bursa, reported with code 20605 without ultrasound guidance. Code 20606 reports the procedure with ultrasound guidance, with permanent recording and reporting. • Major joint or bursa—such as knee joint, hip, shoulder, or subacromial bursa, reported with code 20610 without ultrasound guidance. Code 20611 reports the procedure with ultrasound guidance, with permanent recording and reporting.
20612 and 20615	Aspiration and/or injection procedures for treatment of ganglion cysts and bone cysts are reported with code 20612 for ganglion cyst(s), any location, and with code 20615 for bone cyst.
20650–20694	Insertion, application, and removal of wires, pins, and halo devices are coded to this range of codes. Coders must be able to determine the following: • Site of the procedure • Type of device used—e.g., wires, pins, halo • Type of procedure—application versus removal versus adjustment or revision
20696–20705	Applications of multiplane, unilateral, and external fixation with stereotactic computer-assisted adjustment, including imaging, are reported with codes 20696 to 20697. Code 20696 is reported for the initial and subsequent alignments, assessments, and computation(s) of adjustment schedules, while code 20697 reports the exchange of each strut or the removal and replacement. Code 20697 is not reported with codes 20692 or 20696 and is modifier 51 exempt Codes 20700 to 20705 are add-on codes. Review the CPT manual for the definitions of the codes and for a listing of the codes that these codes are used in conjunction with.

Replantation (20802–20838)

This range of codes, 20802–20838, is used to report the replantation of a part of the upper extremities or a foot following complete amputation. Codes are differentiated by site as follows:

- Code 20802—Arm, includes surgical neck of humerus through elbow joint. The reattachment occurs between the elbow and shoulder.

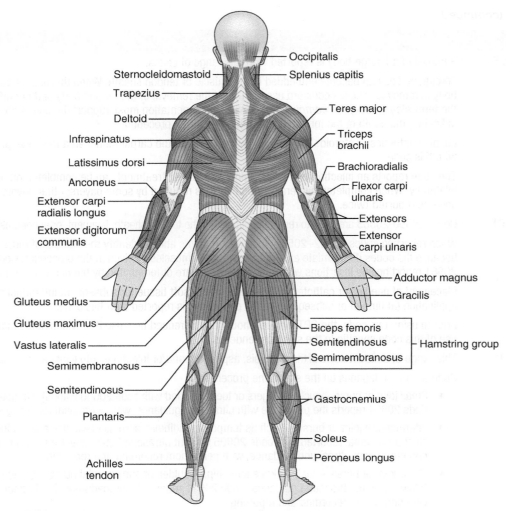

FIGURE 6-5 Posterior View of the Major Muscles of the Body

- Code 20805—Forearm, includes radius and ulna to radial carpal joint. The reattachment occurs between the wrist and elbow.
- Code 20808—Hand, includes hand through metacarpophalangeal joint(s). The reattachment of the hand occurs between the wrist and fingers.
- Code 20816—Digit, excluding thumb, includes metacarpophalangeal joint to insertion of flexor sublimis tendon. The reattachment of one finger, excluding the thumb, occurs at or near the finger's articulation with its corresponding metacarpal bone.
- Code 20822—Digit, excluding thumb, includes distal tip to sublimis tendon insertion. The reattachment of one finger, excluding the thumb, between the fingertip and the attachment of the finger to the hand.
- Code 20824—Thumb, includes carpometacarpal joint to MP joint. The reattachment of the thumb to the hand.
- Code 20827—Thumb, includes distal tip to MP joint. The reattachment of the thumb distal to where the thumb attaches to the hand.
- Code 20838—Foot. The reattachment of the foot at or near the ankle.

Following each one of these codes, a notation appears that instructs the coder as how to report an incomplete amputation for each site described in the code. Locate these notations in the CPT manual.

For example, for code 20802, the following notation appears: "To report replantation of incomplete arm amputation, see specific code[s] for repair of bones[s], ligament[s], tendons[s], nerves[s], or blood vessels[s] with modifier 52." The use of modifier 52 indicates that there is a reduced service.

Because of the process of replantation, the surgery can take up to 12 hours to complete and is performed under general anesthesia. Prior to performing the surgery, the amputated body structure is kept cold (see Figure 6-6). Replantation involves the repair of soft tissue and tendons, bone approximation, and blood vessel repair.

FIGURE 6-6 Preservation of a Digit for Replantation

Grafts or Implants (20900–20939)

Codes 20900–20939, Grafts (or Implants), are used to code cartilage, bone, fascia lata tendon, and tissue grafts of the musculoskeletal system. Coders should note that the notation found in the CPT manual following the heading for this subsection instructs coders not to assign modifier 62 with this code range. Table 6-3 summarizes the codes in this range.

TABLE 6-3 Grafts or Implants (20900–20939)

Code(s)	Description
20900 and 20902	These codes report bone grafts from any donor site. The codes differentiate between minor or small (code 20900) versus major or large (code 20902). Provider documentation must justify code selection.
20910 and 20912	Grafting of cartilage is reported with this code range. The site of the graft is the determining factor for code assignment. Use code 20910 for costochondral and code 20912 for the nasal septum. It should be noted that ear cartilage grafting is not coded to this subsection, but to 21235. In the CPT manual locate the notation that appears after code 20912 that gives direction for the use of code 21235.
20920 and 20922	This range reports fascia lata grafting. The codes are differentiated by the use of a stripper (code 20920) or by incision and area exposure (code 20922).
20924	This code reports tendon grafts from a distance. During this procedure, a tendon is dissected and removed.
+20930	This code reports a **morselized allograft** for spine surgery or placement of osteopromotive material. During this procedure, small pieces of bone are harvested to form the graft from a source other than the patient. This is an add-on code. The CPT manual should be referenced with regard to primary codes that this code would be reported with.

(continues)

TABLE 6-3 (*continued*)

Code(s)	Description
+20931	A **structural allograft** for spine surgery only is reported with this add-on code. This procedure involves a large segment of bone being harvested from a donor source, other than the patient, and placed into the interspace of the spine. This is an add-on code. The CPT manual should be referenced with regard to primary codes that this code would be reported with.
+20932 +20933 +20934	These three codes are all add-on codes for allografts, which includes templating cutting, placement, and internal fixation when performed. These codes are futher differentiated as follows: code 20932 includes an osteoarticular graft including articular surface and contiguous bone, code 20933 includes a partial hemicortical intercalary graft, while code 20934 includes a complete intercalary graft. Prior to assigning these codes, the coder must reference the instructional notations that follow each code that delineate the codes that should not be reported with codes 20932, 20933, and 20934.
+20936	A **local autograft** for spine surgery is reported with this code. During this procedure, only one incision is used to harvest the graft and to complete the procedure. The graft is from the ribs, spinous process, or laminar fragments. This is an add-on code. The CPT manual should be referenced with regard to primary codes that this code is reported with.
+20937	This code is used to report a **morselized autograft** for spine surgery that is completed by harvesting small pieces of the patient's own bone through a separate incision. A common harvest site is the iliac crest. This is an add-on code. The CPT manual should be referenced with regard to primary codes reported with this code.
+20938	A **structural autograft** for spine surgery is reported with this code. During this procedure, a bicortical or tricortical graft is harvested through a separate incision. This is an add-on code. The CPT manual should be referenced with regard to primary codes reported with this code.
20939	This code is used for spine surgery only, to report a bone marrow aspiration for bone grafting through a separate skin or fascial incision. This code is an add-on code and is to be listed separately in addition to the code for the primary procedure completed. Coders should reference the instructional notations that appear in the CPT manual after the code description for additional instructions that impact the assignment of code 20939.

Other Procedures (20950–20999)

Other general procedures that are related to the musculoskeletal system are coded with code range 20950–20999, titled "Other Procedures." Procedures in this range include the following:

- Monitoring of interstitial fluid pressure
- Bone grafts with microvascular anastomosis
- Free osteocutaneous flaps with microvascular anastomosis
- Electrical stimulation and ultrasound stimulation to aid bone healing
- Ablation of bone tumors
- Computer-assisted surgical navigational procedures, with or without images

It should be noted that several guidance notes appear in this section of the CPT manual.

Exercise 6.1—Check Your Understanding

Other General Procedures, Code Range 20000–20999

Fill in the Blank

Enter the appropriate term(s) to complete each of the following statements. Reference the CPT manual.

1. Code 20251 is used to code an open biopsy of a vertebral body in the _____ or _____ area.

(*continues*)

Exercise 6.1 – *continued*

2. Codes 20100–20103 are used to code the exploration of penetrating wounds and are differentiated by the following sites: neck, _____, abdomen/flank/back, and _____.

3. A(n) _____ autograft for spine surgery is completed by harvesting small pieces of the patient's own bone through a separate incision.

4. Electrical stimulation to aid bone healing is coded by using codes 20974 and 20975. Code 20974 is for a(n) _____ approach, whereas 20975 is for a(n) _____ approach.

5. Code 20206 is used to report a biopsy of a muscle using a(n) _____.

6. A diagnostic procedure performed on the sinus tract is known as a(n) _____.

7. When selecting codes for biopsies of muscle or bone, the coder needs to know the site of the biopsy and whether the procedure was performed as an open procedure or by using a percutaneous needle. The coder also needs to know _____.

8. The use of radiological techniques or procedures to visualize the placement of a needle, catheter, or other device is known as _____.

9. Code _____ is used to report placement of a needle or catheter in muscle and/or soft tissue for subsequent interstitial radioelement application.

10. The determining factor for code assignment of cartilage grafting is _____.

Procedures for Musculoskeletal System by Body Site

As mentioned at the beginning of this chapter, the codes for the musculoskeletal system are organized predominantly from head to toe. Table 6-4 lists the subsections and the codes for each.

TABLE 6-4 Musculoskeletal Code Ranges According to Body Site

Title of Code Range	Code Range
Head	21010–21499
Neck (Soft Tissues) and Thorax	21501–21899
Back and Flank	21920–21936
Spine (Vertebral Column)	22010–22899
Abdomen	22900–22999
Shoulder	23000–23929
Humerus (Upper Arm) and Elbow	23930–24999
Forearm and Wrist	25000–25999
Hand and Fingers	26010–26989
Pelvis and Hip Joint	26990–27299
Femur (Thigh Region) and Knee Joint	27301–27599
Leg (Tibia and Fibula) and Ankle	27600–27899
Foot and Toes	28001–28899

Within each subsection, the codes are then organized by types of procedures, mainly staying within the following outline:

1. Incision
2. Excision
3. Introduction or Removal
4. Repair, Revision, and/or Reconstruction
5. Fracture and/or Dislocation
6. Other Procedures

Additional procedural headings are added when necessary, but most of the subsection is organized as outlined here. Because the organization is repetitive, coders need to understand the main terms that relate to each procedural heading.

Incision

Incisions are made into musculoskeletal structures for a variety of reasons:

- Exploration for diagnostic purposes
- Drainage of an abscess, with or without bone removal
- Drainage of a hematoma, with or without bone removal
- Removal of calcareous deposits
- Removal of foreign bodies

These procedures are easily located in the CPT manual by referencing the terms *incision* or *incision and drainage* in the index and then locating the site into which the incision was made or the reason for the incision. These procedures also can be located in the index by referencing the procedure name. For incisions made into a joint, physicians record the medical term arthrotomy. This term also can be referenced in the index.

> **EXAMPLE:** Dr. Smith completed an incision and drainage of the hip joint area because of a hematoma. The coder should reference the terms incision and drainage in the index and then locate the reason for the incision and drainage (I&D), hematoma, and then the site hip. Code 26990 would be found in the index.

Remember to always check the main section of the code book to verify the code selection!

Exercise 6.2—Check Your Understanding

Incision

For each procedure listed, select the appropriate CPT code.

1. Fasciotomy of toe _____
2. Open tenotomy of hip flexor of right side _____
3. Drainage of abscess of finger _____
4. I&D of bursa of left wrist _____
5. Arthrotomy of elbow with removal of foreign body _____
6. Incision and drainage of deep abscess of the soft tissue of the thorax _____
7. Temporomandibular joint arthrotomy _____
8. Incision of bone cortex of shoulder _____
9. I&D of elbow for deep abscess _____
10. Incision of flexor tendon sheath of wrist _____

Excision

An **excision** is the surgical removal of tissue or a structure. Excisions within the musculoskeletal system include removals of soft tissue, soft tissue tumors, bursa, bone cysts or benign tumors, bone, cartilage, synovium, tendon, and other joint structures. The musculoskeletal excision codes are differentiated by:

- Anatomical site
- Structure excised
- Partial versus complete excision
- Accompanying procedures

To locate these codes in the index, the coder should reference the term *excision* or the medical name of the procedure. Coders must read the operative notes carefully to determine the extent of the excision and whether any accompanying procedures were performed. Common excisional procedures of the musculoskeletal system include:

Fasciectomy—Removal of fascia

Osteoectomy—Removal of bone

Synovectomy—Removal of the synovial membrane of a joint

Curettage—The process of removing tissue by scraping

Exercise 6.3—Check Your Understanding

Excision

For the following procedures, select the appropriate CPT code.

1. Interphalangeal joint excisions of the proximal end of two toes _____

2. Metatarsectomy _____

3. Radical resection for tumor of ulna _____

4. Partial acromionectomy with release of coracoacromial ligament _____

5. Excision of mandible _____

6. Radical resection of tumor of the phalanx of the toe _____

7. Arthrotomy of ankle with synovectomy _____

8. Hamstring muscle neurectomy _____

9. Ischial bursa excision _____

10. Radical resection of sarcoma of the soft tissue of the hand—3.5 cm _____

Introduction and Removal

Codes that fall into the range titled Introduction and Removal include the following types of procedures:

- Removal of foreign bodies
- Injection procedures for radiological procedures
- Application of fixation devices
- Impression and custom preparation of prosthesis
- Implant or prosthesis removal

Codes for removals can be located in the index by referencing the term *removal* and then locating the site.

EXAMPLE: Dr. Jones completed the removal of a left wrist prosthesis. To locate this procedure in the index, the coder should reference the term *removal,* then *prosthesis,* and then the term *wrist.* Code range 25250–25251 is listed. Locate the codes in the body of the CPT text; the correct code to select would be 25250.

Other index entries that are applicable to this range of codes include the following:

- Injection
- Application
- Application of external fixation device
- Fixation device, application
- Implant removal
- Prosthesis

Exercise 6.4—Check Your Understanding

Introduction and Removal

For each procedure listed, select the correct CPT code.

1. Impression and custom preparation of orbital prosthesis _____

2. Injection procedure for shoulder arthrography _____

3. Deep removal of a foreign body in the foot _____

4. Removal of implant of hand _____

5. Injection for temporomandibular joint arthrography _____

6. Exploration of the wrist with removal of a deep foreign body _____

7. Therapeutic injection of sinus tract _____

8. Deep removal of a foreign body in the shoulder_____

9. Removal of humeral and ulnar components of a prosthesis _____

10. Manipulation of wrist under anesthesia _____

Repair, Revision, and Reconstruction

Repair, revision, and reconstruction procedures are completed to correct an anomaly or injury to an anatomical structure. These codes are differentiated by:

- Site
- Type of procedure; for example, reconstruction, reduction of muscle and bone, and muscle and tendon transfers and repairs
- Accompanying procedures; such as bone grafts, resection of ribs, tendon grafts, fixation, and plastic repairs

To locate these codes in the index, reference the following terms:

- Reconstruction, then the anatomical site
- Repair, then the anatomical site
- Tendon
- Muscle, then repair or revision
- The specific name of the muscle, tendon, joint, or anatomical site

EXAMPLE: Dr. Hand performs a repair of the carpometacarpal joint. This can be located in the index under the term *carpometacarpal joint*, then *repair*. The correct code is 25447.

Coders should also have an understanding of certain terms when coding in the various repair, revision, and reconstruction sections of the musculoskeletal system. Table 6-5 summarizes medical procedures and their definitions, and code examples for repairs, revisions, and reconstructions completed on the musculoskeletal system.

TABLE 6-5 Repair, Revision, and Reconstruction of the Musculoskeletal System

Term	Definition	Code Examples
Genioplasty	Plastic surgery of the chin These codes are differentiated by the type of approach and the additional procedures that occur, such as augmentation, sliding osteotomy, and grafts.	21120–21123
Augmentation	Surgically increasing the size of an anatomical structure Codes 21125–21127 are used to report mandibular body or angle augmentation. The codes are differentiated by the use of prosthetic materials or bone grafts.	21125 and 21127
Reconstruction	Surgical rebuilding of an anatomical structure Multiple types of reconstructions are completed in the musculoskeletal system. The term *reconstruction* means that the structure was surgically rebuilt to attempt to repair the structure. For example, reconstructions of fractures to the maxilla are relatively common. A common type of maxillar fracture is a **Le Fort fracture**, a bilateral fracture of the maxilla. Le Fort fractures are differentiated according to Le Fort I, Le Fort II, and Le Fort III, depending on the degree of injury. Figure 6-7 illustrates a reconstruction of a Le Fort I fracture.	21141–21160 Le Forts
Arthroplasty	Plastic repair of a joint Common arthroplasty procedures include • **Hip arthroplasty**—the surgical repair or reconstruction of the hip • **Knee arthroplasty**—the surgical repair or reconstruction of a knee Figure 6-8 illustrates a total hip arthroplasty with a prosthesis in place, and a knee arthroplasty with polyethylene and metal components to replace the surfaces of the knee joint. When coding for knee arthroplasty, the coder must reference the operative report to determine the extent of the procedure and the compartments in which the surgery was performed. The codes are differentiated by medial *or* lateral compartments versus medial *and* lateral compartments.	27130- Arthroplasty—total hip 27440–27447 Arthroplasty—knee

Exercise 6.5—Check Your Understanding

Repair, Revision, and Reconstruction

For the following procedures, select the appropriate CPT code.

1. Arthroplasty of the patella with prosthesis _____

2. Whitman's acetabuloplasty _____

3. Fascial defect repair of the leg _____

4. Lengthening of the flexor tendon of the left hand _____

5. Release of thumb contracture _____

6. Open hamstring tenotomy of single tendon, knee to hip _____

7. Repair of dislocating peroneal tendons with fibular osteotomy _____

8. Midtarsal capsulotomy _____

9. Osteotomy of femoral neck _____

10. Anterior tibial tubercleplasty _____

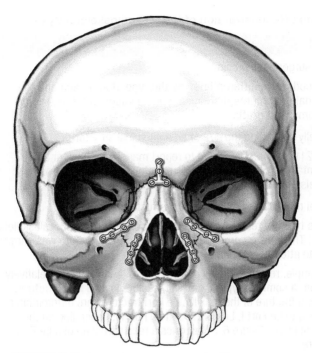

FIGURE 6-7 Reconstruction of a Le Fort
I Fracture

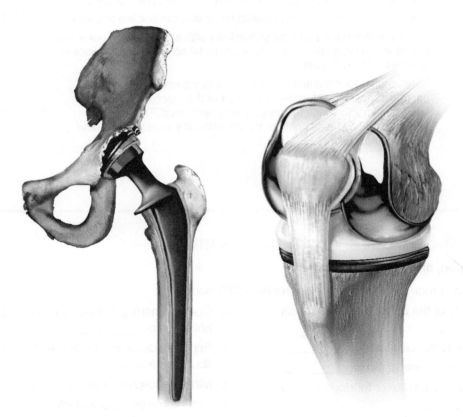

FIGURE 6-8 Total Hip Replacement and Total Knee Replacement
with Prosthesis

Fracture/Dislocation

Fractures and **dislocations**, a displacement of a structure, are treated in a variety of fashions. In order to select a code properly, the coder must be able to determine the following:

1. Location of the fracture
2. Whether or not manipulation occurred
3. Whether the treatment was open or closed or involved percutaneous skeletal fixation
4. Whether internal or external fixation devices were used

The fracture and dislocation codes include the application of a cast or strap and the removal of the initial cast or strap. Many of the descriptions of the treatment of fractures and dislocations include the term *each*. This means that a code is reported for each fracture or dislocation that is treated.

> **EXAMPLE:** Dr. Smith completes a closed treatment of two metatarsal fractures with manipulation. The correct codes to report include the following:
>
> For facilities, the procedure code is reported twice: listing 28470 and 28470.
>
> For physician billing, the procedure code is listed twice, and the 51 modifier is appended to the second code: 28470, 28470-51.

Manipulation

Manipulation or **reduction** of a bone or dislocation is performed to realign the bone or joint. This procedure is completed by open or closed reduction. **Closed reduction** occurs by manually applying force to the injured area without making an incision into the skin. **Open reduction** occurs when the site is surgically opened to realign the area. Figure 6-9 illustrates a closed reduction of a fractured left humerus.

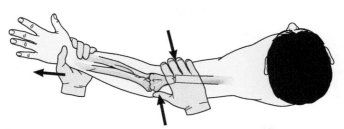

FIGURE 6-9 Closed Reduction of a Fractured Left Humerus

Fixation Devices

Fixation devices are used to immobilize fracture sites to allow for healing. There are two types of fixation used for fracture treatment. **External fixation** involves the placement of pins through soft tissue and into the bone in order to hold an external appliance in place. External fixation appliances are removed. Figure 6-10 illustrates a fracture of the epiphysis of a femur and the use of external fixation.

Internal fixation, also known as **open reduction internal fixation (ORIF)**, occurs when pins or a plate are internally placed into the bone to hold the fracture. The pins or plates are not typically removed after the fracture has healed. Figure 6-11 illustrates a fracture of the femoral neck and the use of internal fixation pins to correct the fracture.

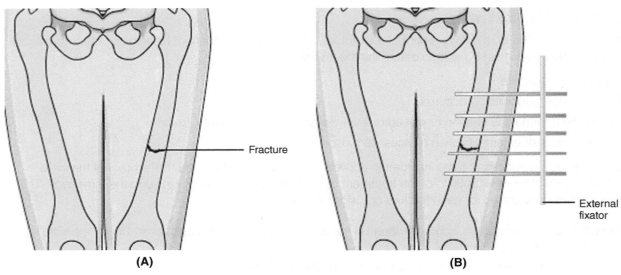

(A)   **(B)**

FIGURE 6-10 Fracture of the Femur and External Fixation to Stabilize the Bone

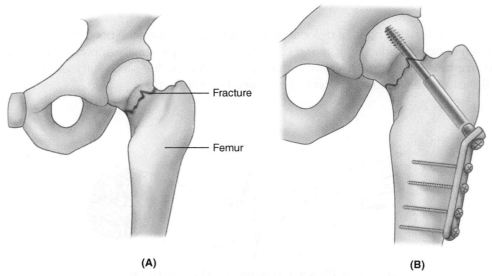

(A)   **(B)**

FIGURE 6-11 Internal Fixation of Fractured Hip   (A) Fracture of the femoral neck.
(B) Internal fixation pins are placed to stabilize the bone. These pins
are not removed after the bone has healed.

Detailed Skeletal Anatomy

When selecting codes for the repair of fractures and dislocations, coders must be able to identify the site of
the fracture and, at times, the exact area of the bone that is treated. Codes 28470–28485 are used to code the
treatment of fractures of the metatarsal bones. Codes 28490–28525 are used to code the treatment of fractures
of the great toe, phalanx, or phalanges.

Coders must have a working knowledge of the skeletal system to code the treatment of fractures. Figure 6-12
illustrates the dorsal view of the bones of the lower arm, wrist, and hand. Figure 6-13 illustrates the superior and
medial views of the bones of the right ankle and foot. Figure 6-14 illustrates the structures of the proximal end
of the femur.

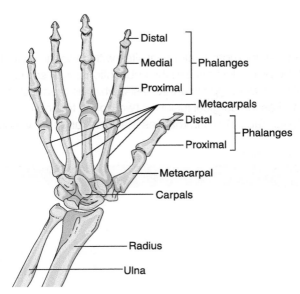

FIGURE 6-12 Dorsal View of the Bones of the Lower Left Arm, Wrist, and Hand

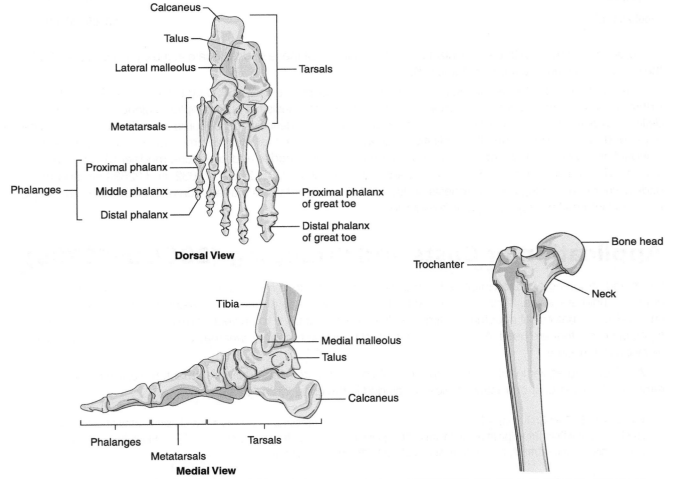

Dorsal View

Medial View

FIGURE 6-13 Superior View of the Bones of the Right Ankle and Foot

FIGURE 6-14 Structures of the Proximal End of the Femur

Arthrodesis

Earlier in the chapter it was stated that for most anatomical sites within the musculoskeletal system, the CPT manual follows a standardized outline of the procedures within the subsections, with some subsections having additional procedures. One such additional procedure type is arthrodesis, which is reported in various subcategories with the CPT manual. Arthrodesis is defined as the surgical fusion of two bones to bind or tie them together. Arthrodesis is also referred to as surgical ankylosis. Table 6-6 summarizes the code range for various arthrodesis procedures.

TABLE 6-6 Code Ranges for Arthrodesis

Anatomical Site of Arthrodesis	Code Range
Spine	22532–22819
Shoulder	23800–23802
Humerus	24800–24802
Forearm and Wrist	25800–25830
Hand and Fingers	26820–26863
Pelvis and Hip Joint	27279–27286
Femur	27580
Leg and Ankle Joint	27870–27871
Foot and Toes	28705–28760

To become familiar with the organization and description of these codes, locate in the CPT manual each of the code ranges that are found in Table 6-6.

In the CPT manual, locate the information that is found prior to code 22532 and follows the heading of Arthrodesis. This section of the CPT manual explains that arthrodesis may be completed alone or with other definitive procedures. When arthrodesis is performed with other definitive procedures a modifier of 51 should be appended to the code for the other definitive procedure to indicate that multiple procedures were completed. It should also be noted that some arthrodesis codes are add-on codes and, therefore, modifier 51 is not to be appended to the add-on code. For example, arthrodesis codes 22585, 22614, 22632, and 22634 are add-on codes. Prior to assigning any arthrodesis codes read all of the notations that are contained in the CPT manual for additional information regarding code assignment.

Application of Casts and Strapping (29000–29799)

Casts and strapping are used in order for fractures to heal and to immobilize an area. **Casts** are fiberglass or plaster rigid dressings. **Strapping** an area is done by using tape or bandage material to bind, protect, or immobilize an anatomical structure. At times, splints are also applied to prevent or limit mobility. There are two types of splints that are used. A **static splint** is used to prohibit mobility, whereas a **dynamic splint** is used to allow limited mobility.

As discussed earlier in this chapter, when casts or straps are used during treatment, the application and removal of the first cast or traction device is included in the code for the treatment.

> **EXAMPLE:** Tom Smith has a fracture of the femoral shaft. The procedure performed is a closed treatment of the femoral shaft fracture without manipulation and with cast application. The code to report would be 27500. Since the cast is applied during this initial treatment, a code from series 29000–29799 is not reported.

Therefore, physicians who apply the initial cast, strap, or splint and follow the patient for subsequent care of the fracture, dislocation, or other injury cannot use code series 29000–29799.

However, codes 29000–29799 are used to report the application of casts and strapping in the following situations:

- When the casting or strapping is the initial casting or strapping, and no other treatment or procedure is performed or is expected to be performed by the same physician completing the casting or strapping.
- When the casting or strapping is the initial service that is performed without any restorative treatment or procedure performed to stabilize or protect the injured area, which could include a fracture or dislocation, and/or to minimize or prevent pain.
- To report an initial cast or strapping when another physician has provided or will provide restorative treatment at a separate time.
- To report a replacement of a cast or strapping during or after the postoperative period from the original care.

EXAMPLE: Jim Banks injured his right arm during a construction accident. He is seen by Dr. Jones, a primary care provider. Dr. Jones immobilized the fracture by placing a long arm splint from the patient's shoulder to his hand.

This would be coded using code 29105—"Application of long arm splint (shoulder to hand)."

Cast Removals or Repairs (29700–29750)

This range of codes is used only when the cast removal is performed by a different physician from the physician who applied the cast. These codes are differentiated by removals, repairs, and wedging of casts. Further code differentiation occurs per type of cast.

Exercise 6.6—Check Your Understanding

Fracture/Dislocation and Application of Casts and Strapping

Indicate whether the following statements are true (T) or false (F).

1. _____ A static splint is used to allow for mobility.
2. _____ Code range 29000–29799 is used to report a cast replacement during the operative period.
3. _____ Dr. Smith casted the left arm of his patient. The cast was from the elbow to the finger. This service was performed after Dr. Jones performed a manipulation of the fracture site two days ago. Dr. Smith should report code 29075.
4. _____ The correct code for the strapping of a finger is 29280.
5. _____ Codes 29700–29750 are always reported for cast removals.

Coding Assignments

Assign the correct code(s).

6. Closed treatment of greater trochanteric fracture _____
7. Open treatment of femoral shaft fracture with placement of screws _____
8. Ankle dislocation treatment by open repair with internal fixation _____
9. Closed treatment of interphalangeal toe joint dislocation under anesthesia _____
10. Application of body cast from shoulder to hips including both thighs _____
11. Application of calf-to-foot leg splint _____
12. Open treatment of traumatic hip dislocation _____
13. Open treatment of ulnar styloid fracture _____
14. Manipulation and percutaneous skeletal fixation of medial humeral condylar fracture _____
15. Acute shoulder dislocation open treatment _____

Endoscopy/Arthroscopy (29800–29999)

An **endoscope**, an optic illuminated instrument used for the visualization of an internal body organ or cavity, is commonly used for procedures completed on the musculoskeletal system. The common endoscopic instrument used for visualization of the interior of a joint is an **arthroscope**. The process of viewing a joint via an arthroscope is referred to as an **arthroscopy**. Figure 6-15 illustrates the use of an arthroscope to view the knee, and Figure 6-16 shows the internal view of the knee during an arthroscopy.

Endoscopic procedures completed in the musculoskeletal system are divided into diagnostic and surgical endoscopies. A **diagnostic endoscopy/arthroscopy** is completed to determine the extent of an injury or disease process and to establish a diagnosis. A **surgical endoscopy/arthroscopy** is performed to surgically treat an injury or condition or abnormality of a joint.

Diagnostic endoscopic codes are included in their surgical endoscopic code counterparts. In other words, a diagnostic arthroscope is included in a surgical arthroscope in the same area. Therefore, if a diagnostic arthroscopy is started, and then a surgical arthroscopic procedure is completed, the diagnostic arthroscope is not reported because it is included in the code for the surgical arthroscopic procedure.

The endoscopy/arthroscopy codes, 29800–29999, are differentiated by the following factors:

- Anatomical site
- Diagnostic versus surgical scope
- Additional procedure(s) performed

Coders should also note when arthroscopic procedures are performed in conjunction with an arthrotomy. When this occurs, the code for the arthrotomy should be appended with modifier 51. This instruction is given in the CPT manual following the heading Endoscopy/Arthroscopy.

To locate an endoscopic/arthroscopic procedure in the index, perform the following steps. (This process should be used for locating all endoscopic procedures, regardless of the body system. This will be referred to in subsequent chapters when additional endoscopic procedures are reviewed.)

1. Reference the term *endoscopy* in the index. (Please note that in the CPT manual, after the heading Endoscopy, the following notation appears: "See Arthroscopy; Thoracoscopy.")
2. Locate the organ/body system being viewed, examined, or treated using a scope.

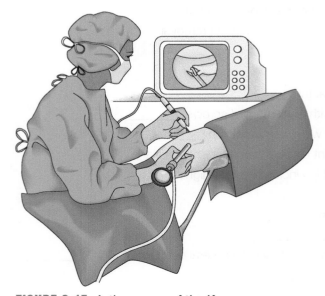

FIGURE 6-15 Arthroscopy of the Knee

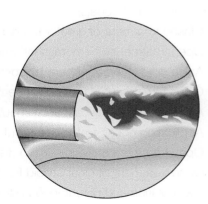

FIGURE 6-16 Internal View of the Knee during Arthroscopy

3. If there is no endoscopy heading, reference an index entry with a descriptor that includes the suffix "-oscopy." In the case of the musculoskeletal system, this entry would be the heading "Arthroscopy."

4. The "-oscopy" heading in the index most likely will be divided by diagnostic, surgical, and unlisted services and procedures or by body site. In the case of arthroscopy, the codes are indexed according to diagnostic, surgical, and unlisted. Select the appropriate subheading.

5. If, after you try to locate the procedure by the preceding method, you find no heading for *endoscopy*, you can be certain that the CPT manual does not have a specific code for the procedure using an endoscopic approach.

6. Query the provider who completed the procedure to determine whether the procedure was completed endoscopically.

7. After querying the provider, if it is determined that the procedure was completed endoscopically, use an unlisted procedure code in the section where the service applies. For arthroscopic procedures, for example, the appropriate code would be unlisted service code 29999—unlisted procedure, arthroscopy. The unlisted codes are always found at the end of the code section. Remember that unlisted codes should be used only after the procedure has been reviewed with the provider. When unlisted codes are used, payers review the claims carefully and usually ask for supporting documentation.

Exercise 6.7—Check Your Understanding

Endoscopic/Arthroscopic Procedures

For the following procedures listed, select the appropriate CPT code.

1. Surgical arthroscopy of the shoulder with capsulorrhaphy _____

2. Arthroscopy of knee with synovial biopsy _____

3. Endoscopic release of the transverse carpal ligament of the wrist _____

4. Arthroscopic removal of a foreign body in the elbow _____

5. Extensive debridement of shoulder via arthroscope _____

6. Athroscopic partial shoulder synovectomy _____

7. Lateral release via arthroscopy of knee _____

8. Endoscopic plantar fasciotomy _____

9. Subtalar joint arthroscopy with removal of foreign body _____

10. Arthroscopy of wrist for internal fixation of fracture _____

Summary

- CPT codes for the musculoskeletal system include codes 20100–29999.
- Wound exploration is completed to determine the extent of the injury and includes surgical exploration of the wound area with enlargement of the wound.
- Many procedures completed on the musculoskeletal system are completed with imaging guidance.
- Replantation involves the repair of soft tissue and tendons, bone approximation, and blood vessel repairs.
- External fixation involves the placement of pins through soft tissue and into the bone in order to hold an external appliance in place.

- Internal fixation, also known as *open reduction internal fixation (ORIF)*, occurs when pins or a plate are internally placed into the bone to hold the fracture.
- The common endoscopic instrument used for visualization of the interior of a joint is an arthroscope.
- A diagnostic endoscopy/arthroscopy is completed to determine the extent of an injury or disease process and to establish a diagnosis.
- A surgical endoscopy/arthroscopy is performed to surgically treat an injury, condition, or abnormality of a joint.

Internet Links

To learn more about foot and ankle conditions and treatments for these conditions, visit *https://www.verywellhealth.com/foot-ankle-surgical-procedures-4012819*.

For information about knee arthroscopies, visit *https://arthroscopy.com*.

To learn more about musculoskeletal disorders overall, visit *https://bmcmusculoskeletdisord.biomedcentral.com/*.

Chapter Review

True/False

Instructions: Indicate whether the following statements are true (T) or false (F).

1. _____ Tendons are thin sheets of fibrous connective tissue.

2. _____ Debridement of the wound area is included in traumatic wound exploration codes 20100–20103.

3. _____ Local anesthetics are injected into the carpal tunnel area to relieve pain.

4. _____ An osteotomy is the completion of plastic surgery on a bone.

5. _____ Diagnostic and therapeutic arthroscopies are coded using the same code.

Coding Assignments

Instructions: Using a CPT manual, select the appropriate code for each of the following procedures.

1. Single tendon tenotomy of shoulder
   _____

2. Correction of claw finger _____

3. Superficial biopsy of soft tissue of back
   _____

4. Reinsertion of spinal fixation device
   _____

5. Open treatment of chronic sternoclavicular dislocation _____

6. Finger sesamoidectomy _____

7. Closed treatment of coccygeal fracture
   _____

8. Knee arthrodesis _____

9. Diagnostic arthroscopy of wrist with synovial biopsy _____

10. Surgical arthroscopy of knee with medial meniscal transplantation _____

11. I&D in shoulder area for deep abscess
    _____

12. Arthrotomy of elbow with capsular excision for capsular release _____

13. Removal of humeral and ulnar prosthesis components with debridement and synovectomy

_____

14. Arthrotomy with exploration of midcarpal joint

_____

15. Phalangectomy of three toes

_____

16. Partial excision of ulna for osteomyelitis

_____

17. Olecranon bursa excision _____

18. Injection procedure for hip arthrography

_____

19. Removal of woodlike item deep in the knee area

_____

20. Flexor tenolysis, foot, single tendon

_____

21. Manipulation of trimalleolar ankle fracture with closed treatment _____

22. Excision of two interdigital neuromas

_____

23. Arthroscopy of shoulder with synovial biopsy

_____

24. Subtalar joint arthroscopy with subtalar arthrodesis

_____

25. Application of long arm cast

_____

26. Strapping of wrist _____

27. Closed treatment of talus fracture

_____

28. Radical resection of tumor of the calcaneus

_____

29. Primary suture of infrapatellar tendon

_____

30. Bilateral pelvis osteotomy _____

31. Application of shoulder to hand cast

_____

32. Wrist arthroscopy with synovial biopsy

_____

33. Shoulder arthroscopy for complete synovectomy

_____

34. Triple arthrodesis _____

35. Superficial biopsy of soft tissue of leg

_____

Case Studies

Case 1

Preoperative and postoperative diagnosis: Left knee arthrosis

Procedure: Arthroscopy and debridement

The patient was prepped and brought into the operating room, where general anesthesia was administered. The knee was prepped, and a video arthroscopy was performed using the anterolateral and anteromedial portals. The scope confirmed the diagnosis. In the medial compartment, the degenerative meniscus was debrided with a shaver. The large osteophytes were removed with a bur. After removal, it was noted that there was improved extension. In the lateral compartment, a small anterior horn of the tear was debrided and shaved back to the meniscal tissue. The portals were sutured with nylon sutures. Sterile dressings were applied. The patient was in stable condition and was sent to the recovery room.

CPT code(s): _____

Case 2

Diagnosis: Right radial shaft fracture

Procedure: Open reduction internal fixation of radius

The patient was placed in the supine position with an armboard extension. A nonsterile tourniquet was placed on the right arm. An incision was made proximal to the distal palmar crease and then extended to the level of the elbow crease through the subcutaneous tissue until the flexor carpi radialis tendon was identified. Further dissection of the area revealed that the fracture was at the insertion of the FPL tendon. The fracture was reduced with bone forceps and clamps. A 12-hole DC plate was fitted to the normal curvature of the volar aspect of the radius. The plate was fixed to the shaft. The screw holes were filled, and there was adequate reduction of the radial shafting. Full supination and pronation were achieved. Hemostatis was achieved, and the wound was irrigated to remove all debris. The subcutaneous tissue was closed using 2-0 Vicryl sutures, and a 3-0 nylon suture was used to close the skin. Sterile dressings were applied, and the patient's arm was placed in a sugar-tong splint. The patient was taken to the recovery room in good condition.

CPT code(s): _____

Case 3

Preoperative and postoperative diagnosis: Painful bunion of the right foot

Operation performed: Correction of bunion—Silver bunionectomy

After being placed in the supine position, the patient was prepped and draped. IV sedation with a local consisting of 15 cc of 1:1 mixture of 0.5% Marcaine plain with 2% Xylocaine with epinephrine was administered. A 5-cm curvilinear incision was made over the first MPJ and carried deep through the subcutaneous tissue, with dissection down to the deep fascia. The prominent medial bunion was exposed, and the bunion was excised at the sagittal groove. The wound area was flushed with normal saline, and the deep structures were closed with 3-0 and 4-0 Vicryl. The skin was closed with 4-0 nylon in a horizontal mattress fashion. The wound was then dressed. The patient tolerated the procedure and was sent to the recovery area.

CPT code(s): _____

Case 4

Preoperative and postoperative diagnosis: Painful left index finger due to previous crush injury

Procedure: Amputation of left index finger

The patient was placed under general anesthesia, and a 1% Lidocaine and 0.5% Marcaine with epinephrine was administered to perform a digital block for the left index finger. A tourniquet was inflated on the left arm. An incision was made over the mid aspect of the proximal phalanx of the left index finger with dissection of the subcutaneous tissue. The digital nerves were cut, and then sharp dissection was taken down to the bone, dividing the flexor and extensor tendons. A bone cutter was used to was taken down to the bone, dividing the flexor and extensor tendons. A bone cutter was used to divide the bone, and the finger was removed. The vessels and nerves were ligated, and the bone was smoothed off with a rongeur. The skin was closed with 5-0 nylon sutures and a dressing applied. The tourniquet was deflated. There was minimal blood loss, and the patient was taken to the recovery room in satisfactory condition.

CPT code(s): _____

Case 5

Indication for surgery

This 49-year-old female patient sustained a proximal tibial plateau fracture three years ago, which was repaired with both internal and external fixation. Since that time, she has developed significant pain due to degenerative disease in the previous fracture area. She presents today for hardware removal.

Postoperative diagnosis: Retained hardware right knee

Surgical procedure: Removal of hardware from right knee proximal tibia

Procedure:

The patient was placed in the supine position. The right leg was prepped and draped after the patient was placed under general anesthesia. High on the right thigh a tourniquet was placed, and the leg was exsanguinated using an Esmarch bandage. An incision was made and carried down through the skin and subcutaneous level down to the level of the hardware. Removal of the screws and plates occurred. The fracture was united at the time of closure. The wound was closed with staples and 2-0 Dexon. The patient tolerated the procedure and was taken to the recovery area.

CPT code(s): _____

Case 6

Preoperative diagnosis: Mass on right middle finger, middle phalanx

Pathology: Benign tumor from middle phalanx

Operation: Excision of benign tumor of middle phalanx of finger

The patient was prepped, and a digital block was achieved using 2.5 cc of 0.25% Marcaine and 1% Xylocaine. The finger was exsanguinated, and a tourniquet was placed. An incision was made over the mass and carried through the subcutaneous tissue. The mass was removed via curettes to scrape the mass from the bone. The specimen was labeled and sent to pathology. Irrigation of the wound occurred, and the skin was closed in layers. A sterile dressing was applied, and the patient was taken to the recovery area in stable condition.

CPT code(s): _____

Case 7

Operative diagnosis: Carpal tunnel syndrome of the right hand

Procedure: Endoscopic carpal tunnel release

The patient was anesthetized with local anesthesia and IV sedation. After the patient was placed in the supine position, a tourniquet was placed on the right arm. A 1.5-cm horizontal incision was made at the wrist, and the subcutaneous tissue was dissected to gain entrance for the endoscope. The operative area was visualized on the monitor. The transverse carpal ligament was released. The scope was removed, and the wound was irrigated and closed with 3-0 Prolene in a running subcuticular stitch. Additionally, Steri-Strips and a sterile dressing were applied, and the tourniquet was deflated. Blood loss was minimal. Patient was stable and sent to recovery.

CPT code(s): _____

Case 8

This 84-year-old patient presented today for an injection with ultrasound guidance with permanent recording and reporting due to degenerative arthritis of the left hip.

Procedure:

After MAC sedation, the left hip was prepped. The puncture site was injected with 1% Lidocaine with epinephrine. A 20-gauge, extra-long spinal needle was placed at the neck–head junction, and Isovue was injected. Additional injections of Lidocaine, Marcaine, and Depo-Medrol 80 mg were given. A Band-Aid was placed on the injection site. There were no complications of the procedure, and the patient was sent to recovery.

CPT code(s): _____

Case 9

Procedural Note

This patient presents with a subfascial soft tissue abscess for incision and drainage of the right upper arm.

After local anesthesia was administered, an incision was made over the abscess on the right arm and continued down to the fascia until the abscessed area was visualized below the deep fascia. The deep abscess was viewed, debrided, and then drained. The area was irrigated, and packing was placed. The patient tolerated the procedure and was instructed to follow up with me in one week.

CPT code(s): _____

Case 10

Procedural Note

Preoperative diagnosis: Possible malignancy on muscle of left thigh

After local anesthesia, a percutaneous bore needle was used to pierce the skin and fascia into the muscle to obtain a biopsy of the muscle tissue. The needle was removed with minimal blood. A bandage was placed on the site. The tissue sample was sent to pathology. The patient was in satisfactory condition after the procedure.

CPT code(s): _____

Respiratory System

Chapter Outline

Learning Objectives

At the conclusion of this chapter, you should be able to:

1. Define key terms related to coding procedures performed on the respiratory system.
2. Define abbreviations related to the respiratory system.
3. Describe the basic anatomy and functions of the respiratory system.
4. Define common procedures performed on the respiratory system.
5. Apply specific guidelines for the respiratory system to this chapter.
6. Select CPT codes for procedures completed on the respiratory system.
7. Identify and code procedures for the respiratory system from case studies.

Key Terms

arytenoidectomy

backbench work

bronchi

bronchoscopy

chemical pleurodesis

choanal atresia

diagnostic nasal endoscopy

direct laryngoscopy

drainage procedures

endotracheal intubation

epiglottidectomy

ethmoidectomy

ethmoid sinuses

extensive nasal polyp excision

extraperiosteal pneumonolysis

flexible bronchoscope

frontal sinuses

frontal sinusotomy

hemilaryngectomy

indirect laryngoscopy

initial rhinoplasty

intranasal biopsy

laryngectomy

larynx

lateral nasal wall reconstruction

lungs

maxillary sinuses

maxillary sinusotomy

maxillectomy

microlaryngoscopy

nasal polyps

nasal vestibular stenosis

open-tube bronchoscope

partial laryngectomy

pharyngolaryngectomy

pharynx

pleurectomy

pneumonectomy

pneumothorax

primary rhinoplasty

revision rhinoplasty

rhinectomy

rhinophyma

rhinoplasty

rhinotomy

rigid bronchoscope

secondary rhinoplasty

septoplasty

simple nasal polyp excision

sinus

sphenoid sinuses

sphenoid sinusotomy

spreader grafting

surgical nasal endoscopy

synechia

thoracoscopy

thoracostomy

thoracotomy

trachea

tracheostomy

Introduction

Procedures performed on the respiratory system include procedures that involve the nose, sinuses, pharynx, larynx, trachea, bronchi, and lungs. The range used for the respiratory system includes codes 30000–32999. The respiratory system consists of a number of organs that allow air to enter the body and waste gases to leave the body.

Guidelines Related to the National Correct Coding Initiative (NCCI)

Reference the following website to obtain the most current NCCI guideline information related to the Respiratory System.

1. Log on to *http://www.cms.gov/Medicare/Coding/NationalCorrectCodInitED/index.html*.
2. Scroll to the section titled "Downloads."
3. Click the link for the most current "NCCI Policy Manual for Medicare Services."
4. A box will appear that requires you to click "Open."
5. Click on "Chapter 5" for guidelines specific to the Respiratory System coding.

Abbreviations Related to the Respiratory System

Abbreviations	Definitions
ARD	acute respiratory distress
ARF	acute respiratory failure
BAL	bronchial alveolar lavage
COLD	chronic obstructive lung disease
COPD	chronic obstructive pulmonary disease
CPAP	continuous positive airway pressure
CXR	chest x-ray

(continues)

(continued)

Abbreviations	Definitions
DOE	dyspnea on exertion
LLL	left lower lobe (of lung)
LUL	left upper lobe (of lung)
PFT	pulmonary function testing
RF	respiratory failure
RLL	right lower lobe (of lung)
RUL	right upper lobe (of lung)
SOB	shortness of breath
TLC	total lung capacity
V/Qscan	ventilation-perfusion scan

Anatomy of the Respiratory System

Coders must understand the anatomy of the respiratory system to assign codes accurately. Figure 7-1 illustrates the anatomy of the upper respiratory system, and Figure 7-2 illustrates the lower respiratory system. Table 7-1 is a summary of common terms related to the respiratory system.

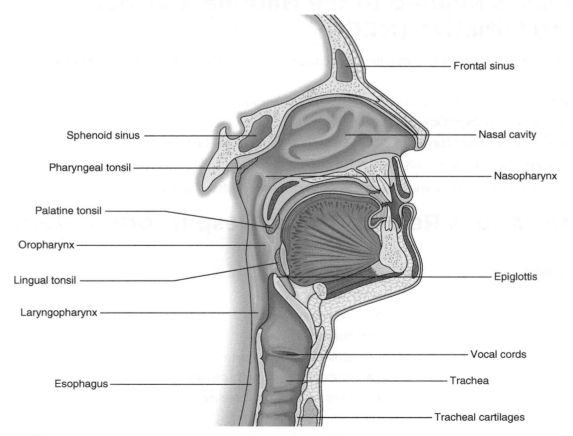

FIGURE 7-1 View of the Nasal Cavity and Structures of the Upper Respiratory System

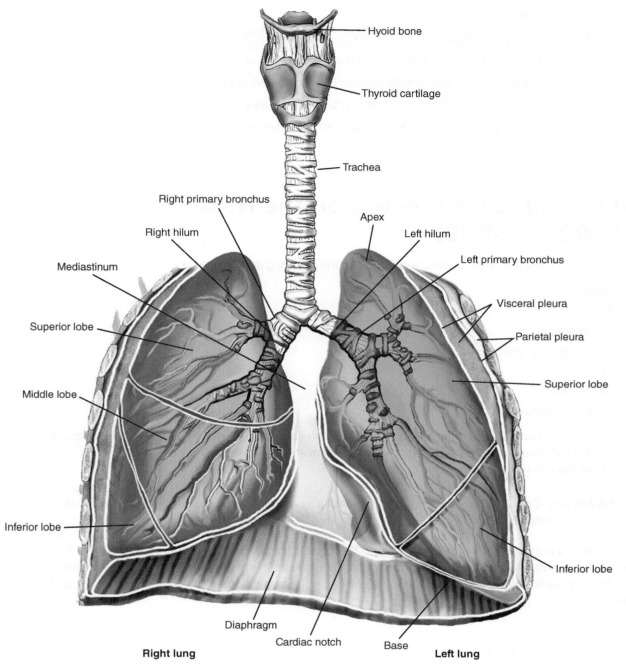

FIGURE 7-2 Structures of the Lower Respiratory System

TABLE 7-1 Respiratory System Terms

Term	Description
bronchi	Large air passages in the lung through which air is inhaled and exhaled
laryngectomy	Surgical removal of the larynx
larynx	The voice organ that connects the pharynx with the trachea

(continues)

TABLE 7-1 (*continued*)

Term	Description
lungs	Pair of organs that are located in the thorax that constitute the main organ of the respiratory system
pharynx	Tubular structure that extends from the base of the skull to the esophagus
sinus	Cavity that is located in the skull close to the paranasal area
trachea	Tube-shaped structure in the neck that extends from the larynx to the bronchi

Procedures Completed on the Nose (30000-30999)

Procedures completed on the nose are divided into the following subcategories:

- Incision
- Excision
- Introduction
- Removal of foreign body
- Repair
- Destruction
- Other procedures

When coding procedures completed on the nose, the coder must determine whether the procedure was completed unilaterally or bilaterally. Code descriptions must be reviewed because notations will specify the correct manner in which to report the codes.

> **EXAMPLE:** Code 30110 is used to report an excision of a nasal polyp, simple. This code is considered a unilateral procedure. To report a bilateral excision of nasal polyps, the 30110 code would be reported with modifier 50.

There is a notation in parentheses following the code listing in the CPT manual that instructs the coder to use the modifier. Within this subcategory of procedures completed on the nose, the coder should review carefully all the notations that are present because specific instructions are given for the various codes found in this section.

Incision (30000, 30020)

Two codes are found in CPT for incisional procedures completed on the nose. Code 30000 is used to code the drainage of an abscess or hematoma of the nose using an internal approach. Code 30020 is used to code the drainage of an abscess or hematoma of the nasal septum. **Drainage procedures** are completed to remove a fluid from an area—in the case of these codes, abscess material or blood.

Excisions (30100-30160)

This subcategory includes biopsies, excisions, and destructions. Table 7-2 summarizes this range of codes.

TABLE 7-2 Excisions (30100–30160)

Code	Description
30100	This code is used to report an intranasal biopsy, which is a biopsy that is completed within the nasal cavity. If the biopsy is completed on the skin of the nose, the CPT manual instructs the coder to reference codes 11102–11107.
30110 and 30115	Nasal polyps are growths in the nasal cavity that are commonly associated with rhinitis. Excisions of nasal polyps are differentiated by simple and extensive excisions. During a simple nasal polyp excision, the polyp's shape allows it to be removed easily because it is usually hanging from a stalk. During an extensive nasal polyp excision, the polyp's shape or thickness, or the number of polyps present, may require more skill and effort for removal. The physician should document that the removal was more than simple, to justify the selection of the code. To report bilateral excisions, use modifier 50.
30117 and 30118	These codes are used to report the excision or destruction of an intranasal lesion. The codes are differentiated by internal or external approaches. Code 30117 reports the internal approach and code 30118 reports the external approach or a lateral rhinotomy.
30120	This code is used to report an excision or surgical planing of the skin of the nose for rhinophyma. Rhinophyma is a rosacea condition of the skin of the nose. The skin appears red, swollen, and distorted with sebaceous hyperplasia.
30124 and 20125	This code range is used to report the simple or complex excision of dermoid cysts of the nose. Code 30124 reports a simple excision, whereas code 30125 reports a complex excision that extends under the bone or cartilage.
30130 and 30140	Excision or submucous resection of the inferior turbinate is reported using these codes. These codes report the removal of part or all of the inferior turbinates. Code 30140 is used when the resection of the inferior turbinate extends into the submucosal layer of tissue. It should be noted that, for the excision or submucous resection of the superior or middle turbinate, code 30999 is assigned.
30150 and 30160	A rhinectomy is the removal of the nose and is differentiated in CPT by partial or total removal by reporting code 30150 for a partial rhinectomy and code 30160 for a total rhinectomy.

Introduction (30200–30220)

There are only three codes in this subcategory of the CPT manual:

- Code 30200—Used for the therapeutic injection of a substance into the turbinates
- Code 30210—Displacement therapy, which would include Proetz type
- Code 30220—Nasal septal prosthesis insertion

Removal of Foreign Body (30300–30320)

Codes 30300–30320 are used to report the removal of a foreign body from the intranasal area. Codes are differentiated by the complexity of the procedure:

- Code 30300—This code is reported for the removal of a foreign body from the intranasal area when the procedure is an office-type procedure.
- Code 30310—When general anesthesia is used during the removal of a foreign body from the intranasal area, code 30310 is reported.
- Code 30320—Report code 30320 when the removal of a foreign body requires the completion of a lateral rhinotomy. A rhinotomy is a surgical procedure in which an incision is made along one side of the nose.

Exercise 7.1—Check Your Understanding

Incisions, Excisions, Introduction, and Removal of Foreign Bodies of the Nose

Using the CPT manual, select the appropriate code for each of the following procedures.

1. Total rhinectomy _____
2. Drainage of hematoma of the nasal septum _____
3. Laser destruction of intranasal lesion via internal approach _____
4. Removal of foreign body from nasal cavity, under general anesthesia _____
5. Excision of nasal polyp _____
6. Nasal septal prosthesis insertion _____

7. Bilateral extensive excision of multiple nasal polyps _____
8. Removal of a foreign body in the nose by lateral rhinotomy _____
9. Surgical planing of the skin of the nose for rhinophyma _____
10. Simple excision of a dermoid cyst of the nose involving the skin and subcutaneous layers _____

Repair (30400-30630)

Surgical repair of the nose is known as **rhinoplasty** and is reported in CPT by using codes 30400–30630. Most rhinoplasty procedures are considered cosmetic in nature, and third-party payers may not reimburse physicians for the completion of these procedures. However, there are times when rhinoplasty procedures are completed because of a congenital anomaly or an injury to the nose. When noncosmetic procedures are completed, it is important for the provider to document this clearly in the operative report because the report can be used to justify the need for the procedure.

During rhinoplasty, incisions are usually created within the nose; however, some surgeons perform the procedure by making external incisions at the base of the nostrils or along the columella. Figure 7-3 illustrates this approach.

To select codes from this subcategory, coders should reference the following entries in the index:

- Rhinoplasty
- Repair, then nose, then vestibular stenosis
- Repair, then nasal septum

Table 7-3 summarizes the codes in the range 30400–30630.

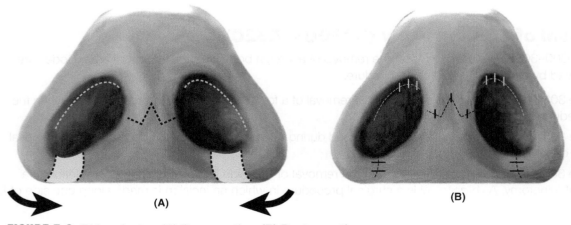

FIGURE 7-3 Rhinoplasty   (A) Preoperative; (B) Postoperative

TABLE 7-3 Repair (30400–30630)

Code	Description
30400–30420	This range of codes is used to report **primary rhinoplasty**, also known as **initial rhinoplasty**, which is the surgical repair of the nose. These codes are differentiated according to the extent of the repair. Code 30400 is used to report a rhinoplasty that involves the lateral and alar cartilages and/or elevation of the nasal tip, whereas code 30410 reports a complete rhinoplasty. Code 30420 is used to report a rhinoplasty that includes a major septal repair, also known as a **septoplasty**. Code 30420 includes rhinoplasty and septoplasty, so it is not necessary to report the septoplasty separately.
30430–30450	**Secondary rhinoplasty**, also known as **revision rhinoplasty**, is differentiated in CPT according to the following: • Minor revisions—including only a small amount of nasal tip work • Intermediate revisions—including bony work with osteotomies • Major revisions—including nasal tip work and osteotomies Coders must read the operative report carefully to select the appropriate code based on provider documentation of the procedure.
30460 and 30462	Codes 30460–30462 are used to code rhinoplasty procedures completed due to a nasal deformity that is secondary to a congenital cleft lip and/or palate. Code selection is based on repair of the tip only, versus repair of the tip, septum, and osteotomies.
30465	This code reports the bilateral repair of **nasal vestibular stenosis**, which is the narrowing of the nasal vestibule. This procedure also is referred to as **spreader grafting** or **lateral nasal wall reconstruction**. During this procedure, an incision is made in the upper lateral cartilage of the nose and continued into the medial aspect of the nasal bones. A graft is inserted to widen the nasal vestibule area. Code 30465 is a bilateral procedure; therefore, when this procedure is performed unilaterally, modifier 52 should be used.
30520	Code 30520 is used to report a septoplasty or submucous resection with or without cartilage scoring, contouring, or replacement with graft. During a septoplasty, cartilage may be removed as grafting material. When this occurs, do not assign an additional code for the harvesting of the graft because it occurred through the same incision. However, when the graft is secured through a separate incision, an additional code from code range 20900–20926 should be assigned to report the harvesting of the graft.
30540–30630	The remaining codes in the Repair subcategory are used to report the following procedures: • Repair of choanal atresia with codes 30540 and 30545—**Choanal atresia** occurs when there is an occlusion of the openings between the nasal cavity and the pharynx. Typically, this is a congenital defect, but it also can be acquired. Code 30540 reports an intranasal choanal atresia repair while code 30545 reports a transpalatine choanal atresia repair. • Lysis intranasal synechia with code 30560. **Synechia** is an adhesion. • Repair of fistula with code 30580—During this procedure, an opening between the mouth and the maxillary sinus is closed. • Septal or other intranasal dermatoplasty with code 30620—It should be noted that this code does not include obtaining the graft. • Repair of nasal septal perforations with code 30630—If a large defect exists, the physician has to complete a separately reportable autogenous graft, in addition to the local flaps that are routinely completed during this procedure.

Destruction and Other Procedures (30801–30999)

The final range of codes that are used to report procedures on the nose include the following:

• Codes 30801 and 30802—These codes are used to report the cautery or ablation of the mucosa of the inferior turbinates, and are differentiated by whether the extent of the procedure was superficial or intramural. Instructional notations are given that direct the coder to use code 30999 for the ablation of the superior or middle turbinates. The additional instructional notations that appear after code 30802 need to be reviewed by the coder prior to code assignment as these notations give instruction as to codes that should not be used with code 30802.

- Codes 30901–30906—These codes are used to report procedures that are completed to control nasal hemorrhages. Codes are differentiated by:
  - Simple or complex cautery.
  - Simple or complex packing.
  - Anterior versus posterior packing.

It should be noted that these codes are not used when the control of bleeding is performed during a procedure. In these cases, the control of the bleeding is considered part of the procedure.

- Codes 30915 and 30920—These codes are used to report ligation of arteries and are differentiated by the artery ligated.
- Code 30930—This code is used to report the therapeutic fracture of the nasal inferior turbinates.
- Code 30999—This is the unlisted procedure code for procedures completed on the nose. It should be noted that there are multiple notations within the subcategory for the nose that instruct coders to assign this code. Coders should be sure to read the notations that appear after the code description entries. Some procedures that are reported with this code include:
  - Therapeutic fracture of superior or middle turbinate.
  - Ablation of superior or middle turbinate.
  - Excision of superior or middle turbinate.
  - Submucous resection of superior or middle turbinate.

Exercise 7.2—Check Your Understanding

Repair (30400–30630) and Destruction and Other Procedures (30801–30999)

Using the CPT manual, select the appropriate code for each of the following procedures.

1. Septal dermatoplasty _____
2. Superficial bilateral cautery of mucosa of inferior turbinates _____
3. Primary rhinoplasty with elevation of nasal tip _____
4. Ethmoidal artery ligation _____
5. Lysis intranasal synechia _____
6. Septoplasty with cartilage scoring _____
7. Anterior, simple control of nasal hemorrhage _____
8. Therapeutic fracture of nasal inferior turbinate _____
9. Intranasal repair of choanal atresia _____
10. Repair of nasal septal perforation _____

Procedures Completed on the Accessory Sinuses (31000–31299)

There are four pairs of sinuses that are named according to the bone that encloses the particular sinus area. Figure 7-4 illustrates these sinuses:

- **Frontal sinuses**—These sinuses are located within the frontal bone behind the eyebrows.
- **Ethmoid sinuses**—These are located between the eyes.
- **Sphenoid sinuses**—These are located directly behind the nose at the center of the skull.
- **Maxillary sinuses**—These are located below the eye and lateral to the nasal cavity.

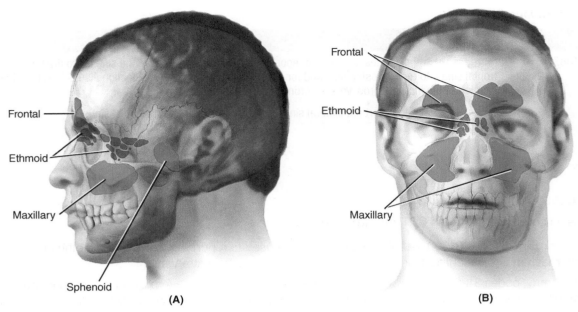

FIGURE 7-4 Sinuses (A) Lateral view; (B) Anterior view

Code range 31000–31299, titled Accessory Sinuses, is used to report procedures that are completed on the sinuses. There are four types of procedures found in this subcategory of CPT:

- Incision
- Excision
- Endoscopy
- Other procedures

Incisions (31000–31090)

Incisions are made into the sinuses for a variety of reasons, including drainage, biopsy, and other reasons. To code in this section, coders need to identify the sinus in which the procedure was completed. The codes are differentiated by the specific sinus and the procedure completed. Table 7-4 summarizes the procedures that are coded by using this section.

TABLE 7-4 Incisions (31000–31090)

Code	Description
31000 and 31002	These codes are used to report lavage by cannulation of the maxillary or sphenoid sinus. Code 31000 reports a lavage by cannulation of the maxillary sinus (antrum puncture or natural ostium) and code 31002 reports the same procedure completed on the sphenoid sinus.
31020–31032	**Maxillary sinusotomy**, an incision made into the maxillary sinus, is reported with this range of codes. These codes are for unilateral procedures; therefore, if a bilateral procedure is completed, the code is reported with modifier 50. The codes are differentiated by intranasal or radical procedures.
31040	Pterygomaxillary fossa surgery, any approach, would be reported using this CPT code.
31050 and 31051	**Sphenoid sinusotomy** codes, which code incisions made into the sphenoid sinus, are differentiated according to the following: • With or without biopsy or • With mucosal stripping or removal of polyps

(continues)

TABLE 7-4 (*continued*)

Code	Description
31070–31087	**Frontal sinusotomy** codes are used to report incisions made into the frontal sinuses to drain the frontal sinus, to remove osteomas, and for other reasons. Proper code selection also is based on the location of the incision: brow versus coronal.
31090	This code is used to report a unilateral sinusotomy of three or more paranasal sinuses.

Excisions (31200–31230)

Sinus excision codes are divided in CPT into two areas:

- **Ethmoidectomy**, codes 31200–31205—These codes are used to report the removal of the ethmoid sinus. The approach must be identified for code selection: intranasal versus extranasal.
- **Maxillectomy**, codes 31225 and 31230—These codes are used to report the removal of the maxillary sinus and are differentiated by the completion of the maxillectomy without or with an orbital exenteration.

Endoscopy (31231–31298)

Codes 31231–31298 are used to report endoscopic procedures completed on the sinuses. Codes 31233–31298, unless otherwise specified, are used to report unilateral procedures, therefore, when the procedure is completed bilaterally, modifier 50 is added to the code. To complete these procedures, a physician uses an endoscope to visualize, examine, and magnify the internal structure of the sinus. A diagnostic sinus endoscopy is included with the surgical endoscopy. A surgical endoscopy also includes a sinusotomy if it is performed.

Diagnostic nasal endoscopy codes use code range 31231–31235 and include the inspection of the entire nasal cavity, the meatus, the turbinates, and the sphenoethmoid recess. Therefore, only one code is needed to report the inspection of all of these areas.

Exercise 7.3—Check Your Understanding

Accessory Sinuses (31000–31299)

Using the CPT manual, select the appropriate code for each of following procedures.

1. Sinus endoscopy with maxillary antrostomy _____

2. Sphenoid sinusotomy with biopsy _____

3. Maxillectomy with orbital exenteration _____

4. Repair of cerebrospinal fluid leak of the sphenoid region via endoscope _____

5. Nasal endoscopy with sphenoidotomy _____

6. Endoscopic balloon dilation of sphenoid sinus ostium _____

7. Unilateral sinusotomy of four paranasal sinuses _____

8. Maxillary sinus lavage by cannulation _____

9. Radical maxillary sinusotomy _____

10. Total extranasal ethmoidectomy _____

Surgical nasal endoscopy procedures are reported using codes 31237–31298 and are used when a nasal endoscope is used to complete a surgical procedure. When coding surgical nasal endoscopy procedures, the coder must read the operative report to ensure that the procedure was completed endoscopically, and then the report must be reviewed to determine the procedure that was completed. Prior to code assignment the coder should review the numerous instructional notations that follow codes in the code range 31240–31297. Locate and review these instructional notations in the CPT manual.

Procedures Completed on the Larynx (31300–31599)

Procedures completed on the larynx are divided into the following subcategories:

- Excision
- Introduction
- Endoscopy
- Repair
- Other procedures

Figure 7-5 illustrates the larynx and related structures.

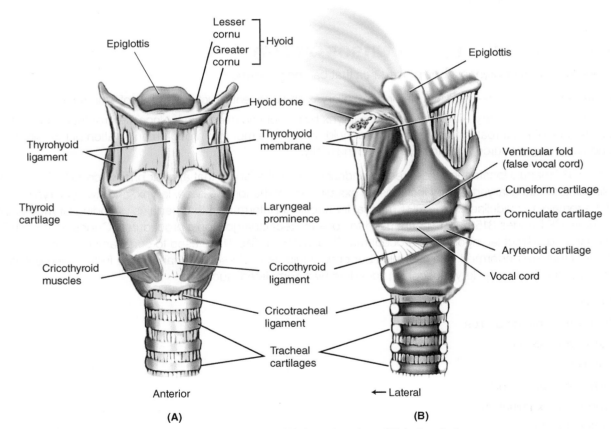

FIGURE 7-5 Larynx and Related Structures   (A) Anterior view; (B) Lateral view

Excision and Introduction (31300–31502)

Excisions and introduction, or insertion, of tubes completed on the larynx are coded by using this range of codes. Table 7-5 summarizes codes found in this range.

TABLE 7-5 Excision and Introduction (31300–31502)

Code	Description
31300	This code is reported when the physician performs a laryngotomy (thyrotomy, laryngofissure), with removal of tumor or laryngocele, cordectomy.
31360–31368	Codes 31360–31368 report a laryngectomy. Code selection is determined by whether the procedure was total or subtotal and whether radical neck dissection occurred.
31370–31382	A **partial laryngectomy**, also known as a **hemilaryngectomy**, is the partial removal of the larynx. Code selection is based on the approach.
31390–31420	This range of codes includes: • **Pharyngolaryngectomy**—Surgical excision of the hypopharynx and larynx, reported with codes 31390 or 31395. These codes are differentiated by without reconstruction (Code 31390) or with reconstruction (Code 31395). • **Arytenoidectomy**—Surgical excision of the arytenoid cartilage, which is the cartilage to which the vocal cords are attached, reported with code 31400. • **Epiglottidectomy**—Surgical excision of the epiglottis, reported with code 31420.
31500	This code is used to code an emergency procedure called an **endotracheal intubation**. In this procedure, an endotracheal tube is placed into the trachea to keep it open.
31502	This code is used to report the changing of a tracheotomy tube prior to the establishment of a fistula tract.

Endoscopy of the Larynx (31505–31579)

There are two types of laryngoscopy procedures that can be performed:

- **Direct laryngoscopy**—The direct viewing of the larynx and adjacent structures by use of a laryngoscope.
- **Indirect laryngoscopy**—The viewing of the larynx by use of two mirrors: a laryngeal mirror that is placed in the back of the throat, and a second mirror held outside the mouth. Through manipulation of the mirrors and using a light source, the larynx is viewed indirectly.

In the CPT manual locate the guidelines for endoscopies of the larynx that appear prior to code 31505. These guidelines state that a laryngoscopy includes an examination of the tongue base, larynx, and hypopharynx. Read the remaining guidelines in the CPT manual for additional information that pertains to coding laryngoscopy procedures. CPT codes 31505–31513 are used to code indirect laryngoscopic procedures. Codes 31515–31571 are used to code direct laryngoscopic procedures. Codes 31575–31579 are used to code laryngoscopic procedures that are performed using flexible fiber-optic equipment. These code ranges are further differentiated according to the reason the laryngoscopic procedure was completed, such as:

- Biopsy
- Removal of foreign bodies
- Removal of lesions
- Injections
- Insertion of obturator
- Diagnostic examinations
- Arytenoidectomy
- Reconstruction

Therefore, when reading through an operative report, the coder should identify the type of laryngoscope used, as well as the reason for the laryngoscopy.

Some codes (for example, code 31536) identify the use of an operating microscope or telescope. If documentation states that the procedure was completed using an operating microscope or telescope, these specialized codes should be used. If both an operating microscope and a telescope was used during the same operative session, the code should be reported only once. Use of an operating microscope is also identified by the physician stating the performance of a **microlaryngoscopy**.

Repair and Other Procedures Completed on the Larynx (31580–31599)

The remaining codes, 31580–31599, are used to report repairs and other procedures completed on the larynx. The repair codes are located in the index by referencing the terms *repair* and then *larynx,* or by referencing the term *laryngoplasty.* Codes 31580–31592 contain numerous instructional notations that follow the codes that must be reviewed by the coder prior to code assignment. Review this range of codes to become familiar with the instructional notations that appear for these codes.

Code 31599 is used to report unlisted procedures that are completed on the larynx.

Exercise 7.4—Check Your Understanding

Procedures Completed on the Larynx (31300–31599)

Using the CPT manual, select the appropriate code for each of the procedures listed.

1. Partial horizontal laryngectomy _____

2. Direct operative laryngoscopy with biopsy _____

3. Indirect laryngoscopy with foreign body removal _____

4. Flexible laryngoscopy with removal of lesion _____

5. Direct laryngoscopy with stripping of vocal cords _____

6. Laryngoplasty for laryngeal web with indwelling keel _____

7. Laryngeal reinnervation by neuromuscular pedicle _____

8. Epiglottidectomy _____

9. Indirect laryngoscopy for diagnosis _____

10. Flexible laryngoscopy with removal of foreign body _____

Procedures Completed on the Trachea and Bronchi (31600–31899)

Procedures completed on the trachea and bronchi are found in code range 31600–31899. Figure 7-6 illustrates the trachea and the bronchi. The code ranges in this subsection include:

- Incision
- Endoscopy
- Bronchial Thermoplasty
- Introduction
- Excision, Repair
- Other procedures

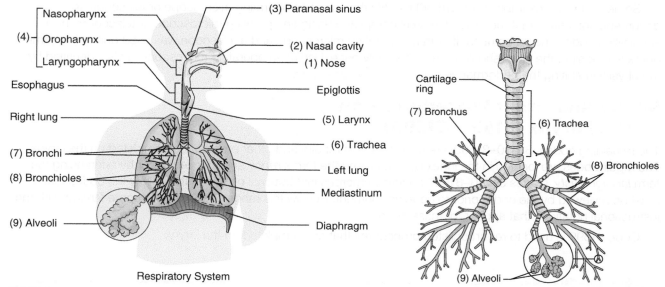

FIGURE 7-6 **Trachea and Bronchi**

Incision (31600–31614)

An incision made into the trachea is referred to as a **tracheostomy**. Codes 31600–31610 are used to report tracheostomies. These codes are differentiated according to whether the procedure was:

- Planned
- An emergency procedure
- A fenestration procedure

EXAMPLE: Dr. Jones has just performed a tracheostomy on a 1-year-old.

When submitting this charge, the coder in his office reports code 31601.

Endoscopy of Trachea and Bronchi (31615–31654)

A commonly completed procedure of the respiratory system is a **bronchoscopy**, an examination of the bronchi using an endoscope. Figure 7-7 illustrates a bronchoscopy. During a bronchoscopy, the scope is inserted

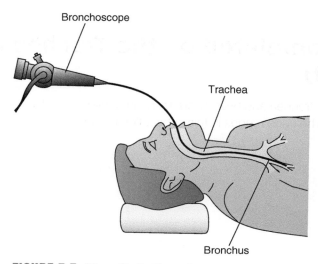

FIGURE 7-7 **Fiber-Optic Bronchoscopy**

through the oropharynx, or mouth, past the vocal cords, and beyond the trachea into the bronchi. A **rigid bronchoscope**, often referred to as an **open-tube bronchoscope**, is inserted through the mouth, whereas a **flexible bronchoscope** is inserted through the mouth or nose. CPT does not differentiate between the scopes for code selection.

At the start of this subsection in the CPT manual, a notation appears that informs the coder that a surgical bronchoscopy always includes a diagnostic bronchoscopy. The note elaborates that for codes 31622–31651, 31660, and 31661, fluoroscopic guidance is included in the code when performed with the procedure listed. Therefore, it is not necessary to code the fluoroscopic guidance separately.

To select a code for a bronchoscopy properly, the coder must read the operative report to determine why the bronchoscopy was performed. The codes are differentiated by the following:

- With or without cell washing
- Brushing or protected brushings
- Bronchial alveolar lavage
- With biopsy (or biopsies), according to various types of biopsies
- Dilation
- Placement of stents
- Removal of foreign bodies
- Excisions or destruction of tumors
- Placement of catheters
- Therapeutic aspiration
- Injection of contrast material

To locate these codes in the index, the coder should reference the term *bronchoscopy* and then reference the subterm that describes the procedure that was completed. Complete services that include sampling of lymph node(s) or adjacent structure(s) using endobronchial ultrasound (EBUS) are reported separately using codes 31652 and 31653. Code 31654 is an add-on code that reports the identification of one or more peripheral lesion(s) using transendoscopic ultrasound. Review the instructional notation found in the CPT manual following code 31654 for additional information about the use of this code. Codes 31652, 31653, and 31654 are reported only once per session.

Bronchial Thermoplasty (31660–31661)

Codes 31660 and 31661 report a rigid or flexible bronchoscopy with bronchial thermoplasty, including fluoroscopic guidance when performed. The codes are differentiated by the number of lobes viewed. Bronchial thermoplasty is a therapeutic procedure generally used to treat patients with severe asthma that is not controlled by medications. A bronchoscope is used with a radiofrequency ablation device to reduce smooth muscle tissue in all central airways.

Introduction, Excision Repair, and Other Procedures Completed on the Trachea and Bronchi (31717–31899)

The introduction codes in this subsection include codes for the catheterization of the area and the instillation of contrast material. Codes are differentiated by site, such as trachea versus bronchi, and by any additional procedures that may be performed.

The repair codes, 31750–31830, also are differentiated by site (trachea versus bronchi) and are further defined according to the type of repair completed. Operative reports must be read to determine:

- The site of the repair
- The type of repair—graft versus fistulization

- The reason for the repair, such as the excision of a tumor or carcinoma
- Whether there was a revision of a tracheostomy scar

Exercise 7.5—Check Your Understanding

Procedures Completed on the Trachea and Bronchi (31600–31899)

Using the CPT manual, select the appropriate code for each of the following procedures.

1. Tracheostoma complex revision with flap rotation _____

2. Flexible bronchoscopy with brushing _____

3. Tracheobronchial catheter aspiration done with a fiberscope at the bedside _____

4. Suture of cervical tracheal wound _____

5. Excision of thoracic tracheal carcinoma _____

6. Intrathoracic tracheoplasty _____

7. Bronchoplasty graft repair _____

8. Tracheobronchoscopy through established tracheostomy incision _____

9. Nasotracheal catheter aspiration _____

10. Surgical closure tracheostomy with plastic repair _____

Procedures Completed on the Lungs and Pleura (32035–32999)

Code range 32035–32999—Lungs and Pleura—is used to code procedures completed on the lungs and pleura. Figure 7-2, shown earlier in this chapter, illustrated the location of the lungs and pleura in relation to other structures of the respiratory system. This subsection is divided into the following areas:

- Incision
- Excision/Resection
- Removal
- Introduction and removal
- Destruction
- Thoracoscopy (Video-assisted thoracic surgery [VATS])
- Stereotactic radiation therapy
- Repair
- Lung transplantation
- Surgical collapse therapy: thoracoplasty
- Other procedures

Incision (32035–32225)

Incisions are made into the lungs and pleura space for a variety of reasons, including to remove air or fluid from the area, control hemorrhaging, repair a tear, or remove a foreign body. The codes found in this area of CPT are summarized in Table 7-6.

TABLE 7-6 Incisions (32035–32225)

Code	Description
32035 and 32036	A thoracostomy, an incision made into the chest wall, is differentiated in CPT with two codes. Code 32035 is used when rib resection for empyema occurs, and code 32036 is used when an open flap drainage for empyema is completed.
32096–32160	This range of codes is used to report thoracotomy, a surgical opening into the thoracic cavity. The codes are differentiated by accompanying procedures or the reason for the thoracotomy.
32200–32225	This range of codes is used to report pneumonostomy, pleural scarification, and decortication.

Excision/Resection, Removal, Introduction and Removal, and Destruction (32310–32562)

Excisions, removals, introductions and removals, and destructions that are performed on the lungs and pleura are coded in CPT by using code range 32310–32562. Codes for this range are summarized in Table 7-7.

TABLE 7-7 Excision/Resection, Removal, Introduction and Removal, and Destruction (32310–32562)

Code	Description
32310–32320	Pleurectomy, the surgical removal of the pleura, is coded in CPT by use of one of two codes. Code 32310 reports a parietal pleurectomy, which is considered a separate procedure in CPT, and decortication and parietal pleurectomy are reported with code 32320.
32400 and 32405	Percutaneous needle biopsies of the pleura, lungs, or mediastinum is report with code 32400 for the pleura and code 32405 for a biopsy of the lung or mediastinum. The CPT manual instructs the coder to see codes 76942, 77002, 77012, and 77021 if imaging guidance is used with percutaneous needle biopsies. Additional instructions are also present that coders must adhere to for these codes.
32440–32491	This range of codes is used to report the removal of a lung, known as a pneumonectomy. Coders must determine whether the procedure was a total pneumonectomy or other than a total pneumonectomy, because this affects code selection. If the procedure was not a total pneumonectomy, code selection is based on the removal of a single lobe, of two lobes, or of a single segment. Codes in this range are divided further according to accompanying procedures.
+32501	This is considered an add-on code. This code is used only in conjunction with code 32480, 32482, or 32484. These codes are the primary codes, and code 32501 is added when a resection and repair of a portion of the bronchus is performed at the time of a lobectomy or segmentectomy.
32503 and 32504	A resection of an apical lung tumor is reported by these codes. The codes are differentiated between the procedure being performed, with or without chest wall reconstruction.
32505 +32506 +32507	Code 32505 reports an initial thoracotomy with therapeutic wedge resection. Codes 32506 and 32507 are add-on codes. Code 32506 reports each additional ipsilateral therapeutic wedge resection after the initial resection for a thoracotomy. Code 32507 reports a thoracotomy with diagnostic wedge resection followed by anatomic lung resection. In the CPT manual, review the instructional notations that follow codes 32506 and 32507 identify the primary procedures for which these codes are used.
32540	This code reports an empyemectomy, which is also known as an extrapleural enucleation of empyema.
32550	This code is used to report the insertion of an indwelling tunneled pleural catheter with cuff. Coders should note the notation found in the CPT manual that instructs the coder that code 32550 should not be reported with codes 32554, 32555, 32556, and 32557 when performed on the same side of the chest.
32551	This is a separate procedure code for tube thoracostomy, with or without water seal. This procedure is commonly completed for abscess removal, hemothorax, or empyema.
32552 and 32553	Code 32552 is used to report the removal of an indwelling tunneled pleural catheter with cuff. Code 32553 reports the placement of interstitial devices for radiation therapy guidance. Coders should look at the notations that follow this code, which direct them to report the supply of the device separately and to report the imaging guidance.

(continues)

TABLE 7-7 (*continued*)

Code	Description
32554 and 32555	These codes report a needle or catheter thoracentesis aspiration of the pleural space. The codes are differentiated as to whether imaging guidance is used or not.
32556 and 32557	Percutaneous pleural drainage with the insertion of an indwelling catheter is reported with these codes. These codes are also differentiated as to whether imaging guidance is used or not. Coders should look at the notation that follows code 32557, which provides guidance on the use of codes 32554–32557.
32560–32562	These codes are used to report destructions. Chemical pleurodesis is coded with code 32560. In this procedure, a chemical is placed into the pleural space to cause inflammation and thereby reduce the effusion of the area. This procedure is commonly completed for persistent or recurrent pneumothorax, an accumulation of air or gas in the pleural cavity. Code 32561 is used to report the instillation of an agent for fibrinolysis on the initial day of treatment. Code 32562 is used to report the instillation on a subsequent day. Although the instillation of a fibrinolytic agent can be performed multiple times on the same day, code 32561 or 32562 is reported only once per day, depending on whether it is the initial or a subsequent day of treatment.

EXAMPLE: Tom Jones had a chest x-ray that revealed a tumor-like spot on his right lung. Dr. Smith performed a percutaneous needle biopsy of the lung.

This procedure would be coded using code 32405-RT.

Thoracoscopy (Video-Assisted Thoracic Surgery [VATS]) (32601–32674)

Code range 32601–32665 is used to report **thoracoscopy**, the examination of the pleura, lungs, and mediastinum using an endoscope to visualize the area. As noted in the CPT manual, a surgical thoracoscopy always includes a diagnostic thoracoscopy. Codes 32601–32609 report diagnostic thoracoscopy, whereas codes 32650–32674 are used to report surgical thoracoscopy.

Diagnostic thoracoscopy codes are differentiated by site, and then by biopsy or without biopsy. Coders must read the operative report carefully to locate the site and determine whether a biopsy was performed.

EXAMPLE: Steven Ashton underwent a diagnostic thoracoscopy of the pericardial sac without biopsy. This would be given the code 32601.

Susan Paign underwent a diagnostic thoracoscopy of the pericardial sac with biopsy. This would be given the code 32604.

Surgical thoracoscopy codes are differentiated according to the type of procedure performed via the scope. To locate these codes in the index, the coder would reference the terms *thoracoscopy,* then *surgical,* and then the type of procedure.

EXAMPLE: Dr. Carl performed a therapeutic wedge resection, initial unilateral, via a thoracoscope.

To code Dr. Carl's procedure, a coder should reference *thoracoscopy* in the index, then *surgical,* then search code range 32650–32674. This would be coded using code 32666.

Stereotactic Radiation Therapy (32701)

Code 32701 reports thoracic target delineation for stereotactic radiation therapy. During this procedure a surgeon and radiation oncologist may work together. The surgeon will determine the targeted treatment area for therapy reported with code 32701, while the radiation oncologist will perform services that relate to radiation oncology. Code 32701 should be reported only once per the entire course of treatment regardless of the number of treatment sessions. Coders should become familiar with the extensive notes for code 32701 that appear before the code in the CPT manual.

Repair (32800-32820)

There are only four codes that are used to code repairs completed on the lungs. The four codes are as follows:

- Code 32800—used to report a repair of a lung hernia through the chest wall.
- Code 32810—used to report a Clagett-type procedure, which is the closure of the chest wall following open flap drainage for empyema. ,
- Code 32815—used to report the open closure of a major bronchial fistula. When using this code, make sure that the operative reports describe an open procedure.
- Code 32820—used to report major reconstruction of the chest wall.

Lung Transplantation (32850-32856)

During a transplantation of a lung or lungs, three distinct components are performed. Codes 32850–32856 are used to report these components. Coders should reference and read the notations that appear under the heading "Lung Transplantation" and before the codes.

Code 32850 is used to report the first component of the transplantation. This is the donor pneumonectomy, or the removal of the lung or lungs from the cadaver. The physician removes the lung and places the organ in cold preservation.

Codes 32855–32856 are used to report the **backbench work**, in which the physician prepares the donor organ prior to transplantation. Remember, the organ has been preserved for a period of time, especially if the organ has had to be transported to another site. Backbench work includes the preparation of the donor lung, including the dissection of the tissue to prepare the pulmonary venous/atrial cuff, pulmonary artery, and bronchus. If the procedure to be performed is a unilateral transplant, code 32855 is used to report the backbench work. If the procedure to be performed is a bilateral transplantation, code 32856 is used to report the backbench work.

The transplantation of the lung or lungs into the recipient is reported using codes 32851–32854. Codes 32851–32852 are used to report the transplant of a single lung and are differentiated by the procedure being performed without or with a cardiopulmonary bypass. Codes 32853–32854 are used to report the transplantation of two lungs and are also differentiated by the procedure being performed, without or with a cardiopulmonary bypass.

Surgical Collapse Therapy, Thoracoplasty, and Other Procedures (32900-32999)

Code range 32900–32960 reports various procedures that are completed for therapeutic purposes to treat pulmonary conditions. Table 7-8 summarizes these codes, as well as codes that fall within code range 32997–32999.

TABLE 7-8 Surgical Collapse Therapy, Thoracoplasty, and Other Procedures (32900–32999)

Code	Description
32900	This code is used to report the extrapleural resection of the ribs. During this procedure, the rib is resected via an incision in the skin without entering the chest cavity. To prevent air from entering the chest cavity, the pleural membrane on the inside surface of the rib is not punctured. The portion of the rib is then removed.
32905 and 32906	These codes are used to report the performance of an extrapleural thoracoplasty or Schede-type thoracoplasty. This procedure is performed to treat thoracic empyema. During this procedure, the chest wall skeletal support is removed to create an area, previously filled with the accumulation of pus in the chest cavity which will fill in with granulation tissue during the healing process. If closure of a bronchopleural fistula occurs, code 32906 is reported.
32940	This code reports **extraperiosteal pneumonolysis**, which is the separation of the surface of the lung from the inside surface of the chest cavity.

(continues)

TABLE 7-8 (*continued*)

Code	Description
32960	Therapeutic pneumothorax, the partial collapsing of the lung by the intrapleural injection of air, is reported with this code. Note that the physician is intentionally collapsing the lung for therapeutic reasons.
32997	This code reports a unilateral total lung lavage to treat specific lung diseases or injuries.
32998 and 32994	The 32998 code is used to report the unilateral ablation therapy of one or more pulmonary tumor(s) including pleura or chest wall when involved by tumor extension, percutaneous, including imaging guidance when performed, via radiofrequency. High-frequency radio waves create heat that destroys the tumors in the lung, pleura, or chest wall. Code 32994, an out of sequence code, reports the procedure via cryoablation.
32999	This code is used to report unlisted procedures completed on the lungs and pleura.

Exercise 7.6—Check Your Understanding

Procedures Completed on the Lungs and Pleura (32035–32999)

Using the CPT manual, select the appropriate code for each of the following procedures.

1. Percutaneous needle biopsy of lung
   _____

2. Pneumonostomy with open drainage of cyst
   _____

3. Thoracotomy for postoperative complications
   _____

4. Repair of a lung hernia via the chest wall
   _____

5. Thoracoscopy with removal of a clot from the pericardial sac _____

6. Parietal pleurectomy _____

7. Thoracostomy with rib resection for empyema
   _____

8. Open biopsy of pleura _____

9. Removal of indwelling tunneled pleural catheter with cuff _____

10. Thoracotomy for exploration
    _____

Summary

- Procedures completed on the nose are divided into the following subcategories: incision, excision, introduction, removal of a foreign body, repair, destruction, and other procedures.
- Drainage procedures are completed to remove a fluid from an area.
- Nasal polyps are growths in the nasal cavity that are commonly associated with rhinitis.
- A rhinotomy is a surgical procedure in which an incision is made along one side of the nose.
- Surgical repairs of the nose are known as *rhinoplasty* and are reported in CPT by using codes 30400–30630.
- A primary rhinoplasty, also known as an *initial rhinoplasty*, is the surgical repair of the nose.
- Secondary rhinoplasty is differentiated in the CPT manual according to minor revisions, intermediate revisions, and major revisions.

- There are four groups of sinuses: frontal, ethmoid, sphenoid, and maxillary.
- A partial laryngectomy, also known as a *hemilaryngectomy*, is the partial removal of the larynx.
- The *direct* viewing of the larynx and adjacent structures by use of a laryngoscope is known as a *direct laryngoscopy.*
- The viewing of the larynx by use of a laryngeal mirror that is placed in the back of the throat with a second mirror held outside of the mouth is known as an *indirect laryngoscopy.*
- A bronchoscopy is an examination of the bronchi using a flexible endoscope.
- To perform a thoracentesis, a physician inserts a needle through a patient's skin and chest wall into the pleural space.
- Pneumocentesis is the surgical puncturing of a lung.
- A thoracoscopy is the examination of the pleura, lungs, and mediastinum using an endoscope to visualize the area.
- Lung transplantation involves three components: cadaver donor pneumonectomy, backbench work, and recipient lung allotransplantation.

Internet Links

To research diseases of sinuses and nose and their treatments, visit *https://ent.weill.cornell.edu /patients/clinical-specialties/nose-sinus-disease*

To view information about thoracentesis, visit *http://www.fpnotebook.com*, and search for thoracentesis.

Chapter Review

Fill in the Blank

Instructions: Fill in the blanks in the statements that follow.

1. A primary rhinoplasty is also known as a(n) _____ rhinoplasty.

2. A(n) _____ is a surgical procedure in which an incision is made along one side of the nose.

3. Secondary rhinoplasty is also known as _____ rhinoplasty.

4. The narrowing of the nasal vestibule is called _____.

5. The sinuses that are located within the frontal bone behind the eyebrows are the _____ sinuses.

6. The sinuses that are located directly behind the nose at the center of the skull are the _____ sinuses.

7. There are two types of nasal endoscopies: _____ and _____.

8. The removal of a lung is known as a(n) _____.

9. Surgical repairs of the _____ are known as rhinoplasty.

10. The surgical puncturing of a lung for aspiration is a(n) _____.

Coding Assignments

Instructions: Using a CPT manual, select the appropriate code for each of the following procedures.

1. Transpalatine repair of choanal atresia
   _____

2. Initial posterior control of nasal hemorrhage with posterior cautery _____

3. Intranasal biopsy _____

4. Complete excision of inferior turbinate
   _____

5. Medial orbital wall decompression via nasal endoscopy _____

6. Diagnostic nasal endoscopy with maxillary sinusoscopy _____

7. Maxillary antrostomy using a sinus endoscope
   _____

8. Cervical tracheoplasty _____

9. Transtracheal tracheostomy, emergency procedure
   _____

10. Rigid bronchoscopy with fluoroscopic guidance with bronchial alveolar lavage
    _____

11. Cricoid split laryngoplasty _____

12. Single segment removal of lung
    _____

13. Removal of lung, pneumonectomy
    _____

14. Diagnostic thoracoscopy with biopsy of the mediastinal space _____

15. Thoracic sympathectomy via thoracoscope
    _____

16. Unilateral diagnostic nasal endoscopy
    _____

17. Maxillectomy _____

18. Excision of an intranasal lesion via internal approach _____

19. Intranasal maxillary sinusotomy
    _____

20. Pneumonostomy with open drainage of abscess
    _____

21. Revision of tracheostomy scar
    _____

22. Extrapleural pneumonectomy
    _____

23. Unilateral total lung lavage _____

24. Total intranasal ethmoidectomy
    _____

25. Rigid bronchoscopy, one lobe, with bronchial thermoplasty _____

26. Catheterization with bronchial brush biopsy
    _____

27. Suture of intrathoracic tracheal wound
    _____

28. Thoracentesis, needle, for aspiration of the pleural space _____

29. Planned tracheostomy _____

30. Laryngoscopy, flexible fiberoptic with removal of lesion _____

31. Submucous resection of superior turbinate
    _____

32. Total rhinectomy _____

33. Secondary rhinoplasty, minor revision
    _____

34. Indirect diagnostic laryngoscopy
    _____

35. Direct operative laryngoscopy with biopsy using operating microscope _____

Case Studies

Instructions: Review each case and indicate the correct code(s).

Case 1

Preoperative diagnosis: Mass on larynx

Postoperative diagnosis: Pending pathology report

Procedure: Laryngoscopy

The patient was prepped and draped in the usual fashion and placed in the supine position. The operating table was turned to 90 degrees, and a donut headrest was used for stabilization. Mirrors were placed for indirect visualization. A laryngoscope was inserted and suspended for visualization. The larynx and the surrounding area were inspected, and a biopsy of the larynx was taken. Hemostasis was verified, and the scope was extracted. The patient tolerated the procedure and was sent to the recovery room.

CPT codes: _____

Case 2

Preoperative diagnosis: Foreign body in bronchus

Postoperative diagnosis: Foreign body in bronchus

Procedure: Removal of a foreign body in the bronchus of the left lung via scope

The patient was consciously sedated, and a bronchoscope was introduced into the left nasal passage. There were no abnormal structures noted as the scope was placed into the left bronchial tree. In the left bronchial tree, there was a foreign body, and the bronchial tree appeared slightly inflamed. The foreign body was removed and sent to pathology for inspection. The scope was removed, and the patient tolerated the procedure and was sent to recovery in stable condition.

CPT codes: _____

Case 3

Procedure Note

This 32-year-old female was brought to the emergency department by her sister with right-side chest pain. Patient states that pain is between 9 and 10 on the pain scale. She has been having shortness of breath for the last four hours. She was fine yesterday except for a little fatigue. The pain started when she woke up this morning. A chest x-ray showed some suspicious area at the left base. At this time it was determined that a percutaneous needle biopsy of the left lung should be completed. This procedure was performed, and the patient is resting.

CPT codes: _____

Case 4

This 24-year-old patient was brought to the emergency room with difficulty breathing after being stung by a bee. The patient is experiencing a severe reaction to the bee sting. She was able to administer the EpiPen but she is still in need of breathing assistance. An emergency transtracheal tracheostomy was performed, after which the patient was resting comfortably.

CPT codes: _____

Case 5

Preoperative diagnosis: Small unidentified mass in the right lung

Postoperative diagnosis: Same

Procedure: Bronchoscopy with biopsy with washings

Conscious sedation of Fentanyl, 20 mcg, and 2 mg of Versed was administered to this patient. A bronchoscope was introduced through the left nostril and moved down past normal vocal cord structure and into the bronchial tree on the right side. There were no ulcerations of the mucosa. Fluoroscopic guidance allowed for the bronchoscope to move into the upper lobe of the right lung. Endobronchial biopsy of a small mass was noted, and washings and brushings were taken. The sample was sent for histology. The patient tolerated the procedure well.

CPT codes: _____

Case 6

Physician Office Procedure Note

This 76-year-old patient is being seen today because of spontaneous nasal hemorrhages. This patient has leukemia and is experiencing frequent bleeding from his nose. He was seen on Monday of this week, and I packed his nose with posterior nasal packing. He returned today and is still bleeding, and I again posteriorly packed his nose to control the nasal hemorrhage. He was instructed to go directly to the emergency department if the bleeding increases at any point.

CPT codes: _____

Case 7

Endoscopy Report

Preprocedure diagnosis: Rule out malignant lesion of right upper lobe of bronchus

Postprocedure diagnosis: Pending pathology report

Procedure: Under conscious sedation, this 82-year-old female was sedated. The airway was anesthetized, and a flexible bronchoscope has advanced through the oral cavity through the larynx using fluoroscopic guidance. The bronchus was viewed, and a lesion was identified. A biopsy of the tissue was taken from the right upper lobe of the bronchus. No other lesions were visualized. Bleeding was found to be minimal, and the scope was removed. The tissue sample was sent to pathology. The patient was sent to the recovery area in stable condition.

CPT codes: _____

Case 8

Preoperative and postoperative diagnosis: External and internal nasal deformity

Procedure: Septorhinoplasty with major septal repair

The patient was placed in the supine position under general anesthesia. This is the first time that this patient has undergone rhinoplasty. A cocaine-soaked pledget was placed in the nasal cavity, and the nasal septum and cartilaginous regions were exposed. After the blood vessels shrank, 1% Lidocaine with 1:100,000 epinephrine was injected into the nasal mucosa. The deformity was visualized via incisions noting the concave of the nasal septum. The cartilage was trimmed, and fat was removed from the subcutaneous regions. The dorsum was reshaped with files, and the periosteum was incised at the caudal aspect of the nasal bones, with a small portion of the bone resected. A vertical incision was made in the septal mucosa, and the cartilage was removed. All incisions were closed in single layers. The nose was dressed with the standard rhinoplasty dressing, and a Denver splint was placed to support the changes in the bone. Estimated blood loss was minimal. The patient was taken to the recovery area in stable condition.

CPT codes: _____

Case 9

Ambulatory Surgery Center Report

Patient history: This 34-year-old male patient was in an accident five years ago, and at that time had a permanent tracheostomy due to the extent of the injury. He now presents with scar tissue in the area of the tracheostomy.

Preoperative and postoperative diagnosis: Redundant scar tissue surrounding a tracheal stoma

Procedure: Repair of the tracheal stoma

The patient was placed under general anesthesia, and the airway was established for proper ventilation during the procedure. An incision was made to resect the redundant scar tissue that had formed around the tracheal stoma. The skin was reanastomosed and closed in sutured layers. Blood loss was minimal. The patient was sent to the recovery area in satisfactory condition.

CPT codes: _____

Case 10

Endoscopy Report

Preoperative diagnosis: Foreign body in larynx

Postoperative diagnosis: Same as above; material sent to pathology

Procedure: This 69-year-old female was brought to the endoscopy suite and topical anesthesia was applied to the oral cavity and pharynx. The laryngoscope was then placed through the oral cavity into the laryngeal area. An aspirator device was fed through the scope and cleared of all saliva to better visualize the foreign body that was present. The foreign body was then removed and sent to pathology. The patient was stable and sent to the postprocedure area. There were no noted complications.

CPT codes: _____

Cardiovascular System

Chapter Outline

Introduction

Guidelines Related to the National
   Correct Coding Initiative (NCCI)

Abbreviations Relating to the
   Cardiovascular System

Anatomy of the Cardiovascular System

Coding Cardiovascular Procedures

Coronary Artery Bypass Grafts

Arteries and Veins

Vascular Injection Procedures (36000–36598)

Arterial and Arteriovenous Procedures
   (36600–37799)

Summary

Internet Links

Chapter Review

Coding Assignments
   Case Studies

Learning Objectives

At the conclusion of this chapter, you should be able to:

1. Define key terms related to coding procedures on the cardiovascular system.
2. Define abbreviations related to the cardiovascular system.
3. Describe the basic anatomy and functions of the respiratory system.
4. Define common procedures performed on the cardiovascular system.
5. Apply specific coding guidelines for the cardiovascular system.
6. Select CPT codes for procedures performed on the cardiovascular system from case studies.

Key Terms

aneurysm	atrioventricular node (AV node)	coronary artery bypass grafts (CABG)	insertion
angioplasty			ligation
angioscopy	bundle of His	dual-chamber system	mitral valve
anomaly	cardiac pacemaker	electrode	myocardium
aortic valve	cardiovascular system	endarterectomy	nonselective placement
arteries	central venous access device (CVA device)	endocardium	pacing cardioverter-defibrillator
atria		epicardium	
	complete replacement	heart	parietal pericardium

partial replacement	pericardium	serous pericardium	veins
percutaneous ventricular assist device (pVAD)	pulmonary valve	single-chamber system	venous access device
	pulse generator	sinoatrial node (SA node)	ventricles
pericardial fluid	removal	thromboendarterectomy	vessels
pericardial sac	repair	tricuspid valve	visceral pericardium
pericardiocentesis	selective placement		

Introduction

The **cardiovascular system** is the system that pumps blood through the body via the heart and blood vessels. Oxygen and nutrients are carried through the body by the blood, and waste products are transported for disposal from the body. The code range for the coding procedures performed within the cardiovascular system is 33016–37799. Within the CPT manual are two subsections with the following headings: Heart and Pericardium and Arteries and Veins.

Guidelines Related to the National Correct Coding Initiative (NCCI)

Reference the following website to obtain the most current NCCI guideline information related to the Cardiovascular System.

1. Log on to *http://www.cms.gov/Medicare/Coding/NationalCorrectCodInitED/index.html*.
2. Scroll to the section titled "Downloads."
3. Click the link for the most current "NCCI Policy Manual for Medicare Services."
4. A box will appear that requires you to click "Open."
5. Click on "Chapter 5" for guidelines specific to the Cardiovascular System coding.

Abbreviations Relating to the Cardiovascular System

The following is a list of the most common abbreviations related to the cardiovascular system.

Abbreviations	Definitions
AED	automated external defibrillator
A-fib	atrial fibrillation
AICD	automated implantable cardioverter-defibrillator
AS	aortic stenosis
ASD	atrial septal defect
ASHD	arteriosclerotic heart disease
BBB	bundle-branch block
CABG	coronary artery bypass graft

CAD	coronary artery disease
CC	cardiac catheterization
CCU	coronary care unit
CHD	coronary heart disease
CHF	congestive heart failure
DVT	deep vein thrombosis
EKG	electrocardiogram
HTN	hypertension
MI	myocardial infarction
MVP	mitral valve prolapse
PAD	peripheral artery disease
pVAD	percutaneous ventricular assist device
PVD	peripheral vascular disease

Anatomy of the Cardiovascular System

The **heart** is a large muscle that acts like a pump, moving blood through the arteries and veins. It is the major organ of the cardiovascular system. It is located between the lungs in the thoracic cavity. Figure 8-1 illustrates the location of the heart and associated structures that are found within the thoracic cavity.

The heart is enclosed in the **pericardium**, or **pericardial sac**, a double-walled sac composed of membranous tissue that surrounds the heart. The **parietal pericardium**, also known as the fibrous pericardium, is the outermost layer. The **visceral pericardium**, also known as the **serous pericardium**, is the inner layer of this double-walled sac. Between the two pericardial layers is a space that is filled with **pericardial fluid**, which prevents the two layers from rubbing against each other. There are three layers of the heart. The outermost layer of the heart is the **epicardium**. The middle layer is the **myocardium**, which is the thickest layer and is the cardiac muscle. The innermost layer is the **endocardium**, which is sometimes referred to as the *lining of the heart*. Figure 8-2 illustrates the linings and layers of the heart.

The heart is divided into four chambers. The upper chambers, called the **atria**, receive blood from the veins. The lower chambers, called **ventricles**, send blood to the arteries. Blood enters the right atrium through the superior vena cava from the upper part of the body and through the inferior vena cava from the lower part of the body. Blood leaves the heart through the aorta and the pulmonary artery. Figure 8-3 illustrates the blood flow through the heart.

The heart pumps blood rhythmically through the body. The rhythm of the pumping is the job of cells that generate and conduct electrical impulses. The **sinoatrial node (SA node)** is found where the superior vena cava and the right atrium meet. Impulses from the SA node move across the atria, causing contractions, pushing the blood into the ventricles of the heart.

When the impulse reaches the junction of the atria and the ventricles, the **atrioventricular node (AV node)**, directs the impulses to the ventricles, causing them to contract. The conduction fibers that cause contraction are called the **bundle of His**.

A coder who is trying to code procedures performed on the cardiovascular system needs to have at least a basic understanding of the anatomy of the heart and how the blood flows through it.

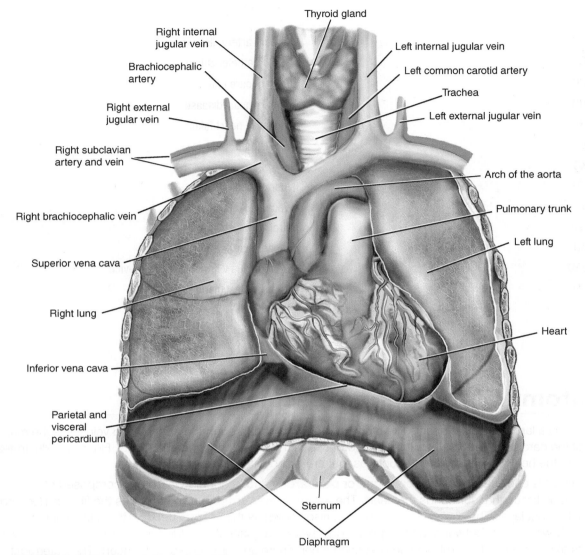

FIGURE 8-1 Heart and Associated Structures

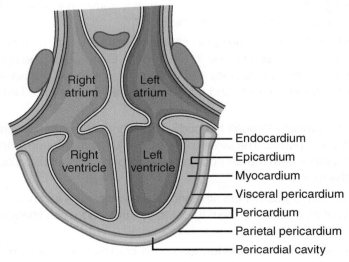

FIGURE 8-2 Linings and Layers of the Heart

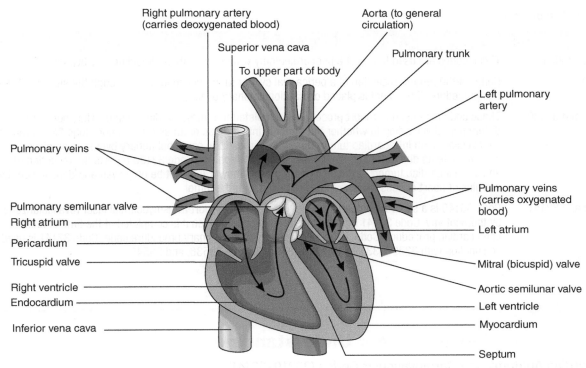

Right pulmonary artery
(carries deoxygenated blood)

Aorta (to general
circulation)

Superior vena cava

Pulmonary trunk

To upper part of body

Left pulmonary
artery

Pulmonary veins

Pulmonary semilunar valve

Right atrium

Pericardium

Tricuspid valve

Right ventricle

Endocardium

Inferior vena cava

Pulmonary veins
(carries oxygenated
blood)

Left atrium

Mitral (bicuspid) valve

Aortic semilunar valve

Left ventricle

Myocardium

Septum

FIGURE 8-3 Blood Flow of Normal Heart

Coding Cardiovascular Procedures

At the start of the section in the CPT manual for the Cardiovascular System, a notation appears that all new coders should be familiar with. This notation discusses the coding of selective vascular catheterizations.

Pericardium, Cardiac Tumor, and Transmyocardial Revascularization (33016–33141)

The first major section of codes discussed in the cardiovascular section is related to the heart and pericardium. The code range 33016–33141 begins the chapter. These codes encompass procedures on the pericardium, cardiac tumor excision, and transmyocardial revascularization. Table 8-1 summarizes the codes in this range.

TABLE 8-1 Cardiovascular Procedures (33016–33141)

Code(s)	Description
33016–33019	A **pericardiocentesis** is a procedure in which the physician removes fluid from the pericardial space by insertion of a fine needle to aspirate the fluid. In the CPT manual prior to code 33016 an extensive notation appears that applies to these codes. Review this notation in the coding manual.
33020	This code is used to report the removal of a clot or foreign body from the pericardium via a pericardiotomy.
33025	At times, the pericardial fluid needs to be drained into the pleural space. This code is used to report the creation of an opening for drainage.

(continues)

TABLE 8-1 (*continued*)

Code(s)	Description
33030–33031	These codes are used to report a pericardiectomy without or with cardiopulmonary bypass.
33050	Code 33050 reports resection of a pericardial cyst or tumor via an incision through the sternum. During this procedure, the patient is placed on cardiopulmonary bypass.
33120 and 33130	These codes are used to report procedures completed to remove cardiac tumors. The codes are differentiated according to whether the tumor is intracardiac or an external tumor. Code 33120 reports the excision of an intracardiac tumor. During the procedure, cardiopulmonary bypass is employed, and any defects due to the removal of the tumor are repaired. Code 33130 reports the resection of an external cardiac tumor. Cardiopulmonary bypass may or may not be employed and depends on the margins of heart or vessel tissue that is removed with the tumor.
33140 and 33141	Code 33140 is a separate procedure code that is used to report transmyocardial laser revascularization by thoracotomy. Code 33141 reports the same procedure when it is completed at the time of another open cardiac procedure. Code 33141 is secondary to the primary procedure code. Code 33141 is used in conjunction with 33390, 33391, 33404–33496, 33510–33536, and 33542.

Exercise 8.1—Check Your Understanding

Cardiac Anatomy and Cardiovascular Codes (33010–33141)

Fill in the blanks in the statements that follow.

1. When the impulse reaches the junction of the atria and the ventricles, the _____ directs the impulse to the ventricles, causing them to contract.
2. The heart is divided into _____ chambers.
3. The middle layer of the heart is the _____.
4. Blood enters the right atrium through the superior vena cava from the upper part of the body and through the _____ from the lower part of the body.
5. The heart is enclosed in the _____, a double-walled sac.
6. The "AV" in the term "AV node" means _____ node.
7. Fluid is drained from the pericardial space by a long needle. The needle is exchanged for an indwelling catheter. This procedure is called _____.
8. The _____ is found where the superior vena cava and the right atrium meet.

Coding Assignment

Select the correct CPT code.

9. Resection of pericardial tumor _____
10. Resection of external cardiac tumor _____
11. Pericardiocentesis with imaging guidance _____
12. Complete pericardiectomy _____

Pacemaker or Pacing Cardioverter-Defibrillator (33202–33275)

A **cardiac pacemaker** is used to correct and manage heart dysrhythmias. The pacemaker is made up of a **pulse generator** that contains a lithium battery as its source of power. In most cases, it lasts six to ten years before it needs to be surgically replaced. The generator controls the heart's rate, the energy output, and the pacing modes. The other part of the pacemaker is the electrodes. An **electrode** is inserted into the heart through the subclavian vein and advanced to the right ventricular apex. If a second electrode, or lead, is needed, it is fixed in the right atrial appendage. The electrodes are then attached to the pulse generator. The pulse generator is implanted internally under the skin (considered permanent) or temporarily attached externally. To place the generator below the skin, an incision is made to create a pocket into which it is placed. The pacemaker system is referred to as either a *single-chamber* or a *dual-chamber* system. The **single-chamber system** has one electrode in either the right atrium or the right ventricle. The **dual-chamber system** has two electrodes: one in the right atrium and one in the right ventricle.

Also coded in this section of the CPT manual are procedures completed for pacing cardioverter-defibrillators. A **pacing cardioverter-defibrillator** differs from a pacemaker in that it emits defibrillating shocks that stimulate the heart and treat ventricular fibrillation or ventricular tachycardia. See Table 8-2.

TABLE 8-2 Pacemaker or Pacing Cardioverter-Defibrillator (33202–33249)

Code(s)	Description
33202–33213	This range of codes is used to report insertion or replacement of pacemaker, single or dual chamber. When coding the insertion or replacement of pacemakers, coders must determine the following: • Is the pacemaker temporary or permanent? • Was the pacemaker inserted with transvenous leads? • What approach was used, thoracotomy, median sternotomy, subxiphoid approach versus endoscopic approach? • Was the device single or dual chamber? Figure 8-4 illustrates the placement of a pacemaker that is implanted under the skin. It should be stated that this section of codes contains instructional notations after the codes. For example, after code 33203, a notation instructs the coder of the following: When epicardial lead placement is performed with insertion of the generator, report 33202, 33203 in conjunction with 33212, 33213, 33221, 33230, 33231, and 33240. Notations also appear after codes 33208 and 33221.
33214	Code 33214 reports the upgrade of implanted pacemaker system, conversion of single-chamber system to dual-chamber system (includes removal of previously placed pulse generator, testing of existing lead, insertion of new lead, insertion of new pulse generator).
33215	Repositioning of previously implanted transvenous pacemaker or implantable defibrillator (right atrial or right ventricular) electrode is reported using this code. The electrode is repositioned because the system is not functioning correctly due to improper placement of the electrode wire.
33216	Code 33216 codes the insertion of a single transvenous electrode, permanent pacemaker, or implantable defibrillator.
33217	Code 33217 codes the insertion of 2 transvenous electrodes, permanent pacemaker, or implantable defibrillator. It should be noted that codes 33216 and 33217 are not reported with numerous codes that are listed in the CPT manual after the description of codes 33216 and 33217. Reference these instructional notations for clarification.
33218–33220	Repair of transvenous electrode(s) for pacemakers is reported with these codes. Code 33218 reports the repair of a single transvenous electrode for a permanent pacemaker or implantable debibrillator, whereas code 33220 reports the repair of two electrodes for a permanent pacemaker or implantable defibrillator.
33222–33223	Procedures completed on skin pockets for pacemakers are reported using these codes. Code 33222 is for the relocation of a skin pocket for a pacemaker, while code 33223 reports the relocation of a skin pocket for an implantable defibrillator.
33224	This code reports the insertion of pacing electrode, cardiac venous system, for left ventricular pacing, with attachment to a previously placed pacemaker or implantable defibrillator pulse generator (including revision of pocket, removal, insertion, and/or replacement of the existing generator). This code is used to report the placement of an additional left ventricular electrode to a previously placed pacemaker or implantable defibrillator.

(continues)

TABLE 8-2 *(continued)*

Code(s)	Description
33225 (must be used in conjunction with codes listed in the CPT manual)	This code is considered an add-on code that is used to report the insertion of a pacing electrode, cardiac venous system, for left ventricular pacing, at time of insertion of implantable defibrillator or pacemaker pulse generator. This code can include an upgrade to a dual-chamber system. This code is listed as secondary to the primary procedure code. The CPT manual lists the primary codes that are used with this code.
33226	At times, it is necessary to reposition a previously implanted cardiac venous system. This code is used to report this procedure for a left ventricular electrode (including removal, insertion, and/or replacement of existing generator).
33233–33238	Code range 33233–33238 is used to report the removal of a permanent pacemaker pulse generator and electrode(s). The codes are differentiated according to the items that are removed. The coder needs to read the operative report to determine which items were removed.
33240	This code is used to report the insertion of an implantable defibrillator pulse generator only with an existing single lead.
33241	During this procedure, the removal of an implantable defibrillator pulse generator occurs. It should be noted that only the pulse generator is removed.
33243–33244	Codes 33243–33244 are used to report the removal of a single- or dual-chamber implantable defibrillator electrode(s). The codes are differentiated by thoracotomy or transvenous extraction of the electrodes. It is common for the physician to attempt to remove the electrodes by transvenous extraction. During this procedure, the electrode wire is disconnected from the generator and then is withdrawn from the site. This is reported with code 33244. If the wire cannot be removed by the transvenous extraction technique, then a thoracotomy is required to gain access to the electrode for removal. Code 33243 reports removal by thoracotomy.
33249	The final code in this section reports the insertion or replacement of permanent implantable defibrillator system with transvenous lead(s) for single- or dual-chamber systems. This procedure is commonly completed using conscious sedation.

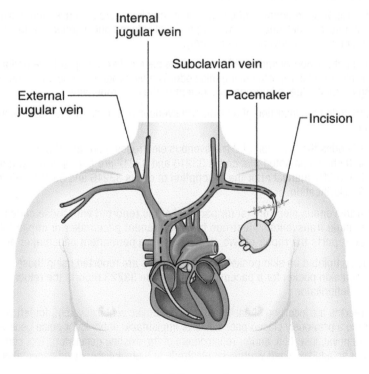

FIGURE 8-4 Implanted Pacemaker

Additional coding guidance for the reporting of this code range includes the following:

- Radiological supervision and interpretation related to pacemaker or implantable defibrillator procedure is included in codes 33206–33249, 33262, 33263, 33264, 33270, 33271, 33272, 33273, 33274, and 33275. It should also be noted, as stated in the instructional notation for pacemaker or implantable defibrillator procedures that fluoroscopy (76000, 77002), ultrasound guidance for vascular access (76937), right ventriculography (93566), and femoral venography (75820) are included in 33274, 33275, when performed. To report fluoroscopic guidance for diagnostic lead evaluation without lead insertion, replacement or revision procedures use code 76000.

- In the CPT manual locate instructional notations that follow the heading Pacemaker or Implantable Defibrillator, which precedes code 33202. In this section of the CPT manual, the coding for the replacement of a pulse generator is discussed. The replacement of a pulse generator is also known as the changing of the battery of a pacemaker or implantable defibrillator. When selecting codes, the coder needs to determine which devices (pacemaker, lead pulse generator, etc.) are removed and/or replaced. Various codes exist for different scenarios. For example, if the pulse generator for a pacemaker is removed without replacement, code 33233 is reported. However, if the pulse generator for a pacemaker is removed with replacement of a pulse generator for only a single-lead system, then code 33227 is reported. If there is a removal of a pacemaker pulse generator with replacement of a pacemaker pulse generator for a dual-lead system, then code 33228 is reported.

Exercise 8.2—Check Your Understanding

Pacemaker or Pacing Cardioverter-Defibrillator (33202–33249)

Using the CPT manual, select the appropriate code for each of the following procedures.

1. Insertion of epicardial electrodes by thoracotomy _____

2. Insertion of a permanent pacemaker with transvenous electrode; atrial _____

3. Relocation of a skin pocket for pacemaker _____

4. Removal of a permanent epicardial pacemaker and electrodes by thoracotomy; dual-lead system _____

5. Upgrade of an implanted pacemaker system with conversion of a single-chamber system to a dual-chamber system _____

6. Repositioning of a previously implanted transvenous pacemaker electrode _____

7. Removal of a permanent transvenous electrode by thoracotomy _____

8. Replacement of a temporary transvenous single-chamber cardiac electrode _____

9. Thoracotomy for removal of a dual-chamber implantable defibrillator _____

10. Replacement of temporary transvenous dual-chamber pacing electrodes _____

Electrophysiologic Operative Procedures, Subcutaneous Cardiac Rhythm Monitor, Implantable Hemodynamic Monitors, and Wounds of the Heart and Great Vessels (33250–33340)

Electrophysiologic operative procedures are reported using codes 33250–33261. This range of codes is used to report procedures that are completed to treat dysrhythmias surgically. During these procedures, tissue ablation, disruption, and reconstruction occurs. The terms *limited* and *extensive* are utilized in this code range. Limited operative ablation and reconstruction include operative ablation that isolates the pulmonary veins or other anatomically defined areas in the left or right atrium. Extensive operative ablation and reconstruction include the services that are included in the limited procedure and additional ablation of atrial tissue, such as the right atrium, atrial septum, or left atrium with the atrioventricular annulus. The notations that appear in the CPT manual prior to code 33250 should be referenced. Codes 33265 and 33266 report surgical endoscopies consisting of operative tissue ablation and reconstruction of atria without cardiopulmonary bypass. Code 33265 reports the limited procedure, while code 33266 reports the extensive procedure based on the definitions in the CPT manual.

Codes 33285 and 33286 report the insertion and removal of subcutaneous cardiac rhythm monitors. These monitors are also known as a cardiac event recorder or an implantable or insertable loop recorder (ILR). These procedures involve the physician inserting an event recorder at the subcutaneous level. The recorder keeps a continuous record of the heart's electrical activity. In the CPT manual, locate code 33285 and read the instructional notation that precedes it. This notation provides additional detail about codes 33285 and 33286. Also note the instructional notation that follows code 33286, which states that the initial insertion of the monitoring device includes the programming of the device. If subsequent electronic analysis and/or programming is needed, the coder is instructed to see codes 93285, 93291, 93298, or 93299.

The transcatheter implantation of an implantable hemodynamic monitor is reported with code 33289. As stated in the code description, the monitor is a wireless pulmonary artery pressure sensor implanted for long-term hemodynamic monitoring. This code also includes the deployment and calibration of the sensor, a right catherization, radiological supervision and interpretation, and pulmonary artery angiography, when performed. In the CPT manual following code 33289, an instructional notation appears that states code 93264 is used to report the remote monitoring of an implantable wireless pulmonary artery pressure sensor. An additional instructional notation also lists the codes that should not be reported in conjunction with code 33289. Reference the CPT manual for the complete listing of these non-reportable codes.

The repair of wounds of the heart and great vessels is reported using codes 33300–33340. This code range contains codes used to report the repair of cardiac wounds, cardiotomy, and the insertion of a graft, aorta, or great vessel. When coding from this range of codes, it is important for the coder to identify whether the procedures were completed with or without bypass. Many of the codes are differentiated by various types of bypass, such as cardiopulmonary bypass or shunt bypass.

Cardiac Valve Procedures (33361–33496)

Procedures on the cardiac valves and other valvular procedures are reported using codes 33361–33496. These codes are summarized in Table 8-3.

TABLE 8-3 Cardiac Valve Procedures (33361–33496)

Code(s)	Description
33361–33366	These codes are used to report transcatheter aortic valve replacement with a prosthetic valve. Since these procedures require two physicians, all components of the procedures are reported by adding modifier 62, which denotes that two surgeons are working together as primary surgeons performing distinct parts of the procedure. In the CPT manual, preceding code 33361, an extensive notation appears that lists the work components of these codes. When performed, the following are included: percutaneous access, placing the access sheath, balloon aortic valvuloplasty, advancing the valve delivery system into position, repositioning the valve if needed, deploying the valve, insertion of a temporary pacemaker, and closure of the arteriotomy. Prior to assigning these codes, the coder should read the notations. Note that the codes in this code range are differentiated according to the approach.
33367–33369	These codes are all add-on codes that are added to codes 33361 to 33366, codes 33418, 33477, 0483T, and 0484T. Only one of these add-on codes can be reported per primary code assignment. This is noted following each add-on code. For example, following code 33367, a notation appears that states, "Do not report 33367 in conjunction with 33368, 33369." Reference the CPT manual to identify these codes and notations.
33390 and 33391	Codes 33390 and 33391 report an open valvuloplasty of the aortic valve with cardiopulmonary bypass. These codes are differentiated as simple or complex.

(continues)

TABLE 8-3 (*continued*)

Code(s)	Description
33404–33417	This code range is used to report services performed on the **aortic valve**. The aortic valve sits between the aorta and the left ventricle and is one of the main valves of the heart. The procedures in this section include valvuloplasty, valve replacement, valve repair, resection, incision, and ventriculomyotomy. It should be noted that in this range of codes an out of sequence code (code 33440) appears. Code 33440 reports an aortic valve replacement by translocation of autologous pulmonary valve and transventricular aortic annulus enlargement of the the left ventricular outflow tract with valved conduit replacement of the pulmonary valve. This is known as a Ross-Konno procedure. In the CPT manual following code 33440 an instructional notation appears that lists the codes that are not be be used in conjunction with code 33440. Reference the CPT manual for the complete listing of these codes.
33418–33430	These procedures report services performed on the **mitral valve**. The mitral valve is the valve between the left atrium and left ventricle. It is also called the *bicuspid valve*. Valvotomy, valvuloplasty, transcatheter mitral valve repair (TMVR), and mitral valve replacement are reported using these codes.
33460–33468	The **tricuspid valve** is the valve that lies between the right atrium and right ventricle. The procedures on the tricuspid valve, such as a valvotomy, valvuloplasty, or valve replacement, are reported using these codes.
33470–33478	This code set involves procedures regarding the **pulmonary valve**. The pulmonary valve is one of the main valves of the heart and sits between the pulmonary artery and the right ventricle. The procedures on the pulmonary valve, such as a valvotomy, valvuloplasty, or valve replacement, are reported using these codes.
33496	This code reports a repair of nonstructural prosthetic valve dysfunction with cardiopulmonary bypass (separate procedure). This code would be used to report the repair of a malfunctioning prosthetic valve that may be leaking around the valve or malfunctioning because of a clot or growth.

Coronary Artery Anomalies and Endoscopy (33500–33508)

Procedures completed on coronary artery anomalies are reported using code range 33500–33507. Codes in this series include endarterectomy or angioplasty. An **endarterectomy** is a procedure used to remove the

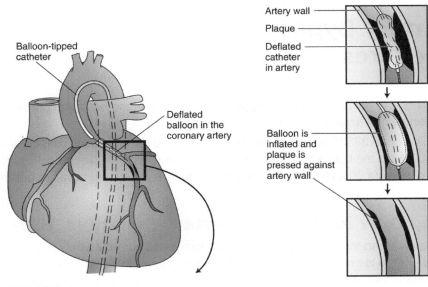

FIGURE 8-5 Angioplasty

plaque deposits from blood vessels. An **angioplasty** is a procedure in which a balloon is inflated in the vessel to push and flatten plaque against the vessel wall. Figure 8-5 illustrates an angioplasty. Code 33508 is used to report a surgical endoscopy including a video-assisted harvest of a vein(s) for a coronary artery bypass procedure. This code is used in conjunction with codes 33510–33523 as an add-on code in addition to the code for the primary procedure.

Exercise 8.3—Check Your Understanding

Coronary Artery Anomalies (33250–33507)

Using the CPT manual, assign the correct code to each of the following.

1. Replacement, pulmonary valve
   _____

2. Valvuloplasty, aortic valve; open, with cardiopulmonary bypass
   _____

3. Repair of anomalous coronary artery from pulmonary artery origin; by graft, without cardiopulmonary bypass
   _____

4. Valvotomy, pulmonary valve, closed heart; via pulmonary artery _____

5. Replacement, mitral valve, with cardiopulmonary bypass
   _____

6. Modified maze procedure for operative tissue ablation and reconstruction of atria
   _____

7. Aortoplasty completed for supravalvular stenosis _____

8. Tricuspid valve valvectomy with cardiopulmonary bypass
   _____

9. Incision of subvalvular tissue for discrete subvalvular aortic stenosis
   _____

10. Infundibular stenosis corrected by right ventricular resection _____

Coronary Artery Bypass Grafts Procedures

Coronary artery bypass grafts (CABG), are types of grafts performed on the heart that are completed using a vein, an artery, or a combination of a vein and an artery.

As discussed previously, code 33508 is an add-on code and is used in conjunction with code range 33510–33523. This code reflects the harvesting of a vein for bypass surgery. The procedure is performed using an endoscope to visualize the area on a monitor. A harvesting cannula is used to remove the portion of the vein to be used for bypass.

Venous Grafting Only for Coronary Artery Bypass (33510–33516)

The 33510–33516 codes are used for reporting coronary artery bypass surgery when *only* veins are used for the bypass. This code range is *not* used to report bypass procedures that use arterial grafts *and* venous grafts during the same procedure. A saphenous vein is typically used, but a vein from the arm, the back of the leg, or a cadaver may also be used. Harvesting of any vein other than the saphenous is separately reportable. To report the harvesting of an upper extremity vein, use code 35500. To report the harvesting of a femoropopliteal vein segment, use code 35572. Harvesting the saphenous vein in the bypass procedure is included in the code reported for the bypass. After the vein is harvested, the heart is stopped and the bypass is performed. The code selection is based on the number of coronary venous grafts. For example, code 33510 reports a coronary artery bypass using a single coronary venous graft, whereas code 33511 is used when two coronary venous grafts are used.

Combined Arterial-Venous Grafting for Coronary Bypass (33517–33530)

Codes 33517–33530 are used to report bypass procedures using both venous and arterial grafts that are done during the same operative session. Because codes from this range are add-on codes, they need to be reported with a primary code that is listed in the instructional notations that follow each code in code range 33517 to 33530. The codes read as combination codes and guide the coder to locate the additional code. An example can be found by referencing CPT code 33522—"Coronary artery bypass, using venous graft(s) and arterial graft(s); five venous grafts (list separately in addition to code for primary procedure)."

The coder needs to pay close attention to the operative report when assigning these codes, not only to be sure the correct number of grafts are captured, but also when there are grafts involving veins and arteries. The coder should also pay attention to who is harvesting the graft: in some cases, one surgeon will harvest the graft, and another surgeon will perform the bypass. In these instances, the surgeon performing the harvest should report his or her service as an assistant surgeon by appending the 80 modifier to the bypass procedure code.

Arterial Grafting for Coronary Artery Bypass (33533–33548)

The 33533–33548 codes would be used to report coronary artery bypass surgeries with the use of arteries or a combination of arterial-venous grafts. The arterial-venous grafts require the reporting of codes from this code range and the 33517–33523 code range, for a total of two codes for this service. Like venous grafting, harvesting the artery is included and is not reported separately except when the artery is taken from the upper extremities; when this occurs, code 35600 is reported in addition to the code for the bypass procedure. When an upper-extremity vein is harvested, code 35500 is additionally reported. When a femoropopliteal vein segment is harvested, code 35572 is also reported.

When a coronary artery bypass graft procedure is performed with a coronary endarterectomy, add-on code 33572 should be reported with the primary procedure code from the 33510–33516 and 33533–33536 code sets.

Anomaly Repair and Other Procedures (33600–33926)

Code range 33600–33926 is used to report procedures completed on various cardiovascular structures and to report procedures to correct a heart anomaly. An **anomaly** is an abnormality or a deviation from the norm in a structure.

The coding in this subsection includes repairs, closures, shunting procedures, transections, and other complex procedures on the heart. The codes involve procedures performed on the aorta, on the pulmonary artery, and on septal and ventricular defects. Because of the complexity of this coding, it is essential that a coder have all appropriate documentation, along with input from the surgeon if needed, to assign the proper code(s) for the services rendered.

Many of the procedures that code to this range can be located in the CPT manual index by referencing the name of the procedure and the anomaly that is being corrected.

EXAMPLE: To code a complete repair of Tetralogy of Fallot without pulmonary atresia, the following could be referenced in the index:

The term *repair*, then *heart*, then *Tetralogy of Fallot*. The index instructs the coder to use code range 33692–33697.

Alternatively, the coder could reference the following:

The term *Tetralogy of Fallot*. When referencing this term, the coder is instructed to reference codes 33692–33697, 33924.

Using either of these approaches, the coder will find the correct code.

Exercise 8.4—Check Your Understanding

Venous and Arterial Grafting, Anomaly Repair, and Other Procedures (33508–33926)

Using the CPT manual, assign the proper code(s) to each of the following:

1. Repair of pulmonary artery stenosis by reconstruction with patch

   _____

2. Blalock-Hanlon procedure

   _____

3. Repair, by ligation, of patent ductus arteriosus _____

4. Descending thoracic aorta graft, with bypass _____

5. Repair of atrial septal defect and ventricular septal defect with patch closure

   _____

6. Repair of pulmonary venous stenosis

   _____

7. Pulmonary artery embolectomy

   _____

8. Sinus of valsalva fistula repair with repair of ventricular septal defect via cardiopulmonary bypass

   _____

9. Division of aberrant vessel

   _____

10. Reimplantation of an anomalous pulmonary artery _____

Heart/Lung Transplantation (33927–33945)

Only corneal and kidney transplants are more common than heart transplants. The patient who presents for heart transplant surgery has had heart damage caused by coronary artery disease, cardiomyopathy, congestive heart failure, or severe congenital heart disease.

Heart/lung transplants are usually performed on patients who will not survive unless both organs are replaced. End-stage lung disease that involves the heart is typically what leads to a heart/lung transplant. The documentation will guide the coder as to what organs were transplanted.

The coder will need to take into consideration whether the organs were harvested from a cadaver donor or if the transplanted heart was an artificial heart. As noted in Chapter 7, Respiratory System, donor transplants involve three distinct components of physician work. The components for a cadaver donor heart/lung transplantation include:

- Cadaver donor cardiectomy with or without pneumonectomy

- Backbench work, including the preparation of the donor organ(s) prior to transplantation

- Transplantation of heart, with or without lung allotransplantation

During the transplant procedure, the heart is inspected while being packed in ice-cold saline. Code 33930 is used to report the removal of the heart and lung(s) from a donor cadaver, and code 33940 is used to report the removal of only the heart. Both codes include the cold preservation of the organ(s).

Backbench work is reported by using code 33933 or code 33944. Code 33933 reports the backbench work for a heart and lung transplant, while code 33944 is used to report the backbench work for a heart transplant.

The transplant is coded by use of code 33935 for a heart/lung transplant with recipient cardiectomy-pneumonectomy or by code 33945 for a heart transplant with or without recipient cardiectomy. Figure 8-6 illustrates the procurement of a donor heart, and Figure 8-7 illustrates a transplanted heart.

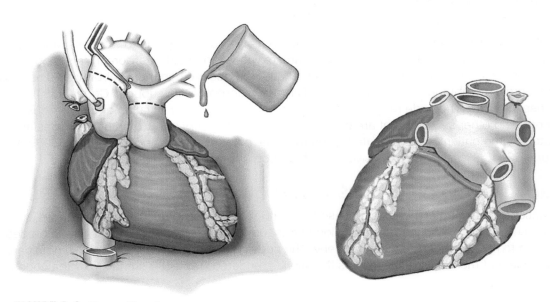

FIGURE 8-6 Donor Heart

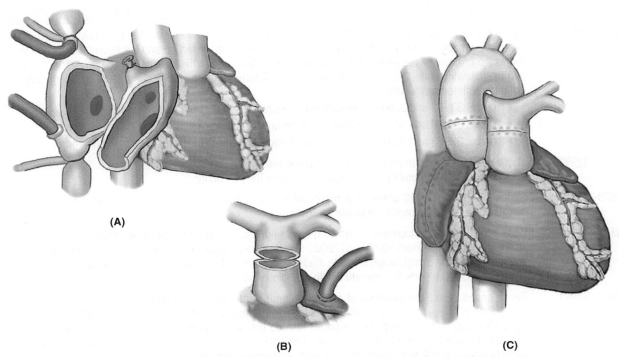

(A)

(B)   **(C)**

FIGURE 8-7 Transplanted Heart   (A) The heart and valves are brought into place. (B) The valves are attached. (C) The heart is secured.

Codes 33927 to 33929 are used to report procedures in which an artificial heart is implanted, removed or replaced. Code 33927 reports the implantation of a total replacement heart system, (artificial heart), with a recipient cardiectomy. The removal and replacement of a total replacement heart system is reported with code 33928. Code 33929 is an add on code and is reported for the removal of a total replacement heart system for heart transplantation. Code 33929 is to be used in conjunction with primary code 33945.

Extracorporeal Membrane Oxygenation or Extracorporeal Life Support Services (33946–33989)

At times when a patient's heart and/or lungs are not functioning correctly due to sickness or injury, the patient has to be placed on extracorporeal membrane oxygenation or extracorporeal life support services, which allow the heart or lungs to rest and recover. These services are commonly abbreviated as ECMO for extracorporeal membrane oxygenation or ECLS for extracorporeal life support. Codes 33946 to 33989 reports these services. The code range is differentiated according to the initiation of the services, daily management, and other services that are component parts of the services. Some of the codes are also differentiated by the patient's age. Locate the instructional notes for code range 33946 to 33989 that appear prior to code 33946. Read these extensive notes to become familiar with this range of codes.

Cardiac Assist (33967–33993) and Other Procedures (33999)

This subsection of the chapter includes the insertions and removals of ventricular assist devices, extracorporeal circulation, and intra-aortic balloon assist devices. These cardiac assist device procedures are performed to help the heart function properly. The coder will need to read the operative note carefully to assign the code that most accurately reflects the service rendered. Table 8-4 summarizes the codes found in this section.

TABLE 8-4 Cardiac Assist (33967–33999)

Code(s)	Description
33967–33974	This group of codes is used to report the insertion and removal of intra-aortic balloon assist devices. The codes are grouped in pairs, with the first code used to report the insertion and the second code used to report the removal of the device. For example, code 33967 reports the insertion of an intra-aortic balloon, and the following code, 33968, reports the removal. There are three groups of codes in this range, and they are differentiated as follows: • Codes 33967 and 33968—percutaneous approach • Codes 33970 and 33971—insertion and removal of device involving the femoral artery • Codes 33973 and 33974—insertion and removal of device involving the ascending aorta
33975–33978	These codes are used to report the insertion and removal of a ventricular assist device. The codes are differentiated by the number of ventricles involved in the procedure.
33979–33980	Codes 33979 and 33980 are used to report the insertion and removal of an implantable intracorporeal ventricular assist that involves a single ventricle.
33981–33983	Code 33981 reports replacement of extracorporeal ventricular assist device for single or biventricular, pump(s), single or each pump. Codes 33982 and 33983 report the replacement of ventricular assist device pump(s); implantable intracorporeal, single ventricle. Code 33982 reports this procedure without cardiopulmonary bypass, while code 33983 reports the procedure with a cardiopulmonary bypass.
33990–33991	These codes report the insertion of a percutaneous ventricular assist device. A **percutaneous ventricular assist device (pVAD)** is inserted to assist a weakened heart in ejecting blood to the body via a mechanical pump. These codes include the radiological supervision and interpretation and are differentiated according to the access. Code 33990 reports the arterial access, and code 33991 reports both arterial and venous access with transseptal puncture.

(continues)

TABLE 8-4 *(continued)*

Code(s)	Description
33992	Code 33992 is used to report the removal of a percutaneous ventricular access device when it occurs separate and distinct from the session in which the device was inserted.
33993	This code reports the repositioning of a percutaneous ventricular access device that occurs at a separate and distinct session from the insertion of the device. The imaging guidance is included in the code.
33999	Code 33999 is used to report cardiac surgery procedures that are not listed in the CPT manual. Prior to reporting this code, the coder should query the provider to ensure that codes within the CPT manual do not represent the procedure completed because reporting this code most likely will trigger a review by the third-party payer.

Arteries and Veins

It is just as important to understand the anatomy of the vessels as it is to understand the anatomy of the heart when you are selecting codes in the cardiovascular system. **Vessels** are structures that move fluid through the body. Arteries and veins are considered vessels. **Arteries** move oxygen-rich blood from the heart to the rest of the body (with the exception of the pulmonary artery). **Veins** move the deoxygenated blood back to the heart (with the exception of the pulmonary vein). Arteries usually have one vein accompanying them throughout the vascular system. Figure 8-8 illustrates arteries, and Figure 8-9 illustrates veins of the body.

Embolectomy/Thrombectomy (34001–34490)

Codes from the 34001–34490 series are used to report embolectomy/thrombectomy procedures completed on arteries or veins, with or without catheter placement. The object of these procedures is to remove a clot in the vessel. The code selection is made by vessel, as well as by approach or method of entry.

Exercise 8.5—Check Your Understanding

Embolectomy/Thrombectomy (34001–34490)

Using the CPT manual, note whether each procedure is being performed in a vein or artery, and then note the approach for each of the codes given. The student can assume that in each example, the surgeon is performing either an embolectomy or a thrombectomy.

Code	Vein/Artery	Approach
1. 34451	_____	_____
2. 34471	_____	_____
3. 34201	_____	_____
4. 34051	_____	_____
5. 34203	_____	_____

Venous Reconstruction (34501–34530)

Codes 34501–34530 are the codes used to report reconstruction of a vein. The type of reconstruction dictates code assignment. Transposition, grafts, anastomosis, and sutures are used for reconstruction.

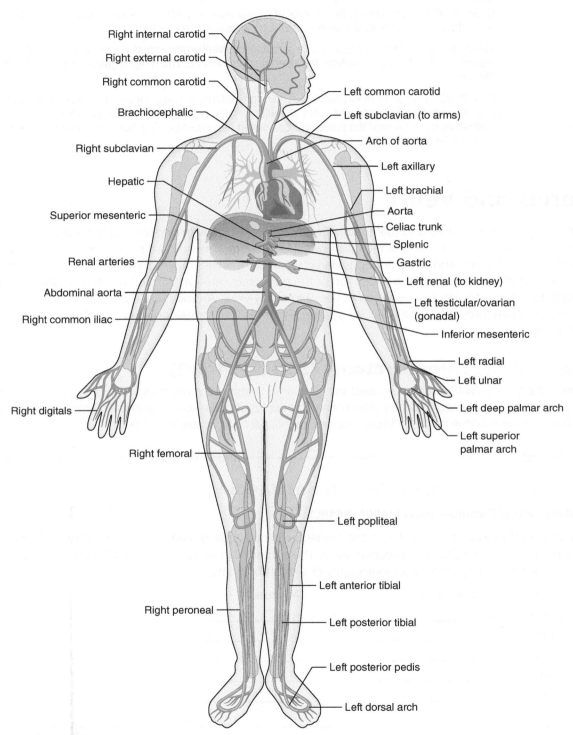

FIGURE 8-8 Arterial Circulation

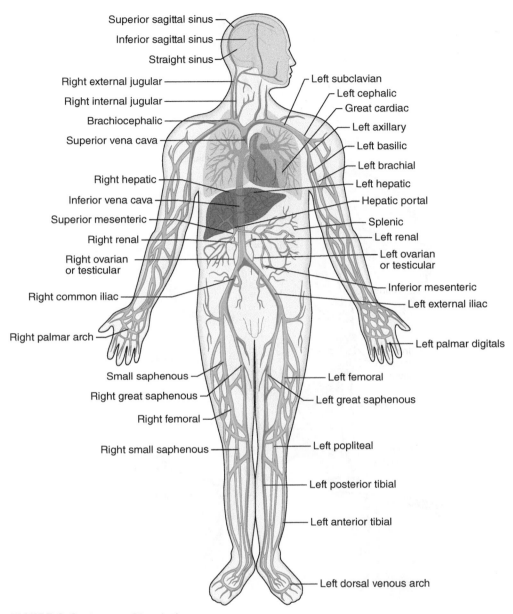

FIGURE 8-9 Venous Circulation

Endovascular Repair of Abdominal Aortic Aneurysm (34701–34834) and Fenestrated Endovascular Repair of the Visceral and Inferenal Aorta (34839–34848)

Codes 34701–34834 are the codes used to report endovascular repair of an abdominal aortic aneurysm. An **aneurysm** is an area in an artery that becomes weakened. With each pulse of blood through the artery, the weakened area balloons out, or expands, causing more weakness of the vessel. Figure 8-10 illustrates the placement of iliac and aortic clamps prior to procedures to address an abdominal aortic aneurysm.

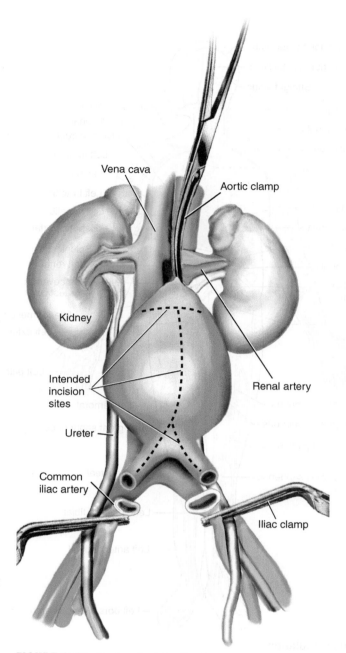

FIGURE 8-10 Abdominal Aortic Aneurysm

This type of coding has several components. Coders must read the notations that appear before code 34701 in the CPT manual to understand fully the coding for this section. Review the instructional notation that states that fluoroscopic guidance and radiological supervision and interpretation in conjunction with endograft repair is not separately reported. Guidance on the coding of wireless physiologic and pressure sensors is also given.

Table 8-5 summarizes the codes in range 34701–34834. Codes 34841 to 34848 report the placement of a fenestrated endovascular graft in the visceral aorta, either separately or in combination with the infrarenal aorta. The graft is placed to repair an aneurysm, pseudoaneurysm, dissection, penetrating ulcer, intramural hematoma, or a traumatic disruption.

TABLE 8-5 Endovascular Repair of Abdominal Aortic Aneurysm (34701–34834)

Code(s)	Description
34701–34718	These codes are used to report the endovascular repair of an aortic and/or iliac artery(ies). The code descriptions are very detailed and must be read carefully prior to code assignment.
34808	This code is an add-on code. Code 34808 is used with code 34701, 34702, 34707, 34708, 34709, 34710, 34813, 34841, 34842, 34843, or 34844 to report the endovascular placement of an iliac artery occlusion device. Within the CPT manual, following the codes, coders should reference the notations regarding codes that these codes should not be assigned with and notations regarding code assignment for radiological supervision and interpretation.
34812–34813	These add-on codes are used for procedures completed on the femoral artery. Code 34812 is used to report an open femoral artery exposure for delivery of endovascular prosthesis by groin incision. If this procedure is completed bilaterally, modifier 50 should be added to 34812. Code 34813 is an add-on to code 34812 and codes the placement of a femoral-femoral graft during endovascular aortic aneurysm repair.
34820	This add-on code is used for unilateral open iliac artery exposure for delivery of endovascular prosthesis or iliac occlusion during endovascular therapy, by abdominal or retroperitoneal incision. If the procedure is performed bilaterally, modifier 50 should be added.
34830–34832	Open repair of an infrarenal aortic aneurysm or dissection, plus the repair of an associated arterial trauma following the unsuccessful endovascular repair, are coded using this range of codes. The codes are differentiated by the type of prosthesis used: tube, aorto-bi-iliac, or aorto-bifemoral.
34833	A unilateral open iliac artery exposure with creation of a conduit for the delivery of an endovascular prosthesis or for establishment of cardiopulmonary bypass, by either an abdominal or retroperitoneal incision is reported using this code. To report a bilateral procedure, add modifier 50 to code 34833. Review the instructional notations that follow code 34833 in the CPT manual to reference the codes that code 34833 are used in conjunction with and codes that 34833 are not to be used in conjunction with. Please note that code 34833 is an add-on code.
34834	Code 34834 is used to report a unilateral open brachial artery exposure for delivery of endovascular prosthesis. The bilateral procedure is reported using modifier 50. Please note that code 34834 is an add-on code.

Exercise 8.6—Check Your Understanding

Endovascular Repair of Abdominal Aortic Aneurysm (34701–34834)

Using the CPT manual, assign the proper code(s) or add-on codes to each of the following:

1. List the add-on code for an open iliac artery exposure for delivery of endovascular prosthesis by abdominal incision, unilateral _____

2. Endovascular repair of infrarenal abdominal aortic aneurysm using aorto-uni-iliac prosthesis _____

3. List the add-on code for an unilateral open brachial artery exposure for delivery of endovascular prosthesis _____.

4. Open repair of infrarenal aortic aneurysm in addition to repair of associated arterial trauma following unsuccessful endovascular repair with aorto-bi-iliac prosthesis _____

5. List the add-on code for an open femoral artery exposure for delivery of endovascular prosthesis by groin incision, bilateral _____

6. List the add-on code for an open brachial artery exposure to assist in the deployment of aortic endovascular prosthesis by incision into the right arm _____

7. List the add-on code for an open femoral artery exposure for delivery of endovascular prosthesis, by groin incision, unilateral _____

8. Open repair of infrarenal aortic aneurysm plus repair of associated arterial trauma, following unsuccessful endovascular repair, aorto-bifemoral prosthesis _____

Direct Repair of Aneurysm or Excision (Partial or Total) and Graft Insertion for Aneurysm, Pseudoaneurysm, Ruptured Aneurysm, and Associated Occlusive Disease (35001–35152)

Code range 35001–35152 includes the artery preparation when an anastomosis is to be completed and includes the endarterectomy. This range reports direct repair of an aneurysm, a pseudoaneurysm, or excision and graft insertion in the various arteries of the body. Knowledge of the site of surgery is essential to select a code properly from this range because the codes identify the artery repaired. For example, code 35002 is for the carotid subclavian artery, and code 35005 is for a vertebral artery. The codes are also differentiated by whether the repair was for:

- An aneurysm and associated occlusive disease

- A ruptured aneurysm

- An aneurysm, pseudoaneurysm, and associated occlusive disease

Careful reading of the operative report must occur to identify the necessary elements for code selection.

Repair of Arteriovenous Fistula (35180–35190)

Code range 35180–35190 is used to report the repair of an arteriovenous fistula. Codes 35180–35184 are used to report the repair of a congenital arteriovenous fistula. These codes are differentiated by the site of the procedure. Codes 35188–35190 are used to code the repair of an acquired or traumatic arteriovenous fistula. These codes are also differentiated by site.

Repair of a Blood Vessel for Reasons Other Than Fistula (35201–35286)

Code range 35201–35286 is used to report the repair of a blood vessel for reasons other than a fistula, with or without patch angioplasty. There are three groupings of codes in this code range:

- Direct repair of a blood vessel—Differentiated by site; codes 35201–35226

- Repair of a blood vessel with a vein graft—Differentiated by site; codes 35231–35256

- Repair of blood vessel with a graft other than a vein—Differentiated by site; codes 35261–35286

Thromboendarterectomy (35301–35390)

Code range 35301–35390 is used to code a **thromboendarterectomy**, a surgical incision that is made into an artery to remove a thrombus or plaque and the arterial lining. This procedure can occur with or without a patch graft. The codes in this range are differentiated according to the artery on which the procedure was completed. Code 35306 is an add-on code that is additionally reported for each additional tibial or peroneal artery. This code is to be listed as an additional code to the primary procedure code 35305. In the CPT manual following code 35306, a notation instructs the coder that codes 35304, 35305, and 35306 are not to be reported with codes 37229, 37231, 37233, and 37235.

Angioscopy (35400)

The angioscopy code, 35400, is an add-on code and is used in conjunction with a code for the therapeutic intervention. **Angioscopy** is a procedure in which a fiber-optic scope is used to visualize the interior of a noncoronary vessel.

Exercise 8.7—Check Your Understanding

Code Range 35001–35400

Using the CPT manual, identify and assign the correct code to each of the following procedures:

1. Direct repair of blood vessel of the neck
   _____

2. Repair of congenital arteriovenous fistula of head and neck
   _____

3. Repair of blood vessel with vein graft, intra-abdominal
   _____

4. Repair, acquired arteriovenous fistula, thorax and abdomen
   _____

5. Direct repair of aneurysm with patch graft by arm incision for ruptured aneurysm of the axillary-brachial artery
   _____

Bypass Graft—Vein (35500–35572) and In-Situ Vein (35583–35587)

This code range reports bypass grafts that are completed using veins. The codes are differentiated according to the location of the vein graft anastomosis. For example, code 35571 reports a procedure whereby the surgeon creates a bypass around the popliteal artery using a vein that is then sutured to the tibial artery. It should be noted that in the CPT manual, prior to code 35500, notations give directions for code assignment. For code range 35501–35587, procurement of the saphensous vein graft is included in the codes and, therefore, is not reported as a separate service. Codes 35583 to 35587 report in-situ vein bypass. The codes are differentiated according to the veins sutured.

Bypass Graft—Other Than Vein (35600–35671)

Sometimes veins are not used for bypass. An artery or other material might be used. If this is the case, the coder would reference the Bypass Graft—Other Than Vein subsection of the cardiovascular chapter of the CPT manual. Codes 35600–35671 offer other reporting options for bypass grafts done with materials other than a vein.

Composite Grafts, Adjuvant Techniques, and Arterial Transposition (35681–35697)

Composite grafts are made from donor and synthetic materials. Codes 35681–35683 are add-on codes and need to be used in conjunction with the codes that are listed in the CPT manual after each code. The harvesting and anastomosis of multiple vein segments from distant sites for use as an arterial bypass graft conduit is reported with codes 35682 and 35683. It should also be noted that, following codes 35681, 35682, and 35683, notations state the codes that are not to be reported together and the codes that these codes should be reported in conjunction with.

Adjuvant technique codes, codes 35685 and 35686, are add-on codes that are used with various codes as listed in the CPT manual. The adjuvant technique involves the surgeon placing a vein patch, placing a cuff at a distal arterial anastomosis site, or creating a fistula between artery and vein during bypass surgery. These adjuvant techniques are used to improve the patency of the lower extremity autogenous or synthetic bypass graft.

Codes 35691–35697 report arterial transposition procedures that are completed to improve blood flow within the arteries. The codes are differentiated according to whether the arteries were anastomosed. Code 35697 is an add-on code.

Excision, Exploration, Repair, and Revision (35700–35907)

Codes 35700–35907 report excision, exploration, repair, and revision of bypass surgery. Code 35700 is an add-on code that reports the return of the patient to the operating room more than one month after an original operation was completed on the femoral-popliteal or femoral anterior tibial, posterior tibial, peroneal artery, or other distal vessel.

Codes 35701–35703 report the exploration of an artery not followed by surgical repair. Exploration for postoperative hemorrhage, thrombosis, or infection is reported with codes 35800–35860. Codes 35870–35884 report repairs, excisions, and revisions. Excisions of infected grafts are reported with codes 35901–35907 and are differentiated according to anatomical site.

Vascular Injection Procedures (36000–36598)

The coding for this subsection of the cardiovascular chapter is difficult for new coders. Two terms that a coder needs to understand in this type of coding are *selective* and *nonselective*. The terms refer to catheter placement. **Nonselective placement** of a catheter means the catheter is functioning in the vessel punctured and does not go into any other vessel or vascular family. **Selective placement** means that the catheter moves into one of the great vessels off the aorta, not including the vessel punctured for access. This is a simplified version, but it is the basic concept for this coding.

Movement of the catheter from one vascular family to another should be reported separately. Radiological services performed in conjunction with catheter movement should also be reported separately. CPT identifies services that are included and those that are not included. Careful attention to these details can make a significant difference in the reimbursement that your surgeon does or does not receive for these services.

Code sets begin with intravenous procedures (36000–36015). The intra-arterial/intra-aortic procedures follow and are reported using codes 36100–36299.

Venous procedures, including venipuncture or intravenous therapy, are reported using codes 36400–36598. Included in the venous procedures are the central venous access (CVA) procedures. A **venous access device** is a device or catheter that allows access to the venous system. It can be used for intravenous medications or fluid delivery and is typically used for patients who require these services for more than 24 hours. A **central venous access device (CVA device)**, is a catheter classified as such if the tip ends in the subclavian, brachiocephalic, superior or inferior vena cava, or right atrium. The device can be inserted into the jugular, subclavian, femoral vein, or inferior vena cava to be considered centrally inserted. If the device is inserted peripherally, it is inserted in the basilica or cephalic vein.

There are five categories for procedures involving these devices. When a catheter is placed in a newly established venous access, it is considered an **insertion**. The **repair** procedures involve fixing, not replacing, either the catheter or port/pump. The repair is one that is other than a pharmacologic or mechanical repair of a intracatheter or pericatheter occlusion. **Partial replacement** involves replacement of only a catheter component, not the whole device. Replacement of the whole device at the same access site is considered a **complete replacement**. The final category, **removal**, involves the removal of the entire device.

When coding the replacement of an existing CVA device, the coder should code for the removal of the old device and assign a code for the new device if it is placed in a separate venous access site.

Arterial and Arteriovenous Procedures (36600–37799)

The next group of codes in the CPT manual is used for procedures that involve arteries and veins. Many involve accessing an artery or a vein for a variety of purposes.

Arterial and Intraosseous Codes (36600–36680)

Codes 36600–36680 are used to report services that involve arterial and intraosseous procedures such as:

- Arterial puncture, code 36600, for withdrawal of blood for diagnosis
- Arterial catheterization, codes 36620–36640, for sampling or for prolonged infusion therapy
- Catheterization of an umbilical artery, code 36660, for diagnosis or therapy on a newborn
- Placement of needle, code 36680, for intraosseous infusion

Hemodialysis Access, Intervascular Cannulation for Extracorporeal Circulation or Shunt Insertion (36800–36861)

Code range 36800–36861 is used to report procedures completed for:

- Hemodialysis access

- Intervascular cannulation for extracorporeal circulation

- Shunt insertion

Numerous notations are present in this range of codes that must be referenced for proper code selection. For example, a notation appears under code 36818 that instructs the coder that this code is not to be reported with codes 36819, 36820, 36821, or 36830 during a unilateral upper-extremity procedure. It should also be noted that many of the procedures in this range are separate procedure codes and are reported only if no other procedure is completed.

Dialysis Circuit (36901–36909)

Code ranges 36901–36909 reports angioplasty, stent placement, thrombectomy, and embolization within dialysis circuit procedures. In the CPT manual prior to these codes, extensive guidelines and definitions are listed that impact the selection of codes in this range. In the CPT manual, review the definitions including dialysis circuit, peripheral dialysis segment, central dialysis segment, and so on.

Codes 36901 to 36906 are built as progressive hierarchies that include less intensive services, and only one code from 36901 to 36906 is to be reported for the service provided in a dialysis circuit. This is highlighted in the guidelines that are found in the CPT manual prior to the codes.

Codes 36907 to 36909 are add-on codes. Following each code there are extensive instructional notations in the CPT manual that outline the codes used in conjunction with these add-on codes. It is essential that coders read all of the guidelines, definitions, and instructional notations that are present in the CPT manual for this range of codes. Locate all of these items and read them prior to code selection.

Portal Decompression Procedures (37140–37183)

Code range 37140–37183 is used to report portal decompression procedures. These procedures, which include venous anastomosis, insertion of shunts, and revision of shunts, are completed to manage venous pressures. Like other sections of this chapter, all notes need to be referenced before codes are assigned.

Transcatheter Procedures (37184–37218)

Transcatheter procedures are completed by using a catheter to complete the following:

- Perform arterial mechanical thrombectomy—codes 37184–37186.

- Perform venous mechanical thrombectomy—codes 37187–37188.

- Inject a drug into the vessel—codes 37195 and 37211–37214.

- Obtain a biopsy sampling—code 37200.

- Retrieve a foreign body—code 37197.

- Transcatheter therapy procedures for thrombosis—codes 37211–37214.

- Placement of intravascular stents—codes 37215–37218.

Coders need to read the notations that are present at the start and end of this code range in the CPT manual for additional instructions on selecting codes from this range.

Endovascular Revascularization (Open or Percutaneous, Transcatheter) (37220-37239)

Code range 37220–37235 reports endovascular revascularization procedures performed on the lower extremities for occlusive disease. When reporting these codes, the coder should report only one primary code from 37220 to 37235 for each extremity vessel treated because the codes are inclusive of all the services provided for that vessel. Therefore, the code for the most intensive service provided should be reported.

As discussed in the CPT manual, in the paragraphs preceding these codes, the codes include the following:

- Accessing and selectively catheterizing the vessel
- Traversing the lesion
- Radiological supervision and interpretation directly related to the intervention
- Embolic protection
- Closure of the arteriotomy
- Imaging completed
- Balloon angioplasty, if performed
- Atherectomy
- Stenting

The organization of the codes is divided into three arterial vascular territories: iliac, femoral/popliteal, and tibial/peroneal. There are specific guidelines for each of the three territories. Prior to code selection, coders must read the notations in the numerous paragraphs before the code descriptions. The guidelines give instructions for coding when multiple territories are treated, coding for lesions that extend across margins of one vessel into another, and for the use of modifier 59, to name a few. It should also be noted that, following individual codes in this section, notations are present in relation to codes used in conjunction with other codes. Codes 37246 to 37249 are out of sequence codes. These codes report transluminal balloon angioplasty, open or percutaneous, and related radiological imaging. These codes are, therefore, considered bundled codes, and the instructional notations that precede and follow the codes must be read and understood prior to assigning these codes. Locate and read the instructional notations that precede and follow these codes. Codes 37236–37239 report transcatheter placement of an intravascular stent(s) for vessels other than in the lower extremities, cervical carotid, extracranial vertebral or intrathoracic, carotid, intracranial, or coronary. These procedures can be performed as an open or percutaneous approach.

Vascular Embolization and Occlusion (37241-37244) and Intravascular Ultrasound Services (37252-37253)

Codes 37241–37244 are used to report vascular embolization and occlusion procedures, excluding the CNS and the head and neck, as well as ablation and sclerotherapy procedures for venous insufficiency/telangiectasis of the extremities/skin. Codes 37252 and 37253 are add-on codes and report intravascular ultrasound of a noncoronary vessel during diagnostic evaluation and/or therapeutic intervention. These codes include radiological supervision and interpretation. Code 37252 reports the initial noncoronary vessel while code 37253 reports each additional noncoronary vessel. Review the instructional notations following code 37253 for additional guidance for reporting these codes.

Endoscopy (37500-37501)

Two endoscopy codes are used for coding in the cardiovascular system. They are code 37500, surgical vascular endoscopy with ligation of perforator veins, subfascial (also known as SEPS); and code 37501, unlisted vascular endoscopy procedures.

Ligation and Other Procedures (37565–37799)

Ligation, the act of tying off blood vessels and dividing and stripping vessels, is reported using code range 37565–37785. These codes are differentiated by the type of procedure and the site of the procedure—in other words, the vein or artery on which the procedure was performed. Codes 37788–37799 are referenced for other procedures that would fall into this subsection of the surgery section, and they include code 37788, penile revascularization; and code 37790, penile venous occlusive procedure.

Summary

- The cardiovascular system is the system that pumps blood through the body via the heart and blood vessels.
- The sinoatrial node, or SA node, is found where the superior vena cava and the right atrium meet.
- At the junction of the atria and the ventricles, the atrioventricular node, or AV node, directs the cardiac impulses to the ventricles, causing them to contract.
- Pericardiocentesis is a procedure in which the physician removes fluid from the pericardial space by insertion of a fine needle.
- A cardiac pacemaker is used to correct and manage heart dysrhythmias.
- A pacemaker is made up of a pulse generator and electrodes.
- Pacemaker systems are referred to as either a *single-chamber* or a *dual-chamber system*.
- An endarterectomy is performed to remove plaque deposits from blood vessels.
- An angioplasty is a procedure in which a balloon is inflated in a vessel to push and flatten plaque against the vessel wall.
- A surgical incision that is made into an artery to remove a thrombus or plaque and the arterial lining is known as a *thromboendarterectomy.*
- A venous access device is a device or catheter that allows for access to the venous system.
- A central venous access device, or CVA device, is a catheter classified as such if the tip ends in the subclavian, brachiocephalic, superior or inferior vena cava, or right atrium.

Internet Links

To learn more about coronary angioplasty, visit ***http://www.nhlbi.nih.gov*** and search on coronary angioplasty.

To learn about various vascular procedures, such as thrombectomy, placement of vascular stents, endarterectomy, and other vascular stenting, visit ***http://vasculardiseasemanagement.com***.

For information on the history of and reasons for heart transplantation, visit ***http://www.texasheart.org***.

Chapter Review

Fill in the Blank

Instructions: Fill in the blanks in the statements that follow.

1. Codes 35180–35184 are for the repair of congenital arteriovenous fistula, whereas codes 35188–35190 are the codes for the repair of a(n) _____ or traumatic arteriovenous fistula.

2. The act of tying off blood vessels is known as _____.

3. The node found where the superior vena cava and the right atrium meet is called the _____ or _____ node.

4. The part of the pacemaker that controls the heart rate, the energy output, and the pacing modes is known as the _____.

5. A pacemaker system that has one electrode in either the atrium or ventricle is called a _____ system.

6. A procedure in which a physician removes fluid from the pericardial space by inserting a fine needle is known as _____.

7. The lower chambers of the heart are the _____.

8. Plaque deposits are removed from blood vessels by the completion of a(n) _____.

9. When an angioplasty is completed, a(n) _____ is inflated in a vessel to push and flatten plaque against the vessel wall.

10. A device or catheter that allows access to the venous system is known as a(n)_____.

11. A central venous access device, or CVA device, is a catheter classified as such if the tip ends in the subclavian or brachiocephalic vein, superior or inferior vena cava, or _____.

12. Intravascular ultrasound services are performed for _____ or therapeutic purposes on a noncoronary artery or vein.

13. The heart is enclosed in a double-walled sac called the _____.

14. Vessels that move oxygen-rich blood from the heart to the rest of the body are _____.

15. Deoxygenated blood is moved back to the heart by _____, with the exception of the pulmonary _____.

Coding Assignments

Instructions: Using the CPT manual, select the appropriate CPT code for each of the following procedures.

1. Thrombectomy of the radial artery by arm incision _____

2. Excision of pericardial cyst _____

3. Suture repair of aorta with shunt bypass _____

4. Coronary artery bypass using three coronary venous grafts, saphenous vein graft _____

5. Banding of pulmonary artery _____

6. Closure of pulmonary semilunar valve by patch _____

7. Repair of patent ductus arteriosus by division of a 14-year-old patient _____

8. Division of vascular ring with reanastomosis _____

9. Femoral vein valvuloplasty _____

10. Repair of blood vessel of upper extremity with vein graft _____

11. Stab phlebectomy of varicose veins in left leg; 12 stab incisions completed _____

12. Ligation of common iliac vein _____

13. Catheterization of umbilical artery of newborn _____

14. Extracorporeal photopheresis _____

15. Saphenopopliteal vein anastomosis _____

16. Ligation, major artery of the abdomen _____

17. Ligation of angioaccess arteriovenous fistula _____

18. Ligation of inferior vena cava _____

19. Direct thrombectomy, vena cava, iliac vein by abdominal incision _____

20. Coronary artery bypass, vein, two coronary venous grafts _____

21. Repositioning of pVAD with imaging guidance, separate session _____

22. Ligation of common carotid artery _____

23. Penile revascularization, artery with vein graft _____

24. Repair of supravalvular mitral ring by resection of left atrial membrane _____

25. Complete repair of tetralogy of Fallot with transannular patch _____

Case Studies

Instructions: Review each case and indicate the correct code(s).

Case 1

Procedure: Replacement of pacemaker generator

The patient was brought to the operating room and was prepped and draped in the usual fashion. The patient was consciously sedated. The previous subcutaneous right infraclavicular skin pocket was identified, and an incision was made in this area to remove the previously inserted generator. The atrial and ventricular leads were checked. Since the pocket was clean, it was determined that the same pocket could be used for the reinsertion of a new generator. A pulse generator was placed and tested. Noting no complications, the physician sutured the site. The patient was found to be in stable condition and was returned to the recovery room in satisfactory condition.

CPT code(s): _____

Case 2

Preoperative diagnosis: Leukemia, in remission

Postoperative diagnosis: Same

Procedure: Tunneled venous access port removal

Reason for procedure: This 8-year-old male completed chemotherapy.

The patient was prepped and draped in the normal sterile fashion. His right side was anesthetized, and an incision was made above the port area. The port was a tunneled device with a subcutaneous port that was peripherally inserted. The incision was taken down to the device, which was freed. The retention sutures were identified and cut. After confirmation that the device was free, it was removed. Hemostasis was obtained, and the wound was closed in layers using 3-0 nylon. A sterile dressing was applied to the area. Patient vitals were taken, and the patient was noted to be stable. He was sent to the recovery room in stable condition.

CPT code(s): _____

Case 3

Preoperative and postperative diagnosis: Excessive fluid in pericardial sac

Procedure: Initial removal of fluid from pericardial sac

After the patient was prepped and draped in the usual fashion, general anesthesia was administered. Using the sternum as an anatomical landmark, a long needle was placed below the sternum. The needle was advanced into the pericardial sac, and 5 cc of fluid were aspirated and sent to pathology for review. The patient was stable, and the wound was dressed. The patient was sent to the recovery area in satisfactory condition.

CPT code(s): _____

Case 4

Preoperative diagnosis: Malignant carcinoma of breast

Postoperative diagnosis: Same

This 39-year-old female presents today for insertion of catheter for central venous access for chemotherapy.

The patient was placed in the supine position and sterile prep occurred. Lidocaine was injected into the right clavicular area. A needle was inserted into the right subclavain vein, and a J-wire was then passed into place. A tunnel was created from the area over the clavicle to the venotomy site, and a dilator was placed over the wire and then dilated. The catheter was then placed into the subclavian vein and secured. The area was flushed, and incisions were sutured. There was minimal blood loss, and the patient was stable and sent to the recovery area.

CPT code(s): _____

Case 5

Preoperative diagnosis: Possible hemorrhage

Postoperative diagnosis: Abdominal hemorrhage of previous operative area

This patient underwent abdominal surgery 36 hours ago. An exploration of the abdominal incision site is planned.

After being placed under general anesthesia, the original abdominal incision site was reopened. A small bleeding site was noted, and electrocautery was used. The wound was closed. The patient tolerated the procedure and was sent to the recovery area.

CPT code(s): _____

Case 6

Preoperative diagnosis: Chest wound

Postoperative diagnosis: Foreign body on the surface of the heart

Anesthesia: General

Procedure: Exploratory cardiotomy

This 59-year-old patient sustained an injury to his chest while loading logs onto a truck at work. He was brought to the ER, and imaging showed a chest wound with a possible foreign body on the surface of the heart. He was then taken to the operating room for exploration of the area. An incision was made in the sternum, and the heart was exposed. A foreign body was visualized on the heart and was removed. There were no penetrating cardiac wounds to be sutured. The operative wound was closed, and the patient was sent to the recovery area in stable condition.

CPT code(s): _____

Case 7

Preoperative and postoperative diagnosis: Cardiac ischemia

Procedure: Thoracotomy for transmyocardial laser revascularization

Anesthesia: General

The patient was prepped and draped in the usual sterile fashion and placed under general anesthesia. A 12-cm incision was made on the left side of the chest. The incision was made between the ribs and was carried down to expose the heart's surface. An ischemia was visualized on the right side of the heart. The laser was inserted into the cardiac area, and between heartbeats, 15 channels were made and pressure was applied to close the opened areas. Prior to closure of the incision, there was no significant bleeding from the cardiac tissue. The laser was removed, the incision was closed, and dressings were placed on the wound. The patient tolerated the procedure with no complications and was sent to the recovery area in stable condition.

CPT code(s): _____

Case 8

Preoperative and postperative diagnosis: Bleeding from pacemaker site

Procedure: Relocation of skin pocket for pacemaker

With the patient under general anesthesia, the previous skin pocket was opened, and the generator was removed. The skin pocket was explored and bleeding stopped in the area. The generator was then relocated, and the pocket was closed with sutures. A sterile dressing was applied. The patient was in stable condition.

CPT code(s): _____

Case 9

Preoperative and postoperative diagnosis: Thrombus and atherosclerosis of iliac artery

Procedure: Iliac thromboendarterectomy

The patient was prepped and draped in the usual sterile fashion and placed under general anesthesia. An abdominal incision was made, and dissection past the large and small bowel occurred to expose the iliac artery. Clamps were placed to isolate the iliac area. A longitudinal incision was made in the artery, and the thrombus and plaque were removed. Then the area was sutured. The diameter of the artery was significantly improved after the procedure. Blood loss was minimal, and the wounds were closed and dressed. No complications were noted. The patient was sent to recovery.

CPT code(s): _____

Case 10

Neonatal Intensive Care Unit Note

This 4-day-old neonate is suspected to be anemic. A blood sample was ordered by the attending, who completed the collection due to the size of the neonate.

Procedure: Venipuncture for collection of venous blood, nonroutine, upper-extremity vein

CPT code(s): _____

Hemic and Lymphatic Systems

Chapter Outline

Introduction

Guidelines Related to the National Correct Coding Initiative (NCCI)

Structures of the Hemic and Lymphatic Systems

Procedures Completed on the Spleen (38100–38200)

General Procedures and Transplantation and Post-Transplantation Cellular Infusions (38204–38243)

Procedures Performed on the Lymph Nodes and Lymphatic Channels (38300–38999)

Summary

Internet Links

Chapter Review

Coding Assignments

Case Studies

Learning Objectives

At the conclusion of this chapter, you should be able to:

1. Define key terms related to coding procedures on the hemic and lymphatic systems.
2. Describe the basic anatomy and functions of the hemic and lymphatic systems.
3. Define common procedures performed on the hemic and lymphatic systems.
4. Apply specific coding guidelines to the hemic and lymphatic systems.
5. Select CPT codes for procedures performed on the hemic and lymphatic systems from case studies.

Key Terms

allogenic bone marrow transplants

autologous bone marrow transplants

axillary lymph nodes

cervical lymph nodes

deep biopsy

deep removal

hematopoietic progenitor cell (HPC) boost

inguinal lymph nodes

lymphadenitis

lymphangiotomy

lymphatic channels

lymphatic vessels

lymph glands

lymph nodes

radical lymphadenectomy

spleen

splenectomy

splenorrhaphy

submandibular lymph nodes

superficial biopsy

superficial removal

Introduction

The hemic and lymphatic systems often are viewed as subsystems of the circulatory system. The unique functions of the hemic and lymphatic systems connect them to the circulatory system. CPT code range 38100–38999 is used to report procedures completed on the hemic and lymphatic systems.

Guidelines Related to the National Correct Coding Initiative (NCCI)

Reference the following website to obtain the most current NCCI guideline information related to the Hemic and Lymphatic System.

1. Log on to *http://www.cms.gov/Medicare/Coding/NationalCorrectCodInitED/index.html*.
2. Scroll to the section titled "Downloads."
3. Click the link for the most current "NCCI Policy Manual for Medicare Services."
4. A box will appear that requires you to click "Open."
5. Click on "Chapter 5" for guidelines specific to the Hemic and Lymphatic System coding.

Structures of the Hemic and Lymphatic Systems

Structures included in CPT for the hemic and lymphatic systems are the spleen, bone marrow, lymph nodes, and lymphatic channels. The **spleen**, the largest organ of the lymphatic system, is located in the left upper quadrant of the abdomen, behind the stomach and just below the diaphragm. The main role of the spleen is to filter blood. Figure 9-1 illustrates the location of the spleen in the abdominal cavity.

The **lymphatic channels** or **lymphatic vessels**, also illustrated in Figure 9-1, transport fluid away from the tissues of the body and toward the thoracic cavity. Lymphatic vessels transport fluid in only one direction.

Lymph nodes, also known as **lymph glands**, are located at various areas along the lymphatic vessels. The nodes are a collection of lymphatic tissue.

Procedures Completed on the Spleen (38100–38200)

Codes 38100–38200 are used to report procedures completed on the spleen. There are four subsections:

- Excision
- Repair
- Laparoscopy
- Introduction

Excisions (38100–38102)

This subsection is used to report a **splenectomy**, the surgical removal of the spleen. Codes 38100 and 38101 are considered separate procedure codes and, therefore, would not be reported if another procedure was completed. Code 38100 is used to report a total splenectomy, and code 38101 is used to report a partial splenectomy. Code 38102 is considered an add-on procedure and is reported when a total splenectomy is completed in conjunction with another procedure. Code 38102 is listed as the secondary code, with the code for the primary procedure listed first. Figure 9-2 illustrates a splenectomy.

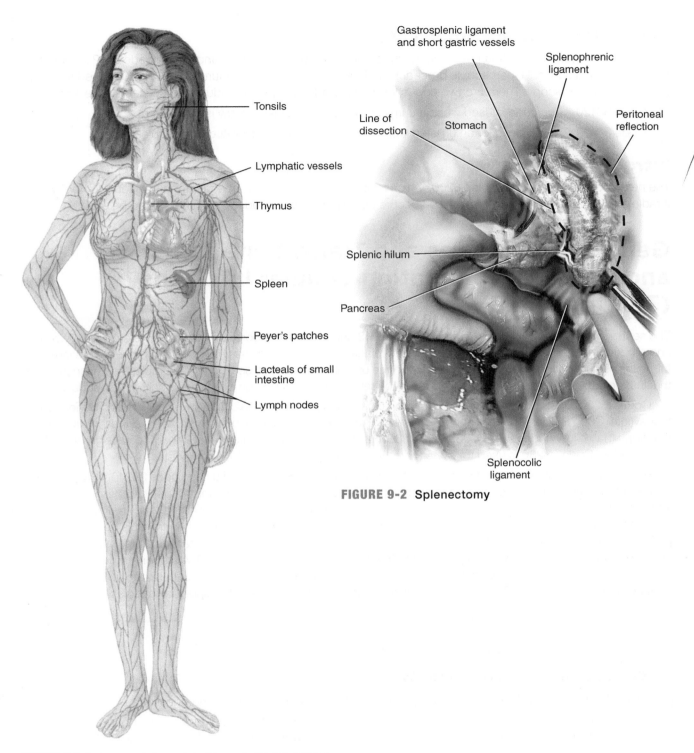

FIGURE 9-2 Splenectomy

FIGURE 9-1 Spleen and Associated Lymphatic Structures

Repair (38115)

There is only one code in this subsection: code 38115. This code is used to report the repair of a ruptured spleen, which also is known as a **splenorrhaphy**. This code does not differentiate between a splenorrhaphy that is completed with a partial splenectomy and one that is completed without it. Therefore, if a repair of a ruptured spleen occurs with a partial splenectomy, it is necessary to report only code 38115 because it includes the partial splenectomy.

Laparoscopy of the Spleen (38120 and 38129)

Coders should read the notation that appears under the heading Laparoscopy and before code 38120. It informs the reader that a surgical laparoscopic procedure includes a diagnostic procedure. Code 49320 is used to report a diagnostic laparoscopy. There are two codes for surgical laparoscopic procedures completed on the spleen:

- Code 38120—This code is used when a surgical laparoscopic splenectomy is completed.
- Code 38129—This code is for an unlisted laparoscopic procedure completed on the spleen.

Introduction (38200)

The next code in this subsection is 38200, which is used for the injection procedure for a splenoportography. If radiological supervision and interpretation occurs for this procedure, code 75810 should also be used.

General Procedures and Transplantation and Post-Transplantation Cellular Infusions (38204–38243)

The section titled General includes codes 38204–38243 and is used to report bone marrow or stem cell services and procedures, and transplantation and post-transplantaion cellular infusions. There are a number of notations found in this subsection that instruct the coder on the use of codes for this section. For example, a notation appears that instructs the coder that each of the codes in the range 38207–38215 can be reported only once per day.

Code 38220 reports diagnostic bone marrow aspiration(s), and code 38221 reports a diagnostic bone marrow biopsy(ies). Code 38222 reports diagnostic bone marrow biopsy(ies) and aspiration(s). Refer to the instructional notations that follow codes 38220, 38221, and 38222 for additional instructions that impact the assignment of these codes. Code 38230 is used for bone marrow harvesting for transplantation; allogenic.

Bone marrow or blood-derived peripheral stem cell transplantation is coded using codes 38240–38243. These codes are differentiated by allogenic transplantation, autologous transplantation, and allogenic donor lymphocyte infusions. In **autologous bone marrow transplants**, cells are cultivated from the patient's own marrow, whereas in **allogenic bone marrow transplants**, cells are taken from a donor and then transplanted into the patient needing the cells. It should be noted that following code 38242, numerous notations direct the coder to additional codes for various types of procedures that involve bone marrow. Code 38243 reports a **hematopoietic progenitor cell (HPC) boost**. During this procedure the patient receives an infusion of hematopoietic progenitor cells from the original donor. This can be completed to treat a relapse or post-transplant cytopenias.

Exercise 9.1—Check Your Understanding

Codes for the Hemic and Lymphatic System

Using the CPT manual, select the appropriate response to each of the following questions.

1. The four subcategories for procedures completed on the spleen are

   _____, _____,

   _____, and _____.

2. A surgical laparoscopy of the spleen always includes a(n) _____ laparoscopy.

3. Bone marrow aspiration is coded using code _____.

4. True or false: Interpretation of a bone marrow biopsy is included in code 38221

   _____.

5. Code 38100 is considered a(n) _____ procedure code; therefore, it is not reported with another code but is reported when the splenectomy is the only procedure completed.

Procedures Performed on the Lymph Nodes and Lymphatic Channels (38300–38999)

Procedures completed on the lymph nodes and lymphatic channels, codes 38300–38999, are divided into the following subsections:

- Incision
- Excision
- Limited Lymphadenectomy for Staging
- Laparoscopy
- Radical Lymphadenectomy (Radial Resection of Lymph Nodes)
- Introduction
- Other Procedures

At times, the coder must identify the site of the lymphatic duct or node to select a code properly. Figure 9-3 illustrates the location of lymphatic ducts and nodes. There are two lymphatic ducts: the right lymphatic duct and

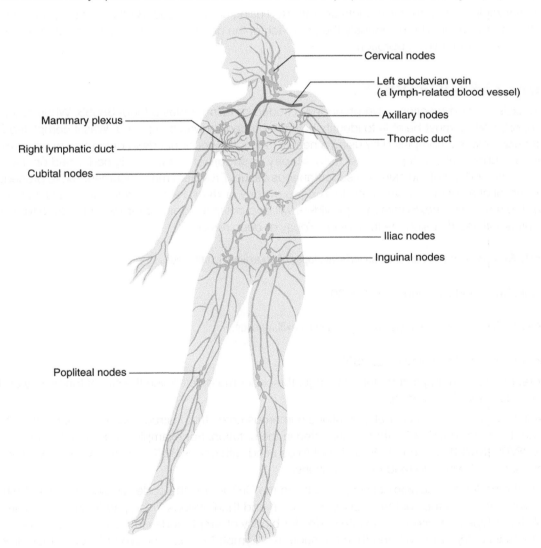

FIGURE 9-3 Lymphatic Ducts and Nodes

the thoracic duct. Although lymph nodes are located throughout the body, there are four major concentrations of lymph nodes:

- **Cervical lymph nodes**—Located in the neck area
- **Submandibular lymph nodes**—Located under the mandible or lower jaw
- **Axillary lymph nodes**—Located in the armpit
- **Inguinal lymph nodes**—Located in the upper femoral triangle of the thigh

Incision (38300-38382)

Incisions completed on the lymph nodes and lymphatic channels are reported using codes 38300–38382. Codes 38300 and 38305 are used to report the drainage of a lymph node abscess or drainage of an enlarged or inflamed lymph node, known as **lymphadenitis**. These codes are differentiated by the terms *simple* and *extensive*. When code 38305—"Drainage of lymph node abscess or lymphadenitis, extensive"—is reported, the patient's record must document the reason for and the description of the extensive treatment.

Lymphangiotomy, an incision made into a lymph node, or other operations on the lymphatic channels are coded using code 38308.

Suturing and/or ligation of thoracic ducts are reported using codes 38380–38382. For the proper selection of a code, the operative report must identify the approach of the procedure. The codes are differentiated by the cervical, thoracic, or abdominal approach.

Excisions (38500-38555)

The biopsy, excision, or dissection of lymph nodes is coded by using codes 38500–38555. When reading an operative report, coders must be able to identify how the procedure was completed. Was it completed as an open procedure, or was it completed by using a needle? Also, the coder needs to determine whether the biopsy or removal was superficial or deep. A **superficial biopsy** or **superficial removal** is performed on a lymph node that is close to the surface of the skin and subcutaneous tissue. Providers may document these procedures as a biopsy or removal of a superficial lymph node. A **deep biopsy** or **deep removal** refers to nodes that are located by or below the muscle tissue. Sometimes providers will document a biopsy or removal of a deep lymph node. Codes are differentiated by using the term *deep biopsy* or *deep removal*.

> **EXAMPLE:** Mary Smith had an open superficial biopsy of an axillary lymph node.

This would be coded by using code 38500.

> **EXAMPLE:** Tom Jones had an open biopsy of a deep axillary node.

This would be coded by using code 38525.

Therefore, before selecting a code for this range, the coder must determine the site of the biopsy and how deep the node is: superficial or deep.

The Excisions subsection of CPT also contains numerous notes that instruct the coder that some of these codes are not to be assigned with other codes listed in the notation. For example, code 38500 is not to be used with codes 38700–38780, and code 38530 is not to be used with codes 38720–38746. When selecting codes from this subsection, be sure to read these notations.

To locate the codes for excisions of lymph nodes in the CPT Index, the coder would reference the main entry, "Excision," and then the subterm, "Lymph System" and then "Nodes." Here, additional codes are listed by anatomical site or type of excision. To locate codes for biopsy of lymph nodes in the CPT Index, the coder would reference the main entry, "Biopsy," and then the subterm, "Lymph Nodes." The type of biopsy then divides the listing.

Limited Lymphadenectomy for Staging (38562, 38564)

There are two codes for limited lymphadenectomy for staging: 38562 and 38564. Both of these codes are separate procedure codes. The codes are differentiated by location. Code 38562 is for the pelvic and para-aortic area, whereas code 38564 is for the retroperitoneal area. Following code 38562, coders should read the notations that state, "When combined with prostatectomy, use 55812 or 55842" and "When combined with insertion of radioactive substance into prostate, use 55862." This notation directs the coder to another section in the CPT manual.

Laparoscopy (38570–38589)

Laparoscopic procedures completed on the lymph nodes are coded to range 38570–38589. As seen in previous sections of the CPT manual, a completed surgical laparoscopic procedure always includes a diagnostic laparoscopic procedure. It should be noted that in the CPT manual, a notation appears that instructs the coder that if a diagnostic laparoscopic procedure is completed as a separate procedure, code 49320 should be reported. The codes found in this subsection are summarized in Table 9-1.

TABLE 9-1 Laparoscopy of Lymph Nodes (38570–38589)

Code	Description
38570	This code is used to report a surgical laparoscopy with a biopsy of the retroperitoneal lymph nodes. This is for a single biopsy or multiple biopsies. Therefore, if two or more samples of tissue are biopsied, report the code only once.
38571	When a bilateral total pelvic lymphadenectomy is completed using a laparoscope, this code should be reported.
38572	This code is used to report a bilateral total pelvic lymphadenectomy that is completed with a periaortic lymph node biopsy. This is for a single biopsy or multiple biopsies.
38573	This code is used to report a surgical laparoscopy with a bilateral total pelvic lymphadenectomy and periaortic lymph node sampling, peritoneal washings, peritoneal biopsy(ies), omentectomy and diaphragmatic washings, including diaphragmatic and other serosal biopsy(ies), when performed.
38589	Unlisted laparoscopy of the lymphatic system is reported using this code.

Radical Lymphadenectomy (Radical Resection of Lymph Nodes) (38700–38780)

Codes 38700–38780 are used to report the radical resection of lymph nodes, which is commonly referred to as a **radical lymphadenectomy**. To code from this range, the lymphadenectomy must be a radical procedure, not a limited one. When these radical procedures are completed, all the lymph nodes are dissected and removed, in addition to the tissue under the skin. To select a code from this section, coders must be able to identify the site of the lymph nodes and the extent of the removal. It should also be noted that in the CPT manual, notations appear that instruct coders to add modifier 50 for bilateral procedures. So, when reading through the operative note, the coder should determine whether the procedure was completed unilaterally or bilaterally. Codes for this range are summarized in Table 9-2.

TABLE 9-2 Radical Lymphadenectomy (38700–38780)

Code(s)	Description
38700	Removal of lymph nodes in the suprahyoid area is reported with this code. If this is a bilateral procedure, modifier 50 is added for some payers.
38720	A complete cervical lymphadenectomy done unilaterally is reported with code 38720. It is reported as a bilateral procedure with the addition of modifier 50.
38724	A modified radical neck dissection of the cervical lymph nodes, also known as a cervical lymphadenectomy, is coded by using code 38724.

(continues)

TABLE 9-2 *(continued)*

Code(s)	Description
38740 and 38745	These codes are used to report axillary lymphadenectomy. The codes are differentiated by a superficial or a complete procedure. The term *complete* refers to the removal of all the nodes.
38746 and 38747	These are considered add-on codes and are listed separately in addition to the code for the primary procedure. Code 38746 reports a thoracic lymphadenectomy by thoracotomy, mediastinal and regional lymphadenectomy; and code 38747 reports an abdominal lymphadenectomy, regional.
38760	When lymph nodes are removed in the inguinofemoral area, including Cloquet's node, code 38760 is listed for the unilateral procedure. Modifier 50 is added for a bilateral procedure. It should be noted that this is also a separate procedure code.
38765	A superficial inguinofemoral lymphadenectomy that is performed in continuity with a pelvic lymphadenectomy is reported as a unilateral procedure with code 38765 and as a bilateral procedure with code 38675-50. This procedure also includes the removal of the external iliac, hypogastric, and obturator nodes. This is also a separate procedure code.
38770	This separate procedure code is used to report a pelvic lymphadenectomy that can include the removal of the external iliac, hypogastric, and obturator nodes. Modifier 50 is added for a bilateral procedure.
38780	Extensive retroperitoneal transabdominal lymphadenectomy is coded with this code. Reporting this code also includes the removal of the pelvic, aortic, and renal nodes. Note that this is a separate procedure code.

Exercise 9.2—Check Your Understanding

Codes from Code Range 38300–38780

Using the CPT manual, select the appropriate CPT code for each of the following.

1. Suture and ligation of the thoracic duct via the abdominal approach _____

2. Limited lymphadenectomy for staging in the pelvic and para-aortic region _____

3. Laparoscopic bilateral total pelvic lymphadenectomy _____

4. Complete axillary lymphadenectomy _____

5. Superficial inguinofemoral lymphadenectomy including Cloquet's node _____

Introduction and Other Procedures (38790–38999)

The last two subsections include the following codes:

- Code 38790—An injection procedure for a lymphangiography

- Code 38792—An injection procedure of a radioactive tracer for the identification of sentinel nodes

- Code 38794—The cannulation of the thoracic duct

- Code 38900—Intraoperative identification of sentinel lymph nodes. Code 38900 includes the injection of a non-radioactive dye when it is performed. This is an add-on code used with numerous codes. Reference the CPT manual for the primary codes in which code 38900 is used as an add-on code. The primary codes are listed after the description of code 38900.

- Code 38999—Unlisted procedures on the hemic or lymphatic system

Summary

- The hemic and lymphatic systems are often viewed as subsystems of the circulatory system.
- The repair of a ruptured spleen is also known as a *splenorrhaphy*.
- The spleen is located in the left upper quadrant of the abdomen, behind the stomach and just below the diaphragm.
- The lymphatic channels, or vessels, transport fluid away from the tissues of the body and toward the thoracic cavity.
- Lymph nodes, also known as *lymph glands*, are located at various areas along the lymphatic vessels.
- In an autologous bone marrow transplant, cells are cultivated from the patient's own marrow.
- In an allogenic bone marrow transplant, cells are taken from a donor and then transplanted.
- There are four major concentrations of lymph nodes: cervical lymph nodes, submandibular lymph nodes, axillary lymph nodes, and inguinal lymph nodes.

Internet Links

To learn more about a splenectomy, visit ***http://www.mayoclinic.org/tests-procedures/splenectomy /basics/definition/PRC-20014837***.

To learn more about lymph and lymph nodes, visit ***http://www.breastcancer.org***.

To learn more about bone marrow transplantations, visit ***http://www.stjude.org*** and search for "bone marrow transplant."

To learn more about bone marrow transplantations from the National Institutes of Health (NIH), visit ***http://www .nlm.nih.gov*** and search for "bone marrow transplant."

Chapter Review

Fill in the Blank

Instructions: Fill in the blanks in the statements that follow.

1. The largest organ of the hemic and lymphatic systems is the _____.

2. A patient's own cells are cultivated to perform the transplant in a(n) _____ bone marrow transplant.

3. A biopsy of a superficial lymph node is completed close to the skin and _____.

4. Code 38505 is used to report a biopsy or excision of a superficial lymph node performed by use of a(n) _____.

5. Cells are taken from a donor and then transplanted into the patient who needs the cells in a(n) _____ bone marrow transplant.

6. An enlarged or inflamed lymph node is known as _____.

7. The repair of a ruptured spleen is also known as a(n) _____.

8. Lymph nodes that are located by or below the muscle tissue are referred to as _____ nodes.

9. Cervical lymph nodes are located in the _____.

10. Inguinal lymph nodes are located in the _____ triangle of the thigh.

Coding Assignments

Instructions: Using the CPT manual, select the appropriate code for each of the following procedures.

1. Open excision of deep cervical node

   _____

2. Splenorrhaphy _____

3. Partial splenectomy _____

4. Laparoscopic splenectomy

   _____

5. Thoracic approach for ligation of the thoracic duct _____

6. Deep jugular lymph node dissection

   _____

7. Suprahyoid lymphadenectomy

   _____

8. Lymphangiography injection procedure

   _____

9. Cannulation of thoracic duct

   _____

10. Complete cervical lymphadenectomy

    _____

11. Axillary excision of cystic hygroma with deep neurovascular dissection _____

12. Thawing of previously frozen cells harvested for transplant without washing _____

13. Bone marrow transplantation from autologous marrow _____

14. Harvesting of bone marrow for transplantation; allogenic _____

15. Drainage of abscess of cervical lymph node

    _____

Case Studies

Instructions: Review each case and indicate the correct code(s).

Case 1

Preoperative diagnosis: Enlarged lymph node in left axillary area

Postoperative diagnosis: Left axillary lymphadenitis

Procedure: Excision of one axillary lymph node

The patient was prepped and draped in the usual fashion and sedated via IV. The left axillary area was cleansed with Betadine, and 1% Xylocaine was injected. An incision was made through the skin, and the enlarged node was identified deep in the fascia. The surrounding vessels in the area were clamped, and the deep node was excised. The node, measuring 2.3 by 2.5 cm, was sent to pathology for further analysis. The subcutaneous tissue and skin were closed. There was minimal blood loss, and the patient tolerated the procedure in good condition and was sent to the recovery room.

CPT code(s): _____

Case 2

Preoperative diagnosis: Pain over spleen after falling down stairs

Postoperative diagnosis: Ruptured spleen

Indications for surgery: This 78-year-old male fell while completing yard work. It is believed that his spleen was ruptured due to this injury.

Procedure: This 78-year-old male was prepped and draped in the usual fashion. General anesthesia was administered, and he was placed in the supine position. An incision was made in the upper midline area. Retractors were then placed. The splenic ligaments and the gastric veins were located and divided so that the left upper quadrant of the abdomen could be viewed. The spleen was ruptured. The splenic hilum was dissected, and the splenic artery and vein were identified and double-ligated. They were then suture-ligated and divided. Removal of the spleen occurred, and hemostasis was achieved. A drain was placed, and the area was closed in layers. There was minimal blood loss. The patient's vitals were taken, and then he was sent to the postop recovery room in stable condition.

CPT code(s): _____

Case 3

Preoperative diagnosis: Non-Hodgkin's lymphoma

Postoperative diagnosis: Non-Hodgkin's lymphoma

Procedure: Bone marrow biopsy and bone marrow aspiration

Indications for surgery: Non-Hodgkin's lymphoma

Procedure: This 25-year-old male was placed in the prone position on the operating table. Posterior superior iliac spines were prepped and draped in the usual sterile fashion. 1% Lidocaine was administered to anesthetize the area. The needle was inserted into the left iliac spinal region, rotated to the right, then left, and removed. The needle was then inserted into the left iliac spinal region at a 45-degree angle, and the procedure was repeated. Bone marrow aspiration and biopsy were performed and sent for contingent flow and contingent cytogenetics. The patient tolerated the procedure well and will return for follow-up and results.

CPT code(s): _____

Case 4

This 42-year-old female presents today with an abscess in the right inguinal area. The patient is not suffering from fever or chills but is in pain in this area from the abscess. The options were explained to the patient, and she decided to proceed with an incision and drainage of the lymph node. All risks and benefits were explained, after which the patient signed the consent form for the procedure.

Procedure: After the patient was made comfortable on the procedure table, the right inguinal area was prepped and draped in the usual sterile fashion. An incision was made over the abscess and carried down until the lymph node was visualized. The lymph node was identified, and the syringe was inserted. At this time, 6 cc of fluid was removed from the node and sent to pathology. Pressure was applied to the area until the bleeding stopped, and the area was closed with Steri-Strips. The patient tolerated the procedure well and will return in 10 days for follow-up.

CPT code(s): _____

Case 5

This 54-year-old male presents with an enlarged cervical lymph node that is deep within the fat pad. The node has been enlarged for the last six months and has been painful. Various treatments occurred with no success.

Procedure: The cervical area was anesthetized, and an incision was made to identify the node. The node was deep within the fat layer and enlarged. The node was excised with additional excision of the scalene fat pad. After bleeding was controlled, the area was sutured. The patient was sent to the recovery area in stable condition.

CPT code(s): _____

Mediastinum and Diaphragm

Chapter Outline

Learning Objectives

At the conclusion of this chapter, you should be able to:

1. Define key terms related to coding procedures on the mediastinum and diaphragm.
2. Explain the location of the mediastinum and diaphragm.
3. Define common procedures performed on the mediastinum and diaphragm.
4. Select CPT codes for procedures completed on the mediastinum and diaphragm from case studies.

Key Terms

anterior mediastinotomy

cervical mediastinotomy

diaphragm

imbrication of the
   diaphragm

mediastinoscope

mediastinotomy

mediastinum

transthoracic
   mediastinotomy

Introduction

The Mediastinum and Diaphragm subsection of the CPT surgery section is used to code procedures completed in the mediastinum and on the diaphragm. The **mediastinum** is the space in the thoracic cavity behind the sternum and in between the two pleural sacs that contain the lungs and pleurae. The **diaphragm** is a dome-shaped muscle that separates the thoracic cavity from the abdominal cavity. Figure 10-1 illustrates the location of the mediastinum and diaphragm.

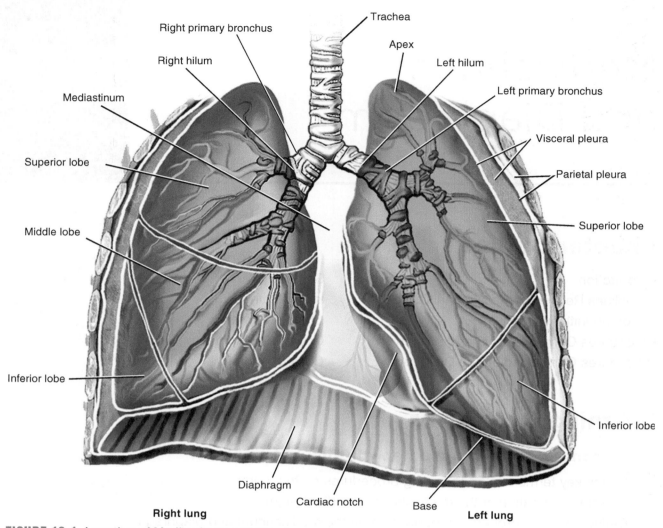

FIGURE 10-1 Location of Mediastinum and Diaphragm

Guidelines Related to the National Correct Coding Initiative (NCCI)

There is no coding guideline information related to this chapter at this time.

Procedures Completed in the Mediastinum (39000–39499)

The Mediastinum section, code range 39000–39499, is used to code procedures completed in the mediastinum. Codes are located in one of four groups, depending on the procedure performed:

- Incision
- Excision/Resection
- Endoscopy
- Other Procedures

Table 10-1 summarizes this code range.

TABLE 10-1 Code Range 39000–39499

Code(s)	Description
39000	This code is used to report a mediastinotomy that is completed with exploration, for drainage, for removal of a foreign body, or for biopsy. A mediastinotomy is a procedure in which an incision is made to open the mediastinum. A cervical approach can be used for this procedure. When the procedure is completed using the front of the body approach, it is known as a cervical mediastinotomy or anterior mediastinotomy. The anterior mediastinotomy is sometimes referred to as the Chamberlain approach or procedure. This is when an incision is made to expose the area, and then a drain is placed, a foreign body is removed, or a biopsy is taken. The area is then sutured closed.
39010	When a transthoracic approach is used for a mediastinotomy that is completed with exploration, for drainage, for removal of a foreign body, or for biopsy, this code is used. During a transthoracic mediastinotomy, the incision is made in the fourth intercostal space to enter the mediastinum. This code also includes either a transthoracic or median sternotomy.
39200 and 39220	Code 39200 is used to code a resection of a mediastinal cyst, whereas code 39220 is used to code a resection of a mediastinal tumor. For both of these procedures, an incision is made in the axilla and is extended below the tip of the shoulder blade. The muscles are then moved or retracted to expose the rib cage, and a rib spreader is used to enter the thoracic cavity to view and remove the cyst or tumor. The rib spreader is removed, and the site is closed using either sutures or staples.
39401 and 39402	These codes are used to code a mediastinoscopy, with code 39401 reporting a mediastinoscopy that includes a biopsy(ies) of mediastinal mass (eg, lymphoma), when performed, and code 39402 reporting a mediastinoscopy with lymph node biopsy(ies). When these procedures are performed, a small incision is made in the area above the sternum. The lighted scope, known as a mediastinoscope, is inserted and is used to visually examine the mediastinum, trachea, and the major vessels found in this area. At times, biopsies are also completed. After the scope is removed, the surgical wound is closed with Steri-Strips or sutures.
39499	Code 39499 is used to report unlisted procedures completed in the mediastinum. Caution should be used before assigning this code. Because this is an unlisted procedure code, most payers will request additional information and require that documentation be submitted to justify the selection of this code.

Procedures Completed on the Diaphragm (39501–39599)

Code range 39501–39599 is used to code procedures completed on the diaphragm. Codes 39501–39561 are used to report repairs, imbrications, and resections of this area, and code 39599 is used to report unlisted procedures completed on the diaphragm. Table 10-2 summarizes the codes found in this section.

It should be noted that the only hernia repair codes that are not located in the digestive-system range of codes are the diaphragmatic hernia repair procedures.

TABLE 10-2 Procedures Completed on the Diaphragm

Code(s)	Description
39501	This code is used to code a repair of a laceration of the diaphragm using any approach that could include an abdominal or chest incision. The incision is completed to expose the tear in the diaphragm, which is repaired using sutures and at times is reinforced by an artificial patch.
39503	This code is used to report a repair of a diaphragmatic hernia that is completed on a neonate. This code includes the repair with or without chest tube insertion and with or without the creation of a ventral hernia. Following the code description, a notation appears stating that modifier 63 should not be used with code 39503.
39540 and 39541	These codes are used to report a diaphragmatic hernia repair that has occurred because of trauma. These codes are not used for neonates. The codes are differentiated by acute hernia (code 39540) and chronic hernia (code 39541). Because the abdominal organs are protruding into the chest cavity, the physician makes an incision into the chest or abdomen to draw the organs back into the abdominal cavity. The opening in the diaphragm is repaired by suturing or by inserting a patch.

(continues)

TABLE 10-2 *(continued)*

Code(s)	Description
39545	This code is used to report the imbrication of the diaphragm. During this procedure, the physician makes a transthoracic or transabdominal incision to draw back the abdominal organs. Folds or tucks are then made in the connective tissue, suturing the tissue to the diaphragm to restore the diaphragm to its correct anatomical position.
39560 and 39561	These two codes are used to report the resection of the diaphragm. Code 39560 is used to report the procedure when a simple repair closes the site. Code 39561 is used to report the procedure when a complex repair closes the site. A complex repair involves repairing the site with a local muscle flap or synthetic material to patch the area.
39599	This code is used to report unlisted procedures completed on the diaphragm.

Summary

- The mediastinum is the space in the thoracic cavity behind the sternum and between the two pleural sacs that contains all the viscera of the chest except the lungs and pleurae.
- The diaphragm is a dome-shaped muscle that separates the thoracic cavity from the abdominal cavity.
- A mediastinotomy is a procedure in which an incision is made to open the mediastinum.
- A cervical or anterior mediastinotomy is completed from the front of the body.
- During a transthoracic mediastinotomy, the incision is made in the fourth intercostal space to enter the mediastinum.
- A mediastinoscope is a lighted instrument that is used to visually examine the mediastinum.
- A transabdominal approach occurs when an incision is made across the abdomen.

Internet Links

For information on symptoms and treatment of diaphragmatic hernias, visit *http://www.umm.edu*.

Chapter Review

Fill in the Blank

Instructions: Fill in the blanks in the statements that follow.

1. During a(n) _____ of the diaphragm, the physician makes a transthoracic or transabdominal incision to draw back the abdominal organs, and then makes folds in the connective tissue, suturing the tissue to the diaphragm to restore it to its correct anatomical position.

2. Code _____ is used to report the repair of a traumatic (acute) diaphragmatic hernia.

3. A lighted scope, known as a(n) _____, is used to examine the mediastinum visually.

4. When performing a transthoracic mediastinotomy, the surgeon makes an incision in the _____ to enter the mediastinum.

5. Code 39503 is used to report a repair of a diaphragmatic hernia that is completed on a(n) _____.

True/False

Instructions: Indicate whether the following statements are true (T) or false (F).

6. _____ When a biopsy is performed in the mediastinum using a cervical approach, CPT code 39200 is reported.

7. _____ A laparoscopic repair of a diaphragmatic hernia and fundoplication are reported using CPT code 39540.

8. _____ CPT code 39560 is used to report a simple resection of the diaphragm.

9. _____ The diaphragm is a dome-shaped ligament that separates the thoracic and abdominal cavities.

10. _____ A cervical mediastinotomy is completed by an approach from the front of the body.

Coding Assignments

Instructions: For each of the following procedures, select the appropriate CPT code.

1. Mediastinoscopy with biopsy of mediastinal mass
   _____

2. Excision of a cyst of the mediastinum
   _____

3. Exploration of the mediastinum with mediastinotomy for drainage via the cervical area
   _____

4. Diaphragmatic hernia repair due to acute trauma
   _____

5. Endoscopy of mediastinum _____

6. Imbrication of the diaphragm for eventration
   _____

7. Resection of the diaphragm with complex repair
   _____

8. Repair of chronic diaphragmatic hernia
   _____

9. Repair of diaphragmatic hernia with chest tube insertion, 23-hour-old newborn
   _____

10. Mediastinal cyst resection _____

Case Studies

Instructions: Review each case and indicate the correct code(s).

Case 1

Preoperative diagnosis: Carcinoma of the mediastinum

Postoperative diagnosis: Tumor of mediastinum, carcinoma

Reason for procedure: Two weeks ago, the patient had a biopsy of a mass found in the mediastinum. Pathology confirmed that the mass was a carcinoma of the mediastinum.

Procedure: The patient was prepped and draped in the usual sterile fashion. General anesthesia was administered. An incision was made in front of the left axilla area just below the nipple. The incision was then extended to below the tip of the left shoulder blade. The muscles were resected to expose the rib cage, and all bleeding points were controlled. The

(continues)

(continued)

rib cage was entered by using a rib spreader that revealed a 2.2 cm by 1.4 cm mass. The mass and surrounding tissue were resected. The wound was closed in a layered fashion with sterile dressings applied. The mass was sent to pathology. The patient tolerated the procedure well and was taken to the recovery room in stable condition.

CPT code(s): _____

Case 2

Preoperative and postoperative diagnosis: Diaphragmatic hernia

Procedure: Repair of a neonatal diaphragmatic hernia

The patient was prepped and draped in the usual sterile fashion, and general anesthesia was administered. An abdominal incision was made under the upper ribs to view the abdominal cavity. The herniated stomach tissue was pulled through the opening in the diaphragm and returned to the correct anatomical position. The diaphragmatic opening was sutured to reduce the size of the opening. A chest tube was inserted. The patient tolerated the procedure and was sent to the recovery room in satisfactory condition.

CPT code(s): _____

Case 3

Procedure: Mediastinoscopy

Reason for procedure: Lymph node biopsy-staging procedure

Diagnosis: Lung cancer

Patient was brought into the operating suite after all consents had been discussed and signed. Patient is aware that this is a lymph node biopsy being performed for staging of his recently diagnosed lung cancer.

Patient was prepped and draped in the usual sterile fashion. General anesthesia was administered. An incision was made approximately 1 cm above the suprasternal notch of the breast bone. Dissection was then carried down to the cartilaginous ridge within the trachea at the tracheal bifurcation. A mediastinoscope was then introduced, which provided good visualization of the mediastinum and its structures.

Lymph nodes 2, 4, 5, and 7 were removed and sent to pathology. The scope was removed, and the incision was closed. The patient was removed from the operating suite with minimal blood loss and in good condition.

CPT code(s): _____

Digestive System

Chapter Outline

Learning Objectives

At the conclusion of this chapter, you should be able to:

1. Define key terms related to coding procedures on the digestive system.
2. Define abbreviations related to the digestive system.
3. Describe the basic anatomy and functions of the digestive system.
4. Define common procedures performed on the digestive system.
5. Select CPT codes for procedures completed on the digestive system.
6. Identify and code procedures for the digestive system from case studies.

Key Terms

abdomen

adenoids

alimentary canal

allotransplantation

alveolus

anastomosis

anoscopy

anus

appendix

ascending colon

bariatric surgery

biliary tract

cheiloplasty

colonoscopy

combined hemorrhoids

descending colon

digestive system

dilation

direct inguinal hernia

duodenotomy

endoscopic procedure

endoscopic retrograde
cholangiopancreatography (ERCP)

enteroenterostomy

enterolysis

enterotomy

esophagogastroduode-
noscopy (EGD)
procedures

esophagus

external hemorrhoids

frenum

gastric bypass surgery

gastrotomy

glossectomy

hemorrhoid

hernia

hiatal hernia

incisional hernia

indirect inguinal hernia

inguinal hernia

internal hemorrhoids

intestine

island flap

laparoscopy

large intestine

ligation

lingual

lingual tonsils

liver

manipulation

Meckel's diverticulum

mesentery

mixed hemorrhoids

nasopharyngeal tonsils

nasopharynx

omentum

open colectomy

palate

palatine tonsils

palatoplasty

pancreas

parotid glands

peritoneum

pharyngeal flap

pharyngoplasty

pharyngostomy

pharynx

proctosigmoidoscopy

prolapsed hemorrhoid

pyloromyotomy

rectum

salivary glands

sigmoid colon

sigmoidoscopy

small intestine

stoma

stomach

strangulated hemorrhoid

strangulated hernia

sublingual

sublingual glands

submandibular glands

thrombosed hemorrhoid

tonsils

tracheostomy

transverse colon

ulcerated hemorrhoid

uvula

vagotomy

ventral hernia

vermilion

vestibule of the mouth

V-excision

Introduction

This subsection of the surgical section of the CPT manual codes procedures performed on the digestive system. The **digestive system** performs numerous functions that include the intake of nourishment, breakdown of food during digestion, absorption of nutrients, and elimination of waste products.

The digestive system begins at the lips when food is taken in and chewing starts. The food then moves to the oral cavity (mouth), the pharynx (throat), and the esophagus, and then on to the stomach, small intestine, large intestine, rectum, and anus. The procedures in this subsection of the CPT manual follow the same order. The procedures of the lips and mouth begin the subsection and move on to the pharynx, esophagus, stomach, intestines, rectum, and anus. The coder should be able to locate a code easily by knowing the area or structure the particular procedure was performed on. It is also helpful if the coder recognizes that the digestive system is sometimes referred to as the **alimentary canal**. Figure 11-1 illustrates the structures of the digestive system.

The digestive system section also includes procedure codes for services pertaining to the liver, biliary tract, pancreas, abdomen, peritoneum, and omentum.

Guidelines Related to the National Correct Coding Initiative (NCCI)

The student will need to perform the following steps to obtain the most current coding guideline information related to this chapter online:

1. Log on to *www.cms.hhs.gov/NationalCorrectCodInitEd.*
2. Scroll to the section titled "Downloads."
3. Click the link for the most current "NCCI Policy Manual for Medicare Services."
4. A box may appear that requires you to click "Open."
5. Click "Chapter 6" for guidelines specific to the digestive system.

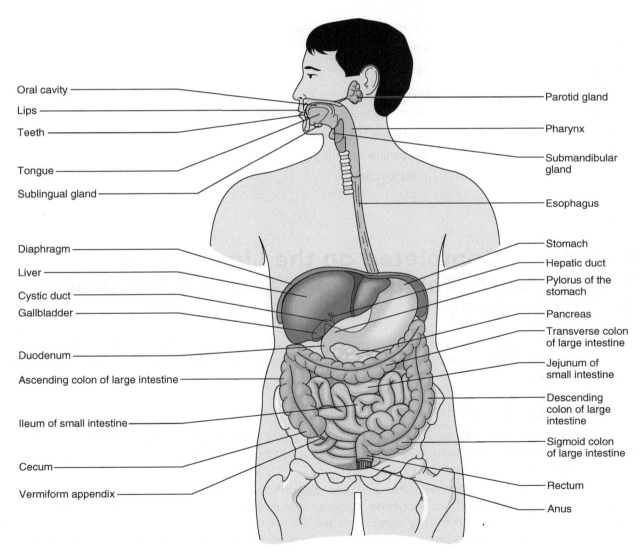

FIGURE 11-1 Organs of the Digestive System

Abbreviations Related to the Digestive System

The following are some of the most common abbreviations related to the digestive system:

Abbreviations	Definitions
BE	barium enema
COL	colonoscopy
EGD	esophagogastroduodenoscopy
GERD	gastroesophageal reflux disease
GI	gastrointestinal
IBD	inflammatory bowel disease
IBS	irritable bowel syndrome
NG tube	nasogastric tube
NPO	nothing by mouth
PEG tube	percutaneous endoscopic gastrostomy tube
SBF	small bowel follow-through
TPN	total parenteral nutrition
UC	ulcerative colitis

Procedures Completed on the Lips, Mouth, Tongue, Teeth, Palate, Uvula, and Salivary Glands (40490–42699)

Figure 11-2 illustrates the oral cavity and many of the structures discussed in this subsection of the chapter. As in other subsections of the Surgery section, the organization of this subsection includes incisions, excisions, repairs, and other procedures.

Lips (40490–40799)

This section begins with codes for excision procedures. A term that coders should be familiar with is **vermilion**, the pinkish border of the lips. Codes 40490–40530 reflect the procedures performed on and around the lips. Table 11-1 summarizes codes from this range.

Codes 40650 to 40761 reports repairs that are completed on the lips. The term **cheiloplasty** refers to the repair of the lips. This section of codes should be reviewed carefully before codes are assigned. The coder needs to be aware of the type of deformity being corrected. Partial, complete, unilateral, and bilateral repairs are reported using the codes from this range of codes. There are several notes that are present for codes in this code range. Review the notes that are found in the CPT manual to become familiar with the instructional notations. The coder also needs to know whether a rhinoplasty was performed in addition to or separate from the repair of the lip. Attention to documentation is imperative. Table 11-2 summarizes codes in this section.

Code 40799 is used to report other unlisted procedures that are completed on the lips.

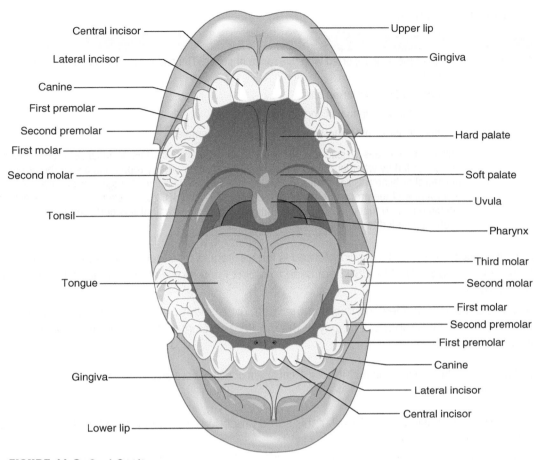

FIGURE 11-2 Oral Cavity

TABLE 11-1 Lips (40490–40530)

Code(s)	Description
40490	This code is used to report a biopsy of the lip.
40500	Vermilionectomy, also known as lip shave, is reported with this code, which also includes the mucosal advancement during the procedure.
40510–40527	This range of codes is used to report excisions of the lip. The codes are differentiated by the type of excision and type of closure or reconstruction. Coders must read the operative report to determine the type of closure or reconstruction completed. A term that coders should be familiar with is **V-excision**, a V-shaped cut made by the doctor.
40530	Code 40530 reports a resection of the lip. This code specifies that "more than one-fourth" of the lip is involved. There is usually layered closure involved in this procedure. Be sure to reference the documentation for support of the use of this code. It should also be noted that an instructional notation follows code 40530 that instructs the coder that for reconstruction the coder should see code range 13131 et seq.

Vestibule of the Mouth (40800–40899)

The mucosal tissue and submucosal tissue of the lips and cheeks comprise the **vestibule of the mouth**. Keep in mind that the teeth and the alveolar process are not part of the vestibule.

This code range begins with codes used to report incision procedures, codes 40800–40806. Codes 40800 and 40801 report the drainage of an abscess, cyst, or hematoma and are differentiated by whether the case is

TABLE 11-2 Lips (40650–40761)

Code(s)	Description
40650–40654	Repair of the lip is reported with this range of codes. The codes are differentiated by the amount of the lip repaired: Code 40650—vermilion only Code 40652—up to half vertical height Code 40654—over one-half vertical height, or complex
40700–40761	This range of codes is used to report the plastic repair of a cleft lip or nasal deformity. The codes are differentiated by whether the repair is the primary or secondary repair and also if the procedures are unilateral or bilateral. The codes are also defined by the number of stages for the procedure: code 40701 is for a one-stage procedure, whereas codes 40702 and 40720 represent a two-stage procedure. It should be noted that code 40720 is a unilateral procedure and, if it is performed bilaterally, modifier 50 should be added to the code.

simple or complicated. Here, the term *complicated* is interpreted as treatment of larger lesions or the completion of multiple incisions. Codes 40804–40805 are used to report the removal of an embedded foreign body from the vestibule of the mouth.

Excision and destruction of lesions found in the vestibule of the mouth are coded using code range 40808–40820. Code 40808 reports a biopsy of the mouth. Excisions in this range are differentiated by the type of repair completed.

> **EXAMPLE:** Dr. Smith completes an excision of a 1-cm lesion of the mucosa and submucosa on the vestibule of the mouth with a simple repair.

This should be coded using code 40812. If this same procedure was completed but the repair was complex, code 40814 should be reported.

Repair codes are reported using codes from the 40830–40845 code range. Knowing whether the procedure was complex and whether the procedure was done bilaterally or unilaterally is necessary when you are coding from this code range. Knowledge of whether the procedure was done in the posterior or anterior portion is also necessary.

The last code in this subsection is code 40899, used for unlisted procedures completed on the vestibule of the mouth. This code should be used only if no other procedure code is appropriate.

Tongue and Floor of Mouth (41000–41599)

Understanding terminology is very important in selecting the correct code from this subcategory. **Lingual** refers to the tongue, and at times, the physician will refer to a procedure being done in the sublingual area. The **sublingual** area refers to the area under the tongue.

Code range 41000–41599 is organized into the following groups of codes:

- Incision—code range 41000–41019
- Excision—code range 41100–41155
- Repair—code range 41250–41252
- Other Procedures—code range 41510–41599

Incision (41000–41019)

Codes 41000–41009 are used to report intraoral incision and drainage of an abscess, cyst, or hematoma of the tongue or the floor of the mouth. The codes are differentiated by the area of the tongue or the floor of the mouth treated. Code 41010 reports an incision of the lingual frenum, or tongue. The **frenum** is a connection. In this case, the connection is between the tongue and the floor of the mouth. The coder should always use as many references as necessary to be sure that a proper code assignment is made and that the documentation supports that code assignment.

Codes 41015–41018 report extraoral incision and drainage of an abscess, cyst, or hematoma of the floor of the mouth. These codes are also differentiated by the site of the procedure.

Code 41019 reports the placement of needles, catheters, or other devices that are used for subsequent interstitial radioelement application. If imaging guidance, stereotactic insertion of intracranial brachytherapy radiation sources, or interstitial radioelement application occurred, the notations that follow code 41019 in the CPT manual should be referenced prior to code assignment.

Excision (41100–41155)

This range is used to report excision codes and biopsies of the tongue and floor of the mouth. Codes 41100 and 41105 are used to report a biopsy of the tongue. When selecting a code from this range, the coder must be able to identify the area of the tongue from which the biopsy was taken. Code 41108 reports a biopsy taken from the floor of the mouth. Codes 41110–41114 report the excision of lesions of the tongue. The coder must determine the extent of the excision when reading the operative note for the procedures. A biopsy that is performed during the same operative session as an excision will affect code selection. Code 41115 reports a frenectomy, which is an excision of the lingual frenum, while code 41116 is used to report an excision of a lesion from the floor of the mouth.

A **glossectomy** is a procedure in which there is a partial or complete removal of the tongue. It is reported using code range 41120–41155. The glossectomy procedures are based on how much of the tongue is removed and whether a tracheostomy is performed. A **tracheostomy** is a surgical opening into the trachea through the neck. This code range also identifies whether there is any radical neck dissection.

Repair and Other Procedures (41250–41599)

After incision and excision codes, the repair codes and other procedures are listed in the CPT manual. Repair of lacerations (code range 41250–41252) is differentiated by the size of the laceration repaired and the site of the repair.

Other procedures that are completed on the tongue are reported with codes 41510–41599. These codes include the following procedures:

- Suture of the tongue to lip for micrognathia—code 41510
- Tongue base suspension—code 41512. Review the instructional notations that follow this code in the CPT manual.
- Frenoplasty—code 41520. Review the instructional notation that follows this code in the CPT manual.
- Submucosal ablation of tongue base—code 41530
- Unlisted procedure—code 41599

Dentoalveolar Structures (41800–41899)

This code range contains procedures performed on the gums and alveolus. The **alveolus** is the socket where the tooth sits. Like the other code ranges, this code set begins with incisions. Code 41800 reports the drainage of an abscess, cyst, or hematoma from dentoalveolar structures. Codes 41805 and 41806 code the removal of an embedded foreign body from dentoalveolar structures and are differentiated by the removal from the soft-tissue area or bone.

Excisions and destructions are coded with code range 41820–41850. Terms that are referenced in the index to select codes from this range include:

- Gingivectomy
- Operculectomy
- Excision, then lesion, then gum
- Alveolectomy
- Destruction, then lesion, then gum

The remaining codes, 41870–41899, report other procedures completed on the dentoalveolar structures. Code 41870 is used for grafting around the teeth. Code 41872, gingivoplasty, and code 41874, alveoloplasty, are reported for each quadrant in which the procedure is completed. Prior to assigning code 41874 coders need to review the instructional notations that follow the code for additional guidelines. Code 41899 reports an unlisted procedure of dentoalveolar structures.

Palate and Uvula (42000–42299)

The **palate** is more commonly called the *roof of the mouth*. The **uvula** is located in the posterior border of the soft palate. It is a small, cone-shaped mass of flesh that hangs from the soft palate. Code range 42000–42299 is divided into the following:

- Incision
- Excision, Destruction
- Repair
- Other Procedures

There is only one incision code in this code range: 42000, drainage of abscess of palate, uvula. Code 42100 is used to report a biopsy of the palate or uvula. The next code range, 42104–42107, reports the excision of a lesion of the palate or uvula. The codes are differentiated by whether a closure was completed. If a closure was completed, the coder must determine whether the closure was a simple primary closure or a local flap closure. Code 42120 reports a resection of the palate or extensive resection of a lesion. Following this code an instructional notation appears providing guidance in the reporting of reconstructions of the palate with extraoral tissue. Review this notation in the CPT manual. Code 42140 reports an excision of the uvula and code 42145 reports a palatopharyngoplasty. In the CPT manual review the instructional notation that follows code 42145. Code 42160 reports the destruction of a lesion on the palate or uvula by thermal, cryo, or chemical means.

Repair codes are found in the 42180–42281 code range. Repairs of lacerations of the palate, codes 42180 and 42182, are differentiated by the length of the repair and whether the repair is complex. Palatoplasty for a cleft palate is reported with codes 42200–42225. A **palatoplasty** is a repair of the roof of the mouth. Also found in the repair section of this code range, codes 42226–42235, are pharyngeal and island flap codes. A **pharyngeal flap** is formed by making an incision through the soft palate to the posterior pharyngeal wall. The incision is advanced to the muscle, and the flap is formed. The **island flap** is made using subcutaneous tissue with nutrient vessels. A maxillary impression for palatal prosthesis is reported with code 42280 while code 42281 reports an insertion of a pin-retained palatal prosthesis. Code 42299 reports unlisted procedures completed on the palate and uvula.

Salivary Glands and Ducts (42300–42699)

The **salivary glands** secrete saliva, which contains an enzyme that aids in digestion. There are actually three pairs of salivary glands. The first are called the **parotid glands** and are located in front of each ear. The **sublingual glands** are located under the tongue. The third set is the **submandibular glands**, which are found on the floor of the mouth.

This code range begins with incision codes that report the following:

- Drainage of abscess—differentiated by site: parotid versus submaxillary or sublingual (codes 42300–42320)
- Sialolithotomy—differentiated by site and whether the case was complicated or uncomplicated (codes 42330–42340)

Code range 42400–42450 then follows, which reports the excisional procedures completed on the salivary glands and ducts. Table 11-3 summarizes the codes in this range.

TABLE 11-3 Salivary Glands, Excision 42400–42450

Code(s)	Description
42400 and 42405	Biopsies of the salivary gland are reported by using these codes, which are differentiated by needle biopsy in code 42400 and incisional biopsy in code 42405.
42408	Excision of sublingual salivary cyst is reported with this code.
42409	Marsupialization of sublingual salivary cyst is reported with this code.
42410–42450	This group of codes reports the excisions of various tumors or glands. To select a code, the coder must determine the location of the procedure: parotid, submandibular, or sublingual gland area. For codes 42410–42426, the coder must also determine the lobes involved and any accompanying procedures, such as en bloc, unilateral radical neck dissection, and others.

Exercise 11.1—Check Your Understanding

Understanding Code Range 40490–42699

Using a CPT manual, locate the correct code for each procedure given, and make note of the subcategory in which the code was found (i.e., Lips, Vestibule of Mouth, Tongue and Floor of Mouth, Dentoalveolar Structures, Palate and Uvula, or Salivary Gland and Ducts). The first one is done for you.

1. Drainage of abscess; parotid, simple
   42300; Salivary Gland and Ducts

2. Palatoplasty for cleft palate, with closure of alveolar ridge; soft tissue only _____

3. Unilateral posterior vestibuloplasty
   _____

4. Excision of lingual frenum _____

5. Resection of lip, more than one-fourth, without reconstruction _____

6. Excision of sublingual salivary cyst _____

7. Biopsy of lip _____

8. Biopsy of floor of mouth _____

9. Periodontal mucosal grafting _____

10. Closure of salivary fistula _____

This code range finishes with repair codes, which include plastic repair and diversion codes of the salivary glands. The other procedure codes in this code set include injection procedures, dilation, and ligation of the salivary duct, along with the unlisted procedure code for salivary glands or ducts.

Procedures Completed on the Pharynx, Adenoids, and Tonsils (42700–42999)

The **pharynx** is the passageway that connects the oral cavity to the esophagus for the digestive system but also connects to the larynx as part of the respiratory system. This structure is part of both the digestive and respiratory systems. The pharynx is also called the *throat*.

The **tonsils** are located in the posterior wall of the **nasopharynx**. The nasopharynx is the part of the pharynx that is located posterior to the nasal cavity. The tonsils are made up of lymphatic tissue and are considered the first line of defense for the respiratory system.

There are actually three pairs of tonsils in the body: the **nasopharyngeal tonsils**, which are also referred to as the **adenoids**; the **lingual tonsils**, which are located at the base of the tongue on the posterior surface; and the **palatine tonsils**, which are the pair that are most commonly referred to as the *tonsils*. This pair of tonsils comes off the soft palate to the base of the tongue. Figure 11-3 illustrates the location of the tonsils.

Code range 42700–42999 is divided as follows:

- Incision
- Excision, Destruction
- Repair
- Other Procedures

The incision codes are listed first, and report the incision and drainage of abscesses, which are differentiated by location: peritonsillar, retropharyngeal or parapharyngeal (intraoral approach), or retropharyngeal or parapharyngeal (external approach).

Codes 42800–42894 follow and are used to report excisions and destructions of the pharynx, adenoids, and tonsils. The codes for tonsillectomy and adenoidectomy, codes 42820–42836, are found in this code range and are assigned according to the age of the patient. It should be noted here that these procedures are implied to be bilateral, so the addition of the 50 modifier is not appropriate for these codes.

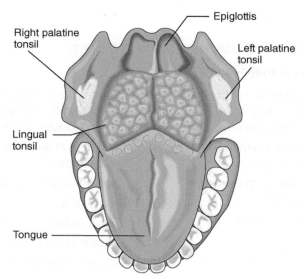

FIGURE 11-3 Types of Tonsils

Repair codes and other procedures on the pharynx are listed next in the CPT manual. Codes that fall into this range include the following:

- Suture of pharynx for wound or injury—code 42900. Medical documentation must support that the suture occurred because there was a wound or injury to the pharynx.
- **Pharyngoplasty**—code 42950. This is for plastic surgery or a reconstructive operation on the pharynx.
- Pharyngoesophageal repair—code 42953.
- **Pharyngostomy**—code 42955. This term is used to identify a procedure in which an artificial opening is made into the pharynx.
- Control of oropharyngeal or nasopharyngeal hemorrhage—codes 42960–42972. These codes are differentiated by whether the procedure was simple, complicated, or involved secondary surgical intervention.
- Unlisted procedures completed on the pharynx, adenoids, or tonsils—code 42999. Remember that this code should be used only when a more specific code is not found.

Procedures Completed on the Esophagus (43020–43499)

The **esophagus** is a muscular structure that moves food from the pharynx to the stomach. The procedures in this code range follow the same format as previous code ranges beginning with incision codes. Codes here report the esophagotomy cervical approach with removal of a foreign body (Code 43020), cricopharyngeal myotomy (Code 43030), and the esophagotomy thoracic approach with removal of a foreign body (Code 43045).

Codes 43100–43135 report excisions completed on the esophagus. Table 11-4 summarizes the codes found in this range.

Please remember that excision codes are determined by how much of the esophagus is removed, so attention to detail in the operative report is necessary.

Endoscopy Procedures (43180–43278)

Code range 43180–43278 reports endoscopic procedures completed via the esophagus. An **endoscopic procedure** involves insertion of a flexible or rigid instrument called an *endoscope*, which is used to view the internal structures.

TABLE 11-4 Esophagus, Excision 43100–43135

Code(s)	Description
43100 and 43101	Excisions of lesions of the esophagus are reported with these codes. For proper code selection, the coder must identify the approach: cervical versus thoracic or abdominal.
43107–43113	Total or near-total esophagectomy are reported with these codes. Codes 43107 and 43108 are for procedures without thoracotomy, and codes 43112 and 43113 are for procedures with thoracotomy. The codes are also further differentiated by other procedures performed at the time of the surgery. Coders must pay close attention to the details of the procedures noted in the operative report for code selection.
43116–43123	Partial esophagectomy is reported with this range of codes. Because there are various types of approaches that can be used, the coder must identify the approach in the operative report to select a code. The coder must also identify other procedures that may accompany the partial esophagectomy that may affect code assignment. For example, code 43123 also includes the accompanying procedure of a colon interposition or small-intestine reconstruction, including intestine mobilization, preparation, and anastomosis(es).
43124	This code reports a total or partial esophagectomy without reconstruction, with cervical esophagostomy.
43130 and 43135	This range of codes reports a diverticulectomy of hypopharynx or esophagus with or without myotomy. Code 43130 reports a cervical approach, while code 43135 reports a thoracic approach.

These procedures may be diagnostic, which determines whether an abnormality is present. If an abnormality is found, a determination should be made as to the extent of the abnormality. If the surgeon is doing anything more than a visual examination, the procedure then becomes a surgical procedure. A diagnostic endoscopy should not be reported in addition to a surgical endoscopy because the diagnostic endoscopy is bundled into the surgical endoscopy. When an endoscopic procedure turns into an open procedure, the endoscopic procedure can be reported separately with modifier 58 to indicate a staged or related procedure.

Codes 43180–43232

The endoscope can be moved down the esophagus for visualization or obtaining biopsies of the esophagus. Code 43180 reports a rigid esophagoscopy, transoral with diverticulectomy of hypopharynx or cervical esophagus with a cricopharyngeal myotomy with or without the use of a telescope or operating microscope. Code 43191 reports a diagnostic esophagoscopy using a rigid scope. Codes 43192 to 43196 report the use of a rigid esophagoscope for therapeutic procedures, such as removal of a foreign body or other procedures.

Code 43197 reports the use of a flexible esophagoscope for diagnostic purposes. Codes 43198 to 43232 reports the use of a flexible esophagoscope for diagnostic and therapeutic procedures.

EXAMPLES:
1. Mr. George presented for a biopsy of a lesion on the esophagus. Dr. Dennis moved the flexible esophagoscope to the area of the lesion, and a biopsy was taken of the lesion in question, along with a biopsy of another lesion viewed during the procedure.
2. Mr. George presented for a biopsy of a lesion on the esophagus. Dr. Dennis moved the flexible esophagoscope to the area of the lesion and decided to remove the whole lesion by bipolar cautery, along with removing another lesion viewed during the procedure using the same bipolar cautery technique.

In the first example, a simple biopsy was performed on each lesion. This procedure would be reported using code 43202. The second procedure would be reported using code 43216 because a more extensive procedure was performed.

For some codes, such as codes 43216–43217, the documentation should note what specific method or technique was used to remove a lesion. The different techniques are noted in the code descriptions and should be reviewed carefully. If necessary, the surgeon should be consulted to ensure that the proper code is selected.

Codes 43200–43232 report the use of an endoscope to view the esophagus or to perform a surgical procedure via the scope. Codes that report surgical endoscopy procedures completed on the esophagus include the following:

- Code 43215—esophagoscopy, flexible, with removal of foreign body
- Code 43211—esophagoscopy, flexible, with endoscopic mucosal resection
- Code 43226—esophagoscopy, flexible, with insertion of guidewire followed by passage of dilator(s) over guide wire
- Code 43231—esophagoscopy, flexible, with endoscopic ultrasound examination

The preceding list is not all-inclusive of the codes in this range. It is used to demonstrate the types of procedures that are completed via the endoscope. To become familiar with all the codes in this section, a new coder should read the codes found in code range 43180–43232. It should also be noted that there are codes within this code range that are out of numerical sequence. Review the notes that are found in the CPT manual following code 43206 for the listing of codes that are out of numerical sequence within this code range of CPT.

Codes 43233–43259 and Codes 43210, 43270, and 43266

Codes 43233 through 43259 and codes 43210, 43270, and 43266 are used for endoscopic procedures in which the scope is moved down the esophagus into the stomach, and then into the duodenum with the possibility of the scope entering into the upper part of the jejunum. Once the endoscope passes through the diaphragm, the procedure becomes an esophagogastroscopic procedure.

Codes 43233–43259 and codes 43210, 43270, and 43266 are used to report **esophagogastroduodenoscopy (EGD) procedures**. During this procedure, the scope is passed to view the esophagus and upper portion of the gastrointestinal tract, including the stomach, upper duodenum, and/or jejunum. This procedure is also known as an *upper gastrointestinal endoscopy*. To locate these codes in the index, the coder would reference the term *endoscopy* and then *gastrointestinal, upper*. It should be noted that there are codes that are out of numerical sequence in this range of codes. For example code 43233 is out of numerical sequence. Be guided by the notes that appear in the CPT manual for the location of codes that are out of numerical order.

Reviewing the CPT manual in this section, the coder should note that there are instructional notes that need to be reviewed before codes are selected from this range. These notations instruct coders about accompanying codes or combinations of codes that are not reported together.

EXAMPLE: By referencing CPT code 43238, the coder will find a notation that says not to report code 43238 in conjunction with numerous codes that are listed, including codes 76942 or 76975. Locate the listing of codes in the CPT manual following code 43238. Ultrasound procedure codes 76942 and 76975 cannot be reported separately, as these services are bundled into code 43238.

As can be noted from reviewing codes 43233–43259 and codes 43210 and 43270 and 43266, there are numerous endoscopic procedures performed on the upper gastrointestinal area. New coders must read operative notes carefully to identify the procedure completed and match it with the correct code from this range, reporting only the procedures completed via the scope. Coders should review documentation to determine the following before assigning codes for endoscopies:

1. Was the procedure diagnostic or surgical?
2. How was the scope inserted? In other words, what was the approach?

3. What was the reason for the endoscopy?

4. To what location was the scope advanced?

Codes 43260–43289

The next range of codes is for **endoscopic retrograde cholangiopancreatography (ERCP)**, codes 43260–43278. ERCP is an endoscopic procedure that combines a retrograde cholangiography and a transhepatic cholangiography. Other procedures performed at the same time as the ERCP determine code assignment. Other procedures include the insertion of a tube or stent into the pancreas, pressure measurement, biopsies, and ablation of polyps or tumors. If separate approaches are used, modifier 51 can be used to indicate multiple procedures at the same operative session. When assigning codes from code range 43260–43278, make sure all notations are read, as instructions for code assignment are given there.

Take your time when assigning codes to make sure that all notes are read and all additional codes are assigned as necessary. Code 43273 is an add-on code that can be used in conjunction with codes 43260–43265 and 43274–43278 when there is also endoscopic cannulation of papilla with direct visualization of the common bile duct(s) and/or pancreatic duct(s) occurring in the same operative session.

Code range 43279–43289 is used to report **laparoscopy**, a procedure using a scope much like an endoscope, which views the interior structures of the abdomen. Laparoscopic surgical procedures always include diagnostic procedures.

Repairs (43300–43425)

The various types of repairs of the esophagus are reported by the 43300–43425 code range. The approach will guide the coder as to the proper code selection. Types of approaches for esophagoplasty help differentiate the codes by noting whether the approach is abdominal, cervical, or thoracic. These codes are also differentiated by any procedures that are performed in addition to the esophagoplasty. These additional procedures include repairs of tracheoesophageal fistulas, both acquired and congenital, and the repair of a paraesophageal hiatal hernia.

Codes 43320–43328 are used to report esophagogastrostomy and esophagogastric fundoplasty. When reporting codes 43330–43352, for esophagomyotomy, esophagojejunostomy, and esophagostomy, the coder must be able to identify the approach, which could be abdominal, thoracic, or cervical. Codes 43360 and 43361 report a gastrointestinal reconstruction for a previous esophagectomy, for an obstructing esophageal lesion or fistula, or for a previous exclusion. Code 43360 reports the reconstruction of a stomach with or without pyloroplasty, while code 43361 is for the reconstruction of a colon interposition or small intestine reconstruction, including intestine mobilization, preparation, and anastomosis(es).

The remaining codes report the following types of procedures:

- **Ligation**—codes 43400 and 43405. This is a procedure that ties or binds something together with catgut, cotton, wire, or silk.

- Suture of esophageal wound or injury—codes 43410 and 43415. The suturing of this type of wound is differentiated by the type of approach used.

- Closure of esophagostomy or fistula—codes 43420–43425. These closure codes are differentiated by the type of approach used.

Manipulation Codes and Other Procedures (43450–43499)

Manipulation codes (43450–43460) and Other Procedures (codes 43496–43499) finish the range of codes for procedures completed on the esophagus. **Manipulation** is a maneuver by hand to treat or perform therapy.

Exercise 11.2—Check Your Understanding

Vocabulary

Fill in the blanks in the statements that follow.

1. _____ is performed when an expansion or stretching is necessary.

2. A(n) _____ endoscopy would not be reported in addition to a surgical endoscopy.

3. The _____ is a muscular structure that moves food from the pharynx to the stomach.

4. A(n) _____ can be rigid or flexible and is used to view internal structures.

5. _____ is a procedure that ties or binds something together with catgut, cotton, wire, or silk.

6. The _____ are located in the posterior wall of the nasopharynx.

7. An endoscopic procedure that combines a retrograde cholangiography and transhepatic cholangiography is known as a(n) _____.

8. A(n) _____, or maneuver by hand, is used to treat or perform therapy.

Dilation procedures are also coded by using this range of codes. **Dilation** is performed when an expansion or stretching is necessary. When a dilation of the esophagus occurs, the provider dilates the esophagus using a balloon or dilator.

Stomach (43500-43999)

The **stomach** is a pouchlike structure that aids in the breakdown and digestion of food. The stomach is positioned at the base of the esophagus on one end and connects to the duodenum on the other end. It is found in the upper left quadrant of the abdomen. Figure 11-4 illustrates the positioning of the stomach in relation to the liver and intestines.

Procedures completed on the stomach are grouped in CPT according to the following:

- Incision
- Excision
- Laparoscopy
- Introduction
- Bariatric Surgery
- Other Procedures

Incision (43500-43520)

Codes 43500–43510 would be used to report **gastrotomy** procedures, surgical incisions made into the stomach. The reasons for the completion of a gastrotomy differentiate the codes as follows:

- Exploration or foreign body removal
- Suture repair of bleeding ulcer
- Suture repair of preexisting esophagogastric laceration
- Esophageal dilation and insertion for permanent intraluminal tube

The final code in this range is code 43520, which reports a **pyloromyotomy**, the cutting of the pyloric muscle.

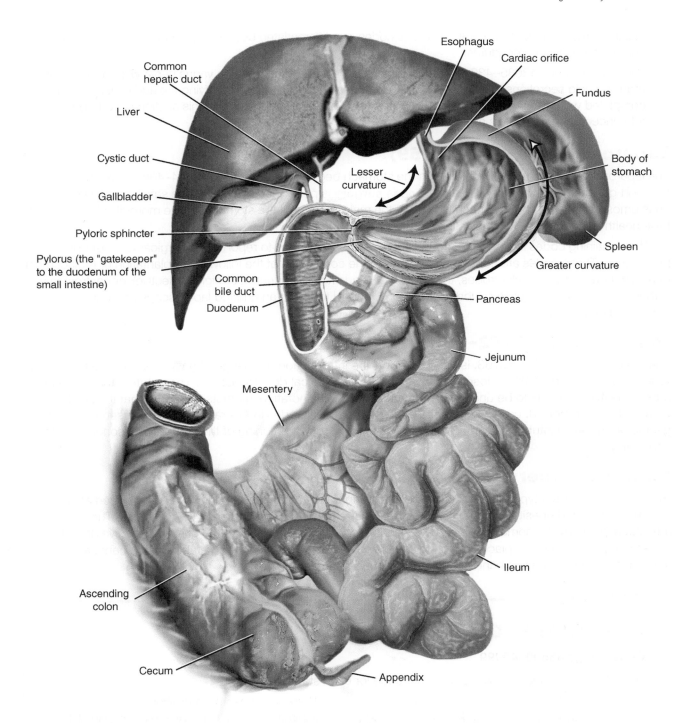

FIGURE 11-4 Position of the Stomach, Liver, and Intestines

Excision (43605–43641)

Biopsies and excisions completed on the stomach are reported using code range 43605–43641. Terms that would be referenced in the CPT index to select codes from this section include:

- Biopsy, then stomach—code 43605
- Excision, then tumor, then stomach—codes 43610–43611

- Gastrectomy—codes 43620–43634. These codes are differentiated between total and partial gastrectomy and accompanying procedures.

- Vagotomy—codes 43635–43641. A **vagotomy** is the surgical cutting of the vagus nerve with the intent of reducing acid secretions in the stomach. These codes are assigned by identifying the additional procedures completed with the vagotomy. Code 43635 is an add-on code, so all notes in this section need to be referenced before a code is assigned.

Laparoscopy (43644–43659)

The laparoscopic procedures completed on the stomach begin with code range 43644–43645, which is used to report gastric bypass surgery. **Gastric bypass surgery** is performed by dividing the small bowel with anastomosis to the proximal stomach to bypass the major portion of the stomach. Some morbidly obese patients have health issues that can be indications for this type of surgery.

The remaining codes in the range, codes 43647–43659, are used to report other surgical laparoscopic procedures. These codes are assigned according to the completion of the following: implantation or replacement of gastric neurostimulator electrodes, transection of vagus nerves (selective or highly selective), or gastrostomy without construction of a gastric tube. Code 43659 is used to report an unlisted laparoscopy procedure completed on the stomach.

Introduction (43752–43763)

The next code set, 43752–43763, is used to report the introduction or change of gastric or nasogastric tubes. When assigning code 43752, closely review the patient's medical documentation. The notation that appears after code 43752 needs to be understood by the coders. This notation instructs the coder that if critical care codes are reported, code 43752 should not be reported. Codes in this range would be used to report gastric or duodenal intubation and aspiration. The change or repositioning of these tubes is also found in this code range.

Bariatric Surgery (43770–43775)

Bariatric surgery is a type of operative procedure using bands and port insertion, and is performed as a treatment of morbid obesity. The bariatric procedures are reported using code set 43770–43775. These codes are differentiated by the components of the procedure completed in relation to the gastric restrictive device. These components include placement of adjustable gastric band, revision of adjustable gastric band, and removal of adjustable gastric band and subcutaneous port components.

Exercise 11.3—Check Your Understanding

Code Range 43500–43999

Using the CPT manual, assign the correct code for each statement given.

1. Pyloroplasty _____

2. Open gastrotomy with suture repair of bleeding ulcer _____

3. Gastrectomy, partial, distal, with Roux-en-Y reconstruction _____

4. Selective transection of vagus nerves done laparoscopically _____

5. Revision of gastroduodenal anastomosis with vagotomy and reconstruction _____

6. Therapeutic gastric intubation and aspiration(s), including lavage (physician skill needed) _____

7. Open gastric restrictive procedure with removal of subcutaneous port component only _____

8. Vagotomy including pyloroplasty, with gastrostomy, truncal _____

9. Gastroduodenostomy _____

10. Surgical closure of gastrostomy _____

Other Procedures Completed on the Stomach (43800–43999)

Other procedure codes used to report gastric procedures are reported using the 43800–43999 code set. Some of the gastric restrictive procedures that cannot be reported with the bariatric or gastric bypass codes are found in this code range. Revision codes and repair codes that are not found elsewhere are coded from this code range as well.

Intestines, Except Rectum (44005–44799)

The **intestine** is a membranous tube that begins at the pyloric opening of the stomach and ends at the anus. It is divided into the small and large intestine. The **small intestine** begins at the pyloric sphincter and moves through the duodenum, jejunum, ileum, and the ileocecal sphincter. It is approximately 20 feet long and encompasses most of the abdominal cavity. Most of the nutrient absorption and digestive process is completed in the small intestine before waste is moved into the large intestine.

The **large intestine** begins with the cecum and then moves to the colon, rectum, and anus. The large intestine further breaks down food and holds it until it can be further broken down and expelled from the body. Liquid is absorbed in both the large and small intestine. The longest part of the large intestine is the colon.

The colon is made up of four specific sections. The first is the **ascending colon**, which begins at the ileocecal junction; at the undersurface of the liver, it becomes the transverse colon. The **transverse colon** moves in a horizontal direction, and at the splenic flexure, it makes a downward turn to the **descending colon**. The descending colon moves down the left side of the abdomen to the **sigmoid colon**, which connects to the rectum. The coder will need to be familiar with the parts of the colon, as well as the intestines, in order to assign the correct code described in an operative note.

Figure 11-5 illustrates the structures of the small intestine, and Figure 11-6 illustrates the anatomy of the large intestine.

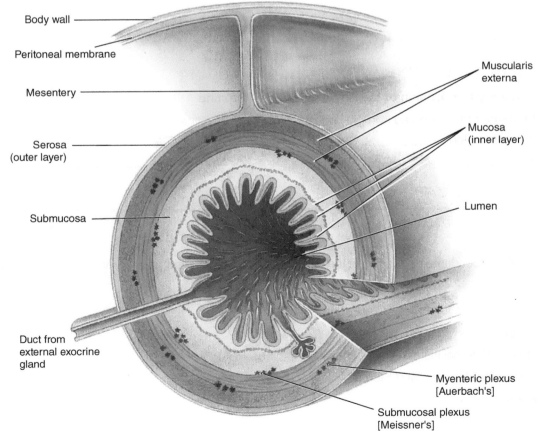

FIGURE 11-5 Small Intestine

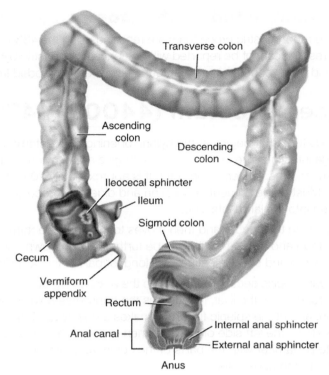

FIGURE 11-6 **Large Intestine**

Exercise 11.4—Check Your Understanding

Understanding the Division of the Small and Large Intestine

Indicate whether the site noted is in the large (L) or small (S) intestine.

1. Transverse colon _____

2. Jejunum _____

3. Ileum _____

4. Cecum _____

5. Ascending colon _____

Coding for the procedures performed in the intestines is organized into the following groups of codes:

- Incision
- Excision
- Laparoscopy
- Enterostomy—External Fistulization of Intestines
- Endoscopy, Small Intestine and Stomal
- Introduction
- Repair
- Other Procedures

Incision (44005–44055)

Procedures that are reported using code range 44005–44055 include the following:

- **Enterolysis**, code 44005, is the freeing of intestinal adhesions. This is a separate procedure code and is reported only when no other procedure is performed. It should also be noted that code 44005 is not to be reported with code 45136.
- **Duodenotomy**, code 44010, is the process of making an incision into the duodenum. This procedure is completed to explore the area, to obtain biopsies, or to remove a foreign body.
- Tube or needle catheter jejunostomy for enteral alimentation, code 44015, is an add-on procedure. This is an intraoperative procedure, and this code can be added to any primary procedure. Code 44015 is always reported as a secondary code to a primary procedure.
- **Enterotomy**, codes 44020–44021, is the process of making an incision into the intestines. These codes are differentiated by the reason for the procedure.

Excision (44100–44160)

Code range 44100–44160 is used to report excisions completed on the intestines. A term that coders will see associated with these procedures is **anastomosis**, which is the process of surgically connecting two structures that are usually hollow tubular parts, such as the intestines. Codes 44100–44130 report the following procedures:

- Biopsy of intestine—code 44100.
- Excisions of one or more lesions of small or large intestines—codes 44110–44111.
- Enterectomy, resection of small intestine—codes 44120–44128. These codes are differentiated according to the accompanying procedures and the reason for the enterectomy.
- **Enteroenterostomy**—code 44130. This is a separate procedure code that is used to report the surgical anastomosis of two parts of the intestine with the creation of an opening between the two areas.

Also included in this range are codes for excision procedures that are completed for intestinal transplant surgery. As in other sections of CPT, these codes involve three distinct components of work associated with the transplantation:

- Donor enterectomy—either from a cadaver (code 44132) or from a living donor (code 44133)
- Backbench work—codes 44715 and 44720–44721
- Recipient intestinal allotransplantation with or without recipient enterectomy—codes 44135 and 44136

Codes 44140 to 44160 are used to report an **open colectomy**, an excision of all or part of the colon by making an incision into the area. These codes are differentiated according to whether the colectomy was partial, codes 44140–44147 and 44160, or whether the procedure was a total colectomy, codes 44150 to 44158. The codes are further differentiated by accompanying procedures. Therefore, when selecting codes from this area, the coder needs to determine the following:

- Was the colectomy partial or total?
- What were the accompanying procedures (such as coloproctostomy, ileostomy, or mucosectomy)?

Figure 11-7 illustrates various colectomy options.

Laparoscopy (44180–44238)

Laparoscopic enterolysis of adhesions, code 44180, allows surgeons the ability to report extensive removal of adhesions that have to be passed through to get to the operative site. Most insurance carriers will not reimburse separately for this procedure because they consider it bundled into the other, more complex operative services provided. However, in some instances, there are such extensive adhesions that the destruction of these

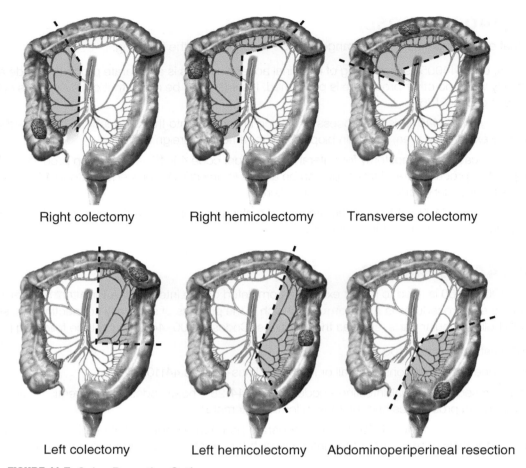

Right colectomy   Right hemicolectomy   Transverse colectomy

Left colectomy   Left hemicolectomy   Abdominoperiperineal resection

FIGURE 11-7 Colon Resection Options

adhesions adds more time to the other surgery being performed. If the surgeon documents this additional time and why this is above and beyond the norm for the service being provided, an appeal may be successful if the claim is rejected by the insurance company.

As with other laparoscopic procedures, a diagnostic laparoscopy is always included in the surgical laparoscopy. However, in this section of CPT, the diagnostic laparoscopy is reported using code 49320, which does not fall within this range of codes. Codes 44180 to 44238 include only surgical laparoscopic procedures and are divided into the following groups of codes:

- Incision—code 44180
- Enterostomy—External Fistulization of Intestines—codes 44186–44188
- Excision—codes 44202–44213
- Repair—code 44227
- Other Procedures—code 44238

In reviewing these codes further, note that all of these laparoscopic procedures are also completed as open procedures. After each of the codes in this section, a notation appears that references the open procedure.

EXAMPLES: Code 44204 is used to report a surgical laparoscopy with a partial colectomy with anastomosis. Code 44140 is used to report a partial colectomy with anastomosis that was completed as an open procedure.

Therefore, it is of utmost importance that, when reading the operative report, the coder identify whether the procedure was completed via a laparoscope or as an open procedure.

Enterostomy—External Fistulization of Intestines (44300–44346)

The Enterostomy section, codes 44300–44346, is next. This section is used to report ileostomy, jejunostomy, or colostomy procedures. The coder needs to know which part of the intestine is being worked on and the division of each so that proper code assignment can be made. Procedures that are coded to this range include:

- Enterostomy or cecostomy—code 44300. This is a separate procedure code.
- Ileostomy or jejunostomy—code 44310. This is for the open procedure.
- Revision of ileostomy—codes 44312 and 44314. These codes are differentiated by simple and complicated.
- Continent ileostomy—code 44316. This is a separate procedure code and is also known as a *Kock procedure.*
- Colostomy—codes 44320 and 44322. These codes are differentiated by whether multiple biopsies were completed. These are open procedures.
- Revision of colostomy—codes 44340–44346. These codes are all separate procedure codes and are differentiated as simple, complicated, or with repair of paracolostomy.

Endoscopy, Small Intestine and Stomal (44360–44408)

Codes 44360–44408 are used to report endoscopic procedures of the small intestine. This code range is also used to report endoscopic procedures through a stoma. In this case, the **stoma** is a surgical opening between a part of the intestine and the outside surface of the skin of the abdomen. Code selection is based on the scope placement, the type of procedure performed, and how it is performed.

The codes in this section are grouped into the following areas:

- Small intestinal endoscopy, enteroscopy beyond the second portion of the duodenum, not including the ileum—codes 44360–44373. These codes are differentiated by the reason for the procedure, such as biopsy, removal of a foreign body, control of bleeding, and stent placement.
- Small intestinal endoscopy, enteroscopy beyond the second portion of the duodenum, including the ileum—codes 44376–44379. These codes are also differentiated by the reason for the procedure.
- Ileoscopy—codes 44380–44384. Code selection is based on whether the procedure was diagnostic, completed with a biopsy, or for placement of a transendoscopic stent.
- Endoscopic evaluation of a small intestinal pouch—codes 44385–44386. Codes are differentiated by a diagnostic procedure or by a biopsy.
- Colonoscopy—codes 44388–44408. These codes are selected based on whether the colonoscopy was diagnostic (code 44388) or whether the colonoscopy was completed to perform a procedure (codes 44389 to 44408) such as a biopsy, removal of a foreign body, or stent placement.

Codes 44500 to 44799

Introduction of a long gastrointestinal (GI) tube is reported with code 44500. This GI tube placement is not the same as the nasogastric tube placement (43752). This procedure is typically referred to as a Miller-Abbott, in which a mercury-filled balloon is swallowed that carries it to the small intestine. The patient is seated lower than the person performing the service. The balloon is then inflated slightly and pulled outward until the obstruction is encountered. The procedure may be done with or without fluoroscopy.

Repair codes and other procedures complete this subsection. The services reported with codes 44602 to 44680 include closure procedures of the large or small intestine. Procedures reported from this range include:

- Suturing of small intestine
- Closure of enterostomy
- Closure of intestinal fistula
- Intestinal plication

Other procedures are reported with codes 44700 to 44799 and include codes for backbench work. Remember that backbench work is the work completed to prepare for a transplant.

Exercise 11.5—Check Your Understanding

Code Range 44005–44799

Using the CPT manual, assign the proper code to each of the following statements.

1. Enterorrhaphy for perforated ulcer small intestine, single perforation _____
2. Revision of colostomy, simple _____
3. Ileoscopy, through stoma, with biopsy _____
4. Laparoscopic lysis of adhesions of the abdomen _____
5. Simple revision of ileostomy _____
6. Duodenotomy for biopsy _____
7. Laparoscopic nontube ileostomy _____
8. Complete removal of transplanted intestinal allograft _____
9. Kock procedure _____
10. Closure of intestinal cutaneous fistula _____

Meckel's Diverticulum and the Mesentery (44800–44899)

Meckel's diverticulum is a form of diverticulum of the ileum. The **mesentery** is the membranous attachment of an organ to the body wall. The codes found in this subcategory include excision codes 44800 and 44820, and a code for the suturing of the mesentery, code 44850. Code 44899 is used to report unlisted procedures completed on Meckel's diverticulum and the mesentery.

Appendix (44900–44979)

The **appendix** is a small, twisted, tubelike structure located at the blind end of the cecum. Figure 11-6 illustrates the location of the appendix in relation to the cecum.

The appendix does not serve any known purpose in the digestive system. The coding begins with incision and excision codes and moves on to laparoscopic codes. An open appendectomy is code 44950 if performed on its own and *not* in conjunction with any other abdominal procedure. If the removal is performed in addition to another major procedure for a clinically indicated reason, add-on code 44955 should be used to report the removal of the appendix. Code 44970 is used to report an appendectomy performed laparoscopically. If this is done at the time of a diagnostic procedure, the diagnostic procedure is considered inclusive to the surgical procedure and is not reported separately.

Colon and Rectum (45000–45999)

At the distal end of the large intestine is the **rectum**, which aids the removal of waste from the body.

The 45000–45020 code range is used to report incision procedures. Procedures reported with this range of codes include incision and drainage of abscesses that are located in the rectum.

Excision procedures are reported using code range 45100–45172. The terms to reference in the index to locate codes from this section include:

- Biopsy, then rectum—code 45100
- Myomectomy, then anorectal—code 45108

- Proctectomy, then partial (open) or total (open)—codes 45110–45123
- Rectum, then prolapse, then excision—codes 45130–45135
- Rectum, then stricture, then excision—code 45150

Destruction of a rectal tumor by electrodesiccation, electrosurgery, laser ablation, laser resection, or cryosurgery via a transanal approach is recorded using code 45190.

Endoscopic procedures can be either surgical or diagnostic in nature and are reported using codes 45300–45398.

Endoscopic procedures are determined by how far into the large intestine the scope is moved. Codes for this subcategory are set up in the order of examinations, which go from least invasive to most invasive.

Examination of the rectum with scope advancement into the sigmoid colon is called a **proctosigmoidoscopy**. The code range for proctosigmoidoscopy is 45300–45327.

A **sigmoidoscopy** is a procedure in which the endoscope is moved all the way through the rectum and sigmoid colon and may even advance slightly into the descending colon. The code range for sigmoidoscopy procedures is 45330–45350.

An examination in which the entire colon, from the rectum to the cecum, is visualized is known as a **colonoscopy**. A colonoscopy may include examination of the terminal ileum as well. The endoscope may be flexible or rigid. The procedure codes used to report a colonoscopy are 45378–45398. Coding guidelines for endoscopic procedures dictate that only the most extensive procedure performed should be reported.

EXAMPLE: Dr. Dodd performed a sigmoidoscopy for lesion removal on his patient, but because of his findings, it was determined that he needed to perform a colonoscopy for polyp removal by snare technique farther up in the large intestine and proximal to the splenic flexure.

Dr. Dodd should be using code 45385—colonoscopy, flexible, proximal to splenic flexure; with removal of polyps, by snare technique. The sigmoidoscopy should not be reported, since the colonoscopy is more extensive and includes the sigmoidoscopy.

Laparoscopy, repairs, manipulation, and other procedures complete this subcategory of the digestive system. A coder uses code range 45395–45999 for surgical laparoscopic procedures, proctoplasty, protopexy, and unlisted procedures completed on the rectum. The coder needs to review the operative notes carefully to be sure that the service was captured correctly.

Repair codes are reported using codes 45500 to 45825. When coding from this range, the coder needs to note the approach that was used in order to select codes from 45540 to 45550. It should also be noted that codes from range 45562–45825 are differentiated by whether a colostomy was performed.

Manipulation procedures of the rectum are reported with codes 45900–45915. These codes are used to report the following procedures:

- Reduction of procidentia
- Dilation of anal sphincter or rectal stricture
- Removal of fecal impaction or a foreign body

Dilation in the rectum is reported using codes 45905 and 45910. Dilation procedures are performed digitally or by using a dilating instrument and are typically done under some type of anesthesia.

Anus (46020-46999)

The **anus** is the most distal structure of the digestive system. The anus is typically where hemorrhoids appear. A **hemorrhoid** is an enlarged varicose vein in or near the anus.

Understanding terminology related to types and complications of hemorrhoids is important in assigning the correct CPT code. Hemorrhoid types can be internal, external, combined, or mixed. **Internal hemorrhoids** are located in the superior vein. **External hemorrhoids** are found outside of the external sphincter. **Combined hemorrhoids** or **mixed hemorrhoids** are found in both places and are usually dilated.

Some of the complications that a coder might need to take into consideration when choosing the correct code are notations from the provider that the hemorrhoid might have been diagnosed as a **prolapsed**, **thrombosed**, **strangulated**, or **ulcerated hemorrhoid**.

When a hemorrhoid becomes prolapsed, it has descended past the anal sphincter. A thrombosed hemorrhoid is one that contains a blood clot and is extremely painful. When the anal sphincter causes the blood supply to be occluded in a hemorrhoid, it is referred to as a *strangulated hemorrhoid*. A hemorrhoid that is inflamed and may have necrotic changes in surrounding tissue is referred to as an *ulcerated hemorrhoid*.

Because of the complications and types of hemorrhoids, code assignment can be tricky, and coders should take these things into account, as well as the type of treatment used and any other modifying factors, such as a fissure or fistula. The guidelines that start this code range have additional information that is extremely helpful and should be referenced prior to code assignment.

Codes in this subcategory include incision (codes 46020 to 46083) and excision (codes 46200 to 46320). Codes 46221, 46945, and 46946 and codes 46250–46262 report hemorrhoidectomy. The codes are differentiated by whether the hemorrhoids are internal versus external, and by accompanying procedures. The coder should note that there is resequencing in the Excision code range. Attention to detail is essential prior to assigning a code.

Endoscopy procedures completed on the anus, known as **anoscopy**, are reported using codes 46600–46615. Code 46600 reports a diagnostic anoscopy, and the remaining codes report anoscopy procedures that are completed for the following reasons: dilation, biopsy, removal of a foreign body, removal of tumors and polyps, control of bleeding, and ablation of lesions.

Codes 46700–46761 and code 46947 are used to report repairs completed on the anus. Terms to reference in the index for code selection in this range include:

- Anoplasty
- Anus, then repair
- Repair, then anal
- Sphincteroplasty, then anal

Exercise 11.6—Check Your Understanding

Vocabulary

Fill in the blanks in the statements that follow.

1. The examination in which the entire colon, from the rectum to the cecum, is visualized is known as a(n) _____.

2. A(n) _____ hemorrhoid is one that contains a blood clot and is extremely painful.

3. The _____ is the most distal structure of the digestive system.

4. The _____ is a small, twisted, tubelike structure located at the blind end of the cecum.

5. _____ is a form of diverticulum of the ileum.

6. A _____ is an enlarged varicose vein near the anus.

7. A _____ is a procedure in which the endoscope is moved all the way through the rectum and sigmoid colon.

8. The _____ is located at the distal end of the large intestine.

Destruction codes are reported by using code range 46900–46942. These codes include the destruction of lesions of the anus by various methods. The coder must be able to identify the method of destruction for code selection: chemical, electrodesiccation, cryosurgery, laser, or surgical excision.

Liver (47000-47399)

The **liver** filters red blood cells, stores essential vitamins, contains enzymes that break down poisons in the body, and produces bile that helps break down fats.

The code selection depends on the service provided and whether the procedure was performed as an open procedure or a laparoscopic procedure. Incision and excision codes start the subcategory and then move into the codes for liver transplantation procedures. The coder should refer to operative notes to see whether imaging guidance was used because additional codes may be necessary for some of the procedures listed.

Liver transplantation codes begin with code 47133 and go through code 47147. These transplant codes have three components encompassing the physician work involved. The harvesting of the graft, including preservation, is the first component. The codes used to report the harvesting are 47133–47142. The next component reflects the physician's part in the benchwork. The codes used for this component are 47143–47147. Code 47135 reports the final component, which is recipient liver allotransplantation. **Allotransplantation** is a transplant that occurs between like species. Allotransplantation includes the recipient hepatectomy (partial or whole) and the transplantation of the allograft (partial or whole), along with care of the recipient patient.

The subcategory continues with repair codes, laparoscopic procedures, and other procedures, including ablation of liver tumors with radiofrequency. Repair codes 47300–47362 include repair of liver hemorrhage. Code 47361 includes wound exploration with extensive debridement, coagulation, and sutures with or without packing. If packing is used, code 47361 should be used. Some types of packing are removed within three days of placement. When the patient returns for removal of the packing, code 47362 should be used to report this service.

Biliary Tract (47400-47999)

The **biliary tract** is composed of organs and ducts that are involved in the processing and movement of bile into the duodenum. The organs and ducts include the liver, gallbladder, and bile ducts. Knowing the approach that the surgeon used is very important to determine the correct code selection.

The codes for incision of these structures are 47400–47480. This range includes such procedures as:

- Hepaticotomy
- Hepaticostomy
- Choledochotomy
- Choledochostomy
- Transduodenal sphincterotomy or sphincteroplasty

Introduction codes begin with code 47490, percutaneous cholecystostomy complete procedure (including imaging guidance, catheter placement, cholecystogram when performed and radiological supervision and interpretation), and include codes 47531–47544 for various biliary procedures that include stent or catheter placement, exchange and/or removal. Codes 47542–47544 are add-on codes. The entire range of codes 47490–47544 include numerous notations prior to the listing of codes and within the code description listings. Read all of the notations that are listed in the CPT manual for these codes.

Endoscopic and laparoscopic procedures are covered by the next set of codes. These codes can be reported as surgical or diagnostic, but as coding guidelines note, surgical procedures include diagnostic ones, so the diagnostic procedures should not be reported separately if a more extensive surgical procedure is being performed at the same operative session on the same problem. These codes are differentiated according to accompanying procedures, such as biopsy, removal of calculus, dilation, cholangiography, cholecystectomy, and types of exploration. A very common procedure is a laparoscopic cholecystectomy. Figure 11-8 illustrates a lateral view of a laparoscopic cholecystectomy, whereas Figure 11-9 illustrates the cross-sectional view.

Excision codes are reported using code range 47600–47715. This code range includes codes for various types of cholecystectomies, excision of a bile duct tumor, and portoenterostomy and other excision procedures.

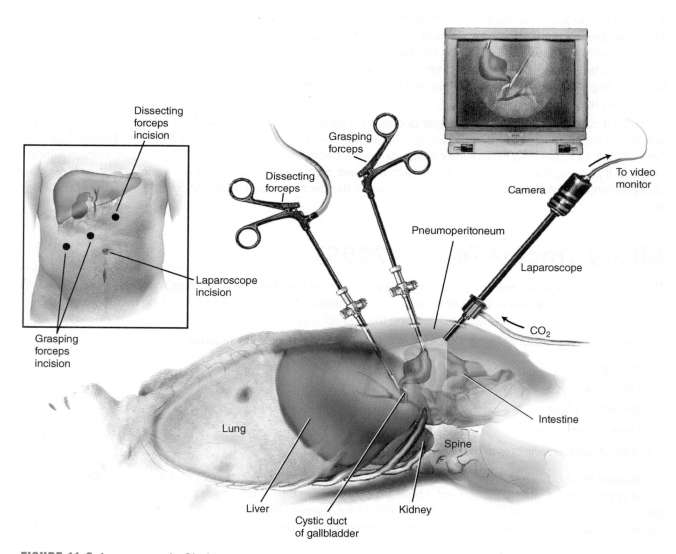

FIGURE 11-8 Laparoscopic Cholecystectomy—Lateral View

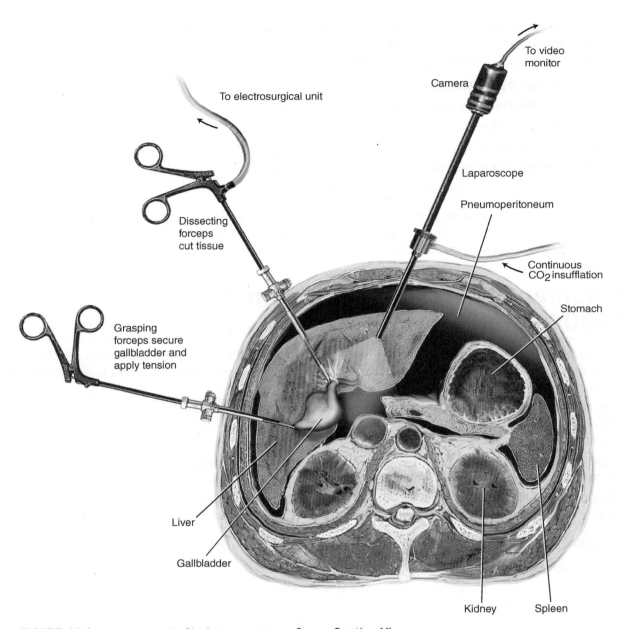

To electrosurgical unit

Camera

To video monitor

Dissecting forceps cut tissue

Laparoscope

Pneumoperitoneum

Continuous CO_2 insufflation

Grasping forceps secure gallbladder and apply tension

Stomach

Liver

Gallbladder

Kidney

Spleen

FIGURE 11-9 Laparoscopic Cholecystectomy—Cross-Section View

Attention to detail is necessary because anastomosis procedures are also found in the Repair section. Repair codes as they relate to the biliary tract are reported with codes 47720–47900. The code 47999 would be used to report unlisted procedures in relation to the biliary tract.

Pancreas (48000–48999)

The **pancreas** is an organ that is located behind the stomach and is connected to the gallbladder and liver by way of the common bile duct. The pancreas secretes juices necessary for digestion but also regulates blood sugar levels with the secretion of the hormone insulin.

Incisions are reported using code set 48000–48020, and excisions are reported using code set 48100–48160.

There is one introduction code, which is code 48400. This is an add-on code and should not be used alone. This code should be used in conjunction with a primary procedure code, as well as a radiological code if appropriate. Codes 48500–48548 report repairs completed on the pancreas and include:

- Marsupialization of pancreatic cyst
- Open external drainage of pseudocyst of pancreas
- Direct internal anastomosis of pancreatic cyst to gastrointestinal tract
- Pancreatorrhaphy for injury
- Duodenal exclusion with gastrojejunostomy for pancreatic injury
- Pancreaticojejunostomy, side-to-side anastomosis

Codes 48550–48556 are used to report pancreas transplant procedures. Like the liver transplant services, pancreatic transplants also have three components: harvesting, backbench work, and transplant. It is essential that the coder review operative notes to be sure all services are captured.

Abdomen, Peritoneum, and Omentum (49000–49999)

The **abdomen** is the area of the body that lies between the thorax and the pelvis. The **peritoneum** is the membranous lining of the abdomen. The **omentum** is the part of the peritoneum that connects the stomach to other structures of the abdomen.

This subcategory of codes begins with incision, excision, and destruction codes. The code range is 49000–49255. The services reported from this code range include drainage, peritoneocentesis, excision, and biopsies.

Laparoscopic procedures are reported with codes 49320–49329. As with any laparoscopic procedure, diagnostic laparoscopic procedures are included in the surgical procedures.

Introduction, revision, and/or removal codes are reported using code set 49400–49465. Insertion of a cannula and peritoneal-venous shunt are reported from this code set.

Repair—Hernioplasty, Herniorrhaphy, Herniotomy, Suture, and Other Procedures (49491–49999)

A **hernia** is a protrusion or bulge through the tissue that normally contains a structure. Hernioplasty, herniorrhaphy, and herniotomy are all terms used when referring to hernia repair. Repairs are usually made with sutures, mesh, or wire. Unless the code states otherwise, the code is for unilateral repair. If a bilateral repair is performed, the coder needs to append modifier 50 to the CPT code.

Hernia repairs are coded according to the type of hernia. There are several types of hernias, and a coder needs to be able to distinguish the differences to be able to assign the correct code. An **inguinal hernia** (codes 49491–49525) is a bulging at the inguinal opening. An **indirect inguinal hernia** is a sac that extends through the inguinal ring and into the inguinal canal, sometimes descending into the scrotum. A **direct inguinal hernia** is a type of inguinal hernia that protrudes into the abdominal wall by the Hesselbach triangle. A **hiatal hernia** is a type of hernia that pushes the stomach upward into the mediastinal cavity through the diaphragm. An **incisional hernia** is a hernia that develops through a surgical scar or scar tissue. A **strangulated hernia** is a hernia that develops gangrene because the sac is tightly constricted. A **ventral hernia** is a hernia that protrudes through an abdominal scar where the abdominal wall is protected only by scar tissue.

Some of the hernia repair codes are further distinguished as initial or recurrent based on whether the hernia has previously been repaired. For some of the codes, the patient age and clinical presentation is a factor in code selection. The clinical presentation of the hernia can be reducible, incarcerated, or strangulated.

Surgical hernia repair completed laparoscopically is reported using code range 49650–49659. Secondary repair of abdominal wall evisceration or dehiscence is reported with code 49900. Other procedures not located elsewhere for this subcategory are reported using codes in the 49904–49999 code range.

Summary

- The digestive system is sometimes referred to as the *alimentary canal*.
- The procedure codes begin with procedures on the mouth and oral cavity and move through the entire digestive system.
- The vestibule of the mouth is the mucosal tissue and submucosal tissue of the lips and cheeks.
- *Lingual* refers to the tongue, and the *sublingual area* refers to the area under the tongue.
- A tracheostomy is a surgical opening in the trachea through the neck.
- An endoscopic procedure involves insertion of a flexible or rigid instrument called an *endoscope*, which is used to view internal structures.
- Endoscopic and laparoscopic procedures are frequently completed on the digestive system.
- Manipulation is a maneuver by hand to treat or perform therapy.
- Dilation is performed when expansion or stretching is necessary.
- Enterolysis is the freeing of intestinal adhesions.
- Duodenotomy is the process of making an incision into the duodenum.
- A hemorrhoid is an enlarged varicose vein in or near the anus and includes the following types: internal, external, combined, and mixed.
- Meckel's diverticulum is a form of diverticulum in the ileum.
- A proctosigmoidoscopy is the examination of the rectum with scope advancement into the sigmoid colon.
- A sigmoidoscopy is a procedure in which the endoscope is moved all the way through the rectum and sigmoid colon and may even advance slightly into the descending colon.
- The examination in which the entire colon, from the rectum to the cecum, is visualized is known as a *colonoscopy*.

Internet Links

To learn more about the digestive system and surgical procedures associated with this system, visit *http://www.health.harvard.edu*.

Also, if you type "digestive system" into a search engine, more information will be available.

Chapter Review

True/False

Instructions: Indicate whether each of the following statements is true (T) or false (F).

1. _____ The nasopharynx is part of the pharynx and contains the tonsils.

2. _____ Cheiloplasty refers to repair of the lips.

3. _____ The digestive system aids the body in eliminating waste.

4. _____ The mouth, throat, intestines, and anus are all structures of the digestive system.

5. _____ For surgical endoscopy, the diagnostic endoscopy should be reported separately because it indicates where the surgery needed to take place.

Fill in the Blank

Instructions: Fill in the blanks in the following sentences.

6. The abdomen is also referred to as the _____.

7. A procedure that is performed by dividing the small intestine with anastomosis to the proximal stomach in the treatment of obesity is known as _____.

8. A type of hernia that pushes the stomach upward into the mediastinal cavity through the diaphragm is called a(n) _____ hernia.

9. The anatomical structure that is positioned at the base of the esophagus on one end and connects to the duodenum on the other end is the _____.

10. An examination of the entire colon, from the rectum to the cecum, is known as a(n) _____.

Coding Assignments

Instructions: For each of the following procedures, select the appropriate CPT code.

1. Free omental flap with microvascular anastomosis _____

2. Ligation of internal hemorrhoids _____

3. Incision and drainage of perirectal abscess _____

4. Single resection of small intestine with anastomosis _____

5. A 1.3-cm laceration repair, vestibule of mouth _____

6. Biopsy of the lip _____

7. Periodontal mucosal grafting _____

8. Lengthening of palate, and pharyngeal flap _____

9. Frenoplasty _____

10. Cricopharyngeal myotomy _____

11. Total esophagectomy with thoracotomy with cervical esophagogastrostomy, without pyloroplasty _____

12. Diagnostic esophagoscopy, flexible, no collection of specimen, transoral _____

13. Upper gastrointestinal flexible endoscopy, from esophagus to stomach through jejunum, with collection of specimen by brushing _____

14. Retrograde cholangiopancreatography, diagnostic endoscopic with collection of specimen using brushing technique _____

15. Transrectal drainage of pelvic abscess _____

16. Appendectomy _____

17. Proctosigmoidoscopy with removal of three polyps by snare technique _____

18. Flexible colonoscopy proximal to splenic flexure; diagnostic, no specimen, no colon decompression _____

19. Umbilical hernia repair of 17 year old, incarcerated _____

20. Repair lumbar hernia _____

21. Secondary suture of abdominal wall for dehiscence _____

22. Open drainage of retroperitoneal abscess _____

23. Laparoscopic cholecystectomy with cholangiography _____

24. Cryosurgery of malignant rectal tumor _____

25. Biopsy of intestine by capsule, three specimens _____

26. Removal of esophageal sphincter augmentation device _____

27. Removal of transplanted pancreatic allograft _____

28. Resection of omentum _____

29. Open drainage of subphrenic abscess _____

30. Marsupialization of abscess of liver _____

Case Studies

Instructions: Review each case and indicate the correct code(s).

Case 1

Preoperative and postoperative diagnosis: Chronic calculus cholecystitis

Anesthesia: General

Procedure: Cholecystectomy via scope

This 12-year-old patient was brought to the operating room and placed on the operating table, and general anesthetic was induced. The abdomen was prepped and draped. An infraumbilical incision was made, and dissection was made down to the fascia, which was lifted and cut. The blunt port trocar was placed, and the abdomen was insufflated with carbon dioxide. Additional 5-mm trocars were placed in the upper abdomen. The gallbladder was identified and retracted. At the level of the Calot triangle, dissection was started, dissecting the peritoneum and adipose tissues from the underlying cystic duct. The cystic artery was taken down with shears. The gallbladder was dissected to free it from the liver bed. The cystic duct was ligated on its proximal and distal aspects with a 0 Vicryl endoloop. The cystic duct was transected and brought through the umbilical site. The area was inspected, with no complications noted. The trocars were removed, and no hemorrhage was noted. Deflation of the abdomen occurred. The umbilical site at the fascia was closed with interrupted 0 Vicryl sutures, and the skin was closed with 4-0 Vicryl sutures. The patient tolerated the procedure well and was sent to the recovery room in stable condition.

CPT code(s): _____

Case 2

Preoperative diagnosis: Bilateral hernias

Postoperative diagnosis: Bilateral inguinal hernias

Anesthesia: MAC

Procedure: Bilateral inguinal hernia repair

This 54-year-old patient was prepped and draped in the usual fashion, and sedation was introduced. The left inguinal region was anesthetized, and an incision was made with a scalpel. Dissection was carried through to the subcutaneous tissue with Bovie electrocautery. The ilioinguinal nerve was identified and was separated from the operative field. The spermatic cord was surrounded with a Penrose drain, and the cord was dissected. A small hernia sac was seen and ligated near its base, and a large Bard PerFix plug was placed into the defect and sutured to the edges. At the floor of the canal, a patch was placed and sutured to the shelving edge of the inguinal ligament midway through the canal and transversalis fascia. The spermatic cord structures were returned to the canal. The underlying tissue was closed with 3-0 Vicryl sutures. The skin was closed with 4-0 Vicryl sutures in a running subcuticular fashion. Next, the same procedure was completed on the right side after seeing a small indirect hernia. A Bard PerFix plug and a large patch were used. Closure was completed in the same fashion. The patient tolerated the procedure well and was sent to the recovery room in satisfactory condition.

CPT code(s): _____

Case 3

This 58-year-old female presented with a history of bleeding hemorrhoids. Today, her chief complaint was some rectal bleeding. We discussed the risks and benefits of an anoscopy to see what was going on. The patient agreed and was prepped for the procedure. She was accompanied by her husband. She had high anxiety about the procedure but was more nervous about the bleeding, so we administered 10 mg of Versed to help her get through this.

Procedure: The anascope was introduced to the rectum, and visualization was performed for the entire rectum. A small polyp appeared to have ruptured. This was not a hemorrhoid and did not look threatening. Another polyp was visualized and appeared to be inflamed. Using snare technique, this one polyp was removed. Samplings were taken and sent for pathology. Patient tolerated the procedure well and was scheduled to return in one week for pathology report results.

CPT code(s): _____

Case 4

Preoperative diagnosis: Gastrointestinal bleeding, chronic calculus cholecystitis

Postoperative diagnosis: Same

Procedure: Gastroscopy with biopsy

Indications: This 32-year-old female had some GI bleeding. A colonoscopy was performed last week that showed no abnormalities, so it was decided that the upper GI tract should be viewed as well.

Procedure: The patient was brought to the procedure suite, at which time she received 10 mg of intravenous Versed and 50 mg of intravenous Demerol for sedation. We used Cetacaine spray to anesthetize the oropharynx. An Olympus video gastroscope was then passed through the oropharynx and into the esophagus, which was unremarkable. The stomach was next visualized. There, multiple gastric ulcers were seen in the antrum and pyloric area. There was some evidence of bleeding, but nothing active at this time. Biopsies of these lesions were taken for histology. The scope was moved to the duodenum, which was clear. The patient tolerated the procedure well.

CPT code(s): _____

Case 5

This 10-year-old male suffered from recurrent strep throat. It was decided by his parents that a tonsillectomy would be the best course to take for this young man.

Procedure: The child was placed supine on the operating table. General endotracheal anesthesia was administered. The patient was prepped and draped in the usual sterile fashion. The right tonsil was grabbed near the superior pole and was retracted medially and inferiorly. The anterior pillar was incised with Bovie cautery, and dissection was carried from the superior to inferior direction and anterior to posterior with care to preserve the posterior pillar. The left tonsil was removed in a similar fashion. The adenoids were left intact.

CPT code(s): _____

Case 6

Preoperative and postoperative diagnosis: Acute abdominal sepsis

Procedure: Exploratory laparotomy with partial excision of colon with end-to-end anastomosis

Description of procedure: The patient was brought to the operating room, and general endotracheal anesthesia was administered. The abdomen was prepped and draped in the usual sterile fashion. A midline abdominal incision was placed. Reaching the fascial area, the omentum was pulled up from over the top of the small intestine. The bowel was greatly distended, and exploration was difficult. The small bowel was then removed from the peritoneal cavity. A Bookwalter retractor was placed to expose the pelvis. A segment of the colon was resected, and the remaining ends of the colon were reapproximated with sutures, thus creating an end-to-end anastomosis. The retention sutures were tied in place, and the wound was packed with saline moistened gauze.

The patient tolerated the procedure well and was sent to the recovery room in good condition.

CPT code(s): _____

Case 7

Preoperative diagnosis: Small bowel obstruction due to extensive bowel adhesions

Postoperative diagnosis: Same

Procedure: Lysis of adhesions with side-to-side ileocolostomy

Description of procedure: The 68-year-old female patient was taken to the operating room and, after induction of general anesthesia, was placed in a supine position. The abdomen was prepped with Betadine solution and draped in the usual sterile fashion. A midline incision was made over the old incision from a previous surgery. The incision extended from the umbilicus down to the pubis. Upon entering the abdominal cavity, adhesions were found anterior to the abdominal wall. These adhesions were removed, and the area was cleaned up, allowing for the small bowel to be better visualized. The obstruction appeared secondary to the distal ileum, being slightly twisted and wedged into the pelvis. In total, there was about 3 feet of small bowel involved. It was possible to bring some of the bowel proximal to the obstruction, and it would easily reach the cecum, which was mobilized. Approximately 2 feet from the ileocecal valve, the small bowel was anastomosed side to side to the cecum by firing a TX 60 stapler distal to the anastomosis and transecting its attachment. Once this was completed, the bowel was able to be brought up through the opening in the abdominal wall.

(continues)

(continued)

The midline incision was closed with #1PDS sutures first; then retention sutures were tied in place. The stoma was matured to the skin, and an appliance was placed.

The patient tolerated the procedure well and was sent to the recovery room in stable but serious condition.

CPT code(s): _____

Case 8

Preoperative diagnosis: Retroperitoneal abscess

Postoperative diagnosis: Same

Description of procedure: This 47-year-old female was taken to the operating room and placed in a supine position. The right flank was prepped with Betadine and draped in a sterile fashion. The previous incision was taken down to the retroperitoneum, which allowed immediate visualization of the abscess. The abscess was opened and drained, yielding about 15 cc of exudate, which was sent to pathology for culture. A Jackson-Pratt was placed within the abscess, and another was placed along the retroperitoneum. They were brought out through two separate puncture sites and sutured in place. The wounds were closed in layers of running #1 PDS, and the skin was closed using staples. All sites were dressed, and the patient was sent to recovery in good condition.

CPT code(s): _____

Case 9

Procedural Notes

This 75-year-old patient was placed in the upright position for placement of a nasogastric tube. The left nostril was examined, and there was no obstruction or foreign body present. The nostril was sprayed to numb the area. The tube was inserted into the nostril and advanced and viewed via fluoroscopic guidance. The tube was advanced into the stomach, and air was injected; using a stethoscope, the air sounds were then heard in the stomach. Tape was placed on the nostril to hold the tube in place.

CPT code(s): _____

Case 10

This 67-year-old male patient has been experiencing chronic anal pain for the last six months. Previous colonoscopy, performed three months ago, was negative. The patient has been treated medically with no pain relief. Today, an examination of the anus and rectum under anesthesia is scheduled.

After obtaining sedation with anesthesia, the patient was prepped and draped in the usual fashion and placed in the lithotomy position. A digital rectal examination was found to be negative. Following the manual rectal examination, a rigid proctoscope was introduced into the anus and the scope was advanced. The anal canal and distal rectal mucosa were visualized and carefully examined. No hemorrhoids, polyps, fistula, or fissures were visualized, and no other pathology was identified. The proctoscope was removed. The patient tolerated the procedure and was taken to the recovery area in satisfactory condition.

CPT code(s): _____

Urinary System

Chapter Outline

Introduction

Guidelines Related to the National Correct
Coding Initiative (NCCI)

Abbreviations Related to the Urinary
System

Anatomy of the Urinary System

Procedures Completed on the Kidneys
(50010–50593)

Procedures Completed on the Ureter
(50600–50980)

Procedures Completed on the Bladder
(51020–52700)

Procedures Completed on the Urethra
(53000–53899)

Summary

Internet Links

Chapter Review

Coding Assignments

Case Studies

Learning Objectives

At the conclusion of this chapter, you should be able to:

1. Define key terms related to coding procedures on the urinary system.
2. Define abbreviations associated with the urinary system.
3. Describe the basic anatomy of the urinary system.
4. Define common procedures completed on the urinary system.
5. Apply specific coding guidelines to this chapter.
6. Select CPT codes for procedures completed on the urinary system.
7. Identify and code procedures for the urinary system from case studies.

Key Terms

cystotomy

cystourethroscopy

external sphincter

kidneys

nephrectomy

nephrolithotomy

nephrorrhaphy

nephrotomy

open drainage of a
perirenal abscess

open drainage of a renal
abscess

partial nephrectomy

pyeloplasty

pyelotomy

renal endoscopic
    procedures

symphysiotomy for
    horseshoe kidney
ureterectomy

ureters
urethra

urinary bladder
urodynamics

Introduction

CPT code range 50010–53899 is used to code procedures completed on the urinary system. The codes are divided into four sections based on the structures that comprise the urinary system. The urinary system removes waste from the body.

Guidelines Related to the National Correct Coding Initiative (NCCI)

The student should follow these steps to obtain the most current coding guideline information related to this chapter.

1. Log on to *http://www.cms.gov/Medicare/Coding/NationalCorrectCodInitED/index.html*.
2. Scroll to the section titled "Downloads."
3. Click the link for the most current "NCCI Policy Manual for Medicare Services."
4. A box may appear that requires you to click "Open."
5. Click "Chapter 7" for guidelines specific to the urinary system.

Abbreviations Related to the Urinary System

Abbreviation	Description
ARF	acute renal failure
BPH	benign prostatic hypertrophy
BUN	blood, urea, nitrogen
CRF	chronic renal failure
C&S	culture and sensitivity
cysto	cystoscopy
ESRD	end stage renal disease
ESWL	extracorporeal shock-wave lithotripsy
IVP	intravenous pyelogram
IVU	intravenous urography
KUB	kidneys, ureters, bladder
PD	peritoneal dialysis
RP	retrograde pyelogram
TURP	transurethral resection of the prostate
U/A	urinalysis
UTI	urinary tract infection
VCUG	voiding cystourethrogram

Anatomy of the Urinary System

The structures found in the urinary system include bilateral kidneys, bilateral ureters, the urinary bladder, and the urethra. Figure 12-1 illustrates these structures.

The **kidneys** are located in the back of the abdominal region of the body on either side of the vertebral column. The main functions of the kidneys are to remove waste products from the blood and to regulate the volume and composition of the blood by allowing the reabsorption of water and other substances into the bloodstream. An adult kidney weighs about 5.5 ounces and is 10 cm long by 5.5 cm wide and 3 cm thick.

Leading from the kidneys are muscular tubes known as **ureters** that are lined with a mucous membrane. The ureters, which measure approximately 30 cm, move urine from the kidneys into the urinary bladder by means of peristalsis.

The **urinary bladder** is located in the pelvic cavity and serves as a temporary reservoir for the urine. An average-sized bladder can hold about one quart of urine.

A single structure known as the **urethra** is a mucous membrane–lined tube that transports the urine from the bladder to be excreted from the body. The length of the urethra is different for males and females. In the female, the urethra is approximately 3 to 5 cm long, whereas in the male, the urethra is approximately 18 to 20 cm long.

Below the neck of the bladder is an **external sphincter** that controls the release of the urine from the bladder. The sphincter contracts around the urethra, sending a message to the bladder to relax and not release urine. When the sphincter relaxes, the bladder neck contracts and releases urine from the body. Figure 12-2 illustrates this process.

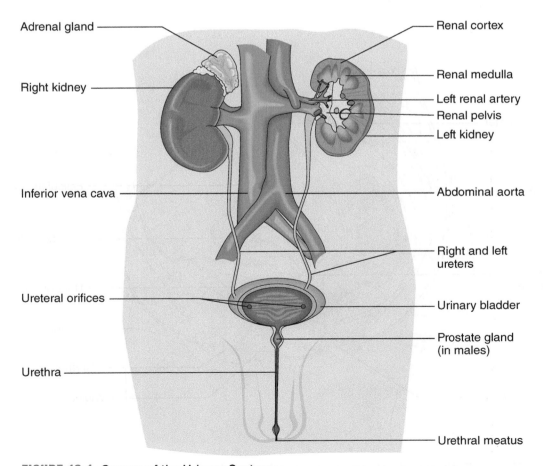

FIGURE 12-1 Organs of the Urinary System

In males and females, the placement of the ureters and bladder is also different because of the reproductive organs. Figure 12-3 illustrates the location of the urinary bladder in females.

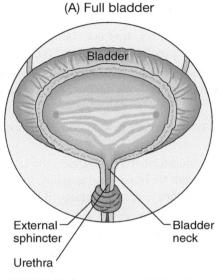

(A) Full bladder

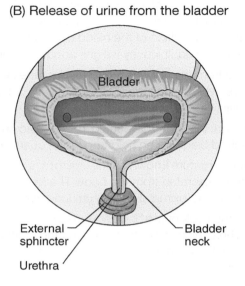

(B) Release of urine from the bladder

FIGURE 12-2 Release of Urine Process

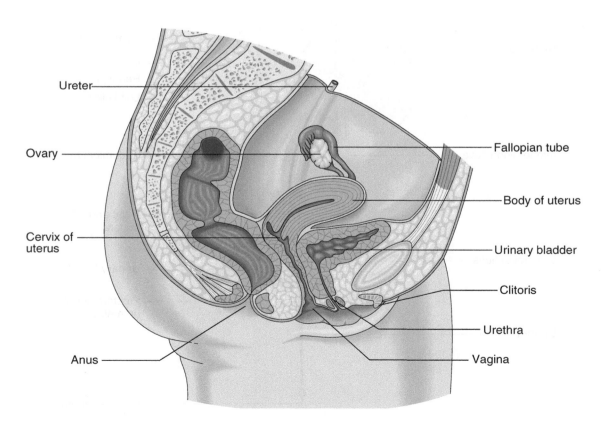

FIGURE 12-3 Position of the Urinary Bladder in the Female

Procedures Completed on the Kidneys (50010-50593)

Codes 50010–50593 are used to report procedures completed on the kidneys. There are eight subsections:

- Incision
- Excision
- Renal Transplantation
- Introduction
- Repair
- Laparoscopy
- Endoscopy
- Other Procedures

Incision (50010-50135)

Codes 50010–50135 are used to report procedures in which an incision is made into the kidney. Table 12-1 summarizes codes from this subsection.

TABLE 12-1 Incision (50010–50135)

Code(s)	Description
50010	This code is used when no other specific procedure is completed on the urinary system and there is renal exploration.
50020	At times, it is necessary to drain an abscess that is located in the renal or perirenal area. Code 50020 reports the open drainage of a perirenal or renal abscess. When an **open drainage of a perirenal abscess** or **open drainage of a renal abscess** is completed, an incision is made into the area, the site is irrigated, and drain tubes are placed.
50040	This code is used to report a nephrostomy, nephrotomy with drainage. During this procedure, an incision is made through the skin and then through the muscles, fat, and other tissue structures to the kidney. An incision is made into the kidney, and a catheter tip is placed. The physician then inserts a drain tube, and the area is closed.
50045	A **nephrotomy** with exploration is reported by using this code. During this procedure, an incision is made into the kidney, and the physician explores the interior area.
50060–50075	These codes are used to code **nephrolithotomy**, the removal of a kidney stone by making an incision into the kidney. The codes are differentiated by whether the procedure is a primary or secondary operation for calculus, complicated by kidney abnormality, or for removal of a large staghorn calculus.
50080 and 50081	These codes are differentiated by the size of the calculus removed by percutaneous nephrostolithotomy or pyelostolithotomy. The procedures can include a dilation, endoscopy, lithotripsy, stenting, or basket extraction. It is imperative that the size of the calculus be recorded in the medical documentation to allow you to select a code accurately.
50100	This is a separate procedure code that is used to report the transection or repositioning of renal vessels.
50120–50135	**Pyelotomy**, an incision made into the renal pelvis, is reported by this range of codes. The codes are differentiated by the reason for the incision: exploration, drainage, removal of calculus, secondary operation, and complications such as a secondary operation or a congenital kidney abnormality.

Excision (50200-50290)

An excision completed on a kidney is known as **nephrectomy**. There are various techniques and reasons why a nephrectomy is completed. Table 12-2 summarizes the codes found in code range 50200–50290.

TABLE 12-2 Excision Procedures (50200–50290)

Code(s)	Description
50200 and 50205	There are two codes that report a renal biopsy. Code 50200 reports a percutaneous renal biopsy completed by a trocar or needle. Code 50205 codes a renal biopsy by surgical exposure of the kidney.
50220–50230	This range of codes is used to report a nephrectomy, a removal of a kidney, that includes a partial ureterectomy, the removal of a ureter. The codes are differentiated by other issues that influence the case: rib resection, previous surgery on the same kidney, regional lymphadenectomy, and so on.
50234 and 50236	When a nephrectomy is completed through the same incision, with a total ureterectomy and bladder cuff, code 50234 is used to report the case. When different incisions are made, code 50236 is reported.
50240	A partial removal of the kidney, known as a partial nephrectomy, is coded using this code. During this procedure (illustrated in Figure 12-4), part of the kidney is removed, and the area is then closed. It should be noted that if this procedure is performed via a laparoscope, code 50543 should be used.
50250	An open ablation of one or more renal mass lesions by cryosurgery is reported with this code. This code also includes intraoperative ultrasound if the ultrasound was performed.
50280 and 50290	These codes are used for excisions of cysts. The codes are differentiated by the location of the cyst. Code 50280 is used for excision or unroofing of a kidney cyst, and code 50290 is used for excision of a perinephric cyst.

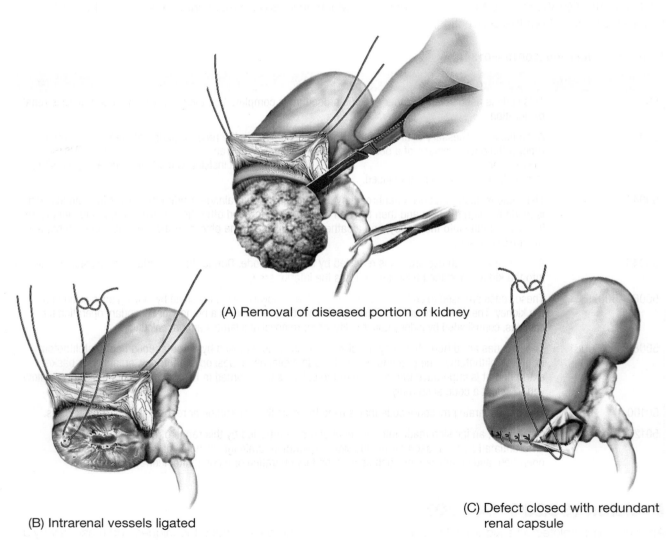

(A) Removal of diseased portion of kidney

(B) Intrarenal vessels ligated

(C) Defect closed with redundant renal capsule

FIGURE 12-4 Partial Nephrectomy

Renal Transplantation (50300–50380)

Code range 50300–50380 is used to report renal transplantation that involves three components of physician work. The three components are as follows:

- Harvesting of kidney—this can include a cadaver donor nephrectomy, unilateral or bilateral, or the harvesting of a graft from a living donor. This phase includes the harvesting of the graft and the preservation of the kidney.
- Backbench work—this includes the preparation of the harvested graft prior to transplantation.
- Recipient renal allotransplantation—during this component of the surgery, the transplant occurs and the recipient is cared for.

Codes from this range are summarized in Table 12-3.

TABLE 12-3 Codes for Renal Transplantation (50300–50380)

Code(s)	Description
50300 and 50320	These codes are to report a donor nephrectomy and are differentiated by whether the kidney is from a cadaver or from a living donor. Code 50300, used for a cadaver donor, is for a unilateral or bilateral kidney removal. It is important that code 50320 is assigned only when the nephrectomy is for a kidney donation. Do not confuse code 50320 with codes 50220 to 50236, which are used for nephrectomies that are performed for reasons besides kidney donation. Figure 12-5 illustrates a simple nephrectomy. The procedural technique is the same, but the reason for the procedure is different; therefore, the codes fall into different code ranges.
50323–50329	The backbench work for a renal transplantation is reported using this range of codes.
50340	Code 50340 is used to code the recipient nephrectomy (the removal of the diseased kidney) when it occurs as a separate procedure. Code 50340 is reported with modifier 50 when the procedure is performed bilaterally.
50360 and 50365	When the kidney graft is implanted and performing the recipient nephrectomy is not completed at the same time, code 50360 is used to report the kidney transplantation. When the transplantation occurs at the same time as the recipient nephrectomy, code 50365 is used.
50370	At times, it is necessary to remove a transplanted renal graft. When this procedure occurs, code 50370 is reported.
50380	This code is used to code a renal transplantation, reimplantation of kidney.

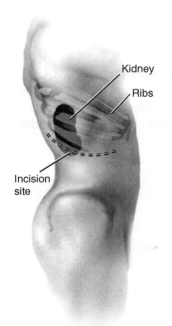

(A) Subcostal incision

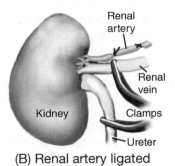

(B) Renal artery ligated

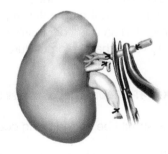

(C) Renal artery transected

FIGURE 12-5 Simple Nephrectomy

Introduction (50382–50396 and 50430–50437)

Code range 50382–50396 and codes 50430–50437 are used to code the introduction of catheters into the renal area and other introduction, injection, change, and removal procedures of the renal pelvis. Codes 50382–50386 report the removal or the removal and replacement of an internally dwelling stent, whereas codes 50387 and 50389 report the removal of an externally accessible stent. When assigning codes, coders should read the notations that appear throughout this section. Many of these codes can be reported bilaterally, and a modifier would be added.

Other introduction procedures are coded by using code range 50390–50396 and codes 50430–50437. Codes 50430 and 50431 are diagnostic procedures that report the injection procedure for an antegrade nephrostogram and/or ureterogram. Codes 50432 to 50435 report therapeutic procedures. Review these codes and note that these codes include imaging guidance. Also review the numerous notations that appear prior to code 50390 and throughout the code descriptions. Codes 50436 and 50437 are out of sequence codes. Code 50436 reports a percutaneous dilation of existing tract for an endourolgic procedure including the imaging guidance and all associated radiological supervision and interpretation with postprocedure tube placement, when it is performed. Code 50437 reports the same procedural components for code 50436 with the addition of a new access into the renal collecting system. For additional information regarding the reporting of these codes, reference the notations following code 50437.

Repair (50400–50540)

This range of codes is used to report repairs that are completed on the kidneys. To select these codes from the index, the coder should reference the following terms:

- **Pyeloplasty**—codes 50400 and 50405. This is plastic surgery that is completed on the renal pelvis of the kidney.
- **Nephrorrhaphy**—the suturing of a kidney wound or injury. Use code 50500.
- Fistula, then the subterm kidney—code range 50520–50526.
- Symphysiotomy, then horseshoe kidney—a **symphysiotomy for horseshoe kidney** is completed to correct a horseshoe kidney, a condition in which there is an abnormal union of the kidneys. Code 50540 should be reported.

Laparoscopy (50541–50549)

As in the other sections of Surgery, a diagnostic laparoscopy is always included in a surgical laparoscopy. This also holds true for code range 50541–50549, laparoscopic procedures involving the renal area. It is important for the coder to read the operative reports carefully before assigning codes from this section. Many procedures can be completed as open or laparoscopic procedures. Therefore, before assigning codes from this range, the coder needs to verify that the procedure was completed via laparoscope.

EXAMPLE: Dr. Jones completes a partial nephrectomy as an open procedure.

This should be coded using code 50240.

EXAMPLE: Later in the day, he completes surgery on another patient in which he completes a laparoscopic partial nephrectomy.

This should be assigned a different code because of the use of a laparoscope. The correct code assignment is 50543.

The coder is reminded of the different code assignments by the presence of notations in the CPT manual. Following the code descriptions for codes 50240 and 50543, notations are present that reference the other codes. Make sure that all notations are read for accurate code assignment.

Endoscopy (50551–50580)

Code range 50551–50580 is used to report endoscopic procedures completed on the kidney. These procedures are known as **renal endoscopic procedures**. Codes in this range are differentiated according to the reason for the endoscopy, such as a biopsy, removal of a foreign body, or other accompanying procedures that can include catheterization, fulguration, or endopyelotomy.

Other Procedures (50590–50593)

A common procedure completed to break up urinary calculi is extracorporeal shock wave lithotripsy. This procedure is noninvasive and uses two x-ray beams to shock the calculi repeatedly, causing the calculi to fracture. This is done through a liquid medium. One technique used is to submerge the patient into degassed, deionized water and direct shock waves through the liquid to the stone. A second, more common technique directs the shock waves through a water cushion to the stone. Code 50590 is used to report this procedure (illustrated in Figure 12-6).

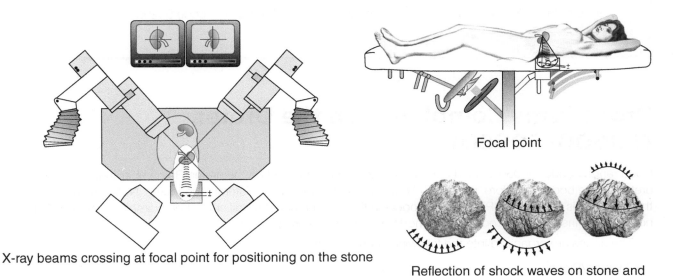

X-ray beams crossing at focal point for positioning on the stone

Focal point

Reflection of shock waves on stone and surrounding fluid with fracture of the stone

FIGURE 12-6 Extracorporeal Shock Wave Lithotripsy

Exercise 12.1—Check Your Understanding

Laparoscopic Procedures Completed on the Kidneys

Using the CPT manual, provide the appropriate responses to the following questions.

1. Code 50230 is used to code a radical nephrectomy with regional lymphadenectomy. The correct code to use if this procedure is performed via a laparoscope is code

   _____.

2. True or false: A laparoscopic ablation of a renal cyst includes the diagnostic laparoscopic procedure, if performed. The coder should use code 50541 to report this service.

   _____

(continues)

Exercise 12.1 – *continued*

3. An unlisted laparoscopy procedure completed on the kidneys should be reported with
   code _____.

4. True or false: Code 50547 is used to report a nephrectomy from a cadaver and includes cold
   preservation. _____

5. True or false: Dr. Smith performed a laparoscopy and a radical nephrectomy. In addition to this,
   he completed an adrenalectomy. Code 50545 should be reported with an additional code for the
   adrenalectomy. _____

6. A nephrotomy with exploration for calculus is reported using CPT code _____.

7. A removal of a transplanted renal allograft is reported with CPT code _____
   components associated with the physician's work.

8. An excision of a cyst of the kidney is reported using CPT code _____.

9. True or false: A laparoscopic nephrectomy is reported using CPT code 50240.
   _____

10. True or false: An excision of a perinephric cyst is reported using CPT code 50290.
    _____

Procedures Completed on the Ureter (50600–50980)

Code range 50600–50980 is used to report procedures completed on the ureter. Remember that there are two ureters in the body. Therefore, modifier 50 may have to be added for bilateral procedures. Notations are found throughout this section of CPT to guide coders in the assignment of modifier 50. For example, code 50715 has a notation that instructs the coder to add modifier 50 for a bilateral procedure.

The codes are organized into the following subsections:

- Incision/Biopsy
- Excision
- Introduction
- Repair
- Laparoscopy
- Endoscopy

Incision, Excision, and Introduction (50600–50695)

Terms that are used to locate these codes in the index include the following:

- Ureterotomy—codes 50600 and 50605. Separate codes are present for exploration or drainage and for insertion of an indwelling stent.
- Ureterolithotomy—codes 50610–50630. When selecting a code from this range, the coder must identify the section of the ureter on which the procedure was completed: upper one-third, middle one-third, or lower one-third.

Locate code 50606 in the CPT manual. Code 50606 is an add-on code that reports an endoluminal biopsy of the ureter and/or renal pelvis, nonendoscopic. In the CPT manual review code 50606 for the full code description and for the primary codes that this add-on code is used with. Also note the codes that should not be reported in conjunction with code 50606. There are two excision codes (codes 50650 and 50660), and these codes are located in the index by referencing the term *ureterectomy*. Injection procedures, manometric studies, and the changing of ureterostomy tubes are coded by using codes 50684 to 50690, titled Introduction.

Codes 50693 to 50695 report the percutaneous placement of a ureteral stent. Code differentiation is based on whether there was a pre-existing nephrostomy tract or whether new access was established, as well as whether or not a separate nephrostomy catheter was used. Review these codes in the CPT manual and note the instructional notation that follows code 50695.

Repair (50700–50940)

Code range 50700–50940 is used to report repairs that are completed on the ureter. Codes 50705 and 50706 are add-on codes. Review their full descriptions in the CPT manual and note the instructional notations that follow each of the codes to determine which primary codes can be used with these add-on codes. Terms to reference in the index to locate codes from this code range include:

- Ureteroplasty
- Ureterolysis
- Ureteropyelostomy
- Ureteroneocystostomy
- Ureteroenterostomy
- Ureterosigmoidostomy
- Ureterostomy

Many of these procedures are performed as unilateral procedures; however, they also may be performed as bilateral procedures. Therefore, coders must read the operative report to determine the extent of the procedure and make the determination regarding the need for modifier assignment.

Laparoscopy and Endoscopy Procedures (50945–50980)

Surgical laparoscopic procedure codes for procedures completed on the ureters include a diagnostic laparoscopy. These codes, 50945–50949, are differentiated according to the type of procedure performed, such as ureterolithotomy, ureteroneocystostomy with or without cystoscopy, and ureteral stent placement.

Endoscopy codes for ureteral procedures completed through an established ureterostomy are found in code range 50951 to 50961. It is important that the coder identify that the endoscopy was performed through an established ureterostomy and also identify the reason for the endoscopy, such as biopsy, ureteral catheterization, fulguration, or removal of a foreign body or calculus.

Code range 50970 to 50980 is used to report ureteral endoscopy through a ureterotomy. The codes are differentiated by the reason for the procedure: ureteral catheterization, biopsy, fulguration, or removal of a foreign body or calculus.

Procedures Completed on the Bladder (51020–52700)

The next section reports procedures completed on the bladder: codes 51020–52700. This range contains numerous subsections of codes:

- Incision
- Removal
- Excision
- Introduction

- Urodynamics
- Repair
- Laparoscopy
- Endoscopy—Cystoscopy, Urethroscopy, Cystourethroscopy
- Transurethral Surgery
- Vesical Neck and Prostate

Incision, Removal, Excision, and Introduction (51020–51720)

Codes 51020–51102 are used to code incisional and removal procedures completed on the bladder that include bladder aspiration, cystotomy or cystostomy, transvesical ureterolithotomy, and drainage of an abscess. Many of these procedures include the insertion of ureteral catheters. An alternate method of catheterizing the bladder for drainage is completed by performing a **cystostomy**. During a cystostomy, an incision is made in the midline and carried through until the bladder is incised. A tube is then inserted and sutured in place. Figure 12-7 illustrates an open cystostomy.

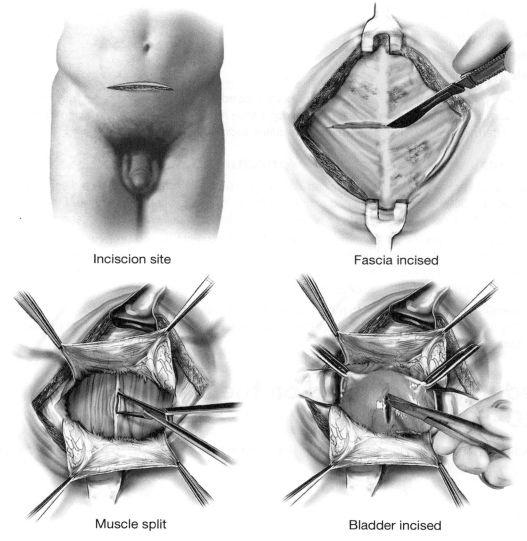

Inciscion site

Fascia incised

Muscle split

Bladder incised

FIGURE 12-7 Open Cystostomy

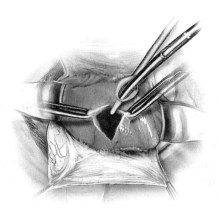 

Cystostomy tube inserted   Cystostomy tube secured with sutures

FIGURE 12-7 (*continued*)

Excision codes 51500–51597 report excisions completed on the bladder. Terms to reference in the index to locate codes from this section include:

- Cystotomy—codes 51520–51535. These codes are differentiated by the reason that the cystotomy was completed.
- Cystectomy—codes 51550–51596. To select codes from this range, the coder needs to identify whether the cystectomy was partial or complete. The coder should then identify any other accompanying procedures that were completed, such as reimplantation of ureters, lymphadenectomy, and others.
- Pelvic exenteration—code 51597

Codes 51600–51720, titled Introduction, report the following procedures:

- Injection procedures completed on the bladder
- Bladder irrigation, lavage, and instillation
- Insertion of bladder catheters
- Changes of cystostomy tubes
- Endoscopic injection of implant material into the submucosal tissues of the urethra and/or bladder neck
- Bladder instillation of an anticarcinogenic agent

Urodynamics (51725–51798)

Urodynamics is the study of the holding and storage of urine in the bladder, the motion and rate of the movement of the urine, and the analysis of how the bladder empties. It should be noted that an extensive notation appears in the CPT manual with regard to coding from this section. Many of these procedures are performed at the same time. When this occurs, modifier 51 should be used with the codes. The codes from this section also reflect that the services were performed by the physician reporting the codes and that all supplies were provided by the physician. If a physician only interprets the results as a result of the testing and/or only operates the equipment, the physician should report the appropriate code with modifier 26. Modifier 26 designates that only the professional component of the service was provided.

Repair (51800–51980)

Code range 51800–51980 codes repairs that occured on the bladder. Terms to reference in the index include:

- Cystoplasty
- Cystourethroplasty

- Urethropexy
- Cystorrhaphy
- Closure, then cystostomy
- Enterocystoplasty

These codes are differentiated by accompanying procedures and by the reason for the procedure.

Laparoscopy and Endoscopy (51990–52010)

Laparoscopic procedure codes 51990 and 51992 are surgical laparoscopy codes and are differentiated by whether the procedure was performed for a urethral suspension for stress incontinence or for a sling operation for stress incontinence. Code 51999 reports an unlisted laparoscopic procedure of the bladder.

Codes 52000 to 52010 are used to report endoscopic procedures completed on the bladder. Code 52000 is a separate procedure code and is used to report a cystourethroscopy. Codes 52001–52010, cystourethroscopy, are differentiated according to the procedure performed through the scope. Procedures include:

- Irrigation and evacuation of multiple obstructing clots
- Ureteral catheterization
- Biopsy
- Ejaculatory duct catheterization

Figure 12-8 illustrates the completion of a cystourethroscopy on a male patient.

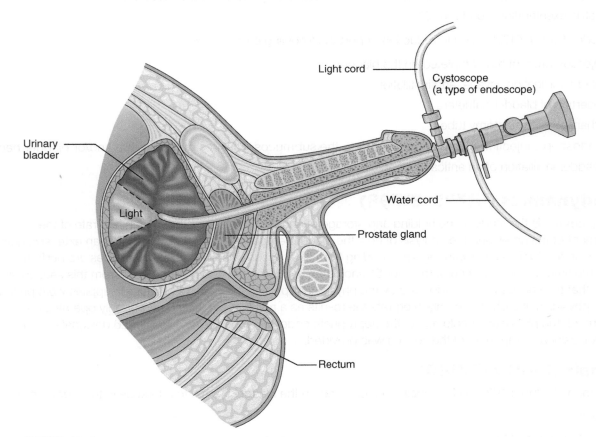

FIGURE 12-8 Cystourethroscopy of Male Patient

Transurethral Surgery (52204–52356)

Code range 52204–52356 is used to report transurethral surgery that is completed by the use of a cystourethroscope. This code range is divided into two subsections:

- Codes 52204 to 52318 for procedures that are completed on the urethra and bladder
- Codes 52320 to 52356 for procedures that are completed on the ureter and pelvis

These codes are further differentiated by the type of accompanying procedures. Coders also need to note the sex of the patient, as some codes specify the sex of the patient.

EXAMPLE: Code 52270 is used to report a cystourethroscopy with internal urethrotomy for a female patient.

To report this procedure for a male patient, code 52275 should be used.

An extensive notation appears prior to code 52320 that affects the coding of a cystourethroscopy of the ureter and pelvis. Coders are given guidance as to codes that cannot be reported together, and the use of modifier 50 when the insertion of bilateral indwelling ureteral stents occurs. New coders need to read and understand the instructions given.

Vesical Neck and Prostate (52400–52700)

This range of codes is used for male patients to report procedures completed on the vesical neck and prostate. Procedures included in this range of codes include:

- Cystourethroscopy for the resection or incision of ejaculatory ducts
- Transurethral procedures performed on the prostate
- Laser coagulation, laser vaporization, and laser enucleation of prostate
- Drainage of prostatic abscess

Exercise 12.2—Check Your Understanding

Procedures Completed on the Ureters and Bladder

Using the CPT manual, select the appropriate responses to the following questions.

1. True or false: Ureteroplasty is a type of repair _____.

2. The correct code for a ureterolithotomy completed on the middle one-third of the ureter is _____.

3. True or false: All procedures performed on the ureters are bilateral procedures _____.

4. Code 51580 is found in the _____ section of codes for procedures completed on the bladder.

5. True or false: Code 52000 can be reported when other procedures are completed _____.

6. A procedure in which an incision is made into the bladder is called a(n) _____.

7. An injection procedure and placement of a chain for contrast and chain urethrocystography are reported using CPT code _____.

8. A cystourethroscopy with a direct vision internal urethrotomy is reported using CPT code _____.

9. An ureterotomy for the insertion of an indwelling stent is reported with code _____.

10. Aspiration of bladder by trocar is reported with code _____.

Procedures Completed on the Urethra (53000–53899)

The final range of codes for procedures completed on the urinary system is code range 53000–53899. This range is divided into the following:

- Incision
- Excision
- Repair
- Manipulation
- Other Procedures

Incision, Excision, and Repair (53000–53520)

Incision codes can be located in the index by referencing terms such as *urethrotomy, urethrostomy, meatotomy,* and *incision* then *urethra*. Excision codes are located in the index by referencing *urethrectomy, excision* then *urethra,* or *excision* then *polyps* then *urethra*.

Repair codes are located in the index by referencing the terms *urethroplasty, sling operation, urethromeatoplasty, urethrolysis,* and *urethrorrhaphy*.

Manipulation and Other Procedures (53600–53899)

Code range 53600–53665 includes codes to report the dilation of the urethra. These codes are differentiated by procedures completed on males and procedures completed on females.

Code range 53850–53854 reports transurethral destruction of prostate tissue. These codes are differentiated by one of three methods: microwave thermotherapy, radiofrequency thermotherapy, or radiofrequency generated water vapor thermotherapy. Code 53855 is used to report the insertion of a temporary prostatic urethral stent. Transurethral radiofrequency microremodeling of the female bladder neck and proximal urethra for stress urinary incontinence is reported with code 53860. To report this code, the diagnosis of stress urinary incontinence must be recorded in the patient's record.

Summary

- The structures that are found in the urinary system include bilateral kidneys, bilateral ureters, the urinary bladder, and the urethra.
- The external sphincter controls the release of the urine from the bladder.
- The kidneys are located in the back of the abdominal region of the body on either side of the vertebral column.
- The ureters are muscular tubes that transport urine from the kidneys to the bladder.
- The urinary bladder is located in the pelvic cavity and serves as a temporary reservoir for the urine.
- The urethra is a mucous membrane–lined tube that transports urine from the bladder to be excreted from the body.
- A pyelotomy is an incision made into the renal pelvis.
- Endoscopy codes for ureteral procedures completed through an established ureterostomy are reported with codes 50951 to 50961.
- Code range 50970 to 50980 is used to report ureteral endoscopy through a ureterotomy.
- An alternate method of catheterizing the bladder for drainage is completed by performing a cystostomy.
- Code range 52400–52700 is used for male patients to report procedures completed on the vesical neck and prostate.

Internet Links

To learn more about kidney stones and their treatment and about the completion of a cystoscopy and ureteroscopy, visit *http://kidney.niddk.nih.gov*.

To research various kidney diseases and the treatment of the diseases, visit *http://www.kidney.org*.

Chapter Review

Fill in the Blank

Instructions: Fill in the blanks in the statements that follow.

1. The removal of a kidney stone by making an incision in the kidney is known as a(n) _____.

2. During a percutaneous drainage of a renal abscess, a CAT scan or _____ is used to guide the placement of a drainage needle.

3. A single structure known as the _____ is a mucous membrane–lined tube that transports urine from the bladder to be excreted from the body.

4. A partial removal of the kidney is known as a(n) _____.

5. Plastic surgery that is completed on the renal pelvis of the kidney is known as _____.

6. Nephrorrhaphy is _____ of the kidney.

7. Surgical laparoscopic procedure codes for procedures completed on the ureters always include a(n) _____.

8. Codes 50951 to 50961 are used to report endoscopy ureteral procedures completed through an established _____.

9. The study of the holding and storage of urine in the bladder, the motion and rate of the movement of the urine, and the analysis of how the bladder empties is called _____.

10. Code 52000 is a separate procedure code and is used to report a(n) _____.

Coding Assignments

Instructions: Using the CPT manual, identify the appropriate code for each of the following procedures.

1. Ureterolithotomy involving the upper one-third of the ureter _____

2. Ureterectomy with bladder cuff _____

3. Percutaneous needle biopsy of the kidney _____

4. Excision of perinephric cyst _____

5. Open drainage of renal abscess _____

6. Partial nephrectomy _____

7. Unroofing of cyst of kidney _____

8. Partial cystectomy _____

9. Ureteral endoscopy by means of ureterotomy with removal of calculus _____

10. Cystourethroplasty with bilateral ureteroneocystostomy _____

11. Cystourethroscopy _____

12. Drainage of deep periurethral abscess _____

13. Insertion of tandem cuff of urethra _____

14. Urethromeatoplasty with partial excision of distal urethral segment _____

15. Bladder lavage _____

16. Complex uroflowmetry _____

17. Ureterotomy with drainage _____

18. Extracorporeal shock wave lithotripsy

    _____

19. Ureterolysis for ovarian vein syndrome

    _____

20. Closure of pyelocutaneous fistula

    _____

21. Cystourethroscopy with transurethral resection of ejaculatory ducts _____

22. Initial dilation of female urethra, including suppository and installation _____

23. Excision of Skene's gland _____

24. Closure of vesicovaginal fistula; abdominal approach _____

25. Cystotomy with insertion of ureteral catheter

    _____

26. Percutaneous unilateral radiofrequency ablation for two renal tumors _____

27. Insertion of non-indwelling bladder catheter

    _____

28. Cystourethroscopy with transurethral resection

    _____

29. Biopsy of urethra _____

30. Fulguration of carcinoma of urethra

    _____

Case Studies

Instructions: Review each case and indicate the correct code(s).

Case 1

Preoperative and postoperative diagnosis: Ureteral calculus

Anesthesia: General

Procedure: Ureteroscopy of left ureter for removal of calculus; stent placement

The patient was taken from the presurgery area to the operating room and prepped and draped in the usual fashion. General anesthesia was administered. The endoscope was placed into the urethra, which appeared to be inflamed. The scope was then carefully passed through the bladder, which appeared normal. The guidewire was introduced, and a balloon was used to dilate the left ureter. The scope was advanced to view the ureter, where a small stone was extracted and a stent was placed. The area was checked for bleeding, and the scope was then removed. The stent was attached to a string, which was in the correct position. Blood loss was minimal, and the patient was sent to the recovery room in good condition.

CPT code(s): _____

Case 2

Preoperative and postoperative diagnosis: Urethral stricture

Procedure: Dilation of urethra, first attempt

This 45-year-old male patient was brought to the operating room and prepped and draped in the usual fashion. After the patient was anesthetized, a urethral dilator was inserted into the

(continues)

(continued)

urethra. The urethra was then dilated to normal range. The dilator was removed, and no bleeding was noted. The patient tolerated the procedure well and was taken to the recovery room.

CPT code(s): _____

Case 3

The patient is a 70-year-old female with a history of bladder cancer. She presents today for a cystoscopy, biopsy, and fulguration of an erythematous area that appeared suspicious in previous testing. The area is the right trigone.

The patient was placed in the supine position, where spinal anesthesia was administered. She was then turned to the dorsal lithotomy position, where she was prepped and draped in the usual sterile manner. A #22 French cystoscopy sheath was passed in atraumatic fashion per the urethra. The bladder was resected with the 70-degree lens, and the right trigone area was found slightly erythematous and hypervascular and was fulgurated. No tumors were found, and no mucosal abnormalities were noted. A biopsy of the area was taken and sent for pathology.

Pathology findings: Chronic cystitis with squamous cell metaplasia

CPT code(s): _____

Case 4

A 68-year-old male presents today for laser coagulation of the prostate due to urinary retention with urgency and difficulty urinating.

Procedure: The patient was placed on the operating table in the lithotomy position. Spinal anesthesia was administered, and external genitalia was prepped and draped. A 21-French cystoscope was introduced into the bladder. Upon inspection, there was no evidence of a tumor. Mild trabeculations were observed on both ureteral orifices. The retroscope was introduced with a resection of the lateral lobes of the prostate being done; complete opening of the prostatic urethra was allowed. The bladder was examined, and all prostatic chips were removed. The bladder was coagulated and smoothed out with the VaporTrode. An indwelling Foley catheter was inserted into the bladder.

CPT code(s): _____

Case 5

Preoperative diagnosis: Sigmoid diverticulitis

Postoperative diagnosis: Same

Procedure: Ureteral catherization via scope

Patient was placed in the lithotomy position after administration of general anesthesia. A size 22 cystoscope with a 30-degree lens was placed with care under direct visualization. A lighted catheter was placed to the side for the scope, and then the left ureteral orifice was visualized. The lighted catheter was moved to the ureteral orifice and then advanced into the left renal pelvis without any problems or difficulty. After this, the cystoscope was removed. The lighted catheter was then connected to the light source. A size 18 Foley catheter was inserted into the bladder without any difficulty, and in balloon, the fluid was 10 cc. There was no blood loss during surgery, and the patient was taken to the recovery area in good condition.

CPT code(s): _____

Case 6

Preoperative diagnosis: Neurogenic bladder with urinary retention

Postoperative diagnosis: Same

Procedure: Bladder aspiration with suprapubic tube placement

Blood Loss: < 10 mL

Indications for procedure: This is a mentally challenged 49-year-old white male who is currently a resident in a long-term care facility who presents today for placement of a suprapubic tube due to erosion of the Foley catheter drain his neurogenic bladder.

Procedure: The patient was brought to the operating room and placed in the supine position. Anesthesia was administered, and the patient was then moved to the dorsal lithotomy position. He was prepped and draped in normal sterile fashion after the Foley catheter was removed. A cystoscopy was used to explore the bladder for tumor or other foreign bodies. None were identified. The bladder was then filled with about 500 cc of sterile water, which allowed for identification of the tract needed to insert the Rauch suprapubic trocar. The skin was anesthetized with Marcaine and Lidocaine. A needle was then inserted through the lower abdominal wall into the bladder, and the trocar was advanced until the sheath of the trocar was in the bladder. A 16 French catheter was placed through the sheath into the bladder, and the balloon was inflated with 10 cc of sterile water. The sheath was then removed, and we noted good placement of the suprapubic tube in the bladder. The tube was then secured with a 0 Prolene suture, and the skin incision was cauterized and hemostasis was achieved. The patient was transferred to the recovery room in good condition.

CPT code(s): _____

Case 7

History: This is a 67-year-old female who has a history of bladder cancer. She has been in remission from grade II superficial transitional cell carcinoma for 18 months now. During her follow-up visit, a cystoscopy was performed, which identified a suspicious area on the right lower portion of the trigone.

Today, she presents for a cystoscopy, biopsy, and fulguration of this area.

Procedure: The patient was placed on the procedure table in supine position with conscious sedation of Versed given. The patient was then placed in the lithotomy position. She was prepped and draped in normal sterile fashion. A #22 French cystoscopy sheath was passed through the urethra in atraumatic fashion. The bladder was resected with the 70-degree lens. The urethra was normal, the bladder was 1+ trabeculated, the lower-right portion of the trigone were erythematous and hypervascular. No papillary tumors or masses were found. No mucosal abnormalities were noted. A total of three cup biopsies were taken using forceps from the erythematous area of the trigone and sent to pathology. This area was fulgurated with the Bugby electrode, no active bleeding was encountered. The pathology came back as chronic cystitis.

CPT code(s): _____

Case 8

Preoperative and postoperative diagnosis: Right renal calculus, 5 mm

Anesthesia: Conscious sedation under supervision of urologist for 45 minutes

Procedure: Extracorporeal shock wave lithotripsy

This twenty-five-year-old patient was placed on the treatment table, and a water cushion was placed over the location of the kidney stone. X-rays were then taken to determine the exact location of the stone, which was then treated with a total of 3,200 shocks. Films confirmed that the stone was pulverized into small fragments. There were no complications, and the patient was sent to the recovery area.

CPT code(s): _____

Case 9

Preoperative and postoperative diagnosis: Transitional cell carcinoma of the bladder

Anesthesia: General

Procedural Notes:

After the patient was prepped, draped, and anesthetized, he was placed in the lithotomy position. A cystourethroscope was inserted through the urethra into the bladder. In the bladder, there was a large amount of tumor that was then fulgurated via electric current. The tumor was noted to be 3 cm in size. There was minimal blood loss. The patient tolerated the procedure well and was sent to recovery in stable condition.

CPT code(s): _____

Case 10

Preoperative diagnosis: Possible recurrence of bladder cancer

Postoperative diagnosis: No findings

Indications for procedure: This 56-year-old female patient had bladder cancer three years ago that was treated. She is undergoing this procedure to determine if the cancer has returned.

Procedural Notes:

A cystourethroscope was passed through the urethra into the bladder. The urethra, bladder, and ureteric openings were carefully visualized for any evidence of cancer recurrence. The examination showed all structures to be normal with no evidence of cancer at this time. The scope was withdrawn, and the patient was sent to the recovery area in satisfactory condition.

CPT code(s): _____

Male Genital System

Chapter Outline

Learning Objectives

At the conclusion of this chapter, you should be able to:

1. Define key terms related to coding procedures on the male genital system.
2. Define abbreviations associated with the male genital system.
3. Describe the basic anatomy and functions of the male genital tract.
4. Define common procedures completed on the male genital organs.
5. Apply specific coding guidelines for the male genital system.
6. Select CPT codes for procedures completed on the male genital organs.
7. Identify and code procedures for the male genital organs from case studies.

Key Terms

circumcision

corpora cavernosa

cryosurgical ablation of prostate

epididymis

foreskin

glans penis

hypospadias

orchiopexy	prostate gland	sperm	tunica vaginalis
penis	scrotum	spermatic cord	vas deferens
Peyronie's disease	seminal vesicle	spermatozoa	vasectomy
prepuce	shaft	testes	

Introduction

The procedures performed on the male genital organs are reported using CPT codes 54000–55899. The organs and structures of the male genital system include the penis, testes, epididymis, tunica vaginalis, scrotum, vas deferens, spermatic cord, seminal vesicles, and prostate. These structures are illustrated in Figure 13-1.

The male genital system is primarily for reproduction, but it also functions as part of the urinary system. When a coder is making a selection that reports a service performed as part of urinary system surgery, the codes in this subsection should be reviewed, as well as those found in the urinary system, to be sure that the proper code is selected. Code descriptions may indicate unilateral or bilateral procedures. If the description does not specify unilateral or bilateral, the coder should assume that the code is for a unilateral procedure; if performed bilaterally, it may need modifier 50 appended to it. Also discussed in this chapter is Reproductive System Procedures (55920) and Intersex Surgery, codes 55970 and 55980.

Guidelines Related to the National Correct Coding Initiative (NCCI)

Perform the following steps to obtain the most current coding guideline information related to this chapter.

1. Log on to *http://www.cms.gov/Medicare/Coding/NationalCorrectCodInitED/index.html*.
2. Scroll to the section titled "Downloads."
3. Click the link for the most current "NCCI Policy Manual for Medicare Services."
4. A box may appear that requires you to click "Open."
5. Click "Chapter 7" for guidelines specific to the male genital system.

Abbreviations Related to the Male Genital System

The following is a list of the most common abbreviations related to the male genital system.

Abbreviation	Definition
BPH	benign prostatic hyperplasia
DRE	digital rectal examination
TRUS	transrectal ultrasound
TUIP	transurethral incision of the prostate
TUMT	transurethral microwave thermotherapy
TUNA	transurethral needle ablation
TURP	transurethral resection of the prostate

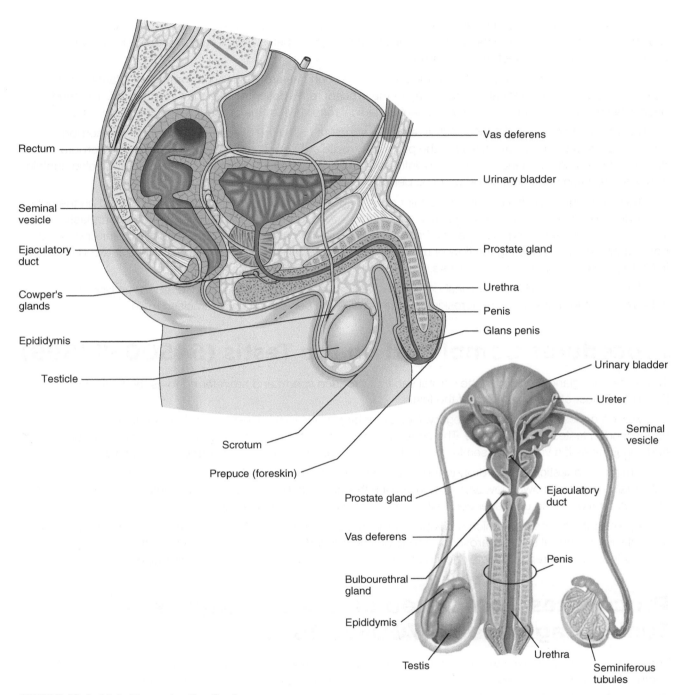

FIGURE 13-1 Male Reproductive System

Procedures Completed on the Penis (54000–54450)

The **penis** is the organ through which the urethra passes to allow urine to be expelled from the body as part of the urinary system. As part of the reproductive system, the penis delivers spermatozoa to the female reproductive tract. The distal end of the penis is known as the **glans penis**. The loose skin covering the glans penis is referred to as **foreskin** or **prepuce**. The glans penis connects to the **shaft**, which is the proximal end of the penis.

The procedures performed on the penis should be reported using codes 54000–54450. Incision, destruction, and excision codes begin this subsection of the male genital system codes.

Codes for reporting a circumcision are found in the Excision subsection. A **circumcision** is an elective procedure used to remove the foreskin completely from the glans penis. The surgical method should be documented, which will affect the code selection.

The coder should be aware that even though these procedures are typically performed on infants (newborn to 28 days), there is a code that allows reporting of the procedure for patients more than 28 days old. The medical necessity should be documented in the patient's medical record when the procedure is done later in life.

The introduction codes (54200–54250) refer to a structure called the **corpora cavernosa**. The corpora cavernosa refers to the erectile tissue of the penis. **Peyronie's disease** is a condition in which the corpora cavernosa becomes hardened. It can be painful and cause deformity if not treated. This code range also contains codes for injection and irrigation procedures performed on the corpora cavernosa.

The next range of codes consists of repair codes (54300–54440). If plastic surgery is performed on the penis, the codes to be referenced are found in this subcategory. Also found in this subcategory are urethroplasty codes. These are codes used to report repair of the penis when it is abnormally curved, or when the ureter opening is not properly located, affecting the flow of urine out of the body. The medical term (and the term the coder will find in CPT for this condition) is **hypospadias**.

Manipulation code 54450 is the last code in this subcategory. This code is used to report the lysis of adhesions that form between the foreskin and the head of the penis in an uncircumcised male.

Procedures Completed on the Testis (54500–54699)

The **testes** are glands located in the scrotal sac that produce sperm and are referred to as the *testicles*. Figure 13-2 illustrates the anatomy of the testis.

Excision codes begin this subcategory. Codes for biopsy, excision of lesions, and exploration for undescended testes are found here. The code for biopsy of the testes contains notes that guide the coder to additional codes if a vasogram, seminal vesiculogram, or epididymogram is performed at the same time.

Sometimes a testicle fails to drop to the scrotum during development. As a male child grows, the testicle will usually drop on its own; however, in some cases this does not happen, and surgical intervention is required. Open exploration for an undescended testis is reported with CPT codes 54550–54560.

Repair codes are next, in which orchiopexy procedures are reported. An **orchiopexy** is a surgical fixation of the testis in the scrotal sac. Laparoscopic repair of a hernia performed at the same time as the orchiopexy would be reported with two repair codes, one indicating the hernia repair and one for the orchiopexy.

Procedures Completed on the Epididymis and Tunica Vaginalis (54700–55060)

The **epididymis** is a tubular structure that is found at the posterior border of a testis and carries sperm to the ductus deferentia (vas deferens). The **tunica vaginalis** is the membranous sac within the scrotum that covers the sides and front of the testis and epididymis.

The coding for these subsections begins with incision and excision codes. Note that there is a notation that follows code 54800 that states for fine needle aspiration biopsy see codes 10004, 10005, 10006, 10007, 10008, 10009, 10010, 10011, 10012, 10021.

Code 54865 is used to report exploration of epididymis with or without biopsy. The subsection for epididymis concludes with code 54900 for a unilateral epididymovasostomy, anastomosis of epididymis to vas deferns and code 54901 for a bilateral epididymovasostomy, anastomosis of epididymis to vas deferns.

Codes 55000 to 55060 report codes for procedures on the tunica vaginalis. There are three subsections: incision, excision, and repair procedures.

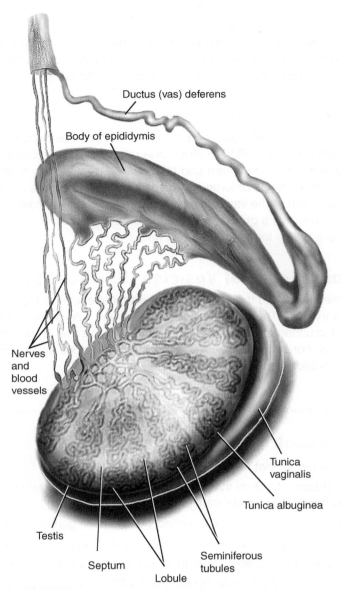

Ductus (vas) deferens

Body of epididymis

Nerves and blood vessels

Testis

Septum

Lobule

Seminiferous tubules

Tunica albuginea

Tunica vaginalis

FIGURE 13-2 Anatomy of the Testis

Procedures Completed on the Scrotum, Vas Deferens, Spermatic Cord, and Seminal Vesicles (55100–55680)

The subsection for procedures completed on the scrotum contains codes for incisions, excisions, and repairs. The vas deferens subsection includes codes for incisions, excisions, introduction, and repairs.

The spermatic cord subsection has codes for excisions, using codes 55500 to 55540, and codes for laparoscopic procedures using codes 55550 and 55559 to report these procedures. Codes for procedures completed on the seminal vesicles include codes 55600 and 55605 for incisions and codes 55650 and 55680 for excisions.

Scrotum (55100–55180)

Understanding the terminology is essential to being able to code these procedures. The **scrotum** encloses, protects, and supports the testicles. The code range for procedures performed on the scrotum consists of codes 55100–55180, which include drainage, exploration, resection, and scrotoplasty.

Vas Deferens (55200–55400)

The **vas deferens** is also referred to as the *ductus deferens* or the *seminal duct*. Procedures completed on the vas deferens are coded from the 55200–55400 code range. The vas deferens is a tube that starts as the epididymis. The epididymis moves upward and takes a turn over the top of the urinary bladder. At the turn, the epididymis becomes the vas deferens. The vasectomy procedures are coded from this code range. A **vasectomy** is the excision of the vas deferens that prevents sperm from moving outside the system, which renders a man sterile. **Sperm** is a germ cell secretion of the testicles. Vasotomy, vasovasostomy, and vasovasorrhaphy procedures are also found in this code range.

Spermatic Cord and Seminal Vesicles (55500–55680)

The **spermatic cord** is a covering around the nerves and vessels that encloses the seminal duct. The **seminal vesicle** is part of the ejaculatory duct. The seminal vesicle and the vas deferens come together to form the ejaculatory duct posterior to the urinary bladder. The surgeon may report that at the time of an inguinal hernia repair, a lipoma of the spermatic cord was also excised. This is typically done and is considered bundled into the hernia repair, so code 55520 would not be reported separately.

Exercise 13.1—Check Your Understanding

Fill in the blanks in the statements that follow.

1. The _____ is a tubular structure that is found at the posterior border of a testis and carries sperm to the ductus deferentia (vas deferens).
2. Code 54512 is found in the _____ subcategory of the male genital system code set.
3. The _____ is a covering around the nerves and vessels that encloses the seminal duct.
4. Laparoscopic orchiopexy for intra-abdominal testis is reported using CPT code _____.
5. A repair of an incomplete circumcision is reported with CPT code _____.
6. Irrigation of corpora cavernosa for priapism is coded using CPT code _____.
7. A surgical fixation of the testis in the scrotal sac is known as a(n) _____.
8. A condition in which the corpora cavernosa becomes hardened is known as _____.
9. The seminal vesicle and the vas deferens form the _____.
10. When performing a circumcision without a dorsal penile or ring block, modifier _____ should be used.

Procedures Completed on the Prostate (55700–55899)

The **prostate gland** secretes fluid that is part of the semen and aids in the motility of sperm. It is located below the urinary bladder and on the upper end of the urethra.

The Prostate subcategory contains notes that the coder will need to pay close attention to when selecting a proper code for the service rendered. Incision codes (55700–55705) instruct the coder to report imaging guidance if appropriate. Needle aspiration and transurethral drainage are also noted for the most specific code assignment possible.

Excision codes (55801–55865) follow the incision subsection. Prostatectomy, transperineal placement of catheters, and exposure of the prostate for insertion of a radioactive substance are found in this code range. The excision codes also contain instructional notes regarding the frequency of the procedure being done. Careful attention to detail must be paid here to be sure that the proper codes and any necessary modifiers are assigned to convey the service properly.

Laparoscopic and other procedures finish this group of codes. Diagnostic procedures are always included in surgical procedures, so the coder must read the operative note to be sure that the code assignment is correct.

Code 55870—electroejaculation is assigned when the physician uses an electrovibratory device that stimulates ejaculation for semen collection, usually for artificial insemination. The actual artificial insemination is not reported with this code.

Code 55873, **cryosurgical ablation of the prostate**, is a surgical procedure used for the ablation of the prostate. Ultrasonic guidance and monitoring is included in the code. Care is taken that the scrotum and ureter are not affected.

Reproductive System Procedures (55920) and Intersex Surgery (55970–55980)

At this time there is only one code listed for Reproductive System Procedures. Code 55920 reports the placement of needles or catheters into pelvic organs and/or genitalia (except the prostate) for subsequent interstitial radioelement application. Following code 55920 the coder should note the instructional notations that provide the coder guidance in reporting the placement of needles or catheters into the prostate (code 55875), the insertion of uterine tandems and/or vaginal ovoids for clinical brachytherapy (code 57155), and the insertion of Heyman capsules for clinical brachytherapy (code 58346). Codes 55970–55980 reflect a series of staged procedures when a patient is undergoing a sex-change operation. These surgical codes are used to report the removal and creation of genital organs. Code 55970 reports male-to-female surgery. Code 55980 reports female-to-male surgery.

Summary

- The procedures performed on the male genital organs are reported using CPT codes 54000–55899.
- The organs and structures of the male genital system include the penis, testes, epididymis, tunica vaginalis, scrotum, vas deferens, spermatic cord, seminal vesicles, and prostate.
- Some structures of the male genital system are also part of the urinary system.
- The coder needs to understand whether a procedure was performed unilaterally or bilaterally.

Internet Links

Using the search field on the following website, search by name of the procedure that you wish to research: *http://www.aafp.org*.

Chapter Review

True/False

Instructions: Indicate whether the following statements are true (T) or false (F).

1. _____ The male genital system is primarily for reproduction, but it also functions as part of the urinary system.

2. _____ Diagnostic procedures are always included in surgical procedures in the laparoscopic section of prostate procedures.

3. _____ The vas deferens is also referred to as the *seminal deferens* and is coded from the 55200–55550 code range.

4. _____ If the code does not state unilateral or bilateral, it is assumed that the procedure is bilateral.

5. _____ Laparoscopic repair of a hernia performed at the same time as the orchiopexy would be reported with two repair codes, one indicating the hernia repair and one for the orchiopexy.

Fill in the Blank

Instructions: Fill in the blanks in the statements that follow.

6. The distal end of the penis is also known as the _____.

7. The erectile tissue of the penis is called the _____.

8. The structure that is located below the urinary bladder and on the upper end of the urethra is the

    _____.

9. The germ cell secretion of the testicles is called _____.

10. An elective procedure used to remove the foreskin completely from the glans penis is called

    _____.

Coding Assignments

Instructions: Using the CPT manual, assign the correct code to the following procedures.

1. Vasovasostomy _____

2. Exposure of prostate for insertion of a radioactive substance _____

3. Destruction of a lesion on the penis using cryosurgery _____

4. Repair of hypospadias—fistula stricture—by simple closure method

    _____

5. Removal of all components of an inflatable penile prosthesis—no replacement

    _____

6. Lysis of post-circumcision adhesions

    _____

7. Needle biopsy of testis

    _____

8. Corpora cavernosa—saphenous vein shunt—unilateral _____

9. Radical orchiectomy with abdominal exploration

    _____

10. Puncture aspiration of hydrocele, tunica vaginalis—no medication was injected

    _____

11. Scrotoplasty, simple _____

12. Excision of varicocele of spermatic veins
    _____

13. Exploration for undescended testis with
    abdominal exploration _____

14. Insertion of testicular prosthesis
    _____

15. Urethroplasty for second-stage
    hypospadias repair—2.5 cm
    _____

16. Deep I&D of the shaft of the penis
    _____

17. Plastic surgery on the penis following a
    car accident _____

18. Surgical reduction of torsion of testis
    with fixation of contralateral testis
    _____

19. Needle biopsy of epididymis
    _____

20. Excision of spermatocele without
    epididymectomy _____

21. Partial amputation of penis
    _____

22. Excision of spermatocele with
    epididymectomy _____

23. Incisional biopsy of testis
    _____

24. Scrotal resection _____

25. Unilateral excision of hydrocele of spermatic
    cord _____

26. Laser destruction of three lesions on penis
    _____

27. Irrigation of corpora cavernosa for priapism
    _____

28. Excision of bilateral hydrocele
    _____

29. Fixation of contralateral testis
    _____

30. Foreskin manipulation including lysis
    of preputial adhesions and stretching
    _____

Case Studies

Instructions: Review each case and indicate the correct code(s).

Case 1

Procedure: Circumcision

This 23-hour-old male was brought to the operating room and prepped and draped in the usual fashion for a circumcision. General anesthesia was administered. An incision was made in the preputial foreskin at the coronal sulcus and extended. The foreskin was retracted, and a second incision was made on the mucous part of the foreskin. The skin was dissected with sharp dissection. After this, electrocoagulating current was used to obtain hemostasis, and the frenum was approximated with sutures. The skin was then closed with 3-0 chromic catgut sutures. Blood loss was minimal. The newborn was taken to the recovery room in good condition.

CPT code(s): _____

Case 2

Preoperative and postoperative diagnosis: Left hydrocele

Procedure: Hydrocelectomy

This 39-year-old male was brought to the operating room and prepared and draped in the usual fashion. General anesthesia was administered, and the patient was placed in the lithotomy position. On the left scrotum, a 3.4-cm incision was made. A hydrocele was visualized, and by dissection, it was freed and removed through the incision site. After removing the hydrocele, sutures were used to close the site. A drain was placed, and the wound was closed in layers. The patient was returned to the recovery suite in satisfactory condition. Blood loss was minimal.

CPT code(s): _____

Case 3

Preoperative diagnosis: Prostate tumor

Postoperative diagnosis: Same

Anesthesia: Conscious sedation

Procedure performed: Needle biopsy of the prostate

Procedure: Moderate sedation was administered, and all precautions were taken and documented on the surgical flow sheet. Verification of the questionable site using transabdominal and prostate ultrasound was performed. The biopsy needle was inserted into the skin of the perineum. The biopsy needle was guided to the area of the prostate in question, and the sheath was advanced over the needle and twisted to obtain the sample. This procedure was repeated two more times to be sure that we had adequate sampling. All samples were sent to pathology for testing.

CPT code(s): _____

Case 4

Preoperative diagnosis: Undescended testis on the right

Postoperative diagnosis: Undescended testis on the right

Anesthesia: General endotracheal

Indications: This 7-year-old male presents with a right inguinal testis, which is palpable to the brim of the scotum.

Procedure: The patient was brought to the operating suite, and general endotracheal anesthesia was administered. The patient was prepped and draped in a sterile fashion. 5 cc of 0.5% Marcaine was injected as an ilioinguinal nerve block on the right side.

A transverse groin incision was made on the right, midway between the distal iliac spine and the pubic tubercle. Dissection was carried down, and the ilioinguinal nerve was identified and preserved. The tunica vaginalis was opened, and the testis appeared normal. Movement went up the cord approximately 2 cm, where a small hernia sac was identified and taken down. Once the hernia sac was repaired, there was adequate room for the testis to be brought down into the scrotum. The inguinal incision was irrigated with normal saline, and closure, using continuous 4-0 Monocryl, was performed. Steri-Strips were applied, and the patient was returned to the recovery room. Patient tolerated the procedure well.

CPT code(s): _____

Case 5

Indications for procedure: This is an elective procedure being done at the request of the patient. This is a 37-year-old male who presents with his wife today for elective vasectomy. All risks, benefits, and techniques were discussed with both husband and wife. We discussed the possibility of reversal if he so chooses in the future; however, he was adamant that this would not be the case.

Procedure: The patient's penis was taped out of the way, and the scrotum was then prepped and draped in the usual sterile fashion. Lidocaine was then injected into the skin along the median raphe. After the Lidocaine numbed the area, blunt dissection was used to divide the subcutaneous tissue. The left side was addressed first. The vas clamp was used to elevate the vas, which was injected with local anesthesia. An incision was made using cautery, at which time blunt dissection was used to isolate the vas. The vas was elevated more, clamped proximally and distally where the segment was then removed and sent for pathology. Each end was then ligated with 3-0 silk sutures, and the remaining exposed mucosa was cauterized. Exactly the same procedure was performed on the right side.

The skin was rinsed with saline, and the midline incision was then closed with interrupted 4-0 Vicryl sutures. The skin was sealed with Histoacryl glue. The patient tolerated the procedure well and left the procedure room in good condition.

CPT code(s): _____

Case 6

Indications: This is a 53-year-old male who presents today for simple destruction of two lesions that appear to be molluscum contagiosum on the shaft of the penis. The risks, benefits, and methods of destruction were discussed in detail with this patient. The patient has elected for surgical excision of the lesions.

Procedure: The patient was brought to the surgical suite in the supine position. The genital area, including the penile shaft, was prepped and draped in sterile fashion. The area was anesthetized using 1% Lidocaine. The first lesion, which was 0.3 cm, was removed using a scalpel. This lesion was located on the underside of the shaft. Once the lesion was removed and sent to pathology, two sutures were placed to close the area. The second lesion, located on the lateral aspect of the penis, was removed in a similar fashion. This lesion was 0.2 cm and was also sent to pathology. This area was also closed using two sutures. Pathology confirmed the diagnosis of molluscum contagiosum.

CPT code(s): _____

Case 7

Indications: This is a 75-year-old male who presents today for a laparoscopic orchiectomy on the left side due to a small precancerous lesion found in the testicle.

Procedure: Under general anesthesia, a trocar is inserted at the umbilicus into the retroperitoneal space, and the abdominal cavity is insufflated. Additional trocars are placed on either side of the abdomen. The left testicle is identified and lifted up from the scrotum. All nerves and vessels in the area are relocated until the testicle is freed. The testicle, once freed, is removed through the retroperitoneal space. No damage to any nerves or vessels is noted. The scrotum is then packed and flushed with normal saline. The patient has opted not to undergo prosthetic surgery at this time. The scrotum is then closed carefully in layers. The trocars are removed, and the incision is closed in layers using 3-0 Vicryl. The patient tolerated the procedure well.

CPT code(s): _____

Case 8

Preoperative and postoperative diagnosis: Deep abscess on penis

Procedural Notes:

After local anesthesia was injected into the penal area, an incision was made. The incision was carried down from the skin into the deeper layers where the abscessed cavity was found. The abscessed area was drained, and a drain was left in place to promote further drainage. The patient tolerated the procedure well, with minimal blood loss.

CPT code(s): _____

Case 9

Preoperative diagnosis: Lesion on penis

Postoperative diagnosis: Pending pathology report

Procedure: Biopsy

After anesthetizing the penis, a small incision was made to remove a small portion of a lesion that was on the left side of the penis. The wound did not require closure. The removed tissue was sent to pathology for examination.

CPT code(s): _____

Case 10

Preoperative and Postoperative diagnosis: Post-circumcision adhesions

Anesthesia: General

Procedure: Lysis of adhesions

The patient was prepped and draped in the usual fashion, and general anesthesia was administered. The foreskin was retracted, and the adhesions were released and the glans was cleansed. The area was examined and no fibrous rings were noted. The defect area was closed using three interrupted sutures. The patient tolerated the procedure and was sent to the recovery room in stable condition.

CPT code(s): _____

Female Genital System

Chapter Outline

Learning Objectives

At the conclusion of this chapter, you should be able to:

1. Define key terms related to coding procedures on the female genital system.
2. Define abbreviations associated with the female genital system.
3. Describe the basic anatomy and functions of the female genital system.
4. Define common procedures completed on the female genital system.
5. Apply specific coding guidelines for the female genital system.
6. Select CPT codes for procedures completed on the female genital system.
7. Identify and code procedures for the female genital system from case studies.

Key Terms

abdominal hysterectomy	colpocentesis	colposcopy	endometrium
Bartholin's glands	colpocleisis	colpotomy	enterocele
cerclage	colpopexy	conization	fallopian tubes
cervix uteri	colporrhaphy	corpus uteri	fulguration

hymen	myomectomy	perineum	vaginectomy
hymenectomy	omentectomy	pudendum	vestibular glands
hysterectomy	oophorectomy	salpingo-oophorectomy	vulva
hysteroscope	ovaries	sling procedures	vulvectomy
introitus	paravaginal	trachelectomy	
in vitro fertilization	Pereyra procedure	vagina	

Introduction

Procedures performed on the female genital system may be performed endoscopically, laparoscopically, or as open procedures. The structures of the female genital system include the vulva, perineum, introitus, vagina, cervix uteri, corpus uteri, and ovaries. Accessory organs include the uterus and fallopian tubes.

Terminology and knowledge of anatomy are essential when you are choosing a code that accurately reflects the service performed. Internal and external genitalia of the female body are involved in the reproductive process. Hormones play a large role in the female system because the female reproductive system needs to be able to sustain a developing fetus during pregnancy. Figure 14-1 illustrates the female reproductive system.

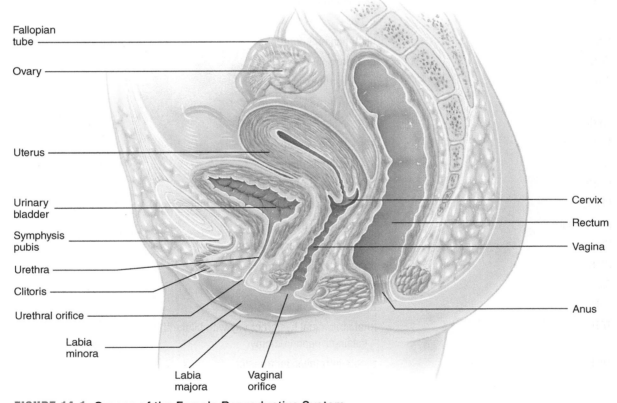

FIGURE 14-1 Organs of the Female Reproductive System

Guidelines Related to the National Correct Coding Initiative (NCCI)

Perform the following steps to obtain the most current coding guideline information related to this chapter online.

1. Log on to *http://www.cms.gov/Medicare/Coding/NationalCorrectCodInitED/index.html*.

2. Scroll to the section titled "Downloads."

3. Click the link for the most current "NCCI Policy Manual for Medicare Services."

4. A box may appear that requires you to click "Open."

5. Click "Chapter 7" for guidelines specific to the female genital system.

Abbreviations Associated with the Female Genital System

The following are some of the most common abbreviations associated with the female genital system:

Abbreviation	Definition
AB	abortion
CIN	cervical intra-epithelial neoplasia
CIS	carcinoma in situ
Cx	cervix
D&C	dilatation and curettage
ECC	endocervical curettage
EMB	endometrial biopsy
GIFT	gamete intrafallopian transfer
GYN	gynecology
IUD	intrauterine device
IVF	in vitro fertilization
LEEP	loop electrosurgical excision procedure
LLETZ	large-loop excision of the transformation zone
Pap smear	Papanicolaou smear
PID	pelvic inflammatory disease
PMS	premenstrual syndrome
SAB	spontaneous abortion
TAB	therapeutic abortion
TAH-BSO	total abdominal hysterectomy with bilateral salpingo-oophorectomy
ZIFT	zygote intrafallopian transfer

Vulva, Perineum, and Introitus (56405–56821)

The **vulva** is an inclusive term used to describe the external genitalia of the female body. The vulva may also be referred to as **pudendum**. The structures that make up the vulva are the mons pubis, labia majora, clitoris, labia minora, vestibule, urinary meatus, vaginal orifice, Bartholin's glands, and perineum. Figure 14-2 illustrates the structures that make up the vulva.

The **perineum** is the diamond-shaped area of skin between the upper area of the vaginal orifice and the anus. The purpose of the perineum is to support pelvic structures. The term **introitus** refers to an opening or space.

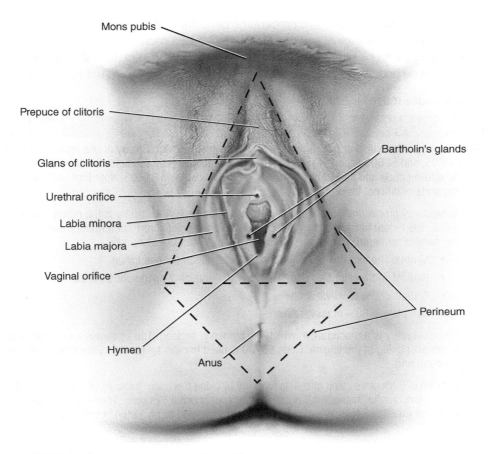

Mons pubis

Prepuce of clitoris

Glans of clitoris

Urethral orifice

Labia minora

Labia majora

Vaginal orifice

Bartholin's glands

Perineum

Hymen

Anus

FIGURE 14-2 Female External Genitalia

This code range begins with incision codes and then moves to destruction codes; see Table 14-1.

TABLE 14-1 Incision and Destruction Codes (56405–56515)

Code(s)	Description
56405–56442	Incision and drainage codes are coded from this range. The incision and drainage of an abscess of the vulva, perineal, or **Bartholin's glands** would be coded from this range. Bartholin's glands, illustrated in Figure 14-2, are glands that secrete lubricating mucous in the vagina. Bartholin's glands may also be referred to as the **vestibular glands**.
56501 and 56515	Destructions of lesion(s) of vulva, differentiated as simple or extensive, are coded from this code range. Attention to detail is necessary when coding destructions. As stated in the instructional notations that follow code 56515, if a destruction of a Skene's gland cyst or abscess or a cautery destruction of a urethral caruncle is performed, this code range would not be referenced.
	For an extensive destruction code to be used, multiple lesions or complicated lesion removal need to be performed. The procedure note would need to be referenced for supporting documentation.

The next code range is used to report excision procedures (see Table 14-2). The approach used to perform the procedure is important to understand when coding excisions.

Codes 56800–56810 reports repairs. This code range includes plastic repair of the introitus (code 56800), clitoroplasty for intersex state (code 56805), and perineoplasty for nonobstetrical injury that is completed as a separate procedure (code 56810). The operative note should be reviewed carefully before a code is assigned. Coders should note the instructional notation below code 56810.

Codes 56820 and 56821 report endoscopic procedures performed on the vulva. A **colposcopy** is a procedure in which a scope is used to view the vaginal and cervical area. The two codes would not be reported together, as 56821 includes a colposcopy with biopsy(s). The coder also needs to keep in mind that if a diagnostic colposcopy is performed to assess the area prior to a surgical procedure, the colposcopy should not be separately reported.

TABLE 14-2 Excision Codes (56605–56740)

Code(s)	Description
56605 and 56606	A biopsy of the vulva or perineum is coded from this code set. Biopsy of one lesion is reported using code 56605, and 56606 is used to report a biopsy of each additional lesion after the first one. Code 56606 is an add-on code and should be used only in conjunction with 56605. Note that code 56606 is for each separate additional lesion that is biopsied.
56620–56640	Vulvectomy procedures are reported with these codes. A **vulvectomy** is the removal of all or part of the vulva. The extent of the excision determines the code selection. To determine the code that best reflects the service rendered, you must understand the extent of the excision: • Simple: The excision of skin and superficial subcutaneous tissue. • Radical: More extensive than simple, with removal of deep subcutaneous tissue. • Partial: <80% of vulvar area • Complete: >80% of vulvar area
56700	**Hymenectomy** is a procedure in which the hymen is excised. The **hymen** is a membrane that covers the external opening of the vagina. Code 56700 is used to report a partial hymenectomy or a revision of the hymenal ring.
56740	Excision of Bartholin's gland or cyst is reported by using this code. It should be noted that in the CPT manual, there are numerous instructional notations that appear under this code. These instruct the coder to use other codes for excisions of Skene's gland, urethral caruncle, and so on. Reference the notes for more information.

Exercise 14.1—Check Your Understanding

Code Range 56405–56821

Indicate whether each statement is true (T) or false (F).

1. _____ One lesion excised from the vulva is reported using code 56606. Code 56610 is used to report a biopsy of each additional lesion of the vulva after the first one.

2. _____ The hymen is a membrane that covers the external opening of the vagina.

3. _____ Vulva repair is reported using codes 56800–56810.

4. _____ If a destruction of a cyst, abscess, or a cautery destruction of a urethral caruncle is performed, the code set used to report this service is 56700–56740.

5. _____ Procedures performed on the female genital system may be performed endoscopically, laparoscopically, or open.

6. _____ A complete radical vulvectomy is reported using code 56633.

7. _____ A partial vulvectomy procedure is the removal of greater than 80% of the vulvar area.

8. _____ A simple vulvectomy procedure is the removal of the skin and superficial subcutaneous tissue.

9. _____ A radical procedure, as it relates to the vulvectomy codes, is defined as the removal of less than 80% of the vulvar area.

10. _____ A colposcopy of the vulva with biopsy is reported using CPT code 56821.

Procedures Completed on the Vagina (57000–57426)

The **vagina** is a fibromuscular structure that connects with the external genitalia and ascends in a tubelike structure to the cervix uteri. The vagina has several functions as a passageway in the female body. The vagina is a passageway for the penis during sexual intercourse. It is also a passageway for menstrual flow and is part of the birth canal, through which the baby passes during a vaginal birth.

An understanding of terminology helps when you are reading the operative reports. When you see the prefix *colp/o* or the prefix *vagin/o*, realize that this is a term relating to the vagina.

Incision procedures are listed first in this subcategory. Codes 57000–57023 are used to report open surgical procedures of the vagina. Colpotomy and colpocentesis are both reported using codes from this code range. A **colpotomy** is a procedure using an open approach, in which the fallopian tubes are identified and then occluded at vascular points. A **colpocentesis** is the aspiration of fluid through the vaginal wall into a syringe.

Destruction of vaginal lesions using cryosurgery, laser surgery, or electrosurgery is reported using codes 57061 and 57065.

Excision codes are reported with CPT codes 57100–57135. Table 14-3 outlines the excision code range.

TABLE 14-3 Excision (57100–57135)

Code(s)	Description
57100 and 57105	Biopsy of vaginal mucosa, either simple or extensive, is reported with these codes.
57106–57109	Vaginectomy, partial with removal of vaginal wall, is reported with this range of codes. **Vaginectomy** is a procedure in which the vagina is excised. In this code range, only partial removal is performed.
57110–57112	Codes 57110–57112 are used to report vaginectomy, the complete removal of the vaginal wall. The codes in this range are differentiated by additional procedures that are completed with the complete vaginectomy.
57120	Colpocleisis procedures are reported with this code. **Colpocleisis** is a surgical closure of the vagina. The operative report may state that a Le Fort–type procedure was performed. This procedure is reported using this code.
57130 and 57135	Excision of vaginal septum, a cyst, or a tumor is reported with this range of codes.

Introduction codes are reported using the 57150–57180 code range. This code range includes the fitting and insertion of a pessary device, a diaphragm, or a cervical cap. The introduction of hemostatic agents for nonobstetrical vaginal hemorrhage is reported using code 57180.

Repairs of the vagina are reported using the 57200–57335 code range (see Table 14-4). The codes in this code range for repair procedures are determined based on the type of repair and the approach.

TABLE 14-4 Repair (57200–57335)

Code(s)	Description
57200–57265	Colporrhaphy procedures are reported with this range of codes. **Colporrhaphy** is the surgical repair of the vagina.
57267	This is an add-on code for insertion of mesh or other prosthesis for repair of pelvic floor defect. This code should not be used alone but needs to be used in conjunction with codes 45560, 57240–57265, and 57285.
57268 and 57270	Repair of **enterocele**—code assignment depends on the surgical approach. *Enterocele* is another term for vaginal hernia.
57280–57283	Colpopexy procedures are reported from this code range. **Colpopexy** is a procedure in which the vagina is sutured to the abdominal wall. Surgical approach determines code selection.

(continues)

TABLE 14-4 (*continued*)

Code(s)	Description
57284 and 57285	**Paravaginal** defect repair is reported using these codes. *Paravaginal* refers to the area around the vagina. Code 57284 is used to report an open abdominal approach, while code 57285 is used to report a vaginal approach. These procedures help restore normal anatomical positions of the vagina, bladder, and urethra.
57287 and 57288	These codes report **sling procedures**. Slings are used to help correct urinary-stress incontinence. These procedure codes are used to report the initial repair, removal, or revision of the sling.
57289	A **Pereyra procedure**, including anterior colporrhaphy, is reported with this code. This is a procedure in which sutures are laced through the Pereyra ligature carrier, and the urethrovesical junction is raised.
57291–57296	Construction or revision of a vagina is reported with this range of codes. Distinction is made by whether the revision is completed with or without a graft and by the approach that is used.
57300–57335	Code 57300 to 57330 report the closure of fistulas in the vaginal area. A fistula is an abnormal passage. Code 57335 reports a vaginoplasty for intersex state.

Manipulation of the vagina includes dilation, examination, and removal of a foreign body with manipulation. The code range for reporting these services is 57400–57415. If removal of the impacted vaginal foreign body is not performed with anesthesia, this code range should not be used; the procedure should be reported using an evaluation and management code. When you are reporting vaginal approach procedures, dilation of the vagina (57400) should not be reported separately, as it is a routine part of the surgical field encountered.

Endoscopic and laparoscopic procedures of the vagina are reported using CPT codes 57420–57426. Code 57420 reports a colposcopy of the entire vagina with the cervix, if the cervix is present. Code 57421 reports a colposcopy of the entire vagina with the cervix, if present, with biopsy(s) of the vagina/cervix. Reference the CPT manual following code 57421 for instructional notations that relate to these two codes. Code 57423 reports a laparoscopic repair of a paravaginal defect. Code 57423 is not to be reported with the codes that are listed in the CPT manual following code 57423. A surgical laparoscopic colpopexy is reported with code 27425, while a laparoscopic revision of a prosthetic vaginal graft is reported with code 57426. When reading operative or procedural notes it is essential that coders identify the approach, such as the use of a laparscope, to ensure that proper code selection occurs.

Exercise 14.2—Check Your Understanding

Vocabulary

Fill in the blanks in the statements that follow.

1. A procedure in which the vagina is sutured to the abdominal wall is called _____.

2. The vagina is a(n) _____ for the penis during intercourse, for menstrual flow, and for a baby to travel through during the birth process.

3. Enterocele is another term for _____.

4. The aspiration of fluid through the vaginal wall into a syringe is called a(n) _____.

5. Repairs of the vagina are reported using the _____ code range.

6. A surgical repair of the vagina is called a(n) _____.

7. A biopsy of the vaginal mucosa would be reported using the _____ code range.

8. Paravaginal defect repairs are reported using the _____ code range.

9. The structure that connects with the external genitalia and ascends to the corpus uteri is the _____.

10. Procedures that are used to help correct urinary stress incontinence are called _____ procedures.

Procedures Completed on the Cervix Uteri (57452–57800)

The **cervix uteri** lies between the ostium uteri and the isthmus. A colposcope is used to view the cervix and portions of the vagina. Biopsies are reported using selected codes from code range 57452–57461. The code selection for biopsies is based on the technique used to perform the biopsy or biopsies. Figure 14-3 illustrates the uterus and other structures.

Excision codes are reported using code range 57500–57558 (see Table 14-5). These procedures are performed as open procedures rather than by using a scope.

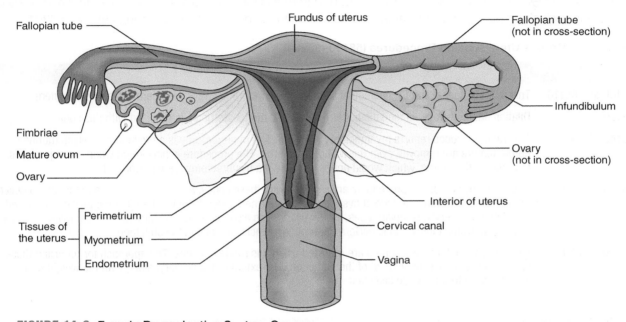

FIGURE 14-3 Female Reproductive System Organs

TABLE 14-5 Excision (57500–57558)

Code(s)	Description
57500	Biopsy, single or multiple, or local excision of lesion, with or without fulguration (separate procedure), are reported with this code. **Fulguration** is the use of an electric current to destroy living tissue, usually to control bleeding.
57505	This code reports endocervical curettage (not done as part of a dilation and curettage). The opening of the cervix into the uterine cavity is scraped.
57510 and 57513	Cautery of the cervix is reported with this range of codes. The codes are differentiated based on cautery technique.
57520 and 57522	Conization of the cervix is reported with this code range. **Conization** is a procedure performed on the cervix in which a cold knife is used to surgically cut a cone-shaped portion of tissue for examination.
57530 and 57531	Trachelectomy procedures are reported with these codes. A **trachelectomy** is the removal of the cervix uteri.
57540–57556	Excision of cervical stump—code selection depends on approach and other repairs performed at the same time.
57558	This code is used to report the dilation and curettage of a cervical stump.

Repair codes (57700–57720), along with the manipulation code (57800), finish this range of codes. Found in the repair code section is code 57700—Cerclage of uterine cervix, nonobstetrical. **Cerclage** is a technique of encircling the cervix uteri with a wire, ligature, or loop. It should be noted here that this is *not* the correct code to be used when an obstetrician is performing the procedure to prevent a spontaneous abortion. When you are reporting vaginal approach procedures, dilation of the cervix (57800) should not be reported separately, as it is a routine part of the surgical field encountered.

Procedures Completed on the Corpus Uteri (58100-58540)

The **corpus uteri** is the area of structures that begins at the fundus of the uterine cavity and moves down to encompass the cervical canal or the external os.

There is an extensive list of excision services reported from this range of codes. Understanding terminology is important in assigning the proper code. Table 14-6 describes the codes found in code range 58100–58294.

TABLE 14-6 Corpus Uteri Excision Procedures (58100–58294)

Code(s)	Description
58100 and 58110	This range of codes reports endometrial sampling. The **endometrium** is the innermost layer of the uterus.
58120	Dilation and curettage, diagnostic and/or therapeutic (nonobstetrical), is reported with this code.
58140–58146	This range of codes reports myomectomy procedures. A **myomectomy** is a procedure in which uterine fibroid tumors are removed from the wall of the uterus. The procedure is performed when the objective is to preserve the uterus, which would not be possible if a hysterectomy were performed.
58150–58240	Abdominal hysterectomy procedures are reported with these codes. A **hysterectomy** is a procedure in which the uterus is removed. The type of hysterectomy performed depends on whether just the uterus is removed or whether the cervix, fallopian tubes, and/or ovaries are also removed. The term **abdominal hysterectomy** refers to a hysterectomy that is performed through an incision made in the abdomen.
58260–58294	Vaginal hysterectomy procedures are reported using this range of codes. The approach for reporting these procedures is the vagina instead of the abdomen. The extent of the surgery, along with the weight of the uterus, will determine code selection.

Introduction procedures are reported with code set 58300–58356. This includes insertion and removal of intrauterine devices (IUDs), insertion of Heyman capsules for clinical brachytherapy, and endometrial ablation. Careful attention to the procedure notes and the verbiage within CPT will determine code assignment.

Repair codes are reported using code range 58400–58540. Hysterorrhaphy and hysteroplasty are found in this code range.

Exercise 14.3—Check Your Understanding

Vocabulary

Fill in the blank with the correct term(s) to complete each statement.

1. The term for the removal of the cervix uteri is _____.

2. The area of structures that begins at the fundus of the uterine cavity and moves down to encompass the cervical canal or the external os is the _____.

3. The term used for the technique of encircling the cervix uteri with a wire, ligature, or loop is _____.

4. Insertion of an IUD is reported with code _____.

5. The removal of uterine fibroid tumors from the wall of the uterus is reported using code range _____.

(continues)

Exercise 14.3—*continued*

6. The innermost layer of the uterus is the _____.

7. A term for the procedure in which uterine fibroid tumors are removed from the wall of the uterus is _____.

8. The code range used to report the cautery of the cervix is _____.

9. A procedure in which the uterus is removed is known as a(n) _____.

10. The term used for a procedure in which a cold knife is used to surgically cut a cone-shaped portion of tissue from the cervix is a _____ procedure.

Laparoscopy and Hysteroscopy (58541–58579 and 58674)

Many gynecological procedures are performed using a laparoscope. As explained in earlier chapters, diagnostic laparoscopic procedures are included in surgical laparoscopic procedures and should not be billed separately.

A **hysteroscope** can be a fiber-optic-type scope or a rigid-type scope. It can be used for diagnostic and surgical procedures. Like the laparoscopic procedure, the diagnostic hysteroscopic procedure is included in the surgical procedure and should not be billed separately. Table 14-7 summarizes the laparoscopic and hysteroscopic procedures.

TABLE 14-7 Laparoscopic and Hysteroscopic Procedures (58541–58579)

Code(s)	Description
58541–58554	Laparoscopic procedures are reported with this range of codes. These procedure codes include excision of myomas, the uterus (hysterectomy), fallopian tube(s), and ovary(ies). The weight in grams is a factor in coding from this code range.
58555–58565	Hysteroscopic procedures are reported with these codes. These procedure codes include diagnostic hysteroscopy, biopsy samplings, resection, ablation, and removal of impacted foreign bodies.
58570–58573	This code range reports surgical laparoscopy with total hysterectomy. The codes are differentiated by the weight of the uterus in grams, along with how extensive the procedure was.
58578	This code is used to report an unlisted laparoscopy procedure, uterus.
58579	Unlisted hysteroscopy procedure, uterus.

Code 58674 is an out of sequence code that is listed first in the CPT manual after the heading entitled Laparoscopy/Hysteroscopy and before the code 58541. Code 58674 reports a surgical laparoscopy completed for an ablation of uterine fibroid(s) and includes intraoperative ultrasound guidance and monitoring, radiofrequency.

Procedures Completed on the Oviduct and Ovary (58600–58960)

This range of codes is divided into oviduct and ovary. This code range includes procedures performed on the fallopian tubes and ovaries. The **fallopian tubes** are bilateral tubes that open at one end in the uterus and at the other end into the peritoneal cavity.

The **ovaries** are also referred to as female gonads and function in producing eggs, which are released during ovulation. The ovaries also produce the female hormones estrogen and progesterone.

TABLE 14-8 Prefixes

Combining Form	Meaning
hyster/o, metr/o	Uterus
men/o	Menstruation
o/o, ov/o	Egg, ovum
oophor/o, ovari/o	Ovary
salping/o	Fallopian tubes

Understanding word parts are essential when you are trying to select the correct code assignment. Being able to apply this knowledge will help you in understanding and translating an operative note and is key to choosing the correct code. Table 14-8 lists prefixes that coders will encounter in operative documentation.

The coding for this section begins with incision codes. Incision codes for the oviduct/ovary area begin with the ligation or transaction of the fallopian tube. The approach can be either vaginal or abdominal, but there needs to be a determination as to whether the procedure was done at the time of a cesarean delivery. The code set 58600–58611 should be referenced for reporting these services. The codes apply equally for both unilateral and bilateral procedures. This would mean that if the procedure was performed on one side or both sides, code selection would be the same, and the quantity would always be one.

If open occlusion of the fallopian tubes is performed, code 58615 would be used to report this service. If the occlusion is done laparoscopically, code 58671 would be used to report the service.

Laparoscopic procedures on the ovaries and oviduct are reported with code set 58660–58679. The procedure codes listed here are surgical laparoscopic procedures and include lysis of adhesions, fulguration or excision of lesions, occlusion of oviducts, and salpingostomy. Excisional procedures reported with code 58700 (reports salpingectomy, complete or partial, unilateral or bilateral) and code 58720 (reports salpingo-oophorectomy, complete or partial, unilateral or bilateral) are separate procedure codes that are not completed via a scope.

The repair codes for fallopian tubes are reported using code range 58740–58770. The repairs are done as open procedures. The coder would reference the laparoscopic section of codes for procedures done through the scope. Open procedures performed on the ovaries begin with incision codes (58800–58822) for the drainage of an ovarian abscess or cyst. The transposition of the ovary is reported using code 58825.

The ovary excision services are reported using code set 58900–58960. Table 14-9 lists the codes for code range 58900–58960.

TABLE 14-9 Ovary Excisions (58900–58960)

Code(s)	Description
58900	Biopsy of ovary, unilateral or bilateral (separate procedure), is reported with this code.
58920	This code reports wedge resection or bisection of ovary, unilateral or bilateral. In this procedure, the surgeon makes a very small, pie-shaped (or wedge) incision into the ovaries. This wedge is taken to reduce the size of the ovaries.
58925	Ovarian cystectomy, unilateral or bilateral, is reported with this code. This procedure code is used to report the removal of ovarian cysts.
58940–58943	Oophorectomy—a partial or total removal of the ovary, unilateral or bilateral, is reported with these codes.
58950–58952	Resection of ovarian, tubal, or primary peritoneal malignancy with bilateral salpingo-oophorectomy and omentectomy. Through abdominal incision, the malignancy is surgically removed, along with any affected structures. A salpingo-oophorectomy refers to fallopian tubes and ovaries. An omentectomy is the removal of part of the omentum.

(continues)

TABLE 14-9 *(continued)*

Code(s)	Description
58953–58956	These codes report bilateral salpingo-oophorectomy. Code selection is based on the reason for the surgery. Coders should note the instructional notation that appears after code 58956.
58957 and 58958	Code 58957 reports a resection or tumor debulking of a recurrent ovarian, tubal, primary peritoneal, uterine malignancy with omentectomy, if performed. Code 58958 reports the same procedure as code 58957 with the addition of a pelvic lymphadenectomy and limited para-aortic lymphadenectomy being completed.
58960	Laparotomy, for staging or restaging of ovarian, tubal, or primary peritoneal malignancy (second look), with or without omentectomy, peritoneal washing, biopsy of abdominal and pelvic peritoneum, diaphragmatic assessment with pelvic and limited para-aortic lymphadenectomy.

In Vitro Fertilization (58970–58976) and Other Procedures (58999)

In vitro fertilization is a process in which a mature egg is exposed to sperm in a laboratory setting. The ova are then implanted into the uterus.

The procedure codes are used to report the retrieval of the egg, the placement of the fertilized egg into the uterus, the gamete intrafallopian transfer (GIFT) procedure, and finally the zygote intrafallopian transfer (ZIFT) procedure.

The last code, code 58999, in this section of the CPT manual is used to report an unlisted procedure for the female genital system (nonobstetrical).

Summary

- Procedures performed on the female genital system may be performed endoscopically, laparoscopically, or as an open approach.
- Terminology and knowledge of anatomy are essential for choosing a code that accurately reflects the service performed.
- Multiple structures of the female genital system are coded from this subsection of the surgery chapter of CPT.
- *Vulva* is an inclusive term used to describe the external genitalia of the female body.
- The vagina is a fibromuscular structure that connects with the external genitalia and ascends in a tubelike structure to the cervix uteri.
- The cervix uteri lies between the ostium uteri and the isthmus.
- The corpus uteri is the area of structures that begins at the fundus of the uterine cavity and moves down to encompass the cervical canal or the external os.
- The fallopian tubes are bilateral tubes that open on one end in the uterus and open at the other end into the peritoneal cavity.
- The ovaries are also referred to as *female gonads* and function in producing eggs, which are released during ovulation.
- The ovaries produce the female hormones estrogen and progesterone.

Internet Links

To learn more about procedures completed on the female genital system, visit *http://www.acog.org*, *http://www.obgyn.net*, and *http://www.reproductive.org*.

Chapter Review

True/False

Instructions: Indicate whether the following statements are true (T) or false (F).

1. _____ If open occlusion of the fallopian tubes is performed, code 58627 should be used to report this service.

2. _____ A colpocentesis is the aspiration of fluid through the vaginal wall into a syringe.

3. _____ Code 56606 is an add-on code and should be used only in conjunction with 56605.

4. _____ Endoscopic and open procedures of the vagina are reported using CPT codes 57420–57425.

5. _____ When you are reporting vaginal approach procedures, dilation of the cervix (57800) should be reported separately, as it is a routine part of the surgical field encountered.

Fill in the Blank

Instructions: Fill in the blanks in the statements that follow.

6. The term _____ refers to an opening or space.

7. The use of an electric current to destroy living tissue, usually used to control bleeding, is known as a(n) _____.

8. A(n) _____ is an abnormal passage.

9. The surgical closure of the vagina is a(n) _____.

10. Another term for vaginal hernia is _____.

Coding Assignments

Instructions: Using the CPT manual, assign the correct code to the following procedures.

1. Radical partial vulvectomy
   _____

2. Simple biopsy of the vaginal mucosa
   _____

3. Colposcopy of vulva with biopsy
   _____

4. Sling procedure for stress incontinence
   _____

5. Electrosurgery for extensive destruction of vulva lesions _____

6. Simple hymenotomy _____

7. Colpotomy with exploration
   _____

8. Thermal cautery of cervix
   _____

9. Plastic repair of urethrocele
   _____

10. Closure of rectovaginal fistula using the abdominal approach _____

11. Pelvic examination under general anesthesia
    _____

12. Pereyra procedure, including anterior colporrhaphy
    _____

13. Vaginal hysterectomy with total vaginectomy

   _____

14. Total abdominal hysterectomy with removal of tubes and ovaries _____

15. Lysis of adhesions of ovaries, laparoscopic procedure _____

16. Drainage of ovarian abscess using open vaginal approach _____

17. Follicle puncture for oocyte retrieval

   _____

18. Bilateral salpingo-oophorectomy with omentectomy, total abdominal hysterectomy, and radical dissection for debulking

   _____

19. Wedge resection of right ovary

   _____

20. Tubotubal anastomosis

   _____

21. Electrosurgery destruction of vulva lesion

   _____

22. Revision of hymenal ring

   _____

23. Laser ablation for cautery of cervix

   _____

24. Pelvic floor repair following excision of a cervical stump via the abdominal approach

   _____

25. Vaginal transection of fallopian tubes

   _____

26. Excision of Bartholin's cyst

   _____

27. Nonobstetrical perineoplasty

   _____

28. I&D of vaginal hematoma due to spontaneous bleeding. The patient is not pregnant.

   _____

29. Vaginal repair of enterocele

   _____

30. Cervical cap fitting with discussion of instructions for use _____

Case Studies

Instructions: Review each case and indicate the correct code(s).

Case 1

Preoperative diagnosis: Vaginal pain

Postoperative diagnosis: Vaginal cyst, pathology pending

The patient was brought to the operating suite and prepped and draped in the usual fashion. After general anesthesia, a speculum was inserted into the vagina. There was one 3-cm cyst on the vagina. Using a CO_2 laser set, the cyst was excised by the laser, and part of the cyst was sent to pathology for further review. Bleeding of the site was controlled, and the patient tolerated the procedure and was sent to the recovery area in satisfactory condition.

CPT code(s): _____

Case 2

Preoperative diagnosis: Pelvic pain preventing pelvic exam

Postoperative diagnosis: Vulvar adhesions

The patient was placed under general anesthesia and placed in the supine lithotomy position. Examination of the pelvis revealed multiple adhesions in the vulvar area. The vagina and cervix were examined and found to be normal. The patient tolerated the procedure and was sent to recovery. Additional therapeutic procedures will be discussed with the patient.

CPT code(s): _____

Case 3

Preoperative diagnosis: Vaginal stricture

Postoperative diagnosis: Vaginal stricture

Procedure: Repair of introitus

The patient was brought to the operating room and prepped and draped in the usual fashion. General anesthesia was given, and the surgical site was cleansed. Three V-shaped incisions were made in the area of the vaginal stricture. Because of the amount of scar tissue present, the tissue was excised. To obtain hemostasis, the mucosa was sewn with sutures, thus repairing the area. The patient tolerated the procedure with minimal blood loss.

CPT code(s): _____

Case 4

Preoperative and postoperative diagnosis: Heavy menstrual bleeding

Procedure: Thermal endometrial ablation

This 53-year-old female patient was brought to the operating room and was prepped and draped for surgery. The patient has been experiencing extensive menstrual bleeding and has elected to undergo an ablation at this time. The patient was placed in the dorsal lithotomy position under general anesthesia. A resectoscope was inserted, and an endometrial ablation was completed, removing tissue and coagulating the area via a fulguration current. Hemostasis was obtained with minimal blood loss. The patient was found to be in satisfactory condition and was sent to the recovery room.

CPT code(s): _____

Case 5

Preoperative and postoperative diagnosis: Uterine fibroids

Procedure: Total abdominal hysterectomy with BSO

Anesthesia: General

This 59-year-old female patient was taken to the operating room and prepped and draped for surgery. The abdomen was opened and explored. A retractor was placed, and the operative field was prepared. Division of the round ligaments occurred, and an incision was made in the anterior peritoneum. The posterior peritoneum was incised, and the uterine vessels were grasped and sutured. Clamps were placed, and the vagina was entered anteriorly while the cervix was excised in toto. The vaginal cuff was sutured with sutures, and the cuff was then sutured. Hemostasis was obtained. Closure of the fascia and fatty layers was completed. The skin was closed with staples. There was marginal blood loss, and the patient tolerated the procedure and was sent to the recovery room in stable condition. Tissue samples were sent to pathology.

CPT code(s): _____

Case 6

Preoperative diagnosis: Cervical lesion

Postoperative diagnosis: Squamous intraepithelial lesion of the cervix

Indications for procedure: This is a 27-year-old female who presented for her annual Pap and pelvic examination. The results of the Pap smear identified an abnormality. The follow-up Pap confirmed the abnormality, and an ultrasound was performed, after which surgery was scheduled to get a definitive diagnosis.

Procedure: The patient was placed in the supine position and administered general anesthesia. She was placed in cane stirrups and then prepped and draped in the usual fashion, although her vaginal vault was not prepped in any way. A coated speculum was inserted, and the cervix was exposed. It was painted with Lugol, and the entire active cervix was nonstaining with the clearly defined margins where the stain began to pick up. Approximately 6 cc of Lidocaine with 1% epinephrine was then injected into the cervix. A large loop wire was then used to excise the anterior cervical lesion. Conization of the cervical 4.5-cm lesion was performed. All specimens were sent to pathology at this time. Hemostasis was achieved using cautery and then Monsel. All instruments were removed and accounted for. The patient was sent to the recovery room in good, stable condition.

CPT code(s): _____

Case 7

Preoperative and postoperative diagnosis: Perineal abscess

Procedural Notes:

After local anesthesia was injected into the perineal area, the area was examined and the abscessed area was visualized between the vulva and the anus. An incision was made into the abscess, and purulent contents were drained. The abscessed cavity was examined and flushed with an antibiotic wash, and the site was packed with medicated gauze. The patient tolerated the procedure and was given discharge instructions and is to follow up in two weeks.

CPT code(s): _____

Case 8

Preoperative diagnosis: Polymenorrhea

Postoperative diagnosis: Benign endometrial polyp

Anesthesia: General

Indication for procedure:

This 49-year-old female has been experiencing polymenorrhea and menorrhagia for the past eight months. Diagnostic examination is necessary to rule out any pathology.

Procedural Notes:

The patient was brought to the operating suite, and general anesthesia was given. The patient was then prepped and draped in the usual fashion while in the dorsal lithotomy position. A speculum was placed, and a tenaculum was used to grasp the cervix, which was dilated to 7 mm. The hysteroscope was placed through the vagina and into the cervical os to visualize the uterine cavity. An endometrial polyp was visualized, and a polypectomy was completed. A small amount of uterine contents were removed via sharp curettage. Specimens were sent to pathology. The tenaculum was taken off the cervix and the scope was withdrawn. The patient was sent to the recovery area in satisfactory condition.

CPT code(s): _____

Maternity Care and Delivery

Chapter Outline

Introduction

Guidelines Related to the National Correct Coding Initiative (NCCI)

Abbreviations Associated with Maternity Care and Delivery

Antepartum and Fetal Invasive Services (59000-59350)

Vaginal Delivery, Antepartuwm and Postpartum Care (59400–59430), and Cesarean Delivery (59510–59525)

Delivery after Previous Cesarean Delivery (59610–59622)

Abortion and Other Procedures (59812–59899)

Summary

Internet Links

Chapter Review

Coding Assignments

Case Studies

Learning Objectives

At the conclusion of this chapter, you should be able to:

1. Define key terms related to coding maternity care and delivery procedures.
2. Define abbreviations associated with maternity care and delivery procedures.
3. Define common maternity care and delivery services and procedures.
4. Apply specific coding guidelines for maternity care and delivery.
5. Select CPT codes for maternity care and delivery procedures.
6. Identify and code procedures for maternity care and delivery from case studies.

Key Terms

abortion

amniocentesis

amnioscopy

antepartum

cesarean section delivery

chorionic villus

cordocentesis

curettage

ectopic pregnancy

embryo

episiotomy

hydatidiform mole

hysterorrhaphy

incomplete abortion

legally induced abortion

missed abortion

| multifetal pregnancy reduction (MPR) | oligohydramnios | septic abortion | vaginal birth after cesarean (VBAC) |
| obstetrics | perinatal period | spontaneous abortion | |

Introduction

The procedure codes used to report obstetric care begin with code 59000 and end with code 59899. This chapter contains information on procedure codes relating to maternity care and delivery, also known as obstetrics. **Obstetrics** is the specialty that treats women during pregnancy, childbirth, and the period of time immediately following childbirth. During the second week through the eighth week of pregnancy, the embryo grows and develops into a fetus. The **embryo** is referred to as the *fetus* from nine weeks until birth, usually at 40 weeks. The period immediately following the birth up to 28 days after birth is considered the **perinatal period**.

Guidelines Related to the National Correct Coding Initiative (NCCI)

Perform the following steps to obtain the most current coding guideline information related to this chapter online.

1. Log on to *www.cms.hhs.gov/NationalCorrectCodInitEd*.
2. Scroll to the section titled "Downloads."
3. Click the link for the most current "NCCI Policy Ma nual for Medicare Services."
4. A box may appear that requires you to click "Open."
5. Click "Chapter 7" for guidelines specific to maternity care and delivery.

Abbreviations Associated with Maternity Care and Delivery

The following abbreviations are most commonly used in relation to maternity care and delivery:

Abbreviation	Definition
CPD	cephalopelvic disproportion
C-section	cesarean section
DUB	dysfunctional uterine bleeding
EDC	estimated date of confinement
EDD	estimated date of delivery
FHT	fetal heart tones
G	gravida
LMP	last menstrual period
multip	multipara

(continues)

(continued)

NB   newborn
OB   obstetrics
PIH   pregnancy-induced hypertension
SAB   spontaneous abortion

Antepartum and Fetal Invasive Services (59000-59350)

Antepartum care is the care rendered during the time prior to childbirth. Antepartum care is usually reported with a "no charge" visit code for a normal pregnancy check because this period of time is part of the global period reimbursed at the time of delivery. Those services rendered during the antepartum period that are unrelated to the pregnancy or childbirth would be reported with an Evaluation and Management (E/M) code.

> **EXAMPLE:** Sara is 22 weeks pregnant and has presented today with an earache. After a brief and problem-focused examination, it was determined that she had otitis media, and an antibiotic was ordered.

Due to the fact that Sara's visit was totally unrelated to her pregnancy, her visit would be coded with an Evaluation and Management code from the 99211–99215 code set. The diagnosis code would clearly indicate that the visit was unrelated to the pregnancy. Normal prenatal care would include visits once a month for up to 28 weeks. A high-risk pregnancy may require more frequent visits. From 29 weeks through 36 weeks, biweekly visits would be considered normal. From 37 weeks until delivery, weekly visits are the norm. Table 15-1 identifies the CPT codes related to antepartum and fetal invasive services.

TABLE 15-1 Antepartum and Fetal Invasive Services (59000–59076)

Code(s)	Description
59000 and 59001	Amniocentesis—diagnostic and therapeutic procedures are reported using code 59000 for a diagnostic amniocentesis and code 59001 for a therapeutic amniocentesis completed for amniotic fluid reduction (includes ultrasound guidance). An **amniocentesis** is a procedure in which a needle is inserted into the amniotic sac to withdraw fluid for examination. Figure 15-1 illustrates an amniocentesis and preparation of a specimen for analysis.
59012	Cordocentesis (intrauterine), any method—**cordocentesis** is a procedure in which an amniocentesis needle is inserted into the umbilical vessel to obtain blood from the fetus. The procedure is not done until the second or third trimester.
59015	This code reports chorionic villus sampling, any method—**chorionic villus** is the medical term for the placenta.
59020 and 59025	These codes report fetal stress testing. The codes in this series are used to report stress or nonstress testing of the fetus. The fetal heart rate and the contractions are monitored. Contractions may or may not be present during testing.
59030	This code reports fetal scalp blood sampling. This procedure is performed in some cases as a way of determining fetal distress.

(continues)

TABLE 15-1 (*continued*)

Code(s)	Description
59050 and 59051	Fetal monitoring during labor by consulting physician (i.e., nonattending physician) with written report and supervision and interpretation is reported with this series of codes. This service is *not* reported by the attending physician, as the service is not separately reportable when the physician is getting reimbursed for global services.
59070	This code reports transabdominal amnioinfusion, including ultrasound guidance. This procedure is performed in cases where there is less than sufficient amniotic fluid present, or **oligohydramnios**, is diagnosed.
59072	Fetal umbilical cord occlusion, including ultrasound guidance, is reported by using this code. This is a procedure that may need to be done in cases of multiple gestation. One of the fetuses may be getting too much fluid while the other is not getting enough, and the exchange of blood between the fetuses needs to be stopped in an effort to save both fetuses.
59074	Fetal fluid drainage (e.g., vesicocentesis, thoracocentesis, paracentesis), including ultrasound guidance, is reported with this code.
59076	This code reports fetal shunt placement, including ultrasound guidance.

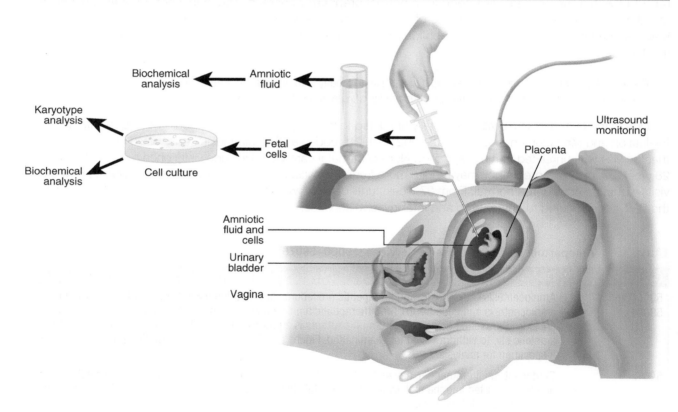

FIGURE 15-1 Amniocentesis and Preparation of Specimen for Amniotic Fluid Analysis

Many of these procedures are performed with scopes. **Amnioscopy** is a scope procedure used to view the fetus in the amniotic sac. A fetoscope or laparoamnioscope may also be used.

The excision procedures are reported with the 59100–59160 code set. These procedures may be reported if there is an abnormal pregnancy and the pregnancy needs to be terminated. Terminology is key and is explained in Table 15-2, which also notes the codes for excisions.

TABLE 15-2 Excision Codes (59100–59160)

Code(s)	Description
59100	This code reports a hysterotomy, abdominal (e.g., for hydatidiform mole, abortion). A **hydatidiform mole** is a grapelike grouping of cysts that is really the ova that cannot develop properly.
59120–59140	Surgical treatment of ectopic pregnancy; tubal or ovarian, requiring salpingectomy and/or oophorectomy, an abdominal or a vaginal approach is reported with this range of codes. An **ectopic pregnancy** is a pregnancy that occurs outside the uterus. Code assignment is based on the extent of the procedure performed.
59150 and 59151	This range of codes reports laparoscopic treatment of ectopic pregnancy. Code assignment is based on the extent of the procedure performed.
59160	This code reports a curettage, postpartum. A **curettage** is a surgical scraping; in this case, the endometrial lining of the uterus would be scraped after childbirth.

Antepartum introduction and repair codes are reported using codes from the 59200–59350 code range. Prior to inducing labor, the physician may need to insert a cervical dilator to chemically stimulate the cervical canal to dilate. Insertion of the cervical dilator would be reported using code 59200.

Codes 59300 to 59350 report repairs. Repair codes are used to report the repair of a ruptured uterus, also referred to as a **hysterorrhaphy**. An episiotomy or vaginal repair completed by a provider other than the attending provider is reported with code 59300. An **episiotomy** is an incision made at the vaginal opening to prevent tearing during delivery. A vaginal or abdominal cerclage of the cervix during pregnancy is completed when the cervix appears to be incompetent or unable to hold the pregnancy and needs reinforcement until it is time to deliver the baby. This procedure is reported using code 59320 for vaginal cerclage or code 59325 for an abdominal cerclage.

Exercise 15.1—Check Your Understanding

Coding Assignments and terms that relate to maternity care and delivery

Indicate whether the following statements are true (T) or false (F).

1. _____ Antepartum introduction and repair are reported using codes from the 59200–59350 code range.

2. _____ Normal maternity care includes monthly visits up to 36 weeks of gestation.

3. _____ Services unrelated to pregnancy should be reported using the Evaluation and Management codes.

4. _____ *Chorionic villus* is another term for *placenta*.

5. _____ Obstetrics is the specialty that deals with women during pregnancy, childbirth, and the period immediately following childbirth.

6. _____ The embryo is referred to as the fetus from the first six weeks of pregnancy until birth.

7. _____ Vesicocentesis is reported using 59012.

8. _____ Code 59076 is used to report fetal shunt placement, including ultrasound guidance.

9. _____ Code 59030 would be used to report fetal monitoring during labor.

10. _____ Code 59325 is used to report a hysterorrhaphy of a ruptured uterus.

Vaginal Delivery, Antepartum and Postpartum Care (59400–59430), and Cesarean Delivery (59510–59525)

Codes found in this code range report antepartum care, delivery of the fetus, and postpartum care. Delivery services include any workup performed relative to the admission and management of labor.

Delivery services also include management of a vaginal or cesarean section delivery. A **cesarean section delivery** is a delivery in which there is a surgical procedure (incision) performed through the abdominal wall to extract the fetus. Postpartum services include hospital care and office visits from immediately following birth to six weeks. It should be noted that if your provider renders only part of the care to the mother, the services should not be billed as global and should be broken out to accurately reflect the portion of the services provided.

> **EXAMPLE:** Dr. Carter monitored Mrs. Black's antepartum care for the first five months, which included four visits. Mrs. Black then relocated to another town.

In this example, Dr. Carter would report code 59425 for antepartum care only.

Services such as fetal monitoring during labor, delivery of the placenta, and episiotomy are included in most delivery services and should not be coded separately. Ultrasound, amniocentesis, and other visits for conditions unrelated to the pregnancy are separately billable. Table 15-3 identifies the codes found in code range 59400 to 59430.

TABLE 15-3 Vaginal Delivery, Antepartum Care, and Postpartum Care (59400–59430)

Code(s)	Description
59400	Routine obstetric care, including antepartum care, vaginal delivery (with or without episiotomy and/or forceps), and postpartum care, is reported by this code. Figure 15-2 illustrates the stages of labor and a vaginal delivery.
59409 and 59410	These codes are used to report vaginal delivery.
59412	This code reports external cephalic version, with or without tocolysis. This procedure is performed when a fetus is presenting breech instead of head down. The fetus is turned within the uterus to a cephalic presenting position.
59414	Delivery of placenta is reported with this code. This is a separate procedure code.
59425 and 59426	These codes report antepartum care only, four visits or more. Fewer than four visits would be reported with an Evaluation and Management code.
59430	Postpartum care only—the physician reporting this code would not have performed any of the antepartum care or the delivery. These services would be reported by another physician. This is a separate procedure code.

Table 15-4 identifies the codes that are used to report delivery by cesarean section and associated services.

TABLE 15-4 Cesarean Delivery Services (59510–59525)

Code(s)	Description
59510	Routine obstetric care, including antepartum care, cesarean delivery, and postpartum care.
59514 and 59515	Cesarean delivery only is reported with code 59514 while a cesarean delivery including postpartum care is reported with code 59515.
59525	Subtotal or total hysterectomy after cesarean delivery. Since this is an add-on code, the primary procedure code must be reported first, with this code to follow. This code must be used in conjunction with codes 59510, 59514, 59515, 59618, 59620, and 59622.

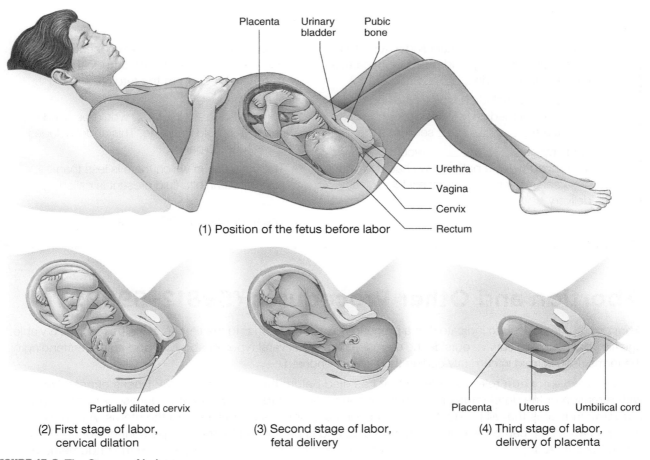

(1) Position of the fetus before labor

Placenta   Urinary bladder   Pubic bone

Urethra
Vagina
Cervix
Rectum

Partially dilated cervix

(2) First stage of labor, cervical dilation

(3) Second stage of labor, fetal delivery

Placenta   Uterus   Umbilical cord

(4) Third stage of labor, delivery of placenta

FIGURE 15-2 The Stages of Labor

Delivery after Previous Cesarean Delivery (59610-59622)

As explained earlier in this chapter, a cesarean delivery is the delivery of a fetus through a surgical incision. Some cesarean deliveries are planned; some are emergency.

The 59610–59614 code range is used to report services rendered to patients who successfully complete a vaginal delivery after a previous cesarean section. The services may also be referred to as **vaginal birth after cesarean (VBAC)**. If the attempt at a vaginal birth is unsuccessful, codes 59618–59622 would be used instead.

Exercise 15.2—Check Your Understanding

Code Range 59000–59622 and terms related to maternity care and delivery

Fill in the blanks in the statements that follow.

1. A delivery in which there is a surgical procedure (incision) performed through the abdominal wall to extract the fetus is called a(n) _____.

2. A hysterectomy performed after a cesarean delivery is reported using CPT add-on code _____.

3. Delivery of the placenta is reported using CPT code _____.

(continues)

Exercise 15.2—*continued*

4. Routine obstetric care, including antepartum care, vaginal delivery, and postpartum care, is reported using code _____.

5. Services that include hospital care and office visits from immediately following birth to six weeks are _____ services.

6. Code range _____ would be referenced when a patient who had a previous cesarean delivery has a successful vaginal delivery.

7. A procedure in which an amniocentesis needle is inserted into the umbilical vessel to obtain blood from the fetus is a(n) _____.

8. CPT code _____ would be used to report fetal fluid drainage. This code includes ultrasound guidance.

9. The condition in which there is less than sufficient amniotic fluid present is called _____.

10. The abbreviation EDC means _____.

Abortion and Other Procedures (59812–59899)

Abortion is a term used to indicate that a pregnancy was ended prior to the time that a fetus reached a viable age (i.e., being able to survive outside the uterus). There are several types of abortion, and an understanding of the terms used will aid in correctly coding the service rendered.

A **missed abortion** refers to a fetus that has died before the completion of 22 weeks of gestation, with retention of the dead fetus or products of conception up to four weeks after demise. An **incomplete abortion** indicates that all products of conception have not been expelled from the uterus. A **legally induced abortion** can be elective or therapeutic, and is performed by medical personnel working within the law. A **septic abortion** is one in which fever and infection are present and the endometrium around the uterus is inflamed. This infection can be life threatening to the mother as well as to the fetus. A **spontaneous abortion** is the complete or incomplete expulsion of the products of conception before a pregnancy goes beyond 22 weeks of gestation. Table 15-5 identifies the codes used to report these services.

Another procedure that may be reported from this code set is **multifetal pregnancy reduction (MPR)**. MPR is a procedure in which one or more fetuses are removed from the uterus in order to increase the chances of the survival of the strongest one. Removal of cerclage suture under anesthesia, uterine evacuation for hydatidiform mole, and unlisted maternity and delivery codes are all found in the 59866–59899 code range.

TABLE 15-5 Abortion Services (59812–59857)

Code(s)	Description
59812	Treatment of incomplete abortion, any trimester, completed surgically—the physician would evacuate any products of conception.
59820 and 59821	Treatment of missed abortion, completed surgically—based on trimester.
59830	Treatment of septic abortion, completed surgically.
59840–59857	Induced abortion—code selection is based on the technique used, as well as whether there was any other procedure performed at the same time.

Summary

- An understanding of the global package for obstetric care is necessary to select the proper codes for services rendered.
- An understanding of terminology is important to proper code assignment.
- Complications that typically would not be part of the regular maternity care should be coded separately using Evaluation and Management codes.
- Cesarean section deliveries can be either planned or emergency.
- VBAC deliveries are those in which a vaginal birth is successfully performed following a cesarean section during a prior pregnancy.
- Abortion treatment can be elective or for treatment following a spontaneous, incomplete, or missed abortion.
- An understanding of the different types of abortion is essential for proper code assignment.

Internet Links

To learn more about pregnancy, childbirth, and postpartum care, visit Dr. Donnica's Women's Health site at *http://www.drdonnica.com*, and the American Congress of Obstetricians and Gynecologists at *http://www.acog.org*.

Chapter Review

True/False

Instructions: Indicate whether the following statements are true (T) or false (F).

1. _____ Antepartum care is the care rendered during the time prior to childbirth.

2. _____ A spontaneous abortion can be elective or therapeutic, and is induced by medical personnel working within the law.

3. _____ Services such as fetal monitoring during labor, delivery of the placenta, and episiotomy are not included in most delivery services and should be coded separately.

4. _____ During the second week through the eighth week of pregnancy, the embryo grows and develops into a fetus.

5. _____ Delivery services include any workup performed relative to the admission and management of labor, as well as ultrasounds performed before the mother goes home from the hospital.

Fill in the Blank

Instructions: Fill in the blanks in the following sentences.

6. The procedure codes used to report obstetric care begin with _____ and go through _____.

7. The acronym VBAC stands for _____.

8. Another term for placenta is a(n) _____.

9. Services that include hospital care and office visits immediately following birth, up to six weeks are called _____ services.

10. A procedure in which one or more fetuses are removed from the uterus in order to increase the chances of the survival of the strongest one is a(n) _____.

Coding Assignments

Instructions: Using the CPT manual, assign the correct code to the following procedures.

1. Fetal nonstress test _____

2. Hysterorrhaphy of ruptured uterus _____

3. Laparoscopic treatment of ectopic pregnancy with salpingectomy _____

4. Vaginal delivery only, with episiotomy _____

5. Treatment of incomplete abortion, second trimester, completed surgically _____

6. Uterine evacuation and curettage for hydatidiform mole _____

7. Induced abortion by dilation and evacuation _____

8. Routine obstetric care, including antepartum care, vaginal delivery, and postpartum care after previous cesarean delivery _____

9. Removal of cerclage suture under general anesthesia _____

10. Multifetal pregnancy reduction _____

11. Fetal shunt placement, including ultrasound guidance _____

12. Antepartum chorionic villus sampling, any method _____

13. Hysterotomy, abdominal _____

14. Transabdominal amnioinfusion, including ultrasound guidance _____

15. Insertion of cervical dilator during obstetric care _____

16. Cerclage of cervix, during pregnancy, vaginal _____

17. Diagnostic amniocentesis _____

18. Routine obstetric care, including antepartum care, cesarean delivery, and postpartum care _____

19. External cephalic version, with tocolysis _____

20. Cesarean delivery only, following attempted vaginal delivery after previous cesarean delivery, including postpartum care _____

21. C-section delivery only _____

22. Antepartum care, five visits _____

23. Postpartum care _____

24. Surgical treatment of missed abortion, first trimester _____

25. Postpartum curettage _____

Case Studies

Instructions: Review each case and indicate the correct code(s).

Case 1

Woman presents in active labor and is admitted for delivery at 41 weeks gestation. Dr. Martin is the covering OB and has never seen the patient until today. Upon check of the cervix, dilation is at 10, and baby is ready to deliver. No type of anesthesia has been given. The fetal monitor is showing a strong, viable fetus. After several pushes, the head appears, and the baby is suctioned immediately. A healthy male child is delivered at 10:08 p.m. Apgar score is 8. Placenta is delivered, no forceps, no episiotomy. Mother and child are doing well. Dr. Martin will not be completing the postpartum care.

CPT code(s): _____

Case 2

A 28-year-old female presents to the emergency room with severe abdominal pain. Upon examination, it is determined that the patient is pregnant, but it is an ectopic pregnancy. The tube is unruptured at this time, so the decision is made to do a laparoscopic resection of the ectopic pregnancy. Laparoscopic technique is used to get to the site. When the area is found, an incision is made in the tube using an electrosurgical technique. Using forceps, the trophoblastic tissue is removed, bleeding is controlled, and the procedure is finished in the usual manner.

CPT code(s): _____

Case 3

Office Note

Diagnosis: Pregnancy at 30 weeks

This 29-year-old patient is 30 weeks pregnant and has been seen by me since she was 8 weeks pregnant. She is moving out of town and is going to be seen by Dr. Nicon in Atlanta, Georgia. Her prenatal records will be sent. At this time, her pregnancy is normal with no complications. She has been seen seven times by me.

Note to billing staff: Please bill patient's insurance at this time.

CPT code(s): _____

Case 4

Office Note

Diagnosis: Normal pregnancy and vaginal delivery

Mrs. Smith delivered a 6-pound, 10-ounce baby girl on 1/10/XX at 1:23 a.m. This is her final postpartum visit. See OB flow sheet for physical findings and record of the antepartum care visits that I completed during her pregnancy.

Note to billing staff: Please bill patient's insurance at this time.

CPT code(s): _____

Case 5

Office Note

Diagnosis: Normal pregnancy followed by attempted vaginal delivery after previous C-section delivery

Mrs. Williams delivered an 8-pound, 12-ounce baby boy on 4/15/XX at 11:11 a.m. via C-section after attempting to deliver the child vaginally. This is her final postpartum visit. See OB flow sheet for physical findings and antepartum visit record.

Note to billing staff: Please bill patient's insurance at this time.

CPT code(s): _____

Case 6

This is a 24-year-old female who has been in active labor for the past 17 hours. The hope was that the labor would progress to a vaginal delivery, but the baby has now turned and is breech. After close observation of the baby through monitoring, the decision was made to perform the cesarean section. I have never seen this patient; she is here visiting from out of town. She is three weeks prior to her due date.

A low transverse abdominal incision was made with a sharp scalpel. The incision was carried through the subcutaneous tissue and the superficial fascia where the incision extended bilaterally. Fascia was grasped with Kocher clamps and undermined with sharp and blunt dissection using Mayo scissors.

Forceps were used to grasp the preperitoneal fascia, which was incised with Metzenbaum scissors until the peritoneal cavity was entered, and the incision extended superiorly and inferiorly.

(continues)

(*continued*)

The Mezenbaum was used to incise a low uterine segment after the bladder was moved to safety with a bladder retractor. Inferior to the peritoneum was then undermined and the bladder retractor replaced in the flap. The low uterine segment was then incised with a sharp scalpel until the intrauterine cavity was entered. The infant was guided to the incision and delivered from the uterus with fundal pressure. The legs were delivered by flexion of the knees, and arms were delivered by rotation of the body. Then the head was delivered. The baby scored 7 on Apgar at 1 minute, and 9 at 5 minutes. Closure of the abdominal incision on the mother was made in layers. Mother and baby were sent to recovery in good condition.

CPT code(s): _____

Case 7

Preoperative diagnosis: Hydatidform mole

Postoperative diagnosis: Same

Indications for surgery: This is a 23-year-old female who presented thinking she might be miscarrying. Her last menstrual cycle was eight weeks ago. She has noted some abdominal pain and now some bleeding. After a pregnancy test, a brief pelvic exam, and ultrasound study, it was determined that she is not pregnant but suffering from a hydatidform mole. The patient is bleeding quite heavily at this time, and there was identification of a hydatid cyst.

Procedure: The patient was taken to the operating room where general anesthesia was administered. She was prepped and draped in the normal sterile fashion, then placed in the dorsal lithotomy position. A weighted speculum was placed in the posterior vagina, and a Deaver retractor was placed anteriorly. At this time, a single-tooth tenaculum was placed in the anterior cervix for retraction. The cervix was then dilated with Hanks dilators to 25 French. A #7 suction curette was inserted without incident. The suction machine appeared to evacuate all cysts, but a curette was manually used with gentle scraping to be sure that all cysts were removed. The curette was gently removed. All instruments were accounted for, and the patient left the operating room in good condition.

CPT code(s): _____

Case 8

Preoperative and postoperative diagnosis: Incomplete spontaneous abortion

Procedure: Treatment of incomplete abortion

This 16-week-pregnant patient was brought to the operating suite and prepped and draped in the usual fashion. A speculum was placed to view the cervix. The cervix was grasped with a tenaculum, and a dilator was inserted into the endocervix. A cannula was passed into the uterus, and a suction machine was used to evacuate the contents by rotating the cannula. To ensure that the uterus was emptied of all contents, a sharp curette was used to scrape the uterine wall. The patient tolerated the procedure and was sent to the recovery area in satisfactory condition.

CPT code(s): _____

Endocrine System

Chapter Outline

Learning Objectives

At the conclusion of this chapter, you should be able to:

1. Define key terms related to coding procedures on the endocrine system.
2. Define abbreviations associated with the endocrine system.
3. Describe the basic anatomy and functions of the endocrine system.
4. Define common procedures completed on the endocrine system.
5. Apply specific coding guidelines for the endocrine system.
6. Select CPT codes for procedures completed on the endocrine system.
7. Identify and code procedures for the endocrine system from case studies.

Key Terms

adrenal glands	hormones	pancreas	thymus gland
endocrine system	hypothyroidism	parathyroid	thyroid gland

Introduction

The **endocrine system** consists of several different internal groups of glands and structures that produce or secrete hormones. **Hormones** are chemical substances produced by the body to keep organs and tissues functioning properly. When structures of the endocrine system are not functioning properly and the hormones are not released as they should be, illness occurs that may require intervention by a physician. The main function of the endocrine system is to keep the body in balance and working properly.

Some of the major structures of the endocrine system and their locations are noted in Figure 16-1. The hormones and their functions are summarized in Table 16-1.

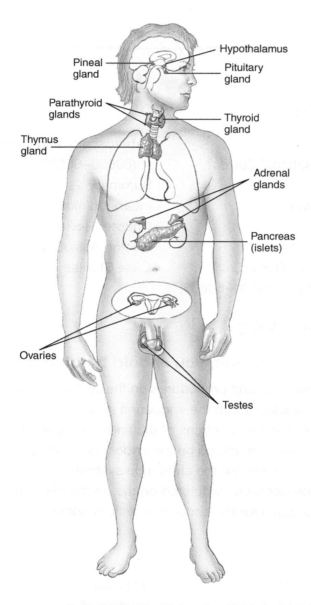

Endocrine system Pituitary, thyroid, parathyroid, thymus, adrenal, and pineal glands, as well as portions of the hypothalamus, pancreas, liver, kidneys, skin, digestive tract, ovaries, testes, and placenta. Also included are hormonal secretions from each gland.

FIGURE 16-1 Endocrine System

TABLE 16-1 Hormones and Functions

Hormone	Functions
Adrenocorticotropic hormone (ACTH)	Stimulates the growth and secretions of the adrenal cortex.
Aldosterone	Aids in regulating the levels of salt and water in the body.
Androgens	Influence sex-related characteristics.
Antidiuretic hormone (ADH)	Helps control blood pressure by reducing the amount of water that is excreted.
Calcitonin	Works with the parathyroid hormone to regulate calcium levels in the blood and tissues.
Cortisol	Regulates the metabolism of carbohydrates, fats, and proteins in the body. Also has an anti-inflammatory action.
Epinephrine	Stimulates the sympathetic nervous system.
Estrogen	Develops and maintains the female secondary sex characteristics and regulates the menstrual cycle.
Follicle-stimulating hormone (FSH)	In the female, stimulates the secretion of estrogen and the growth of ova (eggs). In the male, stimulates the production of sperm.
Glucagon	Increases the level of glucose in the bloodstream.
Growth hormone (GH)	Regulates the growth of bone, muscle, and other body tissues.
Human chorionic gonadotropin (HCG)	Stimulates the secretion of the hormones required to maintain pregnancy.
Insulin (In)	Regulates the transport of glucose to body cells and stimulates the conversion of excess glucose to glycogen for storage.
Lactogenic hormone (LTH)	Stimulates and maintains the secretion of breast milk.
Luteinizing hormone (LH)	In the female, stimulates ovulation. In the male, stimulates testosterone secretion.
Melatonin	Influences the sleep–wakefulness cycles.
Norepinephrine	Stimulates the sympathetic nervous system.
Oxytocin (OXT)	Stimulates uterine contractions during childbirth. Causes milk to flow from the mammary glands after birth.
Parathyroid hormone (PTH)	Works with calcitonin to regulate calcium levels in the blood and tissues.
Progesterone	Completes preparation of the uterus for possible pregnancy.
Testosterone	Stimulates the development of male secondary sex characteristics.
Thymosin	Plays an important role in the immune system.
Thyroid hormones (T4 and T3)	Regulates the rate of metabolism.
Thyroid-stimulating hormone (TSH)	Stimulates the secretion of hormones by the thyroid gland.

Guidelines Related to the National Correct Coding Initiative (NCCI)

Perform the following steps to obtain the most current coding guideline information related to this chapter online.

1. Log on to *www.cms.hhs.gov/NationalCorrectCodInitEd*.
2. Scroll to the section titled "Downloads."
3. Click the link for the most current "NCCI Policy Manual for Medicare Services."
4. A box may appear that requires you to click "Open."
5. Click "Chapter 8" for guidelines specific to the endocrine system.

Abbreviations Associated with the Endocrine System

The following abbreviations are most commonly used in relation to the endocrine system:

Abbreviation	Description
ADH	antidiuretic hormone
ALD	aldosterone
DI	diabetes insipidus
DM	diabetes mellitus
FA	fructosamine test
FBS	fasting blood sugar
GD	Grave's disease
HG	hypoglycemia
IDDM	insulin-dependent diabetes mellitus
NIDDM	non-insulin-dependent diabetes mellitus
TSH	thyroid-stimulating hormone

Thyroid Gland (60000–60300)

Understanding structures of the endocrine system and their particular function in this system will help determine code selection. The **thyroid gland** secretes hormones that regulate growth and metabolism. The thyroid gland is an organ located in the neck with a lobe on either side of the larynx and the trachea. The two lobes are connected by the isthmus. Sometimes the thyroid is not as active as it should be, and a condition known as **hypothyroidism** occurs. The procedure coding for the thyroid gland contains incision, excision, and removal codes. These codes are summarized in Table 16-2.

TABLE 16-2 Thyroid Gland (60000–60300)

Code(s)	Description
60000	This code is used to report the incision and drainage of a thyroglossal duct cyst that is infected. A thyroglossal cyst is also known as a *thyrolingual cysts*.
60100	This code is used to report a biopsy of the thyroid completed via a percutaneous core needle. It should be noted that the CPT manual contains instructional notations that pertain to the assignment of this code when imaging guidance is performed with this procedure, as well as notations that pertain to fine needle aspiration and evaluation of the fine needle aspirate.
60200	Excision of cyst or adenoma of thyroid, or transection of isthmus is reported by use of this code.
60210 and 60212	To report a partial thyroid lobectomy, this range of codes is used. The codes are differentiated by accompanying procedures.
60220 and 60225	Total thyroid lobectomy, unilateral, is reported with these codes, which are differentiated by accompanying procedures.
60240	This code is used to report a thyroidectomy, total or complete.

(continues)

TABLE 16-2 *(continued)*

Code(s)	Description
60252 and 60254	Thyroidectomy, total or subtotal for malignancy, is reported with these codes, which are differentiated by limited neck dissection and radical neck dissection.
60260	Thyroidectomy, removal of all remaining thyroid tissue following previous removal of a portion of thyroid, is reported with this code which is used for the unilateral procedure. For a bilateral procedure, report code 60260 with a modifier of 50.
60270 and 60271	Thyroidectomy, including substernal thyroid, is reported with these codes, which are differentiated by a sternal split or transthoracic approach and a cervical approach.
60280 and 60281	Excision of thyroglossal duct cyst or sinus is reported with these codes. Before code assignment can occur, the coder must be able to determine whether this is a recurrent procedure.
60300	This code is used to report aspiration and/or injection of a thyroid cyst. It should be noted that there are notations following the code that affect code selection.

Parathyroid, Thymus, Adrenal Glands, Pancreas, and Carotid Body (60500–60605)

The **parathyroid** is located along the posterior of the thyroid. There are two parathyroids on each lobe of the thyroid. The parathyroid is another structure that secretes hormones that regulate serum calcium levels. Another structure that should be mentioned is the **pancreas**. The pancreas functions in both the digestive and the endocrine system. In the endocrine system, the pancreas secretes insulin, which is a hormone that regulates blood sugar levels. When the pancreas is not functioning properly, or in some cases not functioning at all, the patient is diagnosed with diabetes mellitus.

The **thymus gland** is located in the middle of the chest, just underneath the sternum. The function of the thymus is to secrete thymosin, which is a hormone that the bone marrow needs to produce T cells that work with the immune system.

The **adrenal glands** sit atop the kidneys. Their function is to regulate electrolytes and help in the metabolism of glucose and adrenaline, which plays an important role in heart and lung function. Procedures that are completed on the parathyroid, thymus, adrenal glands, pancreas, and carotid body are assigned to code range 60500–60605 and are summarized in Table 16-3.

TABLE 16-3 Parathyroid, Thymus, Adrenal Glands, Pancreas, and Carotid Body (60500–60605)

Code(s)	Description
60500–60505	Parathyroidectomy or exploration of parathyroid(s) is assigned to these codes. The codes are divided according to whether the procedure was initially completed, completed for reexploration, or with mediastinal exploration, sternal split, or transthoracic approach.
60512	This code reports a parathyroid autotransplantation and is an add-on code that is listed separately, in addition to the code for the primary procedure completed. Code 60512 can be used with codes 60500, 60502, 60505, 60212, 60225, 60240, 60252, 60254, 60260, 60270, and 60271.
60520–60522	A thymectomy, partial or total, is reported with these codes. All of these codes are separate procedure codes and therefore should not be reported with any other code from the endocrine system. The codes are differentiated by the approach.
60540 and 60545	An adrenalectomy, partial or complete, or exploration of adrenal gland with or without biopsy, transabdominal, lumbar or dorsal, is assigned to these codes. Code 60540 is a separate procedure code. It should be noted that there are numerous instructional notations that appear in the CPT manual in regard to these codes. Review these instructional notations in the CPT manual.
60600 and 60605	Codes 60600 and 60605 are used to report the excision of a carotid body tumor. The codes are differentiated by whether there was also an excision of a carotid artery.

Laparoscopy and Other Procedures (60650–60699)

There are two codes that are used to report laparoscopic procedures completed on the endocrine system. Code 60650 is used to report a surgical laparoscopy:

- With adrenalectomy, partial or complete. During this procedure, a laparoscope is used to view or remove the adrenal gland.
- The exploration of an adrenal gland with or without biopsy, transabdominal, lumbar, or dorsal.

Code 60659 is the second laparoscopic procedure code. This code is used to report any other laparoscopic procedure that is completed on the endocrine system.

The final code in the endocrine system section is code 60699, which is used to report any unlisted procedure not found in this subsection.

Summary

- The endocrine system consists of several different internal groups of glands and structures that produce or secrete hormones.
- Procedures completed on the endocrine system are assigned to CPT codes 60000–60699.
- The thyroid gland secretes hormones that regulate growth and metabolism.
- The parathyroid, located along the posterior of the thyroid, is another structure that secretes hormones that regulate serum calcium levels.
- The thymus gland is located in the middle of the chest, just underneath the sternum, and secretes thymosin.
- The function of the adrenal glands is to regulate electrolytes, help in the metabolism of glucose, and perform an important role in heart and lung function.

Internet Links

To learn more about the endocrine system and procedures completed on this system, visit the sites below and search on procedures discussed in this chapter:

- *http://www.medterms.com*
- *http://www.endocrine.org*
- *http://www.mayoclinic.com*

Chapter Review

Fill in the Blank

Instructions: Fill in the blanks in the statements that follow.

1. Chemical substances produced by the body to keep organs and tissues functioning properly are known as

   _____.

2. The gland that sits atop the kidneys is called the _____.

3. In the endocrine system, the pancreas secretes a hormone that regulates blood sugar levels. This hormone is called _____.

4. The function of the thymus is to secrete a hormone that the bone marrow needs to produce T cells that work with the immune system. This hormone is called _____.

5. Code 60500 is used to report an exploration of the parathyroid(s) or a(n) _____.

True/False

Instructions: Indicate whether the following statements are true (T) or false (F).

6. _____ Cortisol stimulates uterine contractions during childbirth.

7. _____ Norepinephrine stimulates the somatic nervous system.

8. _____ The thymus gland sits in the middle of the chest just under the sternum.

9. _____ The code used to report a complete thyroidectomy is 60240.

10. _____ A parathyroid autotransplantation is reported using 60300.

Coding Assignments

Instructions: Using the CPT manual, assign the correct code to each of the following procedures.

1. Excision of a carotid body tumor without excision of the carotid artery _____

2. Transcervical partial thymectomy _____

3. Complete thyroidectomy _____

4. Aspiration of thyroid cyst _____

5. Excision of thyroid cyst _____

6. Excision of thyroglossal duct cyst _____

7. Dorsal complete adrenalectomy _____

8. Exploration of parathyroid with transthoracic mediastinal exploration _____

9. Total unilateral thyroid lobectomy _____

10. Sternal split thyroidectomy, including substernal thyroid _____

11. Laparoscopic adrenalectomy _____

12. Total thyroidectomy with radical dissection of neck to treat malignancy _____

13. Partial thymectomy with radical mediastinal dissection, sternal split approach _____

14. Unilateral thyroidectomy following previous removal of a portion of the thyroid _____

15. Partial unilateral thyroid lobectomy with isthmusectomy _____

Case Studies

Instructions: Review each case and indicate the correct code(s).

Case 1

Patient presents with pain and swelling in the neck area, abnormal TSH, and other symptoms of an abnormally functioning thyroid. After examination, the physician is unclear as to what the problem is and sends the patient to a surgeon.

(continues)

(*continued*)

The surgeon reviews tests, finds an area of swelling, and suspects a tumor. A biopsy is performed, and a stat pathology report confirms that there is a malignant mass forming on the thyroid. A complete thyroidectomy is performed, leaving the parathyroid glands intact. The wound is closed, and the patient tolerates the procedure well.

CPT code(s): _____

Case 2

Patient presents, after study, with a mass on the thyroid. It was determined that a biopsy of the thyroid should be completed. The thyroid was located by palpation. A large, hollow percutaneous core needle was passed through the skin into the thyroid. The needle was used to remove the tissue. The tissue was sent to pathology for examination. The patient tolerated the procedure well and was sent to the recovery area.

CPT code(s): _____

Case 3

Preoperative diagnosis: Small mass on left adrenal

Postoperative diagnosis: 5-cm malignant neoplasm, left adrenal

Procedure: Adrenalectomy, left

Patient was prepped and draped in the usual sterile fashion. A 5-mm, 30-degree scope was used in conjunction with two more 5-mm ports and one 11-mm port. Spleen, colon, and pancreas were all carefully checked and showed no signs of disease. The adrenal was identified, and all vessels leading to the adrenal were taken down carefully and without incident using a Harmonic scalpel. The mass was identified. The left adrenal was carefully dissected and dropped easily into the bag, which was removed through the 11-mm port site. The kidney was examined, and no sign of disease was noted, so we left the area. The port sites were closed, and the patient was taken to the recovery area in good condition.

CPT code(s): _____

Case 4

Preoperative diagnosis: Hyperparathyroidism, primary

Postoperative diagnosis: Same

Procedure performed: Parathyroidectomy, left side

Procedure: The patient was prepped and draped in the usual sterile fashion. We proceeded with a transverse collar incision on the left. Dissection went through the subcutaneous tissue until the platysma muscles were identified. A subplatysma flap was created, and strap muscles were divided along the midline. The thyroid gland was identified and slightly rotated into position so that the parathyroid on the left was easily identified. The parathyroid was enlarged and somewhat calcified. This calcification allowed for easy removal of the parathyroid without damage to the thyroid gland itself. The surrounding structures were left in good condition, and the neck wound was closed in a layered fashion. The patient left the surgical suite in excellent condition and was taken to recovery.

CPT code(s): _____

Case 5

Preoperative diagnosis: Right thyroid nodule

Postoperative diagnosis: Same

Procedure: Right thyroid lobectomy

Procedure performed: This 42-year-old female was placed supine on the operating table. General anesthesia was induced, after which the neck was prepped and draped with Betadine. A transverse incision was made in the skin fold on the right side of the neck, and was carried down through the skin and subcutaneous tissues. The platysma and strap muscles were divided, and subplatysmal flaps were then raised. The 4.5-cm thyroid nodule was encountered posteriorly on the nerve. It was then necessary to ligate the inferior thyroid artery and vein, the middle thyroid vein, and the superior thyroid artery and vein. The gland was then rotated medially for better access to the nodule. A Harmonic scalpel was used to remove the nodule encompassing the right lobe, which was sent for pathology. The pathology came back as a benign colloid goiter. The left side of the thyroid as well as the parathyroids were left intact. The strap muscles were closed with 3-0 Vicryl, as was the platysma. The skin was then closed with subcuticular 4-0 Vicryl, Benzoin, Steri-Strips, and dressings were applied.

The patient left the operating room in good condition for the recovery room.

CPT code(s): _____

Case 6

Preoperative diagnosis: Thyroglossal duct cyst

Postoperative diagnosis: Same

Anesthesia: General

Procedural Notes:

This 34-year-old male patient was placed in the supine position. He was then placed under general anesthesia, and his neck was prepped and draped in the usual fashion and then flexed for the procedure. The skin around the cyst was circumferentially incised, and the cyst and duct were dissected free to the level of the hyoid bone. The midpoint of the hyoid bone was then excised. A 3-0 plain catgut triple-strand suture was then used to ligate the thyroglossal duct. Iris scissors were used to remove the cyst, and hemostasis was obtained. The wound site was closed in layers. No significant blood loss occurred. The patient was in stable condition and sent to the recovery area.

CPT code(s): _____

Nervous System

Chapter Outline

Learning Objectives

At the conclusion of this chapter, you should be able to:

1. Define key terms related to coding procedures on the nervous system.
2. Define abbreviations associated with the nervous system.
3. Describe the basic anatomy of the nervous system.
4. Define common procedures completed on the nervous system.
5. Apply the specific coding guidelines for the nervous system.
6. Select CPT codes for procedures completed on the nervous system.
7. Identify and code procedures for the nervous system from case studies.

Key Terms

arachnoid mater

autonomic nervous
    system

brain

brain stem

burr hole
    procedures

central nervous system

cerebellum

cerebral cortex

cerebrum

craniectomy

craniotomy

diencephalon

dura mater

endovascular therapy

meninges

mesencephalon

midbrain

peripheral nervous
    system

pia mater

somatic nervous system

spinal nerves

trephine

Introduction

The nervous system is composed of the brain, spinal cord, and peripheral nerves. Within CPT, procedures that are completed on these structures, as well as the skull, meninges, extracranial nerves, and autonomic nervous system, are assigned to codes in the 61000–64999 code range.

Guidelines Related to the National Correct Coding Initiative (NCCI)

The student will need to perform the following steps to obtain the most current coding guideline information related to this chapter online:

1. Log on to *http://www.cms.hhs.gov/NationalCorrectCodInitEd*.
2. Scroll to the section titled "Downloads."
3. Click "NCCI Policy Manual for Medicare Services."
4. A box may appear that requires you to click "Open."
5. Click "Chapter 8" for guidelines specific to the nervous system.

Abbreviations Associated with the Nervous System

These abbreviations are the more common abbreviations used for the nervous system:

Abbreviation	Definition
ANS	autonomic nervous system
CNS	central nervous system
CSF	cerebral spinal fluid
CT	computed tomography
EEG	electroencephalogram
EMG	electromyogram
ICP	intracranial pressure
LP	lumbar puncture
PNS	peripheral nervous system
TENS	transcutaneous electrical nerve stimulation

Anatomy of the Nervous System

The structures that comprise the nervous system are responsible for the communication and control of the body. The nervous system is divided into two systems: the **central nervous system**, which comprises the brain and spinal cord, and the **peripheral nervous system**, which comprises the nerves that connect the body organs to the central nervous system.

The peripheral nervous system is divided into two systems:

- **Somatic nervous system**, which connects the central nervous system to the skin and skeletal muscles via the cranial and spinal nerves.
- **Autonomic nervous system**, which connects the central nervous system to the visceral organs via the cranial and spinal nerves.

Figure 17-1 illustrates the central nervous system and the peripheral nervous system.

The **brain** has more than 100 billion neurons that are connected by means of electrochemical pulses, and it is responsible for all physical and mental functions of the body. The protective tissue that covers the brain and

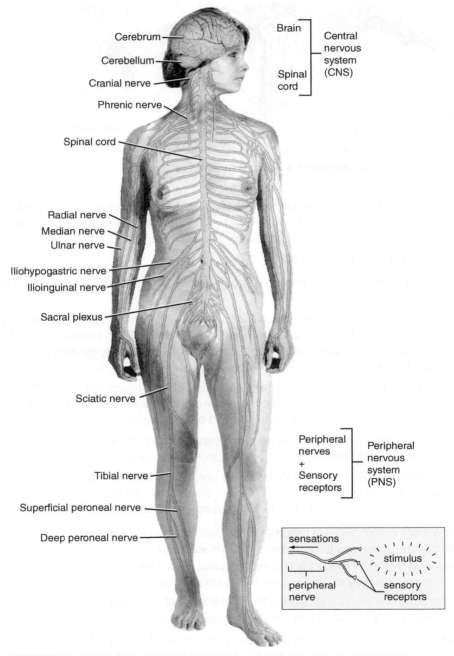

FIGURE 17-1 The Peripheral Nervous System Connects the Central Nervous System to the Structures of the Body

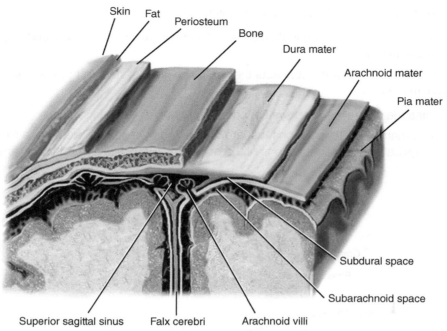

FIGURE 17-2 **Meninges and Related Structures**

spinal cord is the **meninges**. The outermost layer of the meninges is the **dura mater**, the middle layer of the meninges is the **arachnoid mater**, and the innermost layer is the **pia mater**. Figure 17-2 illustrates the meninges and related structures.

The brain is composed of the following areas:

- **Cerebral cortex**—consists of a layer of neurons on the surface of the brain. The cerebral cortex is made up of gray matter.
- **Cerebrum**—the largest part of the brain, which is separated by depressions and grooves and is divided into separate hemispheres by a groove called the *longitudinal fissure.* Each hemisphere is divided into four lobes. Each lobe has a different functional distinction. Figure 17-3 illustrates the lobes and functions of the cerebrum, brain stem, and cerebellum.
- **Cerebellum**—the second-largest part of the brain, separated from the cerebrum by the transverse fissure and the tentorium cerebelli. This part of the brain coordinates skeletal muscle movements and learning new motor skills. Injury to the cerebellum may affect coordination and balance depending on the severity of the trauma.
- **Diencephalon**—this structure is located between the cerebrum and the midbrain. The primary structures found in this area include the thalamus, hypothalamus, posterior pituitary gland, and pineal gland.
- **Brain stem**—connects the diencephalon to the spinal cord. Structures of the brain stem include the medulla oblongata, pons, and midbrain. The **midbrain**, also known as the **mesencephalon**, is located between the diencephlon and the pons. Figure 17-4 illustrates the brain stem.

The spinal cord is a column of nervous tissue that runs within the vertebral canal of the vertebra. The spinal cord's function is to conduct impulses to and from the brain and to serve as a reflex center for the body. The spinal cord is surrounded by the meninges and cerebral spinal fluid. When cross-sectioned, the spinal cord reveals areas of both white and gray matter. Figure 17-5 illustrates the white and gray matter of the spinal cord.

There are 31 pairs of **spinal nerves** located in the spinal area. Most spinal nerves are named for the corresponding vertebrae. Figure 17-6 illustrates the spinal cord and the spinal nerves.

There are 12 pairs of cranial nerves that originate from underneath the brain. The cranial nerves are named for the area or function that they serve and are identified by Roman numerals. Figure 17-7 identifies the Roman numerals and names used for each cranial nerve.

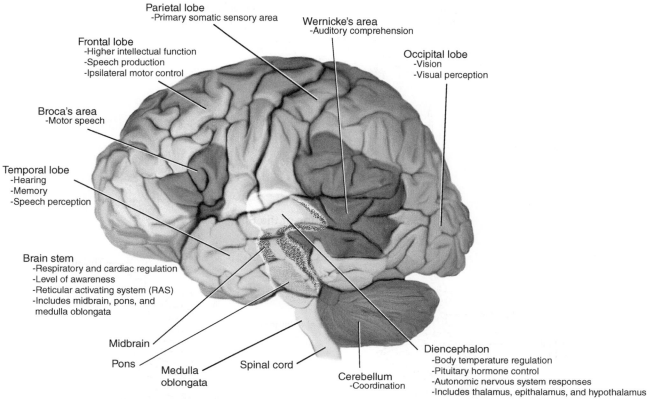

FIGURE 17-3 Functions of the Cerebrum, Brain Stem, and Cerebellum

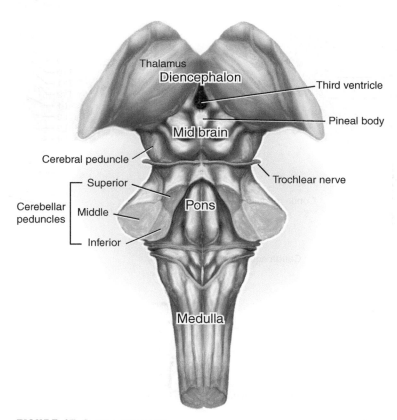

FIGURE 17-4 The Brain Stem

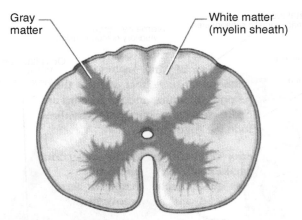

FIGURE 17-5 Cross-Section of the Spinal Cord

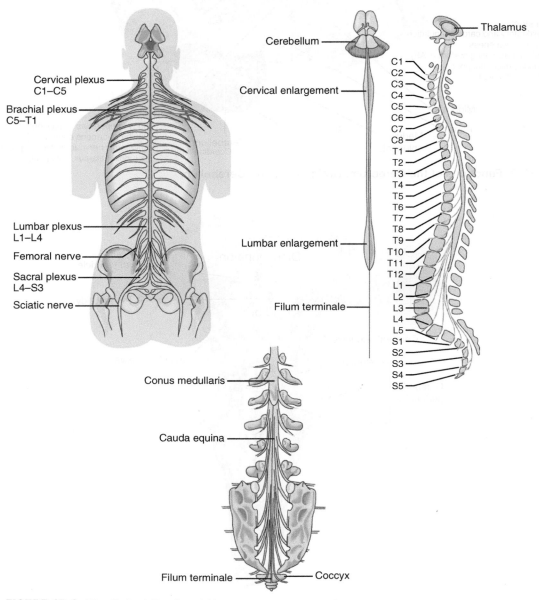

FIGURE 17-6 The Spinal Cord and Nerves

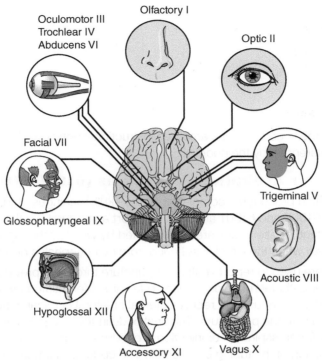

Oculomotor III
Trochlear IV
Abducens VI

Olfactory I

Optic II

Facial VII

Trigeminal V

Glossopharyngeal IX

Acoustic VIII

Hypoglossal XII

Accessory XI

Vagus X

FIGURE 17-7 Cranial Nerves Are Identified by Roman Numerals and Are Named for the Area or Function They Serve

Procedures Completed on the Nervous System (61000–64999)

The codes for the nervous system are divided into three areas:

- Skull, meninges, and brain—code range 61000–62258
- Spine and spinal cord—code range 62263–63746
- Extracranial nerves, peripheral nerves, and autonomic nervous system—code range 64400–64999

Skull, Meninges, and Brain (61000–62258)

This first range of codes, codes 61000–62258, is divided into the following:

- Injection, drainage, or aspiration
- Twist drill, burr holes, or trephine
- Craniectomy or craniotomy
- Surgery of skull base
  - Approach procedures—anatomical area involved
  - Definitive procedures—i.e., biopsy, resection, repair, etc.
  - Repair and/or reconstruction of surgical defects of skull base—reported if certain procedures are performed as outlined in CPT
- Endovascular therapy
- Surgery for aneurysm, arteriovenous malformation, or vascular disease

- Stereotaxis
- Stereotactic Radiosurgery (Cranial)
- Neurostimulators (intracranial)
- Repair
- Neuroendoscopy
- Cerebrospinal fluid (CSF) shunt

Prior to the description of these codes, there are three instructional notations that relate to injection procedures and should be referenced by the coder.

Injections, Drainage, or Aspiration Procedures (61000–61070)

Injections, drainage, or aspiration procedures completed on the skull, meninges, and brain are reported with codes 61000–61070. Codes 61000 and 61001 are used to report a subdural tap through fontanelle, or suture, unilateral or bilateral, for an infant. These codes are differentiated by whether the tap was an initial or subsequent tap. Taps are usually performed when the infant is suffering from hydrocephalus or has a diagnosis of meningitis.

Codes 61020 and 61026 are used to report ventricular puncture through a previous burr hole, fontanelle, suture, or implanted ventricular catheter/reservoir. These codes are differentiated by whether an injection occurred. Codes 61050 and 61055 are used to report cisternal or lateral cervical puncture and are differentiated by whether injections occurred with the procedure. The final code in this section is assigned for puncture for shunt tubing or a reservoir for an aspiration or injection procedure, code 61070. This procedure may be performed to evaluate the function of the tubing or reservoir. The coder is instructed to reference code 75809 for radiological intervention if necessary.

Twist Drill, Burr Hole(s), or Trephine (61105–61253)

Codes 61105 to 61108 are used to report a twist drill hole for punctures. Code 61105 reports a twist drill hole for subdural or ventricular puncture. Codes 61107 and 61108 report twist drill hole(s) for subdural, intracerebral or ventricular punctures and are differentiated by the accompanying procedures that are completed.

Burr hole(s) procedures are reported with codes 61120–61253. During **burr hole procedures**, the physician drills a burr hole in the cranium to complete the procedure, which could include a biopsy of a brain or intracranial lesion, drainage of a brain abscess or cyst, tapping of an abscess or cyst, drainage of a hematoma, and other brain or intracranial procedures. A **trephine** is a surgical instrument that is used to cut a cylindrical shape. This, at times, is used for cutting holes in bone. Figure 17-8 illustrates the creation of burr holes.

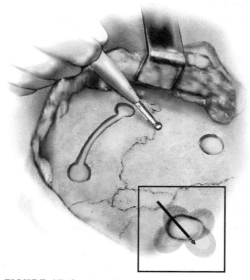

FIGURE 17-8 Burr Holes

Craniectomy or Craniotomy (61304–61576)

A **craniectomy** is completed to remove a skull bone, while a **craniotomy** involves simply making an incision into the skull without removal of bone. Codes 61304 to 61576 are used to report these procedures. CPT codes 61304 or 61305 should not be reported separately when there is a more extensive craniectomy or craniotomy procedure being performed in the same operative session. The codes are differentiated according to the reason for the craniectomy or craniotomy. For example, code 61314 is used to report a craniectomy or craniotomy for the evacuation of a hematoma, while code 61321 is used to report a craniectomy or craniotomy for the drainage of an intracranial abscess located in the infratenorial region. To become familiar with this range of codes, complete the following exercise.

Exercise 17.1—Check Your Understanding

Code Range 61000–61576

Complete the description of each code listed. The first one is completed for you.

Code	Description	Code	Description
1. 61557	Craniotomy for craniosynostosis; bifrontal bone flap	5. 61570	_____
		6. 61105	_____
		7. 61333	_____
2. 61533	_____	8. 61517	_____
3. 61550	_____	9. 61501	_____
4. 61558	_____	10. 61566	_____

Surgery of Skull Base (61580–61619)

Codes 61580 to 61619 are used to report procedures that are completed on the base of the skull. These are extensive procedures that typically involve more than one surgeon. The procedure can have three components: the approach, the definitive procedure, and repair or reconstruction. At times, one physician may complete more than one component. When this occurs, the physician should report the codes and add a modifier of 51 to the secondary and/or additional procedure.

> **EXAMPLE:** Dr. Smith completed the craniofacial approach to the anterior cranial fossa and used code 61580 to report this portion of the procedure. He completed the definitive procedure, an extradural excision of a neoplastic lesion, and reported code 61600-51.

When different surgeons perform different components, each surgeon reports the code for the component that he or she completed.

> **EXAMPLE:** Dr. Smith completed the craniofacial approach to the anterior cranial fossa and reported code 61580.
>
> Dr. Jones completed the definitive procedure, an extradural excision of a neoplastic lesion, and reported code 61600.

The repair codes 61618 and 61619 are reported separately when extensive dural grafting, cranioplasty, local or regional myocutaneous pedicle flaps, or extensive skin grafts are required.

Endovascular Therapy (61623–61651)

Code range 61623 to 61651 is used to report endovascular therapy. **Endovascular therapy** is completed within the vascular system of the head or neck for a specific purpose, such as to control bleeding, destroy a tumor, achieve hemostasis for a bleeding aneurysm, control blood flow during intracranial or extracranial procedures, and for other reasons. These codes are differentiated by the type of endovascular therapy, such as balloon angioplasty or balloon dilation. Some of the codes are further differentiated according to the location or the number of vessels on which the procedure was completed. Codes 61645, 61650, and 61651 report cerebral endovascular therapeutic interventions in any intracranial artery. Code 61651 is an add-on code. Review and follow the instructional notations that appear in the CPT manual after the code description prior to reporting these codes.

Surgery for Aneurysm, Arteriovenous Malformation, or Vascular Disease (61680–61711)

To report surgery for aneurysm, arteriovenous malformation, or vascular disease, codes 61680 through 61711 should be used. To reference these codes in the Alphabetical Index of the CPT manual, the following terms should be located:

- Aneurysm repair, then carotid artery
- Aneurysm repair, then intracranial artery
- Arteriovenous malformation, then cranial repair
- Vascular malformation, then cerebral repair

Codes 61680 to 61692 are used to report surgery of intracranial arteriovenous malformation. For these procedures, the surgeon is resecting an arteriovenous malformation in the brain. To select a code from this range, the coder must determine the tumor location and the complexity of accessing the tumor, simple or complex. Documentation should justify the selection of the codes that describe the procedure completed as complex.

> **EXAMPLE:** Dr. Black performed a craniotomy after angiography located a tumor of the blood vessels. The infratentorial area where the vessels were located was extremely difficult to access. The vessels feeding the tumor took time to ligate. The tumor was removed, bleeding was controlled, and the bone flap was secured.

This procedure is reported using CPT code 61686.

Stereotaxis (61720–61791)

Stereotactic procedures completed on the brain are reported with codes 61720 to 61791. During stereotactic procedures, a computed tomography (CT) or magnetic resonance imaging (MRI) scan is used to scan the brain to locate the area of the brain in which the procedure will be performed. Burr holes are then used to access the brain to insert a needle, electrodes, catheters, or probes. This range of codes is differentiated by the procedure performed and the reason for the procedure.

Stereotactic Radiosurgery (Cranial) (61796–61800)

This range of codes is used to report a procedure that uses externally generated ionizing radiation to eradicate specific targets in the head. No surgical incision is necessary. These codes would be reported by the neurosurgeon. The oncologist would report the appropriate 70000 codes for treatment delivery and management. Extensive instructional notes are present in the CPT manual.

Neurostimulators, Intracranial (61850–61888)

Codes 61850 to 61888 are used to report procedures that involve both simple and complex neurostimulators. The codes are differentiated by the type of approach (twist drill, burr hole or craniotomy, craniectomy, and so on) and the type of neurostimulator placed. This range also contains codes for the insertion, replacement, revision, and removal of neurostimulators. There are coding guidelines located at the beginning of this code range that must be read and followed for proper code assignment.

Repairs (62000–62148)

Repairs completed on the skull and skull vault are reported with codes 62000–62148. Terms to reference in the Alphabetical Index of the CPT manual include:

- Craniotomy, then encephalocele
- Repair, then encephalocele

- Cranioplasty
- Cranioplasty, then encephalocele
- Cranioplasty, then defect
- Cranioplasty, then autograft
- Cranioplasty, then bone graft

Neuroendoscopy (62160–62165)

Neuroendoscopy procedures are reported with codes 62160 to 62165. A diagnostic neuroendoscopy is included in a surgical neuroendoscopy. The codes are differentiated by the reason for the neuroendoscopy, which may include:

- Dissection of adhesions
- Fenestration of septum pellucidum
- Excision of cyst
- Retrieval of foreign body
- Excision of tumor

Cerebrospinal Fluid (CSF) Shunt (62180–62258)

Procedures that involve cerebrospinal fluid shunts are reported with codes 62180 to 62258. Cerebrospinal fluid shunts are placed to drain cerebrospinal fluid away from the brain. Figure 17-9 illustrates a cerebrospinal fluid shunt. This range of codes also reports replacement, irrigation, and removal of CSF shunts.

Spine and Spinal Cord (62263–63746)

Procedures completed on the spine and spinal cord are reported with codes 62263 to 63746. In the CPT manual prior to code 62263 there are extensive instructional notations for the coder to review before assigning codes

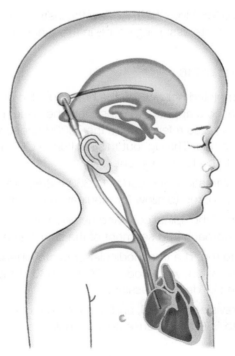

FIGURE 17-9 CSF Shunt

from this section of the manual. Locate and read the instructional notations found in the CPT manual. The codes are divided into the following areas:

- Injection, drainage, or aspiration (including codes for myelography via lumbar injection)—codes 62263 to 62329.
- Catheter implantation—codes 62350 to 62355.
- Reservoir/pump implantation—codes 62360 to 62370.
- Endoscopic decompression of neural elements and/or excision of herniated intervertebral discs—code 62380. Review the definitions that are found in the CPT manual prior to code 62380 before assigning this code.
- Posterior extradural laminotomy or laminectomy for exploration/decompression of neural elements or excision of herniated intervertebral discs—codes 63001 to 63051. Review the definitions that are found in the CPT manual prior to code 63001 before assigning codes from this range of codes.
- Transpedicular or costovertebral approach for posterolateral extradural exploration/decompression—codes 63055 to 63066.
- Anterior or anterolateral approach for extradural exploration/decompression—codes 63075 to 63091. Review the instructional notations that are found in the CPT manual prior to code 63075 before assigning codes from this range.
- Lateral extracavitary approach for extradural exploration/decompression—codes 63101 to 63103.
- Incision—codes 63170 to 63200.
- Excision by laminectomy of lesion other than herniated disc—codes 63250 to 63295.
- Excision, anterior or anterolateral approach, intraspinal lesion—codes 63300 to 63308. Review the instructional notations found in the CPT manual prior to code 63300 before assigning codes from this range of codes.
- Stereotaxis—codes 63600 to 63610.
- Stereotactic radiosurgery (spinal)—codes 63620 and 63621. Review the instructional notations that are found in the CPT manual prior to code 63620 before assigning codes in this range of codes.
- Neurostimulators (spinal)—codes 63650 to 63688. Review the instructional notations that are found in the CPT manual prior to code 63650 before assigning codes in this range of codes.
- Repair—codes 63700 to 63710.
- Shunt, spinal CSF—codes 63740 to 63746.

Many of these procedures are completed not only on the brain but also on the spine and spinal cord. Prior to code 62263, an extensive instructional note appears that instructs the coder in the use of codes 62263 to 62329 for catheter-based treatments. There are also references to the 70000 codes for radiological services that might be used in conjunction with this code range. Throughout this section of CPT, there are numerous instructional notes that should be referenced prior to code assignment.

Codes 62350–62351, catheter implantation, and codes 62360–62362, reservoir/pump implantation, are used to report the placement of a catheter or pump to allow for medication instillation into the spinal area.

Exploration and/or decompression of the spinal cord and nerve roots are reported with codes 63001–63051 and are differentiated by the type of approach and segment of the spinal area in which the procedure occurred.

Codes 63055 to 63066 are used to report a transpedicular or costovertebral approach for posterolateral extradural exploration and/or decompression, while codes 63075 to 63091 report an anterior or anterolateral approach for extradural exploration and/or decompression.

Procedures involving placement, revision, removal, and replacement of neurostimulators in the spinal cord area are reported with codes 63650 to 63688. Because neurostimulators are also placed in the brain, it is important for the coder to read the operative report carefully to determine the site of the neurostimulator. Codes 63700 to 63710 report repairs on the spinal cord. Shunt procedures involving cerebral spinal fluid, such as creation of shunts, and replacement and removals of shunt systems are reported with codes 63740, 63741, 63744, and 63746.

Extracranial Nerves, Peripheral Nerves, and Autonomic Nervous System (64400–64999)

Procedures completed on the extracranial nerves, peripheral nerves, and autonomic nervous system are reported with codes 64400 to 64999. This range of codes is divided into the following areas:

- Introduction/injection of anesthetic agent (nerve block), diagnostic or therapeutic—code range 64400 to 64530. This section of codes is differentiated by procedures completed on the somatic nerves and procedures completed on the autonomic nerves. Codes 64461, 64462, and 64463 are contained within this range of codes but are resequenced codes. These codes report thoracic paravertebral blocks and codes 64461 aand 64462 are differentiated by the number of injection sites, while code 64463 reports a continuous infusion by a catheter. They include imaging guidance when performed.
- Neurostimulators (peripheral nerves)—code range 64553 to 64595. This section is used to report the implantation of neurostimulator electrodes and is differentiated by the type of procedure completed and by the nerve on which the procedure was completed.
- Destruction by neurolytic agent (e.g., chemical, thermal, electrical, or radiofrequency, chemodenervation)—code range 64600 to 64681. This section of codes is differentiated by the destruction of somatic nerves and sympathetic nerves.
- Neuroplasty (exploration, neurolysis, or nerve decompression)—code range 64702 to 64727. These codes are differentiated by the anatomical site of the nerve (e.g., digit, arm, or leg).
- Transection or avulsion—code range 64732 to 64772. These codes are organized according to the nerve location.
- Excision—code range 64774 to 64823. Division of codes in this range is organized according to somatic nerves and sympathetic nerves.
- Neurorrhaphy—code range 64831 to 64876. These codes are used to report the suturing of nerves and are differentiated by the nerve sutured.
- Neurorrhaphy with nerve graft, vein graft, or conduit—code range 64885 to 64913. These codes are used to report nerve grafts and are differentiated by the site and the length of the graft.

When coding procedures that are completed on the nerves, the coder must identify the specific nerve on which the procedure was completed. Coding in this area can be complex, so coders are cautioned to read every detail of medical documentation pertaining to the procedure and all guidelines associated wtih the particular section of this chapter being referenced.

Summary

- The central nervous system is composed of the brain and spinal cord.
- The peripheral nervous system is composed of the nerves that connect body organs to the central nervous system.
- There are 31 pairs of spinal nerves located in the spinal area.
- A craniectomy is completed to remove a skull bone.
- A craniotomy involves making an incision into the skull.

Internet Links

To learn more about the nervous system and procedures completed on the nervous system, visit *http://www.innerbody.com*.

To view information about nerve injections, visit *http://www.spineuniverse.com*.

To learn about multiple types of spinal surgeries, visit *http://www.spinalcompression.com*.

Chapter Review

Fill in the Blank

Instructions: Fill in the blanks in the statements that follow.

1. The diencephalon is connected to the spinal cord by the _____.

2. The outermost layer of the meninges is the _____.

3. The middle layer of the meninges is the _____.

4. The innermost layer of the meninges is the _____.

5. The procedure to remove the skull bone is called a _____.

True/False

Instructions: Indicate whether the following statements are true (T) or false (F).

6. _____ The largest portion of the brain is the cerebellum.

7. _____ The temporal lobe is where the nerves related to hearing, memory, and speech perception are located.

8. _____ The brachial plexus extends from the C1 vertebrae to the T3 vertebrae.

9. _____ Stereotactic procedures completed on the brain are reported using codes 61720 to 61750.

10. _____ The mesencephalon is located between the midbrain and the cerebrum.

Coding Assignments

Instructions: Using the CPT manual, assign the correct code to the following procedures.

1. Craniectomy for drainage of intracranial abscess, infratentorial _____

2. Craniotomy for repair of encephalocele at skull base _____

3. Intradural cervical laminectomy for excision of intraspinal lesion _____

4. Repair of cerebrospinal fluid leak not requiring a laminectomy _____

5. Repair of 6.3-cm myelomeningocele _____

6. Laminectomy for excision of an intraspinal intradural neoplasm in the sacral (intradural) area _____

7. Stereotactic stimulation of spinal cord, percutaneous, separate procedure not followed by other surgery _____

8. Ventriculocisternostomy _____

9. Replacement of ventricular catheter _____

10. Removal of prosthetic plate of skull

_____

11. Craniectomy for implantation of neurostimulator cerebellar electrodes in the cortical area _____

12. Subtemporal cranial decompression

_____

13. Stereotactic implantation of depth electrodes into the cerebrum for the long-term monitoring of seizure activity _____

14. Percutaneous intracranial balloon angioplasty

_____

15. Supratentorial exploratory craniotomy

_____

16. Burr hole for aspiration of intracerebral cyst

_____

17. Puncture of shunt tubing for injection procedure

_____

18. Intracranial craniotomy for hypophysectomy of pituitary tumor _____

19. Craniectomy with excision of foreign body from brain _____

20. Epidural injection of clot patch

_____

21. Transcranial decompression of orbit

_____

22. Reduction of craniomegalic skull

_____

23. Removal of spinal neurostimulator electrode percutaneous array _____

24. Injection of anesthetic agent into maxillary trigeminal nerve _____

25. Facial-spinal accessory nerve anastomosis

_____

26. Infratentorial exploratory craniotomy

_____

27. Craniotomy with elevation of bone flap for selective amygdalohippocampectomy

_____

28. Simple extradural elevation of depressed skull fracture _____

29. Cranioplasty for 3.5 cm diameter skull defect

_____

30. Spinal epidural injection of blood clot

_____

Case Studies

Instructions: Review each case and indicate the correct code(s).

Case 1

Preoperative and postoperative diagnosis: Lower back pain

Procedure: Injection of 6% phenol into L4

The patient was placed in the spinal tap position, and the lumbar area was sterilized. An epidural needle was advanced into the L4 space, 2% Lidocaine was injected, and an epidural catheter was placed; 1.5 cc of 6% phenol was injected into the space. The catheter was removed, and the wound site was dressed. The patient was sent to the recovery area.

CPT code(s): _____

Case 2

Indications for surgery: This 27-year-old male, who was in a motor vehicle accident just prior to arrival, suffered a head injury.

Procedure: Right frontal burr hole placement of ventriculostomy

Operation: After shaving the frontal scalp, the area was prepped and draped. A curvilinear posterolateral concave incision was made in the right frontal scalp, exposing the periosteum. A twist drill burr hole was placed in the right frontal skull. The dura was then opened with a blade knife, as was the pia. A ventricular catheter was placed, and there was good flow of cerebrospinal fluid. This helped relieve the brain edema. A catheter was tunneled out. The scalp was then stitched up, and a sterile dressing was applied. The patient was returned to the recovery room in good condition.

CPT code(s): _____

Case 3

This 79-year-old female had suffered from high-pressure cerebral spinal edema. To take care of this issue, the patient underwent a right cerebrospinal fluid shunt system placement. At this time, she is ready for the shunt system to be removed. The patient was taken to the operating room, and this procedure was performed without incident.

CPT code(s): _____

Case 4

Indications: This patient is a 32-year-old female who presented with a chief complaint of left leg pain radiating from the midcalf to the heel. There is no history of injury, and the use of anti-inflammatory medications, though it offered relief at first, has now stopped working for this patient. She states she has no feeling on the plantar aspect of the left foot at night. She was misdiagnosed several times until recently, when we confirmed the diagnosis of a damaged posterior tibial nerve. Until we do surgery, the extent of the damage is unknown.

Procedure: After induction of general anesthesia, the patient's left leg was prepped and draped in the usual sterile fashion. A vertical incision was made over the medial malleous into the subcutaneous level. Identifying the lacinate ligament overlying the posterior tibial nerve, the ligament was dissected, revealing a slightly damaged posterior tibial nerve. The damaged area was sutured using two sutures. The ligament was then repaired, and layered closure was performed. The patient tolerated the procedure and was sent to recovery in good condition.

CPT code(s): _____

Case 5

Stephen is a 22-year-old male suffering from cerebral palsy. He has been dealing with muscle spasms for the past 2 years, but they have gotten increasingly worse in his right arm. After a brief examination and discussion of risks and benefits, it was decided to try a Botox injection in the right arm to try and offer some relief.

Procedure: The right arm was swabbed with Betadine, and the Botox injection was administered into the brachioradialis muscle. The patient tolerated the procedure well.

CPT code(s): _____

Case 6

Preoperative diagnosis: Herniated disc at the right C7

Postoperative diagnosis: Herniated disc at the right C7

Procedure: Foraminotomy

This patient was administered general anesthesia and moved into the prone position. The cervical area was prepped and draped in the usual sterile manner. A midline incision was made posteriorly over the C7 vertebra. The incision was carried down to the paravertebral muscles through the lamina to reach the spinal cord. A foraminotomy was carried out, giving exposure to the nerve at C7. Once this was completed, the area felt well decompressed. The wound was irrigated out. Some extra bone was removed, and the disc was tapped into place. The wound was irrigated and closed with 3-0 coated Vicryl and 4-0 Vicryl in the skin.

CPT code(s): _____

Case 7

Preoperative diagnosis: Pain in left leg

Postoperative diagnosis: Same

Procedural Notes:

This 43-year-old male patient was placed in the supine position, and his lumbar area was sterilized. An injection of 1.5% Lidocaine was placed into the L2–L3 space, and an additional injection for infiltration was placed into the interspinous ligament. A total of 8 cc was injected. The epidural space was then injected with 12 cc of 0.5% Lidocaine and 80 mg of Aristocort. The needle was removed, and the wound was dressed. There were no complications noted.

CPT code(s): _____

Eye and Ocular Adnexa

Chapter Outline

Learning Objectives

At the conclusion of this chapter, you should be able to:

1. Define key terms related to coding procedures on the eye and ocular adnexa.
2. Define abbreviations associated with the eye and ocular adnexa.
3. Describe the basic anatomy of the eye and ocular adnexa.
4. Define common procedures completed on the eye and ocular adnexa.
5. Apply coding guidelines for the eye and ocular adnexa.
6. Select CPT codes for procedures completed on the eye and ocular adnexa.
7. Identify and code procedures for the eye and ocular adnexa from case studies.

Key Terms

anterior chamber	ciliary body	evisceration	intracapsular extraction
aqueous humor	conjunctiva	exenteration	iris
chalazion	cornea	extracapsular extraction	lacrimal duct
choroid	enucleation	eyelashes	lacrimal gland

lens	optic nerve	retina	tarsorrhaphy
lower eyelid	orbital implants	sclera	upper eyelid
ocular implant	posterior chamber	scleral reinforcement	vitreous humor
optic disc	pupil	suspensory ligaments	

Introduction

The Eye and Ocular Adnexa subsection of the Surgery section of the CPT manual is used to code procedures completed on the eye and ocular adnexa. The eye is mostly contained in the bony orbit of the facial bones and is the structure that allows the transmission of images to the brain for vision to occur. When selecting codes for the eye and ocular adnexa, remember to read the code descriptions and notations that are present in the code manual carefully, as there are many notations throughout this section that have an impact on code assignment.

Guidelines Related to the National Correct Coding Initiative (NCCI)

The student will need to perform the following steps to obtain the most current coding guideline information related to this chapter online:

1. Log on to *http://www.cms.hhs.gov/NationalCorrectCodInitEd*.
2. Scroll to the section titled "Downloads."
3. Click "NCCI Policy Manual for Medicare Services."
4. A box may appear that requires you to click "Open."
5. Click "Chapter 8" for guidelines specific to the eye and ocular adnexa.

Abbreviations Relating to the Eye and Ocular Adnexa

The following abbreviations are commonly used for the eye and ocular adnexa:

Abbreviation	Definition
ARMD	age-related macular degeneration
ECCE	extracapsular cataract extraction
EOM	extraocular movement
ICCE	intracapsular cataract extraction
IOL	intraocular lens
IOP	intraocular pressure
LASIK	laser-assisted in situ keratomileusis
OD	right eye
Ophth	ophthalmology
OS	left eye

(continues)

(continued)

OU	both eyes
PERRLA	pupils equal, round, reactive to light and accommodation
PRK	photorefractive keratectomy
RK	radial keratotomy
VA	visual acuity
VF	visual field

Anatomy of the Eye

There are numerous parts of the eye. The white portion of the eye is known as the **sclera**. This fibrous membrane serves as a protective covering for the eye and maintains the shape of the eyeball. The **iris** is the colored portion of the eye. The **pupil** is in the center of the iris. The pupil controls the amount of light entering the eye. The **conjunctiva** is a colorless mucous membrane that lines the anterior part of the eye.

Tears are produced by the **lacrimal gland** and drain from the eye though the **lacrimal duct**. The lacrimal duct is located at the inner edge of the eye.

The eyes are covered by the **upper eyelid** and **lower eyelid**, which keep the surface of the eyeball lubricated and protected from particles. The **eyelashes** are located along the edge of the eyelids to protect the eye from foreign materials. These structures are identified in Figure 18-1.

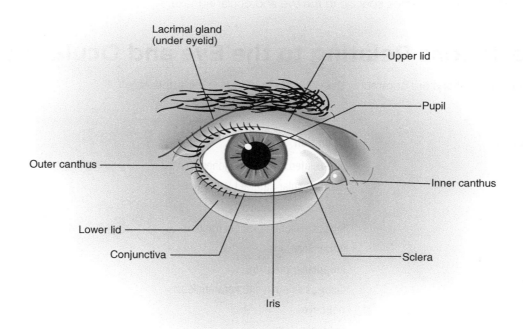

FIGURE 18-1 Front View of the Eye

The **cornea**, a transparent nonvascular structure, is located on the anterior portion of the sclera. The layer just beneath the sclera is the **choroid**, which contains capillaries that provide the blood supply and nutrients to the eye.

Posterior to the iris is the **lens**, which is a colorless structure that allows the eye to focus on images. The structures that are responsible for adjusting the lens are the **ciliary body** and muscle. Attached to the ciliary body and muscle are the **suspensory ligaments**, which attach to the lens and hold it in place.

The nerve cell layer of the eye is the **retina**, which changes light rays into nerve impulses. The impulses are transmitted to the brain by the **optic nerve**. On the optic nerve is a blind spot known as the **optic disc**, which is the point of entry for the artery that supplies blood to the retina.

There are two cavities that make up the interior of the eye, which are filled with a clear, watery fluid known as **aqueous humor**. The **anterior chamber** is located in front of the lens, and the **posterior chamber** is located behind the lens.

The posterior chamber is also filled with **vitreous humor**, a clear, jellylike substance that helps to shape the eye. Figure 18-2 illustrates a lateral cross-section of the eye, showing the relationships among the various structures of the eye.

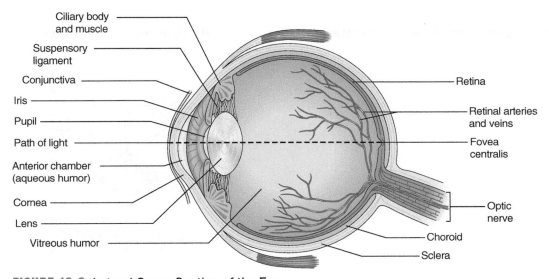

FIGURE 18-2 Lateral Cross-Section of the Eye

Procedures Completed on the Eyeball (65091–65290)

Code range 65091 to 65290 is used to report procedures completed on the eyeball. These codes are divided into the following sections:

- Removal of the eye
- Secondary implant procedures
- Removal of foreign body
- Repair of laceration

Code range 65091 to 65114 is used to report procedures that remove the eye or structures of the eye. To locate these procedures in the Alphabetical Index of the CPT manual, the coder would reference the following terms:

- Evisceration, then ocular contents. **Evisceration** means removal of an organ.
- Enucleation, then eye. **Enucleation** means to remove without cutting into the structure. Figure 18-3 illustrates an enucleation.
- Exenteration, then eye. **Exenteration** means the surgical removal of the contents of a cavity.

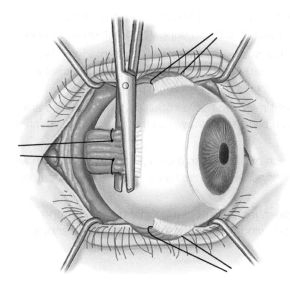

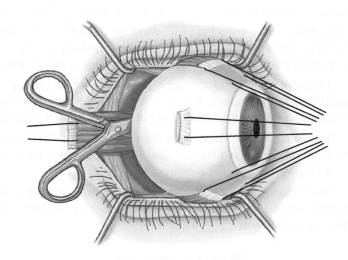

(A) Attachments of the globe are separated

(B) Optic nerve is transected

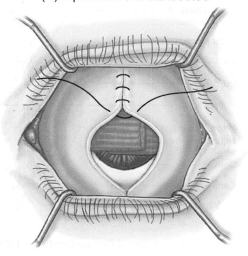

(C) Conjunctiva is approximated

FIGURE 18-3 Enucleation

Codes in the 65091 to 65105 range, Evisceration of the Ocular Contents and Enucleation of the Eye, are differentiated by whether the procedure was performed with or without implants. Codes in the 65110–65114 range, exenteration of the orbit, are differentiated by whether the procedure occurred with the therapeutic removal of bone or with a muscle or myocutaneous flap.

Secondary implant procedures are performed both inside and outside of the muscular cone of the eye. An **ocular implant** is an implant performed inside the muscular cone and is reported with code range 65125–65175. The codes are differentiated according to the type of procedure, including modification of ocular implant, insertion of ocular implant secondary, reinsertion of ocular implant, and removal of ocular implant. Implants that are outside the muscle cone are known as **orbital implants**, and insertion and removal procedures are reported with codes 67550 and 67560. Be sure to look at the instructional notation following code 65175.

Code range 65205–65265 is used to report procedures completed to remove foreign bodies from the external eye or intraocular area. Codes 65205–65222 report procedures completed on the external eye, whereas codes 65235–65265 report intraocular foreign-body removal.

Repairs of lacerations of the conjunctiva and cornea are reported with code range 65270 to 65290. These codes are differentiated by the site of the repair, conjunctiva or cornea, and then by accompanying procedures. A unique feature of codes 65272 and 65273 is that the codes are differentiated by whether the patient was hospitalized.

Procedures Completed on the Anterior Segment (65400–66999)

Code range 65400–66999 is used to report procedures completed on the anterior segment of the eye. This subsection is organized according to the structures found in the anterior segment: cornea, anterior chamber, anterior sclera, iris, ciliary body, and lens. The codes are then further organized according to the type of procedure completed: incision, excision, removal or destruction, or repair or revision. Table 18-1 summarizes some of the codes found in this section.

TABLE 18-1 Anterior Segment (Selected Codes for code range 65400–66999)

Codes	Description
65710–65757	This range is used to report keratoplasty, which is differentiated by whether or not the procedure was completed for aphakia or pseudophakia. During a keratoplasty, also known as a *corneal transplant*, the central part of the cornea is replaced with a graft. Figure 18-4 illustrates a corneal transplantation.
65800–65880	This range of codes is used to report incisional procedures completed on the anterior chamber. Procedures in this range include paracentesis of the anterior chamber of the eye, goniotomy, trabeculotomy, trabeculoplasty, and the severing of adhesions.
65900–65930	This range codes removals that occur in the anterior chamber.
66020–66030	This code range reports the injection of air, liquid, or medication into the anterior chamber of the eye.
66130–66250	Excisions and repairs or revisions completed on the anterior sclera are reported with this range of codes. It is important for the coder to read the operative report carefully to determine any accompanying procedures and the approach of the procedures, as codes are differentiated by this. For example code 66179 reports an aqueous shunt to extraocular equatorial plate reservoir, external approach without graft, while code 66180 reports the same procedure with the accompanying procedure of a graft placement.
66500–66770	This code range is used to report procedures completed on the iris and ciliary body. Procedures include incision, excision, repair, and destruction. When selecting codes for destructions, codes 66700–66770, the coder must be able to identify the method of destruction used, such as diathermy, cyclophotocoagulation, cryotherapy, laser, etc.
66820–66988	This code range is used to code procedures that are completed on the lens. The most common codes used in this section include codes for the removal of cataracts. These codes, 66830–66984, are differentiated by a number of factors that include whether the cataract was secondary; the type of cataract removal, extracapsular or intracapsular; and the removal of lens material according to the type of technique. Coders need to become familiar with the notation that appears in the CPT manual before the code 66830. This notation describes the procedures that are included as part of the code for the extraction of the lens.
+66990	This is an add-on code that is used to report the use of an ophthalmic endoscope. This code should be reported in addition to the code for the primary procedure that was completed. There is a notation immediately following this code description which lists the codes that this add-on code would apply to.
66999	This code reports an unlisted procedure of the anterior segment of the eye.

Extracapsular extraction involves the removal of the lens without removing the posterior capsule. This would include codes 66840 to 66852, 66940, 66982, and 66984. Codes 66920, 66930, and 66983 are used to report the removal of the entire lens with the capsule, which is known as an **intracapsular extraction**. When a cataract is extracted and an intraocular lens prosthesis is inserted during the same operative session, codes 66982, 66983, and 66984 should be reported. Figure 18-5 illustrates an intracapsular and extracapsular cataract extraction.

(A) Trephination

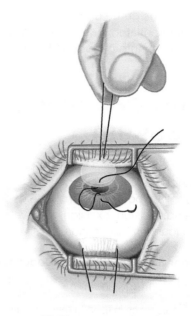

(B) Placement of graft

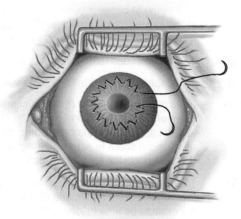

(C) Graft sutured in position

FIGURE 18-4 Corneal Transplant

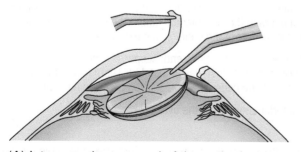

(A) Intracapsular: removal of the entire lens and lens capsule.

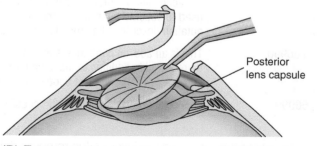

(B) Extracapsular: lens is removed with its anterior capsule, leaving posterior capsule intact.

Posterior lens capsule

FIGURE 18-5 Types of Cataract Extractions

The exchange of an intraocular lens is reported by using code 66986, while the insertion of an intraocular lens after cataract removal is reported by the use of code 66985. The numerous notations found after code 66985 should be referenced.

Prior to completing cataract extraction, a preoperative evaluation needs to occur to determine whether there is justification for the procedure. Medicare has outlined requirements that must be met to justify the surgery, including the following.

There must be documentation of:

- Visual functional status
- Visual impairment
- Informed consent
- Preoperative ophthalmologic testing and medical assessment

It should also be noted that bilateral cataract extraction should not be performed on both eyes on the same day. This is to prevent bilateral vision loss if the procedures were to have complications.

Exercise 18.1—Check Your Understanding

Removal of Cataracts

Read the notation that appears in the CPT manual, under the heading of Removal, prior to code 66830. State yes if the procedure is included as part of the code for the extraction of the lens. State no if the procedure listed is not included as part of the code for the extraction of the lens.

1. Iridectomy _____
2. Repair of iris _____
3. Ciliary body destruction _____
4. Anterior capsulotomy _____
5. Subconjunctival injections

   _____

6. Posterior capsulotomy _____
7. Enzymatic zonulysis _____
8. Lateral canthotomy _____
9. Iridotomy _____
10. Viscoelastic agents _____

Procedures Completed on the Posterior Segment (67005–67299)

Code range 67005 to 67299 is used to report procedures completed on the posterior segment of the eye. This code range is divided into the following sections:

- Vitreous
- Retina or Choroid
- Posterior Sclera
- Other Procedures

Codes that are reported using this range are summarized in Table 18-2.

TABLE 18-2 Posterior Segment (67005–67299)

Codes	Description
67005–67043	This range of codes reports procedures completed on the vitreous. Code 67027 is used to report the implantation of an intravitreal drug-delivery system. During this procedure, an implant is placed in the vitreous that releases medication into the vitreous. Codes 67036–67043 are used to report mechanical vitrectomy completed by a pars plana approach. Before assigning codes 67036–67043, the coder needs to reference the operative report to ensure that the vitrectomy was mechanical. This is usually indicated in the operative report by the use of an ocutome, MicroVit, or daisy wheel probe. The coder will also need to note the extent of the procedure. The numerous notations that follow code 67043 should be referenced.
67101–67121	This code range is used to report repairs completed on the retina or choroid. Diathermy, cryotherapy, and photocoagulation are also methods used to reattach a retina. As instructed by the notation in the CPT manual, when more than one of these approaches are used during the same operative session, the principal modality used should be the therapy reported. Coders should read the operative report carefully and compare the CPT code descriptions to ensure proper code assignment, as many of these codes include multiple components. A detached retina can also be repaired by performing scleral buckling. In this procedure, the retinal breaks are identified and are treated with a cryoprobe, and then the breaks are supported with a scleral buckle. Code 67107 is used to report this procedure. Figure 18-6 illustrates scleral buckling. A complete repair of retinal detachments is reported using CPT code 67113.
67141–67145	Prophylaxis of retinal detachment is reported with these codes, which are differentiated according to the type of therapy used: cryotherapy and/or diathermy or photocoagulation. These procedures are often performed in repetitive sessions, and the codes are intended to include all of the sessions. Various payers have different reporting requirements for these codes. Note the instructional notations that appear after the heading of Prophylaxis.
67208–67229	Destructions of lesions of the retina or choroid, or extensive or progressive retinopathy, are reported with these codes. Codes are differentiated according to the type of therapy used to destroy the lesion or retinopathy, such as cryotherapy, diathermy, photocoagulation, radiation by implantation of source, or photodynamic therapy. Like the prophylaxis codes, these procedures are often performed in repetitive sessions, and the codes are intended to include the sessions. Various payers have different reporting requirements for these codes.
67250–67255	Repairs of the sclera, known as **scleral reinforcement**, are reported with these codes, which are differentiated by whether or not a graft was placed.
67299	This is the Unlisted Procedure code for procedures completed on the posterior segment of the eye.

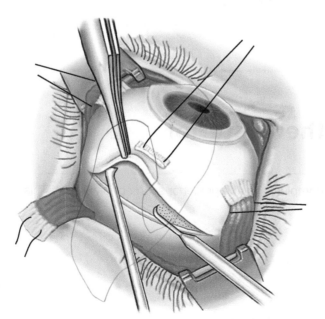

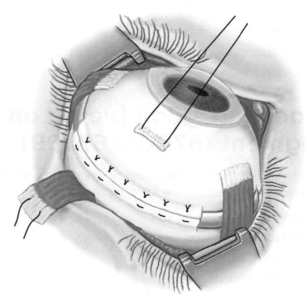

(A) Preparation of sclera for buckle   (B) Scleral buckle sutured in place

FIGURE 18-6 Scleral Buckling for Treatment of Retinal Detachment

Procedures Completed on the Ocular Adnexa (67311–67999)

Code range 67311 to 67999 is used to report procedures completed on the ocular adnexa. The codes are grouped according to the following:

- Extraocular muscles
- Orbit
- Eyelids

There are six muscles that are arranged in pairs surrounding the eye. They are responsible for the ability of the eye to move. The pairs are as follows:

- Superior and inferior rectus
- Superior and inferior oblique
- Lateral and medial rectus

These muscles are illustrated in Figure 18-7. Coders must have an understanding of the muscles of the eye to select codes from code range 67311–67318, strabismus surgery, because specific muscles are identified in the descriptions of the codes. Strabismus surgery is completed to correct a deviation that occurs in one eye. These codes are for unilateral procedures. Code assignment is also based on the number of muscles on which surgery was performed.

Code range 67400–67599 is used to report procedures completed on the orbit that include exploration, excision, and decompression of the orbital area. Terms to reference in the Index of the CPT manual to locate codes in this section include:

- Orbitotomy
- Orbit, then implant
- Orbit contents, then aspiration
- Orbit transplant
- Optic nerve, then decompression

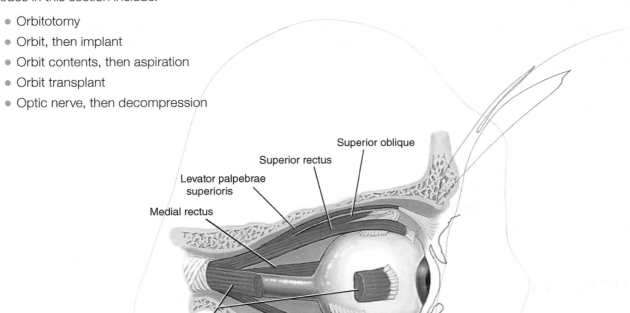

FIGURE 18-7 Muscles of the Eye (the medial rectus muscle is not visible).

Procedures completed on the eyelids are assigned to codes 67700–67999. These codes are divided into the following sections:

- Incision
- Excision, Destruction
- **Tarsorrhaphy**, the entire or partial suturing of the eyelids together
- Repair (Brow, Ptosis, Blepharoptosis, Lid Retraction, Ectropion, and Entropion)
- Reconstruction
- Other Procedures

A common procedure that falls within this code range is an excision of a chalazion of the eyelid. A **chalazion** is a small tumor of the eyelid that is formed by retention of secretions of the meibomian gland. Codes 67800–67808 are assigned to report the excision, which are differentiated by the number of tumors removed, by the eyelids involved, whether general anesthesia was used, and whether hospitalization occurred.

Repairs completed on the eyelids are assigned to codes 67900–67924. Codes are differentiated according to the type of repair and the site of the repair. Reconstruction procedures completed on the eyelids fall into code range 67930–67975. Procedures in this range include suturing of a recent wound of the eyelid, removal of a foreign body embedded in the eyelid, canthoplasty, and reconstruction of the eyelid by full-thickness transfer of a skin flap. Code 67999 is for unlisted procedures completed on the eyelids.

Procedures Completed on the Conjunctiva (68020–68899)

Code range 68020–68899 reports procedures completed on the conjunctiva, including procedures completed on the lacrimal system. Terms to reference in the Index of the CPT manual to locate codes from this section include:

- Conjunctivoplasty
- Conjunctiva, then the type of procedure, such as biopsy, incision and drainage, or lesion destruction
- Conjunctivorhinostomy
- Dacryocystorhinostomy
- Lacrimal duct, then the procedure
- Lacrimal gland, then the procedure
- Lacrimal punctum, then the procedure
- Lacrimal sac, then the procedure

Summary

- The white portion of the eye is known as the *sclera*.
- The iris is the colored portion of the eye.
- The pupil is in the center of the iris.
- The cornea is located on the anterior portion of the sclera.
- The layer just beneath the sclera is the choroid.
- The structures that are responsible for adjusting the lens are the ciliary body and muscle.

- The anterior chamber is located in front of the lens, and the posterior chamber is located behind the lens.
- An ocular implant is placed inside the muscular cone, while an orbital implant is placed outside the muscle cone.
- There are six muscles that are arranged in pairs surrounding the eye.
- Extracapsular extraction involves the removal of the lens without removing the posterior capsule.
- The removal of the entire lens with the capsule is known as *intracapsular extraction*.
- When selecting codes for the eye and ocular adnexa, remember to read the code descriptions and notations that are present in the code manual carefully, as there are many notations throughout this section that have an impact on code assignment.

Internet Links

To learn about conditions of the eye and procedures completed on the eye, visit *http://www.medicinenet.com* and search for the type of procedure, such as keratoplasty. Also visit *http://www.allaboutvision.com* and search for the name of the procedure, such as cataract surgery. Visit *http://www.ascrs.org*, the website of the American Society of Cataract and Refractive Surgery.

Chapter Review

Fill in the Blank

Instructions: Fill in the blanks in the statements that follow.

1. Tears are produced by the _____.

2. Implants that are outside the muscle cone are known as _____.

3. Posterior to the iris is the _____, which is a colorless structure that allows the eye to focus on images.

4. To remove without cutting into the structure is called _____.

5. The posterior chamber is also filled with _____, a clear, jellylike substance that helps to shape the eye.

True/False

Instructions: Indicate whether the following statements are true (T) or false (F).

6. _____ Code 67101 would be used to report a repair of retinal detachment by cryo-therapy, including drainage of subretinal fluid.

7. _____ The retina is a transparent nonvascular structure located on the anterior portion of the sclera.

8. _____ The colored portion of the eyeball is called the *pupil*.

9. _____ Light rays are changed into nerve impulses, which travel to the brain via the optic nerve.

10. _____ Codes in the 65110–65114 code range are differentiated by whether a repair of the cornea or the conjunctiva was performed.

Coding Assignments

Instructions: Using the CPT manual, assign the correct code to the following procedures.

1. Ciliary body destruction by diathermy
_____

2. Diagnostic scraping of cornea for smear sample
_____

3. Removal of blood clot from anterior segment of eye _____

4. Repair of conjunctival laceration, nonperforating laceration sclera, direct closure
_____

5. Radial keratotomy _____

6. Reduction of overcorrection of ptosis
_____

7. Exchange of intraocular lens _____

8. Canthotomy _____

9. Fine needle aspiration of orbital contents
_____

10. Injection of medication into Tenon's capsule
_____

11. Conjunctivoplasty with buccal mucous membrane graft _____

12. Probing of lacrimal canaliculi with irrigation
_____

13. Plastic repair of canaliculi _____

14. Repair of retinal detachment by injection of air
_____

15. Destruction of macular edema by diathermy
_____

16. Scleral reinforcement with graft
_____

17. Biopsy of conjunctiva _____

18. Subconjunctival injection _____

19. Partial dacryoadenectomy _____

20. Destruction of progressive retinopathy by cryotherapy _____

21. Canthoplasty _____

22. Fenestration of optic nerve sheath
_____

23. Iridectomy with corneoscleral section for removal of one lesion _____

24. Diagnostic aspiration of aqueous via paracentesis of the anterior chamber of the eye
_____

25. Repair of scleral staphyloma with graft
_____

26. Keratoprosthesis _____

27. Corneal biopsy _____

28. Removal of epithelial downgrowth of the anterior chamber of the eye _____

29. Iridotomy by stab incision _____

30. Release of vitreous fluid pars plana approach
_____

Case Studies

Instructions: Review each case and indicate the correct code(s).

Case 1

Preoperative diagnosis: Foreign object in right eye

Postoperative diagnosis: Same

Procedure: Removal of foreign body from right eye

(continues)

(*continued*)

The patient was brought to the operating suite, and 2% Lidocaine was injected into the right eye. A slit lamp was used to visualize the area. The object was embedded in the conjunctiva. A V-shaped incision was made to access the foreign object. The object was removed with the side of the beveled edge of an optic needle. An antibiotic was applied to the surface of the eye. The patient tolerated the procedure well and was sent to the recovery area.

CPT code(s): _____

Case 2

Postoperative diagnosis: Lesion on left eye sclera

Procedure: Lesion excision

The patient was prepped and draped in the usual fashion and placed under general anesthesia. An incision was made in the left eye conjunctiva to visualize the lesion. The lesion was 0.5 cm and was removed with scleral scissors. Because of the small incision and the obtaining of hemostasis, sutures were not used to close the site. An antibiotic was used in the eye, and a 24-hour pressure patch was applied. The patient had no complications and was sent to the recovery room.

CPT code(s): _____

Case 3

Preoperative and postoperative diagnosis: Nuclear cataract of left eye

Procedure: Cataract removal with lens implant of left eye

The patient's identification was verified, and a peribulbar block was administered into the left eye. The patient was then prepped and draped in the usual sterile fashion. The placement of a lid speculum occurred, and a paracentesis was made using a diamond blade. Viscoelastic was used to fill the anterior chamber. A triplanar temporal clear-corneal incision was made. A 360-degree capsulorrhexis was completed, and the lens was then hydrated and removed in segments. An aspirator tip was then used to remove the remaining cortical material from the area. Viscoelastic was used to fill the bag, and the lens was then inserted into the bag. After this, the viscoelastic was removed, and the area was hydrated. A Kenalog injection was given. The patient tolerated the procedure with no complications or difficulties. Blood loss was minimal.

CPT code(s): _____

Case 4

Preoperative and postoperative diagnosis: Obscuring vision after cataract, right eye

Procedure: YAG laser discission

The patient was brought into the laser room, and identification was determined. The patient was given Mydfrin 2.5% and Mydriacyl 1% in the right eye prior to the use of the laser at 900. Immediately prior to the use of the laser, Alcaine 0.5% was placed in the right eye. A laser was used to perform a capsulotomy of secondary membranous cataract tissue. The laser was started at 1000 and was finished at 1001. No complications were noted. Alphagan P 0.15% was placed in the patient's right eye following the use of the laser.

CPT code(s): _____

Case 5

Preoperative and postoperative diagnosis: Hemorrhage of vitreous of the right eye and retinal detachment

Procedure: Trans pars plana vitrectomy and cryoretinopexy of right eye

Anesthesia: General

The patient was brought to the operating room and prepped and draped in a sterile fashion. General anesthesia was administered. A speculum was placed in the right eye, and an incision was made into the conjunctiva and Tenon's. Bleeding was present. A complete vitrectomy was performed using a pars plana approach. The patient's retina was then attached via cryoretinopexy. This area was closed and sealed with 6-0 interrupted Vicryl sutures. The conjunctiva and Tenon's were closed with 6-0 plain sutures. Antibiotics and additional topical medications were applied. The patient tolerated the procedure well and was sent to the recovery area in satisfactory condition.

CPT code(s): _____

Case 6

Preoperative diagnosis: Retinal break

Postoperative diagnosis: Same

This 58-year-old male patient presents for a prophylaxis cryotherapy treatment of a retinal break of the right eye. Under conscious sedation, a speculum is used at the lateral aspect of

(continues)

(continued)

the right eyeball, and the cryoprobe is used to seal the break on the lateral aspect of the right eyeball. The patient tolerated the procedure well and was sent home in good condition. He will return in three days for follow-up.

CPT code(s): _____

Case 7

A 15-year-old female presented to the emergency room today complaining of "something in my eye." The irritation started just prior to arrival. She said that she was sitting outside reading when she felt a sensation around her right eye, and then the irritation was present. She tried flushing the eye, but it still feels like something is in there. The patient was lying supine, with her head slightly raised when I inspected the eye. There appears to be some trichiasis. Using a biomicroscope and forceps, several eyelashes were removed, which alleviated the problem. The patient left the emergency room in good condition.

CPT code(s): _____

Case 8

Preoperative diagnosis: Chalazion of left upper eyelid

Postoperative diagnosis: Same

Anesthesia: General

Procedural Notes:

This 3-year-old male patient was placed in the supine position, and general anesthesia was administered. A chalazion clamp was applied to the left upper eyelid to expose the posterior surface of the eyelid with the lid inverted. The chalazion was incised and purulent contents drained. To control hemostasis, the lid was cauterized. Garamycin ointment was applied to the left eye. The clamp was released. There were no complications, and the patient was sent to the recovery area.

CPT code(s): _____

CHAPTER 19
Auditory System and Operating Microscope

Chapter Outline

Learning Objectives

At the conclusion of this chapter, you should be able to:

1. Define key terms related to coding procedures on the auditory system.
2. Define abbreviations associated with the auditory system.
3. Describe the basic anatomy and functions of the auditory system.
4. Define common procedures completed on the auditory system.
5. Apply the specific coding guidelines to this chapter.
6. Select CPT codes for procedures completed on the auditory system.
7. State the code used to report the use of an operating microscope.

Key Terms

auditory ossicles	cerumen	cochlear duct	external auditory canal
auditory tube	ceruminous glands	earlobe	external auditory meatus
auricle	cilia	endolymph	external ear
bony labyrinth	cochlea	eustachian tube	incus

labyrinth	oval window	semicircular ducts	tympanostomy
malleus	perilymph	stapes	utricle
membranous labyrinth	pharyngotympanic tube	tympanic cavity	vestibule
middle ear	pinna	tympanic membrane	
organ of Corti	saccule	tympanic neurectomy	
otoplasty	semicircular canals	tympanoplasty	

Introduction

The auditory system enables a person to hear and to maintain balance when the head and body move. The structures of the ear pick up sound waves for interpretation by the brain. The ear also plays a role in the maintenance of equilibrium by sending messages to the brain about the position and movement of the head.

Guidelines Related to the National Correct Coding Initiative (NCCI)

Perform the following steps to obtain the most current coding guideline information related to this chapter online:

1. Log on to *http://www.cms.hhs.gov/NationalCorrectCodInitEd*.
2. Scroll to the section titled "Downloads."
3. Click "NCCI Policy Manual for Part B Medicare Services."
4. A box may appear that requires you to click "Open."
5. Click "Chapter 8" for guidelines specific to the auditory system.

Abbreviations Associated with the Auditory System

The following abbreviations are used in reference to the auditory system:

Abbreviation	Definition
AD	right ear
AS	left ear
AU	each ear
BC	bone conduction
BOM	bilateral otitis media
dB	decibel
ENT	ears, nose, throat
Oto	otology
PE tube	pressure equalization tube
TM	tympanic membrane

Anatomy of the Auditory System

The structures that comprise the auditory system are divided into three regions: external ear, middle ear, and inner ear. Figure 19-1 illustrates the regions of the ear.

The **external ear** is the visible, outermost part of the ear and is not within the structure of the skull. There are two structures that make up the external ear: the auricle and the external auditory meatus. The **auricle**, also known as the **pinna**, is a flexible cartilaginous flap that has a bottom portion known as the **earlobe**. The auricle allows sound waves to enter the ear canal, which is known as the **external auditory canal** or the **external auditory meatus**. Along the external auditory canal, tiny hairs called **cilia** are present that aid in transmitting sound waves inward to other auditory structures. Also within the external auditory canal are sweat glands, called **ceruminous glands**, that secrete a honey-colored, thick, waxy substance known as earwax or **cerumen**. Cerumen helps to protect and lubricate the ear. In combination with the cilia, the cerumen helps to protect the eardrum from foreign objects. The eardrum, known as the **tympanic membrane**, separates the external ear from the middle ear. The tympanic membrane is a thin, semitransparent membrane, silvery gray in color, that transmits sound vibrations to the inner ear through the auditory ossicles.

The auditory ossicles are part of the **middle ear**. The middle ear, also known as the **tympanic cavity**, is found within the temporal bone and houses the auditory ossicles and the eustachian tube. The **auditory ossicles** consist of three small bones that transmit and amplify sound waves. The bones are named according to their shape:

- **Malleus**—shaped like a hammer
- **Incus**—shaped like an anvil
- **Stapes**—shaped like a stirrup

The tube that connects the bony structures of the middle ear to the pharynx is the **eustachian tube**. The eustachian tube is also known as the **auditory tube** or **pharyngotympanic tube**. The purpose of the eustachian tube is to equalize air pressure within the middle ear.

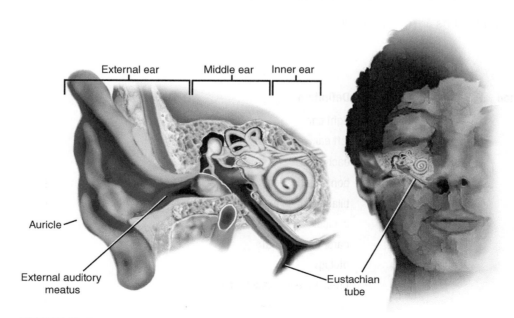

FIGURE 19-1 **External, Middle, and Inner Ear**

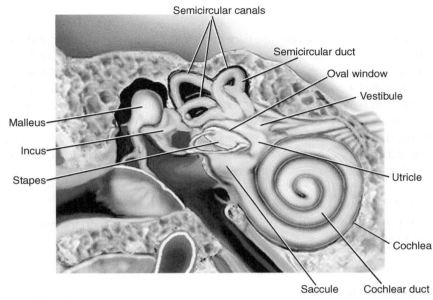

FIGURE 19-2 Structures of the Ear

The middle ear is separated from the inner ear by the **oval window**. Within the inner ear, also known as the **labyrinth**, are bony structures and membranous structures. The bony structures, called the **bony labyrinth**, consist of the following:

- **Vestibule**—the central portion of the inner ear. This structure contains the **utricle** and the **saccule**, which are membranous sacs that aid in maintaining balance.

- **Semicircular canals**—located behind the vestibule, these are three bony structures that are filled with fluid that also help to maintain balance. The **semicircular ducts** are also found in this area and aid in balance.

- **Cochlea**—a snail-shaped, bony structure that contains **endolymph** and **perilymph**, which are auditory fluids that transmit sound. The **organ of Corti**, also found in the cochlea, is the true organ of hearing. The **cochlear duct**, a membranous structure, is found in this area of the ear and aids in the hearing process. The tiny hair cells found in the organ of Corti are stimulated by the sound vibrations. These sound vibrations convert to nerve impulses and are carried to the brain.

The **membranous labyrinth** is a term that is used to describe the utricle, saccule, semicircular ducts, and cochlear ducts, because these structures are all membranous structures.

Figure 19-2 illustrates numerous structures found in the ear.

Procedures Completed on the External Ear (69000–69399)

The first subsection of codes, 69000–69399, is used to report procedures completed on the external ear. These codes are grouped as follows:

- Incision
- Excision
- Removal
- Repair
- Other Procedures

Incision (69000–69090)

This range of codes is used to report drainages that are completed on the external ear and for ear piercing. Codes 69000 and 69005 are used to report the drainage of an abscess or hematoma of the external ear. For both of these procedures, a small incision is made in the skin to drain the contents of the abscess or hematoma. At times, it is necessary to insert a drainage tube and to pack the area. When the physician devotes an extensive amount of time to cleaning the area and the time is documented in the patient's record, it is appropriate to select code 69005, which denotes that the procedure was complicated. Often during this more complicated procedure, antibiotic eardrops are used, and a soft sponge is placed in the ear canal. Code 69020 is used to report the drainage of an abscess of the external auditory canal. At times, packing will occur to absorb abscess material and to promote healing. Ear piercing is reported by code 69090.

Excision (69100–69155)

Code range 69100–69155 is used to report biopsies and excisions completed on the external ear. Table 19-1 summarizes codes 69100 to 69155.

TABLE 19-1 Code Range 69100–69155

Codes	Description
69100 and 69105	These codes report biopsies of the external ear that are completed for diagnostic purposes. During these procedures, the physician uses an instrument to excise a lesion. Code 69100 reports a biopsy on the external ear, while code 69105 reports a biopsy completed on the external auditory canal. If the incisional area is large, a suture closure may be necessary. Packing in the ear canal may be necessary for some biopsies completed in the ear canal.
69110 and 69120	Excisions completed on the external ear are reported with these codes. The codes are differentiated by the size of the area excised. Code 69110 reports a partial excision with a simple repair, while code 69120 reports a complete amputation. After the complete amputation, the site is typically closed during a second procedure that involves a skin flap or graft.
69140 and 69145	Excisions completed on the external auditory canals are reported with these codes. The approach for both of these procedures is to enter the ear canal through the external opening of the ear. The physician will then make an incision to remove the bony growth or the soft-tissue lesion.
69150 and 69155	These codes are used to report a radical excision of an external auditory canal lesion. During both of these procedures, the physician makes a postauricular incision to remove the lesion. Code 69150 is reported when the procedure is completed without neck dissection. When neck dissection occurs, thus removing the lymph nodes from the side of the neck of the procedure, code 69155 is reported.

Removal of Foreign Body (69200–69222)

Code range 69200–69222 is used to report the removal of a foreign body or debridement of the mastoid cavity. Codes 69200 and 69205 report foreign body removal from the external auditory canal. These codes are differentiated by whether or not general anesthesia was used. Unilateral removal of impacted cerumen using irrigation/lavage is reported with code 69209. Unilateral removal of impacted cerumen requiring instrumentation is coded by reporting code 69210. There are numerous instructional notations that follow code 69210 that need to be reviewed prior to assigning code 69210. Locate these notations in the CPT manual and review them.

Codes 69220 and 69222 report debridement of the mastoid cavity. These procedures are completed for patients who have undergone a radical or modified radical mastoidectomy. Because of the extent of this procedure, the site has to be cleaned every three to six months. If the procedure is completed bilaterally, modifier 50 should be reported. When routine cleaning occurs, code 69220 is reported. If anesthesia is used or extensive cleaning occurs, code 69222 is reported.

Repairs and Other Procedures (69300-69399)

Coders should read the notation that is present at the start of this subcategory. The notation instructs the coder to use code range 12011–14302 to report the suturing of a wound or injury of the external ear. This code range, 69300–69320, is used to report only otoplasty and reconstructions of the external auditory canal. Code 69300 is used to report **otoplasty**, plastic surgery of the ear, for a protruding ear. Reconstructions of the external auditory canal are reported with codes 69310 and 69320. The codes are differentiated by whether the reconstruction occurred because of congenital atresia or for another reason. When selecting these codes, the coder must identify the diagnosis on the operative report to justify code selection.

Procedures Completed on the Middle Ear (69420-69799)

The second subsection of codes, 69420–69799, is used to report procedures completed on the middle ear. These codes are divided into the following ranges:

- Incision—codes 69420 to 69450
- Excision—codes 69501 to 69554
- Repair—codes 69601 to 69676
- Other Procedures—codes 69700 to 69799

Incision (69420-69450)

Codes 69420–69421 include procedures that involve the eustachian tubes. These codes are used to report myringotomy that includes aspiration and/or eustachian tube inflation, with or without general anesthesia. Removal of a ventilating tube that is completed using general anesthesia is reported by using code 69424. Since this procedure is often performed bilaterally, the coder would need to add a modifier of 50 to report the bilateral procedure. After code 69424, an instructional notation appears in the CPT manual that lists codes that are not to be reported with code 69424.

Tympanostomy is an incision made into the tympanic membrane to create an opening in the membrane. This procedure is completed using local, topical, or general anesthesia and is reported with codes 69433 or 69436, depending on the type of anesthesia used. Modifier 50 is added for a bilateral procedure.

Code 69440 is used to report the exploration of the middle ear through a postauricular ear canal incision, and code 69450 is used to report a transcanal tympanolysis.

Excision (69501-69554)

Code range 69501 to 69554 is used to report excisional procedures that are completed on the middle ear. To locate these procedures in the Index of the CPT manual, reference the following terms:

- Mastoidectomy, then the type of procedure: complete, revision, radical, simple, and so on
- Resection, then temporal bone
- Excision, then lesion, then middle ear or excision, then tumor, then middle ear

Repair (69601-69676)

Repairs completed on the middle ear are coded with code range 69601–69676. These codes are summarized in Table 19-2.

Other Procedures (69700-69799)

Procedures reported using code range 69700–69799 include:

- Closure of postauricular fistula
- Implantation or replacement of hearing devices and implants

- Removal and repair of devices and implants
- Decompression and suturing of facial nerves

Unlisted procedures completed on the middle ear are coded with code 69799.

TABLE 19-2 Code Range 69601–69676

Codes	Description
69601–69605	This range of codes reports revision mastoidectomy. The codes are differentiated by the intensity of the procedure performed: complete mastoidectomy, modified radical, radical, or the completion of a tympanoplasty or apicectomy.
69610	When a tympanic membrane repair is completed, this code is reported. This code may or may not include site preparation, and may or may not include the placement of a patch.
69620	This code is used to report myringoplasty. This is confined to the drumhead and donor site.
69631–69646	These codes are used to report **tympanoplasty**, the surgical repair of the tympanic membrane. The codes are differentiated by the accompanying procedures that are completed with the tympanoplasty, such as mastoidectomy, antrotomy, etc. Coders must read the operative reports and carefully match the description of the procedure with the description found in CPT because many procedures are grouped into each code found in this section of CPT, thus elevating the need for multiple codes.
69650–69662	Procedures completed on the stapes are reported with this range of codes. Included are stapes mobilization, stapedectomy, and revisions of stapes.
69666 and 69667	Repair and revision of an oval window or round window fistula are reported with these codes.
69670	This is a separate procedure code that is used to report mastoid obliteration.
69676	This code reports a unilateral **tympanic neurectomy**, which is the removal of the Jacobson's nerve that is located in the middle ear. If the procedure is completed bilaterally, add modifier 50.

Exercise 19.1—Check Your Understanding

Matching

Match Column 1 to the definition in Column 2.

Column 1

1. 69210
2. ceruminous glands
3. endolymph
4. 69450
5. middle ear
6. ENT
7. AD
8. AS
9. auditory tube
10. 69105

Column 2

a. transcanal tympanolysis

b. equalizes pressure in the middle ear

c. ears, nose, and throat

d. unilateral removal of impacted cerumen requiring instrumentation

e. sweat glands in the external auditory canal

f. biopsy of external auditory canal

g. left ear

h. an auditory fluid that transmits sound

i. right ear

j. contains the auditory ossicles

Procedures Completed on the Inner Ear and the Temporal Bone, Middle Fossa Approach (69801–69979)

Code range 69801–69979 is used to report procedures completed on the inner ear and the temporal bone. Figure 19-3 illustrates the structures that are found in the inner ear. These codes are divided into the following ranges of codes:

- Incision and/or destruction—code range 69801–69806. This range is used to report such procedures as labyrinthotomy, and endolymphatic sac operations without a shunt or with a shunt. The coder must read the notes found here for proper code assignment.
- Excision—code range 69905–69915. Labyrinthectomy and vestibular nerve section are reported with these codes. The coder must be able to identify the approach used for the labyrinthectomy to properly select a code.
- Introduction—code 69930. Implantation of a cochlear device is reported with this code. The procedure may or may not include a mastoidectomy.
- Temporal bone, middle fossa approach—code range 69950–69979. Procedures reported with this range of codes include vestibular nerve section, facial nerve decompression, decompression of auditory canal, and removal of tumor.

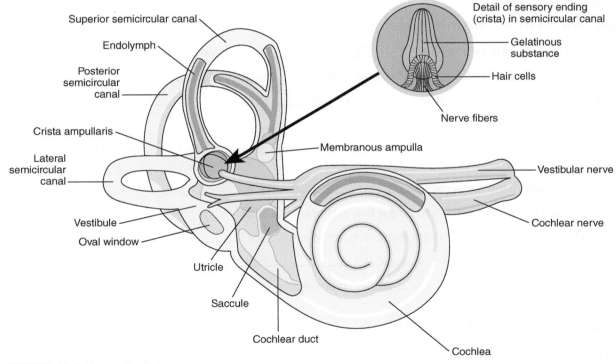

FIGURE 19-3 Inner Ear Structures

Operating Microscope

Following the codes for the auditory system, code 69990 appears in the CPT manual. This code reports the use of an operating microscope with any procedure completed in CPT, except for those codes in which the use of the operating microscope is included. Code 69990 is not reported when the operating microscope is used to magnify or enhance visualization. Code 69990 should not be reported with the codes that are listed in the instructional notation that appears in the CPT manual preceding the description of code 69990. This is an add-on code, so it must accompany another CPT code for the primary procedure.

Summary

- The auditory system is divided into three regions: external ear, middle ear, and inner ear.
- The external ear is composed of the auricle, external auditory meatus, and tympanic membrane.
- The middle ear consists of the malleus, incus, and stapes.
- The inner ear consists of the bony labyrinth and membranous labyrinth.
- The eustachian tube is also known as the *auditory tube* or *pharyngotympanic tube*.

Internet Links

To learn more about the auditory system and procedures completed on the auditory system, visit the following site:

- *http://www.vestibular.org* to reference information on surgical procedures completed on the ear. (Search for descriptions of various ear surgeries.)

Chapter Review

Fill in the Blank

Instructions: Fill in the blanks in the statements that follow.

1. The auditory canal is located in the _____ section of the ear.

2. The external ear and middle ear are separated by the _____.

3. The middle ear is separated from the inner ear by the _____.

4. The middle ear is also known as the _____.

5. An incision made into the tympanic membrane to create an opening in the membrane is known as a(n) _____.

6. Plastic surgery of the ear is called _____.

7. A bony structure found in the middle ear that is shaped like a hammer is the _____.

8. Excisions completed on the middle ear are reported with codes _____.

9. Code 69990 is used to report the use of a(n) _____.

10. The unlisted procedure code for procedures completed on the inner ear is _____.

Coding Assignments

Instructions: Using the CPT manual, assign the correct code to each of the following procedures.

1. Endolymphatic sac operation with shunt placement _____

2. Mobilization of stapes _____

3. Complete mastoidectomy _____

4. Bilateral removal of impacted cerumen requiring instrumentation _____

5. Biopsy of earlobe _____

6. Transtympanic eustachian tube catheterization _____

7. Ventilating tube removal under general anesthesia _____

8. Transcanal tympanolysis _____

9. Patch placed after site preparation with tympanic membrane repair _____

10. Ear canal incision with middle ear exploration _____

11. Excision of aural polyp _____

12. Labyrinthectomy with mastoidectomy _____

13. Revision of stapedotomy _____

14. Implantation of cochlear device with mastoidectomy _____

15. Meatoplasty due to extensive infection _____

16. External auditory canal excision of soft-tissue lesion _____

17. Debridement of the mastoidectomy cavity _____

18. Transnasal eustachian tube inflation with catheterization _____

19. Inner ear fenestration revision operation _____

20. Tympanic neurectomy _____

21. Decompression of internal auditory canal _____

22. Myringotomy with aspiration and eustachian tube inflation _____

23. Transmastoid antrotomy _____

24. Repair of oval window fistula _____

25. Excision aural glomus tumor; transcanal _____

Case Studies

Instructions: Review each case and indicate the correct code(s).

Case 1

Preoperative and postoperative diagnosis: Chronic otitis media in left ear

Procedure: Myringotomy with tube insertion

Anesthesia: General

The patient was prepared and draped in the usual fashion. After the induction of anesthesia, an incision was made in the left tympanic membrane. The cavity was found to contain a thick mucus material, which was removed. A tympanostomy tube was placed in the left ear. There were no complications noted, and the patient was sent to the recovery room in satisfactory condition.

CPT code(s): _____

Case 2

Preoperative and postoperative diagnosis: Foreign object in right ear

Procedure: Foreign body removal

Anesthesia: General

This 3-year-old male was brought to the operating room and placed under general anesthesia for removal of a foreign body from his right ear. Under direct visualization, a forcep was used to

(continues)

(continued)

remove a paper clip that was located in the external auditory canal. There was minimal bleeding in the canal, and no other complications were noted. The patient was sent to the recovery suite.

CPT code(s): _____

Case 3

Preoperative diagnosis: Tinnitus

Postoperative diagnosis: Tinnitus

Procedure: Middle ear exploration through postauricular incision, right ear

Anesthesia: General

Indications: This is a 42-year-old male who has had ringing in his right ear for the past three weeks. Preliminary testing has not revealed any problems, so we will be performing an exploratory procedure on the middle ear.

Procedure: The anesthesiologist administered general endotracheal anesthesia without incident. A curved incision was made just past the postauricular crease. The middle ear canal was exposed after the eardrum was carefully lifted posteriorly. The ossicular chain mobility was tested, and no abnormalities were noted. The eardrum was gently repositioned, and the canal skin was also moved back into place. The ear canal was packed. The incision was then sutured with 4-0 Vicryl. The patient was returned to the recovery room in good condition.

CPT code(s): _____

Case 4

Preoperative diagnosis: Labyrinthitis, worsening, left ear

Postoperative diagnosis: Labyrinthitis, worsening, left ear

Procedure: Labyrinthectomy with mastoidectomy, postauricular incision, left ear

Anesthesia: General endotracheal

Indications: This is a 72-year-old male who has had hearing loss in his left ear for the past three months. Preliminary testing has revealed worsening labyrinthitis of the lining of the labyrinth.

(continues)

(*continued*)

Procedure: The anesthesiologist administered general endotracheal anesthesia without incident. A curved incision was made just past the postauricular crease. Using the drill, the mastoid cavity was drilled out. The posterior ear canal wall looks to be sound and intact. There is a large area of inflammation found to be in the lining of the labyrinth moving into the posterior semicircular canals. Under microscopic guidance the horizontal, posterior, and superior semicircular canals were removed, along with the lining of the labyrinth. The eardrum was gently repositioned, and the canal skin was also moved back into place. The ear canal was packed. The incision was then sutured with 4-0 Vicryl. The patient was returned to the recovery room in good condition.

CPT code(s): _____

Case 5

Preoperative diagnosis: Bilateral persistent T-tubes with small tympanic granuloma

Postoperative diagnosis: Same

Operation: Removal of bilateral T-tubes with bilateral patching of the eardrums.

Indications for surgery: Examination reveals persistent T-tubes in place over the anterior/inferior quadrant with a small amount of tympanic granuloma and no purulence or any granuloma inside the middle ear space. There was a moderate amount of tympanosclerosis over the eardrums bilaterally.

Procedure: Under general ansesthesia, using a laryngeal mask, the ears were scrubbed and draped in the usual manner. Under operating microscope, the ear canals were cleaned, and the eardrums and tubes could be well visualized.

Tubes were removed, along with the small granuloma round them. The eardrums showed some tympanosclerosis bilaterally with no signs of chronic inflammation, granuloma, or any cholesteatoma in the middle ear space. There was drainage on either side.

The edges of the eardrum perforations were refreshed, and the perforation was covered with an EpiDisc. A small piece of Gelfoam was laid carefully over the EpiDisc graft, and the ear canals were filled with Bacitracin ointment.

The patient was awakened and left the operating room in good and stable condition.

Blood loss: less than 1 cc.

CPT code(s): _____

Chapter Outline

Learning Objectives

At the conclusion of this chapter, you should be able to:

1. Define key terms related to coding radiologic procedures.
2. Define abbreviations associated with radiologic procedures.
3. Define common radiologic procedures.
4. Select CPT codes for radiologic procedures and understand documentation requirements.
5. Identify and code procedures for radiology from case studies.

Key Terms

abduction

adduction

A-mode technique

angiography

anteroposterior

aortography

arteriography

arthrography

axial

bone density test

brachytherapy

B-scan

cineradiography

complete study

computed axial
  tomography (CAT)

decubitus

Diagnostic Radiology

Doppler

dosimetry

dual photon
  absorptiometry

echocardiography

endovascular repair

eversion

extension

fluoroscopy

follow-up/repeat study

hyperthermia

inversion

isodose

lateral

limited study

lymphangiography

magnetic resonance imaging (MRI)

mammography

M-mode technique

nuclear medicine

oblique

port

positron emission tomography (PET)

posteroanterior

prone

proton beam treatment

pulmonary perfusion imaging

radiologic technician

radiologist

radiology

radiopharmaceuticals

real-time scanning

scanning

simulation

supine

teletherapy

tomography

ultrasonography

uptake

venography

views

x-ray

Introduction

Radiology is the study of x-rays, high-frequency sound waves, and high-strength magnetic fields, which sometimes includes the use of radioactive compounds, to diagnose and/or treat diseases or injuries. Radiology looks at internal structures of the body. A **radiologist** is a doctor whose specialty is radiology. The person who is specially trained to use the equipment that generates the pictures or studies is known as a **radiologic technician**.

Guidelines Related to the National Correct Coding Initiative (NCCI)

Perform the following steps to obtain the most current coding guideline information related to this chapter online:

1. Log on to *http://www.cms.hhs.gov/NationalCorrectCodInitEd*.
2. Scroll to the section titled "Downloads."
3. Click "NCCI Policy Manual for Medicare Services."
4. A box may appear that requires you to click "Open."
5. Click "Chapter 9" for guidelines specific to radiology.

Terminology Associated with Radiology

An understanding of some of the terminology used in the positioning of a patient as the radiological procedure is performed aids the coder in selecting the appropriate code for the service provided.

Term	Definition
Abduction	To move away from the body
Adduction	To move toward the axis of the body
Anteroposterior	From front to back
Axial	Referencing the axis of a structure or part of the body
Decubitus	Patient is on his or her back or stomach, which helps in localizing fluid

(continues)

(continued)

Term	Definition
Eversion	Turning outward
Extension	Movement that increases an angle of a joint
Inversion	Turning inward or turning inside out
Lateral	On the side
Oblique	Different angles
Posteroanterior	Back to front
Prone	Horizontal position but facedown
Supine	Lying on back

Exercise 20.1—Check Your Understanding

Terminology

Using the terms listed in the preceding box, provide the position described by the example given.

1. Mr. Kasson was lying facedown on the examination table. _____
2. The small boy's ankle was turned inward. _____.
3. Dr. Kelly wanted an x-ray view coming in from the side of Joey's arm. _____
4. Dr. Martin wanted Steven to have the scan done in a position that required him to lie on his back so that fluid would collect in the ankle. _____
5. When Tracy fell, her arm had to be moved away from her body to allow for a better view of her injury. _____

Radiology is not just about x-rays. The specialty of radiology includes CT or CAT scans, MRI, fluoroscopy, echocardiography, and mammography, just to name a few aspects. Because of the vast number of radiological tests that are available, we will define only a few; this list is by no means comprehensive.

Term	Definition
Angiography	X-ray visualization of the heart and blood vessels after intravascular introduction of a contrast medium.
Arteriography	Radiologic visualization of arteries after the introduction of a contrast medium into the bloodstream or into a vessel.
Arthrography	Radiographic visualization of the inside of a joint using a contrast medium.
Cineradiography	A type of x-ray that films at a high speed in order to take a series of images of motion in an organ or system. This technique combines fluoroscopy, radiography, and the use of a camera to film images on a fluorescent screen.

(continues)

(continued)

Term	Definition
Computed axial tomography (CAT)	Cross-sectional images are produced after an ionizing radiational substance is administered. This is a noninvasive test, usually diagnostic.
Doppler	Frequency change in sound, light, or radio waves given off by a source as it moves toward or away from the observer. Often used in determining velocity of blood flow.
Echocardiography	Ultrasound is used to study the structures of the heart.
Fluoroscopy	Immediate serial images are produced using roentgen rays, which allow for examination of the function of a body part or organ.
Magnetic resonance imaging (MRI)	Radio frequency signals are used to examine the soft tissue and bony structures of the body without radiation.
Mammography	Radiographic examination of soft breast tissue for benign or malignant growths.
Positron emission tomography (PET) **scan**	Radioactive substances are administered that allow images of various body structures to be examined in color codes that indicate the degree and intensity of the metabolic process.
Scanning	A study that displays images of body areas by recording and displaying the images for evaluation.
Tomography	A detailed cross-section of tissue structures are produced.
Ultrasonography	Sound waves are passed over body structures to send a signal to a computer, which is then turned into a picture for examination.
X-ray	Electromagnetic waves are used to produce a picture of internal structures of the body.

Exercise 20.2—Check Your Understanding

Vocabulary Understanding

Using the previous box of terms and definitions, match the term to the correct definition.

_____ 1. Tomography

_____ 2. Scanning

_____ 3. X-ray

_____ 4. Echocardiography

_____ 5. MRI

a. A study that displays images of body areas by recording and displaying the images for evaluation.

b. An ultrasound used to study the structures of the heart.

c. A detailed cross-section of tissue is produced.

d. Radio frequency signals used to examine the soft tissue and bony structures of the body without radiation.

e. Electromagnetic waves used to produce a picture of internal structures of the body.

Abbreviations Associated with Radiology

Abbreviation	Definition
AP	anteroposterior
CAT	computed axial tomography
CT	computed tomography
CXR	chest x-ray
ECHO	echocardiogram
Fx	fracture
KUB	kidneys, ureters, and bladder
MRI	magnetic resonance imaging
PET	positron emission tomography
Rad	radiation absorbed dose
Rad Onc	radiation oncology
SPECT	single-photon emission computed tomography
u/s	ultrasound

Coding for Radiology

The radiology specialty is constantly changing, and the coding changes with it. The Radiology chapter of the CPT manual routinely has updates. The coder should review changes and updates frequently to keep up with information that may be critical for reimbursement to the provider.

Like other parts of the CPT manual, the codes in the Radiology chapter are arranged by anatomical site, starting with the head and neck and moving down the body, then by body system. CPT manual divides the chapter into sections that include the following:

- Diagnostic Radiology—e.g., magnetic resonance imaging (MRI) and interventional radiologic procedures
- Diagnostic Ultrasound—e.g., A-mode, B-scan
- Radiologic Guidance—e.g., fluoroscopic guidance
- Breast Mammography
- Bone and Joint Studies
- Radiation Oncology
- Nuclear Medicine—including diagnostic and therapeutic procedures

The CPT codes for the Radiology chapter begin with code 70010 and go through 79999. The radiologist may report services that fall outside this chapter of CPT, such as cardiac catheterizations. Likewise, physicians, surgeons, and other practitioners can select codes from within this chapter when they apply to the services they perform.

Diagnostic Radiology (70010–76499)

Diagnostic Radiology is the section of the Radiology chapter that is used to report a procedure or service rendered during the assessment of a disease for a more definitive diagnosis, as well as its progression or remission.

This section of CPT refers to different **views**, or the position of the patient in relation to the camera or device used to take the pictures. Attention to the way the code reads and how the service is performed is very important.

> **EXAMPLE:** 70210 Radiologic examination, sinuses, paranasal, less than three views

Some codes also mention "with or without contrast." When a code refers to contrast, this means that the patient has been administered a substance that will enhance the image produced. There are different substances, as well as different ways to administer the substance.

> **EXAMPLE:**
>
> 70450   Computerized tomography, head or brain; without contrast material
> 70460   With contrast material(s)
> 70470   Without contrast material, followed by contrast material(s) and further sections

The codes in this subsection of CPT begin with diagnostic imaging codes for the head and neck and then move to the chest, spine, and pelvis, and then the upper and lower extremities. Following these sections, the code selection moves into the abdomen and gastrointestinal tract, urinary tract, gynecological and obstetrical areas, and then the heart and vascular procedures.

Exercise 20.3—Check Your Understanding

Understanding Radiology Coding

Using the CPT manual, code the following from the Diagnostic Radiology subsection of the Radiology chapter.

1. MRI of spinal canal, thoracic; with contrast
   _____

2. X-ray of the femur, one view
   _____

3. CT of the abdomen; without contrast material _____

4. Cholecystography, oral contrast
   _____

5. Urography, infusion, drip technique and/or bolus technique _____

6. Endoscopic catheterization of the biliary ductal system, radiological supervision and interpretation _____

7. Pelvimetry without placental localization
   _____

8. Diagnostic CT colonography including image postprocessing _____

9. CT of the lumbar spine with contrast material _____

10. Single view, frontal, chest x-ray
    _____

Vascular Procedures (75600–75893)

The coding for vascular procedures is extremely difficult for coders because the knowledge of basic anatomy is not enough to code the services rendered correctly. Coding for procedures done on arteries is different than coding for procedures done on veins. Knowledge of the anatomy of a vascular family is essential, as is an understanding of where the surgeon is during each step of an op note. Table 20-1 notes the vascular procedure codes.

Contrast injections, roadmapping, venography, and angiography are services that would be included in the interventional procedure. Separately billable services are identified within the guidelines for this section, so the

CPT manual should be referenced for other services that may or may not be reported. It should also be noted that the radiological procedures are only one component of coding the services rendered. The movement of the catheter is also a service that needs to be reported. Codes from the 36000 code range should be referenced in addition to the codes from this subsection of the chapter.

TABLE 20-1 Vascular Procedures (75600–75893)

Codes	Description
75600–75630	**Aortography**—aorta and branches are injected with contrast material to visualize problems. The site should be referenced to determine the correct code to report the service performed.
75635	Computed tomographic angiography, abdominal aorta, and bilateral iliofemoral lower extremity runoff. This code includes the imaging that is done prior to as well as following the administration of contrast.
75705–75774	Angiography—the site should be referenced to determine the correct code to report the service performed. Introduction of a catheter or injection procedures might be performed at the same time as the angiography. Additional code assignments might need to be reported depending on the documentation.
75801–75807	**Lymphangiography**—examination of the lymphatic system after contrast material has been injected. The site for the procedure, as well as whether the procedure was done unilaterally or bilaterally, needs to be identified to determine the correct code to report the service performed.
75809	Shuntogram for investigation of previously placed indwelling nonvascular shunt (e.g., LeVeen shunt, ventriculoperitoneal shunt, indwelling infusion pump), radiological supervision and interpretation.
75810	Splenoportography, radiological supervision and interpretation. The site should be referenced to determine the correct code to report the service performed.
75820–75880	**Venography**—x-ray image of the veins, also referred to as a *phlebography*.
75885–75887	Percutaneous transhepatic portography with or without hemodynamic evaluation, radiological supervision and interpretation. This is a radiographic exam of the portal vein of the liver.
75889–75891	Hepatic venography, wedged or free, with or without hemodynamic evaluation, radiological supervision and interpretation.
75893	Venous sampling through catheter, with or without angiography (e.g., for parathyroid hormone, renin), radiological supervision and interpretation.

Exercise 20.4—Check Your Understanding

Vascular Procedures

Using Table 20-1 and your CPT manual, select the correct CPT code.

1. Percutaneous transhepatic portography with hemodynamic evaluation, radiological supervision and interpretation _____.

2. Hepatic venography, wedged, without hemodynamic evaluation, supervision and interpretation _____

3. Thoracic aortography injected with contrast material to perform a serialography, radiological supervision and interpretation _____.

4. Phlebography performed bilaterally on an extremity, radiological supervision and interpretation _____.

5. Splenoportography, radiological supervision and interpretation _____.

Transcatheter Procedures (75894–75989)

Transcatheter procedures are addressed in the next subsection of this chapter. Table 20-2 notes the codes that fall within this code set.

TABLE 20-2 Transcatheter Procedures (75894–75989)

Code(s)	Description
75894	Transcatheter therapy—This procedure involves catheter placement for infusion to clinically obstruct blood flow to a clogged vessel or tumor, treat vascular malformations, or control hemorrhaging.
75898	Angiography through existing catheter for follow-up study for transcatheter therapy, embolization or infusion, other than for thrombolysis is reported with this code.
75901–75902	Mechanical removal of pericatheter obstructive material/intraluminal material from central venous device via separate venous access or device lumen, radiologic supervision and interpretation. The notes that appear following the codes in the CPT manual should be followed.
75956–75959	Endovascular repair—repair within the vessel. The site of the repair should be referenced to determine the correct code to report the service performed.
75970	This code reports transcatheter biopsy, radiological supervision and interpretation. Note the instructional notations that follow this code in the CPT manual.
75984	This code is used to report the changing of a percutaneous tube or drainage catheter with contrast monitoring. It includes the radiological supervision and interpretation. There are numerous notations that follow this code that should be read prior to code assignment.
75989	Radiological guidance (e.g., fluoroscopy, ultrasound, or computed tomography) for percutaneous drainage (e.g., abscess, specimen collection), with placement of catheter, radiological supervision and interpretation.

Exercise 20.5—Check Your Understanding

Transcatheter Procedures

Using Table 20-2 and your CPT manual, fill in the blanks in the sentences that follow.

1. To report angiography through existing catheter for follow-up study for transcatheter therapy, embolization or infusion, other than for thrombolysis, use code _____.

2. Repair within the vessel is also known as a(n) _____.

3. To report transcatheter therapy, embolization—any method—radiological supervision and interpretation use code _____.

4. To report radiological guidance for percutaneous drainage with placement of catheter and radiological supervision and interpretation, use code _____.

5. Transcatheter biopsy, radiological supervision and interpretation, would be coded using code _____.

Other Procedures (76000–76499)

The last subsection in the Diagnostic Radiology section of this chapter of the CPT manual covers other procedures. Code 76000 reports a fluoroscopy (separate procedure) for up to 1 hour of physician or other qualified health care professional time. The instructional notation that follows code 76000 needs to be referenced to identify the codes that cannot be reported in conjunction with code 76000. Codes for other procedures performed at the same time as the fluoroscopy may be billed separately, but the NCCI or CPT should be consulted for any additional notes. Table 20-3 lists some of the codes found in code range 76000 to 76499.

TABLE 20-3 Other Procedures

Code(s)	Description
76098	Radiological examination, surgical specimen
	The surgeon will complete the operation once the specimen has been examined.
76100	Radiologic examination, single plane body section (e.g., tomography), other than with urography
76101–76102	Radiologic examination, complex motion (i.e., hypercycloidal) body section (e.g., mastoid polytomography), other than with urography. The code selection is determined by whether the procedure was performed unilaterally or bilaterally.
76120	Cineradiography/videoradiography, except where specifically included
76125	Cineradiography/videocardiology to complement routine examination (list separately in addition to code for primary procedure). This is an add-on code.

Exercise 20.6—Check Your Understanding

Other Procedures

Using your CPT manual, code the following.

1. An unlisted fluoroscopic procedure _____.
2. Cineradiography _____.
3. Radiologic exam of child, looking for foreign body from nose to rectum _____.
4. Computed tomography, with a limited or localized follow up study _____.
5. An unlisted magnetic resonance procedure _____.

Diagnostic Ultrasound (76506–76999)

This subsection of the chapter is organized by anatomical site, beginning with the head and neck and moving down the body to the extremities. If an ultrasound is performed to establish a diagnosis, the technique used and the extent of the study are what drive code selection.

> **EXAMPLE:** 76881 Ultrasound, complete joint (ie, joint space and periarticular soft tissue structures) real-time with image documentation

The extent of the study indicates whether the study was complete, limited, or follow-up/repeat. A **complete study** is a study that encompasses the entire body area. A **limited study** is a partial scan or examination of a body area or quadrant. It also would be used to report a single-organ examination. **Follow-up/repeat study** is a study performed on an area that requires an additional completed, documented study or exam.

Different techniques that a coder might encounter in documentation include A-mode, B-scan, M-mode, real-time, and Doppler. Doppler studies have previously been explained. The **A-mode technique** is a one-dimensional measurement. **B-scan** is a two-dimensional image. The **M-mode technique** is a type of ultrasound technique that takes the measurements of the velocity and amplitude of moving echo-producing structures and allows for one-dimensional viewing. **Real-time scanning** provides a two-dimensional image of both structure and movement.

When reporting services from this subsection, the coder should verify that there is not only an image present in the medical record, but also a written report to accompany this image. Should the record be missing either of these pieces, the service cannot be reported.

Exercise 20.7—Check Your Understanding

Diagnostic Ultrasound (76506–76999)

Using the CPT manual, locate the correct CPT code for the services provided.

1. Ultrasound, chest, real time, with image documentation _____
2. Ultrasound, transvaginal _____.
3. Fetal biophysical profile, without nonstress testing _____.
4. Ultrasound, infant hips, real time with imaging documentation; no manipulation

   _____.

5. Intraoperative ultrasonic guidance _____.

Fill in the blanks in the following sentences, using the information in this text on diagnostic ultrasound.

6. Supporting documentation must include a(n) _____ report along with a(n)
   _____ and must be found in the medical record.
7. The _____ is a one-dimensional measurement.
8. A(n) _____ is a partial scan or examination of a body area or quadrant.
9. This subsection of the chapter is organized by _____.
10. _____ provides a two-dimensional image of both structure and movement.

Radiologic Guidance (77001–77022)

Codes 77001–77022 are used to report fluoroscopic guidance, computed tomography (CT) guidance, magnetic resonance guidance, and other radiologic guidance. Numerous instructional notations appear after the codes. These notations need to be read and followed. For example, code 77001 contains a notation that signals to the coder that code 77001 should not be used with code 77002 and other codes listed. Reference the CPT manual to locate this note. Some insurance payers are no longer paying these codes because they are considering them to be included in the main procedure.

Breast Mammography (77046–77067)

Code range 77046–77067 reports mammography procedures. Code 77065 is used to report a unilateral mammography, whereas code 77066 is used to report a bilateral mammography.

Bone/Joint Studies (77071–77086)

Bone and joint studies are reported using codes 77071–77086. The codes are differentiated by the type of study, such as:

- Bone age studies
- Bone length studies
- Osseous survey
- Joint survey
- Bone mineral density study

Bone studies are found in the diagnostic radiology subsection of the chapter. A bone age study can be done to determine what the skeletal age is by comparing the x-ray of a wrist and hand to a standard equal to chronological age. Code 77072 should be referenced for this study.

Code 77073 is referenced to study the length of the long bones in the skeleton. There are usually four films included in this study, which would include views of the hip, leg, knee, and ankle.

Also found in this area of the Diagnostic Radiology codes are CT scans and dual energy x-ray absorptiometry (DXA) bone density tests. A **bone density test** is used to determine the presence of osteoporosis by looking at the mass or density of the bone.

Radiation Oncology (77261–77799)

Oncology radiology is therapeutic, as opposed to diagnostic, in nature. The patient is typically undergoing treatment for a malignant neoplasm that may respond to radiation by eradicating or shrinking the neoplasm or obstruction, relieving pain. The codes in this chapter of CPT are for actual treatment and should not be used to report consultations or other evaluation and management services that occur between the radiation oncologist and the patient. Services that would be included in these codes are the actual clinical treatment, medical radiation, planning, and the delivery and management of the radiation services.

To determine the best course of treatment, clinical treatment planning comprises planning and simulation. The planning half of the services is reported using codes 77261–77263, which are noted in Table 20-4.

TABLE 20-4   Radiation Oncology

Code	Description
77261	Therapeutic radiology treatment planning; simple
	A simple planning requires a single treatment area of interest encompassed in a single port or simple parallel opposed ports with simple or no blocking. A **port** is a point of entry for treatment.
77262	; intermediate
	The use of this code would require three or more converging ports and two separate treatment areas, multiple blocks or special time dose constraints.
77263	; complex
	Complex planning requires highly complex blocking, custom shielding blocks, tangential ports, special wedges or compensators, three or more separate treatment areas, rotational or special beam considerations, and combinations of therapeutic modalities.

Simulation is the other half of the treatment planning. **Simulation** mimics the disease so that field settings for the size and location of ports to be used can be determined. These codes are reported only once per setup procedure (see Table 20-5). A dedicated simulator, a radiation therapy treatment unit, or a diagnostic x-ray machine can be used.

TABLE 20-5 Therapeutic Radiology Simulation

Code	Description
77280	Therapeutic radiology simulation-aided field setting; simple
	Simple simulation is the simulation of a single treatment area.
77285	; intermediate
	Intermediate simulation involves the simulation of two separate treatment areas.
77290	; complex
	Complex simulation involves three or more treatment areas, or any number of treatment areas if any of the following are involved: particle, rotation or arc therapy, complex blocking, custom shielding blocks, brachytherapy simulation, hyperthermia probe verification, and any use of contrast materials.
77295	3-dimensional radiotherapy plan, including dose-volume histograms
	Some of the tests produce a three-dimensional image of a tumor or associated critical structures. This three-dimensional image is reported using this code. Documentation to report this code must include dose distribution and 3-D volume reconstruction. Add on code 77293 is used with this code and code 77301 to report respiratory motion management simulation in addition to the primary procedure code.

The next section of the Radiation Oncology subsection is medical radiation physics, dosimetry, treatment devices, and special services. The code set is 77295–77370. In order to code from this section, the coder needs to understand some of the terms used. These are defined in the following box:

Term	Definition
Brachytherapy	An internal radiation therapy that is used to treat tissue
Dosimetry	The scientific determination of the rate, amount, and dose of radiation to be administered
Isodose	Equal-intensity doses of radiation to more than one area
Teletherapy	An external radiation treatment where the machine delivers the radiation after being positioned a specified distance from the patient

Radiation treatment delivery encompasses the radiation therapy, as well as the care of the patient throughout his or her treatment. Physician involvement needs to be documented and should include the patient's response to treatment, including any adverse effects. A nonphysician may deliver the treatment, but a physician does need to be involved in the other aspects of the patient's care, such as prescribing and approving the treatment plan.

Radiation and neutron beam treatment delivery codes begin with code 77401, radiation treatment delivery, superficial and/or ortho voltage, and go to 77425. These codes cover the delivery of the radiation and neutron beam treatment.

The next set of codes, 77427, radiation treatment management, five treatments, through code 77499, unlisted procedure, therapeutic radiology treatment management, is used to report radiation treatment management services. The coder should be aware of the instructional notation that follows the heading of Radiation Treatment Management, which is found before code 77427 in the CPT manual. Review the notation and the Radiation Management and Treatment Table that are located in the CPT manual.

Radiation treatment management is reported in units of five fractions or treatment sessions. Sessions are not time driven. Multiple treatment sessions on the same day are counted separately so long as there is a distinct break noted in therapy sessions, and the fractions being counted would typically be rendered on a separate date.

Evaluation and Management (E/M) services related to treatment management should not be billed separately because they are also included in these services. Additional detailed information is found in the instructional note that appears under the heading Radiation Treatment Management.

The next sets of codes involve proton beam treatment delivery and hyperthermia treatments. **Proton beam treatment** delivery is reported using codes 77520–77525. Proton beam treatment is used to treat malignancies by using a high dose of radiation on tumors, but it does not exceed the radiation tolerance of normal healthy tissue. Areas this may apply to include the optic nerves and the spinal cord.

Hyperthermia is a treatment using heat, such as ultrasound, probes, and radiofrequencies, together with radiation therapy, to treat malignancies by speeding up cell metabolism. Speeding up cell metabolism makes the malignancy more vulnerable to the therapy. Hyperthermia treatment is reported using codes 77600–77620.

The radiation oncology subsection of the chapter finishes off with clinical **brachytherapy**. Brachytherapy involves the use of natural or artificial radio elements that are inserted into the body next to or inside the tumor. Treating cancer in this way allows for higher doses of radiation to a smaller, more focused area.

Exercise 20.8—Check Your Understanding

Radiation Oncology

Using information from the Radiation Oncology section, fill in the blanks with the correct term(s) to complete each of the statements that follow.

1. To determine the best course of treatment, clinical treatment planning comprises
   _____ and _____.
2. _____ is a treatment used to treat malignancies by using high doses of radiation on tumors, but it does not exceed the radiation tolerance of normal healthy tissue.
3. _____ is a term used to indicate equal-intensity doses of radiation to more than one area.
4. "A therapeutic radiology simulation-aided field setting; simple" is reported by code
   _____.
5. A treatment using heat is referred to as _____ treatment.

Nuclear Medicine (78012–79999)

Nuclear medicine treats and diagnoses diseases using radioactive isotopes. The subsection on nuclear medicine is broken down by whether the procedure is diagnostic or therapeutic in nature. Then it moves on to classifying by body system. Diagnostic workups and follow-up care are not included in these services unless the code specifies that they are.

The endocrine system starts off the chapter. The code series begins with 78012 and goes through 78099. The codes in this section involve services rendered to organs of the endocrine system, such as the thyroid, parathyroid, and adrenal cortex. Imaging as well as uptake services are found here. An **uptake** looks at the amount and time that a substance takes to draw up or absorb. For example, code 78012—"Thyroid uptake; single or multiple quantitative measurement(s) (including stimulation, suppression, or discharge, when performed)"—measures the thyroid function by determining how much iodine the thyroid takes up and expresses in relation to the amount administered.

Hematopoietic, reticuloendothelial, and lymphatic system codes are next in the Nuclear Medicine section. This code series is 78102–78199. These radiological services are performed on the spleen, lymph nodes, blood, platelets, plasma, and bone marrow.

Radiological services for the gastrointestinal system are reported using codes 78201–78299. The liver, salivary glands, esophagus, and intestines are studied through imaging and function studies. These services are found in this subsection of the Radiology chapter.

The musculoskeletal system is reported using codes 78300–78399. Bone density studies, as well as joint imaging, are located in this part of the subsection. Dual photon absorptiometry is coded to 78351. **Dual photon absorptiometry** is a type of noninvasive bone density test in which low doses of radiation are beamed through the bone, and a computer evaluates the amount of radiation that was absorbed. The summary is interpreted by a physician.

Next is the cardiovascular system subsection, which contains codes that can be reported in addition to stress testing or other procedures as part of the overall service performed on the patient. The code range is 78414–78499. Blood pool imaging, myocardial imaging, venous thrombosis imaging, and cardiac shunt detection are all found in this subsection.

The respiratory system codes begin with 78579 and go through 78599. Pulmonary perfusion imaging is found in this code range. **Pulmonary perfusion imaging** is the imaging of localized radioactive particles and the proportional blood flow that maps lung perfusion. Radioactive macroaggregated albumin particles are injected, which allows a camera to take the images of particles that are too big to pass through pulmonary capillary beds.

Next, we move on to the Nervous System subsection, which includes brain imaging and imaging of cerebrospinal fluid. The codes used for reporting these services are 78600–78699.

The genitourinary system is the last system before the other procedures. The code series is 78700–78799 and includes urinary bladder residual study, kidney function study, and vascular flow studies of the kidneys and testicles.

The last subsection of the nuclear medicine heading is Other Procedures. Radiopharmaceuticals are located in this area of the chapter. **Radiopharmaceuticals** are drugs that are used in testing the cause of a problem by indicating the location, size, or function of organs, tissues, or vessels. Radioactive material aids in the determinations made with regard to the patient's condition. Also found in this subsection is tumor imaging.

The Therapeutic Procedures subsection, which contains the codes to finish the chapter, are reported with codes 79005–79999. This subsection is for radiopharmaceutical services rendered to patients orally, or by intravenous or intra-arterial particulate administration.

Exercise 20.9—Check Your Understanding

Nuclear Medicine

Fill in the blanks in the statements that follow.

1. _____ is a type of noninvasive bone density test in which low doses of radiation are beamed through the bone, and a computer evaluates the amount that was absorbed.

2. Nuclear medicine codes for the nervous system are reported using codes _____.

3. A(n) _____ looks at the amount and time that a substance takes to draw up or absorb.

4. _____ are drugs that are used in testing the cause of a problem by the use of radioactive material.

5. Nuclear medicine codes for the cardiovascular system are reported using codes _____.

Summary

- Radiology is the study of x-rays, high-frequency sound waves, and high-strength magnetic fields, which sometimes includes the use of radioactive compounds to diagnose and/or treat diseases or injuries.
- A radiologist is a doctor whose specialty is radiology.
- Radiology is divided into four sections:
  - Diagnostic Radiology
  - Diagnostic Ultrasound
  - Radiation Oncology
  - Nuclear Medicine

Internet Links

To learn more about radiology and radiologic procedures, visit *http://www.acr.org*, the website for the American College of Radiology, and *http://www.radiologyinfo.org*. Also do a search on radiology at *http://www.mmcradiology.com/procedures/index.html*.

Chapter Review

Fill in the Blank

Instructions: Fill in the blanks in the statements that follow.

1. The study of x-rays, high-frequency sound waves, and high-strength magnetic fields, which sometimes include the use of radioactive compounds to diagnose and/or treat diseases or injuries is known as _____.

2. A physician whose specialty is radiology is a(n) _____.

3. A study that encompasses the entire body area is called a(n) _____.

4. A partial scan or examination of a body area or quadrant is called a(n) _____.

5. A type of noninvasive bone density test in which low doses of radiation are beamed through the bone, and a computer evaluates the amount of radiation that was absorbed, is known as _____.

6. When radioactive isotopes are used to treat and diagnose diseases, the field of medicine that is used is _____ medicine.

7. An internal radiation therapy that is used to treat tissue is known as_____.

8. Drugs that are used in testing the cause of a problem by indicating the location, size, or function of organs, tissues, or vessels are _____.

9. Proton beam treatment is used in treating malignancies by using a high dose of _____ on tumors.

10. A treatment that uses heat, such as ultrasound, probes, and radiofrequencies, together with radiation therapy to treat malignancies by speeding up cell metabolism, is called _____.

Coding Assignments

Instructions: Using the CPT manual, assign the correct code to the following procedures.

1. Splenoportography, radiological supervision and interpretation only _____

2. X-ray of optic foramina _____

3. Two-view x-ray of cervical spine _____

4. Two-view x-ray of hand _____

5. Swallowing function with videoradiography _____

6. Real-time transvaginal ultrasound of pregnant uterus with image documentation _____

7. Thyroid imaging _____

8. Peptide acute venous thrombosis imaging _____

9. Parathyroid imaging _____

10. Gastric empty imaging _____

11. Radiopharmaceutical therapy by intra-arterial particulate administration _____

12. PET scan of the brain for metabolic evaluation _____

13. Proton treatment delivery, simple _____

14. Therapeutic radiology simulation-aided field setting, complex _____

15. Esophageal motility study _____

16. CT scan of the maxillofacial area without the use of contrast material _____

17. Two-view x-ray of the sacroiliac joint _____

18. Radiological exam of the upper GI tract with scout abdominal radiograph and delayed image, single barium contrast study _____

19. Shoulder x-ray, complete, three views _____

20. Perineogram _____

21. Liver and spleen imaging with vascular flow _____

22. Radiopharmaceutical therapy by intravenous administration _____

23. Dacryocystography, nasolacrimal duct, radiological supervision and interpretation

24. Magnetic resonance angiography, neck with contrast _____

25. Radiologic examination of the calcaneus, two views _____

Case Studies

Instructions: Review each case and indicate the correct code(s).

Case 1

Patient: Smith, John

MRN: 58585858

Indication: Possible benign prostatic hypertrophy

Procedure: CT scan of the pelvis with contrast

After oral contrast medium was given, 7-mm helical sections were obtained. Nonionic IV contrast was administered in the right arm. The exam shows no pelvic mass or adenopathy.

(continues)

(continued)

There is a small amount of ascites in the pelvic area. There was also enlargement of the prostate gland. There is no bowel dilation. The bowel wall appears normal. The venous structures are unremarkable.

Impression: Enlarged prostate gland. Small amount of pelvic ascites.

CPT code(s): _____

Case 2

Patient: Latesen, Meg

MRN: 777444

Indication: Pleural effusion

Procedure: Ultrasound of the chest, real time with image documentation

Sonography of the right hemothorax demonstrates right pleural effusion. Magic marker was used on the dorsal surface of the skin at the site of the maximum depth of the pleural fluid.

CPT code(s): _____

Case 3

Patient: Hipston, Harry

MRN: 123456

Indication: Right leg pain, Rule out DVT

Procedure: CT of right leg
            CT of right leg with contrast

Findings: Free vascular flow of all veins, no DVT noted.

CPT code(s): _____

Case 4

Clinical indication: Status postlumbar spine fusion

Orders: X-rays of spine (complete, lumbosacral, six views), flexion/extension

Comparison: Lateral and flexion/extension views, six, of the lumbar spine 8/22/XX

(continues)

(continued)

Findings: This patient is six months status post–L3-L4 discectomy and placement of an intervertebral disc spacer. The patient is also status post–posterior lumbar spin fusion from L3 to L5 with placement of bilateral pedicle screws, joined on each side by vertical rods. There is no evidence of hardware failure or complications on any of the views. Alignment is anatomical. L2–L5 are stable.

Impression: Status post L3–L4 discectomy and placement of an interbody disc spacer. Status post–L3–L5 posterior fusion. Alignment is anatomical, and there is no evidence of abnormal motion on these flexion/extension views. Degenerative changes are stable.

CPT code(s): _____

Case 5

CT scan of the head/brain w/o contrast

Diagnosis: Mental status change.

Technique: Axial images were obtained from the skull base to the vertex. No intravenous contrast was administered for this test.

Comparison study: 3/15/XXXX

Findings: There has been no significant change in one month. There is no evidence of intracranial hemorrhage, large vessel infarction, or mass. There is mild small vessel ischemic disease. This is the same as the last scan. Mild ventriculomegaly is reidentified. The skull is unremarkable accept for atherosclerotic large vessel calcifications. These are unchanged from the last scan.

Impression: No evidence of acute intracranial abnormality.

CPT code(s): _____

Case 6

Technique: Dual-energy x-ray absorptiometry was performed.

Findings: Lumbar levoscoliosis evident with some focally increased density seen at the right side of the L3–L4 junction, likely due to vertebral endplate sclerosis accompanying degenerative disc disease.

Bone mineral density of the lumbar spine is 1.156 g/sq cm with a T score of −0.2.

(continues)

(*continued*)

Bone mineral density of the left femoral neck is 0.754 g/sq cm with a T score of −2.0.

Femoral density of the right femoral neck is 0.818 g/sq cm with a T score of −1.6.

Impression: Osteopenia of right and left femoral necks with moderate fracture risks. Normal bone mineral density of the lumbar spine.

CPT code(s): _____

Case 7

The patient is a normal, healthy 12-year-old male who fell while skateboarding. The patient states that he tried to break his fall by extending his left hand, at which time he experienced immediate pain and deformity. The patient's parents rushed him to the emergency room, where complete views of the wrist were taken by radiology and interpreted by this physician. The findings are as follows:

Findings: Four views of the left wrist show a comminuted fracture of the distal radial metaphysic with angulations and displacement of the fracture fragments. Carpal bones are intact, as is the distal ulna.

At this time, we will be moving the patient to the operating suite, where a closed reduction with casting will be performed.

CPT code(s): _____

Case 8

This 72-year-old female presents today with chest pain, coughing, and wheezing. She has no history of COPD or heart problems. After examination, it appears she has an upper respiratory infection, but she will be sent for a chest x-ray to rule out any other possibilities.

Report: Two views of the chest, frontal and lateral, are submitted for review. No prior studies are available for comparison.

Findings: The cardiac, mediastinal, and hilar shadows are grossly unremarkable. No focal infiltrate or effusions identified. The pulmonary vascularity is grossly normal. The visualized bones demonstrate no abnormalities at this time.

Impression: No active cardiopulmonary disease

CPT code(s): _____

Case 9

Patient: Sunny Jones

MRN: 1092847

Indication: Cough and fever times 15 days

Radiological Report:

Procedure: AP, DEC, LAT, OBL, PA views of chest taken

Impression: There are hypoinflative changes in both lungs.

CPT code(s): _____

Case 10

Patient: Sally Fasto

Indications: Back pain

Procedure: Patient was standing and an AP thoracolumbar junction 2 view x-ray of the thoracolumbar spine was taken.

Impression: Curvature of spine at L1–L2–L3.

CPT code(s): _____

CHAPTER 21

Pathology and Laboratory

Chapter Outline

Introduction

Guidelines Related to the National Correct
   Coding Initiative (NCCI)

Coding for Pathology and Laboratory Services

Abbreviations Associated with
   Laboratory Coding

Sections

Drug Procedures

Summary

Internet Links

Chapter Review

Coding Assignments

Learning Objectives

At the conclusion of this chapter, you should be able to:

1. Define key terms related to coding pathology and laboratory tests.
2. Define abbreviations common to lab testing.
3. Select CPT codes for pathology and laboratory tests.

Key Terms

analyte

cervical intraepithelial
   neoplasia (CIN)

coagulation

cytogenetic

cytopathology

hematology

immunology

microbiology

panel test

transfusion

Introduction

The Pathology and Laboratory section of the CPT manual begins with panel test 80047 and continues through code 89398 and codes 0001U to 0138U. The codes in this section represent testing ordered by providers to rule out a disease or problem, as well as to provide a definitive diagnosis depending on test results and symptoms of the patient. Laboratory testing is also used to monitor a disease process or to measure various substances that might be in the body. Pathology and laboratory codes are more often assigned in an outpatient setting; they are not required for billing inpatient services. However, some hospitals capture the codes for inpatients to keep statistics on the number of tests completed.

In some instances, it is important for a coder to understand how the lab test is performed. Because laboratory services are constantly changing and improving, the coder may need to ask the physician or lab technician for clarification.

This chapter of the CPT manual is further divided into sections, which will be discussed in this chapter. Also addressed in this chapter are consultation codes used only by pathologists that reflect a service, not a test.

Guidelines Related to the National Correct Coding Initiative (NCCI)

Perform the following steps to obtain the most current coding guideline information related to this chapter online:

1. Log on to *http://www.cms.hhs.gov/NationalCorrectCodInitEd*.
2. Scroll to the section titled "Downloads."
3. Click "NCCI Policy Manual for Medicare Services."
4. A box may appear that requires you to click "Open."
5. Click "Chapter 10" for guidelines specific to pathology and laboratory services.

Coding for Pathology and Laboratory Services

Coding for lab testing involves having an understanding of the test being ordered and then being able to assign the code that best reflects the service rendered. Each lab test ordered is assigned its own code unless the group of tests ordered falls under a panel test. A **panel test** is one CPT code that encompasses a group, or panel, of tests.

> **EXAMPLE:** Barb's doctor wanted her cholesterol and triglycerides checked, so he wrote an order for the following tests: serum cholesterol (82465), lipoprotein (83718), and triglycerides (84478).

Each of these tests has its own separate CPT code, but the group of them together can be billed as a lipid panel (80061), which encompasses all the tests requested. If billed separately, the services would be rejected as unbundled and would have to be recoded as a panel test.

Pathology and laboratory services billed together do not require modifier 51 to be used. Coders in an outpatient setting would use this chapter of CPT much more frequently than coders in an inpatient setting. Laboratory tests are itemized for patients in an inpatient setting, but in the outpatient setting, many offices perform their own tests.

The notes at the beginning of each section should be referenced to understand any guidelines specific to that particular section. The coder should read these and become familiar with any specifics before assigning a code.

Abbreviations Associated with Laboratory Coding

Abbreviation	Definition
Barb	Barbiturate
Ca	Calcium
CBC	Complete blood count
CIN	Cervical intraepithelial neoplasia
FBS	Fasting blood sugar
Gu, gu	Guiac

(continues)

(continued)

Hct	Hematocrit
Hgb	Hemoglobin
K	Potassium
Li	Lithium
Mg	Magnesium
mg	Milligram
O2	Oxygen
U/A	Urinalysis
WBC	White blood count

Sections

The CPT manual divides Pathology and Laboratory into sections. Each section begins with the guidelines or notes that are specific to that section.

Organ or Disease-Oriented Panel (80047–80081)

The panel tests have specific components that, when run together, comprise the panel.

EXAMPLE:

80051   Electrolyte panel

This panel must include the following:

Carbon dioxide (82374)

Chloride (82435)

Potassium (84132)

Sodium (84295)

In this example, the electrolyte panel is made up of four different lab tests that, when run together, make up the electrolyte panel.

If other tests need to be run on the same day and are not part of the panel, they are billed separately.

EXAMPLE: If an electrolyte panel was ordered, and the physician also requested a CBC, then the panel test 80051 would be coded for the electrolytes, and then the code 85027 would also be coded for the CBC that was also requested.

CPT guidelines located at the beginning of the panels indicate when certain panels or tests cannot be billed out together. The guidelines also instruct the coder that two or more panel tests that include or duplicate any of the same tests are not to be reported together.

EXAMPLE:

80048   Basic metabolic panel

This panel must include the following:

Calcium, total (82310)

Carbon dioxide (bicarbonate) (82374)

Chloride (82435)

Creatinine (82565)

Glucose (82947)

Potassium (84132)

Sodium (84295)

Urea nitrogen (BUN) (84520)

(Do not use code 80048 in addition to 80053.)

A panel test (80048; basic metabolic panel, Calcium, total) and a comprehensive metabolic panel (80053) would not be billed together. If the coder read the tests included in code 80053, it would be evident that all tests listed in code 80048 are included in 80053, with the addition of albumin (82040), bilirubin, total (82247), phosphatase alkaline (84075), protein, total (84155), transferase, alanine amino (ALT) (SGPT) (84460), and transferase, aspartate amino (AST)(SGOT) (84450). Careful attention to the tests being ordered are necessary to assign the correct code or codes, and attention to any notes surrounding the code assignments is essential.

Exercise 21.1—Check Your Understanding

Panel Tests

Choose the correct panel test code for the following lab tests ordered.

1. Transferase, aspartate amino (AST)(SGOT), albumin, protein (total), transferase, alanine amino (ALT) (SGPT), bilirubin (total), bilirubin (direct), phosphate alkaline panel test _____

2. Albumin, glucose, potassium, creatinine, calcium, phosphate, sodium, carbon dioxide, chloride, BUN panel test _____

3. HDL cholesterol, cholesterol (serum, total), triglycerides panel test _____

4. Carbon dioxide, potassium, glucose, creatinine, sodium, BUN, calcium, chloride panel test

   _____

5. Potassium, sodium, creatinine, calcium, albumin, glucose, phosphatase alkaline, carbon dioxide, chloride, total bilirubin, total protein, alanine amino transferase, aspartate amino transferase, BUN, CBC, TSH, WBC panel test _____

Drug Procedures

Procedures that relate to drug testing, or the presence of a substance within a patient's body, are divided into three subsections in the CPT manual:

- Drug Assay—This includes presumptive drug class screening, and definitive drug testing, which are tests used to identify possible use and non-use of specific drugs or drug classes.

- Therapeutic Drug Assay—These tests are completed to monitor clinical response to a known prescribed medication.

- Chemistry—These tests are completed to determine if a substance, such as amylase, chromium, creatine, and so on is present in the examination material specimen.

Each of these subsections listed above is discussed within this chapter of the book and appears within this chapter according to the code numbers for each subsection. They are not presented in the CPT manual in numerical order.

Drug Assay (80305–80377 and 83992)

In the CPT manual following code 80076, the subsection of Drug Assay appears. Locate this subsection in your CPT manual. Here the definitions appear for the two major categories for drug testing in the Drug Assay subsection, which include:

- Presumptive Drug Class—These tests are completed to identify possible use or non-use of a drug or drug class.
- Definitive Drug Class—These tests are qualitative or quantitative and identify possible use or non-use of a drug.

Reference the subsection in the CPT manual and read the entire notations that appear for this subsection of the manual.

Therapeutic Drug Assays (80145–80299)

Codes from the Therapeutic Drug Assays section reflect testing to monitor the patient's clinical response to a prescribed medication. Whole blood, serum, plasma, or cerebrospinal fluid are used for quantitative testing.

Evocative/Suppression Testing (80400–80439)

Code range 80400–80439 contains panel tests that are used to confirm or rule out a diagnosis and reflect only the technical component of the testing. In the CPT manual, prior to code 80400, coders are instructed to reference Hydration, Therapeutic, Prophylactic, Diagnostic Injections and Infusions, and Chemotherapy and Other Highly Complex Drug or Highly Complex Biologic Agent Administration to report the adminstration of evocative or suppressive agents. The professional component, in which the provider administers the suppressive agent (codes from the Medicine chapter of the CPT manual), is used to report this administration. New coders should be sure to read the text information that appears in the CPT manual in this section.

Another notation that should be noted in this section is "× 2." This alerts the coder to the fact that the test is usually run twice and should not be billed with a quantity of 2.

Consultations (Clinical Pathology) (80500–80502)

The Consultations section of codes comprises consult codes used by the pathologist to indicate that a written report was requested by a primary care physician or other provider. These services indicate the medical interpretation and not a test.

The 80500—"Clinical pathology consultation; limited, without review of patient's history and medical records"—code allows the pathologist to bill at a consultation level for his or her expertise in rendering a medical opinion or judgment within the pathologist's scope of practice. The 80502—"Clinical pathology consultation; comprehensive, for a complex diagnostic problem, with review of patient's history and medical records"—code is available if the pathologist also reviews the patient's medical history and medical records.

Urinalysis (81000–81099)

The Urinalysis section of CPT contains codes for various tests on urine. The coder needs to know how the test was run to properly code in this section. The dipstick or tablet is frequently used in the office, but a microscope or an automated test may also be performed.

Molecular Pathology (81105–81408 and 81479)

This subsection is used to report medical laboratory procedures that are completed to analyze nucleic acid to detect variants in genes. The codes are differentiated based on the specific gene being analyzed. The name of the genes are described as per the gene names approved by the Human Genome Organization (HUGO). Extensive notations appear in the CPT manual prior to code 81170 that apply to the assignment of these codes. They state that these codes include all analytical services performed. Procedures that are performed prior to cell lysis should be reported separately. Read the notations to review these notes and the definitions that apply to these codes.

Genomic Sequencing Procedures and Other Molecular Multianalyte Assays (81410–81471)

Genomic sequencing procedures and other molecular multianalyte assays are DNA or RNA sequence analysis methods that allow for the analysis of the human genome. This analysis helps to determine the patient's DNA or RNA makeup, which can have medical significance or be useful in the medical management of the patient's case.

Multianalyte Assays with Algorithmic Analyses (81490–81599)

Codes 81490 to 81599 report multianalyte assays with algorithmic analyses. The results from the completed assays are analyzed using algorithmic analysis and patient information (if available), and then are scored with a numerical value or probability that is typically unique to a single clinical laboratory or manufacturer. These tests analyze if a patient is at risk for a disease. It should be noted that individual payers may or may not pay for these tests.

Chemistry (82009–84999)

Unless otherwise stated, tests in the Chemistry section are considered quantitative. The sources or specimens can be blood, stool, urine, or blood serum. If the code does not specify a source, any code can be used for any of the sources. Each source is considered a separate specimen, so if the exact same test is run on urine and blood, the coder would use one code for the urine and the exact same code for the blood. The coder may encounter the term **analyte**, which refers to the substance being tested.

Hematology and Coagulation (85002–85999)

Hematology is the study of blood. **Coagulation** is the clotting of blood. The Hematology and Coagulation section contains codes for blood testing such as clotting factors, blood counts, and platelets.

Immunology (86000–86849)

As the name implies, **immunology** is the study of the immune system. The tests in the Immunology section include testing for allergies and sensitivity to a substance.

Tissue-typing procedures are also found in this section. Cross-matching for transplant patients would be found in this section as well.

Transfusion Medicine (86850–86999)

Transfusion is the direct introduction of whole blood or blood components into the bloodstream. Code range 86850–86999 includes codes for antibody screens, antibody identification, and blood typing. Other procedures, such as volume reduction of blood or blood products and leukocyte transfusion, are also coded from this section.

Microbiology (87003–87999)

Microbiology is the study of microorganisms, which involves the identification of organisms. The technique for obtaining the specimen is very important here, as some descriptions in this section are similar to those described in the Immunology section.

Anatomic Pathology (88000–88099)

The Anatomic Pathology section is what physicians use to bill their services for autopsies and postmortem examinations.

Cytopathology (88104–88199)

Cytopathology is the study of cells, especially in the disease process. Codes from this section include Pap smears and cervical screenings.

Codes 88142–88143 may be referred to as "thin prep" codes. The collection of the specimen may be done by aspiration of vaginal fluid, or by cervical or endocervical scraping.

Codes 88150–88153 are used when any method other than the Bethesda system is used to evaluate the specimen. This is where a coder may see designations of **cervical intraepithelial neoplasia (CIN)** of CIN 1, CIN 2, and CIN 3. In this system, 1 designates mild dysplasia and 3 designates severe dysplasia.

Cytogenetic Studies (88230–88299)

Cytogenetic studies address heredity or genes at the cellular level. A chromosome study is coded to the Cytogenetic Studies section of the CPT manual.

Surgical Pathology (88300–88399)

The Surgical Pathology section of the CPT manual contains codes that would be used for gross examination of a specimen. Gross examination involves the collection of a specimen that is bigger than a cell. Microscopic examination may or may not be necessary for the pathologist to determine a diagnosis. The six levels of gross or microscopic examination are identified using codes 88300–88309.

In Vivo (e.g., Transcutaneous) Laboratory Procedures (88720–88749)

Codes in the range 88720–88749 are used to report in vivo procedures.

Other Procedures and Reproductive Medicine Procedures (89049–89398)

Code range 89049–89240 reports procedures that include cell count of miscellaneous body fluids, fat stain, gastric intubation, aspiration, and fractional collections. Codes 89250 to 89398 report reproductive medicine procedures that include the preparation of an embryo for transfer, cyropreservation of embryos, and semen analysis to name a few.

Proprietary Laboratory Analyses (0001U–0138U)

This subsection includes codes that describe proprietary clinical laboratory analyses. The analyses can be provided by a single laboratory or licensed or marketed to multiple providing laboratories. The laboratories must be cleared or approved by the Food and Drug Administration.

Reference the extensive instructional notation that appears after the heading of Proprietary Laboratory Analyses and before the code 0001U.

Summary

- Codes from this chapter represent testing done to assist in diagnosing as well as ruling out various diseases.
- Laboratory testing is constantly changing and improving, so the coder needs to be aware of changes and also have references that will aid in understanding and choosing codes from this section.
- Unlike other chapters in the CPT manual, coding guidelines for this chapter are typically found at the beginning of each section. Careful attention to these notes is necessary.
- The coder may encounter abbreviations within provider notes that will need clarification in order to locate a proper code.
- Attention to detail is essential for performing correct coding in this chapter.

Internet Links

To learn about laboratory tests, visit *http://www.labtestsonline.org*.

To review information on tests, visit *http://www.pathology.washington.edu*, and click the "Diagnostic" tab to learn about various laboratory tests.

Chapter Review

True/False

Instructions: Indicate whether the following statements are true (T) or false (F).

1. _____ Code 89190 is used to report a nasal smear for eosinophils.

2. _____ The abbreviation for magnesium is mg.

3. _____ Pathology codes are broken into panel tests.

4. _____ Code 80055 reports an obstetric panel.

5. _____ Code 80048 reports an electrolyte panel.

Fill in the Blank

Instructions: Fill in the blanks in the statements that follow.

6. One CPT code that encompasses a group of tests is called a(n) _____.

7. A substance being tested is also known as a(n) _____.

8. The direct introduction of whole blood into the bloodstream is _____.

9. The most severe of the cervical intraepithelial neoplasia designations is _____.

10. The abbreviation WBC stands for _____.

Coding Assignments

Instructions: Using the CPT manual, assign the correct code to each of the following.

1. Semen analysis for presence of sperm, including Huhner test _____

2. Lymphocytotoxicity assay, visual crossmatch, with titration _____

3. ANA titer _____

4. Lipase, chemistry test _____

5. Renal function panel _____

6. Aldosterone suppression evaluation panel _____

7. Protein analysis of tissue by Western blot, with interpretation and report _____

8. Level VI Surgical pathology, gross and microscopic examination _____

9. Chromosome analysis; count five cells, one karyotpe, with banding _____

10. Compatibility test; incubation technique _____

11. Obstetric panel _____

12. Lithium assay _____

13. Calcium, total _____

14. CBC, automated _____

15. Clot retraction _____

16. Pinworm microbiology examination

   _____

17. Immune complex assay _____

18. Thrombomodulin _____

19. TSH _____

20. Lipid panel _____

21. Flow cytometry DNA analysis

   _____

22. Rh(D) blood typing _____

23. RBC antibody screen _____

24. Phospholipid platelet neutralization

   _____

25. Cold agglutinin screen _____

26. Amikacin therapeutic drug assay

   _____

27. Limited clinical pathology consultation without review of patient's history and medical record

   _____

28. Urine pregnancy test, by visual color comparison methods _____

29. Aldolase chemistry _____

30. Serum cholinesterase chemistry

   _____

Medicine

Chapter Outline

Learning Objectives

At the conclusion of this chapter, you should be able to:

1. Define key terms related to coding from the Medicine section of the CPT manual.
2. Define procedures that are found in the Medicine section of the CPT manual.

3. Identify the method of administration for common vaccines and toxoids.

4. Select CPT codes for services that are found in the Medicine section of the CPT manual.

5. Identify and code procedures for medicine from case studies.

Key Terms

biofeedback	immune globulin	peripheral arterial disease (PAD) rehabilitation	psychoanalysis
gonioscope	narcosynthesis		refractor
hemodialysis	ophthalmologist	peritoneal dialysis	serial tonometry
hemoperfusion	ophthalmology	psychiatrist	spirometry testing
hypnotherapy	optometrist	psychiatry	vaccine

Introduction

The Medicine section of the CPT manual is found after the Pathology and Laboratory section. The code range in this section begins with code 90281 and goes through code 99607. A wide variety of services are found in the Medicine section. The subsections found in this chapter are as follows:

- Immune Globulins, Serum or Recombinant Products
- Immunization Administration for Vaccines/Toxoids
- Vaccines/Toxoids
- Psychiatry
- Biofeedback
- Dialysis
- Gastroenterology
- Ophthalmology
- Special Otorhinolaryngologic Services
- Cardiovascular
- Noninvasive Vascular Diagnostic Studies
- Pulmonary
- Allergy and Clinical Immunology
- Endocrinology
- Neurology and Neuromuscular Procedures
- Medical Genetics and Genetic Counseling Services
- Adaptive Behavior Services
- Central Nervous System Assessments/Tests
- Health and Behavior Assessment/Intervention
- Hydration, Therapeutic, Prophylactic, Diagnostic Injections and Infusions, and Chemotherapy and Other Highly Complex Drug or Highly Complex Biologic Agent Administration
- Photodynamic Therapy
- Special Dermatological Procedures
- Physical Medicine and Rehabilitation

- Medical Nutrition Therapy
- Acupuncture
- Osteopathic Manipulative Treatment
- Chiropractic Manipulative Treatment
- Education and Training for Patient Self-Management
- Non–Face-to-Face Nonphysician Services
- Special Services, Procedures, and Reports
- Qualifying Circumstances for Anesthesia
- Moderate (Conscious) Sedation
- Other Services and Procedures
- Home Health Procedures/Services
- Medication Therapy Management Services

Guidelines Related to the National Correct Coding Initiative (NCCI)

Perform the following steps to obtain the most current coding guideline information related to this chapter online:

1. Log on to *http://www.cms.hhs.gov/NationalCorrectCodInitEd*.
2. Scroll to the section titled "Downloads."
3. Click "NCCI Policy Manual for Medicare Services."
4. A box may appear that requires you to click "Open."
5. Click "Chapter 11" for guidelines specific to the Medicine, Evaluation, and Management Services section.

Immune Globulins (90281–90399)

An **immune globulin** functions as an antibody for a short period of time. This type of passive immunity occurs as the immune globulin circulates through the body. The basic structure determines the type of immunoglobulin function.

The code range is 90281–90399. Botulism immune globulin, hepatitis B immune globulin, rabies immune globulin, and varicella-zoster immune globulin are all coded from this code range. Most of these immune globulin products are administered intramuscularly, but the coder would need to read the code and determine whether the route of administration listed is reflected accurately in the code selection. The codes in this range are reported in addition to administration codes and are modifier 51 exempt.

Immunization Administration for Vaccines and Toxoids (90460–90474)

The codes in the range 90460–90474 report services provided by a physician when counseling the patient and/or family on any adverse effects related to immunization during administration of a vaccine. These codes are reported separately in addition to the code for the vaccine or toxoid supply. Table 22-1 provides the codes and descriptions.

TABLE 22-1 Immunization Administration for Vaccines/Toxoids

Codes	Description
90460–90461	Immunization administration through 18 years of age. The route of administration (i.e., intramuscular, intradermal, subcutaneous, or percutaneous) does not matter. These two codes are used *only* when the physician or another qualified health-care professional (i.e., nurse) provides face-to-face counseling to the patient or family during administration of the vaccine.
	Code 90461 is an add-on code and is reported with 90460 for each additional vaccine or vaccine component given.
	EXAMPLE
	Mary received an MMR vaccine. The physician provided counseling to her mother just prior to the injection being given by the nurse. The following codes were reported:
	90707—"Measles, mumps, and rubella virus vaccine (MMR), live, for subcutaneous use"
	90460—"Immunization administration—first vaccine (measles)"
	90461 × 2—"Each additional vaccine/toxoid component (mumps, rubella)"
90471–90472	These administration codes are reported for immunization administration for patients over the age of 18 or administration of a vaccine that is not accompanied by face-to-face physician or qualified health-care professional counseling. The route of administration (i.e., intramuscular, intradermal, subcutaneous, or percutaneous) does not matter.
90473–90474	Immunization administration by intranasal or oral route; each vaccine (single or combination vaccine/toxoid)

Vaccines and Toxoids (90476–90756)

A **vaccine** is a dead microorganism that is administered for prevention or treatment of a disease. A toxoid is the actual bacterial exotoxin that has lost its toxic effect but kept its ability to produce antibodies. A live vaccine is one that was prepared from live microorganisms but has been thinned down and that has kept the immunogenic properties.

Adenovirus vaccines, hepatitis A and B vaccines, influenza virus vaccines, and rabies vaccines are all found in code range 90476–90749. Also found in this code range are childhood immunizations such as the diphtheria, tetanus toxoids, and pertussis vaccine; measles, mumps, and rubella (MMR) vaccine; and poliovirus vaccine. The 90476–90749 codes identify vaccine products only and would require an additional code assignment for their administration.

Exercise 22.1—Check Your Understanding

Vaccines and Administrations

Assign the correct CPT code to each of the following vaccines, and indicate the method of administration (i.e., subcutaneous, intramuscular, or intradermal).

1. Tdap for a 14-year-old _____
2. Typhoid vaccine, live _____
3. MMRV, live vaccine _____
4. HepA, pediatric/adolescent dosage 3 dose schedule _____
5. DTaP-Hib-IPV _____
6. Varicella virus vaccine live for subcutaneous use _____
7. Adenovirus type 4 PCV13 live _____
8. HepA, adult dosage _____
9. Anthrax _____
10. Yellow fever vaccine, live, for subcutaneous use _____

Psychiatry (90785–90899)

Psychiatry is the branch of medicine that treats mental disorders, which include emotional and behavioral disorders. A **psychiatrist** is a medical doctor who administers treatment for patients with mental, emotional, and behavioral disorders. A similar mental disorder can manifest itself in different levels of severity in different patients.

Psychiatry codes found in the 90785–90853 code range are illustrated in Table 22-2.

Other psychiatric services or procedures are found in code range 90863–90899. This code range encompasses codes that fall outside the other subcategories noted in this section of the chapter. Table 22-3 notes other psychiatric service codes.

TABLE 22-2 Psychiatry Codes (90785–90853)

Code(s)	Description
90785	This is an add-on code that is reported with codes 90791, 90792, 90832, 90833, 90834, 90836, 90837, 90838, 99201–99255, 99304–99337, 99341–99350, and 90853. This code reports interactive complexity when delivering the primary service. For example, the use of play equipment or other devices during the session. Coders must read the instructional notations that appear before code 90785 for a complete listing of factors that indicate the use of this code.
90791–90792	Psychiatric diagnostic evaluations are reported with these codes. Code 90791 reports a psychiatric diagnostic evaluation, while code 90792 reports a psychiatric diagnostic evaluation with medical services. Extensive notations prior to these codes should be read and understood by the coder prior to code assignment.
90832–90838	This code range reports psychotherapy, which is treatment of mental illnesses and behavioral disturbances through therapeutic communication. The codes are time based and are differentiated by the lengths of time of the therapy and whether an evaluation and management service occurred with the therapy. Codes 90833, 90836, and 90838 are add-on codes that are used with the appropriate Evaluation and Management (E/M) codes to denote that E/M services and psychotherapy occurred on the same date by the same provider. Following each of these add-on codes, notations appear in the CPT manual that will assist the coder in code selection. Also, coders should read the extensive notations that appear prior to code 90832 regarding the assignment of codes from this section.
90839–90840	These codes are time based and are used to report psychotherapy for crisis situations. Prior to code 90839, an extensive notation appears that instructs the coder how to report these codes. The coder should report the total face-to-face time even if the time is not continuous.
90845	**Psychoanalysis**—a form of psychotherapy in which the patient's unconscious thoughts are recognized and analyzed Different techniques might be used for this type of psychotherapy.
90846–90847	Family psychotherapy This procedure may or may not be done with the patient present.
90849	Multiple family group psychotherapy
90853	Group psychotherapy (other than a multiple-family group) This might be a session in which more than one patient participates. The patients involved may or may not have the same problem. This code selection is not a correct choice if the group is made up of the patient and family members.

TABLE 22-3 Other Psychiatric Services (90863–90899)

Code(s)	Description
90863	Pharmacologic management, including prescription, and review of medication, when performed with psychotherapy services. This is an add-on code that is reported with codes 90832, 90834, or 90837.
90865	Narcosynthesis for psychiatric diagnostic and therapeutic purposes (e.g., sodium amobarbital [amytal] interview) **Narcosynthesis** is a form of psychiatry that involves the administering of an intravenous drug that allows the patient to release thoughts that might be suppressed or repressed.

(continues)

TABLE 22-3 (*continued*)

Code(s)	Description
90867–90869	Therapeutic repetitive transcranial magnetic stimulation treatment delivery management. Each code is reported once per session.
90870	Electroconvulsive therapy (includes necessary monitoring) This type of therapy is used to treat patients with chronic or profound depression when all other forms of treatment have been unsuccessful.
90875–90876	Individual psychophysiological therapy incorporating biofeedback training by any modality (face to face with the patient) with psychotherapy (e.g., insight-oriented, behavior modifying, or supportive psychotherapy) Code choice is determined by the approximate time spent with the patient; time must appear in the documentation.
90880	**Hypnotherapy** is a type of psychotherapy that alters the state of consciousness to heighten awareness and opens the patient up to suggestions that may alter the patient's thoughts or behavior.
90882	Environmental intervention for medical management purposes on psychiatric patient's behalf with agencies, employers, or institutions
90885	Psychiatric evaluation of hospital records, other psychiatric reports, psychometric and/or projective tests, and other accumulated data for medical diagnostic purposes
90887	Interpretation or explanation of results of psychiatric or other medical examinations and procedures, or other accumulated data to family or other responsible persons, or advising them how to assist patient
90889	Preparation of report of patient's psychiatric status, history, treatment, or progress (other than for legal or consultative purposes) for other individuals, agencies, or insurance carriers
90899	Unlisted psychiatric service or procedure

Exercise 22.2—Check Your Understanding

Psychiatry (Code Range 90785–90899)

Indicate whether the following statements are true (T) or false (F).

1. _____ Family psychotherapy without the patient present is reported using CPT code 90847.

2. _____ Code 90839 reports 60 minutes of psychotherapy for crisis.

3. _____ Code 90845 is used for the management of the patient's medications.

4. _____ Electroconvulsive therapy and monitoring is reported with code 90870.

5. _____ Code 90885 is described as an environmental intervention for medical management purposes on the psychiatric patient's behalf with agencies, employers, or institutions.

Biofeedback (90901–90913)

Biofeedback deals with involuntary physiological responses and teaches the patient how to consciously manage these responses. The physiological responses that can be treated using biofeedback include high blood pressure and incontinence. The code selected is determined by the modality. Biofeedback may or may not be covered by a particular payer. This should be discussed with the patient prior to treatment.

Dialysis (90935–90999)

The Dialysis subsection is divided into four components in the CPT manual: Hemodialysis, Miscellaneous Dialysis Procedures, End-Stage Renal Disease Services (ESRD), and Other Dialysis Procedures.

Hemodialysis (90935–90940)

Hemodialysis removes waste from the blood but involves a continuous movement of blood from the body to a hemodialyzer for filtering, and then the clean blood is returned to the patient's bloodstream. Figure 22-1 illustrates the hemodialysis machine and process. Table 22-4 lists the codes used for reporting hemodialysis services.

This code range includes all evaluation and management services related to the patient's renal disease on the day of the hemodyalysis procedure.

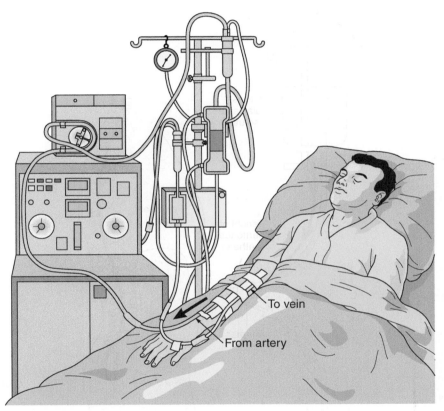

FIGURE 22-1 Hemodialysis

TABLE 22-4 Hemodialysis (90935–90940)

Code	Description
90935	Hemodialysis procedure with single provider evaluation
	The catheter would have already been placed in an artery or vein. This code would be used to report a single treatment that includes the physician evaluation.
90937	Hemodialysis procedure requiring repeated evaluations, with or without substantial revision of dialysis prescription
	The catheter would have already been placed in an artery or vein. This code would be used to report services provided by the physician during the patient's hemodialysis treatment.
90940	Hemodialysis access flow study to determine blood flow in grafts and arteriovenous fistulae by an indicator method

Miscellaneous Dialysis Procedures (90945–90947) and Other Dialysis Procedures (90989–90999)

The procedures found in the 90945–90947 and 90989–90999 code ranges are used to report services that are not found in the other code ranges for dialysis procedures, such as peritoneal dialysis, hemofiltration, and other continuous renal replacement therapies. **Peritoneal dialysis** is another form of cleaning the waste from the bloodstream, but instead of a machine to filter the blood, the peritoneal membrane is used as the filter. Figure 22-2 illustrates peritoneal dialysis.

Also found in this code range are procedure codes that report dialysis training and hemoperfusion. **Hemoperfusion** is a way for toxins to be removed from the blood in which the physician perfuses the blood through activated charcoal or resin and then transfuses the blood back into the patient.

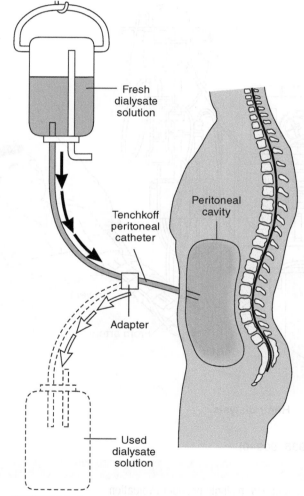

Fresh dialysate solution

Tenchkoff peritoneal catheter

Peritoneal cavity

Adapter

Used dialysate solution

FIGURE 22-2 Peritoneal Dialysis

End-Stage Renal Disease Services (90951–90970)

Code range 90951–90970 is used to report end-stage renal disease services. Codes 90951–90966 are reported once per month. Codes 90967–90970 are for services lasting less than a full month and are billed per day. The codes are differentiated by age-specific services and place of service—outpatient, home, or inpatient setting.

Exercise 22.3—Check Your Understanding

Dialysis Services

Assign the correct code for each of the following.

1. Monitoring and nutrition assessment for the month of May, for a 15-year-old ESRD patient _____

2. Dialysis training, patient, including helper where applicable—completed course _____

3. Hemodialysis access flow study to determine blood flow in grafts and arteriovenous fistulae by an indicator method _____

4. ESRD services for 35-year-old ESRD patient for five days of the month; the rest of the month, he was in the hospital (code only for the outpatient setting) _____

5. Hemoperfusion _____

Gastroenterology (91010–91299)

The services reported in the Gastroenterology code range are for diagnostic procedures performed on the gastrointestinal system. If Evaluation and Management (E/M) services were performed at the same time, these services would be reported separately. The surgical section for procedures of the digestive tract should be referenced before codes from this code range are used.

Procedures of the esophagus are reported first, including intubation and gastroesophageal reflux tests. Gastric intubation, gastric aspiration or lavage, and gastric saline load testing are also reported from this code range.

Gastric physiology is reported using codes 91132 and 91133. These codes report electrical activity generated by the stomach, which enables physicians to detect abnormalities of the stomach.

Ophthalmology (92002–92499)

Ophthalmology is the study of diseases and disorders of the eye. An **ophthalmologist** is a medical doctor who specializes in treatment of these diseases and disorders. An ophthalmologist is able to prescribe medication as part of the treatment plan, as well as conduct tests and issue prescriptions for corrective lenses. An **optometrist** is not a medical doctor and cannot prescribe medication but is able to prescribe corrective lenses.

The codes in the Ophthalmology subsection of the Medicine section of the CPT manual are services reported by an ophthalmologist. General ophthalmological services are divided into new patient and established patient services. The services report the medical examination and evaluation with initiation of treatment. The levels of service reported are intermediate and comprehensive. The code selection is determined by whether the patient is new or established, and whether the service was intermediate or comprehensive.

Intermediate levels of service (codes 92002 and 92012) include patient history, general medical observation, and external examination. Ophthalmoscopy is included, as is biomicroscopy, mydriasis, and tonometry. Initiation of a plan of care is also included in these service codes.

Comprehensive levels of service (codes 92004 and 92014) include all of the same services that are reported in the intermediate service codes, in addition to gross visual field testing and basic sensorimotor examination.

Special ophthalmological services (code range 92015–92145) include refractor testing. A **refractor** is a machine that contains a large series of lenses that are changed quickly during an examination as the patient views an eye chart. Also included in this code range is code 92020 for gonioscopy. A **gonioscope** is a type of scope that examines the eye for signs of glaucoma. Table 22-5 summarizes some of these services.

TABLE 22-5 Specialized Services (92015–92287)

Code(s)	Description
92065	Orthoptic and/or pleoptic training, with continuing medical direction and evaluation This code is used when the patient needs to be trained to perform exercises to correct ocular problems related to the ocular muscles.
92081–92083	Visual field examination, unilateral or bilateral, with interpretation and report. Code selection is based on the extent of the examination.
92100	Serial tonometry (separate procedure) with multiple measurements of intraocular pressure over an extended time period with interpretation and report, same day (e.g., diurnal curve or medical treatment of acute elevation of intraocular pressure) Serial tonometry is a procedure that measures pressure over the course of the day. There are multiple pressure checks that record the significant peaks within a 24-hour period.
92132–92134	These codes report scanning computerized ophthalmic diagnostic imaging (e.g., scanning laser) with interpretation and report, unilateral or bilateral.
92136	Ophthalmic biometry by partial coherence interferometry with intraocular lens power calculation is reported with this code.
92145	This code reports a corneal hysteresis determination, by air impulse stimulation, unilateral or bilateral, with interpretation and report. During corneal hysteresis a measurement is taken that determines the eye(s) response to application and removal of air impulse stimulation thus measuring the biomechanic properties of the cornea. This test can determine ocular abnormalities and eyes that are at risk for diseases. The most common reason to complete this test is for the diagnosis and monitoring of glaucoma. However this test is also completed to identify other corneal pathology or for pre-refractive surgery risk assessment

Other Specialized Services

Opthalmoscopy procedures (code range 92201–92260) are billed separately only if they are not part of a general ophthalmologic service. Fluorescein and fundus procedures are found in this code range.

Other specialized services (code range 92265–92499) include electroretinography, color-vision examination, and fitting of contact lenses. Codes for fitting of spectacles or prosthesis services are located in the 92340–92371 code range and should be reviewed carefully before codes are assigned.

Special Otorhinolaryngologic Services (92502–92700)

The Special Otorhinolaryngologic Services section is provided to report special diagnostic services typically performed by an ear, nose, and throat (ENT) specialist. Screening tests, such as speech evaluations and hearing tests, are found in this code range.

Cardiovascular (92920–93799)

The Cardiovascular section of the Medicine chapter includes codes used to report diagnostic and therapeutic services. Codes 92920–92944 are out of numerical sequence in the CPT manual.

The therapeutic services reported here include such procedures as stent placements, percutaneous transluminal coronary angioplasty (PTCA), and percutaneous transluminal coronary arthrectomy.

- Coronary therapeutic services and procedures are reported with codes 92920–92979, which includes percutaneous transluminal coronary procedures. Attention to documentation is necessary in order to assign the proper codes from this code range. Coders should also note the codes in this range that are add-on codes.
- Cardiopulmonary resuscitation is reported using code 92950.

- Cardiography and cardiovascular monitoring services are reported using code range 93000–93278. Electrocardiograms, cardiovascular stress tests, and Holter monitoring are found in this code range. Some codes in this code range differentiate the technical and professional components. Per the guidelines, an order must be present in the patient's record in addition to the separate written reports. Orders and reports must be authenticated by the provider. Attention to the service the physician actually provides is key in code assignment.

- Implantable insertable, and wearable cardiac device evaluations are reported with codes 93264–93298. These services are diagnostic procedures used to assess device therapy and cardiovascular physiologic data.

- Echocardiography services are reported using codes from the 93303–93356 code range. Documentation is important in billing these services. If the clinically relevant findings are not documented, the service cannot be reported. The documentation must include quantitative measurements, and any abnormalities need to be described.

- Cardiac catheterization is used to view the heart and associated structures, such as great vessels and coronary arteries. It is an invasive procedure and may or may not be performed with other services. Introduction, positioning, gauging pressure, and obtaining samples are included in the codes. When coding cardiac catheterizations, the coder must determine whether the catheterization is being performed for congenital heart disease or other reasons. Extensive detailed guidelines must be followed for proper code assignment. The codes used to report cardiac catheterization services are 93451–93583. It should be noted that endomyocardial biopsy services and repair of a septal defect should be reported from this code range.

- Transcatheter closure of a paravalvular leak is reported with code range 93590–93592. Code 93590 reports the percutaneous transcatheter closure of a paravalvular leak for the initial occlusion device of a mitral valve. Code 93591 reports the percutaneous transcatheter closure of a paravalvular leak for the initial occlusion device of an aortic valve. Code 93592 is an add-on code used to report each additional occlusion device and is to be reported in conjunction with 93590 or 93591.

- Intracardiac electrophysiological procedures and studies are reported using codes from the 93600–93662 code range. The services in this code range report the evaluation of the electrical conduction system of the heart.

- **Peripheral arterial disease (PAD) rehabilitation** is reported using code 93668. The PAD rehabilitation codes refer to patient-monitored exercise until symptoms of the disease lessen and are reported "per session." The exercise session lasts anywhere from 45 to 60 minutes. The patient's claudication threshold is monitored, tracking any symptoms.

- Other cardiac and vascular studies are reported using codes 93701–93799. Electronic analysis of pacemakers and thermograms, as well as determining venous pressure are services that are coded from this code range.

Noninvasive Vascular Diagnostic Studies (93880–93998)

Code range 93880–93998 covers supervision of patient care, as well as studies and interpretation for noninvasive vascular diagnostic studies. The patient record needs to include a hard copy of the vascular study, as well as the interpretation and bidirectional vascular flow or imaging when performed. A handheld screening device does not constitute enough work to report these codes for payment and would be considered part of the physical exam related to the vascular system.

- Cerebrovascular arterial studies are reported using codes 93880–93895.

- Extremity arterial studies (including digits) are reported using codes 93922–93931.

- Extremity venous studies (including digits) are reported using codes 93970 and 93971.

- Visceral and penile vascular studies are reported using codes 93985–93990.

- Extremity arterial–venous studies are reported using code 93990.

Pulmonary (94002-94799)

Pulmonary codes are used to report both diagnostic and therapeutic procedures and services. The coder needs to be aware that these codes include laboratory services as well as physician services, and the codes should not be reported separately. The interpretation of results is also bundled into the codes reported.

Spirometry testing measures lung capacity and is reported using codes 94010–94070.

Bronchospasm evaluations and vital capacity testing are also found in the Pulmonary subsection of the Medicine section. Breathing response testing and aerosol inhalation treatments are found in this code range. It should be noted that referencing documentation is essential to correct code selection. This section is used for code selection when a code from the Respiratory subsection in the Surgery section has been referenced and a better code has not been found.

Allergy and Clinical Immunology (95004-95199)

Code selection from the Allergy and Clinical Immunology code range is based on the patient's history, physical findings, and clinical judgment of the physician or provider of the service. The code description may refer to the number of tests performed. For reimbursement purposes as well as accurate reporting, the quantity should reflect the correct number of tests performed. Allergy testing and immunotherapy does not include any additional evaluation and management services, which means they should be reported separately if applicable.

- Allergy testing is reported using code set 95004–95071. The technique used in testing could be scratch, puncture, prick, or intradermal, and it should be noted in the documentation.

- Ingestion challenge testing is reported using codes 95076 and 95079. During this testing, a patient is given food, a drug, or another substance to ingest, and is then monitored for an allergic reaction. Code 95076 reports the first 120 minutes of testing, and code 95079 reports each additional 60 minutes of testing. The notation in the CPT manual prior to code 95076 states that if testing time is less than 61 minutes, an Evaluation and Management (E/M) code should be reported if appropriate.

- Allergen immunotherapy is reported using code set 95115–95199. Allergenic extracts are administered at specific intervals until therapy levels are reached. The number of injections should be noted, as this will steer code selection.

Endocrinology (95249-95251)

Two codes are found in the Endocrinology subsection that are used to report continuous glucose monitoring of interstitial tissue fluid via a subcutaneous sensor for up to 72 hours. The codes for physician interpretation and report are also found here. When reporting these codes, do not add code 99091. These codes are reported no more than once per month.

Neurology and Neuromuscular Procedures (95700-96020)

Code range 95700 to 96020 is used to report neurology and neuromuscular procedures. It should be noted that codes are out of numerical order. This range of codes is divided into the following sections:

- Sleep Testing—code range 95800–95811 and codes 95782 and 95783. This range of codes is used to report sleep studies and polysomnography to diagnose sleep disorders. Sleep studies are differentiated from polysomnography studies in the selection of codes from this range. Polysomnography studies include the recording of sleep and sleep staging.

- Routine Electroencephalography (EEG)—code range 95812–95830. These codes are differentiated by the monitoring time. Extended EEG includes reporting times longer than 40 minutes. Routine EEG includes 20 to 40 minutes of monitoring time. Code 95829 is used to report an electrocorticogram completed at surgery.

- Electrocorticography—codes 95829 and 95836. These are out of sequence codes that report the recording of an EEG. Code 95829 reports an electrocorticogram at surgery (separate procedure) while code 95836 reports the recording of the electrocorticogram from an implanted brain neurostimular pulse generator/transmitter. Code 95836 includes the recording and interpretation, and written report up to 30 days. Prior to assigning code 95836, the coder should review the instructional notations that follow the code for further coding guidance.

- Range of Motion Testing—code range 95851–95857. This range of codes is used to report muscle and range of motion testing. The codes are differentiated according to the location of the muscle testing (e.g., extremity versus hand).

- Electromyography and Nerve Conduction Tests—code range 95860–95913. This range of codes is differentiated by the location of the testing. For example, code 95860 reports a needle electromyography of one extremity with or without related paraspinal areas, and code 95865 reports needle electromyography of the larynx.

- Intraoperative Neurophysiology—codes 95940 and 95941. These codes report intraoperative neurophysiology monitoring. These codes are add-on codes. Code 95940 requires that the provider is in attendance and reports each 15 minutes of attendance. Code 95941 reports the monitoring from outside the operating room or the monitoring of more than one case while in the operating room, and it reports an hour of time.

- Autonomic Function Tests—code range 95921–95924 and code 95943. These codes report the testing of autonomic nervous system functions and is differentiated according to the nerve that is tested.

- Evoked Potentials and Reflex Tests—code range 95925–95939. This group of codes reports studies completed to obtain information about the functioning of the nerves being tested.

- Special EEG Tests—code range 95954–95967. This code range is used to report special EEG tests that are completed to monitor the brain's electrical activity. Please note that there are numerous codes that are out of sequence.

- Neurostimulators, Analysis—Programming—code range 95970–95984. This range of codes is used to report the testing of neurostimulators. The codes are differentiated by the type of neurostimulator that is analyzed.

- Motion Analysis—code range 96000–96004. A patient's movement is analyzed by the completion of motion analysis.

- Functional Brain Mapping—code 96020. This includes neurofunctional testing selection and administration during noninvasive brain testing.

Medical Genetics and Genetic Counseling Services (96040) and Adaptive Behavior Services (97151–97158)

Medical Genetics and Genetic Counseling Services are reported with code 96040. An extensive notation appears in the CPT manual in front of code 96040. This code is reported for each 30-minute face-to-face service with the patient or family. The time spent must be face-to-face time with the patient. Code range 97151 to 97158 are out of sequence codes that report Adaptive Behavior Assessments (codes 97151 and 97152) and Adaptive Behavior Treatment (codes 97153 to 97158). The CPT manual contains extensive instructional notations for this range of codes. In the CPT manual, review the instructional notations that apply to this range of codes.

Central Nervous System Assessments and Tests (96105–96146), and Health Behavior Assessment and Intervention (96156–96171)

Central nervous system assessments and tests (e.g., neurocognitive, mental status, and speech testing) are reported with code range 96105–96146. Included in this range are codes for psychological testing, assessment of aphasia, developmental testing, and neurobehavioral and neuropsychological testing. Following the completion of the tests, a report is typically generated. The codes require that the time reported to support the code selection is face-to-face time.

Health behavior assessment and intervention is reported with code range 96156–96171. This range is used to report assessments that are completed to identify the various psychological, behavioral, emotional, cognitive, and social factors that have an effect on the patient's physical health problems, and the prevention, treatment, or management of the physical health problems. The codes are differentiated by assessments versus interventions. The assessments are divided into initial assessments and reassessments. The intervention codes identify interventions completed for individuals, groups, or families. Codes 96150 to 96155 represent 15-minute time periods. Code 96160 reports the administration of a patient-focused health risk assessment instrument with scoring and documentation for each standardized instrument. Code 96161 reports the administration of a caregiver focused health risk assessment instrument for the benefit of the patient, with scoring and documentation for each standardized instrument.

Hydration, Therapeutic, Prophylactic, Diagnostic Injections and Infusions, and Chemotherapy and Other Highly Complex Drug or Highly Complex Biologic Agent Administration (96360–96549)

Codes in the 96360–96549 range are used to report the following services:

- Hydration (codes 96360–96361). These codes indicate that prepackaged fluids and electrolytes were administered through an intravenous (IV) infusion. The nurse usually starts these under the orders of a physician, who supervises the service. No special monitoring is required, and the patient is usually at little risk. These codes require that start and stop times be documented for accurate code assignment, as well as to support the service reported. These codes are not intended to be reported by the physician in the facility setting.

- Therapeutic, Prophylactic, and Diagnostic Injections and Infusions (excludes Chemotherapy and Other Highly Complex Drug, or Highly Complex Biologic Agent Administration) (code range 96365–96379). These codes are used to report IV infusions or injections for the administration of substances or drugs for reasons other than hydration. The person administering the treatment usually needs some type of training. The physician usually supervises the administration or performs the service, but in some instances, the physician assesses the patient and writes the order, which allows another qualified person to administer the drug or drugs. Constant presence of a qualified health-care professional is necessary, and time must be documented.

- Chemotherapy and Other Highly Complex Drug or Highly Complex Biologic Agent Administration (code range 96401–96549). This range of codes is divided into the following sections:

  ○ Injection and Intravenous Infusion Chemotherapy and Other Highly Complex Drug or Highly Complex Biologic Agent Administration—code range 96401–96417. This range is used to report chemotherapy administration by various techniques that include subcutaneous or intramuscular, intralesional, push technique, and intravenous infusion.

  ○ Intra-arterial Chemotherapy and Other Highly Complex Drug or Highly Complex Biologic Agent Administration—code range 96420–96425. Intra-arterial chemotherapy administration is coded to this range, which is differentiated by the technique, the length of time of the administration, or the use of a portable or implantable pump.

  ○ Other Injection and Infusion Services—code range 96440–96549. All other types of chemotherapy administration are reported with these codes. The refilling and maintenance of portable pumps, irrigation of devices, and other injections are also reported with this range.

It should be noted that extensive notes in the CPT manual apply to this range of codes.

Photodynamic Therapy (96567–96574)

Code range 96567–96571 is used to report photodynamic therapy. During this type of therapy, the physician applies a photosensitizing agent to treat lesions. It should be noted that some of the codes are reported according to the length of time of the treatment. Medical documentation should be reviewed to ensure that the times that are reported by the codes can be substantiated.

Special Dermatological Procedures (96900–96999)

Code range 96900–96999 is used to report special dermatological procedures. Procedures in this range include actinotherapy, examination of hair, photochemotherapy, and laser treatment for skin disease. Laser treatment codes are divided further according to the total area involved in the treatment.

Physical Medicine and Rehabilitation (97010–97799)

Physical Medicine and Rehabilitation is divided into the following areas:

- Physical Therapy Evaluations—code range 97161–97164. These codes are out of sequence codes when presented in the CPT manual. Codes 97161 to 97163 report physical therapy evaluations ranging from low to high complexity. Code 97164 reports the re-evaluation of a physical therapy established plan of care. Prior to assigning these codes coders need to review the instructional notations and definitions that apply to these codes which appear before the code descriptions. Review these codes in the CPT manual.

- Occupational Therapy Evaluations—code range 97165–97168. These codes are out of sequence codes when presented in the CPT manual. Codes 97165 to 97167 report occupational therapy evaluations ranging from low to high complexity. Code 97168 reports the re-evaluation of an occupational therapy established plan of care. In the CPT manual, prior to the listing of these codes, instructional notations and definitions are listed that pertain to these codes. Review these instructional notations and definitions in the CPT manual.

- Athletic Training Evaluations—code range 97169–97172. These codes are out of sequence codes when presented in the CPT manual. Codes 97169 to 97171 report athletic training evaluations ranging from low to high complexity. Code 97172 reports the re-evaluation of an athletic training established plan of care. Prior to assigning these codes coders need to review the instructional notations and definitions that appear in the CPT manual prior to the listing of these codes. Locate and review these in the CPT manual.

- Modalities—supervised—code range 97010–97028. This includes any physical agent that is used for therapy, including application of hot or cold packs, traction, electrical stimulation, vasopneumatic devices, paraffin baths, whirlpool, diathermy, infrared, and ultraviolet. These services do not require constant one-on-one contact between patient and provider.

- Modalities—constant attendance—code range 97032–97039. To report this range of codes, the provider must be one on one with the patient; thus, the term *constant attendance*.

- Therapeutic Procedures—code range 97110–97546. These codes also require the physician or therapist to be in direct contact with the patient. The codes are differentiated by the therapeutic procedure that is completed. Some of the codes are reported for each 15 minutes of therapy. If time is associated with the code chosen, it must be supported in the documentation.

- Active Wound Care Management—code range 97597–97610. To report these codes, the provider must be in direct contact with the patient. These procedures are completed to promote healing or to remove devitalized and/or necrotic tissue. The coder should know the total surface area in square centimeters to appropriately capture all services.

- Tests and Measurements—code range 97750–97755. Physical performance tests or measurements and assistive technology assessments are reported with these codes. Each code represents 15-minute intervals.

- Orthotic Management and Prosthetic Management—code range 97760–97763. Orthotic management, prosthetic management, and checkout for established patients are reported with this range of codes.

Because most codes in this range are time-based codes, documentation of time in and time out is required by most insurance carriers.

Additional Procedures (97802–99607)

The code range 97802–99607 reports the following procedures:

- Medical Nutrition Therapy—code range 97802–97804
- Acupuncture—code range 97810–97814
- Osteopathic Manipulative Treatment—code range 98925–98929
- Chiropractic Manipulative Treatment—code range 98940–98943
- Education and Training for Patient Self-Management—code range 98960–98962
- Non-Face-to-Face Nonphysician Services—code range 98966–98972
- Special Services, Procedures, and Reports—code range 99000–99082
- Qualifying Circumstances for Anesthesia—code range 99100–99140
- Moderate (Conscious) Sedation—code range 99151–99157
- Other Services and Procedures—code range 99170–99199
- Home Health Procedures/Services—code range 99500–99602
- Medication Therapy Management Services—code range 99605–99607

Summary

- The Medicine section follows the Pathology and Laboratory section.
- There are many sections within the Medicine section.
- Diagnostic and therapeutic procedures are found in the Medicine section.
- Some codes break out the professional and technical components.
- Some codes in the Medicine section are time based.

Internet Links

For more information on some of the topics related to psychiatry covered in this chapter, visit *http://www.aapb.org*. To learn about procedures, navigate to *https://www.nlm.nih.gov/index.html* and search for procedures discussed in this chapter.

Chapter Review

True/False

Instructions: Indicate whether the following statements are true (T) or false (F).

1. _____ The code range for medical nutrition therapy is 97802–97804.

2. _____ The Cardiovascular subsection of the Medicine section includes codes used to report diagnostic and therapeutic services.

3. _____ Cardiopulmonary resuscitation is reported using code 92990.

4. _____ The physiological responses that cannot be treated using biofeedback include high blood pressure and incontinence.

5. _____ An optometrist is not a medical doctor but can prescribe medication and corrective lenses.

Fill in the Blank

Instructions: Fill in the blanks in the statements that follow.

6. The process of taking waste from the blood when the kidneys are not functioning properly to allow the body to do this on its own is called _____.

7. A form of psychiatry that involves the administering of an intravenous drug that allows the patient to release thoughts that might be suppressed or repressed is called _____.

8. A type of scope that examines the eye for signs of glaucoma is called _____.

9. Lung capacity can be measured by _____ testing.

10. Peripheral artery disease (PAD) rehabilitation is reported using code _____.

Coding Assignments

Instructions: For each of the following procedures, select the appropriate CPT code.

1. 15 minutes of upper-extremity prosthetic training initial encounter _____

2. Home visit for intramuscular injections _____

3. Photo tests _____

4. Determination of venous pressure _____

5. Cardiopulmonary resuscitation _____

6. Diagnostic analysis of cochlear implant with programming for 4-year-old patient _____

7. Binaural electroacoustic evaluation for hearing aid _____

8. Live yellow fever vaccine, for a 22-year-old (no counseling), subcutaneous use _____

9. Family psychotherapy with patient present _____

10. 16-year-old, end-stage renal disease service, one day of service _____

11. Duodenal motility study _____

12. Re-evaluation of an occupational therapy established plan of care. (Assume that the documentation meets all of the components for this code.) _____

13. Select picture audiometry _____

14. Auditory rehabilitation for postlingual hearing loss _____

15. Left heart catheterization by transseptal puncture through intact septum _____

16. Initiation and management of continuous positive airway pressure ventilation _____

17. Evaluation of breathing response to CO2 _____

18. Ergonovine provocation test _____

19. Monaural hearing aid check _____

20. Hypnotherapy _____

21. Anorectal manometry _____

22. Electro-oculography with interpretation and report _____

23. Tone-decay test _____

24. Filtered speech test _____

25. Complete transcranial Doppler study of the intra-cranial arteries _____

Case Studies

Instructions: Review each case and indicate the correct code(s).

Case 1

This is an 80-year-old male who has been suffering for the past eight weeks with a nonhealing ulcer on the lateral aspect of the right calf. The ulcer does look better today, having gone from 6 cm to 4.3 cm. It is still oozing, and there is some necrosis around the lower edge of the wound. I debrided the wound with a scalpel into the dermal layer of all devitalized tissue. Bacitracin was applied, and the wound was dressed. The patient was given instructions on how to care for the wound until he presents again in two weeks.

CPT code(s): _____

Case 2

This is a 32-year-old, Type 2 diabetic female. She was diagnosed approximately two weeks ago and now presents for an initial assessment and intervention for medical nutrition therapy. She does not want to have to take insulin, so her doctor agreed that, with some nutrition counseling and exercise, she may be able to avoid it. We spent 30 minutes discussing the American Diabetic Association diet plan and how to implement it. We also discussed exercise and how to work it into her schedule. She will follow up with me in two weeks to see how things are progressing. If she has any problems before then, she will call this office.

CPT code(s): _____

Case 3

Marcus is a 2-year-old child who presents here with his mother. He is running a fever of 101 and is very lethargic for a 2-year-old. He is not eating or drinking, and mom said he has vomited each time he tries. She did get a few drops of water into him prior to this visit, but nothing else. He has not had a wet diaper in the past six hours. An IV of D5-1/2 normal saline + 30 mEq KCl was started. We performed the IV therapy for one hour, after which Marcus was acting much improved. His temp was down to 98. We gave him a popsicle, which he kept down. Mom was instructed to let us know if he does not have a wet diaper over the next few hours or if his condition worsens.

CPT code(s): _____

HCPCS Codes

Chapter Outline

Learning Objectives

At the conclusion of this chapter, you should be able to:

1. Define key terms related to HCPCS coding.
2. Identify who publishes HCPCS Level II codes and when updates are made.
3. Select HCPCS Level II codes.
4. Summarize the contents included in each of the HCPCS Level II appendices.

Note: A Level II HCPCS manual is needed to work through this chapter.

Key Terms

Advance Beneficiary
  Notice (ABN)

advanced life support
  (ALS)

basic life support (BLS)

Certificate of Medical
  Necessity (CMN)

durable medical
  equipment (DME)

durable medical
  equipment,
  prosthetics, orthotics,

and supplies
  (DMEPOS)

enteral

Healthcare Common
  Procedure Coding
  System (HCPCS)

Level II codes

National Drug Codes
  (NDCs)

parenteral

Introduction

The **Healthcare Common Procedure Coding System** is referred to with the acronym **HCPCS**, which is pronounced "hicpics." HCPCS consists of CPT codes, Level I and National Codes, and Level II codes.

The **Level II codes** are published annually by the Centers for Medicare and Medicaid Services (CMS) at the same time the Level I codes or CPT codes are published. The American Medical Association (AMA) maintains the Level I codes, whereas CMS maintains Level II codes (ever since a 2003 mandate by the Secretary of the Department of Health and Human Services). Level II codes report **durable medical equipment (DME)**, such as wheelchairs, crutches, and bandages. These codes are also used to report prosthetics, medications, orthotics, temporary Medicare codes, provider services that are not found in CPT, and temporary National Codes. Because the CPT codes do not cover all services provided, HCPCS codes allow for more accurate reporting of services rendered during a patient encounter. The coder may see DME noted as **DMEPOS (durable medical equipment, prosthetics, orthotics, and supplies)**.

HCPCS codes are alphanumeric, comprising one letter followed by four numbers.

> **EXAMPLE:**
> J0207   Injection, amifostine, 500 mg

The alpha character indicates the section where the code is found. In our example, the *J* indicates this code is found in the section that identifies HCPCS drugs administered by means other than oral.

Level II codes are a standardized coding system that is accepted by Medicare, Medicaid, workers' compensation insurance, and most commercial and private insurances to most accurately reflect the supplies provided to patients at the time of a service. Some payers may not accept certain codes from the HCPCS coding system, but prior to billing a service, the coder may check fee schedules or contact the payer directly to see if the code will be recognized.

Medical record documentation needs to support the medical necessity for billing of items reported with HCPCS Level II codes. The clinical notes need to be clear as to why a DME or DMEPOS is necessary, and a signed and dated order must be provided.

> **EXAMPLE:** Dr. Martin had been treating Sylvia for the past two years for pain and swelling occurring with arthritis. Today she was given a 20 mg injection of methylprednisolone acetate. This visit is for the first injection.

In this instance, Dr. Martin would report J1020 to reflect the injection of the 20 mg of methylprednisolone acetate. The reason for the injection was clearly noted in an effort to support the medical necessity for the injection. Of note is the fact that these codes are *not* used on the inpatient side for facility billing. These services would be included in the reimbursement paid to the facility based on the diagnosis, not on services rendered.

Certificate of Medical Necessity for DME Items and Advance Beneficiary Notice

A **Certificate of Medical Necessity (CMN)** clearly explains why a physician feels that a patient needs the DME item or service. This certificate should be filed in the patient's medical record for certain supplies. Although a CMN may be kept on file, this alone cannot justify the medical necessity for the DME. The CMN can be used in addition to clinical documentation substantiating the service or item rendered. If a DME supplier is audited by Medicare, the original CMN may be requested. Although a faxed copy to the supplier is enough to support the issuance of a supply, there is an understanding that an original CMN is kept on file at the provider's office.

If there is no clinical documentation to support the medical necessity of a service rendered, the provider cannot bill the patient directly unless the provider of the service could not have known that the service would not be paid by Medicare or if the provider had the patient sign an **Advance Beneficiary Notice (ABN)**. An ABN is written notice to the patient that states the patient was made aware of the exact procedure being considered, the dollar amount associated with the procedure, and the possibility that Medicare would not pay for this service. All payers have their own guidelines for payment of the HCPCS codes. Medicare publishes noncovered HCPCS Level II codes in the HCPCS manual.

Organization and Use of HCPCS Level II Codes

HCPCS Level II codes are organized into the following sections:

- A codes—Transportation Services Including Ambulance, Medical and Surgical Supplies
- B codes—Enteral and Parenteral Therapy
- C codes—Outpatient PPS
- E codes—Durable Medical Equipment
- G codes—Procedures/Professional Services (Temporary)
- H codes—Alcohol and Drug Abuse Treatment Services
- J codes—Drugs Administered Other Than Oral Method and Chemotherapy Drugs
- K codes—Temporary Codes, for use by Durable Medical Equipment Administrative Contractors
- L codes—Orthotic and Prosthetic Procedures and Devices
- M codes—Medical Services
- P codes—Pathology and Laboratory Services
- Q codes—Q Codes (Temporary)
- R codes—Diagnostic Radiology Services
- S codes—Temporary National Codes (Non-Medicare)
- T codes—National T Codes Established for State Medicaid Agencies
- V codes—Vision Services and Hearing Services

The HCPCS Level II manual is arranged by code number. Though services are grouped together, the index is set up by the name of the medical or surgical supply, the orthotic or prosthetic, or the service provided. The index may also be referenced by the brand name or the generic name of a drug. In some instances, the actual body part that requires the supply may also be referenced.

> **EXAMPLE:**
> Cervical
>
> collar, L0120, L0130, L0140, L0150, L0170
>
> halo, L0810–L0830
>
> head harness/halter, E0942
>
> helmet, A8000–A8004
>
> orthotic, L0180–L0200
>
> traction equipment, not requiring frame, E0855

The symbols used in the HCPCS Level II code manual are similar to those in the CPT manual. A black circle (●) preceding a code indicates a new code, and a black triangle (▲) indicates revised terminology or rules.

Each of the publishers of HCPCS Level II code manuals has its own color coding, symbols, and level-of-coverage instructions. You will need to read the introduction to your particular manual to be sure you are getting the greatest benefits from it.

Steps in code selection for HCPCS are the same as the steps in locating any other CPT code. The coder first needs to identify the service or procedure performed. The term referenced may be a supply, a route of administration, a body part, or a procedure. After identifying the term necessary to locate the code, the coder references the index. A code is selected and then located in the manual. Check the exact verbiage associated with the code selected. All instructional notations should be reviewed. If necessary, refer to the appendices and identify any modifiers that might need to be applied. After making these references, select and assign a code to the service.

EXAMPLE: The diagnostic statement reads, "Issue a drainable ostomy pouch for use on barrier with locking flange (2-piece system)." The coder follows these steps:

1. Turn to the index and look under the term *ostomy*.
2. Locate the terms listed under the main term.
3. Locate the term *pouch*, and follow indentations under *pouch* to the term *drainable*.
4. Find codes A4412 and A4413 and A5056 and A5057.
5. Locate these codes in the A code section of the code manual.

When the coder reviews the verbiage associated with A4412 and A4413, he or she finds that these codes do not include the term *locking flange*. However, further review of this code section brings the coder to A4426—Ostomy pouch, drainable; for use on barrier with locking flange (2-piece system), each.

Exercise 23.1—Finding a HCPCS Code

Underline the main term that would be referenced in the index to find the correct HCPCS code.

Then assign the proper HCPCS code.

1. Single-vision lenticular lens _____
2. Aluminum crutches _____
3. Food supplement _____
4. Indwelling port _____
5. Breast pump manual _____
6. Wound cleanser _____

7. Elbow splint _____
8. Urine sensitivity study _____
9. Vascular closure device _____
10. Diabetic shoe inlay _____

The coder should be sure that a HCPCS Level I code is not available before assigning a HCPCS Level II code. The coder needs to read the selected code carefully because some codes indicate "each" or "per," so the quantity reported may need to be more than 1. Hospitals and offices can lose revenue if the proper amounts are not reported.

EXAMPLE: Stuart needed new handgrips for his walker. Two hand grips were dispensed. The code reported was A4636 × 2.

The A4636 code reads, "Replacement, handgrip, cane, crutch, or walker, each." The word *each* indicates that for each replacement handgrip given, the code may be reported separately, so the quantity would be 2. Reimbursement is lost if the quantity is reported incorrectly.

Exercise 23.2—Learning HCPCS

Locate the correct code for the statement given.

1. Implantable neurostimulator adaptor
   _____

2. Static finger splint _____

3. Dry pressure mattress _____

4. Urinary incontinence repair device without
   sling graft _____

5. Seat attachment for walker
   _____

6. Clubfoot wedge _____

7. Prolotherapy _____

8. Mental health assessment by nonphysician
   _____

HCPCS Sections

After the index, the sections of the manual begin with the A codes. A codes are used to report transportation services; medical and surgical supplies; and administrative, miscellaneous, and investigational services. It should be noted that there are large gaps in the numbering system for HCPCS Level II codes. The reason for these gaps in numbering is that there is room for growth within a code set, allowing new items to be used by providers.

A Codes—Transportation Services Including Ambulance, Medical and Surgical Supplies

The transportation services are reported using A0021–A0999 and include wheelchair van services, taxi transportation, and ambulance emergency transportation. Also reported using A codes are ground mileage, nonemergency transportation, and air transportation. Some of the codes mention "ancillary" in the code description.

> **EXAMPLE:**
> **A0200**   Nonemergency transportation: ancillary lodging, escort

The ancillary service codes are used to report additional expenses incurred during travel, such as lodging, tolls, and meals. Some of the codes in this section contain abbreviations such as ALS and BLS. **ALS** is used to denote **advanced life support**, **BLS** is used to indicate **basic life support**.

Ambulance services require identification of point of pickup and point of destination. These points of origin and destination are indicated by the use of specific modifiers, which are noted within HCPCS. The arrangement modifiers are placed after the code for the service being rendered. The QM modifier "Ambulance service provided under arrangement by a provider of services," or the QN modifier "Ambulance service furnished directly by a provider of services," would be appropriate. The modifiers describing the origin and destination are listed second.

The Medical and Surgical Supplies section of the A codes comprises the A4206–A9999 code range. The coder should query the local Medicare or primary insurance carrier to verify payment of services rendered or items dispensed that would be coded from this code range. Some items or services, though found here to have a specific code, are considered bundled into other services and are not reported separately.

Exercise 23.3—A Codes

Select the proper A code for the item or service described.

1. Mileage for an ALS patient who needed to be transported 3 miles _____

2. Ostomy irrigation bag _____

3. Blood pressure monitor _____

4. One fistula cannulation kit for hemodialysis _____

5. Nonelastic, below-the-knee compression wrap, right and left _____

6. One sterile eye pad _____

7. One pint of Betadine solution _____

8. Replacement battery for patient-owned ventilator _____

B Codes—Enteral and Parental Therapy

The next section in the HCPCS Level II manual is Enteral and Parenteral Therapy. This chapter is broken down into the enteral formulae and enteral medical supplies, parenteral nutritional solutions and supplies, and enteral and parenteral pumps. The term **enteral** refers to a route of administration involving the gastrointestinal tract. **Parenteral** refers to a route of administration *not* involving the gastrointestinal tract. Some of the pump codes found in this section of HCPCS require the use of an MS modifier, which reads, "Six months' maintenance and servicing fee for reasonable and necessary parts and labor which are not covered under any manufacturer or supplier warranty." Coders should check with local carriers to see if the use of this modifier is appropriate in their area.

C Codes—HCPCS Outpatient PPS

C codes are used to report services that may be used by the outpatient prospective payment system (OPPS) and are not to be used to report any other services. These codes are used for technical services only and may be reported by non-OPPS hospitals; Critical Access Hospitals; Indian Health Service Hospitals; hospitals located in Guam, Saipan, American Samoa, and the Virgin Islands; and Maryland waiver hospitals at their discretion. CMS updates the C codes quarterly. These codes can only be reported for facility (technical) services.

Exercise 23.4—HCPCS B and C Codes

Select the correct B or C code for each of the following services or items.

1. Catheter for hemodialysis patient receiving short-term infusion _____

2. Enteral nutrition infusion pump with alarm _____

3. Nasogastric tubing with stylet _____

4. Transluminal artherectomy rotational catheter _____

5. Clevidipine butyrate injection, 1 mg _____

6. Parenteral nutrition solution; amino acid, 3.5%—home mix _____

7. NOC for enteral supplies _____

8. Ureteral catheter _____

D Codes—Dental Procedures

Dental procedures and services begin with D0000 and go through D9999. This range of codes is copyrighted and modified by the American Dental Association (ADA), not by the national panel responsible for the other HCPCS codes.

The D codes are used for reporting oral evaluations, x-rays, laboratory testing, preventive services, restorative services, and prosthetics. There are also codes included for surgical procedures and orthodontics. The coder should refer to a CPT manual for codes that may be more appropriate for the setting in which the service was performed. D codes are not currently found in the HCPCS manual. The ADA holds the copyright on these codes and has instructed CMS to remove them. D codes are available in other resources.

E Codes—Durable Medical Equipment

E codes are used to report durable medical equipment such as walkers, canes, crutches, respiratory equipment, and pacemakers. A good deal of the equipment used for patients with respiratory disorders is found in this code range. The documentation surrounding the billing of these codes must support the medical necessity of the supply being reported. If the medical necessity is not clear, the service may be denied.

G Codes—Temporary Procedures/Professional Services

G codes are used to report professional procedures and services that have not been assigned a CPT code but would typically be services found in the CPT manual. These national codes are assigned by CMS on a temporary basis.

EXAMPLE:
```
G0156        Services of home health/hospice aide in home health or hospice
             settings, each 15 minutes
```

The services provided by a home health aide are not found within CPT, so the services are reported using code G0156. Should a better code become available within CPT, the CPT code would be the code reported instead of the G code. The G codes may or may not be paid by insurances. The coder should check with the carrier before the service is rendered.

Exercise 23.5—E and G Codes

Match the code in the first column with the correct description in the second column.

1. E0310 _____   **a.** Wheelchair seat cushion
2. E0190 _____   **b.** Home blood glucose monitor
3. G0252 _____   **c.** Direct admission of patient for observation
4. E2610 _____   **d.** Barium enema, for colorectal cancer screening
5. E0160 _____   **e.** Full-length bed rails
6. G0390 _____   **f.** Built-in whirlpool
7. E1310 _____   **g.** Trauma response team
8. G0379 _____   **h.** Portable sitz bath equipment with commode
9. G0106 _____   **i.** Decubitus care pillow
10. E0607 _____   **j.** PET imaging of breast

H Codes—Behavioral Health and/or Substance Abuse Treatment Services

H codes are not recognized by Medicare but are used by Medicaid agencies that are state mandated for reporting mental health services, including behavioral health. Drug and alcohol treatment services are included in this code range.

J Codes—Drugs Administered Other Than Oral Method

J codes are used to report drugs that would typically not be self-administered. J codes can be found by referencing the following terms: *chemotherapy, inhalation,* or *IV solution.* Appendix 1—Table of Drugs can also be used to locate the proper J code. Most of the codes in this chapter are noted by generic names, but the brand names are listed under the code description in some cases.

> **EXAMPLE:**
> J0300   Injection, amobarbital, up to 125 mg
> Use this code for Amytal.

Some payers require the submission of **National Drug Codes (NDCs)** when you report medications using J codes. An NDC number is an 11-digit number that identifies the manufacturer, the product, and the package size. The NDC number can be found on the box, bottle, or other part of the packaging. The NDC numbers can also be found online. It is extremely important that the correct information is reported.

Exercise 23.6—J Codes

Identify the correct J code for the description given.

1. NebuPent Route INH
   _____

2. Hydrocortisone sodium succinate
   _____

3. Dacarbazine, 200 mg
   _____

4. Levalbuterol (compounded) administered through a nebulizer, 0.5 mg
   _____

5. Trilone, 5 mg injection
   _____

6. 1 mg injection of busulfan
   _____

7. Amifostine injection, 500 mg
   _____

8. Maxipime injection, 500 mg
   _____

K Codes—Temporary Codes Assigned to DME Regional Carriers

Next are the temporary K codes that are used to report DME wheelchairs and accessories to DME regional carriers instead of to Medicare. The K codes include wheelchairs and wheelchair accessories and quality measures.

L Codes—Orthotic and Prosthetic Procedures and Devices

Orthotic and prosthetic procedures and devices are reported with L codes. L codes include orthotic devices, halo procedures, and scoliosis procedures. The use of orthotic treatment of scoliosis requires continual adjustments.

When you are coding from this section of HCPCS, it is important to read any notations that might be associated with the codes you are looking at because some codes are classified as "base" codes. Base codes report basic procedures and can be modified by adding codes from the "Additions" section. For example, the procedures in the L6000–L6590 range are considered base procedures and can be modified by adding procedure codes from section L6600–L6698.

Exercise 23.7—K and L Codes

Select the code that best identifies the supply rendered or service performed.

1. Rancho hip action, hip orthotic, custom fabricated _____

2. Group 5, single-power wheelchair for child weighing 85 lb _____

3. One replacement battery for external infusion pump owned by the patient; silver oxide, 1.5 volts _____

4. Transmitting coil for a cochlear implant _____

5. Hallux prosthetic implant _____

6. Cervical, collar, molded to patient model _____

7. Above-knee, molded-socket, single-axis constant friction, knee, shin, SACH foot _____

8. Hallux implant _____

M Codes—Medical Services and Quality Measures

The M codes are used to report cellular therapy, prolotherapy, intravenous (IV) chelation therapy, fabric wrapping of an abdominal aneurysm and quality measures.

P Codes—Pathology and Laboratory Services

Pathology and laboratory services are currently reported using P codes. This code range is used to report chemistry and toxicology tests, pathology screening tests, microbiology, and miscellaneous pathology and laboratory services. This section is also where the coder will find the codes for transfusions and infusions.

Q Codes—Temporary Codes

Q codes are temporary codes used to report various supplies, drugs, and biologicals in instances where no permanent code has been assigned.

R Codes—Diagnostic Radiology Services

Radiology services are currently reported using R codes. As with the M codes, there are very few R codes at this time. The R codes are used to report the transportation of electrocardiogram (EKG) equipment and/or portable x-ray equipment.

S Codes—Temporary National Codes

S codes are non-Medicare codes. These codes are temporary codes that are utilized by Blue Cross/Blue Shield Association (BCBSA) and also the Health Insurance Association of America (HIAA). The codes are used to report supplies, drugs, and services when there are no National Codes.

Along with BCBSA and other private payers, Medicaid also recognizes some S codes. The Medicaid fee schedule should be referenced to identify the S codes that are recognized by Medicaid.

T Codes—Temporary National Codes Established for State Medicaid Agencies

T codes are used by Medicaid state agencies. Like the S codes, T codes are not recognized by Medicare but are recognized by some private payers. Some of the services found in this code range include respite care, sign language or interpretive services, and nursing care in the home. As with the S codes, query the payers as to whether they will pay a service reported by the T code before you bill the code.

V Codes—Vision Services and Hearing Services

HCPCS also contains V codes. The V codes within HCPCS are used to report services that are related to the senses. Vision services are first, followed by services related to hearing, and then speech and language pathology services. This is the last section before the appendices.

Appendices

The appendices of HCPCS contain a great deal of information and are used very frequently. Appendix 1, Table of Drugs, is referenced for medications. Appendix 1 is a four-column table. The first column of drug names is listed in alphabetic order by brand name and generic name. The second column notes the unit dose, the third column identifies the route of administration, and the last column indicates the HCPCS code used to identify the medication. These sample columns are illustrated in Table 23-1.

TABLE 23-1   HCPCS Appendix 1 Table Columns

Drug Name	Unit Per	Route	Code
Adalimumab	20 mg	SC	J0135
Adasuve	1 mg	INH	J2062
Adcetris	1 mg	IV	J9042
Adenocard	1 mg	IV	J1053

Appendix 2 identifies modifiers used with HCPCS codes. HCPCS Level II code modifiers are used in the same manner as HCPCS Level I codes. Modifiers are used to enhance or further identify a service code. The modifiers could be alpha or alphanumeric.

EXAMPLE: The podiatrist performed a trimming of dystrophic nails on the first three toes of the left foot.

The doctor would report a G0127 for the nail trimming and use modifiers to identify the toes treated. The modifiers begin with TA for the great toe, left foot; T1, for the second digit, left foot; and T2 for the third digit.

Appendix 3 in the CPT manual lists abbreviations and acronyms used in HCPCS descriptors. Appendix 4 in the CPT manual is entitled Internet-only Manuals. It identifies the listing of the CMS Web-based system program instruction and provides a very brief description of sections of the CMS manual. This appendix is quite long but does contain good information. Appendix 5 contains new, changed, deleted, and reinstated HCPCS codes. This appendix is used as a quick reference for yearly coding changes. The last appendix is Appendix 6, which is a quick reference for place of service and types of service.

Exercise 23.8—Understanding the Drug Table

Using Appendix 1 in the HCPCS manual, locate the drug noted and complete the table.

Drug Name	Unit Per	Route	Code
Alemtuzumab	_____	_____	_____
Cancidas	_____	_____	_____
Enbrel	_____	_____	_____
Gastromark	_____	_____	_____
Fertinex	_____	_____	_____
Nubain	_____	_____	_____
Wehdryl	_____	_____	_____
Medidex	_____	_____	_____
Panitumumab	_____	_____	_____

Summary

- Level II HCPCS codes are published annually by the Centers for Medicare and Medicaid Services (CMS).
- Level II codes are used to report prosthetics, medications, orthotics, temporary Medicare codes, provider services that are not found in CPT, and temporary National Codes.
- A Certificate of Medical Necessity (CMN) can be used in addition to the clinical documentation to substantiate a service rendered.
- Level II codes are organized into the following sections:
  - A codes—Transportation Services Including Ambulance, Medical and Surgical Supplies
  - B codes—Enteral and Parenteral Therapy
  - C codes—Outpatient PPS
  - E codes—Durable Medical Equipment
  - G codes—Procedures/Professional Services
  - H codes—Alcohol and Drug Abuse Treatment Services
  - J codes—Drugs Administered By Other Than Oral Method including Chemotherapy
  - K codes—Temporary Codes, for use by Durable Medical Equipment Administrative Contractors
  - L codes—Orthotic and Prosthetic Procedures and Devices
  - M codes—Medical Services
  - P codes—Pathology and Laboratory Services
  - Q codes—Temporary Codes
  - R codes—Diagnostic Radiology Services
  - S codes—Temporary National Codes (Non-Medicare)
  - T codes—National T Codes Established for State Medicaid Agencies
  - V codes—Vision Services and Hearing Services

Internet Links

Internet references can be found at the following locations:

http://www.cms.hhs.gov/MedHCPCSGenInfo/

http://www.nd.gov/eforms/doc/sfn00526.pdf (This is a copy of the Certificate of Medical Necessity.)

Chapter Review

Fill in the Blank

Instructions: Complete the following statements.

1. HCPCS Level II codes are published _____ by _____.
   (when)   (who)

2. A document clearly explains why the physician feels the patient needs durable medical equipment or a service, and it must be filed in the patient's medical record for certain supplies. This document is known as a certificate of _____ necessity.

3. HCPCS codes that are used to report transportation services are _____ codes.

4. A written notice to the patient that identifies a provided service that might not be covered by CMS is known as a(n) _____.

5. A postural drainage board is reported with code _____.

True/False

Instructions: Indicate whether the following statements are true (T) or false (F).

6. _____ Appendix 2 identifies modifiers used with category 1 and category 2 codes.

7. _____ The route of administration involving the gastrointestinal tract is called the *parenteral*.

8. _____ When coding for ambulance services, the point of pickup and the destination must both be identified.

9. _____ Level I codes are published by the CMS.

10. _____ Codes related to the senses, such as speech and hearing, are located in the Q code series.

Coding Assignments

Instructions: Assign the correct HCPCS Level II code for each of the following statements.

1. Instruction in initial use of insulin pump

   _____

2. Pelvic sling _____

3. Abdominal aneurysm wrap

   _____

4. Hearing aid battery _____

5. Oxygen stand _____

6. Foot drop splint, prefabricated

   _____

7. Colorectal cancer screening, screening sigmoidoscopy barium enema _____

8. Adult, fiberglass short arm cast

   _____

9. Durable humidifier for extensive supplemental humidification during IPPB treatment

   _____

10. Full-length bedrails _____

11. Dual-chamber, rate-responsive pacemaker _____

12. Durr-Fillauer semi-rigid cervical collar _____

13. CPAP mask _____

14. Heel holder, with ankle strap _____

15. Levine stomach tube _____

16. Food thickener (3 oz) _____

17. Community psychiatric supportive treatment, as needed _____

18. DonJoy knee immobilizer _____

19. Lobar lung transplantation _____

20. 50 mg of Phenergan _____

21. Pelvic belt _____

22. Inversion/eversion correction device _____

23. Annual depression screening, 15 minutes _____

24. Benesch boot, pair, child _____

25. 1 mg of Pertuzumab _____

26. Replacement tubing for breast pump _____

27. Embolization protective system _____

28. Fixed height folding walker _____

29. Portable Sitz type bath _____

30. Cervical overdoor traction equipment _____

Case Studies

Instructions: Review each case and indicate the correct code(s).

Case 1

Sally Smith presented today for a follow-up visit after eye surgery. The wound was examined, and no complications were noted. An occlusive eye patch was placed on her left eye. She was instructed to return in eight weeks.

Note to billing: Visit was postoperative care; bill for supply used.

HCPCS code(s): _____

Case 2

Michelle presented to her doctor's office with a complaint of amenorrhea. A pregnancy test showed that she was pregnant. The doctor gave her prenatal vitamins and told her he would see her in four weeks.

The patient will be charged only for the prenatal vitamins because her pregnancy will fall into a global service.

HCPCS code(s): _____

Case 3

DME Delivery Bill

Patient: Harry Westin

Age: 73 years old

Site of Delivery: Patient's home

Item Delivered: Full-length bedside rails

HCPCS code(s): _____

Case 4

Orthotics Invoice

Name: Mary Jump   DOB: 1/10/57

Diagnosis: Left foot arch deformity

Arch support supplied: Premolded longitudinal left foot arch support, removable

HCPCS code(s): _____

Case 5

Hemodialysis Clinic Note

Ralf Past will be traveling out of town and will be performing his dialysis on his own with the assistance of his wife, who is a nurse. He was given a portable compact travel hemodialyzer system.

HCPCS code(s): _____

Case 6

Sandra was suffering with shoulder pain, which started about six weeks ago, getting progressively worse. Most movement is painful, and the patient states that she is unable to lift anything over her head. We discussed several options. Sandra agreed that the injection would be the best option. 80 mg of Cortimex was injected into the shoulder joint for bursitis.

HCPCS code(s): _____

Billing Forms (CMS-1500 and UB-04)

HEALTH INSURANCE CLAIM FORM

APPROVED BY NATIONAL UNIFORM CLAIM COMMITTEE (NUCC) 02/12

	PICA						PICA		

1. MEDICARE ☐ (Medicare#) MEDICAID ☐ (Medicaid#) TRICARE ☐ (ID#/DoD#) CHAMPVA ☐ (Member ID#) GROUP HEALTH PLAN ☐ (ID#) FECA BLK LUNG ☐ (ID#) OTHER ☐ (ID#)   **1a. INSURED'S I.D. NUMBER**   (For Program in Item 1)

2. PATIENT'S NAME (Last Name, First Name, Middle Initial)   **3. PATIENT'S BIRTH DATE** MM DD YY SEX M ☐ F ☐   **4. INSURED'S NAME** (Last Name, First Name, Middle Initial)

5. PATIENT'S ADDRESS (No., Street)   **6. PATIENT RELATIONSHIP TO INSURED** Self ☐ Spouse ☐ Child ☐ Other ☐   **7. INSURED'S ADDRESS** (No., Street)

CITY   STATE   **8. RESERVED FOR NUCC USE**   CITY   STATE

ZIP CODE   TELEPHONE (Include Area Code) ( )   ZIP CODE   TELEPHONE (Include Area Code) ( )

9. OTHER INSURED'S NAME (Last Name, First Name, Middle Initial)   **10. IS PATIENT'S CONDITION RELATED TO:**   **11. INSURED'S POLICY GROUP OR FECA NUMBER**

a. OTHER INSURED'S POLICY OR GROUP NUMBER   **a. EMPLOYMENT?** (Current or Previous) YES ☐ NO ☐   **a. INSURED'S DATE OF BIRTH** MM DD YY SEX M ☐ F ☐

b. RESERVED FOR NUCC USE   **b. AUTO ACCIDENT?** PLACE (State) YES ☐ NO ☐   **b. OTHER CLAIM ID** (Designated by NUCC)

c. RESERVED FOR NUCC USE   **c. OTHER ACCIDENT?** YES ☐ NO ☐   **c. INSURANCE PLAN NAME OR PROGRAM NAME**

d. INSURANCE PLAN NAME OR PROGRAM NAME   **10d. CLAIM CODES** (Designated by NUCC)   **d. IS THERE ANOTHER HEALTH BENEFIT PLAN?** YES ☐ NO ☐ *If yes*, complete items 9, 9a, and 9d.

READ BACK OF FORM BEFORE COMPLETING & SIGNING THIS FORM.
12. PATIENT'S OR AUTHORIZED PERSON'S SIGNATURE I authorize the release of any medical or other information necessary to process this claim. I also request payment of government benefits either to myself or to the party who accepts assignment below.

SIGNED _____ DATE _____

13. INSURED'S OR AUTHORIZED PERSON'S SIGNATURE I authorize payment of medical benefits to the undersigned physician or supplier for services described below.

SIGNED _____

14. DATE OF CURRENT ILLNESS, INJURY, or PREGNANCY (LMP) MM DD YY QUAL.   **15. OTHER DATE** QUAL. MM DD YY   **16. DATES PATIENT UNABLE TO WORK IN CURRENT OCCUPATION** FROM MM DD YY TO MM DD YY

17. NAME OF REFERRING PROVIDER OR OTHER SOURCE 17a. | 17b. NPI   **18. HOSPITALIZATION DATES RELATED TO CURRENT SERVICES** FROM MM DD YY TO MM DD YY

19. ADDITIONAL CLAIM INFORMATION (Designated by NUCC)   **20. OUTSIDE LAB?** YES ☐ NO ☐ $ CHARGES

21. DIAGNOSIS OR NATURE OF ILLNESS OR INJURY Relate A-L to service line below (24E) ICD Ind.
A. ___ B. ___ C. ___ D. ___
E. ___ F. ___ G. ___ H. ___
I. ___ J. ___ K. ___ L. ___

22. RESUBMISSION CODE   ORIGINAL REF. NO.

23. PRIOR AUTHORIZATION NUMBER

24. A. DATE(S) OF SERVICE From MM DD YY To MM DD YY	B. PLACE OF SERVICE	C. EMG	D. PROCEDURES, SERVICES, OR SUPPLIES (Explain Unusual Circumstances) CPT/HCPCS | MODIFIER	E. DIAGNOSIS POINTER	F. $ CHARGES	G. DAYS OR UNITS	H. EPSDT Family Plan	I. ID. QUAL	J. RENDERING PROVIDER ID. #
1								NPI	
2								NPI	
3								NPI	
4								NPI	
5								NPI	
6								NPI	

25. FEDERAL TAX I.D. NUMBER SSN ☐ EIN ☐   **26. PATIENT'S ACCOUNT NO.**   **27. ACCEPT ASSIGNMENT?** (For govt. claims, see back) YES ☐ NO ☐   **28. TOTAL CHARGE** $ **29. AMOUNT PAID** $ **30. Rsvd for NUCC Use**

31. SIGNATURE OF PHYSICIAN OR SUPPLIER INCLUDING DEGREES OR CREDENTIALS (I certify that the statements on the reverse apply to this bill and are made a part thereof.)
SIGNED _____ DATE _____

32. SERVICE FACILITY LOCATION INFORMATION
a. NPI   b.

33. BILLING PROVIDER INFO & PH # ( )
a. NPI   b.

NUCC Instruction Manual available at: www.nucc.org   *PLEASE PRINT OR TYPE*

Text along right margin: CARRIER — PATIENT AND INSURED INFORMATION — PHYSICIAN OR SUPPLIER INFORMATION

FIGURE A1-1 The CMS-1500 Form

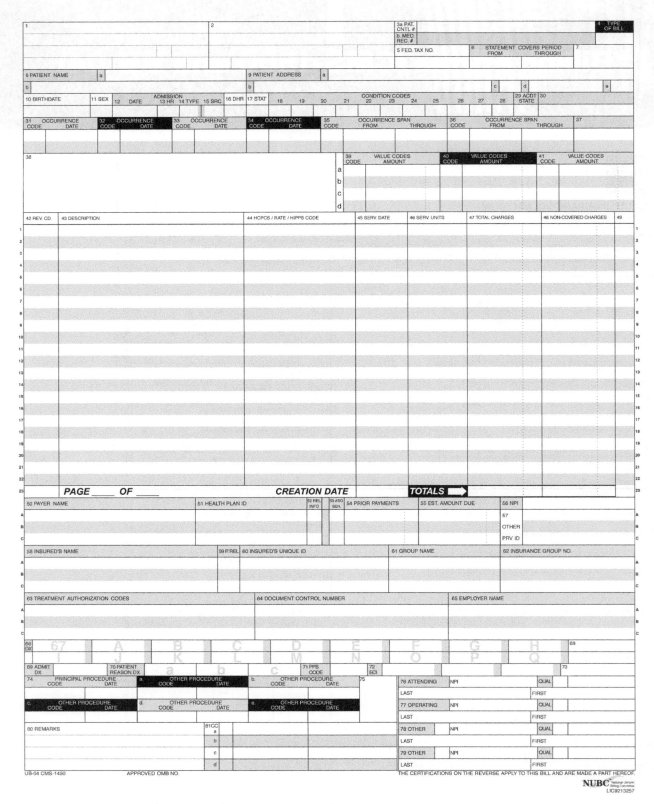

FIGURE A1-2 The UB-04 Form, Also Known as the CMS-1450 Form

APPENDIX II

Surgical Positions

FIGURE A2-1 Supine Position

FIGURE A2-2 Trendelenburg Position

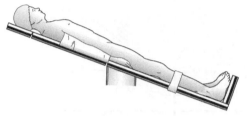

FIGURE A2-3 Reverse Trendelenburg Position

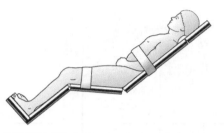

FIGURE A2-4 Fowler's Position

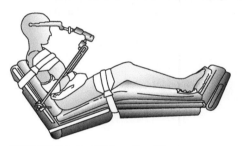

FIGURE A2-5 Sitting Position

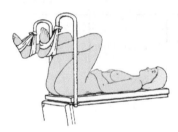

FIGURE A2-6 Lithotomy Position

FIGURE A2-7 Prone Position

FIGURE A2-8 Kraske Position

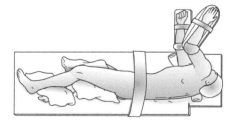

FIGURE A2-9 Right Lateral Position

FIGURE A2-10 Right Kidney Position

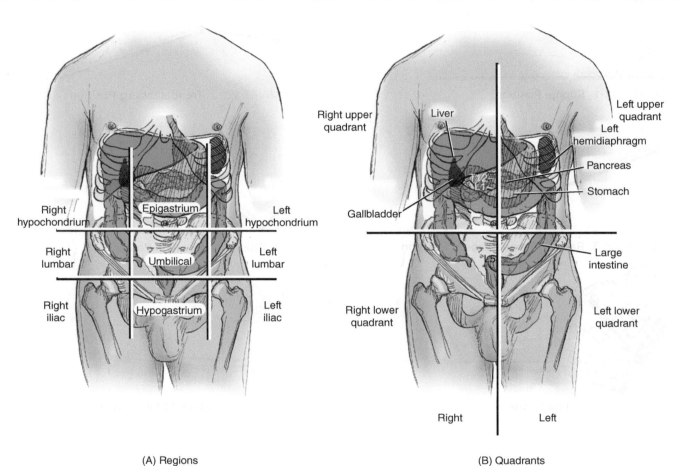

(A) Regions

(B) Quadrants

FIGURE A3-1 Abdominopelvic Divisions

Code	2019 Base Unit	Code	2019 Base Unit	Code	2019 Base Unit	Code	2019 Base Unit
00100	5	00218	13	00537	7	00731	5
00102	6	00220	10	00539	18	00732	6
00103	5	00222	6	00540	12	00750	4
00104	4	00300	5	00541	15	00752	6
00120	5	00320	6	00542	15	00754	7
00124	4	00322	3	00546	15	00756	7
00126	4	00326	7	00548	17	00770	15
00140	5	00350	10	00550	10	00790	7
00142	4	00352	5	00560	15	00792	13
00144	6	00400	3	00561	25	00794	8
00145	6	00402	5	00562	20	00796	30
00147	4	00404	5	00563	25	00797	11
00148	4	00406	13	00566	25	00800	4
00160	5	00410	4	00567	18	00802	5
00162	7	00450	5	00580	20	00811	4
00164	4	00454	3	00600	10	00812	3
00170	5	00470	6	00604	13	00813	5
00172	6	00472	10	00620	10	00820	5
00174	6	00474	13	00625	13	00830	4
00176	7	00500	15	00626	15	00832	6
00190	5	00520	6	00630	8	00834	5
00192	7	00522	4	00632	7	00836	6
00210	11	00524	4	00635	4	00840	6
00211	10	00528	8	00640	3	00842	4
00212	5	00529	11	00670	13	00844	7
00214	9	00530	4	00700	4	00846	8
00215	9	00532	4	00702	4	00848	8
00216	15	00534	7	00730	5	00851	6

(*continues*)

(*continued*)

Code	2019 Base Unit	Code	2019 Base Unit	Code	2019 Base Unit	Code	2019 Base Unit
00860	6	00948	4	01402	7	01680	3
00862	7	00950	5	01404	5	01710	3
00864	8	00952	4	01420	3	01712	5
00865	7	01112	5	01430	3	01714	5
00866	10	01120	6	01432	6	01716	5
00868	10	01130	3	01440	8	01730	3
00870	5	01140	15	01442	8	01732	3
00872	7	01150	10	01444	8	01740	4
00873	5	01160	4	01462	3	01742	5
00880	15	01170	8	01464	3	01744	5
00882	10	01173	12	01470	3	01756	6
00902	5	01200	4	01472	5	01758	5
00904	7	01202	4	01474	5	01760	7
00906	4	01210	6	01480	3	01770	6
00908	6	01212	10	01482	4	01772	6
00910	3	01214	8	01484	4	01780	3
00912	5	01215	10	01486	7	01782	4
00914	5	01220	4	01490	3	01810	3
00916	5	01230	6	01500	8	01820	3
00918	5	01232	5	01502	6	01829	3
00920	3	01234	8	01520	3	01830	3
00921	3	01250	4	01522	5	01832	6
00922	6	01260	3	01610	5	01840	6
00924	4	01270	8	01620	4	01842	6
00926	4	01272	4	01622	4	01844	6
00928	6	01274	6	01630	5	01850	3
00930	4	01320	4	01634	9	01852	4
00932	4	01340	4	01636	15	01860	3
00934	6	01360	5	01638	10	01916	5
00936	8	01380	3	01650	6	01920	7
00938	4	01382	3	01652	10	01922	7
00940	3	01390	3	01654	8	01924	5
00942	4	01392	4	01656	10	01925	7
00944	6	01400	4	01670	4	01926	8

(*continues*)

(*continued*)

Code	2019 Base Unit	Code	2019 Base Unit	Code	2019 Base Unit	Code	2019 Base Unit
01930	5	01951	3	01962	8	01969	5
01931	7	01952	5	01963	8	01990	7
01932	6	01953	1	01965	4	01991	3
01933	7	01958	5	01966	4	01992	5
01935	5	01960	5	01967	5	01996	3
01936	5	01961	7	01968	2	01999	0

APPENDIX

V

Locality-Adjusted Anesthesia Conversion Factors as a Result of the CY 2019 Final Rule

Contractor	Locality	Locality Name	2019 Work GPCI	2019 PE GPCI	2019 MP GPCI	National Anes CF of 22.2730
10112	00	Alabama	1.000	0.890	0.492	21.20
02102	01	Alaska**	1.500	1.117	0.708	30.99
03102	00	Arizona	1.000	0.971	0.834	21.95
07102	13	Arkansas	1.000	0.872	0.576	21.25
01112	54	Bakersfield, CA	1.020	1.074	0.618	22.36
01112	55	Chico, CA	1.020	1.074	0.562	22.29
01182	71	El Centro, CA	1.020	1.074	0.570	22.30
01112	56	Fresno, CA	1.020	1.074	0.562	22.29
01112	57	Hanford-Corcoran, CA	1.021	1.074	0.562	22.30
01182	18	Los Angeles-Long Beach-Anaheim (Los Angeles CNTY), CA	1.046	1.177	0.694	23.28
01182	26	Los Angeles-Long Beach-Anaheim (Orange CNTY), CA	1.046	1.177	0.694	23.28
01112	58	Madera, CA	1.020	1.074	0.562	22.29
01112	59	Merced, CA	1.020	1.074	0.562	22.29
01112	60	Modesto, CA	1.020	1.074	0.562	22.29
01112	51	Napa, CA	1.055	1.256	0.458	23.39
01182	17	Oxnard-Thousand Oaks-Ventura, CA	1.024	1.176	0.673	22.87
01112	61	Redding, CA	1.020	1.074	0.562	22.29
01112	62	Riverside-San Bernardino-Ontario, CA	1.021	1.074	0.753	22.56
01112	63	Sacramento–Roseville–Arden-Arcade, CA	1.027	1.092	0.562	22.47
01112	64	Salinas, CA	1.026	1.101	0.562	22.49
01182	72	San Diego-Carlsbad, CA	1.023	1.116	0.570	22.50
01112	07	San Francisco-Oakland-Hayward (Alameda/Contra Costa CNTY), CA	1.075	1.325	0.421	23.93

(continues)

(*continued*)

Contractor	Locality	Locality Name	2019 Work GPCI	2019 PE GPCI	2019 MP GPCI	National Anes CF of 22.2730
01112	52	San Francisco-Oakland-Hayward (Marin CNTY), CA	1.065	1.291	0.458	23.69
01112	05	San Francisco-Oakland-Hayward (San Francisco CNTY), CA	1.075	1.325	0.421	23.93
01112	06	San Francisco-Oakland-Hayward (San Mateo CNTY), CA	1.075	1.325	0.421	23.93
01112	65	San Jose-Sunnyvale-Santa Clara (San Benito CNTY), CA	1.052	1.214	0.562	23.34
01112	09	San Jose-Sunnyvale-Santa Clara (Santa Clara CNTY), CA	1.083	1.354	0.388	24.13
01182	73	San Luis Obispo-Paso Robles-Arroyo Grande, CA	1.020	1.084	0.562	22.32
01112	66	Santa Cruz-Watsonville, CA	1.030	1.161	0.562	22.77
01182	74	Santa Maria-Santa Barbara, CA	1.032	1.126	0.562	22.68
01112	67	Santa Rosa, CA	1.024	1.130	0.562	22.55
01112	68	Stockton-Lodi, CA	1.020	1.074	0.562	22.29
01112	53	Vallejo-Fairfield, CA	1.055	1.256	0.458	23.39
01112	69	Visalia-Porterville, CA	1.020	1.074	0.562	22.29
01112	70	Yuba City, CA	1.020	1.074	0.562	22.29
01112	75	Rest of California	1.020	1.074	0.562	22.29
04112	01	Colorado	1.000	1.018	1.042	22.39
13102	00	Connecticut	1.021	1.112	1.255	23.38
12202	01	DC + MD/VA Suburbs	1.045	1.205	1.261	24.13
12102	01	Delaware	1.007	1.019	1.119	22.62
09102	03	Fort Lauderdale, FL	1.000	1.012	1.797	23.40
09102	04	Miami, FL	1.000	1.029	2.566	24.50
09102	99	Rest of Florida	1.000	0.952	1.358	22.59
10212	01	Atlanta, GA	1.000	0.997	1.088	22.38
10212	99	Rest of Georgia	1.000	0.899	1.073	22.02
01212	01	Hawaii, Guam	1.001	1.146	0.614	22.28
02202	00	Idaho	1.000	0.902	0.512	21.27
06102	16	Chicago, IL	1.008	1.034	1.925	23.79
06102	12	East St. Louis, IL	1.000	0.936	1.785	23.11
06102	15	Suburban Chicago, IL	1.009	1.053	1.565	23.38
06102	99	Rest of Illinois	1.000	0.919	1.208	22.27
08102	00	Indiana	1.000	0.919	0.379	21.14

(*continues*)

(*continued*)

Contractor	Locality	Locality Name	2019 Work GPCI	2019 PE GPCI	2019 MP GPCI	National Anes CF of 22.2730
05102	00	Iowa	1.000	0.907	0.423	21.16
05202	00	Kansas	1.000	0.911	0.615	21.44
15102	00	Kentucky	1.000	0.880	0.819	21.60
07202	01	New Orleans, LA	1.000	0.966	1.273	22.52
07202	99	Rest of Louisiana	1.000	0.887	1.199	22.15
14112	03	Southern Maine	1.000	1.007	0.670	21.85
14112	99	Rest of Maine	1.000	0.922	0.670	21.55
12302	01	Baltimore/Surr. CNTYS, MD	1.023	1.095	1.295	23.41
12302	99	Rest of Maryland	1.009	1.033	1.082	22.66
14212	01	Metropolitan Boston, MA	1.033	1.179	1.061	23.56
14212	99	Rest of Massachusetts	1.020	1.067	1.061	22.94
08202	01	Detroit, MI	1.000	0.989	1.691	23.17
08202	99	Rest of Michigan	1.000	0.919	1.018	22.01
06202	00	Minnesota	1.000	1.011	0.362	21.44
07302	00	Mississippi	1.000	0.870	0.370	20.96
05302	02	Metropolitan Kansas City, MO	1.000	0.963	1.073	22.24
05302	01	Metropolitan St. Louis, MO	1.000	0.959	1.053	22.20
05302	99	Rest of Missouri	1.000	0.863	0.993	21.78
03202	01	Montana***	1.000	1.000	1.631	23.13
05402	00	Nebraska	1.000	0.910	0.318	21.03
01312	00	Nevada***	1.002	1.017	0.909	22.24
14312	40	New Hampshire	1.000	1.045	1.050	22.50
12402	01	Northern NJ	1.041	1.180	0.938	23.54
12402	99	Rest of New Jersey	1.024	1.123	0.938	23.04
04212	05	New Mexico	1.000	0.921	1.247	22.33
13202	01	Manhattan, NY	1.052	1.180	1.615	24.65
13202	02	NYC Suburbs/Long Island, NY	1.041	1.205	2.149	25.27
13202	03	Poughkpsie/N NYC Suburbs, NY	1.016	1.070	1.313	23.22
13292	04	Queens, NY	1.052	1.200	2.121	25.40
13282	99	Rest of New York	1.000	0.950	0.595	21.55
11502	00	North Carolina	1.000	0.931	0.695	21.62
03302	01	North Dakota***	1.000	1.000	0.540	21.65
15202	00	Ohio	1.000	0.917	1.005	21.99
04312	00	Oklahoma	1.000	0.891	0.954	21.83

(*continues*)

(*continued*)

Contractor	Locality	Locality Name	2019 Work GPCI	2019 PE GPCI	2019 MP GPCI	National Anes CF of 22.2730
02302	01	Portland, OR	1.010	1.054	0.783	22.34
02302	99	Rest of Oregon	1.000	0.967	0.783	21.86
12502	01	Metropolitan Philadelphia, PA	1.022	1.074	1.379	23.43
12502	99	Rest of Pennsylvania	1.000	0.936	1.033	22.09
09202	20	Puerto Rico	1.000	1.007	0.990	22.28
14412	01	Rhode Island	1.027	1.050	0.999	22.92
11202	01	South Carolina	1.000	0.912	0.553	21.36
03402	02	South Dakota***	1.000	1.000	0.389	21.44
10312	35	Tennessee	1.000	0.901	0.526	21.28
04412	31	Austin, TX	1.000	1.021	0.747	22.00
04412	20	Beaumont, TX	1.000	0.924	0.839	21.79
04412	09	Brazoria, TX	1.020	0.997	0.839	22.39
04412	11	Dallas, TX	1.012	1.014	0.768	22.22
04412	28	Fort Worth, TX	1.007	0.986	0.747	22.00
04412	15	Galveston, TX	1.020	1.011	0.839	22.44
04412	18	Houston, TX	1.020	1.012	0.936	22.58
04412	99	Rest of Texas	1.000	0.938	0.796	21.78
03502	09	Utah	1.000	0.927	1.165	22.24
14512	50	Vermont	1.000	1.015	0.595	21.78
11302	00	Virginia	1.000	0.986	0.908	22.10
09202	50	Virgin Islands	1.000	1.007	0.990	22.28
02402	02	Seattle (King CNTY), WA	1.027	1.146	0.931	23.16
02402	99	Rest of Washington	1.000	1.011	0.902	22.18
11402	16	West Virginia	1.000	0.857	1.296	22.17
06302	00	Wisconsin	1.000	0.957	0.347	21.23
03602	21	Wyoming***	1.000	1.000	0.880	22.11

These case studies provide additional coding practice.

Case 1

Preoperative Diagnosis: Recurrent acute otitis media.

Postoperative Diagnosis: Recurrent acute right otitis media and left acute otitis media, right serous otitis media.

Operation Performed: Bilateral myringotomy with PE tube placement.

Anesthesia: General.

Indications: This is a 21-month-old female with a history of recurrent acute otitis media and at this time she presents for bilateral PE tube placement.

Details of Procedure: The patient was taken to OR and underwent uneventful induction of anesthesia. The right ear was examined first. Small amount of cerumen was cleaned. There were obvious air-fluid levels and a diffuse mild negative pressure with mild retraction of pars tensa.

The radial incision was made just anterior to the 6 o'clock position and a #5 suction was used to aspirate thick mucous. We utilized Cipro ophthalmic drops to help mobilize the thick mucous. When that was evacuated, a Reuter-Bobbin tube was placed. It was blue, Medronic style, and had a 1.14 mm inner diameter. This was kept in place with a Rosen pick in usual manner and Cipro drops were placed.

Next the left ear was explored. The left ear was bulging and very thickened and hyperemic. There was a full mucoid effusion there. A radial incision was made and a turbid mucopus came forward from the incision. She was aspirated with #5 suction. The middle ear cleft was well defined. The ear drum remained quite thickened. I was able to uneventfully place a Reuter-Bobbin tube there which was of a 1.14 mm inner diameter.

Ciprofloxacin ophthalmic drops were placed, and then suctioned out, irrigated again, and suctioned again. It looked like lumen of the tube was clear and there was no ongoing bleeding. We put more Cipro drops in and awakened the patient uneventfully having tolerated bilateral tube placement well.

I prescribed Cefzil p.o. for 7 days at 150 mg p.o. b.i.d. and Ciprodex drops for three days b.i.d. I asked the mother to put the Ciprodex in the left ear three times today.

(continues)

(continued)

The patient tolerated the procedure well and I will see her back in the office in approximately 10 days. I will consider getting an audiogram update on her when I review the chart at the post-op visit.

ICD-10-CM Code(s): _____

CPT Code(s): _____

Case 2

Date of Surgery: 10/3/XXXX

Preoperative Diagnosis: NUCLEAR CATARACT OD

Postoperative Diagnosis: Same as above.

Procedure: Cataract Removal Lens Implant OD

Anesthsia: Topical

Surgeon: Samantha Friends

In the preoperative area the anesthesia department applied a topical anesthesia of 2% Xylocaine gel to the patient's right eye.

In the operating room the patient's right eye was prepared and draped in the usual manner. A Barraquer wire speculum was placed between the lids. Ocucoat was applied to the cornea. A side port incision was made at 12 o'clock. Healon 5 was instilled into the anterior part of the anterior chamber. A bent needle with balance salt solution was then placed into the anterior chamber and used to deepen the anterior chamber between the lens and the Healon 5, and was used to produce a continuous circular capsulorhexis. A 1.1 mm diamond incision was made at the limbus about 2mm long temporally. The side port incision was then superiorly increased to 1.1 mm. Hydrodissection of the nucleus was done with a Ryecroft cannula on a syringe containing l/3cc of unpreserved 1% Xylocaine, after clearing a path to the incision. After the fluid wave was completed, the lens was rotated 180 degrees and flipped within the capsular bag. Healon 5 was then placed between the lens and the cornea, the cornea incision temporally and superiorly. An irrigating Bechert nucleus rotator was placed through the superior incision and the Phaco tip was placed through the temporal incision. The lens was emulsified within the capsular bag. An irrigating hand piece with an irrigating solution containing epinephrine, Vancomycin, and Gentamycin was then placed through the superior incision, and an aspiration hand piece through the temporal incision. This was used to remove the cortical remnants and polish the capsule. Healon 5 was then placed into the anterior chamber to plug up the capsulorhexis. Balance salt solution was then placed below this into the capsular bag to deepen the capsular bag. A 2.8 mm diamond keratome was used to

(continues)

(*continued*)

enlarge the 1.1 mm temporal corneal limbal incision. A + 17.0 diopter AMO lens was carefully inspected, irrigated, and loaded into the unfolder and placed through the incision and the leading haptic, placed into the capsular bag followed by the optic and then the trailing haptic. The irrigation aspiration hand pieces were then used to remove the viscoelastic. The lens was carefully inspected and was in good position. The incisions were hydrated with balance salt solution. The anterior chamber was restored to its normal depth with irrigating solution. The incision was checked for leakage. The conjunctiva and cornea were flushed with a Betadine solution. The speculum was removed. Blood loss was minimal. The patient left the operating room in good condition. There were no complications of surgery.

ICD-10-CM Code(s): _____

CPT Code(s): _____

Case 3

Preoperative Diagnosis:

1. Pregnancy, term, undelivered.

2. Fetal intolerance to labor.

Postoperative Diagnosis:

1. Pregnancy, term, delivered (living female infant).

2. Fetal intolerance to labor.

3. Thick green amniotic fluid (3 + meconium).

Name Of Procedure:

1. Primary cesarean section (low transverse).

Operative Findings: The uterus, tubes, and ovaries had a normal appearance.

Time and date of delivery: 1631 hours, 12/12/94 Weight at birth: 7 lb. 5 oz.

Apgar scores were 8 at one minute and 9 at five minutes. ESTIMATED BLOOD LOSS: 600 cc.

Operative Procedure: The patient was prepped and draped under spinal block anesthesia. A Foley catheter was in place. She was in the supine position. A Pfannenstiel incision was made and carried down to the rectus fascia. The bladder was incised transversely, and undermined cephalad and caudad. With sharp and blunt dissection, the rectus and pyramidalis muscles were separated in the midline. The peritoneum was entered, and the defect was extended under direct vision, avoiding the bladder reflection. The uterine incision was made transversely at the cervical area above the bladder reflection, and extended bilaterally using bandage scissors. Thick, green amniotic fluid was noted on entering the uterine cavity. The vertex was delivered from a left occiput posterior presentation. The upper respiratory tracts were suctioned before delivery of the shoulder, torso, and breech, without

(*continues*)

(*continued*)

complication. The cord was doubly clamped, cut, and the infant was handed to Dr. Hawa who attended the delivery. The placenta was manually removed. The uterus was exteriorized. The uterine cavity was cleaned. The uterine incisions were approximated using tfl chromic suture continuously, interlocking. Further suturing was necessary for hemostasis. The uterus was placed back in the abdomen. The wound was irrigated using saline solution. The peritoneum was closed using a 4-0 chromic suture continuously. The rectus fascia was closed using a #0 Vicryl continuously. The subcutaneous tissues were approximated using a 3-0 chromic suture continuously. The skin was approximated using staples.

The patient tolerated the procedure well and was returned to the Recovery Room in good condition. The estimated blood loss was 600 cc. No blood was replaced.

ICD-10-CM Code(s): _____

CPT Code(s): _____

Case 4

Preprocedure Diagnosis: Rule out upper GI pathology and colonic pathology.

Postprocedure Diagnosis: Colonic polyp as well as submucosal deformity of the duodenal bulb with active bleeding.

Procedure Performed: Colonoscopy with polypectomy and panendoscopy with bicap therapy.

Physician: Micelle Cousins, M.D.

Instruments Used:

Anesthesia: Demerol 25 mg IV, Versed 1 mg IV.

Indications: The patient is a 78-year-old male with a history of anemia, and lung carcinoma.

Recent upper GI series revealed some deformity of the duodenal bulb.

Complete history and physical is as per consultation note.

Procedure:

Colonoscopy: The colonoscope was advanced into the cecum. The ileocecal valve was well visualized and within normal limits. Just distal to the cecal valve there was a villous-appearing polyp measuring at approximately 2 × 1 cm. This was resected almost completely and retained for analysis. There are multiple large diverticula in the left colon without active bleeding. There are no other inflammatory changes and/or polyps throughout the colon.

Upper Endoscopy: The endoscope was advanced under direct vision of the esophagus. This appeared unremarkable. The scope was then advanced into the gastric lumen and, again, this revealed no significant abnormalities. Upon entering the duodenal bulb very carefully,

(*continues*)

(*continued*)

there was evidence of recent bleeding with a focal coagulant of blood in the bulb. On closer inspection, with washing of the catheter revealed a submucosal prominence with active bleeding was revealed. A bicap probe was used to coagulate this area and stop the blood loss. No ulceration was seen at this site. This appeared to be a submucosal process. The remaining portion of the duodenum was unremarkable.

Impression:

1. Large polyp in the right colon, most likely villous adenoma.
2. Multiple large diverticula.
3. Submucosal process in the duodenal bulb with secondary active blood loss.
4. Status post bicap therapy to this lesion.

Recommendation:

1. We will place patient on Carafate 1 gm q.i.d. over the next 10 days for this site of the bicap therapy.
2. Obtain a CT scan of the abdomen to rule out extrinsic pathology accounting for this tuberance into the lumen in the bulb. With his history of lung carcinoma this needs to be ruled out for other extrinsic pathology.
3. Will see the patient back in the office in two weeks.

Follow-up: Hematocrit on the current iron therapy.

ICD-10-CM Code(s): _____

CPT Code(s): _____

Case 5

Preoperative Diagnosis: End stage renal disease.

Postoperative Diagnosis: Same.

Operation: Left radial cephalic arteriovenous fistula

Wound Classification: clean

Operative Procedure:

Under satisfactory monitored anesthesia care, the left arm was prepped with Betadine, draped in a sterile fashion. 1% Xylocaine was used for local anesthesia. An incision was made halfway between the radial artery and the cephalic vein. The cephalic vein was mobilized. The vein was on the small side but I still felt it was worth a try to use it for an AV fistula. The radial artery was in excellent condition. The patient was given Heparin, the radial artery was controlled, arteriotomy was made in the radial artery, and the end of the vein was sutured to the side of the artery with running 7-0 Prolene suture. After appropriate flushing, clamps

(*continues*)

(continued)

were released, reestablishing flow through the fistula. Technically the anastomosis appeared to be good. The patient was given Protamine, the wound was closed with running Vicryl in the subcutaneous tissue and 5-0 Monosoft in the skin. Dry sterile dressing was applied. Sponge and needle count was correct. The patient was sent to the day surgery area in satisfactory condition.

ICD-10-CM Code(s): _____

CPT Code(s): _____

Case 6

Preoperative Diagnosis: Urinary retention.

Postoperative diagnosis: Same.

Operation Performed: Cystoscopy transurethral prostatectomy and bladder neck incision.

Anesthesia: General.

Blood Loss: 100 CC.

Drain In Place: A 22-French 3-way Foley catheter with 40 cc in balloon.

Procedure: With the patient in the dorsal lithotomy position under general anesthesia, he was prepped and draped in a routine sterile manner for a cystoscopy. A 23.5 cystoscope was introduced into the bladder under direct vision. There was noted to be a trabeculated bladder with catheter reaction and an obstructing 2.5-cm prostate. At that point, the scope was removed and the 24-French Teflon resectoscope sheath was placed after lubricating it with K-Y jelly and Vaseline. Using a cutting current of 170 and a coagulation current of 70, the procedure was performed.

A groove was cut from the bladder neck to the verumontanum. The left lobe was then resected posteriorly to anteriorly and a similar resection was performed on the right. Additional tissue was removed circumferentially from the apex. Hemostasis was accomplished. The chips were irrigated out of the bladder. There was still tightness of the bladder neck, so bladder neck incisions were made with a Collings knife, which opened up the bladder neck. The bladder was filled, the scope removed, and a 22-French 3-way Foley catheter was inserted, placed on moderate traction on the left leg after inflating it to 40 cc. The catheter irrigated well and the patient was taken to recovery in good condition.

ICD-10-CM Code(s): _____

CPT Code(s): _____

Case 7

Preoperative Diagnosis: Mass

Postoperative Diagnosis: Intracellular neoplasm

Procedure: Biopsy with excision of vulvar area

This 49-year-old patient has been seen by me for the last six weeks. She has had biopsies of lesions that extend from the clitoris on the left. The pathology report taken on 12/31/XX confirmed condyloma and dysplasia that extends to the lateral margins. A pap smear was obtained and the pathology was found to be negative.

Today the patient presents for an excisional biopsy.

Procedure:

The patient was placed in the dorsal lithotomy position and the vagina was prepped and draped in the usual sterile fashion. The condylomatous changes were easily demarcated. The area was prepped with Betadine and 10 cc of 1% Xylocaine. In an elliptical fashion the entire lesion was excised with an addition of a 6 mm margin on both sides. Bleeding was controlled and the skin edges were closed with a continuous locked suture of 4-0 Vicryl. The patient tolerated the procedure and was sent to the recovery area in stable condition. The tissue was sent to pathology for analysis.

ICD-10-CM Code(s): _____

CPT Code(s): _____

Case 8

Preoperative Diagnosis: Missed abortion.

Postoperative Diagnosis: Same.

Operation: Suction Uterine Curettage.

Operative Findings:

The uterus was about ten weeks' size, soft; both adnexae were negative. The tissue removed was consistent with the products of conception.

Operative Procedure:

The patient was placed in the supine position on the operating table. General anesthesia was given by Dr. Tinst. The patient was then placed in the lithotomy position. The vagina, perineum, and abdomen were prepped and draped in the usual fashion. An examination under anesthesia was carried out, which revealed a uterus of ten to eleven weeks' size. The adnexae were negative for masses. The cervix was closed. A weighted speculum was placed. The cervix was visualized and the anterior lip of the cervix was grasped with a single-tooth tenaculum. The

(continues)

(continued)

cervix was dilated until adequate dilation was achieved. Using a 12-mm size suction curette tip, the uterine cavity was emptied of its contents. Confirmation of the completeness of the uterine curettage was done with a sharp curette and no further tissue was obtained.

Estimated Blood Loss: The estimated blood loss was approximately 500 ml.

The tenaculum was then removed and the anterior lip of the cervix was inspected. Adequate hemostasis was present at the tenaculum application site. At the conclusion of the procedure, the uterus was firmly contracted. During the procedure, a dilute solution of Pitocin was infused. The patient was also given Methergine, 0.2 mg, intramuscularly. The patient tolerated the procedure well and left for the Recovery Room in satisfactory condition.

ICD-10-CM Code(s): _____

CPT Code(s): _____

Case 9

Preoperative Diagnosis: Abdominal aortic aneurysm.

Postoperative Diagnosis: Same.

Operation Performed: Abdominal aortic aneurysm repair, retroperitoneal approach.

Anesthesia: General endotracheal with epidural.

Indications For Procedure: The patient is a 51-year-old white male who was found to have an abdominal aortic aneurysm by physical exam. He has some history of glucose intolerance but is otherwise healthy.

He is here for elective aneurysm repair.

Procedure: The patient was taken to the operating room and placed on the table in the supine position and Anesthetized with general endotracheal anesthesia without difficulty. A Foley catheter was inserted and then the patient was positioned with his shoulders in the right lateral decubitus position and his hips as flat as possible to open up the space between his left iliac crest and his left costal margin. The table was also reverse flexed to help open up this space.

We made an incision from the tip of the 11th rib extending medially toward the lateral border of the rectus. We used the knife and then Bovie cautery to go through the subcutaneous tissues, and then through the external and internal oblique muscles and the transversalis muscle. We stayed extraperitoneally and bluntly dissected in this plane, lifting both the kidney and the ureter up with peritoneal cavity, and keeping the retroperitoneal fat down along the psoas muscle. We used the Omni retractor for retraction once we had dissected out this plane. The patient was fairly thin and we were able to easily identify two lumbar veins and the left renal vein. We tied the lumbar vein and retracted the left renal vein superiorly. We were also able to identify the left renal artery and it appeared to have two branches that came off fairly close to the takeoff of the main artery.

(continues)

(continued)

We carefully dissected out the neck of the aneurysm and were able to get completely around it with a finger. We chose a gently curved clamp for the aortic clamp. We then worked our way distally. We were able to identify the left iliac artery very easily. It came up almost directly to the left. We cleared it off circumferentially and planned to place a clamp on this. The right iliac artery we could palpate, but we were not able to dissect out. We planned on using a balloon catheter to occlude this.

We then gave the patient 5,000 units of heparin intravenously and after three minutes we clamped the aorta and the left iliac artery and opened the aneurysm with the 11 blade. Once we had the aneurysm open, we palpated for the orifice of the right iliac artery and placed in the 9 French balloon occlusion catheter down the artery and pulled back gently as the balloon was inflated to occlude the artery. Once we had hemostatic control, we removed other clots, thrombi, and plaque from inside of the aneurysm and used 2-0 silk sutures to suture ligate any backbleeding from the lumbar arteries. We did not see the IMA, but on the patient's preoperative angiogram, all the branches of the IMA, the celiac, and the SMA were opened and visualized. With the aneurysm open, we T'd off the ends to prepare the sewing rings and then chose a #20-mm Hemashield graft for the graft. Because the proximal aorta was somewhat still dilated, we used 2-0 Tycron pledgeted sutures to do an interrupted mattress anastomosis. We completed the anastomosis and slowly released the clamp. It was apparent that there were a few gaps between the sutures. We used about three or four more 2-0 Tycron sutures in order to gain control and finally we had a hemostatic anastomosis.

When we were satisfied with this anastomosis, after placing a clamp on the graft itself, we removed the clamp on the proximal aorta and then stretched the graft to choose the length to do the distal anastomosis. We cut off the graft and then the distal anastomosis with a running 3-0 Prolene suture. We started posteriorly with a mattress stitch and worked our way around from either side. When we were finished, we flushed back the left iliac artery, and then reclamped it and flushed back the right. We removed the balloon occlusion catheter from the right and completed sewing the anastomosis. We then removed the left iliac clamp. We then gradually released the clamp from the graft to open perfusion to the legs. We did this slowly and anesthesia kept up with the volume. The patient's blood pressure did not drop below 100 for more than 20 seconds and was easily resuscitated back up to blood pressures in the 110–120 range. He continued to make urine throughout the case.

Once the clamp was off, we checked again for hemostasis. There was another lumbar which we had to oversew with a 2-0 silk, and we removed more plaque and identified more small branches which required oversewing. We used 2-0 chromic suture to oversew the edge of the aneurysm wall itself, which was oozing slightly. We packed for five minutes and checked again. When we were satisfied with the hemostasis, we removed all the retractors and began to close.We closed the incision in layers of 2-0 Vicryl suture starting with transversalis, then the internal oblique, and then the external oblique. We then irrigated between layers and

(continues)

(continued)

closed the skin with staples. There was approximately 1,500 cc of blood loss and 1,200 cc of Cell Saver, 3 L of LR, 1,000 cc of Hespan, and 500 cc of 5% albumin was given during the case. The patient was taken to the recovery room where he was extubated. He tolerated the procedure well. He will keep his Foley catheter.

ICD-10-CM Code(s): _____

CPT Code(s): _____

Case 10

Preoperative Diagnosis: Chronic osteomyelitis, left second toe.

Postoperative Diagnosis: Chronic osteomyelitis, left second toe.

Operation Performed: Amputation of distal phalanx, left second toe.

Anesthesia: Local with sedation

Procedure: In the supine position, the left foot was prepped with Betadine scrub and was washed and draped in a sterile fashion; 0.5% Xylocaine with 0.5% Marcaine was infiltrated in the dermis of the left second toe, approximately 6 cc was used.

A posterior flap incision was made through the dermis and subcutaneous fat down to bone circumferentially. The bone was cut at the DIP joint with bone cutters, and the articular surface of the proximal phalanx was debrided with rongeurs. Bleeding was good at the tissue level and the tissue appeared quite viable. No purulent material was seen and good healthy bone remained. The area was cauterized in several places and closed with interrupted 4-0 nylon suture; ¼-inch Steri-strips with benzoin were also applied, and sterile dressing was placed.

The patient was taken to the recovery room in good condition. Estimated blood loss approximately 2 cc. Needle and sponge counts correct times two.

ICD-10-CM Code(s): _____

CPT Code(s): _____

Case 11

Preoperative Diagnosis: Bilateral hydroceles

Postoperative Diagnosis: Bilateral hydroceles

Operation Performed: Bilateral Hydrocelectomy

Anesthesia: General

Clinical History: This is a 2-year-old boy with an obvious hydrocele. The left cord was thickened.

Operative Findings: Bilateral communicating hydroceles.

Procedure: With the patient under general anesthesia, the abdomen and groin were prepped and draped in a sterile manner. A transverse incision was made over the right inguinal canal. The external oblique fascia was opened in the direction of its fibers through the external ring. The cord was brought up into the wound and the cord was explored. The hydrocele was identified and separated from the vas and vessels. It was clamped and divided and traced proximally to the internal ring where it was twisted and triply ligated with 2-0 Ethibond sutures. The distal sac was subtotally excised down to the testicle using electrocautery. The external oblique fascia was closed with interrupted 4-0 Vicryl sutures. Scarpa's fascia was closed with interrupted 4-0 Vicryl sutures and the skin was closed with interrupted 5-0 Vicryl in a subcuticular fashion and reinforced with Mastisol and Steri-strips. The left side was explored through a similar incision. The external oblique fascia was identified, and the cord was seen and explored. A small communicating hydrocele was identified, separated from the vas and vessels, and was traced proximally to the internal ring where it was triply ligated with 3-0 Ethibond suture. The distal hydrocele was then taken down to the testicle and removed. The external oblique fascia was closed with interrupted 3-0 Vicryl sutures, the Scarpa's fascia was closed with interrupted 4-0 Vicryl sutures, and the skin was closed with interrupted 5-0 Vicryl in a subcuticular fashion and reinforced with Mastisol and Steri-strips. Blood loss was minimal. There were no operative complications. The child tolerated the procedure well.

ICD-10-CM Code(s): _____

CPT Code(s): _____

Case 12

Preoperative Diagnosis: Status post left distal radius and ulna fractures with gradually worsening apex volar angulation of the radius fracture.

Postoperative Diagnosis: Same

Operation: Closed manipulation or closed osteoclasis, left distal radius fracture and application of a long-arm fiberglass cast.

Wound Classification: Clean

Operative Indications: The indications can be reviewed on my admission History & Physical exam note.

Operative Procedure:

This is a eight-year-old child, right-hand dominant, admitted to Outpatient Surgery at the Sunny View Hospital by me today, 6/4/XX. There being no medical or anesthetic contraindications to surgery, the patient was brought to the operating room. General mask anesthesia was administered per anesthesiologist.

With the patient appropriately anesthetized, I simply manipulated the distal radius. It was largely healed, but I was able to change the apex volar angulation for more than 30 degrees to approximately 10–15 degrees. I really could not move the fracture any further.

Intraoperative radiographs documented the improvement in the apex volar angulation and a long arm, well-padded fiberglass case was applied with elbow flexion at 90 degrees; the forearm in neutral rotation; the carpus in neutral rotation; and the index, little digit metacarpophalangeal joints were left free to allow full, passive and active flexion.

Three-point fixation molds were applied about that distal forearm carpus and proximal hand area.

At the conclusion of the closed manipulation, or osteoclasis, and application of the cast, the patient was simply awakened and brought to the Recovery Room where she arrived in stable condition. The patient tolerated the procedure well.

The patient did not receive fluids perioperatively. It was a closed procedure, hence, no blood loss. There were no pathologic specimens.

ICD-10-CM Code(s): _____

CPT Code(s): _____

Case 13

Preoperative Diagnosis: Lipoma of right posterior shoulder/axilla

Postoperative Diagnosis: Same, pending pathology

Operation Performed: Excision of Lipoma of Right Posterior Shoulder/Axilla

Anesthesia: Local with intravenous sedation and monitoring

Description: With the patient in left lateral decubitus position, the right shoulder and axilla were prepared with Betadine, and draped with sterile drapes. There is a bulging mass at the posterior axillary fold. Margins of this were delineated, 1% xylocaine with epinephrine was infiltrated in the skin over the mass and at the periphery and deep to it. Later, supplementary doses were administered.

A 13 cm long incision was made obliquely from superior posterior to anterior inferior, ending at the posterior axilla. It was carried through the skin and superficial subcutaneous tissue. A multi-lobular fatty mass was encountered. It is invading the surrounding tissue and is partitioned at the periphery in multi-septal fashion. At the posterior aspect of the muscle, the surface is flat and it is the only area which has some sort of delineating capsule. Anteriorly there is a 2.5 × 3.5 cm single bulge extending in the axilla itself. This was dissected out without injuring any of the vessels. The entire lesion is about 11 × 9 cm in size. Multiple bleeders were coagulated. A Jackson Pratt drain was inserted anteriorly/inferiorly through a separate stab incision and secured with #2 silk.

A multilayer repair with interrupted 4-0 and 5-0 polysorb sutures to the subcutaneous tissue and skin, and 5-0 nylon to the superficial skin was performed. A dressing with Xeroflo, dressing sponges, and Hypafix was applied. Blood loss was minimal. Prior to the conclusion of the procedure 10 cc of 0.25% Marcaine was infiltrated in the skin and surrounding tissue for postoperative comfort.

Pathology

Tissue:

A) LIPOMA, RT POSTERIOR SHOULDER

Clinical Diagnosis And History: Lipoma, Rt Posterior Shoulder

Gross Description:

Specimen received in formalin labeled, "lipoma right shoulder" is a lobulated partially encapsulated tan to pink-red 9.5 × 6.0 × 2.5 cm portion of fibroadipose tissue. Sectioning shows a homogeneous yellow-tan lobulated and fatty cut surface. Representative sections are submitted (4 blocks).

Diagnosis:

MATURE FAT, CONSISTENT WITH LIPOMA, RIGHT POSTERIOR SHOULDER

ICD-10-CM Code(s): _____

CPT Code(s): _____

Case 14

Preoperative Diagnosis: Right testicular torsion

Postoperative Diagnosis: Torsion of right testicular appendix

Operation Performed: Exploration of right testicle with excision of right testicular appendix.

Operative Note: With the patient under satisfactory general anesthesia, the scrotum was prepped and draped in the usual sterile manner. An incision was made in the hemi-scrotum, and the testicle was extruded through the incision. The appendix testis was cross clamped and excised. The base was tied with a simple 3-0 Chromic tie. The testicle was fixed in the scrotum with 1 suture of 4-0 Chromic suture extending through the tunica albuginea and into the scrotum. The testicle was returned to the scrotum. The incision was closed with interrupted 4-0 Chromic suture. Neosporin was applied to the incision. The patient was discharged to the Recovery Room in good condition.

ICD-10-CM Code(s): _____

CPT Code(s): _____

Case 15

Preoperative Diagnosis: Right middle finger extensor contracture.

Postoperative Diagnosis: Same

Operative Procedure: Right middle finger extensor tenolysis and partial collateral ligament incision metacarpophalangeal joint.

Indications For Procedure: This is a 25-year-old right dominant painter, who complains of right middle finger pain at the MP joint. He originally underwent a bone grafting of a giant cell tumor in the metacarpal approximately two years ago. Since then, he has had considerable discomfort in the MP joint, with difficulty extending and flexing the finger. He has had extensive therapy without relief of his symptoms.

His physical examination shows flexion to approximately 75 degrees, without full active extension.

Procedure: After adequate median, dorsal, radial, and ulnar sensory nerve blocks with Lidocaine 2% and Marcaine 0.5%, equal volumes, 20 cc total, the right upper extremity was prepped and draped in the usual sterile fashion. The arm was exsanguinated and forearm tourniquet inflated to 250 mm of mercury.

A pre-existing longitudinal surgical scar over the MP joint was extended proximally the distance of 1 cm. This dissection was carried down through the skin and subcutaneous tissues. An extensive amount of scar tissue was encountered just above the sagittal bends. This was resected, and sent to pathology.

(continues)

(*continued*)

The extensor tendon was then identified, firmly adherent to the sagittal band. Tenolysis was begun at this level, which was slightly proximal to the MP joint. A combination of blunt and sharp dissection was used. Primarily scissors were used to free up the sagittal band in the tunnel through which the tendon could pass. At the completion of the tenolysis, the MP joint could be passively and fully extended by placing pressure on the tendon. Passive flexion was achievable to approximately 80 degrees. It was felt to be improved, but not completely resolved.

It was, therefore, elected to perform a partial resection of the collateral ligament. Sharp dissection was placed through the sagittal bands, down to the capsule. A mini-arthrotomy measuring about 4 mm, was extended over the insertion of the collateral ligament, and using a #69 beaver blade, they were resected. The flexion was then improved to approximately 90 degrees. Hyperflexion to 100 degrees was not achievable with this procedure. However, it was felt to be sufficient so that he would have a functional range of motion and a good grip.

The wound was thoroughly irrigated. The tourniquet was released, and hemostasis was achieved after five minutes of digital pressure. The skin was reapproximated with Ethilon 4-0 suture, using the horizontal mattress technique. A light dressing with Coban was applied. The patient tolerated the procedure well, and was taken to the recovery room in stable condition.

ICD-10-CM Code(s): _____

CPT Code(s): _____

Case 16

Preoperative Diagnosis: Anal fissure, class 4 hemorrhoids.

Postoperative Diagnosis: Same.

Operation Performed: Hemorrhoidectomy and sphincterotomy, left lateral.

Procedure: The patient was put in the prone position on the Wilson frame, the buttocks were spread with tape, the perianal area was prepped and draped in normal sterile fashion with 2% lidocaine with Epinephrine being placed in the anal canal. Left lateral, right anterior and right posterior hemorrhoidectomy was performed in the same fashion by making an incision on each side of the lead, lifting the hemorrhoidal tissue off the internal and external sphincter, undermining the mucosa and anoderm then reapproximating with 3-0 chromic suture. The left lateral had some growth-like structure that looked as if they were large papilloma, pathology is pending. A margin was obtained on that lead around the internal sphincter partially, small amount to treat the posterior anal fissure, which had been quite bothersome. All three leads were checked and found to have adequate hemostasis, a dressing was placed after 0.75% Marcaine was placed in the wounds.

ICD-10-CM Code(s): _____

CPT Code(s): _____

Case 17

Diagnosis: Displaced subcapital fracture right hip

Postoperative Diagnosis: Same as above

Operation: Modular Austin Moore femoral head replacement right hip

Wound Classification: Clean

Anesthesia: Spinal

Operative Procedure:

In the laminar flow operating room spinal anesthesia was induced. The patient was positioned supine with a rolled sheet under the right hip, which was scrubbed and prepped with Betadine and sterilely draped. A lateral incision was made with an anterolateral approach to the hip used. Homan retractors were used for exposure. The anterior capsule was exposed and excised. The femoral neck was trimmed with an oscillating power saw to the appropriate level and angle, and the bone fragments and femoral head removed from the acetabulum. This measured exactly 55 mm and a 55 mm femoral head trial prosthesis was found to fit very well within the acetabulum. The remainder of the capsule was excised and the short rotators released at their insertion on the greater trochanter. The leg was then adducted and externally rotated, and the proximal femur was exposed with Homan retractors. The medullary canal was initially opened with a mortis and chisel and a blunt tipped tapered reamer, followed by progressive sizes of rasps to a size large, which provided an excellent press fit. A size large Zimmer modular Austin Moore stem was then inserted into the femur and impacted so that the collar was the calcar, and a 55 mm module chrome cobalt femoral was head placed on the stem. The hip was irrigated well to remove any bone debris or chips within the acetabulum, which was checked carefully, both manually and visually, and the hip reduced. There was excellent stability and motion. Two Hemovac drains were brought out anteriorly through separate stab wounds. The incision was closed using interrupted Vicryl for the deeper tissues and staples for the skin. A dry sterile dressing was applied. The patient tolerated the procedure well and was taken to the recovery room in satisfactory condition.

ICD-10-CM Code(s): _____

CPT Code(s): _____

Case 18

Indications For Procedure: A 70-old male with a recently discovered left hilar mass, probable left upper lobe and lingula. No clinical symptoms except a long history of COPD. Has not smoked in 12 years. Bronchoscopy to be done for evaluation.

Pre-Procedure Diagnosis: Rule out carcinoma of left lung

Post-Procedure Diagnosis: Same

Anesthesia: Topical Cetacaine, and Cyclaine

Procedure Performed: Flexible Bronchoscopy

Findings: After induction of satisfactory anesthesia, the flexible bronchoscope was introduced. There were normal appearing cords, which moved normally. The carina was midline and sharp. The entire right side was examined, and was within normal limits. On the left side, there were some bronchitic changes in the left upper lobe region, no question of narrowing, and there was no sign of any tumor. Washings were obtained from the entire left side including the left upper lobe for cytology and culture. The bronchoscope was removed. The patient tolerated the procedure well and went to the Recovery Room in satisfactory condition.

ICD-10-CM Code(s): _____

CPT Code(s): _____

Case 19

Left Stereotactic Breast Biopsy

Indications: This patient had a prior comparison bilateral mammogram performed at the hospital last week, which demonstrated a mass in the posterior aspect of the left breast. This was suspicious for malignancy. A core biopsy was requested.

Using the stereotactic prone core biopsy device, multiple core samples were obtained through the area of mammographic abnormality.

The patient tolerated the procedure without incident.

Biopsy showed poorly differentiating infiltrating ductal carcinoma, grade III.

Impression: Positive core biopsy for malignancy in the left breast.

ICD-10-CM Code(s): _____

CPT Code(s): _____

Case 20

Preoperative Diagnosis: Urinary retention

Postoperative Diagnosis: Same

Operation Performed: Suprapubic punch cystotomy

Operative Note: With the patient in the supine position, the lower abdomen was prepped and draped in the usual sterile manner. 10 cc of 1% Xylocaine with Epinephrine were instilled into an area two fingerbreadths above the pubic symphysis. A small transverse skin incision was made and a Campbell suprapubic punch trocar was inserted into the bladder. An 18 French Foley catheter was inserted, inflated and secured at skin level. Sterile dressings were applied. The patient was discharged to his room in good condition.

ICD-10-CM Code(s): _____

CPT Code(s): _____

GLOSSARY

A

abdomen   the area of the body that lies between the thorax and the pelvis

abdominal hysterectomy   the removal of the uterus performed through an incision made in the abdomen

abduction   to move away from the body

abortion   the term used to indicate that a pregnancy was ended prior to the time that a fetus reached a viable age and could survive outside the uterus

acellular dermal replacement   replacing skin with a skin substitute that is composed of porous lattice fibers and a synthetic substance

add-on code symbol (+)   used within CPT to list procedures that are completed in addition to the primary procedure or service performed

adduction   to move toward the axis of the body

adenoids   one of three sets of tonsils; also referred to as the *nasopharyngeal tonsils*

adjacent tissue transfer   a procedure in which healthy tissue is manipulated or rearranged from a site close to or next to an area that is open due to disease or injury

adrenal gland   a gland that sits atop the kidney; regulates electrolytes and helps in the metabolism of glucose and adrenaline

Advance Beneficiary Notice (ABN)   a written notice that is signed by a patient to document that the patient has been made aware that a procedure or service to be completed may not be payable through Medicare

advance life support (ALS)   specialized life support services and/or supplies that are used when treating a patient

alimentary canal   another name for the digestive tract

allogenic bone marrow transplants   procedures in which cells are taken from a donor and transplanted to a patient needing the cells

allotransplantation   a type of transplant that occurs between like species

alternative laboratory platform testing   modifier 92

alveolus   socket where the tooth sits

amniocentesis   a procedure in which fluid is withdrawn from the amniotic sac

amnioscopy   a scope procedure used to view the fetus in the amniotic sac

A-mode technique   a radiological technique that takes a one-dimensional measurement

analyte   a substance being tested

anastomosis   the process of surgically connecting two structures that are usually hollow, tubular parts

anesthesia   loss of sensation

anesthesiologist   a physician who is qualified to administer anesthesia and is board certified

aneurysm   an area in the artery that becomes weakened

angiography   imaging of the vessels

angioplasty   a procedure in which a balloon is inflated in the vessel to push and flatten plaque against the vessel wall

angioscopy   a procedure in which a fiber-optic scope is used to see within a noncoronary vessel

anomaly   an abnormality or deviation from the norm in a structure

anoscopy   an endoscopic procedure performed on the anus

antepartum   the time period prior to childbirth

anterior chamber   a chamber located in front of the lens of the eye

anterior mediastinotomy   a mediastinotomy completed from the front of the body

anteroposterior   front to back

anus   the most distal structure of the digestive system

aortic valve   sits between the aorta and the left ventricle and is one of the main valves of the heart

aortography   a test in which contrast material is injected to visualize problems with the aorta and its branches

appendix   a small, twisted, tubelike structure located at the blind end of the cecum

aqueous humor   clear, watery fluid that fills the interior of the eye

arachnoid mater   the middle layer of the meninges

arteries   vessels that move oxygen-rich blood from the heart to the rest of the body (with the exception of the pulmonary vein)

arteriography   imaging of the arteries

arthrodesis   surgical repair or reconstruction fixation of a joint

arthrography   x-ray of the inside of a joint

arthroplasty   plastic surgery of a joint

arthroscope   a scope used to view the joints

arthroscopy   the examination of the interior of a joint by using an arthroscope

arthrotomy   surgical incision of a joint

arytenoidectomy   surgical excision of the arytenoid cartilage

ascending colon   the part of the colon that begins at the ileocecal junction; at the undersurface of the liver, it becomes the transverse colon

aspiration   the surgical removal of fluid from the body

assistant surgeon   modifier 80

assistant surgeon (when qualified resident surgeon not available)   modifier 82

atria   the upper chambers of the heart that receive blood from the veins

atrioventricular node (AV node)   sometimes referred to as the *AV node;* directs the impulses to the ventricles, causing them to contract

auditory ossicles three small bones that transmit and amplify sound waves

auditory tube also called the *eustachian tube;* connects the bony structure of the middle ear to the pharynx

augmentation the surgical increase of the size of a structure

auricle a flexible cartilaginous flap that has a bottom portion known as the *earlobe*

autogenous graft a type of graft in which tissue is taken from one part of a person's body and put on another part of the same person's body

autograft surgical transplantation of a person's own tissue

autologous bone marrow transplants transplants for which cells are cultivated from patient's own marrow

autonomic nervous system connects the central nervous system to the visceral organs via the cranial and spinal nerves

axial an axis of a structure or part of the body

axillary lymph nodes nodes located in the armpit

B

backbench work the physician's preparation of a donor organ

balanced anesthesia anesthesia delivered by a combination of inhalation, injection, and instillation

bariatric surgery a type of operative procedure using bands and port insertion; performed as a treatment of morbid obesity

Bartholin's glands glands that secrete lubricating mucous in the vagina; also referred to as the *vestibular glands*

base unit reflects the usual services attached to anesthesia and the value of the work associated with the anesthesia services provided; also called *basic value* or *relative value*

base unit value reflects the usual services attached to anesthesia and the value of the work associated with the anesthesia services; also called *basic value* or *relative value*

basic life support (BLS) services that are provided for life support that include, but are not limited to, the control of bleeding, immobilization of fractures, treatment of shock, delivering of babies, and cardiopulmonary resuscitation

basic value reflects the usual services attached to anesthesia and the value of the work associated with the anesthesia services provided; also called *relative value*

benign lesion a lesion whose cell growth is abnormal but not life threatening

Bier blocks injections of an anesthetic agent into the arm below the elbow, or in the leg below the knee

bilateral procedure modifier 50

biliary tract organs and ducts that are involved in the processing and movement of bile into the duodenum

biofeedback measurements of physiological responses and patient instruction on how to control these responses

biopsy removal of tissue for pathological examination

block see *block anesthesia*

block anesthesia a type of regional anesthesia in which anesthetic is injected along a major nerve tract, interrupting the nerve conductivity

bone density test a test used to determine the presence of osteoporosis by looking at the mass or density of the bone

bony labyrinth a maze of bony structures within the inner ear

brachytherapy an internal radiation therapy that is used to treat tissue

brain the organ responsible for all physical and mental functions of the body

brain stem a structure that connects the diencephalons to the spinal cord

brief HPI a history of present illness consisting of one to three elements

bronchi large air passages in the lung through which air is inhaled and exhaled

bronchoscopy an examination of the bronchi using a flexible endoscope

B-scan a two-dimensional radiological image

bullet symbol denotes a new code that has been added since the previous edition of CPT

bundled a term indicating that preoperative, postoperative, and the service itself are included in the price the physician receives for the procedure

bundle of His the conduction fibers that cause the contractions of the heart

burn an injury to the body tissue that is a result of heat, flame, sun, chemicals, radiation, and/or electricity

burr hole procedures procedures in which the physician drills a burr hole in the cranium. The acts could include a biopsy of the brain or intracranial lesion, drainage of brain abscess or cyst, tapping of abscess or cyst, drainage of hematoma, and other brain or intracranial procedures

C

cardiac pacemaker a device used to correct and manage heart dysrhythmias

cardiovascular system the system that pumps blood through the body via the heart and blood vessels

care plan oversight services coordinated for a patient over a 30-day period for the purpose of assessment or care decisions

cartilage thin sheets of fibrous connective tissue

case management physician supervision and coordination of direct care received by a patient as part of an interdisciplinary team

casts fiberglass, plaster, or plastic rigid dressing used to immobilize an area to prevent movement

Category I codes from the main sections of CPT

Category II tracking codes; not mandatory

Category III codes for collection of statistical data

central nervous system the system composed of the brain and spinal cord

central venous access (CVA) device a catheter classified as such if the tip ends in the subclavian, brachiocephalic, right atrium, or superior or inferior vena cava

cerclage a technique of encircling the cervix uteri with a wire, ligature, or loop

cerebellum the second-largest part of the brain, which coordinates skeletal muscle movements and the learning of new motor skills

cerebral cortex consists of a layer of neurons on the surface of the brain

cerebrum   the largest part of the brain, which is separated by depressions and grooves and is divided into separate hemispheres by a groove called the *longitudinal fissure*

Certificate of Medical Necessity (CMN)   a document that clearly explains why a physician feels a patient needs the durable medical equipment (DME) item or service; should be filed in the patient's medical record for certain supplies

Certified registered nurse anesthetist (CRNA)   a registered nurse with 36 months of additional training in anesthesiology who is certified to administer anesthesia

cerumen   wax in the ear

ceruminous glands   canal sweat glands that secrete cerumen

cervical intraepithelial neoplasia (CIN)   the Bethesda System used to evaluate the specimen

cervical lymph nodes   nodes located in the neck area

cervical mediastinotomy   a mediastinotomy completed from the front of the body

cervix uteri   the area between the ostium uteri and the isthmus

cesarean section delivery   a delivery in which there is a surgical procedure (incision) performed through the abdominal wall to extract the fetus

chalazion   a small tumor of the eyelid that is formed by the retention of secretions of the meibomian gland

cheiloplasty   repair of the lips

chemical pleurodesis   a process where a chemical is placed into the pleural space to cause inflammation; this reduces effusion of the area

chief complaint   the reason for the patient encounter

choanal atresia   a narrowing or blockage of the nasal airway by tissue; a congenital condition

chorionic villus   the medical term for the placenta

choroid   the layer just beneath the sclera that provides the blood supply and nutrients to the eye

cilia   an external auditory canal with tiny hairs that help in transmitting sound waves

ciliary body   the muscles that are responsible for adjusting the lens of the eye

cineradiography   a type of x-ray that films at a high speed to take a series of images of motion in an organ or system

circumcision   a procedure in which the foreskin is completely removed from the glans penis

class findings   reflect the clinical findings of patients with severe peripheral involvement

clean-contaminated wound   a wound with a low infection rate; involves a minor break in surgical technique, but no inflammation is present

clean wound   a wound with a very low infection rate; involves no inflammation or break in sterile technique

closed reduction   manual application of force to realign an injured area

closed treatment   where a fracture site is not surgically exposed or open

coagulation   clotting of blood

cochlea   a snail-shaped, bony structure that contains auditory fluids that transmit sound

cochlear duct   a membranous structure that aids in the hearing process

colonoscopy   an endoscope is used to examine the entire colon, from the rectum to the cecum

colpocentesis   the aspiration of fluid through the vaginal wall into a syringe

colpocleisis   a surgical closure of the vagina

colpopexy   a procedure in which the vagina is sutured to the abdominal wall

colporrhaphy   the surgical repair of the vagina

colposcopy   a procedure in which a scope is used to view the vaginal and cervical area

colpotomy   a procedure in which the fallopian tubes are identified and then occluded at vascular points

combined hemorrhoid (mixed hemorrhoid)   found in both the superior vein and outside the external sphincter; usually dilated

complete PFSH   the review of at least two areas of the past, family, or social history

complete replacement   replacement of the whole vessel device through the same access site

complete study   a study that encompasses the entire body area

complex repair   repair that involves reconstruction, skin grafting, stents, retention sutures, or time-consuming techniques in addition to a layered closure

comprehensive examination   the highest level of examination; consists of a multisystem examination

comprehensive history   documentation of four or more elements of the history of the present illness (HPI); a complete review of systems; and a complete past, family, and social history (PFSH)

computed axial tomography (CT, CAT)   a procedure in which cross-sectional images are produced after an ionizing radiational substance is administered

conduction anesthesia   a type of regional anesthesia in which anesthetic is injected along a major nerve tract, interrupting the nerve conductivity

conization   a procedure performed on the cervix in which a cold knife is used to cut a cone-shaped portion of tissue surgically for examination

conjunctiva   a colorless mucous membrane that lines the anterior part of the eye

conscious sedation   a method of anesthetizing the patient that causes a controlled state of depressed consciousness; also called *moderate sedation*

consultation   a request to render an opinion or expertise by another provider or appropriate source

contaminated wound   a major break in surgical technique; acute nonpurulent inflammation is present

contributory factors   factors that affect the selection of Evaluation and Management (E/M) codes

coordination of care   activities that are completed by healthcare professional to arrange for patient care; one of the factors that are used to justify the selection of Evaluation and Management (E/M) codes

cordocentesis   a procedure in which an amniocentesis needle is inserted into the umbilical vessel to obtain blood from the fetus

cornea a transparent nonvascular structure located on the anterior portion of the sclera

coronary artery bypass grafts (CABG) types of grafts performed on the heart using veins, arteries, or a combination of veins and arteries

corpora cavernosa the erectile tissue of the penis

corpus uteri the area of structures that begins at the fundus of the uterine cavity and moves down to encompass the cervical canal or the external os

counseling a discussion with a patient about test results, prognosis, and other factors as outlined in the CPT manual; one of the factors used in the selection of Evaluation and Management (E/M) codes

CPT modifier a two-digit code that is appended to the CPT code to indicate that a service or procedure has been altered for some reason, but that the main definition of the code has not changed

craniectomy a procedure to remove the skull bone

craniotomy an incision into the skull without removal of bone

critical care care for a patient who requires constant attention by the provider because of situations related to his or her medical condition, whose illness or injury would put the patient at high risk

cryosurgical ablation of prostate a surgical procedure used for ablation of the prostate

curettage the process of removing tissue by scraping

Current Procedural Terminology (CPT) a coding system developed by the American Medical Association (AMA)

cystourethroscopy examination of the posterior urethra and the urinary bladder with a cystoscope.

cytogenetic studies of heredity or genes at the cellular level

cytopathology the study of cells, especially in the disease process

D

debridement a type of cleansing

decision for surgery modifier 57

decubitus the position of a patient on his or her back or stomach, which helps in localizing fluid

decubitus ulcer an ulcer resulting from continuous pressure in an area that eventually breaks down, causing a sore

deep biopsy the removal of nodes located below the muscle tissue

deep removal see *deep biopsy*

defect site an area that will receive tissue; also called a *recipient site*

dermal autograph a skin graft taken from a patient's own body that involves the dermal tissue.

dermatome an instrument that cuts slices of skin; the thickness is determined by the surgeon

dermis a thick layer of tissue located directly below the epidermis

descending colon the part of the colon that moves down the left side of the abdomen to the sigmoid colon

destruction a procedure that totally destroys or removes something

detailed examination examination of an affected area and other systems or organs related to the problem

detailed history documentation of four or more elements of the history of the past illness (HPI); a review of two to nine systems; and an element from the past, family, and/or social history (PFSH)

diagnostic arthroscope a scope used to view the joints of the body for diagnostic purposes

diagnostic endoscope a scope used to view the body internally for diagnostic purposes

diagnostic nasal endoscopy the inspection of the entire nasal cavity, the meatus, the turbinates, and the sphenoethmoid recess

diagnostic procedures done to determine a diagnosis and establish a care plan

Diagnostic Radiology the section of the Radiology chapter used to report a procedure or service rendered when assessing a disease for a more definitive diagnosis, as well as its progression or remission

diaphragm a dome-shaped muscle that separates the thorax from the abdomen

diencephalon the structure located between the cerebrum and the midbrain

digestive system this system performs the functions that take in and break down food for nutrient absorption and elimination of waste products

dilation a procedure performed when an expansion or stretching is necessary

direct inguinal hernia an inguinal hernia that protrudes into the abdominal wall by the Hesselbach triangle

direct laryngoscopy direct viewing of the larynx and adjacent structures by use of a laryngoscope

dirty and infected wound nonsterile conditions in which infection and inflammation are present and a foreign body may be present; also known as an infected wound

discontinued out-patient hospital/ambulatory surgery center (ASC) procedure after administration of anesthesia modifier 74

discontinued out-patient hospital/ambulatory surgery center (ASC) procedure prior to the administration of anesthesia modifier 73

discontinued procedure modifier 53

dislocation displacement of bone from the normal anatomical position

distinct procedural service modifier 59

donor site the area that provides the tissue used to make the repair

Doppler frequency change in sound, light, or radio waves given off by a source as it moves toward or away from the observer

dosimetry the scientific determination of the rate, amount, and dose of radiation to be administered

drainage procedures procedures completed to remove a fluid from an area

dual-chamber system a pacemaker system that has two electrodes, one in the atrium and one in the ventricle

dual photon absorptiometry a type of noninvasive bone density test in which low doses of radiation are beamed through the bone, and a computer evaluates the amount of radiation that was absorbed

duodenotomy   making an incision into the duodenum

durable medical equipment   medical equipment that is used in a patient's home repeatedly for a specific medical purpose

durable medical equipment, prosthetics, orthotics, and supplies (DMEPOS)   medical equipment, prosthetics, orthotics, and supplies that are repeatedly used by patients for a specific medical purpose

dura mater   the outermost layer of the meninges

dynamic splint   a splint that allows limited mobility

E

earlobe   the bottom portion of the external ear

echocardiography   an ultrasound that is used to study structures of the heart

ectopic pregnancy   a pregnancy that occurs outside the uterus

electrodes   devices attached to the pulse generator in a cardiac pacemaker

elements of examination   system or body areas that are examined

embryo   the fetus from 9 weeks until birth, usually at 40 weeks

emergency department (ED)   an organized hospital-based facility for the provision of unscheduled episodic services to patients who present for immediate medical attention

endarterectomy   a procedure used to remove plaque deposits from blood vessels

endocardium   the innermost lining of the heart

endocrine system   internal glands and structures that produce or secrete hormones

endolymph   an auditory fluid that transmits sound

endometrium   the innermost layer of the uterus

endoscope   an instrument used to visualize an internal body organ or cavity

endoscopic procedure   a procedure involving the insertion of a flexible or rigid instrument called an *endoscope*, which is used to view internal structures

endoscopic retrograde cholangiopancreatography (ERCP)   an endoscopic procedure that combines a retrograde cholangiography and a transhepatic cholangiography

endotracheal intubation   the insertion of an endotracheal tube into the trachea to keep it open

endovascular repair   repair within the vessel

endovascular therapy   a specific procedure to control bleeding, destroy a tumor, achieve hemostasis for a bleeding aneurysm, control blood flow during intracranial or extracranial procedures, and other reasons

enteral   route of administration involving the gastrointestinal tract

enterocele   another term for a vaginal hernia

enteroenterostomy   a procedure used to report the surgical anastomosis of two parts of the intestine with the creation of an opening between the two areas

enterolysis   freeing of intestinal adhesions

enterotomy   a procedure in which an incision is made into the intestines

enucleation   removal without cutting into a structure

epicardium   the inner layer of the double-walled sac around the heart; also known as *visceral pericardium*

epidermal autograft   an autograft that involves the epidermis

epidermis   the outermost layer of the skin

epididymis   a tubular structure that is found at the posterior border of a testis and that carries sperm to the *vas deferens*

epidural anesthesia   the injection of an anesthetic agent into the epidural space above the dura mater that contains the spinal nerves and cerebrospinal fluid

epidural blocks   the injection of an anesthetic agent into the epidural space above the dura mater that contains the spinal nerves and cerebrospinal fluid

epiglottidectomy   a surgical excision of the epiglottis

episiotomy   an incision made at the vaginal opening to prevent tearing during childbirth

escharotomy   the removal of necrosed tissue of severely burned skin

esophagogastroduodenoscopy procedure (EGD)   a procedure in which a scope is used to view the esophagus and the upper portion of the gastrointestinal tract, including the stomach, upper duodenum, and/or jejunum

esophagus   a muscular structure that moves food from the pharynx to the stomach

established patient   a patient who has received professional services from a physician or another physician of the same specialty within the past three years in the same group setting

ethmoidectomy   the partial or total removal of the ethmoid bone or ethmoid cells within the ethmoid sinus

ethmoid sinuses   sinuses located between the eyes

eustachian tube   a tube that connects the bony structures of the middle ear to the pharynx

Evaluation and Management (E/M)   codes that reflect the evaluation by a provider and also the management portion of the patient's care

eversion   turning outward

evisceration   the removal of an organ

excision   the surgical removal of a structure

exenteration   the surgical removal of the contents of a cavity

exostosis   a benign bony growth that projects from the surface of a bone

expanded problem-focused examination   an examination that includes the affected area with other body systems or areas that might also be affected by the problem that brought the patient into the office

expanded problem-focused history   documentation of one to three elements of the history of past illness (HPI), as well as a review of systems directly related to the chief complaint

extended HPI   history of present illness consisting of at least four elements or status of at least three chronic or inactive conditions

extension   movement that increases an angle of a joint

extensive nasal polyp excision a procedure in which a polyp's shape or thickness or the number of polyps present may require more skill and effort for removal

external auditory canal ear canal

external auditory meatus ear canal

external ear the outermost part of the ear that is visible, outside the structure of the skull

external fixation the placement of pins through soft tissue into bone to hold an external appliance in place

external hemorrhoid a type of hemorrhoid found outside the external sphincter

external sphincter a sphincter that controls the release of urine from the bladder

extracapsular extraction extraction that involves the removal of the lens without removing the posterior capsule

extraperiosteal pneumonolysis the separation of the surface of the lung from the inside surface of the chest cavity

eyelashes hairs that work with the upper and lower eyelids to protect the eye from foreign material

F

face-to-face time the provider's time with the patient during an examination

fallopian tubes bilateral tubes that open at one end in the uterus and at the other end in the peritoneal cavity

family history information regarding immediate family members who suffer from a chronic or acute illness, which would affect care of the patient either during current or future encounters

fascia a sheet of fibrous tissue

fasciectomy removal of fasciae

fine needle aspiration an aspiration in which a very fine needle is inserted into a site to withdraw fluid

first-degree burn the least severe kind of burn

fixation the process of suturing; fastening a structure in place

flash symbol indicates codes for vaccines that are pending FDA approval

flexible bronchoscope a scope inserted through the nose or mouth

fluoroscopy the use of a scope to produce immediate serial images using roentgen rays, which allow for examination of the function of a body part or organ

follow-up/repeat study a study performed on an area that requires an additional completed, documented study or exam

forbidden symbol Indicates that a code is exempt from the use of modifier -51 but has not been designated as CPT add-on procedures or services.

foreskin loose skin covering the glans penis; also referred to as *prepuce*

free graft a freeing of tissue from its original site

frenum a connection

frontal sinuses sinuses located within the frontal bone, behind the eyebrows

frontal sinusotomy a procedure that involves incisions made into the frontal sinuses

fulguration the use of an electric current to destroy living tissue

full-thickness graft a surgical transplantation that involves the epidermis and dermis of the donor site

G

gastric bypass surgery division of the small bowel with anastomosis to the proximal stomach to bypass the major portion of the stomach

gastrotomy a procedure that involves surgical incisions into the stomach

general anesthesia anesthesia that affects the whole body, causing a loss of consciousness

genioplasty plastic surgery of the chin

glans penis the distal end of the penis

global days preoperative services, postoperative services, and the procedure; also called the *global package* or *surgical package*

global package preoperative services, postoperative services, and the procedure; also called the *global days* or *surgical package*

glossectomy partial or complete removal of the tongue

gonioscope a type of scope that examines the eye for signs of glaucoma

graft a section of tissue that is moved from one site to another in an effort to heal or repair a defect

guidelines items that are necessary to appropriately interpret and report the procedures and services contained in a section

H

habilitative services modifier 96

Healthcare Common Procedure Coding System (HCPCS) a coding classification system that consists of CPT (Level I codes) and National Codes (Level II codes)

heart the major organ of the circulatory system

hematology the study of blood

hematoma the collection of blood in a particular space or organ

hematopoietic progenitor cell (HPC) boost a procedure in which the patient receives an infusion of hematopoietic progenitor cells from a donor.

hemilaryngectomy partial removal of the larynx

hemodialysis a process that removes waste from the blood but involves a continuous movement of blood from the body to a hemodialyzer for filtering; clean blood is returned to the patient's bloodstream

hemoperfusion a way for toxins to be removed from the blood by perfusing the blood through activated charcoal or resin; the blood is transfused back into the patient

hemorrhoid an enlarged varicose vein in or near the anus

hernia a protrusion or bulge

heterodermic graft a type of graft in which tissue from a different species is used for repair

hiatal hernia a type of hernia that pushes the stomach upward into the mediastinal cavity through the diaphragm

hip arthroplasty plastic surgery to repair the hip

history contains the chief complaint; history of present illness (HPI); review of systems; and past, family, and social history (PFSH)

history of present illness (HPI)   a chronological description of the patient's present illness

hollow circle symbol   indicates a reinstated or recycled code in CPT

homograft   a graft involving tissue from an individual of the same species; also known as a *homologous graft*

homologous graft   a graft involving tissue from an individual of the same species; also known as a *homograft*

horizontal triangles symbol   indicates new or revised text in the CPT manual

hormones   chemical substances produced by the body to keep organs and tissues functioning properly

hydatidiform mole   a grape-like grouping of cysts that are really the ova and cannot properly develop

hymen   the membrane that covers the external opening of the vagina

hymenectomy   a procedure in which the hymen is excised

hyperkeratotic   an overgrowth of skin

hyperthermia   a treatment using heat, such as ultrasound probes, and radiofrequencies together with radiation therapy to treat malignancies by speeding up cell metabolism

hypnotherapy   a type of psychotherapy that alters the state of consciousness to heightened awareness and opens the patient up to suggestions that may alter his or her thoughts or behavior

hypospadias   repair of the penis when it is abnormally curved or when the ureter opening is not properly located, affecting the flow of urine out of the body

hypothyroidism   a condition that results in an underactive thyroid gland

hysterectomy   a procedure in which the uterus is removed

hysterorrhaphy   repair of the uterus

hysteroscope   a fiber-optic–type scope that can be used for surgical or diagnostic procedures in the uterus

I

imaging guidance   a radiologic procedure that assists the physician in locating the area to be addressed

imbrication of the diaphragm   a transthoracic or transabdominal incision to draw back abdominal organs

immune globulin   functions as an antibody for a short period of time

immunology   study of the immune system

incision   a surgical cut made in skin or flesh

incisional hernia   a type of hernia that has developed through a surgical scar or scar tissue

incision and drainage (I&D)   surgically cutting over an area to be drained and then withdrawing or draining the fluid

incomplete abortion   an abortion in which all products of conception have not been expelled from the uterus

increased procedural services   modifier 22

incus   a bone of the ear shaped like an anvil

indirect inguinal hernia   a sac that extends through the inguinal ring and into the inguinal canal

indirect laryngoscopy   viewing of larynx by using a laryngeal mirror that is placed in the back of the throat while a second mirror is held outside the mouth

informational modifier   a statistical modifier; used for informational purposes

inguinal hernia   bulging at the inguinal opening

inguinal lymph nodes   nodes in the upper femoral triangle of the thigh

inhalation   when a substance is moved through the respiratory and/or circulatory systems

initial observation care   the first day of care provided to a patient while in observation

initial rhinoplasty   the surgical repair of the nose; also known as *primary rhinoplasty*

injection   a substance administered directly into the bloodstream, subcutaneous tissue, or intramuscular

insertion   to place a device or substance within the body or body part; a catheter placed in a newly established venous access

instillation   introduction into a body cavity that has a mucous membrane

integumentary system   considered the largest body system, it protects the internal parts of the body; also called the *skin*

intermediate repair   a procedure where laceration is fixed in layers; wound layers do not go deeper than non-muscle fascia

internal fixation   pins or plate internally placed into bone to hold the fracture; also known as *open reduction internal fixation (ORIF)*

internal hemorrhoid   a type of hemorrhoid located in the superior vein

intestine   a membranous tube that begins at the pyloric opening of the stomach and ends at the anus

intracapsular extraction   removal of the entire lens of the eye with a capsule

intranasal biopsy   a biopsy that is completed within the nasal cavity

intraspinal anesthesia   injection of an anesthetic agent within the spinal column

introitus   an opening or space

inversion   turning inward or inside out

in vitro fertilization   a process in which a mature egg is exposed to sperm in a laboratory setting; ova are then implanted into the uterus

iris   the colored portion of the eye

island flap   a flap repair made using subcutaneous tissue with nutrient vessels

isodose   equal-intensity doses of radiation to more than one area

K

kidneys   organs that remove waste products from the blood and regulate the volume and composition of the blood by allowing the reabsorption of water and other substances into the bloodstream

knee arthroplasty   surgical repair of the knee

L

labyrinth   bony and membranous structures within the inner ear that form a maze

lacrimal duct   the duct that tears drain through

lacrimal gland   the gland that produces tears

laparoscopy   a procedure that views interior structures of the abdomen

large intestine   an organ that begins with the cecum and moves to the colon, rectum, and anus

laryngectomy   surgical removal of the larynx

larynx   the voice organ that connects the pharynx with the trachea

lateral   on the side

lateral nasal wall reconstruction   repair of the lateral aspect of the nasal wall

Le Fort fracture   bilateral fracture of the maxilla

legally induced abortion   an abortion induced by medical personnel working within the law; can be elective or therapeutic

lens   a colorless structure that allows the eye to focus on images

Level I codes   CPT codes that are designated as level I within the Healthcare Common Procedure Coding System (HCPCS)

Level I (CPT) modifiers   two-digit numeric codes that are appended to a level I (CPT) code to indicate that a service or procedure has been altered, but the main definition of the code has not changed

Level II codes   codes published annually by Medicare and used to bill for services and procedures; also referred to as National Codes

Level II (HCPCS/National) modifiers   alphanumeric characters that are used to modify a Level II code

ligaments   bands of connective tissue that bind the joints together and connect the articular bones and cartilages to allow movement

ligation   the act of tying off; in vessel procedures, the division and stripping of vessels

limited study   a partial scan or examination of a body area or quadrant

lingual   referring to the tongue

lingual tonsils   one of three sets of tonsils that are located at the base of the tongue on the posterior surface

liver   the organ that filters red blood cells, stores essential vitamins, and contains enzymes that break down poisons and produce bile, which helps break down fats

local anesthesia   when an anesthetic agent is applied topically to the skin or injected subcutaneously

local autograft   a procedure in which one incision is used to harvest a graft from a patient who is the recipient and donor

low birth weight (LBW)   description of an infant with a present body weight of 1,500–2,500 grams

low–complexity medical decision making   decision making that is of low complexity and low risk to patient

lower eyelid   the bottom eyelid; works with the upper eyelid to keep the surface of the eyeball lubricated and protected from particles

lungs   the pair of organs that are located in the thorax and constitute the main organ of the respiratory system

lymphadenitis   having an enlarged or inflamed lymph node

lymphangiography   examination of the lymphatic system after contrast material has been injected

lymphangiotomy   an incision made into a lymph node

lymphatic channels   vessels that transport fluid away from the tissues of the body toward the thoracic cavity

lymphatic vessels   see *lymphatic channels*

lymph glands (nodes)   located at various areas along the lymphatic vessels; collections of lymphatic tissue

lymph nodes (glands)   collection of lymphatic tissue

M

magnetic resonance imaging (MRI)   imaging where radio frequency signals are used to examine the soft tissue and bony structures of the body without radiation

malignant lesion   lesion that has abnormal, cancerous cell growth

malleus   one of the auditory ossicles; shaped like a hammer

mammary ductogram   the study done on the mammary duct to the mammary gland

mandated services   modifier 32

manipulation   reduction of a dislocation or fracture

mastectomy   the excision of the breast or breast tissue

mastotomy   a surgical incision of the breast

maxillary sinuses   sinuses located below the eye and lateral to the nasal cavity

maxillary sinusotomy   an incision made into the maxillary sinus

maxillectomy   removal of the maxillary sinus

Meckel's diverticulum   a form of diverticulum of the ileum

mediastinoscope   a scope inserted into sternum area to visually examine the mediastinum, trachea, and major vessels found in this area

mediastinotomy   a procedure in which an incision is made to open the mediastinum

mediastinum   the space in the thoracic cavity between the lungs

membranous labyrinth   structures within the ear that include the utricle, saccule, semicircular ducts, and cochlear ducts

meninges   protective tissue that covers the brain and spinal cord

mesencephalon   a structure located between the diencephalon and the pons; also known as the *midbrain*

mesentery   the membranous attachment of an organ to the body wall

metastasis   when a malignant growth or tumor spreads from one part of the body into another

microbiology   the study of microorganisms

microlaryngoscopy   the use of an operating microscope on the larynx

midbrain   a structure located between the diencephalons and the pons; also known as the *mesencephalon*

middle ear   a structure found within the temporal bone; houses the auditory ossicles and eustachian tube

minimum assistant surgeon   modifier 81

missed abortion   a fetus that has died before completion of 22 weeks of gestation, with retention of the dead fetus or products of conception up to 4 weeks after demise

mitral valve   the valve between the left atrium and left ventricle

mixed hemorrhoids   see *combined hemorrhoid*

M-mode technique   an ultrasound technique that takes the measurement of the velocity and amplitude of moving echo-producing structures and allows for one-dimensional viewing

moderate-complexity medical decision making   decision making in which the risk factors and complexity of the patient problem are high

moderate sedation   a method of anesthetizing the patient that causes a controlled state of depressed consciousness; also called conscious sedation

modifier 22   increased procedural services

modifier 23   unusual use of general anesthesia

modifier 24   unrelated E/M service, same physician, during postoperative period

modifier 25   significant, separately identifiable E/M service by the same physician on the same day of the procedure or other service

modifier 26   professional component; physician reports only the professional component of a service rendered

modifier 27   multiple outpatient hospital E/M encounters on the same date

modifier 32   mandated services; required or mandated by a peer review organization; insurance company; governmental, legislative, or regulatory agency

modifier 33   preventive service

modifier 47   anesthesia by surgeon when regional or general anesthesia is provided by the same physician or surgeon who is performing the procedure or service

modifier 50   bilateral procedure

modifier 51   multiple procedures; additional procedure(s) or service(s) would be reported with this modifier; not used by facilities

modifier 52   reduced services; procedure is partially reduced or eliminated at the physician's discretion

modifier 53   discontinued procedure; termination of a surgical or diagnostic procedure because of extenuating circumstances that threaten the well-being of the patient

modifier 54   surgical care only

modifier 55   postoperative management only

modifier 56   preoperative management only

modifier 57   decision for surgery

modifier 58   staged or related procedure or service by the same physician during the postoperative period

modifier 59   distinct procedural service

modifier 62   two surgeons; two primary surgeons work together to perform distinct parts of a single reportable procedure

modifier 63   procedure performed on infants less than 4 kilograms

modifier 66   surgical team; several physicians of different specialties, other highly skilled and specially trained personnel, and various types of complex equipment during the operative procedure

modifier 73   discontinued outpatient hospital/ASC procedure prior to the administration of anesthesia

modifier 74   discontinued outpatient hospital/ASC procedure after administration of anesthesia

modifier 76   repeat procedure by same physician

modifier 77   repeat procedure by another physician; basic procedure or service performed by another physician had to be repeated

modifier 78   return to the operating room for a related procedure during the postoperative period

modifier 79   unrelated procedure or service by the same physician during the postoperative period

modifier 80   assistant surgeon

modifier 81   minimum assistant surgeon; second surgeon for a short period of time but not throughout the whole procedure

modifier 82   assistant surgeon when a qualified resident surgeon is not available in a teaching facility; used in a teaching-hospital residency program

modifier 90   references outside laboratory; laboratory procedures are performed by a party other than the treating or reporting physician

modifier 91   repeat clinical diagnostic laboratory test

modifier 92   alternative laboratory platform testing

modifier 95   synchronous telemedicine service rendered via a real-time interactive audio and video telecommunications system

modifier 96   habilitative services

modifier 97   rehabilitative services

modifier 99   indicates that multiple modifiers are needed for an individual CPT code

modifying units   determined by physical conditions and qualifying circumstances that affect the administration of anesthesia

Mohs micrographic surgery   a type of chemosurgery

morselized allograft   a procedure in which small pieces of bone are harvested to form the graft from a source other than the patient

morselized autograft   the harvesting of small pieces of the patient's own bone through a separate incision

multifetal pregnancy reduction (MPR)   a procedure in which one or more fetuses are removed from the uterus to increase the chances of survival of the strongest one or ones

multiple modifiers   modifier 99

multiple outpatient hospital E/M encounters on the same date   modifier 27

multiple procedure   modifier 51

muscle   tissue that is composed of fibers and cells that cause movement and are able to contract

myocardium   the middle layer of the heart

myomectomy   a procedure in which uterine fibroid tumors are removed from the wall of the uterus

N

narcosynthesis   a form of psychiatry that involves the administering of an intravenous drug that allows the patient to release thoughts that might be suppressed or repressed

nasal polyps   growths in the nasal cavity that are commonly associated with rhinitis

nasal vestibular stenosis narrowing of the nasal vestibule

nasopharyngeal tonsils one of three sets of tonsils that are also referred to as the adenoids

nasopharynx the part of the pharynx that is located posterior to the nasal cavity

National Codes codes published annually by Medicare and used to bill for services and procedures; also referred to as *Level II codes*

National Correct Coding Initiative (NCCI) an initiative implemented to standardize proper coding and payment for Medicare Part B claims

National Drug Code (NDC) an 11-digit number that identifies the manufacturer, the product, and the package size of a drug

nature of the presenting problem a factor used to select an Evaluation and Management (E/M) code; indicates the severity of the current problem

nephrectomy an excision completed on a kidney

nephrolithotomy removal of a kidney stone by making an incision into the kidney

nephrorrhaphy suturing of the kidney

nephrotomy an incision made into the kidney so the physician can explore the interior

new patient a patient who has not received professional services within the past three years from a physician or another physician of the same specialty who belongs to the same group practice

nonselective placement where a catheter is functioning in the vessel punctured and does not go into any other vessel

nuclear medicine medicine that treats and diagnoses diseases using radioactive isotopes

number symbol indicates codes that are out of numerical sequence

O

oblique different angles

observation a time period in which a patient is in the hospital for a short-term stay while a plan of care is being determined

observation status see *observation*

obstetrics the specialty that deals with women during pregnancy, childbirth, and the time immediately following childbirth

ocular implant an implant performed inside the muscular cone

oligohydramnios when there is insufficient amniotic fluid present

omentectomy removal of the omentum

omentum the part of the peritoneum that connects the stomach to other structures of the abdomen

oophorectomy a partial or total removal of the ovary, unilateral or bilateral

open colectomy excision of all or part of the colon by making an incision into the area

open drainage of a perirenal abscess a procedure in which an incision is made into the area, the site is irrigated, and drain tubes are placed

open drainage of a renal abscess a procedure in which an incision is made into the area, the site is irrigated, and drain tubes are placed

open reduction a procedure in which a site is surgically opened to realign the area

open reduction internal fixation (ORIF) a procedure in which pins or a plate is internally placed into bone to hold the fracture; also known as *internal fixation*

open treatment a procedure in which a fracture site is surgically exposed and visualized

open-tube bronchoscope a scope inserted through the mouth; also referred to as a *rigid bronchoscope*

ophthalmologist a doctor who specializes in the treatment of diseases and disorders of the eye

ophthalmology the study of diseases and disorders of the eye

optic disc a blind spot on the optic nerve

optic nerve the nerve through which impulses are sent to the brain

optometrist a healthcare professional who prescribes corrective lenses

orbital implants implants that are outside the muscle cone

orchiopexy a surgical fixation of the testis in the scrotal sac

organ of Corti the true organ of hearing

ostectomy a procedure in which bone is removed

osteoclasis the process of creating a surgical fracture of a bone to correct a deformity

osteoectomy a procedure in which bone is removed

osteoplasty surgical repair or reconstruction completed on bone tissue

osteotomy sawing or cutting of a bone

otoplasty plastic surgery of the ear

oval window a structure that separates the middle ear from the inner ear

ovaries structures referred to as *female gonads;* they function in producing eggs, which are released during ovulation

P

pacing cardioverter-defibrillator a device that emits defibrillating shocks that stimulate the heart and treat ventricular fibrillation or ventricular tachycardia

palate roof of the mouth

palatine tonsils one of three sets of tonsils that come off the soft palate

palatoplasty repair of the roof of the mouth

pancreas an organ that secretes juices necessary for digestion and to regulate blood sugar levels

panel test a group of tests reported by one CPT code

parathyroid a structure on the posterior of the thyroid that secretes hormones that regulate serum calcium levels

paravaginal the area around the vagina

parenteral a route of administration not involving the gastrointestinal tract

parietal pericardium the outermost layer of the heart

parotid glands one of three sets of salivary glands that are located in front of each ear

partial laryngectomy the partial removal of the larynx; also known as a *hemilaryngectomy*

partial nephrectomy removal of part of the kidney

partial replacement   replacement of a catheter component, but not the whole device, during a vessel procedure

past, family and/or social history (PFSH)   components of a patient's history that affect the level of history selected for an Evaluation and Management (E/M) code

past history   any past medical information that may affect the medical decision-making process

pedicle flap   a flap of skin that hangs on a stem of skin that contains blood vessels

penis   the male organ through which the urethra passes to allow urine to be expelled from the body as part of the urinary system; also a part of the reproductive system as the male organ that delivers spermatozoa to the female reproductive tract

percutaneous skeletal fixation   a fracture treatment in which a fracture site is neither open nor closed and fixation is placed across the fracture site

percutaneous ventricular assist device (pVAD)   a mechanical pump that assists a weakened heart in injecting blood to the body.

Pereyra procedure   a procedure in which sutures are laced through a Pereya ligature carrier and the urethrovesical junction is raised up

pericardial fluid   fluid that prevents the two layers of the pericardial sac from rubbing against each other.

pericardial sac   a double-walled sac composed of membranous tissue that surrounds the heart

pericardiocentesis   a procedure in which the physician removes fluid from the pericardial space by insertion of a fine needle to aspirate the fluid

pericardium   a double-walled sac that encloses the heart

peridural anesthesia   injection of an anesthetic agent into the epidural space above the dura mater that contains the spinal nerves and cerebrospinal fluid

perilymph   an auditory fluid that transmits sound

perinatal period   the period of time immediately following birth up to 28 days after birth

perineum   the diamond-shaped area of skin between the upper area of the vaginal orifice and the anus

peripheral arterial disease (PAD) rehabilitation   a process comprising patient-monitored exercise until symptoms of the arterial disease lessen

peripheral nervous system   a system composed of the nerves that connect the body organs to the central nervous system

peritoneal dialysis   a form of cleaning waste from the bloodstream; instead of a machine to filter the blood, the peritoneal membrane is used as the filter

peritoneum   the membranous lining of the abdomen

pertinent PFSH   review of the history related to the problem identified in the history of present illness (HPI)

Peyronie's disease   a condition in which the corpora cavernosa becomes hardened

pharyngeal flap   an incision made through the soft palate to the posterior pharyngeal wall and advanced to the muscle to create a flap

pharyngolaryngectomy   a surgical excision of the hypopharynx and larynx

pharyngoplasty   plastic surgery or a reconstructive operation on the pharynx

pharyngostomy   a procedure in which an artificial opening is made into the pharynx

pharyngotympanic tube   a tube within the middle ear that equalizes air pressure; also known as the *eustachian tube*

pharynx   the tubular structure that extends from the base of the skull to the esophagus

physical status modifiers   modifiers used to describe the patient's health status

pia mater   the innermost layer of tissue surrounding the brain

pilonidal cyst   a closed sac, located in the sacrococcygeal area, which contains epithelial tissue with hair nested within the sac

pinch graft   surgical transplantation of a small amount of autograft tissue

pinna   the flexible cartilaginous flap that is located at the base of the ear, known as the *earlobe*

place of service (POS)   the location in which the service is performed, such as the home, office, hospital, or skilled nursing facility

pleurectomy   surgical removal of the pleura

pneumonectomy   removal of a lung

pneumothorax   an accumulation of air or gas in the pleural cavity

port   an area where a treatment beam will enter the skin and focus on a malignant area

positron emission tomography (PET) scan   a scan in which radioactive substances are administered that allow images of various body structures to be examined in color codes that indicate the degree and intensity of the metabolic process

postanesthesia recovery period   the period of time following the completion of surgery, in which anesthesia was administered by an anesthesiologist or other professional administering anesthesia, until the patient is released to the surgeon or to another physician.

posterior chamber   a chamber located behind the lens of the eye

posteroanterior   back to front

postoperative management only   modifier 55

preoperative management only   modifier 56

prepuce   loose skin covering the glans penis; also referred to as *foreskin*

preventive medicine service   a service in which a patient presents for a well visit or a physical examination

pricing modifier   an increase or decrease of the fee for the service provided

primary rhinoplasty   a surgical repair of the nose; also known as *initial rhinoplasty*

problem-focused history   brief history of present illness (HPI), which is related to the problem that brought the patient to the office

procedure performed on infants less than 4 kg   modifier 63

proctosigmoidoscopy   examination of the rectum with scope advancement into the sigmoid colon

professional component   modifier 26

prohibitory symbol   Indicates that a code is exempt from modifier -51 and also has not been denoted as a CPT add-on code

prolapsed hemorrhoid   a hemorrhoid that has descended past the anal sphincter

prone   horizontal position, facedown

proprietary laboratory analyses (PLA) tests symbol   this symbol is used to denote duplicate proprietary laboratory analyses tests.

prostate gland   a gland that secretes fluid that is part of the semen and aids in the motility of sperm

proton beam treatment   a technique used in treating malignancies by using higher doses of radiation on tumors; at the same time, it does not exceed the radiation tolerance of normal healthy tissue

psychiatric residential treatment center   a facility that provides 24-hour care, which includes a therapeutically planned and professionally staffed group living and learning environment

psychiatrist   a medical doctor who administers treatment for patients with mental, emotional, or behavioral disorders

psychiatry   the branch of medicine that deals with mental disorders

psychoanalysis   a form of psychotherapy in which the patient's unconscious thoughts are recognized and analyzed

pudendum   an inclusive term used to describe the external genitalia of the female body; also referred to as the *vulva*

pulmonary perfusion imaging   imaging of localized radioactive particles and the proportional blood flow that maps the lung perfusion

pulmonary valve   a valve that sits between the pulmonary artery and right ventricle

pulse generator   a part of a pacemaker that controls the heart rate, the energy output, and the pacing modes

pupil   a structure located in the center of the iris

pyeloplasty   the plastic surgery completed on the renal pelvis of the kidney

pyelotomy   an incision made into the renal pelvis

pyloromyotomy   the cutting of the pyloric muscle

Q

qualifying circumstances   conditions that are unusual or out of the ordinary and affect the administration of anesthesia

R

radical lymphadenectomy   a procedure in which lymph nodes are dissected and removed in addition to tissue under the skin

radiologic technician   a person who is specially trained to use equipment that generates pictures or studies taking during radiological testing

radiologist   a doctor whose specialty is radiology

radiology   the study of x-rays, high-frequency sound waves, and high-strength magnetic fields in an effort to treat or diagnose disease or injury

radiopharmaceuticals   drugs used in testing the cause of a problem by indicating location, size, or function of organs, tissues, or vessels

real-time scanning   scanning that provides a two-dimensional image of both structure and movement

recipient site   the area that will receive a graft; also known as the *defect site*

reconstruction   surgical rebuilding of a structure

rectum   distal end of the large intestine

reduced services   modifier 52

reduction   an attempt to realign a bone or joint

reference (outside) laboratory   modifier 90

referral   a patient transfer to a specialist for treatment of a condition

refractor   a machine that contains a large series of lenses that are changed quickly during an examination as the patient views an eye chart

regional anesthesia   anesthesia in which a particular body area or region is anesthetized

rehabilitative services   modifier 97

relative value   a value that reflects the usual services attached to anesthesia and the work associated with the anesthesia services provided; also called *basic value*

Relative Value Guide (RVG)   a guide that contains the basic value of each of the anesthesia services and additional codes that act as supplements to the regular CPT codes, along with narratives

removal   to take out an entire structure, lesion, or device

renal endoscopic procedures   procedures performed on the kidneys using a scope

repair   surgical closure of an area that may have been injured as a result of trauma or that was surgically created; procedure involves fixing, not replacing

repeat clinical diagnostic laboratory test   modifier 91

repeat procedure by another physician   modifier 77

repeat procedure by same physician   modifier 76

retina   the nerve cell layer of the eye that changes light rays into nerve impulses

review of systems (ROS)   an inventory of body systems that is obtained from the patient to identify signs and/or symptoms that the patient may be experiencing

revision rhinoplasty   minor, intermediate, or major revisions of the nose; also known as *secondary rhinoplasty*

rhinectomy   removal of the nose

rhinophyma   a rosacea condition of the skin of the nose. The skin appears red, swollen, distorted with sebaceous hyperplasia

rhinoplasty   surgical repair of the nose

rhinotomy   a surgical procedure in which an incision is made along one side of the nose

rigid bronchoscope   referred to as an *open-tube broncho-scope;* inserted through the mouth

S

saccule   like the utricle, this membranous sac aids in maintaining balance

salivary glands   glands that secrete saliva that contains enzymes that aid in digestion

salpingo-oophorectomy   removal of the fallopian tubes and ovaries

scalpel   a small, pointed surgical knife

scanning   a study that displays certain body areas for evaluation

sclera   the white portion of the eye

scleral reinforcement   repairs of the sclera

scrotum   a structure that encloses, protects, and supports the testicles

secondary rhinoplasty   minor, intermediate, or major revisions of the nose; also known as *revision rhinoplasty*

second-degree burn   a partial-thickness burn that forms blisters

selective placement   the placement of a catheter that moves into one of the great vessels off the aorta, not including the vessel puncture for access

semicircular canals   canals located behind the vestibule; three bony structures that are filled with fluid that help to maintain balance

semicircular ducts   ducts located behind the vestibule that help to maintain balance

seminal vesicle   part of the ejaculatory duct posterior to the urinary bladder

septic abortion   an abortion in which fever and infection are present

septoplasty   rhinoplasty that includes major septal repair

serial tonometry   a procedure that measures pressure over the course of the day

serous pericardium   the outermost layer of the pericardial sac

shaft   the proximal end of the penis

shaving   removal of a lesion from the epidermal or dermal layer without incision or slicing into the subcutaneous level of the skin

sigmoid colon   the descending colon moves down the left side of the abdomen to the sigmoid colon, which then connects to the rectum

sigmoidoscopy   a procedure in which the endoscope is moved all the way through the rectum and sigmoid colon and may even advance slightly into the descending colon

significant, separately identifiable E/M service by the same physician on the same day of the procedure or other service   modifier 25

simple nasal polyp excision   a procedure in which a polyp's shape allows it to be removed easily

simple repair   a repair in which there is a single-layer closure, where laceration does not go any deeper than the subcutaneous tissue

simulation   in radiology, it mimics the disease so that field settings for size and location of ports to be used can be determined

single-chamber system   a pacemaker system that has one electrode in either the atrium or the ventricle

sinoatrial node (SA node)   a node that sends impulses across the heart, causing contractions and pushing blood into the ventricles

sinogram   a diagnostic procedure on the sinus tract

sinus   a cavity that is located in the skull, close to the paranasal area

skeletal traction   the application of force to a limb using felt that is applied to the skin

skin tags   small lesions that can be brownish or flesh colored and are raised away from the body

skin traction   the application of a pull on an affected body structure; straps are attached to the skin surrounding the structure

sling procedures   procedures using slings to correct urinary stress incontinence

small intestine   a structure that begins at the pyloric sphincter and moves through the duodenum, jejunum, ileum, and ileocecal sphincter

SOAP note   a provider note that contains a subjective, objective, assessment, and plan

social history   part of the history of past illness (HPI) that records a patient's marital status, use of tobacco, alcohol, and drugs, and other social factors that would influence the care of the patient

somatic nervous system   a system that connects the central nervous system to the skin and skeletal muscles via the cranial and spinal nerves

sperm   a germ cell secretion of the testicles

spermatic cord   a covering around the nerves and vessels that encloses the seminal duct

sphenoid sinuses   sinuses located directly behind the nose at the center of the skull

sphenoid sinusotomy   incisions made into the sphenoid sinus

spinal anesthesia   injection of an anesthetic agent into the spinal area

spinal nerves   31 pairs of nerves located in the spinal area

spirometry testing   testing that measures lung capacity

spleen   an organ that filters blood; the largest organ of the lymphatic system

splenectomy   surgical removal of the spleen

splenorrhaphy   repair of the spleen

split-thickness autograft   a skin graft taken from a patient's own body that contains only part of the dermal layer.

split-thickness graft   a graft in which the tissue is about half or more of the thickness of the skin

spontaneous abortion   the complete or incomplete expulsion of products of conception before a pregnancy goes beyond 22 weeks of gestation

spreader grafting   repair of the lateral nasal wall

staged or related procedure or service by the same physician during the postoperative period   modifier 58

staged procedure   a second procedure that was planned as part of the main procedure

Standby Services   a type of prolonged services in which a physician requests that another physician stand by in the event that the services of the second physician are needed.

stapes   one of the auditory ossicles, shaped like a stirrup

star symbol   denotes codes that may be used to report synchronous (real-time) telemedicine services when modifier -95 is appended to the code

static splint   a splint used to prohibit mobility

statistical modifier   an informational modifier; used for informational purposes

stoma   a surgical opening between a part of the intestine and the outside surface of the abdomen

stomach   a pouchlike structure that aids in the breakdown and digestion of food

straightforward medical decision making   a process with low complexity and low risk to the patient

strangulated hemorrhoid   a hemorrhoid in which the anal sphincter causes blood supply to be occluded

strangulated hernia   a hernia that develops gangrene because the sac is tightly constricted

strapping   taping to bind, protect, or immobilize an anatomical structure

structural allograft   a procedure in which a large segment of bone is harvested from a donor source, other than the patient, and is placed into the interspace of the spine

structural autograft   spine surgery involving a bicortical or tricortical graft that is harvested through a separate incision

subarachnoid anesthesia   injection of an anesthetic agent into the spinal area

subcutaneous   the layer of skin that makes the connection to the muscle surface

sublingual   relating to the area under the tongue

sublingual gland   one of three sets of salivary glands that contain enzymes, which aid in digestion; located under the tongue

submandibular gland   one of three sets of salivary glands, which contain enzymes that aid in digestion; located on the floor of the mouth

submandibular lymph nodes   nodes located under the mandible or lower jaw

superficial biopsy   the removal of lymph nodes located close to the surface of the skin and subcutaneous tissue

superficial removal   see *superficial biopsy*

supine   a sitting position

surgical arthroscopy   a procedure that surgically treats an injury or condition of abnormality of a joint

surgical care only   modifier 54

surgical endoscopy   a procedure that surgically treats an injury or condition of an internal body organ or cavity

surgical nasal endoscopy   a procedure in which a nasal endoscope is used to complete a surgical procedure

surgical package   preoperative services, postoperative services, and the procedure; also called the *global package* or *global days*

surgical team   modifier 66

suspensory ligaments   ligaments that hold the lens of the eye in place

symphysiotomy for horseshoe kidney   correction of a condition of abnormal union of the kidneys

synechia   an adhesion of the iris to either the cornea or lens

synovectomy   removal of the synovial membrane of a joint

T

tarsorrhaphy   the entire or partial suturing of the eyelids

teletherapy   an external radiation treatment in which the machine delivers the radiation after being positioned a specified distance from the patient

tendon   dense fibrous band of connective tissue that attaches muscles to bones

testes   glands located in the scrotal sac that produce sperm and are referred to as the *testicles*

therapeutic procedures   part of the care plan; procedures used as treatment for a diagnosis that has already been rendered

third-degree burn   a burn that goes to the subcutaneous layer or further

thoracoscopy   the examination of the pleura, lungs, and mediastinum using an endoscope to visualize the area

thoracostomy   an incision made into the chest wall

thoracotomy   a surgical opening into the thoracic cavity

thromboendarterectomy   a surgical incision that is made into an artery to remove a thrombus or plaque and the arterial lining

thrombosed hemorrhoid   a hemorrhoid that contains a blood clot and is extremely painful

thymus gland   a gland that functions to secrete thymosin, which is a hormone the bone marrow needs to produce T cells that work with the immune system

thyroid gland   a gland that secretes hormones that regulate growth and metabolism

time unit   anesthesia time or time spent providing anesthesia services

tissue-cultured epidermal autograft   a graft where tissue is harvested in a split tissue autograft and then cultured tissue is grafted back to the donor

tomography   a radiological procedure in which a detailed cross section of tissue structure is produced

tonsils   structures considered the first line of defense for the respiratory system

trachea   a tube-shaped structure in the neck that extends from the larynx to the bronchi

trachelectomy   removal of cervix uteri

tracheostomy   an incision made into the trachea

transfusion   the introduction directly into the bloodstream of whole blood or blood components

transthoracic mediastinotomy   a mediastinotomy performed through the fourth intercostal space

transverse colon   the part of the colon that moves in a horizontal direction, and at the splenic flexure, makes a downward turn to the descending colon

trephine   a surgical instrument used to cut a cylindrical shape; at times, used for cutting holes in bone

triangle symbol   denotes that a code has been revised from the previous edition of CPT with a substantial change in the description of procedure or service

tricuspid valve   the valve between the right atrium and right ventricle

tube pericardiostomy   a procedure in which fluid is drained from the pericardial space by placing a long needle into the pericardial space and then exchanging the needle for an indwelling catheter

tunica vaginalis   the membranous sac within the scrotum that covers the sides and front of the testis and epididymis

two surgeons   modifier 62

tympanic cavity   the cavity in the temporal bone that houses the auditory ossicles and eustachian tube

tympanic membrane   the part of the eardrum that separates the external ear from the middle ear

tympanic neurectomy   removal of the Jacobson's nerve located in the middle ear

tympanoplasty   surgical repair of the tympanic membrane

tympanostomy   an incision made into the tympanic membrane to create an opening

U

ulcerated hemorrhoid   a hemorrhoid that is inflamed and may have necrotic changes in surrounding tissue

ulcers   erosions of the skin in which tissue becomes inflamed and then lost

ultrasonography   a radiological procedure in which sound waves are passed over body structures to send a signal to a computer that is then turned into a picture for examination

unbundling   a coder's selection of more than one code for a procedure when only one code should have been selected

unit/floor time   the time that a provider spends on the patient's unit or floor

unplanned return to the operating room for a related procedure during the postoperative period   modifier 78

unrelated E/M service by the same physician during postoperative period   modifier 24

unrelated procedure or service by the same physician during the postoperative period   modifier 79

unusual anesthesia   modifier 23

upper eyelid   a structure that works with the lower eyelid to keep the surface of the eyeball lubricated and protected from particles

uptake   the amount and time a substance takes to draw up or absorb

ureterectomy   removal of a ureter

ureters   structures that move urine from the kidneys into the urinary bladder

urethra   a mucous membrane–lined tube that leads the urine from the bladder to be excreted from the body

urinary bladder   a structure that serves as a temporary reservoir for urine

urodynamics   the study of the holding and storage of urine in the bladder, motion and rate of the movement of the urine, and analysis of how the bladder empties

utricles   along with the saccule, these are membranous sacs that aid in maintaining balance

uvula   a small, cone-shaped mass of flesh that hangs in the posterior border of the soft palate

V

vaccine   a dead microorganism that is administered for prevention or treatment of a disease

vagina   a fibromuscular structure that connects with the external genitalia and ascends in a tubelike structure to the cervix uteri

vaginal birth after cesarean (VBAC)   an attempt at vaginal delivery after a previous cesarean section

vaginectomy   a procedure in which the vagina is excised

vagotomy   the surgical cutting of the vagus nerve with the intent of reducing acid secretions in the stomach

vas deferens   a tube that starts at the epididymis and goes over the top of the urinary bladder and allows sperm to move outside the system

vasectomy   excision of the *vas deferens* to prevent sperm from moving out of the system; renders a man sterile

veins   vessels that move deoxygenated blood back to the heart (with the exception of the pulmonary veins)

venography   x-ray image of the veins; also referred to as a *phlebography*

venous access device   a device or catheter that allows for access to the venous system

ventral hernia   a type of hernia that protrudes through an abdominal scar where the abdominal wall is protected only by scar tissue

ventricles   the lower chambers of the heart that send blood to the arteries

vermilion   a pinkish border of the lips

very low birth weight (VLBW)   infant weight less than 1,500 grams

vessels   structures that move fluid throughout the body

vestibular glands   glands that secrete lubricating mucous in the vagina; also referred to as *Bartholin's glands*

vestibule   the central portion of the inner ear

vestibule of the mouth   mucosal tissue and submucosal tissue of the lips and cheeks

V-excision   removal of tissue using a V-shaped incision

views   positions of the patient in relation to the camera or device taking pictures

visceral pericardium   the inner layer of the double-walled sac of the heart; also known as the *epicardium*

vitreous humor   a clear, jellylike substance that helps to shape the eye

vulva   external genitalia of the female body; also referred to as the *pudendum*

vulvectomy   removal of all or part of the vulva

W

wedge excision   an excision shaped like a wedge

wound exploration   examination that determines the extent of the injury and includes surgical examination of a wound area

X

xenograft   a graft made up of nonhuman material

x-ray   electromagnetic waves that are used to produce a picture of internal structures of the body

INDEX